The Complete CRYSTAL HANDBOOK

Your Guide to More than 500 Crystals

Disclaimer

—*For Freya my granddaughter and Caitlin my young friend who made writing this such an adventure.*
www.cassandraeason.com

The
Complete
CRYSTAL
HANDBOOK

Your Guide to More
than 500 Crystals

Cassandra Eason

UNION
SQUARE
& CO.

NEW YORK

Contents

Introduction

A book on crystals and gems is like no other book, because it gives access to the fabulous world of nature's most beautiful treasures. Even if you are not a crystal collector, some crystals in the book you may know already or possess as jewellery. Of the 500 minerals in the book, some are relatively rare but are quite magical, such as pale yellow Libyan desert glass, first recorded in Ancient Egypt where it was carved into a scarab on the breastplate of Tutankhamun. Other crystals are not externally dazzling but nevertheless contain healing or restorative properties and become valued like old friends.

Many gems and crystals have acquired myths to explain their perceived properties. Sunstone, the ancients believed, once formed part of the sun and fell to earth during a full solar eclipse. Pearls are said to be tears that fell into the ocean into open oyster shells, the tears of the angels over the sins or sorrows of humankind.

This book explains, for each crystal, traditional uses for physical and emotional healing, and also how they can be used practically in the home and the workplace to give personal power and protection.

Some have quite mundane purposes – a brown jasper worry stone to hold if you are trying to quit smoking and get a craving, or amethyst according to folklore deters animal fleas, while green aventurine brings luck in competitions.

A few of the rarer crystals in their natural form need to be handled carefully because they contain sulphur, lead or other potentially harmful minerals if ingested, but these I have listed. These should be displayed safely away from children or carried wrapped in a small bag.

The book does open the door to the world of wonderful minerals and you may wish to collect your favourites or wear them as jewellery. Even if you do not consider it possible that they have healing powers (and you may change you mind if you try), crystals act as a psychological boost to your energies and self-confidence or give out "do not mess with me" energies that cause others to treat us with more respect. For every crystal works in interaction with the energy field of the user or wearer and so enriches your world every time you use it.

Introducing Crystals

All minerals growing within the Earth have powerful energies, containing the stored natural elemental powers of their formation over millions of years, shaped by volcanic heat and waters seeping deep into the ground. Some, like black obsidian, are not crystals at all but natural glass generated by the sudden cooling of volcano-cascaded lava. Grey or fawn tubes of fulgurite are formed instantly as lightning hits sand. Others are organic, such as pearls, or made of fossils or, like golden amber, from fossilized tree resin, often containing insects or plant material. Green olivine sometimes has extra-terrestrial origins when found in stony and stony iron meteorites.

How a crystal or gem is cut can bring out its true nature. The lustrous moving cat's-eye formation that appears in such gems as yellow chrysoberyl or green alexandrite needs to be skilfully cut into dome-shaped cabochons to display its effect. So do gems that contain a six- or twelve-rayed star, like ruby or sapphire or flash opal with its appearing and disappearing flickers of rainbow colour.

Jewellery is one of the most popular ways to display gems and crystals, and benefit from their healing and empowering qualities directly through skin contact. Traditionally, earrings protect the mind from psychological attack; necklaces and pendants shield the heart from emotional manipulation and bring love; bracelets or arm bands reach out to attract abundance and opportunities. Belt buckles guard and empower the Solar Plexus and Sacral energy centres of the body that control will-power, self-confidence, needs and desires. Rings on any finger symbolize lasting love, friendship and health continuing in a never-ending cycle.

Anniversary stones and birthstones (pp.45 and 47) are ways of using polished and often faceted gems as tokens of deep affection or, if bought for oneself, of self-value, and are invariably luck-attracting. Tumbled or tumblestones are a relatively inexpensive way to collect a variety of stones and can be used as worry stones, displayed around the home or cast for divination (pp.30–37). Geodes of purple amethyst or yellow citrine with numerous tiny, glittering crystals packed inside are natural ornaments, as are large pieces of dendritic limestone as nature's own unique abstract paintings. Carvings of animals or statues appear in many different stones, from creamy soapstone to deep green verdite, and act as power symbols of qualities we wish to attract, such as the courage of the lion or the focus of the hawk.

How crystals are formed

What are minerals?

Minerals are the building blocks of rocks. Most rocks are composed of a mixture of minerals, but a few contain just one kind or species of mineral. For example, granite contains quartz, feldspar and mica.

Most minerals grow as crystals. What makes a crystal a crystal is that the atoms and molecules arrange themselves in a regular and repeated three-dimensional pattern in a process known as atomic bonding.

When one or more minerals are fused through atomic bonding, forming a crystal, it is the structure and quantity of each mineral that determine the final crystal variety. There are families (groups, classifications) of crystals that all have similar properties, and it may be just a minute difference in the amount of one or other mineral that changes its colour or crystalline structure. To identify crystals, we look at their mineral content and their structure (p.11).

Throughout this book you will see references to mineral names. Many of the elements of which they are composed are abundant in the Earth's crust, whilst others can be extremely rare.

Eight elements make up almost 99 per cent of the crust: oxygen, silicon, aluminium, iron, calcium, sodium, potassium and magnesium. Other elements include titanium, boron, beryllium, fluorine, carbon, chromium and manganese.

The composition of a crystal or mineral, if it does not form crystals, is shown by its chemical formula. For example, the chemical formula of iron pyrites shows that for each atom of iron there are two atoms of sulphur. However, occasionally, one element can appear as two minerals. The minerals graphite and diamond both consist of the element carbon. Graphite is soft, shiny grey and used in pencils, whereas diamond is a colourless, sparkling gem, the hardest of minerals. The difference is the different arrangement of carbon atoms in the two.

Most minerals and crystals are silicates, which means a combination of oxygen and silicon, the two most abundant elements in the crust. Other groups include oxides, carbonates, phosphates, borates, sulphides and halides.

What is a gemstone?

Natural processes create beautiful crystals that can be made into gems by cutting and faceting. To be a gemstone, a mineral species is defined as an object of beauty, rarity and durability. Sapphire, emerald, diamond and ruby are considered precious gemstones, but there are many semi-precious gemstones, such as beryl and topaz. There are 3,700 mineral species currently identified but very few are cut as gemstones.

Crystals in history

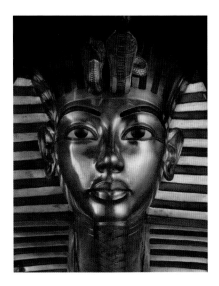

The oldest crystal so far discovered has been dated to 4.4 billion years old and has challenged previous thoughts as to how old the planet was when cooling formed the Earth's crust and life began on Earth. This crystal is one of several tiny zircon specimens extracted from mines in northwestern Australia.

The first known use of crystals by humans was during the early Stone Age, when flint served as tools and weapons. Obsidian was prized many centuries further on by the Mayans, producing a very sharp edge or point for knives and spears, and also forming magical mirrors to see into the future.

Baltic amber is amongst the oldest known amulets, dating back to 30,000 years ago, with discoveries of decorative amber beads in Britain that are more than 10,000 years old.

There is evidence of crystals being used in Ancient Egypt as a source of healing as early as 2000 BC. Lapis lazuli, considered good for eyesight as well as protective against the evil eye, was sacred to Nut the sky goddess, who arched over the whole world covered in stars.

Plato (427–347 BC), the Greek philosopher, claimed that stars and planets converted decayed and decaying material into the most perfect gemstones, which then came under the rule of those planets and stars. The Greek pharmacist Dioscorides described in the fifth volume of his *Materia Medica* over two hundred crystals and gems that could be used for healing and to banish fears.

Ancient China held quartz and nephrite jade in high regard from early times, and India used a variety of crystals in association with astrology as early as 400 BC, for example ruby with the sun and red coral with Mars.

Gems and crystals take their place in religious history throughout civilizations. They are frequently mentioned in the Bible, in particular in Exodus, where 12 were used in the breastplate of the first high priest, Aaron, brother of Moses, representing the 12 tribes of Israel; they also feature in the Koran, as well as other religious texts. Abraham was said in Judaeo-Christian myth to have worn a magnificent sapphire around his neck; when he died it rose to the sun.

Crystals were frequently used during the medieval period for their healing of particular ailments as well as for amulets of protection, and these traditions continue though less visibly. Since the 1960s crystals have enjoyed a huge revival of their use in healing and health therapies, as well as for use during psychic and spiritual development.

How crystals work

Many people find they are instinctively drawn to a particular rock, crystal or gemstone. Some discover that they can physically feel the crystal vibrating with energy; a tingling sensation is experienced whilst holding it. Others find that a crystal or combination of crystals makes them feel better or assists the healing of an ailment. This could be due to some degree to the placebo effect, the mind and the power of positive thinking healing the body. Alternatively, it could be possible that the crystal's energy vibration is having a physical effect on our bodies, balancing and realigning atoms within our own bodily make-up. Whatever the answer, and there are undoubtedly many more theories, we do know that thousands of years of history show a proven and undeniable track record of the powerful healing properties of crystals.

What do the scientists tell us?

Solids (as well as gas and liquid) are made up of atoms, molecules and/or ions. These particles possess energy. They move in all three states – gas, liquid or solid – but differently. In gas they freely and randomly move about and have no particular connection with other particles, and have no regular form. In liquid they are more compressed; they have a "relationship" with neighbouring particles, but still have a certain amount of freedom and space to move about easily – this gives liquid its "flow". Solids are made of particles that are closely compacted together in a regular formation. However, they do have a small amount of space around them, not enough to push or shove past a neighbouring particle, but just enough to allow for a tiny amount of movement, which can cause a vibration, albeit imperceptible to the average human being. Crystals do vibrate, as can all solids.

We all know that quartz has been used to power wristwatches. Quartz is piezoelectric. This means it is capable of generating an electrical charge when under stress. Quartz is commonly used today as a crystal oscillator – an electronic circuit utilizing the mechanical resonance of a vibrating piezoelectric crystal. So, we now know that crystals, at least some of them, have a definite measurable energy.

The huge energy input in the creation of crystals transforms into power for spirituality and healing. Deep within the earth's surface the melting pot of the unknown gives rise to crystals of immense beauty and powerful grounding energies. A collision of material from outer space leaves us its rare and wonderful offspring.

Holding one of these gifts of nature, allowing it to resonate with our own energies and letting it assist us in our healing efforts, whether for our own benefit or to heal another, makes it immediately evident that crystals undoubtedly have powers, even if these simply mean triggering our own inner healing abilities.

The art of using crystals in healing has developed over many centuries. One day, science may be able to give us a definitive answer as to how and why they work as a healing tool. Thousands, if not millions, of people have enjoyed the healing benefits of crystals over the centuries and continue to do so today. If they did not work, people would not continue to use them; perhaps this is a good enough reason to believe in what may seem to sceptics unbelievable.

Crystal shapes and terms

To identify crystals, we look at their mineral content and their structure.

Crystals form in a variety of ways and their resulting structures or "habits" can be grouped into six (or sometimes seven) groups or "systems". Crystals are grouped based on the symmetry (or lack of it) of their three-dimensional structures:

Cubic or isometric

This is the simplest and one of the most common crystal forms, where its three axes meet at 90° angles and all are the same length. There are six faces in parallel pairs. This crystal formation has total symmetry. Within the isometric system however, there are 14 more formations, increasing in complexity, built upon this simple structure, for example the dodecahedron and octahedron.

Examples: diamond, garnet and halite, among many others.

Tetragonal

Similar to the cubic (or isometric) system, having three axes that are at a 90° angle to each other. However, whilst the two horizontal axes are of the same length, the vertical axis is either longer or shorter. Again, there are various formations based on this system, many of which, to the untrained eye, have little resemblance to the simple shape illustrated here.

Examples: scapolite, vesuvianite and zircon.

Hexagonal

In this system there is an additional axis, which gives the crystal six sides. The three horizontal axes meet at 60° angles to each other and

the vertical axis is at a 90° angle to the horizontal axes. Included in the hexagonal system is a sub-system called the trigonal system.

Examples of hexagonal: aquamarine, beryl, emerald and zincite.

Examples of trigonal: quartz, ruby, sapphire and tiger's eye.

Orthorhombic

Here, like the isometric system, the three axes meet at a 90° angle to each other, but they are all different lengths.

Examples: chrysoberyl, peridot, sulphur and topaz.

Monoclinic

In this system all the axes have different lengths as with the orthorhombic system, but with two sides perpendicular and the base at an angle, forming a parallelogram.

Examples: azurite, gypsum, jadeite and malachite.

Triclinic

This crystal system has no symmetry. All axes are different lengths and there are no axial angles of 90°.

Examples: kyanite, labradorite, oligoclase and turquoise.

Finally we have amorphous materials. These are not minerals. They are non-crystalline materials but are usually included within the general subject of crystals and gems. Formed by a variety of natural processes such as volcanic activity or fossilization, they include amber, glass, jet, obsidian and opal.

Crystals and colours

The colour of a crystal is the most important and easiest way of identifying the right crystal for specific healing, personal empowerment or protection purposes. If a colour is hot like red, associated with life blood and fire, its action will be dynamic, fast and go straight to the root of a problem. In contrast, a green crystal represents gradual growth and nature, linked to slow but continuing increase in any area of life. The shade of a crystal will also offer clues: sparkling transparent clear quartz, reflecting sunlight, has different energies from cloudier shimmering white selenite that resembles moonlight.

Enhance the power of a crystal by burning a candle of a similar colour. It is a good idea to build up a collection of crystals in different shades and intensity of brightness within the same colour, such as soothing transparent purple amethyst and brighter opaque purple sugilite that is still gentle but faster acting. You can also use an antidote colour, for example a blue crystal if someone is very angry or a situation is too fast moving and red aura energy field powers are in overload.

The following are traditional colour associations. There is more information in the section on chakras about how different colours are linked to different energy centres and parts of the body (pp.21–23).

White colourless
Originality, new beginnings, clarity, inspiration, developing talents, ambitions, innovations of all kinds, breaking a run of bad luck, good health, vitality, spiritual development, contact with angels and spirit guides. Can be substituted for any other colour.

Healing powers: Whole-body healing, general health, integration of mind, body and soul, brain, neurological disorders, auto-immune system, acute pain relief.
Antidote: Grey.

White cloudy
(translucent) or opaque (solid colour)
Nurturing, slower new beginnings, especially after loss, slower unfolding potential, protection against negativity, mothers and babies, restoring hope, granting wishes and fulfilling dreams, discovering secrets (also grey), calling love from the past or from afar.
Healing powers: Hormones, fluid balance, fertility, pregnancy, gradual recovery from illness, depression or exhaustion, bone marrow, cells.
Antidote: Yellow.

Red
Movement, courage, positive change, strength, action, determination, assertiveness, power, sexual passion, male potency, taking the initiative, competitiveness, protecting loved ones, survival, overcoming obstacles.
Healing powers: Energy, muscles, low blood pressure, poor circulation, blood ailments especially anaemia, feet, hands, skeleton, reproductive organs, lifts depression.
Antidote: Blue.

Orange
Confidence, joy, creativity, female fertility (also red), abundance, independence, self-esteem and image, personal identity, independence, happiness, media, self-employment.

Healing powers: Ovaries, intestines, increases pulse rate, kidneys, bladder, menstruation, menopause, food allergies, arthritis, rheumatism, immune system, food-related addictions.

Antidote: Indigo.

Yellow

Logic, memory, determination, concentration, study, examinations, tests, new technology, clear communication (also blue), job changes, money-making ventures, speculation, short-distance home moves, short holidays, conventional healing, surgery, repelling envy, malice, spite, deception.

Healing powers: Lymphatic system, metabolism, blood sugar (also green and blue), digestion, liver, gall bladder, pancreas, spleen, nervous system, eczema, skin problems, nausea, sickness.

Antidote: Violet.

Green

Love, fidelity, commitment, beauty, horticulture, environment, healing through nature, crystal healing, gradual increase of health, wealth, ultimate luck bringer, winning competitions

Healing powers: Heart, lungs, respiratory system, infections and viruses, especially colds and influenza, high blood pressure (also blue), pollen and fur allergies, addictions and obsessions (also blue).

Antidote: None needed.

Blue

Idealism, leadership, justice, career, promotion, authority, long-distance travel and house moves, marriage, partnerships of all kinds, prosperity, business expansion, peace.

Healing powers: Thyroid gland, throat, fevers, inflammation, teeth, childhood rashes, cuts, bruises, scalds, burns, high blood pressure, eyesight, communication disorders.

Antidote: Red.

Purple

Spirituality, imagination, dreams, psychic powers, intuition, teaching, counselling, healing from higher sources such as angels, energy healing like Reiki, banishing past sorrow or present troublesome influences, psychic protection.

Healing powers: Headaches, migraines, scalp, ears, hair, sinusitis, easing childbirth, addictions, neuroses, phobias, nerve endings and connections, allergies to chemicals and modern living, hyperactivity, insomnia.

Antidote: Orange.

Pink

Reconciliation, mending quarrels, happy family relationships, friendship, gentleness, kindness, children and teenagers, girls entering puberty, young or new love and trust after betrayal.

Healing powers: Glands, ears, stress headaches, PMS, skin, ulcers, psychosomatic and stress-induced illnesses, insomnia, nightmares, family ills, babies, children, abuse and self hatred.

Antidote: Dark blue.

Brown

Practical matters, security, gradual accumulation of money, learning new skills in later years, home, property, financial institutions, officialdom (also blue), older people, animals, finding what is lost or stolen, perseverance, patience.

Healing powers: Feet, legs, bowels, hernia, anus, prostate, all chronic conditions, relief of chronic pain, growths, degenerative conditions in old age, panic attacks.

Antidote: Green.

Grey

Compromise, adaptability, ability to merge into the background, neutralizing unfriendly energies and malice, peace-making, keeping secrets, shielding from psychic attack.

Healing powers: Lesions, wounds, burns, tissue and nerve connections, obsessions and acute anxiety, persistent pain.

Antidote: Clear white.

Gold

Perfection, fulfilling great ambitions, urgent or large infusion of money and resources, long life, recognition and fame, recovery after major setback, healing when the prognosis is not good.

Healing powers: Nervous system, spine, skin, addictions, obsessions and compul-sions, minor miracles, remission, heals whole system.

Antidote: None needed.

Silver

Establishing natural fertility cycles, moon rituals, wishes and good luck, discovering the truth, intuition, female spirituality, unexpected money within a month, attracting love.

Healing powers: Cleanses toxins, visual disturbances, epilepsy, draws out illness or pain; nightmares, eases the passing of a loved one.

Antidote: None needed.

Black

Transformation, peaceful endings, grief, banishing sorrow, guilt and destructive influences, acceptance of what cannot be changed, working within restrictions, blocking a negative or harmful force, all psychic protection.

Healing powers: Pain relief, constipation, IBS, shields from side effects of invasive treatments such as x-rays or chemotherapy.

Antidote: Clear white.

Choosing crystals

Our ancestors looked on hillsides or seashores to find their crystals, and it is still possible to find beautiful pieces of natural jasper, quartz, agate, amber or jet. Working with crystals local to your area is especially magical and powerful.

However, in the modern world there is a huge array of beautifully polished crystals obtainable to anyone, wherever they live, by mail order or via the Internet.

If you do want to collect crystals for healing, personal empowerment or protection, there is no substitute for visiting a specialist crystal store and passing your hand over a tray of similar crystals to feel the one that is right for you. Equally, handling a series of crystal pendulums or gazing within different spheres will reveal which is your special crystal, perhaps not the most externally dazzling but which resonates with your energies.

At a mineral store, too, you can receive accurate advice about the composition of your crystal. Make a trip to a crystal store an occasion; if there are any specimens you do want to buy, email or telephone in advance to make sure they are in stock if you are travelling a long way.

Museums with a geological section are usually a good place to view and buy high-quality mineral specimens

You can also buy crystals by mail order using the images on the Internet site as a guide. If you choose a more personalized site, they will display different examples of the same mineral. Run your hand in front of the page on the screen or make a printout until you feel your palm tingling and know which is the one for you.

This is not so possible with tumblestones, but look on different sites until you find the particular shade or pattern. Real rock hound site owners are happy to correspond.

With crystals, size is not important: what matters is the composition of the crystal. Nor should you feel that you need spend a fortune. There are considerable price variations even in rarer crystals so shop around.

However, it is better to buy, for example, a small piece of natural citrine rather than a much larger, heat-treated specimen. Likewise, less colourful stones are preferable to ones that have been dyed. If in doubt check with images on a mineralogical site to see the raw product.

Cleansing your crystals

There are a number of ways you can cleanse crystals when you first acquire them, before and after a healing session or if you are using a crystal for good luck or protection. Some methods take a minute or two between healing sessions or if you are in a hurry. However, use one of the slower acting techniques at least monthly or more frequently if you are experiencing a lot of stress or negativity. Crystals kept around the home have heavy-duty use and if they appear dull or feel heavier than usual they may need extra cleansing.

Cleansing a crystal when you first obtain it or after use

Citrine and kyanite are the only two crystals that never need cleansing.

Water

Wash crystals under a running tap. This works for most tumblestones except those that are fragile, like selenite, or metallic but not for gems. Lapis lazuli and turquoise can also be damaged by prolonged water contact. Leave crystals to dry naturally or use a soft cloth kept only for your crystals.

Amethyst geodes

You only need a small amethyst geode, clusters of tiny amethysts embedded in a piece of rock. Stand individual crystals or points on the flat part of the geode. Alternatively make a circle of crystals around a large unpolished piece of amethyst. In either case the cleansing will take 24 hours. Citrine, kyanite and apophyllite can be kept with crystals to keep them fresh between more formal cleansing.

Using Mother Earth

Burying crystals in soil for 24 hours is a good way of resting an overworked crystal and is especially effective for crystal points. Choose a deep indoor or outdoor plant pot with a growing plant such as lavender, rose or rosemary or sage herbs. You do not need to bury the crystals very deep as long as they are completely covered. Brush the dirt off the crystal and, if necessary, wipe clean. This works best for unpolished natural stones. For a delicate crystal or gem, rest it on top of the soil in a small ceramic open dish.

Using fragrance

This is suitable for any crystal or gem. Circle a sagebrush or cedar smudge stick or a lemon-grass, pine, juniper, frankincense, lavender or rose incense stick in anti-clockwise spirals in the air over any crystals to be cleansed for three or four minutes. Leave the incense to burn through near the crystals unless you are in a hurry to use the crystals. The smudge or incense will also purify the room and any other healing tools or materials in it. This can be a good way of closing the energies at the end of the day or after you have finished a major healing session.

Using sound

Collect any crystals to be purified and over them ring either a hand bell nine times or strike a small singing bowl over them for about a minute until the sound ceases. Repeat twice more. Sound is an efficient cleanser if you have been working with any intense sorrow or healing when the official medical prognosis of the patient is not good.

Light

Sunlight is the best cleanser for vibrant, richly coloured or sparkling crystals and all gems like topaz or diamond. Leave the crystals from dawn, or when you wake, till noon. If the day is cloudy or it is winter, substitute a small gold-coloured or natural beeswax candle for sunlight and leave your crystals in a circle round the candle in a safe place until the candle burns through or goes out naturally. Aventurine, amethyst, aquamarine, beryl, kunzite, citrine, sapphires, fluorite, rose quartz and smoky quartz do not respond well to sunlight.

Crystals in transparent or translucent softer shades or that have clouds or inclusions within them tend to do better in moonlight, and rose quartz, moonstone, selenite and amethyst are very responsive to lunar energies. The night of the full moon is best of all for cleansing. Leave out all your crystals if possible in a sheltered place outdoors every month all night on full moon night or a night leading up to the full moon or on an indoor window ledge.

Salt

Though salt is a traditional cleansing method, salt is physically abrasive and can damage crystals. If you do use salt rather than immersing the crystals in salt, make three clockwise circles of salt around the crystals. Leave the crystals within the salt circles for about 12 hours, any time of the day or evening and night. Then scoop up the salt from the circles and dissolve the remaining salt in water. Tip the salt water away under a running tap. Alternatively rest the crystals in a ceramic or glass dish or plate on top of a large bowl of salt for 12 hours.

Infusions

This is a very traditional method. Sprinkle a crystal with a few drops of hyssop or rosemary infusion and then wipe it clean with a soft damp cloth. To make the infusion, add a teaspoon of dried hyssop or rosemary herb to a cup of boiling water, stir, cover, leave for ten minutes, then strain. Alternatively, use amethyst elixir: soak an amethyst in cold water for a few hours then remove the amethyst. If working with a gem or delicate crystal, you sprinkle the infusion round the crystal in circles or float it in a small sealed container in the water or infusion overnight. Dried herbs, particularly sage, thyme, rosemary and hyssop, are excellent cleansers and you can place a delicate crystal or gem in a tiny glass or ceramic dish in a larger bowl of herbs for 12 hours.

Crystal Healing

In the sections on chakras (pp.21–23), auras (pp.24–25) and crystal healing layouts (pp.27–28), I have suggested ways you can heal yourself, friends and family or begin more formal healing practices. But crystal healing can be much more spontaneous and informal, and even a beginner can heal themselves or loved ones.

If you have a headache, for example, you could choose a crystal that helps to tackle it, such as rose quartz. Alternatively, if you are not certain of the source of an illness or pain, use your intuition and a crystal pendulum to select the right crystal (see below).

Warm the crystal in your cupped hands to activate your own innate healing powers and press it gently against the point of discomfort or pain, or wherever instinctively your hand guides you. After a minute or two hold the crystal a few centimetres above the spot or, if a more general malaise, pass it slowly over the front of the whole body, feet to head. Healing will pass through to the back. In either case, allow your hand to move the crystal clockwise or anti-clockwise or both in turn, trusting your intuition to direct you. When you sense healing is complete, remove the crystal and cleanse it (p.16).

To choose the right crystal for any purpose

Spread out all the crystals you have in a circle.

At first, you may find it easier to use a crystal pendulum to give you external confirmation that the choice of crystals you sense is right, as you may not trust yourself. You can programme your pendulum, if you are unfamiliar with using one, by moving the pendulum in a clockwise circle and saying, "Let this movement always represent yes for me," and then circle the opposite way and say, "Let this represent no."

Hold your pendulum over each crystal in turn and ask it to give you the yes response if it is the right crystal to relieve the condition and/or to reduce any related pain or unpleasant symptoms.

You may find one crystal is enough, in which case it will give no response over all the others.

If you have two crystals, you can hold one in each hand and pass them in spirals at the same time over the body or relevant place.

If more than two crystals, then sit in the middle of the crystals, making what seems to be a logical crystal layout with them, for example three in a triangle or four in a square.

Making a crystal elixir

What are crystal elixirs?

Crystal-infused elixirs are empowered water that has been filled with the spiritual energy of crystals by soaking a crystal in the water. The infused water acts as a vehicle for vibrations of the crystal which interacts with the person's own energy field.

Making crystal elixirs

Direct infusion method

• A rounded tumbled crystal the size of an average coin will infuse a normal-sized glass or bottle of water. However, you can add two crystals, either of the same kind or with different properties, to quantities of water up to 500 or 600 ml.
• Work with three small crystals, the same kind or mixed, for up to 100 ml. Increase the number of crystals proportionately if you want even bigger quantities.
• Wash the crystal or crystals you intend to use in your elixir under running water.
• Place the crystal/s in the water using a spoon or tongs. Still mineral or distilled/filtered water is good; tap water is fine for animals, plants and around the home or your workspace.
• Cover the container or put the lid back on.
• Hold the sealed container between your hands, stating the purpose of the elixir. Ask that the elixir be "created for the greatest good and purest purpose to bring the healing/help/protection in the way that is right for the person/circumstances".
• Leave the covered water and crystals/in the refrigerator all night.
• Unless you have made a glass of crystal elixir to drink immediately, pour the water into suitable containers when you wake.
• Remove the crystal/s.

Crystal waters keep their full power for about 24 hours or three days in the refrigerator.

Indirect crystal elixir

Use this method for a very concentrated elixir with a larger number of the same crystal (up to seven crystals) or crystals with complementary powers, for extra protection, healing or if results seem slow.

It is also a suitable method to use with one or two crystals if you are concerned about soaking them directly in drinking water; also for safe elixirs with porous, natural (not tumblestones) or delicate crystals or gemstones, but not for toxic ones (see below).
• Half fill a large glass bowl.
• Hold the crystals or gem/s in your cupped hands over the water and stating the purpose of the elixir as in method 1.
• Place the crystal/s or gem/s in a small, fully sealable glass container.
• Close the lid and float the small container in the water in the bowl.
• Cover the bowl or put fine mesh across so it cannot become polluted.
• Leave the bowl for a full 24-hour cycle indoors near a window. Fill bottles with the water and use as needed.

Warning

For crystals listed as toxic, the only safe way to make elixirs is placing a glass or jug of water near a toxic crystal in a sealed container for 48 hours. Make sure the crystal does not come into contact with water or glass.

Crystals and chakras

Chakra power

Chakras are the driving force of our inner energy system, made up of seven main energy centres controlling different parts of the body and mind and energy channels that link them. Chakras are part of our inner spiritual body, described as whirling rainbow vortices of energy that empower the aura, the energy field around us that receives and transmits life force between us and the world.

To feel your chakras, hold the palm of the hand you do not write with over each area. If the chakra is in balance, you will sense a warm swirling sensation. If the sensation feels jarring or unpleasant, the chakra is probably overactive; if you feel nothing, it may be blocked. Each chakra has its own crystals, listed below and in each entry in the directory.

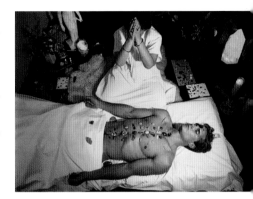

Chakra 1 Root or Base

Colours: Red, brown, grey and black.
Located in the perineum; can also heal through the thighs and minor related chakras in knees, ankles and soles of the feet.
Key qualities: Physical power, strength, immedi-ate action, the physical self, self-preservation.
Balanced: Good health, stamina, perseverance, developed instincts.
Unbalanced: Flight-or-fight reactions, excessive fear, anger or irritability; locked in routine, blunted instincts, stuck in past sorrows.
Rules: Legs, feet and skeleton including teeth (also Throat chakra), base of spine, bones and joints, bowels, large intestine, anus, prostate gland, testes, penis (also Sacral), basic cell structure.
.For balance, move crystals over chakras, anti-clockwise for woman and clockwise for men.

Chakra 2 Sacral or Hara

Colours: Orange, silver.
Located just below navel and womb.
Key qualities: Sexual desire, pleasure, self-esteem, self-image, independent judgment, connection with others through balanced emotions, ability to accept change.
Balanced: Acceptance of, and pleasure in, basic desires for love, approval, food, gut intuitions about others; balance between dependency and independence.
Unbalanced: Doubting own value, over-reliance on authority figures; orally focused addictions; easily unbalanced by stress.
Rules: Abdomen, lower back, female reproductive system (also Root), blood, all bodily fluids and hormones, menstrual and menopausal problems, kidneys, bladder, innermost child, the person we are inside. Move crystals over chakra clockwise for

a woman or anti-clockwise for a man to balance.

Chakra 3 Solar Plexus

Colours: Yellow.

Located around centre of upper stomach.

Key qualities: Integration of experiences; unfulfilled potential; rejection of what is not helpful; self-confidence; intellectual power.

Balanced: Learn from mistakes and take new opportunities; apply thought and determination rather than sentiment in decision-making.

Unbalanced: Feeling at the mercy of fate, restless, indecisive; alternatively workaholic tendencies and obsession with worldly success, compulsive behaviour.

Rules: Digestion, liver, spleen, gall bladder, stomach and small intestine, middle back, autonomic nerve system, metabolism.

Move crystals over chakra anti-clockwise (women) or clockwise (men) to balance.

Chakra 4 Heart

Colours: Green and pink

Located in the centre of the chest; also rules chakras in palms of the hands and fingertips and the minor thymus chakra in upper chest.

Key qualities: Compassion, social identity, appropriate roles for stages of life, self-love, love of and with others, healing powers via hands and arms, healing with herbs and nature, inner harmony, environmental awareness.

Balanced: Giving and receiving love equally; empathizing without drowning in responsibility;, valuing self as you are; appreciation of beauty.

Unbalanced: Over-emotional outbursts, sentimentality, possessiveness, jealousy,

allergies to plants and animals, panic attacks.

Rules: Upper back, rib cage, chest, lymph glands, skin, circulatory system, lower lungs, abdominal cavity, skin.

Move crystals chakras clockwise (women) and anti-clockwise (men).

Chakra 5 Throat

Colour: Sky or light blue.

Located round the base of the throat and the Adam's apple; also at the base of the brain at the back of your neck as minor Brain-stem chakra.

Key qualities: Clear communication with outer world and within self, creativity, ideas and ideals, concentration, ability to deal with the abstract, speaking the truth with kindness, cultural values, listening as well as talking, dreams and unconscious wisdom.

Balanced: Expression of creativity, personally or professionally, leadership qualities, justice, and fair-mindedness; activates the blueprint of your life plan, the ideal person you can become; healing through crystals.

Unbalanced: Communication difficulties, voice loss or stammering, outbursts of inappropriate language when frustrated, minor dishonesty or illusion, alternatively sarcasm, rigid ideas, prejudice.

Rules: Neck, voice mechanism, bronchial passages, jaw, mouth, eyes, passages to ears, Move crystals over these chakras in an anti-clockwise direction for women and clockwise for men.

Chakra 6 Brow or Third Eye

Colour: Indigo (bluish purple) or different shades of purple, tinged with silver.

Located just above the bridge of the nose.

Key qualities: Imagination, clairvoyant and healing powers, ability to communicate with angels and

Crystals and chakras

spirit guides, divergent or inspirational thinking; very active chakra in children.

Balanced: Ability to grasp the whole picture, evolved intuition and imagination, higher spiritual healing abilities through angels and guides.

Unbalanced: Problems accepting life as it is, dreaming life away, headaches and inability to cope with pressures of modern life.

Rules: Ears, visual clarity, sinuses, pituitary gland, face, both hemispheres of the brain, radiating into the central cavity of the brain. Move crystals over chakra clockwise (women) and anti-clockwise (men).

Chakra 7 Crown

Colours: Violet, rich purple merging into pure white and gold.

Located at top of head in the centre where the three main bones of the skull fuse at the anterior fontanelle to several centimetres above the head; merges with higher Soul Star chakra and cosmos.

Key qualities: Integration of mind, body and spirit, prophecy, ability to reach the top in any chosen field, nobility of spirit and actions, seeking perfection; universal energy healing powers such as Reiki.

Balanced: Wisdom, sense of being at home in body, but also able to see beyond the material world; fulfilment of major dreams and ambitions.

Unbalanced: Alienation from life, indefinable recurring mild flu-like illnesses: alternatively obsession with perfection and beauty, leading to inability to value real love or happiness.

Rules: Higher brain functions, skull, auto-immune system, neurological conditions, whole-body health and long life.

Move crystals over chakras anti-clockwise (women) or clockwise (men).

Assessing chakra health

Pass the hand you do not write with a few centimetres away from the body over the seven main chakras. You can assess and heal minor chakras via their ruling one. When assessing someone else's chakras you may feel the chakra sensations in your own body or see images in your mind.

Chakra healing with chakra crystals

You can heal blocked or over-active chakras with small round or oval chakra crystals, by holding the appropriate crystal in turn on the relevant area. The body will take the required amount of healing from each crystal through its chakra. But if any chakra was particularly blocked or in overdrive when you assessed it, you can give it extra input.

Chakra touch healing

Choose a crystal for each chakra; use the hand you write with to hold it. Place your seven chakra crystals on a table nearby. Ask for blessings and guidance from the angels and guides and hold each crystal over the appropriate chakra area in turn, from Root up to Crown. Gently massage the chakra in the direction suggested for each. This will slow down or unblock it. Trust your hand and the crystal. If you do not know the person well, you can hold each crystal a few centimetres away from the body, circling the crystal over the chakra. When you sense the energies are balanced, return the crystal to the table and continue with the next crystal until you have used all seven. If any area seems particularly troublesome, return to the affected chakra with the appropriate crystal. Pass your hands down either side of the body, a few centimetres away from it, to smooth the energies of the aura energy field surrounding the body. Cleanse your pendulum and crystals.

Crystals and the auras

The aura is a rainbow-coloured energy field that surrounds people, animals, plants, crystals and even places. People have an aura made up of seven bands of coloured light that encloses the individual in an ellipse, extending about an arm span all round. This can be seen externally by those with evolved clairvoyant sight and by children and with the inner eye by almost everyone, even with no psychic training.

Each of the seven aura layers is related to and is the same colour as one of the main seven chakras or inner energy centres (pp.21–23) and so shares the same crystals. Each aura layer, like its related chakra, is linked with specific body organs and functions; for everyday crystal work, aura crystals are mainly used for empowerment or protection of the energy field and to cleanse the aura of any negativity or stress clinging to it from everyday living; also from other people's energy fields that constantly interact in daily living.

You will need: a clear crystal pendulum or clear crystal point, 14 aura crystals, two in each of the main seven rainbow colours, one in a vibrant shade to energize a sluggish aura colour and one in a gentler tone to slow overactivity.

Assessing the aura by touch

Aura energies become progressively lighter the further away from the body they are. The innermost red aura layer follows the contours of the body most closely and feels the heaviest. The outermost spiritual violet/gold layer floats relatively formlessly at the exterior of the aura to join the white light of the cosmos. The easiest way to assess the intensity, shade and the smoothness or streakiness of the colours to gain information about the health, personality and current preoccupation of the person whose aura you are studying – or indeed your own aura – is through psychic touch, a natural psychic power we all possess called psychometry. This information reveals when the use of a specific aura crystal will help to restore balance in the aura and so in life.

From the experience of feeling your own aura when you have balanced it, detecting problems due to aura imbalance will become more obvious when you work with the auras of others.

As well as the seven colours of the rainbow that move outwards in order – red, orange, yellow, green, blue, indigo/purple and violet – gold, white and other

colours may appear in the aura. These minor colours are attached to the seven main rainbow bands and empowered by a minor chakra, for example pink is linked to the green Heart chakra. The rainbow and other minor colour crystals are listed in detail with the seven chakra colours on pages 21–23. The easiest place to assess the aura is round the head and shoulders and this is also the best place to empower and seal or protect the aura from stress or negativity. It may be helpful to cleanse and re-empower your aura weekly or more frequently after a bad day or a quarrel.

Working with the aura

• Begin with your own aura or a friend or close family member so you will feel relaxed and able to take your time.

• Take your clear crystal pendulum or a clear single or double terminated crystal point in the hand you write with; pass it through your aura in and out in a weaving movement starting above your head and going right down to your shoulders on either side, including your hair for the innermost layer will reach your scalp.

• Pass the pendulum slowly from a central position several centimetres above the Crown of your head in the air to find the outermost layer limits of your aura. It will be the same distance approximately all round down to your shoulders. Remember the whole aura can be up to an extended arm length from your scalp.

• You will sense in your fingertips a slight buzzing, almost an electric charge and rippling where the outer limits of the aura merge into the cosmos. The outermost limits are quite ethereal and not well defined so take your time. If you cannot detect anything, move your hand slowly inwards as your aura may be temporarily smaller if you are tired, unwell or have felt under pressure.

• Once located, follow this sparkly edge where the aura touches the cosmos round your head and shoulders.

• Once you have found the outermost layer, move your pendulum inwards in small spirals, assessing how the layer feels – vibrant, warm and flowing, or blocked and lifeless. Did it feel too powerful, like putting your hands in very fast-moving water? Did you detect any faded areas where the energy disappeared or a spot where the energy appeared tangled like a knot? These are places to return with your relevant aura crystal.

Crystals and the auras

25

Using crystals for meditation and relaxation

Choosing your crystal

There are many crystals listed throughout this book that are beneficial for mediation and relaxation. Pink rose quartz, purple amethyst, a creamy moonstone, white shimmering selenite or a dark smoky quartz is very effective, as is a purple amethyst pyramid or a clear quartz sphere with inclusions, markings and cloudy areas within. Crystal eggs are ideal for meditation. Alternatively, one of the patterned jaspers has pathways you can follow with your eye to lead you inwards to your mind.

Beginning to relax

Find yourself a quiet place where you will be undisturbed for between ten minutes and half an hour. Unplug the phone and, if you can, any electrical items in the room. Alternatively, you can choose a place outdoors near trees or fragrant flowers, with flowing water or a fountain to shut out everyday noises. Indoors, a CD of the rainforest, ocean sounds or meditation music will make a boundary between you and the everyday world.

• Sit comfortably, or if you prefer, lie down.

• Hold your chosen crystal and cup it in your hands so you make a connection.

• It may be easier at first to close your eyes. Breathe calmly and deeply for a few minutes and let any thoughts drift away.

• As you do this, notice any tension in your shoulders or back, and physically relax the muscles.

• Think only of the here and now, not what you should be doing. Bring your mind to the absolute present.

• If thoughts try to invade your open mind, acknowledge and release them, paying them no attention.

Entering the meditative state

• Slowly open your eyes and gaze into or at your crystal, still holding it in both hands.

• If the crystal is full of patterns or inclusions, let your mind wander without effort or analysis.

• Now slowly allow peace and happiness feelings to fill the empty space. Smile, but at no particular thought.

Returning to the world

When you are ready, allow yourself to come back into the everyday world around you. Do not rush. Gently stretch, get up and walk calmly back to where you need to be. When you get there, breathe slowly and deeply for a few seconds. Smile and feel the warmth of happiness and peace growing inside.

There are many meditation techniques that can follow on from this basic method. Experiment with different crystals (you can find suggestions within the crystal listings for different mediation purposes). Gradually you may start to see images during the relaxation/meditation, within the crystal or in your mind, not related to the everyday world but of other places and times and of your guardian angel and spirit guides. This will follow naturally.

A simple five-minute or ten-minute crystal meditation whenever you are feeling stressed, at the start of your working day or just before sleep will make all the difference to your health and well-being, even within a few weeks.

Creating a crystal layout

Nature has its own healing grids, some created by humans for ceremonial reasons like the ancient stone ship circles of Scandinavia or the Stonehenge circle in England.

By using a number of crystals arranged in a regular geometric formation, called a healing grid or layout, round a person, animal or photograph of a person or place, you can concentrate and focus healing energies in a way that is far more powerful than working with separate crystals. You can work with as few as three crystals to make a healing triangle or use as many crystals as you wish to create radiating stars or wheels with lines of crystals round a patient or a photograph. The crystals need only be small.

Using round crystals

You will need one set of six round pink rose quartz or purple amethyst crystals for bringing calm and removing pain and illness.

Also obtain a second set of either six round yellow citrines or six clear quartz round crystals for any energizing and health-restoring purpose. For removing illness and energizing at the same time, alternate three energizers with three calming pain-removers round the body.

Arrange the six crystals, one over the head and one under the feet as you or the patient lie down, and the others evenly on either side, at elbow and knee height a few centimetres away from the body. Add or substitute crystals from the ailments list to any grid you create. Some people use eight crystals, with three on each side at the shoulder, elbow and knee.

If you or family members suffer from ongoing or recurring conditions, you could purchase a set related to the problem, for example six orange carnelians for menstrual or fertility difficulties. For extra power, place an additional crystal on the body just above the navel of the patient. This should be a crystal related to the ailment or main problem.

Crystal points and crystal grids

As an alternative to rounded crystal grids and for more dynamic, faster healing, you can create your layout entirely from six or eight crystal points.

Use yellow citrine or clear quartz points for maximum power, and for gentler healing and protection amethyst or smoky quartz points – or mix and match. Again, set a round crystal in the centre on the body, related to the ailment.

Single-terminated crystals have a point at one end and the other rounded or square. In a crystal layout, set the point facing outwards to remove any illness, sorrow, addictions, blockages or pain and pointing inwards to energize and to bring healing from the cosmos, earth, angels and spirit guides.

Alternatively, position the points so every other one faces outwards to bring balanced energies. Double-terminated crystals, with a point at both ends, ensure a two-way energy flow (p.343).

For the simplest procedure, having set up the layout and asked the blessings of angels and guides, sit or lie within the crystal grid for between 15 and 20 minutes, playing soft music, and let nature do its work. Afterwards, remove in reverse order of setting, one by one.

The Master crystal

For additional power, join together the individual crystals with what is called a master crystal (p.343). In direct healing this is usually a pointed, thin, clear wand-like quartz crystal. Laser quartz wands are ideal slender crystals that taper inward from base to termination (point), as are the frosted lemurian seed crystal wands (p.380); alternatively, choose an ice-clear Tibetan quartz (p.334) or any beautiful crystal wand that vibrates with energy (p.364 for information about wands).

Touch each crystal with the master crystal wand once you have set the crystal in its grid position and then draw visualized lines of light between that crystal and the next crystal, moving clockwise as if the wand was a crayon of light, to join the grid crystals psychically together.

Join these visualized lines of light as though you were drawing them physically, starting and finishing at the highest point over the head, and then go round a second or even third time until you can feel the vibrating humming connection of the crystals.

Finally, touch the central crystal with the wand and picture straight rays of pulsating light radiating from it like the spokes of the wheel, connecting it to every other crystal.

For absent healing, if using a photo of an animal or person, you can set a larger master crystal cluster in the centre and visualize the rays of light forming a star or wheel with the central crystal as the hub, radiating out to each of the individual crystals in turn as the spokes.

Healing with a layout

You or the person to be healed should lie flat on cushions on the floor with the head slightly propped up on a cushion.

For a shorter treatment, arrange the crystals around a chair and ask the person being treated to hold the central crystal in their cupped hands or set it under the middle of the chair.

If the grid is on the floor, kneel to join the crystals with the visualized light rays using your wand.

If healing yourself, make the shape of crystals round you wider than your body so there is enough room to lie down on the floor within the grid comfortably once you have created the shape. You can sit up within the area as you create the crystal formation round you.

If the layout is round yourself, instead of physically joining the points you have the option of creating the shape in light over your head with the master wand as you sit or lie and visualize the figure of light expanding to enclose you.

Creating a
sacred space

Whether you own a few crystals or have a large collection, a special crystal space in your home will over the weeks spread harmonious, peaceful energies through your home, as well as adding a lightness and brightness.

If you have a family or share a house with friends, you may prefer to create a private crystal space in your bedroom or a quiet spot such as a conservatory where you can

enjoy meditation and carry out personal healing work. However, if you do have your crystal place in the main relaxing area, if you have children they too will be drawn to sit quietly when you light candles and to hold special crystals.

What you will need for your sacred crystal space:

• A white all-purpose candle that you can re-light. This can be lit whenever you or the family or friends sit in the crystal place or just for five minutes at the end of a busy day for a private quiet time.

• A central crystal focus, such as a crystal angel, a crystal sphere, pyramid, a cluster or a crystal geode, all of which integrate and transform energies.

• Fragrance, for example a pot of fragrant herbs, a flowering plant, and a bowl of dried rose petals or lavender heads, some floral incense or a fragrance oil and burner.

• Bowls of varied small crystals.

• A green-ink pen and white paper or an unlined notebook in case you receive any insights or messages as you hold or gaze into your crystals.

• A pointed clear-quartz pendulum. This will allow you to select a particular crystal that may be of help to you or a family member.

Your crystal time should be your special, mobile-free, time when you play your favourite music and let the worries of the day and the future flow into the crystals and the candle flame.

Crystals and Divination

F or thousands of years, people have used crystals for divination, to access, it was believed, information about the future from deities, angels and spirits.

Crystal spheres, the best-known form of crystallomancy or lithomancy (using smaller stones), became popular in Europe during the 1400s among ceremonial magicians and alchemists. Rituals were long and complex. One, in an anonymous manuscript from the 1500s, included complex purification rituals of practitioner and sphere and then invoking protection from God and the good angels: "First say one Paternoster, one Ave Maria, one Creed, then say, 'Vobiscum Spiritu [with or by your spirit], God of Abraham, God of Isaac, God Of Jacob, God of Elias … who hast given virtues to stones, woods and herbs, consecrate this stone'."

Smaller gems were also dropped into a bowl of water to interpret the patterns, ripples and sounds created.

In the modern world we can use crystal spheres, eggs, pendulums and small crystals to access our own inner wisdom and use our innate clairvoyant powers to see not a fixed future but the possibilities that may result from our taking particular actions.

The images we see within or on the surface of crystals are projected by our inner or psychic eye into the crystal, so that we may actually physically see them, though they may be symbolic. However, some people only ever see images in their mind, but with great accuracy stimulated by the reflective surface of the crystal.

Clairvoyant vision that is central to scrying, the word used for seeing or sensing images on or within reflective surfaces such as crystals, is not restricted by the limits of the physical eye range, and so using crystals we can see distant places or people far away or beings from other dimensions by a process called remote viewing. Clairvoyance also enables us to look into past worlds and past lives that may hold clues to present dilemmas, as well as forwards to the future not yet made.

Crystallomancy & lithomancy

There are two traditional ways of using crystals to get answers about our own lives and to help others to discover their best path ahead. You can scry (perceive reflective images within a crystal sphere) or cast a number of small crystals of different colours and types into a circle. The psychic knowledge for both methods will be manifest as a multi-sensory experience, in the form of words in our mind, impressions and feelings, as well as rich visual images in our mind or, in the case of the crystal sphere, within the depths of the ball.

Lithomancy

I have described the colour meanings of small crystals and their planetary associations in the next section so you can create your own lithomancy set using small tumblestones.

Though the crystal colours you pick apparently at random from a drawstring bag are one indication of meaning, what you feel and see as you hold each crystal you have picked is the best source of psychic information.

The method operates on the principle of psychokinesis, the natural but often undeveloped instinct whereby we are drawn by unconscious prompting, in this case to choose the right crystal without looking to give us the precise answer we need.

Creating your crystal casting area
• Draw a circle about a metre in diameter.
• You can create a temporary circle in sand, earth or with stones on grass.
• You can draw it on paper in pen or chalk.
• Sit or kneel facing the circle.

The closer to the centre crystals fall, the greater the significance, either in the immediate or long-term future, and they usually suggest independent action or an original solution. They can also indicate key strengths in your personality that will be of help to you right now.

Crystals that fall mid-way represent the need for co-operation with others and for working within the constraints imposed by the current situation. They indicate negotiations, whether to persuade others of your point of view or to adapt your plans or actions so that you can fulfil at least part of your plans.

Crystals near the edge talk of matters where right now fate or other people are steering the course: you may have to accept that there are obstacles or opposition you must overcome in order to move forward.

The area outside the circle
This represents the unexpected, what has not yet come into your life, both opportunities and new contacts or influences. Waiting a few weeks may be advantageous.

Casting the crystals
Ask a question. As you formulate it in your mind, place your power hand, the one you write with, in the bag of crystals.

Take as much time as you need until you select three crystals that feel right.

Hold these three crystals in your cupped hands over the centre of the circles and then let them fall onto the circles as you open your hands.

Interpreting the reading
Note first the position of the crystals and how they are divided between the circle areas. If they are divided between areas of

the circle then matters are complex and there may be unfinished business before you can move forward. Maybe there are different factors or approaches that need to be brought together.

Next, hold each crystal you cast on the cloth in turn in cupped hands in the order that feels right.

Close your eyes and allow impressions, images and words to form.

Then hold all three together and see what the combined energies tell you.

You can also select a single crystal each morning from your crystal bag without looking, to alert you to the mood of the day ahead and suggest the strengths you will need. Carry it as a talisman in a tiny purse.

Crystal spheres

The circle and sphere are symbols of completeness and it was believed that a crystal sphere was a microcosm of the wider universe. Therefore, within it could be captured information about past, present and future.

Scrying with crystals spheres is a much slower process than casting small crystals and involves stilling the mind and allowing in the quietness, so that images can form almost unbidden in your mind or in the ball.

Choosing a sphere

Use a clear quartz crystal sphere with cracks or inclusions. You will find the cracks inside necessary to allow your physical eye to have a focus so that your inner and intuitive eye can operate.

Reading your crystal ball

Work in natural sunlight or moonlight, or light a candle and work in golden or white

candlelight, so the light is reflected in the crystal sphere.

Either have a specific question in mind or allow your mind to go blank so that your unconscious wisdom provides information on areas of your life that are crucial to your well-being.

Sit for a minute or two, resting the sphere on the table with your hands enclosed over the ball. Keep your eyes closed while you tune in.

Keep a tape recorder running and talk softly as you receive impressions through your fingertips, either as images in your mind or words. Record also any feelings, such as joy or sorrow.

Now open your eyes and look at a point of light near the centre of the sphere. Then allow the cracks in the ball to create images.

The ball will reveal numerous symbols, such as animals, birds, butterflies, mountains and seas.

Finding three key images

As you see an image, ask yourself, if for example it is a bird, where is the bird: flying through the sky, in its nest, in a cage, trapped in a snare? Is it large or small, a predator or a songbird? Are its wings outstretched in flight, poised to swoop or is it beating against the bars of the cage?

You can see what a lot of information you are gaining just from that one image.

Repeat this twice more until you have three images.

In time the process will become more spontaneous and your pictures will appear quite easily.

The first of these three images refers to the past, the second to the present and the third to the future.

Divinatory meanings of crystal colours

The method I use for small crystal lithomancy uses 15 tumblestones (use precious stones like ruby in tumblestone form). This means you need 15 different crystals and a drawstring bag to keep them in. Choose crystals of a similar size, shape and smoothness. I have suggested stones that work well but you can substitute similar ones if you cannot get one of the recommended crystals, though they are common.

The first seven stones represent the seven traditional planetary signs that include the sun and moon and appear in a reading where an issue or question involves essential or major changes or personal opportunities. You have the choices.

Stone 1 The Sun

Colour: Orange or gold.
Crystal: Carnelian or sunstone.
The Sun rules Leo and Sunday.
Areas of concern: Innovation of all kinds and new beginnings, energy, joy, health, prosperity, spiritual awareness and self-confidence, development of unique talents, ambitions, wealth after hardship, good luck replacing bad fathers and authority figures of either sex.

Stone 2 The Moon

Colour: Silver or cloudy white. **Crystals**: Moonstone or selenite.
The Moon rules Cancer and Monday.
Areas of concern: Home and family matters, mothers, children and animals, fertility, protection, travelling, psychic powers, healing, secrets, sexuality, magic.

Stone 3 Mercury

Colour: Yellow.
Crystals: Citrine or yellow jasper
Mercury rules Gemini, Virgo and Wednesday.
Areas of concern: Money-making ventures, communication, adaptability, logic, learning, examinations and tests, mastering new technology, short-distance travel and short breaks, conventional methods of healing, especially surgery, business negotiations, overcoming debt, deceit, envy, malice and spite.

Stone 4 Venus

Colour: Green or pink.
Crystals: Jade or rose quartz.
Venus rules Taurus and Libra and Friday.
Areas of concern: Love, reconciliation, beauty, the arts, crafts, relationships, friendships, blossoming sexuality, the acquisition of beautiful possessions, slow but sure growth of prosperity (Venus rules all matters of growth), fertility and women's health matters, excessive and unwise love affairs, possessiveness.

Stone 5 Mars

Colour: Red.
Crystals: Red tiger's eye, red jasper.
Mars rules Aries and is the co-ruler of Scorpio and Tuesday.
Areas of concern: Courage, change, taking the initiative, independence and separateness from others, overcoming seemingly impossible odds, defeating opposition, improving health, strength and vitality, passion and the consummation of love.

Stone 6 Jupiter

Colour: Blue or turquoise.
Crystals: Chrysocolla or turquoise.
Jupiter rules Sagittarius, and is co-ruler of
Pisces and Thursday.
Areas of concern: Rapid and major increase
in money, career, power or joy, leadership,
creativity, idealism, justice and the law,
authority and altruism, marriage, permanent
relationships (business and personal), fidelity,
loyalty, male potency, excesses.

Stone 7: Saturn

Colour: Brown or grey.
Crystals: Smoky quartz or brown banded
agate.
Saturn rules Capricorn and is co-ruler of
Aquarius and Saturday.
Areas of concern: Property, financial and
official institutions, unfinished business,
endings that lead to beginnings, slow-moving
matters, limitations, overcoming obstacles that
are long-standing or need careful handling,
psychic protection, locating lost objects (also
animals and people), regaining self-control
over bad habits or emotions, older people.

The second seven stones target specific
areas of life and tend to refer to less
immediate issues or those where there may
need to be compromise. Other people and
life make more of the decisions.

Stone 8: Home, family and animals

Colour: Pink.
Crystals: Mangano calcite or pink opal.

Stone 9: Career

Colour: Blue.
Crystals: Lapis lazuli or blue aventurine.

Stone 10: Love

Colour: Red or green.
Crystals: Ruby or any green or red garnet.

Stone 11: Health

Colour: Clear white.
Crystals: Clear quartz crystal or clear
fluorite.

Stone 12 Luck

Colour: Green.
Crystals: Amazonite or green aventurine.

Stone 13: Money

Colour: Brown.
Crystals: Brown tiger's eye or chalcopyrite.

Stone 14: Travel

Colour: Green or blue.
Crystals: Sodalite or blue tiger's eye.

Stone 15: The mystery stone of what is as yet hidden

Colour: Purple or dark gold.
Crystals: Amethyst or rutilated quartz.

The crystal tarot

Choosing crystal substitutes for the 22 major tarot cards combines the living energy of associated crystals with the traditional meaning of tarot cards.

Holding each selected crystal triggers rich clairvoyant images in your mind to answer any question. This is because the crystals chosen from a drawstring bag without looking amplify your innate psychic powers, linking you to the cosmic source of hidden wisdom, past, present and future.

Tarot crystal meanings

The Fool: Clear crystal quartz.
Being true to yourself and new beginnings. Take a leap into the unknown.

The Magician: Carnelian.
Creativity, the entrepreneur. Passion; put ideas and plans into action now.

The High Priestess: Amethyst.
Healing and unique talents. Follow your own path: act independently.

The Empress: Jade.
Mothering and nurturing: care for yourself as well as others.

Emperor: Turquoise or blue howlite.
Fathering, ambitions. Be determined; take the lead.

The Hierophant: Lapis lazuli or sodalite.
Tradition, responsibility. Take the long-term view and play safe.

The Lovers: Rose quartz.
Love, romance and family: choices, reconciliation.

The Chariot: Rutilated quartz or laboradite.
Travel or chosen change: decide and steer your own destiny.

Justice: Banded agate.
Law, officialdom and injustice: stand by your principles.

The Hermit: Desert rose.
Withdrawal from conflict. Listen to your inner voice, not others.

The Wheel of Fortune: Green aventurine.
Good luck, changes in circumstance: turn challenges to opportunity.

Strength: Malachite.
Winning through difficulty; renewed energy. Persevere quietly.

The Hanged Man: Bloodstone/heliotrope.
Letting go; trust. Short-term sacrifice brings long-term gain.

Death: Apache tear or jet.
Endings leading to beginnings: grieve and move on. This never foretells actual death.

Temperance: Blue lace agate.
Harmony, moderation: a time to compromise.

The Devil: Red jasper.
Suppressed anger: express grievances and needs calmly.

The Tower: Leopardskin jasper or snakeskin agate.
Freedom from restrictions: temporary disruption brings liberation.

The Star: Citrine.
Recognition, achieving dreams. Develop hidden talents.

The Moon: Moonstone or selenite.
Fertility, intuition. Avoid illusion and deception.

The Sun: Amber.
Health, prosperity, happiness: life will be good.

Judgment: Hawk's eye/falcon's eye.
Criticism, guilt: accept mistakes and move forward.
The World: Aquamarine.
Relocation, long-distance travel: seize opportunities.

Reading your crystal tarot

• Place the 22 stones in a bag.
• Ask and concentrate on an issue or question.
• Put the hand you write with into the bag, touch each crystal and pull out the crystal that feels right.
• Read its tarot meaning and then hold it in cupped hands.

• Ask to be shown or told as pictures or words in your mind what is unknown to you about the circumstances surrounding the question and the true feelings of other people involved.
• Place each crystal on the table after reading it.
• Choose a second crystal to show the best action to take or change in direction needed.
• Do the same for the third crystal, asking the outcome of any action or change in direction within three months. For a longer-term outcome pick a fourth crystal for the 12 months ahead.

Spell casting with crystals

• Choose a crystal. Each crystal has its own magic meaning, carnelian for courage and confidence, amber for fertility, jade for gentle love, green aventurine for good luck.
• Use a white candle for attracting good things and a dark purple or blue one to bind or banish. If you are binding or want to remove something, you will also need a bowl of earth or sand.
• Light the candle to put the spell energies into motion and say what you seek to attract or want to remove from your life.
• Next, pass the crystal clockwise nine times in a circle above the candle flame, repeating as a short three- or four-word phrase what you want or do not want, three times. For instance, "Bring me money soon" or Stop "(name) from bullying me".
• Toss the crystal up and down rhythmically higher and higher between your hands as you repeat the three or four words louder

and faster and, if you wish, stamp your feet in time. For example, "Take away fear".
• When you feel that the spell power is at its height, call out "Take away fear NOW!" and give the crystal a final toss higher in the air.
• As fast as possible, blow out the candle still holding the crystal to attract your wish.
• To bind or banish something or someone, do not blow out the candle straight away but very rapidly transfer the crystal to the hand you do not write with.
• Push the flame end of the candle into a bowl of earth with the hand you write with.
• Carry the crystal as a symbol of what you wish to attract in the days ahead and repeat the closing words nine times in your mind, picturing the successful outcome.
• For binding and banishing, bury the crystal immediately after the spell. Alternatively, for banishing throw the crystal into running water or for binding keep it in a small lidded container in the coldest part of the freezer.

Using Crystals in Your Life

Although crystals are often associated with healing, they are useful in every aspect of daily life. In each individual crystal entry I have listed everyday purposes and how a crystal can be helpful in the workplace and for spiritual or psychic development. Some crystals are lucky for particular professions. For example, beautiful creamy flower jasper with its colourful swirls that look like flower petals helps florists, beauticians and hairdressers, as well as those who work in aromatherapy or with flower essences.

Flower jasper is also psychologically supportive if worn as jewellery by teenage girls who are teased about their weight or appearance if they do not fit in to the stick-thin model-girl image, to value themselves as they are. Being a strong jasper as well as beautiful, its energies encourage the teenager not be pressurized into crash diets or to become withdrawn and maybe eat more, so getting fat as a reaction to the teasing, which then increases.

The power of crystals involves both psychology and something less definable in the interaction of crystal with user. If we feel confident and powerful or beautiful, then that is the impression we give and so we attract positive reactions that reinforce the new, more open behaviour.

Flower jasper is also good for lightening up a workplace where co-workers are over-serious or have an inflated sense of their own importance. You turn up at work wearing a new flower jasper pendant and because it is so beautiful you feel good, you smile and are more open to those serious people you maybe have stopped communicating with. They respond to your smile, maybe comment on the pendant, and you discover they like flowers; someone comes in with a bunch the next day to brighten the office. That again excites comment and you discover a keen gardener in your midst who brings in some home-grown vegetables for everyone. Gradually, the real people emerge from behind the masks that may have been partly due to insecurity. Maybe you, too, seemed very serious without realizing it.

Crystals to use at home

Crystal grids and formations are one of the most powerful ways to energize and protect your home and, if you share your home, to draw everyone together in harmony.

Place small tumblestones in a variety of different colours, some sparkling, some gentle and some very dense and rich in colour, in glass or ceramic bowls; when not in use they will harmonize and energize your home automatically.

Encourage friends and family to add crystals from the bowls to create an impromptu large crystal wheel or mosaic pattern that is constantly changing with fresh input. Indeed, it can be very calming to work on the grid with family or a lover after a disagreement, as the act of creating new patterns as you talk psychologically eases the tensions.

Leave small crystal points near any crystal grid, and even children will enjoy tracing the patterns of the evolving shapes. Light candles round a grid and let your fingers trace the shapes in and out. Within minutes you will relax and often come up spontaneously with creative solutions to seemingly impossible situations.

In theory you can create a crystal grid or layout anywhere, round the edges of the room where the family gathers or round the outside of your home if you have land all around.

For long-term health, fidelity in love or fertility, make a grid of 13 moonstone crystals, with a circle of the 12 months round a bedroom and one in the centre under the bed, to represent the 13 moons.

Make a sodalite grid round a picture for an elderly relative to help maintain their health, mobility and mental faculties.

A lapis lazuli grid work wonders to bring calm and gentle loving communication if you have temperamental teenagers or a family of drama kings and queens, or where a child has Asperger's syndrome, autism or an attention-deficit condition.

Make a clear quartz grid to empower an item of clothing or school bag to protect a child from bullying, or one of turquoise for a partner who is a regular traveller. A grid around your laptop when not in use helps to preserve it from thieves, viruses and hackers. State your intention as you create the grid.

Keep a circle of amethyst and clear quartz in the kitchen on a work surface to empower and purify food or a jug or water for juice. Leave it in the circle for a few minutes; rose quartz is good for baby milk or food before healing to ease potential colic or feeding difficulties.

Crystals to use at work

Crystals help with work issues in all kinds of ways, for example opening doors to opportunity and making your efforts more favourably noticed so that you are not passed over for promotion or a pay rise. By carrying an empowered crystal or wearing it as jewellery you can ensure that you are protected from spite and malice, and create harmony in your workspace that will spread through the office.

Crystals for power in the office

Green chrysoprase makes finding work easier and is supportive when beginning a new job, a new venture or project.

Herkimer diamond gets you noticed in a positive way and brings prosperity through high achievement; also effective for stabilizing company finances.

Blue lapis lazuli, like turquoise, encourages you to aim high, and brings promotion and increasing success; good for striving for lasting recognition in your own field and, if you desire it, fame in a creative or public-performance-related area.

Turquoise also promotes leadership, assists relocation or regular travel associated with career and regaining a lost opportunity, as well as avoiding unwise investments.

Green and white tree agate brings increasing influence through networking and the gradual expansion of business; for

Internet-based businesses and family firms; for long-term projects and careers.

A clear crystal sphere or a glass paperweight near a telephone or on top of a computer or fax machine brings advantageous business calls and Internet connections, and when it catches the sunlight the quartz radiates fresh energies and clears stagnant ones.

Workplace defence

Green amazonite protects against others taking advantage of you and unfair practices at work, and attracts new customers and new orders to a business.

Blue calcite deters cliques, factions and workplace rivalries, and protects equipment, possessions and premises from theft and the workplace from dishonesty.

Purple fluorite reduces hyperactivity and unnecessary pressure in the workplace and workaholic tendencies; keeps you calm during interviews and assessments.

Have also within your work area a bowl of darker semi-transparent stones to filter out depressing comments or discouraging remarks that can sap energy and enthusiasm. Especially effective are amethyst, grey or brown smoky quartz, golden rutilated quartz, rainbow or gleaming black obsidian or its softer sister, semi-transparent Apache tear.

If there is a lot of hostility or gossip or you have a bullying boss or manager, set darker smoky quartz points or obsidian arrows (narrow arrow-shaped pieces of black obsidian, traditionally used in sevens) pointing outwards on your desk in a semi-circle to create a safe, calm zone within which you can operate.

Crystals to use for travel

Some of the associations are obvious, for example sea crystals such as ocean jasper protect travellers by water. Moonstone guards night travellers. Blue crystals tend to be associated with air travel and grey ones lower our visible presence, while pink may soften anger.

Travel crystals

The following are traditionally associated with safe and happy travel.

Aquamarine (greenish blue): For journeys by sea, fear of water or any long-haul travel that involves flying or driving long distances.

Aventurine (blue): To protect against travel disruption, the loss of luggage or personal items and for safety on holidays or weekends away.

Coral (blue): For safety on water, while swimming and against travel accidents or muggings.

Falcon or hawk's eye (blue) or any cat's eye crystal: Stops you getting lost while driving or being conned while travelling or on holiday, and keeps backpackers or gap-year students safe.

Jade (green): Helps prevent you falling ill while on holiday; for travelling alone and to protect children and animals from straying or being hurt while on a journey.

Kunzite (lilac): Guards against road rage and becoming stressed while driving in traffic or on long journeys; also calms difficult passengers in your vehicle.

Malachite (green and black): For protection if travelling by air or on congested motorways; removes fears of flying and helps jet lag; helps things to go smoothly for business travel.

Moonstones (any colour): Protect travellers, especially those who travel at night and on or over sea. Frequent travellers should keep one in the glove compartment for safe night driving and as protection against road rage.

Ocean jasper (often green with orbs): A lucky charm for all who sail or go fishing, to keep them and their boats safe, and for travellers by sea.

Onyx or Apache tear (black): For safety while travelling at night and against terrorism anywhere. Apache tear that you can see though if held up to light is good for lowering your profile in dangerous places.

Sodalite (dark blue): Prevents fears of flying; hold sodalite on take-off and landing; also counteracts jet lag.

Tiger's eye (red): Protects your money and credit cards and you against being threatened by drunks or drug addicts.

Tree agate (green and white): For car travel especially on fast, heavily polluted or crowded roads, for daily train journeys; helps to combat fatigue on long journeys.

Turquoise (turquoise): For guarding you and your possessions against theft, loss or attack while travelling, for preventing accidents, especially falls; protects pets in transit.

Smoky Quartz (grey or brown): Guards vehicles from theft or mechanical breakdown and the driver against road rage.

Crystals to use for love

Love crystals work by opening our personal energy field or aura to attract and to keep love in our lives and encourage fidelity. They can make a relationship more resistant to outside influences that may seek to come between a couple or family, and help to keep a couple together when times get hard. They also act as a bond and reminder of what was good, if problems cause a temporary parting or one of the partners to be unfaithful.

Soft pink crystals like rose quartz are excellent for new love, particularly after a former breakdown in trust, while deeper green crystals such as jade or emerald represent fidelity. Strong deep red gems, like garnet or ruby, bring love that endures in good times and bad.

Gems such as sapphires and diamonds form traditional pledges of love and are often given as rings at a time of betrothal or major commitment.

Copper, the metal of Venus, goddess of love, as well as the more usual silver, the romantic metal of the moon, and gold, signifying love forever belonging to the sun, are also exchanged as relationship rings. Rare platinum is the ultimate twin-soul, "our love will last forever and a day" metal.

Orange crystals like carnelian are fertility and potency symbols and, as with moonstone or selenite, are linked with conceiving an infant.

Love crystals include:

Amber (orange): Protects against negative outside influences and interference; calls a twin soul.

Amethyst (purple): Heals love quarrels, removing obsessions or addictions by one partner that cause problems in the relationship.

Angelite (blue): Reduces anger in a partner or unnecessary quarrels if both of you have strong opinions; also encourages spiritual love.

Aquamarine (pale blue): Calls a lover back; helps two people with different lifestyles to live together in harmony, reduces the effects of sensitive issues that cause quarrels.

Carnelian (orange and red): Rekindles passion that has faded in an otherwise loving relationship; for the consummation of love.

Chrysoprase (green): Opens you to new love, for overcoming a period of stagnation or a sticking point in a relationship.

Jade (green): The crystal of new love, gentle love and fidelity and love in later life; increases trustworthiness in love.

Jasper (red): Passion helps a woman to overcome a jealous love rival or unfair opposition to a relationship.

Jet (black): Overcomes sorrow for lost love and broken relationships so that you can start again.

Moonstone (cream and shimmering): First or new love and the increase of passion; good if love must be kept a secret.

Moss agate (deep green with pale blue or white inclusions): The gradual increase of love and commitment, love growing from friendship or with a work colleague.

Rose quartz (pink): To attract gentle love and romance or to call a lover to you.

Crystals to use for good luck and prosperity

Prosperity and good-luck crystals are like magnets, working, it would seem, by sending out abundance-attracting energies into the cosmos from your personal aura or psychic energy field amplified through the crystal.

Money crystals

Agate, banded: For restoring financial stability after losses or necessary expenditure, for financial increase or good investments for the future; for any dealings with the bank.

Amethyst (purple): For reducing tendency to over-spend, gambling addictions or unwise investments.

Chalcopyrite (gold): Connected with the powers of growth in business or prospects and resulting prosperity.

Citrine (sparkling yellow): For all fast money ventures and especially for commercial success. Citrine can be kept in a purse or wallet to attract money and stop excessive outflow; also for financial speculation.

Jet (black): In home and business, jet stabilizes finances, for overcoming debt problems; property deals.

For good luck

Not surprisingly, some prosperity stones double up as prosperity crystals, but they also bring good luck in other areas of life. The more you use and carry a good-luck stone, the luckier it becomes. Most green crystals carry a good-fortune-bringing element, as do some golden-yellow stones.

Amazonite (green): For games of chance, competitions and good luck in any financial venture, good with green aventurine.

Apache Gold (gold and black): A natural luck bringer through finding things, whether an antique in your attic that is more valuable than you realize or an unexpected bargain at a garage sale or market.

Aventurine (green): Known as the gambler's stone, the luckiest of all stones in games of chance and competitions, it is often placed in charm bags for good fortune and money.

Jade (green): Both nephrite and jadeite, are luck bringers in every way and reverse bad fortune; bring luck in love and better health.

Green chrysoprase: A luck charm for employment: rub one over the envelope of any applications or letters you send out relating to employment, money or new business; hold over a computer mouse before applying online for a new job or business finance.

Chrysoberyl (yellow or yellowish green): In its cat's eye form chrysoberyl brings luck in the shape of sudden opportunities and unexpected lucky breaks of which you can take advantage.

Anniversary gemstones

Official list of the American Gem Trade Association.

1st	Gold
2nd	Garnet
3rd	Cultured or natural pearls
4th	Blue topaz *(top)*
5th	Sapphire
6th	Amethyst *(second from top)*
7th	Onyx
8th	Tourmaline
9th	Lapis lazuli *(third from top)*
10th	Diamond
11th	Turquoise
12th	Jade
13th	Citrine
14th	Opal
15th	Ruby
16th	Peridot
17th	Carnelian or watches
18th	Cat's eye
19th	Aquamarine
20th	Emerald *(second from bottom)*
21st	Iolite
22nd	Spinel
23rd	Imperial topaz
24th	Tanzanite
25th	Silver
30th	Cultured or natural pearl
35th	Emerald
40th	Ruby
45th	Sapphire *(bottom right)*
50th	Gold
55th	Alexandrite
60th	Diamond

Crystals and children

Children have a natural affinity with crystals. They love handling rocks and crystals and finding natural quartzes on the beach or by rivers. Sometimes they instantly love particular crystals, such as shining gold chalcopyrite or moonstone or selenite that shimmers in moonlight.

Allow them to handle crystals, supervised of course if they are young, from as early an age as possible; let them choose tumblestones instead of sweets or plastic toys so they can build up their own collection in a drawstring bag. This can bring hours of pleasure, and children are remarkably good at putting their hand in the bag and accurately identifying purely by feel the different crystals. What is more, an amethyst geode with its glittering purple jewels is better than any plastic fairy-tale castle.

Certain crystals are beneficial to children, for example lapis lazuli, sodalite or soft blue agate calms hyperactive children. Some, like rose quartz or amethyst, soothe little ones who have trouble sleeping or who have a fear of the dark. Particular crystals that are extra child-friendly include any of the soft chalcedony stones, blue and pink Andean opals, blue lace agate and angel stones such as blue celestite and angelite that a child can hold to feel their guardian angel near when they are afraid or lonely.

Crystal balls and crystal pyramids stimulate a child's imagination. You can weave bedtime stories using these crystals and encourage your children to create their own magical crystalline worlds to bring restful sleep and beautiful dreams.

Older children, particularly those who are studying for exams, may find natural yellow citrine or any of the yellow stones an aid to concentration and memory. Red jasper held before school gives them the strength to resist teasing or bullying. It may or may not be the actual crystal itself having a direct effect, but the power of suggestion associated with it. Either way, the crystal is a physical three-dimensional object your child can hold, treasure and use as a confidence-trigger.

Your birth and month crystals

Crystals correspond with birth months and zodiac signs. You can wear them any time you need strength, protection, luck, healing or just want to be noticed in a positive way. Each zodiacal and birth month crystal is associated with an angel. Your own crystal can connect you with the energies of your angel. In Chinese astrology each animal has a special crystal.

Month	Crystal	Zodiac	Date	Crystal	Chinese	Crystal	Zodiac/Month Angels	Crystal
Jan	Garnet	Capricorn	22 Dec –21 Jan	Onyx	Rat	Emerald, garnet, moonstone, pearl	Cambiel for January and Aquarius	Amethyst, blue bace agate, zircon
Feb	Amethyst	Aquarius	22 Jan – 21 Feb	Turquoise	Ox	Amber, aquamarine, lapis lazuli, topaz	Barakiel for February and Piscies	Bloodstone, coral, fluorite
March	Aquamarine, bloodstone	Pisces	22 Feb – 21 March	Moonstone	Tiger	Alexandrite ruby Sapphire	Machidiel for March and Aries	Carnelian, diamond
April	Diamond, rock crystal	Aries	22 March –20 April	Diamond	Rabbit	Emerald, jade pearl, sapphire	Asmodel for April and Taurus	Emerald, rose quartz
May	Chrysoprase, emerald	Taurus	21 April – 21 May	Emerald	Dragon	Agate, amethyst, garnet, ruby	Ambriel for May and Gemini	Citrine, white sapphire
June	Alexandrite, moonstone, pearl	Gemini	22 May – 21 June	Agate	Snake	Black pearl, opal	Muriel for June and Cancer	Moonstone, pearl
July	Red-brown carnelian, ruby	Cancer	22 June –22 July	Pearl	Horse	Topaz, turquoise	Verchiel for July and Leo	Clear quartz crystal, golden topaz
Aug	Peridot, sardonyx	Leo	23 July – 22 Aug	Ruby	Sheep	Emerald, opal, red coral, sapphire	Hamaliel for August and Virgo	Jade, moss agate, opal, peridot
Sept	Lapis lazuli, sapphire	Virgo	23 Aug – 22 Sept	Sapphire	Monkey	Opal, peridot, tiger's eye, white coral	Zuriel for September and Libra	Blue sapphire, blue topaz,
Oct	Opal, pink tourmaline	Libra	23 Sept – 23 Oct	Opal	Rooster	Citrine, topaz	Bariel for October and Scorpio	Aqua aura, black pearl, coral, obsidian
Nov	Citrine, topaz	Scorpio	24 Oct – 21 Nov	Sardonyx	Dog	Diamond, lapis lazuli, ruby	Adnachiel for November & Sagittarius	Ruby, turquoise
Dec	Blue topaz, turquoise zircon	Sagittarius	22 Nov –21 Dec	Topaz	Pig	Lavender jade, moonstone, ruby	Anael for December and Capricorn	Garnet, ruby, titanium aura

The Crystal Directory

The 500 crystals are listed according to colour so that you can easily find ones for particular purposes. I have given the overall colour meanings on pages 12–14 for fast reference. Colour is a good indication of the basic nature of the crystal. For example red crystals and gems tend to be far more dynamic in their energies and faster acting than more reflective purple ones and more concerned with action in the material world. But within the colour groupings there are variations that partly depend on the chemical composition and partly on the shade or vibrancy of the individual crystal. So opaque red jasper is far more instantly proactive than transparent deep rich ruby that releases more enduring power, particularly in love in bad times and good. Yet both are equally protective. Red aventurine though, like the other two a guardian of the home and family with its more muted red shades, relies more on a slower build up and release of power if, for example, you are a shift worker and have to stay awake all night or to help you whistle and sing through a gathering where there are difficult relatives intent on causing trouble.

Each entry is divided into categories so you can check its individual properties, beginning with the kind of crystal and its physical healing properties. Each crystal is also suitable for different kinds of emotional healing. There are also listings for everyday uses, the workplace and magical significance which include working with a crystal for spiritual or psychic development, in meditation or in rituals and empowerments. Each is related to a specific chakra and on pages 21–23 is information about the different energy centres of the body and how related chakra crystals can be used to bring the body and mind into harmony. There are particular fragrances you can burn as you meditate or relax. The sign of the zodiac associated with the crystal is given as you may find your personal star sign crystals are particularly lucky or empowering. The divinatory meaning explains the essential quality of the crystal. Finally, a short section of information describes what makes that crystal unique and also sometimes the myths and beliefs that have grown up around it to explain those special qualities.

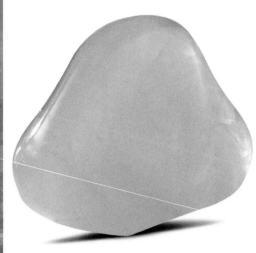

Type: Silicon dioxide; quartz with manganese impurities, sometimes embedded in the form of tiny needles, sometimes crafted or found naturally as heart shapes.

Colours: Pink, translucent, glowing and semitransparent to clear pale or deeper pink; untumbled ice-like chunks of rose quartz are also sold.

Availability: Common.

Physical benefits: Said to help circulation; healing mothers after a complicated birth; skin especially stress-related conditions; headaches, fertility, genitals, female reproductive system, healthy flow of fluids.

Emotional healing: Depression, especially post-natal depression, forgiving mistakes, your own as well as others; the best crystal for overcoming abuse of all kinds.

Chakra: Heart.

Rose Quartz

Candle colour: Pink. **Fragrances:** Lemon balm, lemon verbena, lilac, lily of the valley, rose and ylang ylang.
Practical uses: The best sleep crystal for adults and children: prevents nightmares, night terrors and will bring beautiful dreams. It helps children not to be afraid of the dark. **Workplace:** Use a large piece of unpolished rose quartz in your workspace for ongoing protection against unwanted intrusion and gossip. **Magical significance:** Rose quartz is the crystal of reconciliation. Cast a tiny one in flowing water at sunset and speak words you would like to say. **Divinatory meaning:** Forgive yourself for past mistakes and do not accept the blame others try to offload for their inadequacies. If someone cannot accept the real you, that is their problem. **Zodiac:** Taurus.
Empowerment: I will be as kind to myself as I am to others.

Adonis, lover of the Greek goddess Aphrodite (Venus in Roman lore), was attacked by Ares, god of war, in the form of a boar. Aphrodite rushed to save him and caught herself on a briar bush. Their mingled blood stained the white quartz pink. A mothering crystal, especially if you have lost your own mother, it helps you to mother yourself. It is also a good stone to hold on your stomach during pregnancy to create a bond with your unborn

child. Take the crystal into hospital with you so it is near the baby after birth and will soothe it in the days after birth. Called the heart stone, rose quartz may have been a love token as early as 600 BC.

Twin rose quartz hearts are often placed with pink roses on a private love altar and pink candles are lit nightly to call love or to strengthen a relationship. Alternatively, enclose a photo of yourself and a lover with tiny rose quartz crystals in a heart shape.

Rose Quartz

Type: Layers of platinum (p.181), silver (p.178) and gold bonded to the surface of a quartz crystal.

Colours: Raspberry rose, metallic sheen.

Availability: One of the rarer bonded quartzes.

Physical benefits: May ease onset of puberty in girls and early menstrual difficulties; problems with teenage pregnancy, especially if the young woman is unsupported by a partner; bacterial and fungal infections; internal and external parasites; endocrine system; sciatica, lower back and slipped discs.

Emotional healing: Restores a sense of self-worth and positive body image, particularly among younger women who have suffered from dieting and exercise obsessions to look like celebrities or have been teased about obesity and so have continued to put on weight.

Chakra: Heart.

Rose Aura Quartz

Candle colour: Deep pink. **Fragrances:** Cherry blossom, hibiscus, mimosa, peach, vanilla. **Practical uses:** Rose aura quartz prevents outflow of energies from individuals and the home, whether money, health or good fortune, at the same time drawing in what is of lasting value. **Workplace:** For writers of romantic fiction and all who work with fragrances, beauty products or services, modelling, hairstyling and fashion to combine necessary profit with a desire to make people feel better by maximizing their own unique charisma rather than striving for a stereotype. **Magical significance:** Rose aura is a crystal of transformation, especially transformation in love; hold it every morning and again before going out socially or online to a dating site to flood your aura energy field with 'love find me' or 'love stay with me' vibes. Set rose aura that you have held or worn as jewellery on a picture of a lost or estranged love and allow the power of love to cross the miles to the place your ex-love lives and make telepathic connection. **Divinatory meaning:** Do not let anyone shake your self-image by unfair criticism intended to make you feel bad about yourself and not to help. **Zodiac:** Taurus. **Empowerment:** I am of beauty and of worth.

Rose aura quartz is very similar to ruby aura which is also bonded with platinum and gold or silver and gold and can be fuchsia pink. Bonded or fused quartzes are created by a modern version of alchemy whereby quartz is heated to very high temperatures and the purified metal is added in a vacuum which permanently fuses it to the surface of the quartz. Since gold, silver and platinum are powerful healers when combined

with quartz, the energy of rose aura is uplifting but not overwhelming. Rose is an aura quartz often favoured by younger women, while a number of older women prefer the slightly richer ruby aura.

Keep a rose-aura cluster, or its big sister ruby aura, if you or loved ones have been suffering from cyclical colds or a virus that never fully clears or your children are constantly coming home from school with tummy bugs or head lice, to break the pattern.

Rose Aura Quartz

Type: Silicon dioxide, quartz, often mottled in its natural form. Clear strawberry quartz is artificially produced and is more brittle.

Colours: Natural strawberry quartz is mid pink, sometimes with lighter pink markings, but can occasionally be found in a more translucent strawberry colour, particularly when polished.

Availability: Relatively rare.

Physical benefits: Thought to relieve skin rashes, rosacea, scars and lesions, bruises, food allergies and heart irregularities, excessive blushing and stammering.

Emotional healing: Increases self-esteem in people who come from over-critical families, or have a controlling partner, so making breaking out of the cycle of self-doubt easier.

Chakra: Heart.

Strawberry Quartz

Candle colour: Pink. **Fragrances:** Apple blossom, chamomile, clary sage, mimosa, strawberry. **Practical uses:** A good stone for parents with large families to enjoy the happy special moments and not become overwhelmed by responsibility; for any family where one parent is frequently away. Take on spontaneous days out or weekend trips, especially in summer, to experience joy and a sense of blessing. **Workplace:** For all who work in daycare facilities or care for small children as a childminder, babysitter, au pair or nanny; helpful while training in any form of childcare, child psychology or as a child protection officer if you have little previous personal experience of children, to tune into their unspoken needs. **Magical significance:** Natural strawberry quartz is a gentle introduction to past-life work/out-of-body travel. Hold one in the hand you do not write with while listening to hypnotherapy or psychic journeying CDs or if you visit a professional hypnotherapist or past-lives therapist. **Divinatory meaning:** Time for self-nurturing after a prolonged period of being there for everyone; close the door unless someone is offering you help. **Zodiac:** Taurus. **Empowerment:** I need not fill every moment with activity.

A very gentle comforting crystal associated in modern goddess traditions with the mother goddess. Good for children who hate being away from the home, to feel safe and open to new experiences; keep a strawberry quartz with your baby's travel cot for sleeping in unfamiliar places and rub it over your baby or young child's favourite toy to reassure them if they are staying overnight without a parent.

A bowl of strawberry quartz tumblestones makes temporary accommodation more home-like; carry one on long journeys by plane, bus or train to relax you into sleep and to make hotel rooms feel welcoming if you stay in them a lot on business. A calming stone at home or work to keep a sense of perspective if others create dramas; use with children if they witness an argument or unpleasant event or if someone is nasty to them. Keep strawberry quartz near soft fruits to preserve their freshness and enhance their nutritional powers.

Pink Danburite

Type: Calcium borosilicate.

Colours: Very pale pink and like clear glass (also occasionally yellow, grey or brown).

Availability: Rarer than colourless danburite in all its forms.

Physical benefits: May help heart, heart bypasses and transplants, muscle weakness; even gentler than clear danburite for the young, infirm and very sick animals or birds, particularly small or injured ones; may ease allergies or illnesses aggravated by the fast pace of the world.

Emotional healing: For victim support, for hijack victims or those who have witnessed major disasters

Chakra: Heart.

Candle colour: Deep pink. **Fragrances:** Apple blossom, rose, violet. **Practical uses:** Pink danburite helps children to play together. **Workplace:** The crystal for aid agency and hospice staff. **Magical significance:** Pink danburite calls healing powers from angelic sources; a piece of pink danburite can form the centre of a healing grid with six pieces put around a patient's head, feet, elbows and knees. **Divinatory meaning:** You discover why a friend has been out of touch and may need to offer support. **Zodiac:** Taurus and Aquarius. **Empowerment:** Gentleness is not a sign of weakness but inner strength.

Danburite is a recent discovery, cast up by Mother Earth about the time of the Industrial Revolution to heal ills caused by the frantic pace of modernity; the rarer pink danburite addresses the needs of people forgotten by society; good for anyone caught up in an acrimonious divorce, to feel safe. Danburite clusters in an infant's room soothe a little one who wakes crying in the night. If a partner or close family member is manipulating in the name of love, pink danburite, worn over a period, will bring quiet strength to break free.

Pink Tourmaline

Type: Silicate.

Colours: Pink.

Availability: Common.

Physical benefits: Seen as helpful for spinal problems or injuries, the nervous system, neuralgia and migraines; for boys and girls approaching puberty; all gynaecological conditions, especially to regularize the menstrual cycle to make conception easier.

Emotional healing: Reduces fear and panic; the best crystal for teenage pregnancy and to assist in bonding with baby.

Chakra: Heart and Crown.

Candle colour: Pink. **Fragrances:** Anise, lavender. **Practical uses:** Protective during travel. **Workplace:** A crystal that should be owned by all healers to heal their own problems. **Magical significance:** Use pink tourmaline to call back an estranged lover. Pass through the smoke of a rose incense stick, scatter rose petals round it and sprinkle with rose water, saying, "Through sky, by earth, through fire and across water, may my love not hesitate to return". **Divinatory meaning:** Your inner child is in need of healing – take time to have fun. **Zodiac:** Taurus and Scorpio. **Empowerment:** I welcome and offer love and kindness.

Egyptian legend speaks of how tourmaline made its journey from the centre of the Earth and passed over a rainbow, taking with it all of the colours as its own. Pink came from the early-morning sky. Pink tourmaline is one of the most loving stones, comforting children who have suffered from any form of abuse. Take off pink tourmaline jewellery at night so its shielding effects do not shut out positive energies as well as negative if worn 24/7.

Type: Chalcedony.

Colours: Pink, cream and grey bands, sometimes with an eye formation that is considered especially lucky.

Availability: Common.

Physical benefits: Thought to relieve sexual dysfunctions in both sexes; stomach problems; be good for stimulating the body's immune system; help the body to absorb oxygen so benefiting the circulation; be good for the skin; see as treating underlying causes of illness rather than the symptoms.

Emotional healing: A crystal of infinite possibility and hope, so balancing depression, fears such as agoraphobia and panic attacks, especially in crowded places; helps all who have suffered loss and still grieve; relieves emotional blocks to fertility.

Chakra: Sacral.

Botswana Agate

Candle colour: Pink. **Fragrances:** Cherry blossom, geranium, magnolia, peach. **Practical uses:** Suggests practical solutions rather than dwelling on the reasons for a situation or assigning blame. **Workplace:** Good for all creative projects and ventures, injecting logic, the reality principle and focus to bring plans into actuality. **Magical significance:** The eye formation is both protective and lucky. Hold one while choosing lucky numbers for a lottery or picking a horse for a race. **Divinatory meaning:** You may have to look for an opportunity or solution, but it has been there all the time, hidden by looking too far away and missing the obvious. **Zodiac:** Gemini. **Empowerment:** I call fertility and blessings into my life.

Named after the land in Africa where it was discovered, Botswana agate is called the sunset stone because it retains sunlight which can comfort people through dark, lonely nights.

Traditionally the crystals were used in African fertility ceremonies to encourage potency and the conception of strong, healthy offspring. This crystal is ideal for children and teenagers who are very sensitive and easily hurt by teasing, and will help them to find like-minded friends; good if you are joining a dating agency or embarking on online dating to find someone with whom you are spiritually in tune and who shares your dreams.

The very best crystal if you are trying to give up smoking (drink the elixir, water in which the crystal has been soaked for a few hours, first thing in the morning). A protective crystal for all who work with fire and to protect the home against fires. It also balances the aura and all your inner spiritual energies.

Morganite

Type: Cyclosilicate/beryl.

Colours: Pink, rose-lilac, peach, orange or pinkish yellow, sometimes with colour banding; coloured by manganese and lithium.

Availability: Obtainable from specialist jewellers, crystal stores and online.

Physical benefits: May help larynx, tongue, thyroid gland, lungs and nervous system, heart palpitations and irregularities, burns and scalds.

Emotional healing: For girls entering puberty who do not have a mother and for younger women struggling with eating disorders.

Chakra: Heart.

Candle colour: Pink. **Fragrances:** Apple blossom, lavender, lemon balm, rose. **Practical uses:** Take a piece to meetings with bank managers and accountants to ensure you get fair treatment. **Workplace:** Good for new businesses to get a foothold in the market. **Magical significance:** Opens communication with your guardian angel. **Divinatory meaning:** You may feel a very small fish in a very big pool, but you can speak out over a matter where you know you are right. **Zodiac:** Taurus. **Empowerment:** I will be slow to prejudge others.

Called after its discoverer, John Pierpont Morgan, an American banker who was interested in magic and mineralogy, morganite has been adopted as a stone for lawyers to ensure fairness. Use morganite to show compassion towards people who may have mental or emotional problems or physical illnesses that make them hostile towards others. Wearing morganite for a few weeks helps express emotional needs you have considered unreasonable, but which are necessary to make a relationship more equal. Also known as Pink Beryl.

Sugilite

Type: Cyclosilicate.

Colours: Pale pink to lavender pink to magenta/fuchsia, streaked with black.

Availability: Pink rarer than in violet/purple.

Physical benefits: Believed to assist with pain relief (especially from burns), infections and viruses, functioning of the adrenal, pineal and pituitary glands, dyslexia, autism, Asperger's syndrome.

Emotional healing: Pink sugilite is a stone of the heart and resolves inner hurt; helpful for adopted children rejected by birth-parents they have tracked down.

Chakra: Heart.

Candle colour: Bright pink. **Fragrances:** Carnation, hyacinth, lilac, orchid. **Practical uses:** An excellent crystal for children who find socializing hard. **Workplace:** A stone for all involved in the care of vulnerable people; brings compassion to carers. **Magical significance:** An excellent amulet for children who recall past lives; keeps the balance between everyday practicalities and the spiritual world. **Divinatory meaning:** Loving someone does not mean you have to accept their bad moods. **Zodiac:** Taurus and Aquarius. **Empowerment:** I will not get stuck in self-pity.

Though not considered as valuable as its rich-purple-coloured sister, pink sugilite, especially in magenta or fuchsia shades, is a powerful love crystal; avoids sentimentality in relationships while encouraging commitment in good times and bad. Wear pink sugilite jewellery to attract a kindred spirit; also encourages a love of life and belief in inherent goodness of people. Pink sugilite brings balance to food-related addictions and compulsions such as excessive alcohol, gambling or out-of-control spending.

Type: Calcium carbonate, manganese-rich calcite.

Colours: Very pale pink with white inclusions/bands, occasionally mauve.

Availability: Common.

Physical benefits: Thought to absorb pain; called the Reiki stone because it transmits universal life-force healing energy to wherever in the body it is needed most; seen as especially beneficial for the health of premature babies and their mothers.

Emotional healing: Heals abuse of all kinds; helps mothers to bond with babies, particularly after a difficult birth and for post-natal depression; for mothers, fathers and grandparents who lose a child at any age.

Chakra: Heart.

Mangano Calcite

Candle colour: Pale pink. **Fragrances:** Apple, cherry blossom, lily, sweetgrass. **Practical uses:** Give to children who become afraid of their imaginary friend, are scared about ghosts or when they have been temporarily separated from one or both parents for whatever reason; use to console also very young animals who have been rejected or abandoned by their mother: wrap a tumblestone in a cloth beneath their sleeping place. **Workplace:** For all foster and adoptive parents, for teachers and assistants who work with disabled or abused children, child-protection officers, all medical staff who care for premature babies and sick children, children's hospice workers and children's aid workers. **Magical significance:** Mangano calcite, along with angelite and seraphinite, is one of the best crystals for making connections with angels. Mangano calcite links you to your guardian angel and healing angels who assist your own healing powers to develop. **Divinatory meaning:** Be gentle with yourself and avoid for now anyone who criticizes you or makes you feel bad about yourself. **Zodiac:** Cancer. **Empowerment:** I will allow myself to be vulnerable.

Mangano calcite is the gentlest of the calcites, even softer in energies than its closest sister, pink calcite. It is a female-friendly stone but can be used equally by men who are feeling vulnerable and lost and who need to cherish themselves.

An ideal first crystal for a baby or child; reassuring if they experience separation anxiety when their mother or main carer has to be absent for even for a short time, leaving them at daycare or with a child-minder, relative or friend. Yet it does have the power to break down resistance; if you are estranged from your mother or father, grandparents or adult child, set mangano calcite with their picture.

Every Friday, burn a pale pink candle next to the crystal, asking that the bond will be restored.

Type: Silicate/spodumene with manganese that causes the pink colour.

Colours: Pink, striated, sometimes with streaks of white.

Availability: Relatively common.

Physical benefits: May help with hormone-linked migraines, the reproductive system in women, puberty in girls, PMS, menstrual problems, skin rashes caused by allergies to chemicals, circulation, heart, neuralgia, epilepsy, reducing the after-effects of anaesthesia.

Emotional healing: Relieves heartache and heartbreak, particularly in women; for human and animal mothers who find it hard to care for their young, for whatever reason, or who need mothering themselves; good for sleepless babies and over-active small children.

Chakra: Heart.

Pink Kunzite

Candle colour: Pink. **Fragrances:** Clary sage, magnolia, mimosa, rose, violet. **Practical uses:** Called in its pink shades the woman's stone, kunzite jewellery is an ideal gift for a girl entering puberty to help her love her changing body; for a young or first-time mother and for all single mothers, to feel supported. **Workplace:** A protective stone for men and women if your manager or employer brings personal dislikes or problems to work or uses flirtation or sexual bullying as a power ploy. **Magical significance:** Pink kunzite has been adopted by people in conventional religions and in alternative forms of spirituality to symbolize reverence for a Mother Goddess as the creatrix and nurturer of all living things. **Divinatory meaning:** What a relative or very close friend is saying is not what they mean; ask gentle but probing questions to discover the real problem. **Zodiac:** Pisces and Taurus. **Empowerment:** I am sensitive to my own hidden needs.

Kunzite was named in 1902 after the New York jeweller and gemstone specialist George Frederick Kunz, who catalogued and described its properties.

Wear pink kunzite if you want to find new love after a relationship breakdown or to marry someone you love but who is scared to commit to a relationship. The colour of kunzite, like tourmaline, can vary according to the angle from which you look at it.

This phenomenon is called pleochroism or multi-colouredness, and in a cut stone the best colour is seen from above. Genuine, as opposed to heat-treated, kunzite is generally quite pale in colour, and natural darker shades are therefore the most valuable.

Pink kunzite will calm examination, interview or assessment nerves and is useful in situations where you cannot show irritation, for example with sleepless babies or a very sick or confused relative. Both lilac and pink kunzite are effective for bi-polar disorder, the pink kind being especially helpful for women and younger people.

Type: Manganese inosilicate/chain silicate.

Colours: Pink or salmon pink, usually with varying size of black patches, veins and inclusions; less frequently red or red-brown.

Availability: Common.

Physical benefits: May be useful for insect bites, stings and allergic reactions caused by them, cuts, wounds, scar tissue, birth marks, ulcers, skin conditions caused by allergies, auto-immune conditions, emphysema and other chronic or progressive lung conditions.

Emotional healing: Heals the mental scars of a violent lover; relieves the pain of unrequited love; reduces obsession for a love who would never leave an existing relationship.

Chakra: Heart.

Rhodonite

Candle colour: Rose pink. **Fragrances:** Geranium, hyacinth, magnolia, narcissus, rose. **Practical uses:** Keep rhodonite where you and the family relax, to calm children, teenagers and adults who have trouble controlling their temper, swear or constantly argue; put one by your computer to protect you or family members online. **Workplace:** If colleagues regularly get under your skin or belittle you in front of others, wear rhodonite jewellery to increase your self-assurance and overcome feelings of inadequacy. **Magical significance:** Rhodonite transmits positive energies to service personnel, peacekeepers and aid workers and those who live in war zones. Set a dish of tumbled rhodonites or a rhodonite egg next to a picture of a war-torn area or a loved one serving overseas. Light a rose pink candle, name those you wish to bless and let the candle burn out. **Divinatory meaning:** Examine your innermost emotions to determine what you really want to be and who, if anyone, you want to be with. **Zodiac:** Aries. **Empowerment:** Love is stronger than anger.

In Feng Shui, rhodonite balances yin and yang energies. Even if you know nothing about Feng Shui, hold a rhodonite massage wand in the hand you write with and walk around the home.

If energies are too yang, you will feel a surge in your fingers, if too yin, the wand will feel lifeless; if energies are balanced, you will experience tranquillity. In places that are too yang, set a rhodonite that is more black than pink, and the

reverse if an area feels too yin. Rhodonite is an excellent crystal for many disabilities, since it assists the healing of speech and hearing and is a very balancing crystal for children and adults with

Down's syndrome or cerebral palsy. As a crystal of gentle love, wear rhodonite jewellery after a break-up to learn to love yourself and value your own company, to avoid dashing into the first relationship on offer and maybe repeating old mistakes.

Bustamite

Type: Manganese calcium silicate, sometimes found with sugilite (p.55); related to rhodonite (p.58).

Colours: Predominantly pale to deep pink; also red, brownish red and red-brown.

Availability: Obtainable from specialist crystal stores and online.

Physical benefits: May benefit the heart, especially irregular heartbeat, circulation, keep older people mobile for longer, said to help tumours, melanomas.

Emotional healing: Bustamite is a stone of gentle courage, to give the strength to leave an abusive situation.

Chakra: Heart and Brow.

Candle colour: Pink. **Fragrances:** Almond blossom, honey, neroli, peach. **Practical uses:** Bustamite encourages relaxation and makes any home or workplace welcoming. **Workplace:** For chiropractors and physiotherapists. **Magical significance:** Brings sanctity to weddings, baby blessings and natural burials. **Divinatory meaning:** Care for your health and comfort and ask for any support you need, though you may find this hard if you are normally self-sufficient. **Zodiac:** Taurus. **Empowerment:** I can put down roots wherever I am.

This beautiful and sometimes brightly coloured stone brings connections with others and eases relationships at work with people who may be unapproachable; softens cantankerous family members. Bustamite also increases love in new relationships; grounding for anyone who dreams of the perfect lover and gives up at the first hurdle when a relationship runs into difficulties. Bustamite spreads gentle healing and unblocks the entire body's energy centres if placed on a patient's heart or in the centre of the chest or breasts where the Heart chakra energy centre lies.

Andean Opal

Type: Hydrated silicon dioxide, common opal, displaying no iridescence.

Colours: Pink, pastel-coloured with a pearl-like sheen.

Availability: Relatively rare as true Andean opal (some are dyed substitutes).

Physical benefits: May aid healing children, animals, very old or chronically sick people; skin irritation, dryness or cracking, eyesight, heart, low blood sugar, diabetes.

Emotional healing: Very calming for children and adults who are overwhelmed by life; also for timid animals you have adopted.

Chakra: Heart.

Candle colour: Pink. **Fragrances:** Almond, apple blossom, hibiscus, peach, pink rose. **Practical uses:** If you find it hard to accept help or gifts and are one of life's fixers, pink opal allows you to be more receptive to others' generosity. **Workplace:** Wear pink opal if your mind is always jumping ahead to the next task. **Magical significance:** Pink opal is sacred to Pachamama, the Peruvian earth mother, and considered one of her gifts; wear or carry pink opal to attract love. **Divinatory meaning:** Kindness from a stranger will restore your faith in life. **Zodiac:** Taurus. **Empowerment:** To accept help is not weakness.

A stone to help all to trust again after an attack, abuse or betrayal. Wear pink opal to bring joy into your life if your emotions have become very flat or you feel disengaged. Pink opal is a tough-love stone when life is hard, to prevent sentiment standing in the way of speaking honestly to others if someone is abusing your trust. Good for a reality check in relationships or where one partner is very needy and stifling, to gain emotional completeness and not constantly drag up the past as a weapon to avoid dealing with present issues.

Type: Halide/sodium chloride.

Colours: Pink, white or colourless (the pure form); also orange, yellow and red.

Availability: Common.

Physical benefits: Can help lungs, allergies that cause respiratory problems, sinus, migraines, infections, absorption of necessary minerals, colon and lower intestinal tract disorders, water retention, chemical imbalances in the body or mind.

Emotional healing: Pink halite heals emotional problems connected with relationships, especially those where past ties and responsibilities that still exist prevent a totally fresh start.

Chakra: Heart and Sacral.

Halite/Rock Salt

Candle colour: Pink. **Fragrances:** Acacia, anise, eucalyptus, rose, tea tree. **Practical uses:** Halite is often carved into lamps. The lamps are used as natural air ionizers to counteract the positive (harmful) ions caused by pollution. Place a halite lamp anywhere in the home to improve air quality. It benefits anyone suffering from pet allergies, hay fever or asthma, reduces emissions from electrical items and induces health and well-being. **Workplace:** Orange or red halite is a natural attracter of success and encourages the successful completion of business and contracts and the positive resolution of unsatisfactory situations through renegotiation of basics. **Magical significance:** Leave a small piece of white halite to dissolve undisturbed in cold water; then put a little of the solution to dry out in a warm place; concave or hopper crystals gradually form to act as a talisman of transformation and new beginnings; pour the rest away under running water to increase the flow of good luck and prosperity. **Divinatory meaning:** You may be tempted to abandon a situation but it is better to build on the good aspects that can be salvaged. **Zodiac:** Cancer and Pisces. **Empowerment:** I value and preserve what I have built up.

Halite, isometric crystals formed after the evaporation of briny waters from seas or salt lakes, is a fast-growing crystal; some specimens sold can be less than a year old. It can also, however, be found as deposits in ancient bedrock where once, long, long ago, there were seas or salt lakes.

Some halite is accumulated over millions of years in salt caverns deep underground in the Himalayas and this, in orange or pink, is the kind most often used in rock-salt lamps. Because

of its association with salt, a sacred substance regarded throughout history as a symbol of life, halite is considered to be magical; sometimes large halite clusters enclose treasures that have been dropped into a salt lake as offerings.

Pink halite, particularly, is a crystal for surviving setbacks and starting over again, whether in a relationship, a new love, a new career or a new location, so that you can build on past knowledge. Halite also lifts the bad moods of others.

Type: Cryptocrystalline quartz.

Colours: Varying shades of creamy pink. The pink is due to the presence of manganese or ferrous oxide impurities.

Availability: Relatively common.

Physical benefits: Believed to ease ageing, skin and wrinkles, baby and childhood illnesses, especially rashes; pregnancy problems especially high blood pressure and pre-eclampsia; be good for first-time mothers, those who have had surgical intervention and post-natal problems such as scars and stitches not healing or mastitis that makes breast-feeding difficult.

Emotional healing: Helps with compulsions and obsessions, including obsessive compulsive disorder, fear of germs; also post-natal depression, abuse especially in early childhood.

Chakra: Heart.

Pink Chalcedony

Candle colour: Pink. **Fragrances:** Clary sage, neroli, rose, rosewood, violet. **Practical uses:** Pink chalcedony is known as the baby stone, given to a woman before birth and set on a mother's stomach to increase communication between mother and unborn child. After the birth it was traditionally kept beneath the baby's crib to keep away all harm. **Workplace:** A stone for healing bitterness, rifts or jealousy caused by unfair promotion or sackings, unjust decisions made by impersonal corporate bodies and for softening an over-competitive cut-throat atmosphere. **Magical significance:** A fun stone for releasing or rediscovering your inner child and to connect with the wonders and magic of the natural world, if you have become very serious or weighed down by responsibility. **Divinatory meaning:** A sudden reminder from the past may temporarily shake you, but you can now deal with buried feelings positively once and for all. **Zodiac:** Taurus and Pisces. **Empowerment:** I release old sorrows to make room for joy.

A crystal of kindness, a bowl of tumbled pink chalcedony mixed with mangano calcite and rose quartz tumblestones will bring gentleness, beauty, harmony, homeliness and affection to any apartment or house, no matter how soulless or unlovely its location.

Works wonders as a gift for children who are jealous of a new family member, especially a new baby; helps animal mothers to care for their young and not reject the litter. Pink chalcedony is a goddess stone, worn sometimes as a cross by women who seek the feminine aspects of God within conventional religion.

Pink chalcedony worn as jewellery will ease heartache and heartbreak; buy a piece for yourself to mark your new beginning.

Pink chalcedony is believed to help children to get over a family separation crisis such as divorce, estrangement or bereavement; good, too, for a girl entering womanhood to help her love her changing body, especially if puberty comes early.

Stilbite

Type: Zeolite, tectosilicate, belonging to the zoisite family.

Colours: Pink, creamy pink, peach, white.

Availability: Relatively common in clusters, rarer as tumblestones.

Physical benefits: Thought to be helpful to rid the system of toxins, for laryngitis, sun burn, melanomas, skin pigmentation problems, torn or strained ligaments, bad reaction to prescription drugs.

Emotional healing: Gentle healing of all emotional issues, particularly those connected with a relationship breakdown when a partner walked out or the death or disappearance of a parent, especially the mother.

Chakra: Heart, Throat and Crown.

Candle colour: Pink or white. **Fragrances**: Geranium, honeysuckle. **Practical uses**: Place under a pillow or near your bed to help with sleep problems, helpful if you suffer frequent nightmares. **Workplace**: Use stilbite to assist when clear thinking is required. **Magical significance**: Focus on this crystal by the light of a geranium-scented candle to achieve communication with your guardian angel. **Divinatory meaning**: A period of creativity is indicated that may involve loved ones, working on a long desired and overdue home improvement. **Zodiac**: Aries and Taurus. **Empowerment**: I am filled with love for life.

Stilbite is often found joined to apophyllite crystals (p.142). When it is teamed up with any other crystals, it amplifies their energies and is itself increased in healing powers. If you are new to pursuing psychic development, stilbite guides the subconscious mind to higher realms, where deep insights and intuitive thoughts can be accessed. Place by your child's bedside when you tell a bedtime story to gather loving energies together if you have been working late.

Pink Dolomite

Type: Calcium magnesium carbonate.

Colours: Pink, beige with pink hue, milky white, colourless, reddish white, brownish white, yellowish white, grey.

Availability: Relatively common.

Physical benefits: May help bones, teeth, nails, skin, PMS, menopause, female reproductive problems, urogenital system, asthma, emphysema, kidney stones, lungs, colds, coughs, adrenal glands, heart, circulation, cramps, insomnia.

Emotional healing: Prevents energy from draining away on useless causes or emotionally demanding problems.

Chakra: Heart.

Candle colour: White. **Fragrances**: Almond blossom, apple blossom, hyacinth, lilac, pink roses. **Practical uses**: Attracts resources for voluntary initiatives and fund-raising; supportive for all who care for people with disabilities, serious illnesses or behavioural difficulties. **Magical significance**: A stone of small miracles, when logic has failed; hold dolomite on your navel, focus on the pleasure or relief of the attainment of your need and it may soon happen. **Workplace**: Use for any creative venture or if an original approach is needed. **Divinatory meaning**: Everything happens for a reason so look at a delay as a chance to reassess and maybe adjust your future direction. **Zodiac**: Taurus. **Empowerment**: I do not fear being alone

Discovered in the late 1790s in the Swiss Alps by an explorer called Dolomieu, the crystal is believed in popular folklore to be stored treasure belonging to gnomes who have forgotten to collect it. For this reason dolomite in the home will attract enough for your needs and a little more. An anti-jealousy stone, dolomite soothes those who are insecure about love to enjoy a relationship without fearing constant betrayal or continually testing their partner's loyalty.

Type: Manganese carbonate.

Colours: Rose pink with white or paler pink banding, though it can vary from lighter pink to those that are almost red, opaque; may also contain orange, yellow and brown. Very occasionally transparent pink crystals can be found.

Availability: Common.

Physical benefits: Thought to assist with circulation, heart problems, blood pressure, breathing problems, asthma, stress-related migraines.

Emotional healing: Opens up any blocked psychic chakra energy centres so light and power can flow upwards into the body from the earth via the Root chakra, from the natural world through the Heart chakra and downwards through the Crown from the cosmos; this can help movement towards the future after a period of doubt; assists the expression of love towards others without fear of rejection.

Chakra: Heart/Solar Plexus.

Rhodochrosite

Candle colour: Bright pink. **Fragrances**: Anise, cedarwood, copal, hibiscus, lime, orange, rose, rosewood. **Practical uses**: Helpful for children starting childcare, school, a new school or college so that they will find friends easily and settle in; good also as a gift to new family members such as step-children. **Workplace**: Use in a small workplace setting for friendly non-emotional working relationships where the atmosphere can get claustrophobic and personalities intrude on professional matters. **Magical significance**: A calling-back crystal, whether a lost lover, a friend or family member who has broken off all contact or a missing pet. **Divinatory meaning**: Open your heart to the possibility of love and friendship and you may find that it was close to you or present all the time; choose old valued friends rather than exciting new acquaintances. **Zodiac**: Sagittarius. **Empowerment**: I allow love to flow freely to and from my heart and most of all to love and value myself.

Rhodochrosite is known as the Inca rose because the Native Americans who lived in the Andes believed the crystal contained the blood of great ancestral rulers. If you are seeking news or contact with a lost friend, relative or former love, place the crystal next to a photograph of the missing person: putting your hands on either side of the crystal, say the person's name softly three times and ask the person to send news or get in touch.

Visualize the person where and when you last were together.

Leave the crystal next to the photograph. For an animal, put the crystal where the pet used to love sitting and sleeping.

Holding the crystal between your cupped hands, imagine the animal back in its place. Leave the crystal on a surface near the exit or entrance the animal used most.

Rhodochrosite also increases mind-to-mind or telepathic links between you and your family and animals; very good for new or first-time mothers to learn to trust their maternal instincts.

Type: Fluorine aluminium silicate; occurs naturally but many pink topaz are dyed.

Colours: From pale to brighter or reddish pink.

Availability: Rare in untreated form.

Physical benefits: Thought to reduce toxins in body, breasts and ovaries; may help with early-onset puberty, menopause, HRT treatment, inflammation, burns and fevers, fertility and fertility treatments, insomnia, asthma, haemmorrages, heart palpitations and weakness, hearing and earache.

Emotional healing: For creating a balance between being open to love and trust, and not giving or loving too much or over-identifying with your partner or would-be lover.

Chakra: Heart.

Pink Topaz

Candle colour: Pink. **Fragrances:** Almond blossom, apple blossom, cherry blossom, magnolia, rose. **Practical uses:** Wear pink topaz to take away sadness if you have been hurt in love and have shut yourself away from other people to gradually heal your sorrow; a wonderful gift to a first love from her lover on a birthday or first anniversary to signify affection that will continue to grow through the months and years. **Workplace:** A piece of natural pink topaz in your workspace or pink topaz jewellery helps you to value yourself and to assess your worth so that you can ask for promotion or more money or responsibility; good for working with a love partner or parent in business, for mutual trust and respect. **Magical significance:** Pink topaz brings good luck in love. Write in the air over it in rose incense stick smoke or the index finger of the hand you do not write with, the name of the person you wish to attract or if not known, write "whoever will make me happy and I him/her". Enclose the smoke or visualized words with a smoke- or air-drawn heart shape. **Divinatory meaning:** If you have been hurt before, go slowly in new love so you feel secure at every stage; do not rush from a broken commitment to a new one instantly. **Zodiac:** Taurus. **Empowerment:** I am willing to take a risk and trust again.

Pink topaz that is untreated is one of the most valuable forms of topaz and is found in Pakistan and Russia. The well-known nineteenth-century poet and writer Oscar Wilde (1854–1900), who was enamoured with all topaz, described pink topaz somewhat unpoetically as the eyes of a wood pigeon.

The first artificial pink topaz was created in 1750, when a Parisian jeweller discovered that the much more common yellow topaz turns pink if exposed to moderate heat. Pink topaz is a very hard gem and so is one of the more powerful pink crystals, representing not ideal unattainable love or dreams but realistic love; it eases obsessing over unattainable love or waiting in hope for an indifferent person to soften.

Like all topaz, the pink form helps uncover falsehoods and illusions; if held or worn, it will enable you to distinguish between groundless fears that love will not last or that you are not good or beautiful enough from what are real doubts about fidelity or intention.

Type: Manganese-rich epidote; variety of zoisite (calcium aluminium silicate).

Colours: Pink or reddish.

Availability: Relatively rare, but obtainable through specialist crystal stores and online.

Physical benefits: May facilitate healing of all sexual and reproductive disorders, especially PMS, endometriosis, dysmenorrhoea; assists with gastro-intestinal disorders, lower bowel problems, breathing and fertility; good for weight loss.

Emotional healing: Thulite offers strong support for anyone who has suffered emotional abuse or is experiencing bullying. It helps combat feelings of negativity that could induce self-harm.

Chakra: Heart and Root.

Thulite/Pink Zoisite

Associated candle colour: Pink. **Associated fragrances:** Angelica, chamomile, lavender, rose, rosemary. **Practical uses:** Called the marathon runner's crystal, thulite is helpful for all long-term endeavours and will give stamina when you feel like giving up; good for sports and for getting through long days and nights; wear close to the body. **Workplace:** Thulite as three or more tumblestones or a piece of natural thulite next to a green plant will assist in spreading harmony even to a very large, impersonal or competitive workplace. It will be beneficial to those who are feeling unsupported or left out. **Magical significance:** Use thulite to bring reconciliation after a lovers' quarrel or to call back a love from the past. Put dried rosemary in a pink bag with two thulites and pass the sealed bag over a candle flame three times, saying, "Rosemary is for remembering. I ask you love, remember me." **Divinatory meaning:** There will be a chance of reconciliation with someone from the past, but you may find they have not changed. **Zodiac:** Taurus and Gemini. **Empowerment:** I can forget and move on even if I cannot forgive.

Named after the legendary Norse island of Thule that was believed to be at the most northerly edge of the world, this is a crystal that warms hearts and lives.

Thulite is beneficial to those who require the powers of showmanship or who seek fame. It assists with articulacy, expression, extroversion and leadership. It can be helpful for actors and performers, jugglers and acrobats, amateur as well as professional; give a tumbled thulite to a child in a school play to enable them to overcome

nerves or to a teenager before an oral school examination.

Thulite will assist with problem-solving skills and intellectual resources and the ability to overcome obstacles that are in the way of getting one's message across. It also helps us access the inner child which can be translated into spontaneous pleasure; brings new beginnings at any stage or age and creates a sense that all will be well (which it invariably is); helps us to experience and work with the powers of plants, stones and crystals.

Type: Silicate, microcrystalline quartz, here with a high iron content that makes it red.

Colours: Red to terracotta red-brown, sometimes mixed with other minerals to give black line designs.

Availability: Common.

Physical benefits: May help circulation, anaemia, blood cells and blood toxicity, menstruation, safe childbirth and reduction of labour pains, burns, scalds, arthritis, rheumatism, sense of smell, circulation, fertility especially if undergoing treatment for conception; heart conditions, bypass and transplants, exhaustion.

Emotional healing: Gives men and woman quiet strength to resist bullying or domestic violence; offers emotional stability if a serious illness is in remission or during a long treatment where the outcome is uncertain.

Chakra: Root.

Red Jasper

Candle colour: Red. **Fragrances:** Basil, dragon's blood, garlic, mint. **Practical uses:** A winter or cold-day crystal; wear red jasper jewellery or keep crystals in your gloves when not wearing them and add red jasper elixir to warm drinks. **Workplace:** A power crystal for increasing confidence and respect if you are the new boy or girl or you are a very small cog in a very big wheel. **Magical significance:** Protective against psychic attack or if working with spirit rescue, potentially violent or psychologically disturbed people; wear two or three items of red jasper jewellery or a pouch of three small tumblestones round your neck or waist. **Divinatory meaning:** Be tough but kind with someone close who acts helpless and drains you of money or energy with constant demands. **Zodiac:** Aries. **Empowerment:** I am a high achiever.

According to Viking and German legend, the hilt of the magical sword of Siegfried, the dragon-slayer, was inlaid with red jasper to give him courage. It is therefore a power stone for every man who struggles to make his mark in a competitive and often ruthless world. Called among some Native North Americans the blood of Mother Earth and in Ancient Egypt linked with the fertilizing blood of Mother Isis, the first single parent deity, red jasper strengthens mothers (and indeed fathers) who bring up children alone.

A stone of passion, red jasper is a token of all who consummate love. Red jasper is also the crystal of actors, actresses and all connected with the theatre, television drama, films and drama therapy. Carry red jasper as protection against physical threats and keep in the car to prevent accidents, theft or road rage.

If you work with earth energies, this stone can help you to make a deep and powerful connection when contacting earth spirits and guardians of the leys and sacred sites.

Brecciated Jasper

Type: Silicate, microcrystalline quartz; red jasper that contains haematite.

Colours: Dark or brick reds, patterned with brown, black and beige swirls and/or clear crystal inclusions.

Availability: Relatively common.

Physical benefits: Believed to help allergies, liver, stomach upsets, digestive disorders, eczema, psoriasis and skin problems aggravated by stress.

Emotional healing: Helps to assimilate and calm emotional responses, sexual problems stemming from self-doubt or guilt.

Chakra: Root, Sacral.

Candle colour: Red. **Fragrances:** Benzoin, orange, rosemary. **Practical uses:** Bury small pieces against a boundary fence if you have nasty neighbours; a tumblestone in a child's room can prevent nightmares. **Workplace:** Improves confidence, inspiration and enthusiasm. **Magical significance:** Breaks the psychological/psychic hold of those who seek to manipulate or dominate. **Divinatory meaning:** An unpleasant colleague should not intimidate you. **Zodiac:** Virgo and Scorpio. **Empowerment:** Each dawn brings new inspiration.

Brecciated jasper has strong grounding energies so is useful during periods of instability or for dealing practically with a crisis. It is an excellent crystal to wear if you are involved with animals, especially when a pet is in need of healing. Keep with precious objects to prevent accidents. Brecciated jasper can be used to cleanse the aura and improve dream recall.

It offers a sense of vitality and strength, increasing self-confidence, creative inspiration. It also helps to enhance physical endurance and sports stamina.

Poppy Jasper

Type: Silicate, microcrystalline quartz with mineral or organic inclusions, variation of brecciated jasper (p.67).

Colours: Brick red with shades of brown or black, also golden yellows, cream, or white in a single stone; Morgan Hill jasper has red and yellow orbs resembling poppies.

Availability: One of the less common jaspers.

Physical benefits: May help adrenalin regulation, low energy, certain allergies, anaemia, irregular menstruation, summer colds, infectious illnesses with rashes.

Emotional healing: Caffeine addiction, extreme anxiety.

Chakra: Heart.

Candle colour: Red. **Fragrances:** Carnation, geranium, hibiscus, poppy, red rose. **Practical uses:** The joy bringer, encourages outdoor pursuits and helps to keep plants healthy. **Workplace:** Generates enthusiasm and motivation and is good for marketing; opens opportunities for travel and international presence on the Internet. **Magical significance:** Sit near any ancient site or temple holding poppy jasper to connect with the world chakras and become energized and empowered. **Divinatory meaning:** Enjoy the moment and think about all the good things in your life. **Zodiac:** Aries. **Empowerment:** I am happy with my life.

Wear poppy jasper next to the skin for a regular infusion of happiness and energy; excellent for giving the impetus for a pleasurable, new health regime. Because of the association of poppies with remembrance and peace, poppy jasper makes a good reconciliatory gift or can be set around a map to bring world peace; give tumblestones to friends or family to maintain regular contact.

Poppy jasper overcomes lethargy and depression. It also helps to encourage consideration and communication around the physically disabled.

Type: Beryl, ring silicate, sometimes called the red emerald.

Colours: Red to pinkish red.

Availability: Rare as gem quality, obtainable in specialist crystal stores and jewellers and online.

Physical benefits: Thought to be good for heart, liver, lungs, mouth, throat, stomach, ulcers of all kinds, chilblains and all winter chills, gradually raising and maintaining physical energy levels; good for anyone who is chronically ill or very old who feels the cold.

Emotional healing: A stone to overcome grief and emotional heartbreak, loss and betrayal, to open the Heart chakra energy centre to future love.

Chakra: Heart.

Bixbite/Red Beryl

Candle colour: Red. **Fragrances:** Anise, dragon's blood, hibiscus, poppy, thyme. **Practical uses:** A crystal of warm, affectionate lasting love; wear or carry bixbite to attract someone with whom you are compatible and to keep a relationship caring and supportive even in bad times. **Workplace:** For creating a caring environment, especially if it is a family firm or a small company where personal customer service is the key to success. **Magical significance:** Use in love magic to call your twin soul by holding the bixbite up to candlelight at midnight and asking your other half to find you. Blow out the candle and sleep with bixbite taped close to your heart. **Divinatory meaning:** You may be tempted to act impulsively and unwisely; consider the consequences carefully. **Zodiac:** Aries and Taurus **Empowerment:** I value lasting love and loyalty rather than excitement.

Bixbite is a powerful protector against psychic and psychological vampires and against all who would manipulate or deceive you. Wear bixbite or tape it close to your navel if you know you will be meeting someone whose charms or persuasion you find hard to resist; wear or take it when you make a major purchase to choose wisely and not be swayed by sales talk.

A stone of passion, bixbite will kindle sexual desire if you love someone but are afraid because of previously bad sexual experiences. A good wedding or pre-wedding gift if the arrangements are overwhelming, to remind you of the reason you are marrying. Also a stone of reconciliation if a partner has been unfaithful, to set between you as you talk to find if there is any way back.

Also will help you to heal family coldness if you visit a relative from whom you have been estranged, especially if you quarrelled over a love choice; also helps to create necessary channels if you have to talk to your ex-partner's new love to reach agreement over your children.

Blood Agate

Type: Chalcedony, crypto-crystalline quartz; also known as red agate or pigeon's blood.

Colours: Red and white, translucent and glowing, resembles coagulating blood.

Availability: Relatively common.

Physical benefits: May be useful for blood disorders, circulation, excessive bleeding; menstrual problems, hysterectomy, energy and stamina, fertility, digestive and lymphatic systems; one of the best stones for good health.

Emotional healing: A survival stone, when a person has lost the will to live, or harms or neglects themselves; particularly effective for bulimia and anorexia.

Chakra: Root and Solar Plexus.

Candle colour: Red. **Fragrances:** Allspice, cinnamon, dragon's blood, ginger, hibiscus. **Practical uses:** Restores passion in love and life. **Workplace:** Good for determination, stamina and ingenuity in finding a job and combatting inequality non aggressively. **Magical significance:** Used by the Vikings in axe divination to find lost objects or hidden treasure; hold in closed hands until warm to know where and how to find what you need, whether lost or undiscovered. **Divinatory meaning:** If you really want something, fight for it; if not, let it go. **Zodiac:** Aries. **Empowerment:** Life pulsates within me.

Wearing blood agate or carrying a tiny blood agate egg is powerful in fertility problems where stress spoils lovemaking; it helps girls with late-onset puberty make the transition to womanhood.
Its power lies in the restoration of good health, employment and lasting love. It is helpful in keeping to fitness regimes or persisting with business ventures. As an additional boost for an all-or-nothing moment, combine blood agate with red jasper, but avoid overload. Blood agate overcomes a fear of spiders and discourages them in the home.

Fire Agate

Type: An iridescent form of brownish-red agate consisting of plated crystals of iron or thin layers of limonite over layers of chalcedony; also with goethite inclusions.

Colours: Red with glints and flashes.

Availability: Relatively common.

Physical benefits: Seen as helpful for reducing fever, good for circulation, hot flushes, colon, endocrine system, vision especially at night, increasing metabolic rate.

Emotional healing: Motivation to overcome addictions; gives courage and confidence, prevents exhaustion.

Chakra: Root and Solar Plexus.

Candle colour: Scarlet. **Fragrances:** Allspice, copal, dragon's blood, mint, sage. **Practical uses:** Protects family and home if placed on an outside sill. **Workplace:** A crystal of ambition and high achievement., so place on any proposal or creation you want to sell for 24 hours. **Magical significance:** Traditionally used to connect with fire elementals and spirits. Pass three times over a red candle flame and make a wish but take care as this is very powerful. **Divinatory meaning:** A chance to achieve your heart's desire, but beware of sudden temptation. **Zodiac:** Aries. **Empowerment:** I aim for perfection and will not accept less.

Fire or flame agate was used in alchemy because it was believed to contain the essence of fire. In many traditions sacred to fire deities, such as the Hindu god Agni, it encourages timid adults and shy children to speak up and not be ignored or bullied. Use a picture as your computer screen saver for instant courage. A stone of integrity that encourages high standards of behaviour and intentions in self and others, it allows us to experience passion both in love and life. Set where air circulates round it.

Type: Oxide, quartz.

Colours: Banded gleaming reds.

Availability: Common.

Physical benefits: Seen as assisting anaemia, blood and blood cell disorders, eye infections and night vision, overall body strength and vitality, libido in both sexes, sexual dysfunction and potency in men, menstruation, psychosomatic illnesses, recovery after major surgery.

Emotional healing: Fills its wearer with enthusiasm and optimism if depressed; calms anger and irritability, especially in men.

Chakra: Sacral and Solar Plexus.

Red Tiger's Eye/Ox Eye

Candle colour: Red. **Fragrances:** Allspice, cinnamon, dragon's blood, ginger, hibiscus. **Practical uses:** If you are in a situation or place where tempers are flaring or stress is reaching boiling point, place red tiger's eye tumblestones around the room. Wash them in very cold water afterwards. **Workplace:** Red tiger's eye increases personal power for those downtrodden at work, effective for repelling inappropriate sexual remarks or behaviour; splashing the elixir on your throat will make you speak calmly and with authority. **Magical significance:** For any urgent need light a red candle and surround it with eight small red tiger's eye crystals. Drip a tiny amount of melted wax on each stone; when the candle has burned through, carry the tiger's eyes in a small drawstring bag. **Divinatory meaning:** Your efforts will be positively recognized as long as you do not let anyone else take credit for your ideas or input. **Zodiac:** Aries and Taurus. **Empowerment:** My efforts will bring results as long as I persevere.

Red tiger's eye occurs naturally when the golden-brown variety is exposed to heat, such as by fire or lightning, but most on the commercial market is artificially heat-treated. This does not affect its metaphysical qualities.

Red tiger's eye (as with all colours of this gem) is chatoyant, meaning it reflects iridescent light from its banded surface like that of a cat's eye.

This effect is best when a stone is cut *en cabochon* (shaped and polished). Red tiger's eye makes fabulous jewellery, particularly for women

fighting sexism or trying to break into a male-dominated firm on merit without sacrificing their femininity.

It is associated with the strength and courage of the ox and so is a fierce defence worn round the neck against any kind of bullying.

It also acts as an antidote against anger and so can calm the bullies. Red tiger's eye will help in mediation and in releasing creative blocks. It is excellent if you are normally shy about being noticed and rewarded for your efforts.

Ruby

Type: Corundum (aluminium oxide silicate).

Colours: Pinkish red, purple-red, deep rich to dark ruby red; the most valuable are deep red with a slight blue tinge called pigeon's blood ruby.

Availability: Common to relatively rare, depending on quality and colour.

Physical benefits: May help with infections, circulation, heart, energy, female fertility, male impotence; menstrual problems, early menopause, fibromyalgia, gynaecological operations, pregnancy – particularly for older women.

Emotional healing: Helps the sharing of loving energy despite past hurt; reduces fear of the paranormal and evil.

Chakra: Heart.

Candle colour: Red. **Fragrances:** Allspice, basil, carnation, cinnamon, dragon's blood, red rose. **Practical uses:** Protects the home from fire and intruders; wear discreetly to stay safe at night. **Workplace:** Increases profile and prosperity. **Magical significance:** Guards against psychic and psychological attack (it is said to darken in the presence of a liar); wear during lovemaking to conceive and maintain/restore passion. **Divinatory meaning:** Value friends and family even if they seem temporarily dull. **Zodiac:** Cancer and Sagittarius. **Empowerment:** My fears have no reality and I let them go.

Ruby Star

Type: Corundum (aluminium oxide silicate), displays a six- or even more rarely twelve-ray star-shaped light effect.

Colours: Pinkish red, purple-red to dark ruby red, most perfectly a rich red with a hint of blue.

Availability: Becoming rarer and highly prized.

Physical benefits: As well as the physical healing properties of the mother stone, it is thought to help stress, sexual dysfunction, fertility, vasectomy reversal. migraine.

Emotional healing: Very potent for those inclined to self-harm or self-neglect. Helps overcome the trauma of sexual abuse and suppressed anger.

Chakra: Heart and Brow.

Candle colour: Dark red or burgundy. **Fragrances:** Basil, bay, carnation, cinnamon, rose. **Practical uses:** To radiate confidence when feeling socially disadvantaged. **Workplace:** Wear at interviews and set on important paperwork or products for sale. **Magical significance:** Transforms darkness to light, if you think someone dislikes you or is using magic against you. Press against your brow if you sense danger or reflect outwards if enemies are present. **Divinatory meaning:** Now is the time to let everyone know what you can achieve; luck is with you. **Zodiac:** Cancer and Sagittarius. **Empowerment:** I will follow my star.

The ruby is one of the four precious gemstones (the others are diamond, emerald and sapphire), worn since ancient times to signify high status.

It is most commonly associated with love, especially faithful passionate commitment., and helps older women to value their beauty and life experience. Rubies bring prophetic dreams and banish nightmares; to dream of rubies is a sign of coming prosperity and good fortune.

Tumblestones at home for each family member will maintain loving links wherever they are.

The ultimate star ruby is the Rosser Reeves in the Smithsonian, Washington, DC. There are much larger examples, but this one is the most perfect to date. Star rubies have the same metaphysical properties as rubies but with increased healing and magical energies, and are most powerful at full moon. They amplify internal resources and fortitude. Wear or hold if your energies are at low ebb or you feel unloved. A star ruby will attract a twin soul.

Type: Chalcedony.

Colours: Red-brown, red, reddish orange, the active male energy stone, distinguished by its glowing vibrant colour.

Availability: Common, especially as tumblestone.

Physical benefits: May help with exhaustion, lack of energy, ME, male potency and sex drive; male genital disorders; improve appetite; cleanse the blood; for circulation, the gall bladder, liver, spleen, jaundice, digestive disorders; stimulate self-healing of the body; rheumatism, bone, joint pains and arthritis especially in men.

Emotional healing: Alleviates jealousy and possessiveness in relationships; helps anger management; a dish of vibrant carnelians in the home absorbs fury from toddlers, teenagers and adults of both sexes; assists with the male mid-life crisis: wash crystals weekly.

Chakra: Solar Plexus.

Red Carnelian

Candle colour: Bright orange. **Fragrances:** Cedar, ginger, juniper, pine, sagebrush. **Practical uses:** Protects against poverty and attracts prosperity; wear carnelian when funds are low to draw resources and good luck into your life; good for success in any creative money-spinning ventures. **Workplace:** A crystal of ambition, drive and determination if you are aiming for the top; good for defeating workplace bullies, whether individuals, cliques or large impersonal organizations that exert pressure to meet impossible targets. **Magical significance:** If you have a powerful urgent desire or need courage, light a circle of eight red candles; pass carnelian jewellery or a lucky vibrant carnelian three times over all the candles. Then light a carnelian-fragrance incense stick and draw a lion or a bear over the carnelian in incense smoke to empower it. **Divinatory meaning:** Not a time to back down; ask for what you need and do not settle for second best. **Zodiac:** Leo. **Empowerment:** I will not underestimate myself.

A stone of the sun, male-energy carnelian is ideal for women who need to assert themselves or make a major career or personal leap. Roman carnelian rings or seals engraved with deity images or fierce animals were considered both protective and lucky.

A DIY crystal, carnelian traditionally guards against falling masonry and accidents with tools.

Carnelian assists with renting, selling and buying property. Keep one with a picture of a home

you would like rent or to buy and on a road-facing window ledge to encourage prospective purchasers.

Red carnelia is seen as a stone of passion, place beneath the four corners of the mattress or circled round a red candle in the bedroom before lovemaking. It is also useful for giving confidence for performances on stage or live media work and guards the home from theft, fire, storm, loss or accident.

Type: Calcium carbonate.

Colours: Usually pale red, but can be reddish pink to orangish red with clear streaks.

Availability: Common.

Physical benefits: Thought to assist with all menstrual problems, especially irregular ovulation, ovarian cysts, endometriosis, amenorrhea, painful menstruation; help to improve circulation and cleanse the blood; can help kidneys and pancreas.

Emotional healing: For anyone expressing anger in inappropriate ways, by self-harming or seeking unnecessary medical attention or frequent panic attacks; for people who are hooked on psychic or sex phone lines or who seek love through indiscriminate sex; over-control as in obsessive compulsive disorder.

Chakra: Sacral and Root.

Red Calcite

Candle colour: Pale red. **Fragrances:** Acacia, almond, hibiscus, poppy, rose. **Practical uses:** Gives children and teenagers the courage to stand up to bullies without becoming aggressive themselves; also for timid animals who are bullied by others in the home or streets. **Workplace:** Helpful for mothers returning to work after maternity leave to regain their confidence and to have the stamina to combine work and family life. **Magical significance:** To rekindle passion in a long-standing relationship, light rose scented candles in the bathroom; add a smooth natural red calcite to your bath along with your favourite rose essence; gently massage your body with it, chanting softly, "I call my love with fire and with fragrance, with fragrance and with fire". **Divinatory meaning:** You have every right to be angry with someone close. Consider their good qualities before deciding how to respond. **Zodiac:** Scorpio. **Empowerment:** I will not only survive but thrive.

Associated with the veins of Mother Earth that carry her life blood to her children; in the north of Scandinavia some people still ask permission of the rock before cutting it. Red calcite helps us to understand our karmic patterns and so to avoid repeating the same mistakes or being constantly attracted to the wrong kind of person.

It curbs over-excitable animals that bark, yowl or jump up with misdirected pleasure.

Take some on an outing so children do not become too boisterous and fall over or hurt themselves or others. A good bedside crystal to get you up on cold, dark winter mornings. Slip a small tumblestone in your pocket or glove to touch while waiting in the cold for transport.

Take one to the gym or out walking, cycling or running if you have not exercised for years or are seriously unfit, for stamina and to get the life force flowing. Keep red calcite with you when you consummate a relationship for the first time, particularly after a long period of celibacy or if you are very anxious.

Almandine Garnet

Type: Silicate (iron aluminium silicate); often found combined with pyrope garnet.

Colours: Wine red to purple-red to red-black, brownish red. Precious garnet is deep red, transparent almandine.

Availability: Common unless with a star formation.

Physical benefits: May help with pain, especially in childbirth, metabolism, wounds and cuts, menstruation, circulation, blood clots, haemophilia, gallstones, fertility, sexual potency and libido, DNA, immunity to colds and flu.

Emotional healing: Helps in bereavement

Chakra: Root and Heart.

Candle colour: Red. **Fragrances:** Angelica, bay, copal, rosemary. **Practical uses:** Enduring passion for a person, hobby or cause. **Workplace:** Protective in an emotionally or sexually charged environment; eases the situation where someone resists change. **Magical significance:** Protection against emotional vampires, manipulators and evil spirits. Anyone engaged in spirit rescue should wear it. **Divinatory meaning:** Look at who is draining your emotional energies. **Zodiac:** Capricorn and Aquarius. **Empowerment:** I need not doubt my love will last.

Garnet is the name for a group of silicate minerals crystallized in a cubic system. The Crusaders wore almandine garnet rings to keep them safe.

Some rare almandine crystals from India or Idaho have asbestos inclusions that create a highly-prized, star-like effect when faceted; Almandine garnet prevents anger being directed inwards, which leads to stress-related conditions. Hold over your navel, your Sacral energy centre, and let the anger flow creatively or alternatively dissipate harmlessly outside your energy field.

Pyrope Garnet

Type: Silicate/nesosilicate, magnesium aluminium garnet, often found with the almandine variety.

Colours: Dark red, bright red, violet red, rose-red and reddish orange.

Availability: Relatively common as jewellery.

Physical benefits: Claimed to relieve blood disorders, circulation, epecially in cold weather, heart, arthritis, rheumatism, low blood sugar, gallstones, influenza, nosebleeds, libido, immunity.

Emotional healing: The most fiery of the garnets, pyrope restores the will to live when life has hit an all-time low; relieves anxiety and phobias about blood.

Chakra: Root and Heart.

Candle colour: Bright red. **Fragrances:** Almond, anise, cinnamon, dragon's blood, ginger. **Practical uses:** If you lie awake worrying or feel alone in a strange bed. **Workplace:** Wear for productivity or performance without sacrificing integrity or quality. **Magical significance:** A gem of Mars, used for power and courage; write over it with the index finger, "I am fierce as a wolf" or "brave as a lion." **Divinatory meaning:** Use the fire burning within you creatively and with care but do not let it go out. **Zodiac:** Capricorn and Aquarius **Empowerment:** I will not let my inner fire burn dim.

Bohemia is famously home to pyrope garnets, which can be as big as hens' eggs and were made into lavish jewellery in the 18th and 19th centuries. The Anglo-Saxons made adornments of garnet and gold to accompany them in the afterlife. The pyrope was considered effective against legendary vampires and pyrope bullets were once used in slings in parts of Asia. These protective, courage-inspiring, and beauty-enhancing qualities still make pyrope a multi-purpose gem, that many people prefer to the ruby.

Red Spinel

Type: Magnesium aluminium oxide. Artificially made spinels are not so good for healing or empowerment.

Colours: Red and sparkling.

Availability: Relatively common.

Physical benefits: May improve blood disorders, inflammation; is a gentle energizer; and is seen as a pain reliever for degenerative conditions connected with mobility; believed to generate the body's own self-healing system.

Emotional healing: Red spinel should be worn by people who feel no one ever takes them seriously; good for middle or youngest children in adulthood to become self-reliant and independent.

Chakra: Root and Heart.

Candle colour: Red. Fragrances: Acacia, allspice, cinnamon, dragon's blood, galbanum. **Practical uses:** Sustains love in difficult times or where there is family opposition. **Workplace:** Wear to attract people who can boost your career and to encourage creative ideas; a natural leadership crystal, to take along to job appraisals or interviews. **Magical significance:** Used to ward off negative influences. **Divinatory meaning:** Speak out, as your opinions and ideas will be well received, even if previously ignored. **Zodiac:** Leo and Scorpio. **Empowerment:** Love can last even long distance.

Red spinel is often mistaken for a ruby. Indeed, the famous Black Prince's Ruby in the British crown jewels is red spinel. Henry V wore it on his helmet at Agincourt (the helmet saved his life from an axe blow by the Duke of Alençon). For this reason red spinel is considered protective against physical attack, particularly by women in combat or who work in hazardous jobs. Red spinel will give the strength in any bad situation such as divorce or job loss, to fight on and to obtain your rights without resorting to aggressiveness.

Red Zircon

Type: Silicate/nesosilicate, zircon.

Colours: Rich red, red-orange, red-violet and dark red.

Availability: Relatively common.

Physical benefits: Believed to help with infections and viruses; relieve pain, speeds healing of wounds and bruises; protect against MRS, C. Difficile, Norovirus and modern bugs that spread rapidly; ease insomnia, ear infections, liver, gall bladder and intestines.

Emotional healing: Brings peace after turmoil, sleep after wakefulness, renewed vitality after exhaustion and a sense of personal blessings after misfortune.

Chakra: Root and Heart.

Candle colour: Red. Fragrances: Carnation, cinnamon, hyacinth, saffron, sage. **Practical uses:** Use for official correspondence, job or loan applications to ensure a favourable response. **Workplace:** Increases persuasive power so good for salespersons, press officers or lecturers. **Magical significance:** Use as a love charm and to increase personal charisma; rub a cross shape over your zircon to deter jealous love rivals. **Divinatory meaning:** If you really want something, now is the time to go all-out with power and passion. **Zodiac:** Leo and Sagittarius. **Empowerment:** I feel the surge of renewed enthusiasm, for life.

Jacinth is referred to in the New Testament as one of the foundation stones of the heavenly Jerusalem. It was worn as protection against the Black Death in the 1300s and against the Great Plague of London in 1665. Red zircon is also called hyacinth after the flower created by Apollo when his love Hyakinthos was killed. Red zircon (also called Jacinth) is an anti-theft crystal. It was said to lose its sheen in the presence of plague, so be wary if your zircon becomes dull after spending time with someone, as they may be draining you.

Red Aventurine

Type: Microcrystalline quartz, sometimes containing inclusions of haematite to give a metallic, iridescent glint.

Colours: Red.

Availability: Common.

Physical benefits: May help reproductive system, fertility, speeds metabolism, lower cholestero, be helpful for side effects of radiotherapy, haemophilia, skin conditions especially eczema, fungal conditions, low blood pressure, pulse and irregular heartbeat, fibromyalgia, hernia.

Emotional healing: Restores good humour; increases libido if worn or placed beneath the mattress.

Chakra: Root and Solar Plexus.

Candle colour: Red. **Fragrances:** Allspice, cedar, copal, mint, saffron. **Practical uses:** Good for weight problems. **Workplace:** Helps if you work long hours, and have to produce ideas or talk a lot; good for nightshift workers with families. **Magical significance:** Brings money when carried in a small red bag with a sprinkling of spice such as ginger or cinnamon; for fertility substitute dried rosemary or dried rose petals. **Divinatory meaning:** Your integrity and hard work will bring you success over a ruthless rival. **Zodiac:** Aries. **Empowerment:** As I wish so shall it be, as long as my heart is pure and my intention good.

Traditionally used against theft, fire, and lightning strikes. Protective against traffic accidents; place one in your car if you drive frequently.

Brings good luck when the odds are against you – hold a very small crystal, call out your need, then throw it as far as possible; the finder will be lucky too. A dish of red aventurines creates harmony between brothers and sisters. Wear if organizing a children's party, attending a family social event or meeting relatives who always find fault, to enable you to take everything in your stride.

Harlequin Quart

Type: Quartz crystal with lepidocrocite or haematite inclusions, sometimes at the base of a crystal point.

Colours: Tiny red stars or red clouds within usually clear, colourless quartz.

Availability: Relatively rare.

Physical benefits: Seen as good for heart, blood disorders; assists blood thinning, veins, thymus, thyroid, skin rashes caused by allergies to food, animal hair or dust mites, acne, recurring infections particularly those circulating round a workplace, school or neighbourhood, haemorrhoids, hernia.

Emotional healing: Releases your inner child; gives you permission to be happy and have fun if life is all work.

Chakra: Root and Heart.

Candle colour: Red. **Fragrances:** Anise, cinnamon, dragon's blood, ginger, hibiscus. **Practical uses:** Brings joy to impromptu gatherings and family outings. **Workplace:** Transforms ideas into practical action; wear to obtain resources or financial backing. **Magical significance:** Traditionally used for soul retrieval – hold to your navel and picture a journey in which you collect sparkling gems that represent important parts of yourself. **Divinatory meaning:** Persevere if others are unenthusiastic about a good idea; look for alternative support or funding. **Zodiac:** Aries. **Empowerment:** I give myself permission to have fun.

Harlequin quartz (also known as fire or flame quartz) promotes fun and spontaneity. Keep a natural piece in the home to encourage a spirit of adventure; helps children and pets who do not like to play outdoors. Reduces the need for over-planning every activity; wear to achieve balance beween hard work and social life.

Excellent if you have a secret talent you are afraid to try out in public. Use for enthusiasm and stamina in long-term projects such as house renovation, or major fitness training you have to fit around work or family.

Type: Zinc oxide, the ore of zinc (see also schalenblende).

Colours: Red, red-orange, orange-yellow to deep brown.

Availability: Obtainable from specialist crystal stores and online.

Physical benefits: Thought to assist wound healing, prostate gland, female and male genitalia and reproductive organs, libido, fertility, HIV, AIDS, auto-immune diseases, bronchitis, resistance to colds and influenza.

Emotional healing: Overcomes crippling worries about failure and getting hurt that prevent participation in employment or relationships; good if you have been burned by previous bad experiences.

Chakra: Root, Sacral, Solar Plexus.

Zincite

Candle colour: Orange. **Fragrances:** Carnation, ginger, hibiscus, orange, sage. **Practical uses:** Associated with property, home buying and selling; carry zincite when house hunting to identify the right home for you; keep on display when prospective buyers visit your home. **Workplace:** An excellent crystal when think-tanking or for team projects to increase group dynamics; brings like-minded people together to work towards a common goal and so is excellent for joint-enterprise projects. **Magical significance:** Associated with dragons and dragon energies in magic, empower zincite for good fortune, prosperity or fertility using either candle or fire magic. **Divinatory meaning:** You will meet a useful like-minded person to help get a venture off the ground. **Zodiac:** Taurus and Libra. **Empowerment:** I call creative energies into my life.

Called by indigenous peoples the life blood of the Earth Mother, zincite is abundant in New Jersey, USA, but quite rare elsewhere. It has grown artificially as a result of a fire at an old Polish zinc-smelting works. where the very old smoke stacks had created the perfect environment for growth.

This renders them somewhere between man-made and natural.

Zincite activates the lower chakras of the body that in turn energize the higher ones. A small piece brings a tremendous feeling of wellbeing, energy

and vitality. Even those who are not particularly sensitive to crystal energies will be able to experience and benefit from its charge.

Zincite is a shield and blocker both of harmful energies from the environment and from infections and diseases. It is often used with other crystals, for example malachite or chrysocolla, to halt the progress of an infection or condition.

Enhances all creative energies, whether artistic, writing a novel, growing flowers or starting a family. This crystal should be used with caution as it is so powerful and is not suitable for children or animals.

Red Coral

Type: Organic, branching calcareous skeletons of sea creatures.

Colours: Red, red-orange, also softer shades of pink.

Availability: Relatively common.

Physical benefits: Believed to be good for cells, tissue and bone marrow, circulation, inflammation, rashes (softer pink coral shades); aid female fertility, menstruation, bones, teeth, inner-ear problems, indigestion, wounds, bruises, hiccups, colic, heartburn, kidneys, bladder and parathyroid.

Emotional healing: Red coral is a joy-bringer and restores confidence after previous setbacks.

Chakra: Root and Heart.

Candle colour: Red. **Fragrances:** Acacia, anise, basil, cinnamon, heather, hibiscus. **Practical uses:** Brings courage in confrontational situation; helpful for women in a community or profession where women are not respected. **Workplace:** Hold to determine your goals for the day; touch to get back on track after interruptions. **Magical significance:** Turns paler if you are tired or stressed and in the presence of a harmful person; hold to decide a course of action. **Divinatory meaning:** Do not be put off by previous setbacks as the energies are now favourable. **Zodiac:** Scorpio. **Empowerment:** I can try again and succeed.

Coral comes from the Ancient Greek words for sea daughter or princess. They believed it was formed from the severed head of Medusa, and this has given it protective associations against deceivers and manipulators. It is especially soothing for babies and teething rings of red or pink coral were given in a number of cultures as protection against harm. A stone of calm, pink is good for teenagers while red reassures older people who worry about failing memory and health. Red, like white, coral assuages fears about falling.

Rubellite

Type: Lithium-rich crystalline silicate.

Colours: Red, various shades from deep pink to rich red, resembling a ruby. The redder stones are more powerful.

Availability: Clear inclusion free rubellite is rare, but generally rubellite is relatively common.

Physical benefits: May help heart problems, physical energy, spleen and liver, anaemia, lung complaints, coughs and colds, muscle spasms and weakness.

Emotional healing: A powerful stone that strengthens and harmonizes the feminine within both sexes; makes women strong in emotional challenges. Men should not work with red tourmaline for prolonged periods of time.

Chakra: Root and Heart.

Candle colour: Red or dark pink. **Fragrances:** Chamomile, cherry blossom, gardenia, hyacinth, jasmine. **Practical uses:** Bestows dignity, diplomacy and quiet authority if others are unreasonable or pulling rank. **Workplace:** Keep near a computer to negate harmful electromagnetic effects; helps to deter people from picking fights or disputing your expertise. **Magical significance:** Awakens passion and desire, especially in deeper red. **Divinatory meaning:** There is an emotional challenge ahead; use your femininity to take a calm and gentle approach. **Zodiac:** Libra and Scorpio. **Empowerment:** Love will heal me and guide me.

Rubellite (or Red Tourmaline) is effective in activating the Root chakra, without awakening aggression Circle at the tops of your thighs to restore vitality, libido, stamina and passion for life. You may experience tingling in your knees and feet as you circle your thighs. Keep the crystal moving until you feel a throbbing, rising warmth; do this weekly for vitality especially in winter. A shield against negativity: pass above your hair to clear your aura and make positive plans. Helps learning, and decisions that have long-term benefit.

Mahogany Obsidian

Type: Volcanic glass that has started to crystallize and contains high levels of iron.

Colours: Mahogany, brownish red or orange-brown with black spots or black with brownish spots.

Availability: Rarer than black obsidian.

Physical benefits: Seen as useful for circulation, pain relief, growth, hypothermia, Reynaud's disease, carpel tunnel syndrome, blockages, dust mite allergy, deep skin healing, hormonal problems, menopause, painful teeth and gums.

Emotional healing: Dispels built-up anger.

Chakra: Root, Sacral and Solar Plexus.

Candle colour: Red. **Fragrances:** Cedar, cloves, hyssop, sage, sandalwood. **Practical uses:** Tumblestones shield the home from fires, high winds, earthquakes or subsidence. **Workplace:** Protective against volatile substances, situations or moods. **Magical significance:** For women's spirituality, candle magic and offerings to Mother Earth; both sexes can use it to celebrate moving on naturally to a new life stage. **Divinatory meaning:** You are gentle but can and should stand up for your rights and change the status quo. **Zodiac:** Scorpio. **Empowerment:** I accept the inevitable with grace and dignity.

Use a polished sphere for gazing or scrying, to reflect changes you need to make and insights into helpful influences. Linked with goddesses such as the Viking Edda, the Celtic Cailleach and with the grandmother of Christ, St Anne, it can be worn by women over 50 to draw work opportunities, attract lasting love and bestow serenity about mature beauty; a gift for grandmothers to say 'I appreciate your wisdom'.

Mahogany obsidian makes older pets more tolerant and accepting of young animals and children.

Vanadinite

Type: Part of apatite group of phosphates, barrel-shaped and hollow prismatic crystals; often on rock matrix.

Colours: Red, orange, yellow-brown, can be bright and transparent in natural state.

Availability: Specialist crystal stores and online.

Physical benefits: Thought to treat fatigue, reproductive problems, breathing difficulties; bladder weakness, reduce inflammation and may be helpful for growths of all kinds.

Emotional healing: Helps you to love your body; especially if anorexic, bulimic or prone to self-harming.

Chakra: Root and Sacral.

Candle colour: Red or orange. **Fragrances:** Ginger, lavender, patchouli, pennyroyal, rosemary, vanilla. **Practical uses:** Encourages prioritization when you have demands on your time, resources and money. **Workplace:** Helps to clarify long-term goals and avenues for career development. **Magical significance:** Pass a crystal through your aura, to bring together body, mind and spirit and rise above everyday life while still operating effectively. **Divinatory meaning:** Be careful about over-spending or being over-generous with others. **Zodiac:** Virgo. **Empowerment:** I desire what I need, rather than need what I desire.

Vanadinite is a stone of energy conservation and healing. It enables you to bring order out of chaos, and if you get spaced out or suffer panic attacks, it will bring you back to earth; good for attracting money for a major purchase. Seal a small piece in plastic in your purse when you go impulse shopping or if you are out with shopaholic friends.

WARNING: Vanadinite should not be used to make an elixir (placing it in water) as it is poisonous (lead). Wash hands after touching (unless in a rock matrix). Keep away from children and pets.

Type: Calcium carbonate.

Colours: Light orange to peach to rich orange.

Availability: Common.

Physical benefits: May help with gallstones, liver or spleen, kidneys and bladder, Irritable Bowel Syndrome (IBS), sexual dysfunction or low fertility in either sex, bedwetting in older children, urinary incontinence at any age; wear to increase energy levels, especially in cases of chronic fatigue or ME.

Emotional healing: Heals the psychological scars of sexual attack or abuse of any kind; relieves food-related conditions such as anorexia, bulimia and excessive exercising and any phobias; also shyness.

Chakra: Sacral.

Orange Calcite

Candle colour: Orange. **Fragrances:** Almond blossom, bergamot, neroli, orange, peach. **Practical uses:** For attracting love in later life, turning friendship into love at any age and for rekindling a relationship from the past; sit by orange candle light, hold your calcite, speaking words you would like to say to your chosen partner. Next day initiate or increase actual contact. **Workplace:** The crystal for all in the hospitality trade, especially catering and hotels, party planners, children's entertainers and all who sell or manufacture food; take a tumblestone to business lunches or corporate events to balance business with pleasure. **Magical significance:** Called the problem-solving calcite. Whatever the problem or dilemma, put the crystal next to your blank computer screen or pen and paper. Hold the calcite for a minute or two, put it down and write without thinking. The answer will be in what you have written. **Divinatory meaning:** Beware over-indulgence at a social event as you may be led into unwise temptation. **Zodiac:** Leo **Empowerment:** I feel safe because I am secure in myself.

Orange calcite, the stone of happiness, is regarded in the Baltic world as a gift from the pre-Christian sun goddess Saule on the Winter Solstice in December to remind people that the sun and happiness will always return after a period of darkness or sadness.

For orange calcite is a crystal that promotes optimism and wellbeing; at mealtimes place an orange tumblestone for each person present round an orange calcite polished egg or sphere on the table and light an orange candle. This ensures, whether one or many are present, the atmosphere is congenial and relaxing; carry as a pre-conception crystal if you are planning a baby, especially if you are older or have been using artificial contraception for a long time.

Helpful for house-training pets and indeed toddlers who are slow to leave nappies. Orange calcite gently awakens or reawakens sexual desire and sensuality; good for creativity and self-esteem.

Copper Denrite

Type: Metal, dendrite, looks like copper leaf or made into different forms.

Colours: Golden-red burnished bronze.

Availability: Common.

Physical benefits: Thought to improve blood, circulation, exhaustion, toxicity, rheumatism, arthritis, stiffness and swellings of hands and feet, inflammation, weight loss, fertility, libido, particularly in women, metabolism, balance.

Emotional healing: Removes emotional burdens if worn on the hand you do not write with. Once a week, pass nine times over a green plant to clear energies.

Chakra: Heart.

Candle colour: Green. **Fragrances:** Clary sage, eucalyptus, pine, vervain, vanilla. **Practical uses:** Activates our instinctive radar and ability to find lost items or pets. **Workplace:** Overcomes lethargy and lack of enthusiasm. Wear as jewellery if you are trying to motivate others or work with difficult clients. **Magical significance:** Copper tubing makes the ultimate magic wand as copper conducts energy to and from the spiritual world. Point outwards to call what you need and towards your body to energize you. **Divinatory meaning:** Someone becomes friendlier, including you in a social event. **Zodiac:** Taurus. **Empowerment:** I am worth knowing.

Copper jewellery has been worn since ancient times and is used in sacred offerings and to purify water. It was sacred to love goddesses, including the Greek Aphrodite and her Roman counterpart Venus (it is the metal of her planet). Copper leaves are a good-luck charm, placed in a small green bag – the colour of Venus. Wrap them in cloth, one for health or money, two for love, three for a baby.

Add basil for money, rosemary for fertility and lavender or rose for love, tie with green ribbon in three knots. Protects against love rivals.

Copper Nugget

Type: Metal nuggets.

Colours: Burnished golden-reddish bronze.

Availability: Common.

Physical benefits: May help balance energies, clear blockages, rheumatism, arthritis, stiffness and swellings of hands and feet; helpu with infected wounds, fertility, weight loss; and worn over the navel for travel sickness.

Emotional healing: Helps connections grow with other people if you find it hard to socialize or are necessarily apart from friends and family.

Chakra: Heart.

Candle colour: Green. **Fragrances:** Lilac, lily, mimosa, rose, violet. **Practical uses:** A copper ring on your wedding finger brings love; on the opposite hand it attracts new friends. **Workplace:** For year-round luck, place a nugget in a small bowl as each month passes until you have 12. **Magical significance:** To attract money to your life, place a nugget in a ceramic pot with a lid; add a copper coin every day until full, then give the money to charity. **Divinatory meaning:** Start a dialogue with someone you would like to know better, as the other person would welcome contact. **Zodiac:** Taurus. **Empowerment:** Life flows in and around me harmoniously.

Copper brings good luck to the home: nuggets traditionally insulate against storm, fire and flood and attract good visitors. It opens energy pathways and attracts the right people and resources into your life. Carry when travelling to find the right facilities and to minimize delays. Hold on your Heart chakra to balance your entire energy system, remove any blockages or negativity and to draw up earth energy outdoors. A crystal nugget will amplify the powers of other crystals if placed within a circle of copper nuggets for a few hours.

Amber

Type: Fossilized tree resin. Semi-fossilized resin is called copal; amber may contain plant matter or insects.

Colours: Translucent orange, golden yellow and brown.

Availability: Common.

Physical benefits: Seen as helpful for female fertility and male potency; teething (do not place in mouth) and toothache; stimulating self-healing; believed to ease childbirth and gallstone pain.

Emotional healing: Removes obstacles we put in our own way; improves short-term memory, relieves depression, addiction, anxiety seasonal affective disorder.

Chakra: Solar Plexus.

Candle colour Yellow. **Fragrances:** Chamomile, copal, frankincense, marigold, sunflower. **Practical uses:** An all-purpose detoxifier if worn as jewellery. **Workplace:** Amber melts rigid or confrontational attitudes in others and entrenched, out-of-date practices. **Magical significance:** Encourages past life recall and ancient wisdom. Focus on the fossil in bright sunlight or candlelight. **Divinatory meaning:** A chance for romance or unexpected admiration, but think before giving up reliable love for a sudden flirtation or passion. **Zodiac:** Leo and Sagittarius, . **Empowerment:** I am warmed by my inner fire to express my creativity.

Amber was in legend formed by the rays of the setting sun. In Scandinavia, it is said to be the tears of Freyja, the Viking Goddess of Love and Beauty. In the Far East it is considered to contain the souls of tigers and so bring courage to wearers.

A good-luck talisman to increase natural radiance and attract lasting love. Because of its electrostatic properties, it is considered one of the most healing substances. Scandinavian women had spindles with amber whorls to spin protection into garments or their warrior husbands and sons.

Peach Aventurine

Type: Microcrystalline quartz, sometimes containing mica that gives aventurine a metallic, iridescent glint.

Colours: Soft peach or more glowing orange.

Availability: Common.

Physical benefits: May help urinary, genital and reproductive problems, lungs, heart, adrenal glands, skin problems, including some rashes, nausea, any disfigurement.

Emotional healing: Chronic worry about every aspect of life, obsessive compulsive disorder, fear of heights and lifts, blushing and crippling shyness or distorted and exaggerated anxieties over physical appearance.

Chakra: Sacral.

Candle colour: Peach. **Fragrances:** Apple blossom, cherry blossom, juniper, peach, strawberry. **Practical uses:** Encourages creativity and helps you to market yourself. Wear as jewellery or keep with your emerging creations. **Workplace:** Excellent if you work in the beauty or fashion industry or counsel people with poor self-image. **Magical significance:** The best aventurine for meditation, especially with a fruit-scented candle, incense stick or oil. **Divinatory meaning:** See and project yourself as you really are and not in terms of old criticism. **Zodiac:** Taurus. **Empowerment:** I do not need to hide behind an image.

An excellent stone used alongside Reiki treatment. For healing or general empowerment it should be worn for days or weeks if a condition is chronic. Wear as jewellery or in a small orange bag round your waist or neck. Wearing or carrying peach aventurine regularly will make you feel calmer and more connected with life and others. People will comment how well or radiant you are looking. It is a wonderful stone for self-conscious teenagers, especially if they are worrying about their skin and appearance.

Fire Opal

Type: Hydrated silicon dioxide. Fire opal is a type of opal (the others are common and precious) and is called precious fire opal if it displays iridescent flashes of colours within it when it is moved.

Colours: Bright orange to red, glowing.

Physical benefits: Can help abdomen, lower back, kidneys, genitals, intestines, adrenal glands, libido, orgasm, fertility, iron deficiency and blood disorders.

Emotional healing: Awakens personal power to cope courageously with emotional turmoil or unwelcome change; heals sexual and domestic abuse and trauma.

Chakra: Solar Plexus.

Candle colour: Red. **Fragrances:** Allspice, anise, benzoin, copal, ginger. **Practical uses:** Good for tackling major issues and facing up to people. **Workplace:** Wear to get your career moving, to stir inert colleagues or employees and for all dangerous jobs or life-and-death decisions. **Magical significance:** A focus for candle magic, both to attract money and to bring passion into a relationship. Name the purpose as you pass the opal round a red candle flame nine times (not too close, as heat can damage it). **Divinatory meaning:** Straight talking and decisive actions are necessary. **Zodiac:** Aries. **Empowerment:** I can tackle problems head-on.

In Mexico, fire opal was called by the Aztecs the stone of the bird of paradise after their feathered serpent creator god, Quetzalcoatl. This power to stimulate creativity and new beginnings, as well as necessary destruction, makes fire opal the most active of the opals. It can be worn as a charm by anyone who wants to be independent and live by their own rules, or to make their mark professionally or personally. It is also a stone that gives courage to find passionate, lasting love with someone of whom your family or friends would disapprove.

Orange Selenite

Type: Fibre gypsum, hydrous calcium sulphate, with pearl-like lustre, similar to its sister satin spar (p.149).

Colours: Orange, also sometimes blue or green as well as white (p.157).

Availability: Rarer than white selenite.

Physical benefits: May assist with fertility, nausea, fluid retention, hormones, menstrual problems, gallstones and kidney stones, bladder weakness and prolapsed womb.

Emotional healing: Helpful for self identity and all food obsessions related to self image.

Chakra: Sacral.

Candle colour: Orange or silver. **Fragrances:** Bergamot, cranberry, honey, lemongrass, orange. **Practical uses:** A sphere on a dining table encourages a healthy appetite and a sense of well-being. **Workplace:** Tumblestones encourage creativity and originality, pride and pleasure in work; helpful for flexibility in the workforce. **Magical significance:** Orange selenite is a focus for connecting with moon and Earth divas or higher nature essences. **Divinatory meaning:** A time for hospitality and socializing and for mellowing attitudes towards someone you care for. **Zodiac:** Cancer. **Empowerment:** Socializing can be as important as work.

Orange selenite encourages a friendly, productive atmosphere so is good for persuading children to do their homework and assist with chores. Placed on a market stall it encourages people to buy. It also helps people feel to feel secure at night.

Orange selenite is good for everyday and past life recall and for sending healing to places damaged by deforestation, mining and emissions released into the environment.

Selenite is not suitable for prolonged use outdoors and should not become wet.

Orange Aragonite

Type: Dimorphous calcium carbonate that grows usually as twin crystals in clusters.

Colours: Orange through orangey brown to brown.

Availability: Common.

Physical benefits: May help to keep away winter chills and snuffles, Reynaud's syndrome, chilblains and poor circulation, problems of the ovaries, prostate gland, central nervous system, bones or joints; hair loss and chronic fatigue.

Emotional healing: The stone of moderation, especially in cases of extreme dieting and exercise.

Chakra: Sacral.

Candle colour: Orange. **Fragrances:** Clary sage, ginger, hibiscus, neroli, orange. **Practical uses:** Keep tumblestone next to clocks if you or your family are constantly running late. **Workplace:** Carry or take along a cluster if you are organizing or attending any networking, marketing, sales or training events. **Magical significance:** An earth energy crystal to neutralize geopathic stress in your home. **Divinatory meaning:** Be sure that a current project or relationship merits the time you are spending on it. **Zodiac:** Cancer and Capricorn. **Empowerment:** I value time and so spend it, not waste it.

Aragonite is found in hot springs, volcanic rocks and caves and as the iridescent colors in abalone and mother-of-pearl shells. It is often regarded as the crystal of earth and sea mothers. Good for earth healing rituals and earth-based spirituality.

Keep in your home to gently encourage children towards independence. Place in the centre of a crystal layout to encourage friendships; add tumblestones for absent friends and family in a wheel formation made of small crystals near the centre of your home to send loving energies.

Orange Carnelian

Type: Chalcedony.

Colours: Orange-pinkish and softer paler orange, the receptive or passive female energy stone, also occasionally yellowish orange, pink or almost brown.

Availability: Common, especially as tumblestones.

Physical benefits: Can aid female fertility, IVF and artificial insemination, PMS, menstrual and menopausal symptoms, kidneys, colds, cuts, wounds, blood disorders, heart palpitations, hay fever, recovery after illness, surgery, accident or trauma.

Emotional healing: Overcomes sexual anxieties, vaginismus, failure to reach orgasm; eating disorders.

Chakra: Sacral.

Candle colour: Orange. **Fragrances:** Chamomile, hibiscus, marigold, orange, rosemary. **Practical uses:** Pink-hued carnelian adjusts a couple to parenthood. **Workplace:** A dish of soft-hued crystals fosters a stimulating atmosphere without over-competitiveness. **Magical significance:** Set two carnelians in front of an orange candle, call your twin soul, blow out the candle then cast the crystals into running water or a deep lake. **Divinatory meaning:** You may get the chance to breathe new life into a relationship. **Zodiac:** Virgo and Sagittarius. **Empowerment:** I am as courageous as a lioness.

The Ancient Egyptians called carnelian the setting sun. They associated it with the fertile menstrual blood of the mother goddess Isis. The hieroglyph *tjet* (right), representing the girdle of Isis, was drawn or engraved on carnelian or red jasper by women seeking help from Isis. You can draw the *tjet* in incense-stick smoke over a carnelian if you need help with improving fertility.

Tangerine Quartz

Type: Silicon dioxide, naturally occurring quartz permanently coated with haematite or iron.

Colours: Orange and the clear crystal can be seen within.

Availability: From specialist mineral stores and online.

Physical benefits: Can assist assimilation of iron and minerals, healthy weight loss, reproductive problems, HIV and Aids, sexual dysfunction, recovery after an accident or trauma; abdomen, lower back, Seasonal Affective Disorder.

Emotional healing: Balancing for sex addiction, for those who love too much or who are afraid to make love.

Chakra: Sacral.

Candle colour: Orange. **Fragrances:** Carnation, geranium, hibiscus, neroli, orange. **Practical uses:** A stone of fertility, creativity and ingenuity. Wear if you are short of money to maximize your resources. **Workplace:** Place tumblestones on a meeting table for brainstorming; good for helping those in leisure or hospitality to stay cheerful. **Magical significance:** Encourages passion and fertility. Hold on your navel for five minutes to activate desire and confidence in your sexual charisma; **Divinatory meaning:** Enjoy the present, adapt what you have and breathe new life into it. **Zodiac:** Sagittarius. **Empowerment:** I awaken desire for happiness.

Tangerine quartz grows in enriched soil in lands as far apart as Brazil and Madagascar where it has been called the fruit-of-the-earth stone. However it is worn or used, tangerine quartz enriches life in the here-and-now, encouraging pleasure in what you have and who you are. Give tangerine quartz to anyone who is depressed, down on their luck, or who has been ill to become aware of possibilities and to contact friends and family again.

A natural health-bringer, especially in winter Exotic cat breeds thrive in the presence of this crystal.

Alabaster

Type: Gypsum, hydrous calcium sulphate, fine-grained and translucent, related to selenite (p.157).

Colours: White, colourless or grey, but minerals may tint it also in shades of red, brown and yellow.

Availability: Common.

Physical benefits: Thought to be beneficial for digestive disorders, swallowing mechanisms, regrowth of new cells and tissue, heart problems, pain relief in long-standing conditions.

Emotional healing: Eases the transition at times of unwelcome change or loss.

Chakra: Root and Brow.

Candle colour: Orange, white. **Fragrances:** Anise, chamomile, cloves, cyphi, galbanum. **Practical uses:** Keep an alabaster statue in your home for a week or two before moving; make it the first item set in your new home to transfer good fortune and happiness. **Workplace:** Attracts contacts and helps arrangements. **Magical significance:** Rub a tumblestone gently to activate your inner spiritual spark and transform obstacles into opportunity. **Divinatory meaning:** Your anger at injustice is justified, but focus on what is best for you right now. **Zodiac:** Pisces. **Empowerment:** I will not waste time on what cannot be changed.

Alabaster has been used for more than 2,000 years, notably in the carvings, funerary urns and ornaments of the Etruscans whose culture flourished around 800 BC in central and northern Italy. Alabaster has remained a magical spiritual mineral, created from evaporated inland seas, and is used for power animal statues such as owls and hawks. Alabaster also makes forgiveness easier if bitterness is holding you back or you have to work with or see a person who wronged you for family or social reasons.

Hessonite Garnet

Type: Calcium aluminium silicate. Variety of grossular garnet.

Colours: Orange, from medium to dark brown-orange, reddish brown, due to iron and manganese inclusions.

Availability: Relatively rare.

Physical benefits: Believed to help to regulate the immune, metabolic and hormonal systems; improve fertility, lumbar regions, bone marrow, assimilation of vitamin A, arthritis, rheumatism.

Emotional healing: Good for helping people who have spent much of their lives alone cope with mainstream life.

Chakra: Sacral.

Candle colour: Orange. **Fragrances:** Allspice, basil, cinnamon, copal, frankincense. **Practical uses:** Removes inhibitions and helps in social situations. **Workplace:** Use whenever you have to think on your feet or need creative fast responses; for anyone in the media, or in the hospitality industry. **Magical significance:** Awakens astrological and spiritual ability in any tradition. **Divinatory meaning:** Be careful you do not add to untrue gossip and cause misunderstandings. **Zodiac:** Capricorn and Aquarius **Empowerment:** I enjoy creativity for creativity's sake.

Hessonite is very slightly softer than other garnet varieties. It is nicknamed the cinnamon stone not only because of its colour, but because of the land of spices where it originated – Ceylon, now known as Sri Lanka. Hessonite has been in use since the times of Ancient Rome and Greece as a talisman to attract abundance, joy and health. Hessonite brings success in self-initiated businesses based on an original idea or unfilled market niche. Hessonite garnet inspires and brings out artistic expression, even in the seemingly untalented.

Wulfenite

Type: Sulphates, lead molybdate.

Colours: Orange, red and yellow.

Availability: Common, but with a varying price range as some specimens are highly collectible.

Physical benefits: Seen as being helpful with menopause and menstrual cycles, female reproductive problems, including endometriosis and uterine fibroids, restores appetite and aids digestion and the spleen.

Emotional healing: Balances emotions and invigorates passion to heal failing relationships; enables us to acknowledge our own shadow negative side and that of others without becoming resentful or guilty.

Chakra: Solar Plexus, Sacral and Root.

Candle colour: Orange. **Fragrances:** Bay, lemon, galbanum, geranium, hibiscus, peppermint. **Practical uses:** Encourages environmental awareness. **Workplace:** Separates the personal from the professional. **Magical significance:** Aids psychic development, especially through tuning into nature's forces. **Divinatory meaning:** A chance to express a creative gift in a way that will get tangible positive rewards, but also involves effort and the risk of standing out from the crowd. **Zodiac:** Sagittarius. **Empowerment:** I accept that sometimes I have negative feelings.

First described by Austrian mineralogist Franz Xavier Von Wulfen in 1785, and named after him, wulfenite is the crystal of the Solar Plexus chakra energy centre, associated with the physical sun and our inner sun. It is a crystal of clearing emotional blockages and expressing our true selves so that our inner and outer selves harmonize. This crystal enables us to reach out in our relationships with balanced giving and taking. **WARNING**: Do not use to make elixirs, gem water or massage oil as it contains poisonous lead and molybdate.

Type: Calcium carbonate.

Colours: Pale to golden honey, amber.

Availability: Relatively common.

Physical benefits: Thought to be good for helping to assist cell, skin and tissue regeneration, diabetes and all blood sugar fluctuations, fertility, bites and stings, back, spine, colon, digestion, intestines, liver, gall bladder, pancreas, spleen, nausea; infections when they first appear, bedwetting and stress incontinence, increased libido, for encouraging healthy growth in children

Emotional healing: A nurturing feel-good stone, especially for older women who have had emotional problems and lack self-esteem after the menopause; also for any woman after a hysterectomy who mourns the loss of her fertility and feels she is no longer sexually desirable.

Chakra: Solar Plexus.

Honey/Amber Calcite

Candle colour: Natural beeswax. **Fragrances:** Carnation, cloves, honey, marigold, peach. **Practical uses:** Put honey calcite tumblestones on the table at family parties and celebrations to bring happiness to the gathering and stop old rivalries flaring up; for harmony and a sense of blessings at any mealtime, whether you are alone or eating with friends or family; helpful if a family member has an eating disorder, to prevent mealtimes becoming a battle. **Workplace:** Wear honey calcite if you have been passed over for promotion or had to take a job you did not really want, to overcome feeling cheated even if you were; it restores the optimism and desire to maximize every opportunity, actively cooperate with former rivals and create a dynamic power base for future advancement. **Magical significance:** The ultimate abundance-bringing crystal, especially if you can obtain a small piece of honeycomb crystal; surround it with golden-coloured crystals, flowers, fruit and jewellery, and regularly light beeswax candles to attract abundance or fertility in the way you need. **Divinatory meaning:** Do not worry about not having enough for your needs, for you are entering a golden period where things will manifest as most needed. **Zodiac:** Sagittarius and Pisces,. **Empowerment:** I lack nothing.

As well as ordinary honey calcite, a rare beautiful form of honeycomb calcite is found only in Utah.

This is formed by the growth of long fibrous or tubular cells and looks like petrified honey. White membranes outline each yellow calcite cell and it is a wonder of nature. Because of the honey colour and particularly as natural honeycomb calcite, it is associated in Christian tradition with the Virgin Mary and her mother Anne, who is the patroness of beekeepers. It is also linked with

the Neolithic bee goddess tradition. Animals love honey calcite. A piece of natural honey calcite in the garden will help flowers and herbs to flourish, even in poor soil, and attract bees, butterflies and dragonflies.

Use honey calcite for social or professional networking; especially helpful for setting up websites, blogs, online and making web links with groups or individuals; good for dating sites and cyber love that flourishes in the everyday world.

Type: Hydrated iron oxide, composed mainly of goethite.

Colours: Yellow, yellow-brown, red-brown.

Availability: Common.

Physical benefits: Said to promote the healing of blood, lungs and liver disorders; used in Chinese medicine for intestines, stomach and general digestive disorders; is believed to relieve IBS and chronic diarrhoea.

Emotional healing: Calming and grounding in the fast 24/7 world; for those alone in life, gives a sense of kinship with others, encourages home-making and may guide a mate or like-minded companion to you.

Chakra: Root or Sacral.

Limonite

Candle colour: Yellow. **Fragrances:** Benzoin, cloves, geranium, myrrh, rosemary. **Practical uses:** Protects against psychic, psychological and physical negativity. Used as artists' pigment (ochre) and for ancient cave art and so represents in Australian Aboriginal culture, beauty and creativity given by Mother Earth. **Workplace:** A useful aid for studying and all forms of learning. Promotes motivation and concentration and so is an excellent crystal to aid revision periods. **Magical significance:** Helps to focus psychic abilities and improves visionary skills; used in earth healing rituals and for rites of passage as red (limonite oxide) and yellow; any piece of limonite from any-where in the world carries the ancient genetic memory that enables you to tap into earth power. **Divinatory meaning:** Do not let the negative reaction of someone you hoped would support you deter you from following a slower lifestyle. **Zodiac:** Virgo. **Empowerment:** I welcome the fertility of the earth.

Every newly built or impersonal modern home, soulless hotel room or workplace benefits from a piece of limonite to make it feel more welcoming; if there are threats of redundancies or cutbacks at your place of work or if you have an intrusive landlord or lady, flatmates or neighbours, this crystal creates stability and marks your own territory.

Keep also in the car to hold if your satellite navigation is giving you false information to guide you home or to a chosen destination.

Hold it over the place you need to be on the map and say, "Take me there." Place also near the tank or cage of an exotic pet to help them feel safe; good for researching family history and locating distant family members.

Citrine

Type: Quartz, heated naturally in the earth.

Colours: Yellow and transparent, from pale to golden yellow, honey or almost brown; may contain rainbows and sparkles.

Availability: Relatively rare, but worth obtaining.

Physical benefits: Said to be good for relieving skin problems and allergies, especially those caused by food or chemical intolerances, liver problems and liver transplants, short-term memory loss, bedwetting particularly in young adults; fibromyalgia, nausea and vomiting; morning sickness.

Emotional healing: Effective against being a workaholic, stress leading to over-spending or excessive risk-taking, gambling addictions; neuroses of all kinds.

Chakra: Solar Plexus.

Candle colour: Yellow. **Fragrances:** Almond, lemon balm, orange. **Practical uses:** A pyramid or geode attracts health and abundance to the home and spreads sunshine and happiness. **Workplace:** For all who work in merchant banking, casinos, sports and fitness instructors, the media, medical personnel and healers. **Magical significance:** Natural citrine tumblestones where light catches them clear unfriendly ghosts; sprinkle citrine elixir weekly to prevent negative energies returning. **Divinatory meaning:** A time to communicate your ideas and needs clearly. **Zodiac:** Gemini. **Empowerment:** I attract abundance into my life.

Natural citrine is said to contain solidified sunlight and never to absorb negativity and so never needs cleansing; wear as a shield against spite and jealousy, at the same time benefiting from its wealth- and luck-bringing powers. Natural citrine has all the powers and healing properties of heat-treated citrine but its energies are more powerful if less instant. Give as an angel or sphere to a newborn to bring intelligence, health, happiness, curiosity, money, confidence,, and above all healing wisdom. Carry to attract love and protect against those who would break your heart.

Heat-Treated Citrine

Type: Heat-treated purple amethyst or grey smoky quartz

Colours: Yellow and transparent; colours tend to be brighter, sparkling and may have inclusions.

Availability: Common.

Physical benefits: May help ease problems with the following: pancreas, liver, spleen, gall bladder, digestive system; back, spine, bedwetting, exhaustion, lack of energy; fibromyalgia, metabolism, Crohn's disease.

Emotional healing: Effective against depression, alcohol abuse, addictions, overcoming repressed childhood hurts and for breaking a cycle of worry or guilt.

Chakra: Solar Plexus.

Candle colour: Yellow. **Fragrances:** Bergamot, lemongrass, lime, marigold,. **Practical uses:** Brings happiness to family gatherings; for selling your house, put seven tumble-stones in a row on an indoor window ledge before a buyer comes. **Workplace:** Increases sales, attracts customers and encourages right choices in financial speculation. Keep a tumblestone in a cash register. **Magical significance:** Hold while looking into a mirror in sunlight and say, "I am worthy of admiration, I am worthy of consideration and so I take my place in the sun". **Divinatory meaning:** Take a chance or speculate as luck is with you. **Zodiac:** Gemini. **Empowerment:** I am not afraid to take a chance.

Place on your Solar Plexus energy centre if you have to speak at a meeting or are struggling for ideas. Keep near your computer when installing and learning new software or applying for a loan or credit card online.

Hold close to your mouth and breathe in softly seven times, then blow the citrine breath outwards; repeat for two or three minutes to fill the aura energy field that surrounds you if you are scared or lonely; splash an elixir on your wrist pulse points, throat and brow if you are sleepy, experiencing an unhealthy craving or if you are struggling with facts and figures.

Type: Sulphate (calcium tungstate).

Colours: Yellow or golden, orange, green-grey, brown, white.

Availability: Rare but obtainable from some specialist crystal stores and online.

Physical benefits: Thought to help to balance male and female hormones and reproductive systems, regulate excessive testosterone in its effects in women including facial hair growth, relieve lower back and leg problems, ADHD and hyperactivity, especially if it is manifest as aggressive behaviour.

Emotional healing: Restores emotional and mental balance; reduces mood swings, excessive anger and violence in either sex, particularly young females and all teenagers who join street gangs.

Chakra: Root and Crown.

Scheelite

Candle colour: Yellow or Orange. **Fragrances:** Dragon's blood, grapefruit, hibiscus, honeysuckle, mimosa. **Practical uses:** Use in a predominantly male household or chauvinistic working environment for softer, less competitive energies, if children of either sex or indeed animals play too roughly or teasing gets out of hand. **Workplace:** Scheelite in your workspace helps you to resist psychological pressures from a hostile environment and to think clearly and perform competently if you are being assessed or monitored or are the subject of an official inspection or investigation. **Magical significance:** Scheelite aids those new to meditation or who are easily distracted to enter a deeply relaxed state: carry in a neck pouch during moving meditation, when you meditate while walking or dancing; the best crystal for acquiring trance mediumship skills. **Divinatory meaning:** Keep calm if you are being unfairly pressurized or blamed; your innocence will be soon proved. **Zodiac:** Libra. **Empowerment:** I will not deny but work though anger.

Scheelite is a major tungsten ore and works with our thought patterns, opening our mind to psychic awareness in everyday life. This is because it stimulates the Crown chakra, heightening our mental and spiritual awareness, but its direct connection in the Root chakra keeps us grounded. As a bonus, scheelite aligns all the other chakras in between, so you are neither stuck in the material world nor out of touch. If worn or carried, it will cleanse your aura energy field automatically of pollution and blockages, and reduce the effects of

overload and overstimulation from the daily world.

Golden Chinese faceted scheelite is a fabulous collector's gem but too soft for jewellery.

Scheelite is good for all psychic development work; it helps us connect simultaneously with paranormal and earth energies and so should be part of every ghost-detective's equipment.

Place one in a pocket or shoulder bag as a counterbalance and amplifier when dowsing for minerals, water or ley lines using copper rods or a forked hazel twig.

Anatase

Type: Titanium dioxide.

Colours: Yellow, green/yellow, blue, brown or black.

Availability: Rare, but can be found in some specialist crystal stores or online.

Physical benefits: Believed to help improve sinus problems, memory loss, stress, increase and balance metabolism and for psychosomatic rooted illnesses, tics and stuttering.

Emotional healing: Overcomes a sense of helplessness in the face of obstacles and misfortune, creating a sense that there is always some positive action that can be taken, however small.

Chakra: Solar Plexus.

Candle colour: Yellow. **Fragrances:** Almond, anise, lime. **Practical uses:** Keep on the table during family discussions to get on with sorting out issues. **Workplace:** Set in your workspace to overcome subtle undermining and criticism; good for writing clear, concise emails. **Magical significance:** Good for finding what is lost: hold a pendulum over anatase and visualize what is missing. Follow the swing of the pendulum in the area you know you have mislaid the item or over a map of your house or immediate vicinity. **Divinatory meaning:** Do not let others avoid discussing issues **Zodiac:** Scorpio. **Empowerment:** I am certain I will win through.

Known as the crystal of decisiveness, this a good crystal for those who make policies, laws or judgements or are involved in the legal profession. Also if you are planning a total change of lifestyle but hesitate to take the first step. A crystal for speaking out. It is helpful if you have always tried to please people or your identity has been eroded by the demands of others. Good for research and whenever you need clarity. Take a piece with you to any meetings with authority figures or officials to put your cause or case calmly and firmly, especially if you suspect there is some hidden agenda.

Lemon Chrysoprase

Type: Chalcedony gem variety with nickel; alternatively light yellow magnesite with brown to light tan veining.

Colours: Lemon yellow to yellow-green.

Availability: Common.

Physical benefits: May assist with skin, muscles, mobility, nausea especially in pregnancy, diarrhoea, weight loss, liver, cholesterol, detoxification, hormone imbalance, sexual dysfunction, headaches (food-related), saliva and sweat glands, recovery after illness or surgery.

Emotional healing: Good for breaking free of emotional blackmail, manipulation and mind games.

Chakra: Heart and Solar Plexus.

Candle colour: Lemon yellow. **Fragrances:** Bergamot, grapefruit, lemon. **Practical uses:** Bury by the front door to deter unwanted callers; wear to protect against emotional pressure. **Workplace:** Use to fight unfair dismissal, false accusations or to get a fair hearing. **Magical significance:** Empower to break hexes or attempts to control your mind by naming the perpetrator as you hold the stone; seal in a plastic container in the freezer; bury both after three months. **Divinatory meaning:** You may hear something shocking; do not take it seriously as the teller has a hidden agenda. **Zodiac:** Gemini. **Empowerment:** All will be resolved in its own time.

Wear or carry and touch lemon chrysoprase to deter undesirable people from bothering you at night when travelling home. Give a tumblestone or as jewellery to any family member who is jealous of an addition, or if your new partner resents your children; also makes established pets accept new animals. The crystal benefits from occasional rehydration with water. Will reduce the pains of unrequited love; carry to deter a would-be lover who refuses to take no for an answer.

Encourages honesty; touch one to sense the intention to deceive as you will feel an icy tingling in your fingers.

Type: Cyclosilicate/Beryl.

Colours: Yellow-green, or greenish-yellow to brown

Availability: Relatively common (but flawless specimens less common and more expensive)

Physical benefits: Believed to aid problems with the digestive system, liver, spleen and heart, bilious attacks, nausea, jaundice, diarrhoea, spine, kidney and bladder problems, such as cystitis and for warming stiff or immobile limbs or cold fingers and toes whether caused by cold weather or poor circulation.

Emotional healing: Facilitates understanding of another's needs; a gift for those with for narcissistic personalities or those who are wrapped up in their own problems and blame others in the past for everything.

Chakra: Sacral and Solar Plexus

Heliodor

Candle Colour: Yellow. **Fragrances:** Angelica, chamomile, lavender, peppermint, sweet marjoram. **Practical uses:** Keep heliodor in your home or wear it as a gemstone to increase your levels of happiness and buoyant energy, particularly in winter-time or if your home is naturally dark and has little natural light. **Workplace:** Boosts drive and determination to succeed if your get up and go has waned or others have worn away your enthusiasm; wear or carry heliodor to convince others to back you financially or with resources. **Magical significance:** Hold heliodor in pale sunlight or in dark winter by gold candlelight; look within it to contact your still wise centre and inner sun and fill yourself with certainty of your life path; hold by natural water to connect with water spirits. **Divinatory meaning:** A return of hope and the way ahead at last seems open; a good omen for unexpected holidays abroad and winter sun. **Zodiac:** Leo. **Empowerment:** I seek the light within me.

Heliodor is a greenish-yellow beryl but not, as it is commonly mistaken, golden beryl, though they are similar. In fact, Heliodor is the variety name that includes all yellow, yellow-green, light-green, orange, and brown beryl.

Golden yellow beryl is a variety of heliodor with a golden yellow colour like the sunshine at noon in summer. What is commonly called heliodor is more like early winter sunshine filtering through trees.

The name Heliodor is derived from the Greek language and translates as gift from the sun.

Throughout history, heliodor has been used as a talisman to increase honesty in others and to regain what has been lost in terms of employment, prospects or money. A wonderful stone for the self-employed or those who struggle to balance care of children or elderly or sick relatives with a career. A small piece of heliodor helps tropical animals, birds or fish to live happily in colder climates. You should also use heliodor if you are moving to a colder part of the world to help you acclimatize.

Type: Aluminium oxide containing beryllium, the *official* cat's eye in lustrous eye form.

Colours: Clear yellow, honey, yellowy green or brown.

Availability: Relatively rare.

Physical benefits: Claimed to relieve disorders connected with exhaustion; diarrhoea, IBS, coeliac disease, stomach ulcers and other intestinal disorders, food allergies and intolerances; chest infections; improves resistance to illness; good for eyesight, particularly night vision and clear-sightedness; encourages gentle weight loss by natural means.

Emotional healing: Good for people who adopt the opinions and values of whomever they are with, to see life through their own eyes and develop a personal identity.

Chakra: Solar Plexus.

Chrysoberyl

Candle colour: Yellow or gold. **Fragrances:** Marigold, mimosa, mint, rosemary, thyme. **Practical uses:** Associated traditionally with great leaders, a good gem to wear if you have organize a sports, community, charity or social event such as a wedding or christening if you know there will be interference. **Workplace:** Encourages us to strive for the highest possible standards; therefore excellent both for teaching children values and for good ethics in any workplace if management is non-existent or corrupt. **Magical significance:** Wear or hold to increase telepathic communication with your cat or other intelligent pets such as dogs or horses, particularly if you are late home and want to reassure them. **Divinatory meaning:** Look for long-term advantage and security if contemplating change, and consider if you might be better be off where you are. **Zodiac:** Gemini or Leo. **Empowerment:** I do not need to follow the lead of others.

There are two other gem varieties of chrysoberyl, apart from cat's eye: the faceted transparent yellowish green to green, yellow and brown version and emerald-green alexandrite. Chrysoberyl is different from beryl, which is silicate, whereas these are aluminium oxide containing beryllium.

Most special of the chrysoberyls is the lustrous cat's eye, also known as cymophane. This is not faceted but carved into cabochons, highly polished domed shapes cut to preserve the moving-eye effect. It is a luck-bringer; also, because of its link with cats, it is very protective against accidents and mishaps, particularly those caused by haste.

Chrysoberyl enhances the healing properties of other crystals or alternative remedies, helping to instinctively identify the nature of an illness and whether it needs conventional or spiritual healing remedies or both. All chrysoberyls, especially the yellow ones, are natural prosperity-bringers and were once believed to attract a wealthy partner. They represent the desire and ability to strive for the best and highest standards in ethics, success and achievement.

Andradite Garnet

Type: Calcium iron silicate.

Colours: Yellow, yellowish or emerald-green, grey-green, black, brownish red, brownish yellow.

Availability: Rare to more common, depending on colour.

Physical benefits: Said to improve strength, stamina and vitality; stimulates metabolism, benefits the circulation.

Emotional healing: Brings emotional strength, stability and balance, promoting self-confidence and self-esteem in those who rely too much on the approval and permission of others.

Chakra: Root, Solar Plexus and Heart.

Candle colour: Yellow or burgundy. **Fragrances:** Bay, benzoin, frankincense, juniper, rosemary. **Practical uses:** The yellow and darker forms of andradite counterbalance sentimentality and emotional clinginess, encouraging the equal growth of a relationship. **Workplace:** Helpful for anyone who works alone; encourages networking and ideas-pooling. **Magical significance:** Protective against fears of the darker side of life, and attempts at mind control, particularly through emotional pressures and misuse of sexual power. **Divinatory meaning:** Do not hesitate to ask now you need assistance. **Zodiac:** Capricorn and Aquarius **Empowerment:** I will not be distracted.

Orthoclase

Type: Silicate, potassium feldspar, closely related to moonstone and amazonite.

Colours: Yellow, greenish, colourless, white, grey.

Availability: Rare in transparent gem-quality form; common opaque types available at specialist crystal stores and online.

Physical benefits: Claimed for centuries in different cultures to be a healer of all ills, especially helpful for back, heart conditions and transplants of any organ to assist the host body to accept the new organ.

Emotional healing: A bringer of peace in times of emotional upheaval. If you are suffering from grief, tune into this crystal to help you rise out of the dark.

Chakra: Solar Plexus, but can assist in aligning all the chakras.

Candle colour: Pale yellow. **Fragrances:** Jasmine, lime, mimosa, neroli, poppy. **Practical uses:** Assists in finding unusual ways of achieving dreams; increases unique qualities in a conformist world. **Workplace:** Helpful to transform dissension and achieve consensus; set one in the middle of a meeting table. **Magical significance:** Clarifies messages from other dimensions; assists those who have experienced UFO contact or cryptozoological creatures to integrate their experiences into their everyday world. **Divinatory meaning:** A time of personal growth that may mean you move away from some friends and closer to others. **Zodiac:** Cancer. **Empowerment:** I do not need to fit in.

Andradite garnet has three main sub-varieties of differing colour groups and values. The yellow is called topazolite. The variety of andradite will determine its metaphysical properties, but all possess energies common to all garnets: protection, strength, communication and relationship-building. Yellow andradite is the most powerful and active, operating through the Solar Plexus and adding focus and determination. Boosts creative skills and opens the mind to clearer thinking. Wear any andradite to attract your cosmic equal and life companion.

A crystal that in times of tragedy radiates power to bring consolation; offer to the bereaved or place close to a photograph of someone who is dying for a peaceful passing. Use to mark a pet's grave.

Offer orthoclase to hold if a child has been deeply traumatized; for rape victims or those who have been attacked or are being threatened with violence. If you live in an area where there is serious unrest or is affected by war or terrorism, wear in any unavoidably confrontational situation, close your eyes and let it carry you to a temporary sanctuary to restore inner peace.

Yellow Fluorite

Type: Halide/calcium fluoride.

Colours: Yellow.

Availability: One of the less common fluorites.

Physical benefits: May relieve problems with cholesterol, liver, bile, stomach adhesions, intestinal blockages or growths, stomach-stapling operations, cosmetic surgery, DNA, arthritis, rheumatism, spine, bones, teeth particularly wisdom teeth and gum health, shingles.

Emotional healing: For self-defeating behaviour and constantly comparing oneself unfavourably with others; reduces jealousy through insecurity and lack of self-love.

Chakra: Sacral and Solar Plexus.

Candle colour: Yellow. **Fragrances:** Chamomile, lavender, lemongrass, lemon verbena, sage. **Practical uses:** Counteracts the tendency of caring people to give the coat off their back to every hard-luck story they come across. **Workplace:** Helps dreamy gentle souls gain commercial sense without sacrificing their spiritual nature; for anyone setting up in self-employment to avoid being too ambitious at first. **Magical significance:** Good for paranormal investigations or experiments to maintain objectivity without sacrificing intuition. **Divinatory meaning:** You need to use logic and uncharacteristic toughness to resolve a problem. **Zodiac:** Gemini. **Empowerment:** I can be strong and spiritual.

Carry if you are naturally gentle and spiritual to direct intellect and effort into tangible achievements. If you find it hard to organize your thoughts or produce specifically defined results because your imagination takes off, use as an elixir or wear the crystal. Steers the fine path between attainable dreams and illusions; ideal for young people who are reluctant to begin a career from the bottom. Keep in the workplace or in organizing ventures where cooperation is needed

A crystal to hold when you need to come up with a plausible excuse to avoid an event you are dreading.

Yellow/Golden Opal

Type: Hydrated silicon dioxide, common opal, displaying no iridescence.

Colours: Amber, gold and yellow.

Availability: Found in specialist crystal stores and online.

Physical benefits: Claimed to assist problems with gallstones and kidney stones, infections, absorption, appetite, chronic exhaustion, Parkinson's disease, memory, insulin regulation, diabetes; ease childbirth and assist natural onset of labour, eyes, elixir is a general energizer.

Emotional healing: Increases happiness and makes situations feel better, so creating the impetus to actively seek positive solutions; restores the will to live.

Chakra: Solar Plexus.

Candle colour: Yellow. **Fragrances:** Benzoin, elder blossom, marigold, orange, sunflower. **Practical uses:** A lucky stone to instinctively be in the right place at the right time; attracts friends in unexpected places and makes online chat more real and personal. **Workplace:** A naturally stabilizing stone, worn or set in the workspace spreads good humour and tolerance. **Magical significance:** Hold your opal up to the sun or light at dawn, noon and sunset, best of all on a Sunday; it will hold enough sun power to keep you smiling all week. **Divinatory meaning:** Do something for pleasure not for duty or profit. **Zodiac:** Gemini and Cancer. **Empowerment:** I have all I need to be happy.

Yellow opal is a winning-competitions stone; good for quiz shows and tests of ability and knowledge; carry to enjoy competitive sports rather than obsessing about winning, and for stamina while running marathons or taking part in extreme sports. Also helps to remove limits you put on your own potential through lack of self-belief or opportunity; a good stone if you are returning to study. An anti-jealousy and -spite stone, wear to turn envy or gossip away from you and create a shield of positive energy; give to a teenager who is teased for being too clever and for enjoying study.

Type: Magnesium aluminium oxide. Some spinels are made artificially but are not so good for healing or empowerment.

Colours: From pale to golden yellow; may sometimes be heat-treated.

Availability: One of the less common spinel colours.

Physical benefits: Thought to help to relieve energy deficiencies, clear stagnation, toxins and mercury or lead from the body, digestive blockages, liver, pancreas and gall-bladder infections, Seasonal Affective Disorder, amnesia, short-term memory failings; improve the appetite.

Emotional healing: The sunshine spinel, yellow spinel is a natural anti-depressant; encourages optimism and brings strength to keep going one day at a time in difficult periods; naturally pessimistic people should wear yellow spinel to counterbalance gloom.

Chakra: Solar Plexus.

Yellow Spinel

Candle colour: Yellow. **Fragrances:** Chamomile, cloves, orange, rosemary, sunflower. **Practical uses:** Sunshine spinels attract beautiful things, happy people and chances for spontaneous fun and laughter into daily life; wear yellow spinel on duty at social occasions, family events you are dreading and work events, to have a much better time than anticipated. **Workplace:** Excellent for difficult examinations, assessments or tests or where there is fierce competition for a job or professional award; good for learning difficult languages with unfamiliar lettering systems and for mastering complex technological data or formulae. **Magical significance:** Use yellow spinel at the centre of a healing layout between the person's navel and their upper stomach (approximately waist level), surrounded by six citrine; clears emotional blockages that are standing in the way of physical healing; wear while healing others or during a clairvoyant session to maintain optimism and energy levels. **Divinatory meaning:** Say yes to the chance of a spontaneous outing or treat; the chores will be there tomorrow but the sun may not be. **Zodiac:** Sagittarius. **Empowerment:** I can make my own sunshine.

Yellow spinel is a crystal of personal power and determination to fulfil destiny in a way that will bring happiness rather than just material success. If you feel that you have lost your enthusiasm for life, hold yellow spinel on your Solar Plexus in the centre of your upper stomach and recall the last time you felt excitement or spontaneous joy; then go back to the time before that and keep going back until you have rekindled those feelings.

Yellow spinel is a crystal that also rekindles or inspires a love of learning if you were badly taught at school; keep a natural piece at home to stimulate conversation and encourage curiosity about life and an openness to explore new experiences and places; helpful for anyone who is restricted by circumstances or physical mobility, to develop mind pursuits.

It is an excellent anti-spite crystal against family jealousy and old rivalries that spill over into adulthood and for reducing over-competitiveness between adult siblings that may be carried over to the next generation.

Yellow Jasper

Type: Silicate, microcrystalline quartz.

Colours: Mustard, sandy or burnished yellow.

Availability: Common.

Physical benefits: Seen as useful for improving problems with stomach bloating, liver, gall bladder, gallstones, bile duct and large intestine, nausea, fat intolerance, chronic indigestion, immune system, circulation, for all animal healing.

Emotional healing: Eases chronic worries and self-consciousness about what other people say and think about you; overcomes embarrassment of eating in public.

Chakra: Solar Plexus.

Candle colour: Yellow. **Fragrances:** Angelica, bergamot, fennel, lemongrass, mint. **Practical uses:** Take on holiday to guard against danger, help you make friends and protect you from potential stomach disorders. **Workplace:** Encourages the completion of tasks that have been put off. **Magical significance:** A good anti-spite and -venom crystals if you are the subject of a whispering campaign; keep a bottle of yellow jasper elixir between you and the nasty person and afterwards tip away. **Divinatory meaning:** You will soon receive an invitation to travel. **Zodiac:** Gemini, and Capricorn. **Empowerment:** I am a part of the Earth Mother.

Yellow jasper, if worn for prolonged periods, builds self-confidence, attracting others to help with a goal or offer friendship. Also protects you from negative energy and is beneficial for those living in close-knit communities. Transmits healing and empowering earth energy and connects you with the earth and wildlife. If held outdoors while you sit on the ground, it connects you with the cultures of indigenous people and totem animals through the ages through astral or mind travel.

A crystal of the intellect, yellow jasper encourages steady learning. Wear to protect against false people.

Lemon Quartz

Type: Silicon dioxide/quartz; occurs naturally. Lemon colour caused by iron; also called oro verde.

Colours: Golden yellow-green, lemon.

Availability: Common.

Physical benefits: May relieve issues with nausea, bladder and kidneys, brain functioning, diabetes, lack of energy; for speeding recovery from an operation or prolonged illness, detoxify, increase metabolism and assist any weight-loss programme, clear colds that linger and infections of the skin.

Emotional healing: A a reminder of all the good things in life and blessings to counteract negativity.

Chakra: Solar Plexus.

Candle colour: Lemon yellow. **Fragrances:** Lemon, lemongrass, lime, neroli. **Practical uses:** Brings good luck and a flow of fresh energies. **Workplace:** Wear to work efficiently; use in a workplace where there are relation-ships that interfere with the running of the business, to stay detached and meet deadlines without appearing unsociable. **Magical significance:** Said traditionally to have power against snake venom, worn as a pendant it repels spite; spiral a lemon or lemongrass incense stick over it weekly to clear of human venom. **Divinatory meaning:** Stay detached from an argument between friends. **Zodiac:** Gemini. **Empowerment:** I will use my head as well as my heart.

Lemon quartz is faster-acting than citrine; wear for examinations or interviews. Use for making instant decisions, and for acquiring money fast in an emergency. Often worn by ghost investigators if the nature of a haunting is unknown or there is poltergeist activity.

One of the most effective crystals to wear to break the hold of someone who plays mind games, wear as earrings if the person uses flattering words to break down resistance. Reduces cravings, particularly for cigarettes and for food-related issues where binge and fasting create fluctuating weight; a prosperity-bringer.

Yellow Jade

Type: Silicate/pyroxene, jadeite with mineral inclusions.

Colours: Lemon to brighter yellow.

Availability: Relatively common.

Physical benefits: Said to help with the digestive system, organs that deal with waste, liver, gall bladder, pancreas, spleen, gallstones and kidney stones, calcification of bones, tongue and mouth diseases, ulcers, childhood skin parasites.

Emotional healing: Yellow jade jewellery and tumblestones protect against peer-group or classroom spite; particularly shielding from SMS malice or nastiness on social networking sites such as Facebook.

Chakra: Solar Plexus and Root.

Candle colour: Yellow. **Fragrances:** Chamomile, marigold, sage, sagebrush, sunflower. **Practical uses:** Encourages new friendships to grow and existing ones to flourish; give to become friends with adult children. **Workplace:** Encourages professionalism and high standards of performance and behaviour. **Magical significance:** Keep as your stone of fortune, for attracting luck in career, travel and in making money through speculation or money-spinning ideas. **Divinatory meaning:** Think lucky and you will feel lucky – and will take chances you would otherwise have dismissed. **Zodiac:** Taurus and Gemini. **Empowerment:** I make my own good fortune though endeavour.

Yellow jade is the happiness stone and should be kept around the home to bring sunshine or in the office to cheer everyone up. A travel stone to guide you off the beaten track; a stone of assimilation and discrimination, wear to amplify your internal radar to know a good decision from a bad one; an excellent shield if you are easily hurt by an over-abrasive attitude in someone who means well but makes you feel inferior. Wear at social events where you do not know many people or when going on holiday alone to attract like-minded people and to exude confidence.

Sulphur

Type: A soft natural element mineral, easier and safer to handle as sulphur quartz.

Colours: Yellow, green, yellow-brown, red or greyish yellow, white with yellow streaks in quartz.

Availability: Common.

Physical benefits: Believed to assist in healing infections and inflammations, skin conditions, digestion, fevers and joint inflammation, swellings, cysts and haemorrhoids, detoxify the body, speed wound healing and sinus problems. Use only indirectly as sulphur is poisonous.

Emotional healing: Helps those with a disposition to negativity or anger or who are under stress to overcome this.

Chakra: Solar Plexus.

Candle colour: Yellow. **Fragrances:** Angelica, benzoin, copal, garlic, juniper. **Practical uses:** Carrying sealed sulphur quartz crystal in a small yellow bag diminishes adverse effects of unfamiliar food and water; also helps you to avoid anyone who would cheat you. **Workplace:** Brings focus and mental alertness; carry the mineral wrapped in paper or in a small box in the glove box of a car in bad weather if your job involves driving or commuting. **Magical significance:** Sulphur can be used for banishing and protection. **Divinatory meaning:** Let go of anger even though justified. **Zodiac:** Aries and Leo. **Empowerment:** I release negative thoughts and feelings and fill my self with joy and light.

Sulphur, also called brimstone, will bring anything to the surface into manifestation; keep close when you are asking for help or favours; if put near a job or loan application or when surfing the Net for the right car, you usually end up with something better than hoped for. Use tiny pieces of sulphur to represent what you want to get rid of in your life and put them in the ground beneath a tall rock. **WARNING:** Sulphur is toxic and combustible and should not be put in water. Do not use for elixirs. Wash hands after handling and keep away from children and pets.

Chalcopyrite / Copper Pyrite

Type: Copper iron sulphide; mainly copper ore.

Colours: Brassy gold, sometimes with a slight green or iridescent tint.

Availability: Common.

Physical benefits: May ease problems with brain disorders, meningitis, tumours, DNA and gene therapy.

Emotional healing: Counters a poor self-image and overcomes fear of failure; helps lonely people find friends.

Chakra: Heart and Crown.

Candle colour: Green. **Fragrances:** Apple blossom, clary sage, rose, rosewood, violet. **Practical uses:** Carry a polished stone when you begin a fitness regime, or or participation in vigorous sports. **Workplace:** Connected with the powers of growth in business and resulting prosperity; good for careers in fashion and beauty, and the media or sales. **Magical significance:** To find missing items, hold horizontally at waist height in the hand you write with. Walk from the last place you recall having the item. If the stone vibrates you are on track. **Divinatory meaning:** A period of increased good fortune, also a chance for travel. **Zodiac:** Taurus. **Empowerment:** It is better to go forward in hope than to hold back in fear.

Unpolished chalcopyrite is a stone of fire, believed to warm travellers in lonely places by generating heat in the body when placed inside outer garments. Eight tumblestones in a circle round a patient strengthen the effects of acupressure, acupuncture and shiatsu, and a pointed natural chalcopyrite, its point towards the patient's feet, assists reflexology. A shielding crystal against the effects of prolonged medication, treatment or repeated surgical intervention. The stone of mystical experiences, it aids an instinctive understanding of the past and spiritual connection with ancestors.

Yellow/Peach Moonstone

Type: Feldspar.

Colours: Yellow, yellow-brown or peach.

Availability: Relatively common.

Physical benefits: Thought to help with hormonal cycles, connected with fertility, menstruation, the menopause, PMS, fibroids, IVF and surrogate mothering; stomach acid, indigestion, nausea and vomiting, gallstone pain, pancreatic problems, fluid retention, food allergies.

Emotional healing: A consoling crystal for anyone who feels helpless because of weight problems; wear to love and value yourself as you are now and to separate food from emotional needs.

Chakra: Sacral.

Candle colour: Peach. **Fragrances:** Chamomile, peach, ylang ylang. **Practical uses:** Wear all month and make love on the night of the full moon to trigger your fertility cycle. **Workplace:** Helpful for farmers, gardeners, florists, food production and distribution workers, artists, dancers, musicians and singers; medical staff involved in fertility. **Magical significance:** Most powerful on the full moons of later summer and autumn, and still effective on the night of any full moon for major wishes or empowerments. **Divinatory meaning:** What you work for is coming to fruition. The results may be better than hoped. **Zodiac:** Cancer. **Empowerment:** I acknowledge my potential for growth.

Yellow and peach moonstones make impersonal situations more welcoming;; helps to bring out the best in people who are unpleasant due to sorrow or shyness. Attracts prosperity and success; generates enthusiasm in lethargic family members, and is the most active moonstone in preserving dreams but focusing them in the real world. Good gardening crystals: bury one in the three days leading up to the full moon in land you wish to cultivate; place one in soil of delicate plants. A good gift for a girl entering puberty early.

Type: Native element/precious metal.

Colours: Metallic yellow and gleaming.

Availability: Common.

Physical benefits: Called a master healer because it is said to help almost every condition and will amplify the strength of any other crystals, metal or substance used; particularly arthritis, heart and spine, circulation, nervous system and digestion, tissue regrowth.

Emotional healing: Dispels negative thoughts, reduces excessive, harmful actions and reactions; even the smallest amount of gold provides the incentive to dig oneself out of an emotional or life-situation hole.

Chakra: Brow and Crown.

Gold

Candle colour: Gold or yellow. **Fragrances:** Benzoin, cinnamon, frankincense, orange, rosemary. **Practical uses:** Gold rings, even very thin ones, bring fidelity to those in a relationship "as long as the sun lasts", it is said, and protection from jealous rivals; if you are unattached, a gold ring endows courage and confidence to approach the person you want to be with and, if necessary, fight to win the right love. **Workplace:** Wear gold to attract power, prosperity, promotion and success, and to bring happiness and fulfilment in career; gold lucky charms attract positive attention at interviews or auditions if you seek fame. **Magical significance:** Gold is the metal of the sun, especially at noon, the time of the sun's greatest power, and at midsummer; used as offerings to the deities for thousands of years. On Midsummer Day at noon, drop a thin gold ring or earring in sunlit water for success during the year ahead in the way most needed. **Divinatory meaning:** Now is the time to apply for a television reality show, attend an audition or major job interview, or submit a creative work; success is around you. **Zodiac:** Leo **Empowerment:** I am pure gold.

Gold has been associated in many lands and ages with the deities and immortality. The Ancient Egyptians believed that the skin of the deities was made of gold, and for this reason some Pharaohs, most notably the boy king Tutankhamun, was given a gold mask after death and his mummy set in three gold coffins.

Incredibly malleable, gold can be beaten into the finest of layers, called leaf, that is used for decorative and artistic proposes.

Pure gold is yellow in colour but is often alloyed with other minerals, such as silver or copper, to make it harder. Pure 24-carat gold is quite soft.

Gold helps to clear emotional and psychic blockages throughout the body and mind caused by negativity. Used in conjunction with angel crystals such as seraphinite, opal aura or angelite during meditation, gold can help you to connect with the higher angelic realms, especially the Archangel Michael, whose special metal is gold.

Golden/ Yellow Calcite

Type: Calcium carbonate.

Colours: From pale yellow through shades of yellow to gold.

Availability: Common.

Physical benefits: Seen as aiding the detoxification of all digestive organs.

Emotional healing: Self-esteem that has been damaged by abuse, coldness or neglect in childhood or later in life by a destructive or controlling relationship; assists body-image issues.

Chakra: Solar Plexus and Sacral.

Candle colour: Gold. **Fragrances:** Anise, copal, frankincense, sandalwood, sage. **Practical uses:** Melts resentment and estrangement and, if worn, attracts friendships and social opportunities. **Workplace:** A crystal of learning that is helpful to anyone with learning difficulties, with dyslexia or who freezes in panic in test situations. **Magical significance:** Write down the names of anyone spiteful, fold the list as small as possible and tie it with three knots with a piece of yellow calcite in a yellow scarf. Keep in a drawer. **Divinatory meaning:** A routine social event will be better than expected. Accept the invitation. **Zodiac:** Sagittarius and Pisces **Empowerment:** I will make today golden.

Use for healing pets or for soothing rescued or lost animals; add the natural crystal to pet water for a few hours; also helps pets who are jealous of a new family member to minimize aggression. Set tumbled stone in healing or home empowerment/protection layouts to spread the energy through the grid and into the patient or the home. The more golden the stone, the more powerful its properties; a golden calcite sphere expands the boundaries of what is possible through our own efforts rather than luck. An excellent crystal if you are a mature student or want to retrain.

Libyan Desert Glass

Type: Natural glass, pure silica (98 percent), very smooth.

Colours: Pale yellow, can be clear, milky or bubbly.

Availability: Relatively common.

Physical benefits: Said to be excellent for whole-body healing, heal nervous system, tumours and growths, thymus; stimulate the body's immune system; encourage gentle but thorough scans and investigations.

Emotional healing: Wearing insulates sensitive adults from developing physical symptoms as a reaction to stress; heals trauma or abuse from childhood and loss of parents in infancy.

Chakra: Solar Plexus and heart

Candle colour: Pale yellow, straw yellow or pale apple green. **Fragrances:** Chamomile, cyphi, musk, sage. **Practical uses:** Soothes children who have problems fitting in. **Workplace:** Attracts money, business and profitability. Keep in your store or by your computer for drawing new business and for building up a business. **Magical significance:** A powerful focus for group healing to send strength to an absent person, animal or place; each person in a healing circle holds their piece to catch the light of a circle of golden candles, then directs the rays through the glass to the subject; this can also be done alone with a candle. **Divinatory meaning:** Present problems will not affect or delay your future success. **Zodiac:** Aries. **Empowerment:** I feel at home on the Earth.

Worn over the heart, Libyan Desert glass opens the Heart energy centre, allowing love to flow, both in close relationships and towards humanity.

Because of the inclusion in some pieces of Libyan glass of the extra-terrestrial meteoric mineral iridium, it is speculated it was created by the airborne explosion of a comet or asteroid landing on Earth. Libyan glass is estimated to be over 28 million years old and so is a natural focus for exploring ancient wisdom and for mind-travel to ancient places and past lives.

Apache Gold

Type: Pyrite with steatite or chalcopyrite with black schist.

Colours: Brown or black and gold.

Availability: Relatively rare, but very beautiful.

Physical benefits: Seen as helping digestion, stomach and intestines, bowels, constipation, diarrhea, IBS, Crohn's disease, wheat and dairy intolerances and food allergies caused by additives, ear problems, teeth, jaw, bones, alimentary canal; appetite, absorption of nutrients, vitamins and minerals.

Emotional healing: Brings out the good side even of difficult people and assists those who are depressed to focus and develop their strengths and coping strategies.

Chakra: Root and Solar Plexus.

Candle colour: Gold. **Associated fragrances:** Cedar, copal, pine, sweetgrass. **Practical uses:** Wherever you place a piece or if you wear a polished form, energy, confidence, optimism and determination will be activated. **Workplace:** Good for youth unemployment where a someone is losing motivation; wear to fight to keep your job at any age; for all involved in recruitment. **Magical significance:** Wear or buy as tribute to the Earth Mother in rituals for healing the earth and for working with Medicine wheels, labyrinths, shamanism and any indigenous forms of spirituality. **Divinatory meaning:** Do not worry about failing. You have talent and luck is on your side. **Zodiac:** Aries. **Empowerment:** Good times are ahead.

Golden Labradorite

Type: Plagioclase feldspar (tectosilicate)

Colours: Transparent gold or champagne-coloured.

Availability: Quite rare, but available through some specialist crystal stores and online; well worth tracking down.

Physical benefits: May be good for digestion, kidneys, bedwetting, gall bladder, spleen, detoxification.

Emotional healing: For anyone haunted by unfinished business, missing family members of whom there is no news and for recovery after a major tragedy.

Chakra: Solar Plexus.

Candle colour: Gold. **Fragrances:** Benzoin, copal, sandalwood. **Practical uses:** Each month surround yourself with 12 small pieces; lie in sunlight or gold candlelight for 15 minutes to recharge. Afterwards hold and name the monthly goal. **Workplace:** Boost your confidence by wearing every day will make your talents shine. **Magical significance:** On the first of the month, place one in a glass bowl and do so every day for a week, saying seven times, "Gold and silver I have none, into my life good fortune come." Keep lottery tickets or competition entries in the bowl; repeat every month. **Divinatory meaning:** An unexpected windfall will arrive. **Zodiac:** Leo **Empowerment:** I make my own fortune.

Apache gold is good for turning life around and bringing joy. A natural abundance-giver, it can be worn to stop the drain of money and resources and to bring abundance into your life. It is a good grounding and earthing stone if you are healing others, to reinforce the healing and at the same time to protect the healer from absorbing illness or tension. In mediumship or ghost hunting, Apache gold acts as a channel for benign ghosts, family ancestors and spirit-guide teachers and shields against mischievous low level spirits. Wear for happy adventures. A natural luck bringer.

Golden labradorite removes blocks in the Solar Plexus chakra, the home of willpower, personal identity, confidence and the ability to achieve. Spiral through and above your hair to mend tears in your aura energy field by filling them with energizing golden light. Meditate with golden labradorite to open up the channels to the higher realms of archangels. This stone helps you see a way through difficulties and gives the willpower to push forward.

A crystal if you have been having counselling for a while to rely on yourself more.

Golden Beryl

Type: Beryl, ring silicate, also known as heliodor especially in its yellow-green variety.

Colours: Canary yellow to golden yellow.

Availability: Common.

Physical benefits: May help with liver, stomach, spleen, pancreas, small intestine, gallstones, glands, nausea and vomiting, diarrhoea and chronic constipation, preserve youthfulness, heart, for concussion and skull damage, Seasonal Affective Disorder, exhaustion.

Emotional healing: The ultimate confidence and wellbeing gem, often called the sunshine stone.

Chakra: Solar Plexus.

Candle colour: Bright yellow. **Fragrances:** Chamomile, copal, marigold, sage, sunflower. **Practical uses:** Increases the capacity to recall new information; good for study, especially for reluctant students. **Workplace:** A wise stone if your business is in trouble; helps you to keep cheerful and focused. **Magical significance:** Enables you to discover secrets about people's intentions. Close your eyes, hold between your hands, ask what you need to know and the names and information will come to you. **Divinatory meaning:** Anything is possible right now with determination and effort. **Zodiac:** Sagittarius. **Empowerment:** I am motivated to succeed in any challenge.

Protects against the psychological and emotional manipulation of others and from unfriendly ghosts, and general dark energies. A dish of tumblestones where sunlight will shine on them disperses spookiness and attracts angelic energies; good for couples whose relationship has lost its sparkle. Wear if you are impatient with others to develop empathy; for healers, medical personnel, call-centre staff, therapists, care workers and parents to hold in natural form towards the end of a long day to keep smiling. A good naming-day or christening gift for a child as a good-fairy gem.

Gold Scapolite/ Wernerite

Type: Silicates. Wernerite is the old name still used describe the mineral.

Colours: Pale gold to yellow, translucent even in its natural state; also white and purple.

Availability: Found in specialist crystals stores or online.

Physical benefits: May assist eye problems, arthritis and bone problems; may help relieve effects of Alzheimer's and dementia.

Emotional healing: Enables the carrier to break self-destructive patterns; good for post-natal depression and PMS; for counsellors and psychotherapists to achieve lasting results.

Chakra: Solar Plexus.

Candle colour: Gold, yellow. **Fragrances:** Chamomile, orange, pine, sage. **Practical uses:** Good for multi-taskers to remember what needs to be done and to find creative solutions. **Workplace:** Soothes the body, releasing tension in the neck and shoulders; helpful to those who work at computers, constantly answer the phone or are desk-bound; absorbs and disperses electromagnetic emissions from electrical equipment. **Magical significance:** A versatile healing stone that emits the energies needed for each individual to achieve a fulfilling outcome. **Divinatory meaning:** Take a leap of faith. Make happiness your goal. **Zodiac:** Taurus. **Empowerment:** Today will be the best day ever.

Can be confused with varieties of citrine and golden beryl. But hold the happiness stone as it is called and you may want to laugh aloud or smile continually and so it feels different energy-wise. Gold scapolite will offer ongoing positivity that can lift any situation that requires a positive energy boost, such as Christmas, weddings or family events where you know certain people arrive with the intention of spreading doom and gloom or things can go wrong with arrangements; helps you and those round you to release any resentments or grievances, real or imagined, from the past.

Golden Barite

Type: Barium sulphate.

Colours: Yellow to golden.

Availability: Found in specialist crystal stores and online.

Physical benefits: May help to cleanse toxins; relieve stress-related stomach disorders, spleen, liver, gallstones, strengthen body after radiotherapy or chemotherapy, energize the whole system and promote whole-body health, said to increase resistance to chills, infections and viruses.

Emotional healing: Reduces addictions and cravings by creating a feel-good factor and increasing self-control.

Chakra: Solar Plexus.

Candle colour: Gold. **Fragrances**: Frankincense, patchouli, sage, sunflower. **Practical uses**: Hold and questions can be answered by sudden insight; excellent for calming worriers as it induces a sense of well-being; good for making a little money go a long way. **Workplace**: Encourages friendly workplace interactions and cooperation. **Magical significance**: Hold and picture in your mind an animal whose qualities you admire; imagine yourself becoming the creature and you will be filled with their power. **Divinatory meaning**: You will feel in top form and will be able to persuade others to cooperate. **Zodiac**: Leo and Aquarius. **Empowerment**: I feel good about my life.

Golden barite creates a feeling of contentment and so helps us appreciate the life we have. Its gentle continuous release of energies enables you to pace yourself. Brings dream recall and creative solutions in dreams if you focus on a problem before sleep as you hold the crystal. Then put the crystal by the bed and forget the problem. Encourages the belief that anything is possible if you act with enthusiasm and confidence.

It also frees you from the need for the permission others to follow your path. Leave from first light to noon on the midsummer solstice around to empower.

Imperial/ Golden Topaz

Type: Silicate.

Colours: Golden yellow to orange-yellow.

Availability: Easily obtainable in all its forms.

Physical benefits: Thought to improve metabolism, the nervous system; ease problems with gallbladder; haemorrhoids, hormones; promote tissue regeneration, travel sickness.

Emotional healing: A bringer of balance, golden topaz overcomes lack of motivation and enthusiasm; traditionally worn or carried on the left side of the body to replace any free-floating anger and irritability with calm, good humour and self-confidence.

Chakra: Solar Plexus.

Candle colour: Yellow or gold. **Fragrances**: Benzoin, copal, frankincense, heather, marigold. **Practical uses**: Increases self-worth but prevents inflated ego and self-importance in ourselves and others. **Workplace**: Brings money, success and fame. **Magical significance**: Hold up to golden candlelight and connect with fire essences and spirits to fill you with inspiration to see into the future. **Divinatory meaning**: You have as much right to aim high as anyone else. **Zodiac**: Scorpio and Sagittarius. **Empowerment**: I am proud of my achievements.

A gem associated with nobility of spirit as well as status and the stone of the sun. The Ancient Egyptians considered it contained the golden rays of Ra, their sun god, and they used it to help prevent injury. The Romans believed it would cure eye problems and the Greeks thought it made the invisible. Imperial or golden topaz is associated with soul love. Use this crystal to attract the right love into your life or improve existing relationships. All topaz increases in power from the crescent to the full moon and enables you to detect a fraud in love or money during this period. Use to protect your home.

Cacoxenite

Type: Usually forms within a host crystal, commonly amethyst or quartz, and is a major mineral in the powerful Super Seven crystal; phosphate.

Colours: Golden or brown, yellow, yellowish brown, reddish yellow to greenish yellow.

Availability: Relatively rare.

Physical benefits: Believed to assist with cell disorders, thyroid, hormonal imbalances, parasites, growths and tumours, warts, verrucas and moles, stomach and digestive problems; be good for whole body healing.

Emotional healing: An anti-stress crystal that helps to remove the causes of stress.

Chakra: Solar Plexus, Brow and Crown.

Candle colour: Silver or gold. **Fragrances:** Anise, copal, ginger, hibiscus. **Practical uses:** Encourages courtesy, have cacoxenite in amethyst on the table at mealtimes and gatherings to avoid confrontations. **Workplace:** Promotes the highest good in a company; good for deterring dirty tricks. **Magical significance:** Carry on the night of the crescent and full moon to tune in to the rising energies. Light a silver candle and burn a written wish to be fulfilled by the following full moon. **Divinatory meaning:** Beware someone offering you a service or favour who is less than honest. **Zodiac:** Sagittarius. **Empowerment:** I seek only the highest good.

Cacoxenite or cacoxitite takes on different energies according to its host crystal. In quartz it is more active, dynamic and instant than when in gentle, soothing amethyst. It is believed to raise the spiritual awareness of the human race and increase awareness of the significance of random events to guide us on the right path; also encourages a sense of the essence of the creator manifest in the beauty of nature and the kindness of people. This then leads to the realization that everyone has a divine spark. Good in times of emotional upheaval.

Yellow Zircon

Type: Silicate/nesosilicate, zircon.

Colours: Pale yellow, greenish yellow, canary yellow to gold; sometimes heat-treated.

Availability: Relatively common.

Physical benefits: Seen as relieving stomach weakness, pain relief particularly of any gastric or liver problems; may assist with jaundice, hepatitis, nausea, vomiting, varicose veins, high cholesterol; thought to be protective against tropical diseases, encourage successful surgery on the stomach, gall bladder, spleen or liver.

Emotional healing: An excellent stone for adults who are bullied verbally or constantly undermined at work or home and feel to blame, to see through the perpetrator's control and manipulation and break the cycle of abuse.

Chakra: Solar Plexus.

Candle colour: Yellow. **Fragrances:** Chamomile, fennel, lemon, lemongrass. **Practical uses:** Considered to attract prosperity through ingenuity and money-spinning ideas; wear if you plan to start up a home-based industry. **Workplace:** Ideal for those who struggle to process precise information. **Magical significance:** Protective against nasty paranormal energies; give to anyone who has used a Ouija board or called up spirits using mediaeval formulae they do not understand. **Divinatory meaning:** Do not put off the groundwork to launch your ideas so you do not fall foul of officialdom at the first hurdle. **Zodiac:** Gemini. **Empowerment:** I will think first and act afterwards.

The noblest of the zircons, the more golden shades are associated with detachment from pettiness and self-seeking; good for all who want to fulfil their destiny by inventions, research or making a difference globally, or who want to work abroad on humanitarian aid projects. It assists in replacing what is or outworn with the minimum of and disruption and in exploring wider-ranging alternatives.

Encourages good humour and spontaneity; wear it to spread joy and to boost your own energy levels; prevents nightmares and unpleasant psychic dreams.

Type: Volcanic silica glass.

Colours: Dark brown to black with gold sheen.

Availability: Obtainable from specialist crystal stores and online.

Physical benefits: Claimed to improve digestion and impotence, especially stress-related, burn away destructive whole-body genetic illnesses., provide relief for acute pain. Also cited as aiding remission, particularly to neurological conditions, glaucoma and progressive eye problems.

Emotional healing: Shields against ongoing effects of abuse of power, allowing expression of calm resistance with courage and honour.

Chakra: Root, Solar Plexus.

Gold Sheen Obsidian

Candle colour: Gold. **Fragrances:** Copal, cyphi, frankincense, hyssop, sandalwood. **Practical uses:** Carry a golden sheen obsidian sphere or large round crystal and a lighted gold candle from room to room once a week to instantly clear any negativity or stagnation and to attract health and happiness. **Workplace:** Gives access to the root of any problem; wear or carry in a pouch for any diagnostics work from medical or psychological to finding faults in machinery or circuits; a favourite with Reiki healers and those practising psychic surgery. **Magical significance:** A gold sheen obsidian sphere held in candlelight connects a series of images on the surface of the ball in a timeline from past (including past lives) to the root of any problem revealing what is hidden in the present and future potentials. **Divinatory meaning:** The answer is there once you move beyond the "What is the point of it all?" stage. **Zodiac:** Scorpio and Sagittarius **Empowerment:** I see beauty even in the darkest moments.

Golden sheen obsidian is created when small bubbles of air are aligned along layers of obsidian as the molten rock is flowing just before meeting water and instantly cooling.

Use gold sheen obsidian either in a sphere or polished slab as a magic mirror to connect with spirit guide teachers at times when some important knowledge or breakthrough is eluding you. Shine a light for a few moments on the golden sheen obsidian as you look into it, close your eyes, open them; in the obsidian or your mind you will faintly see *your* teacher guardian and be given the missing information as words or images in your mind.

Placed in the wealth area of your home or office if you use Feng Shui or kept with financial papers, near your business computer or in your purse or wallet, this crystal will attract fast money growth and bring achievement of your longer-term financial goals. If worn, it will deter those who try to thwart your ideas or obstruct your path to success and prosperity, usually through jealousy.

Type: Oxide, quartz.

Colours: Brown and gold striped; gleaming and chatoyant, reflecting light in wavy bands (see red tiger's eye, p.70).

Availability: Common.

Physical benefits: May help to ease stomach and gallbladder problems, ulcers, sprains, rheumatism; increase energy levels and strength, restore balance to the body.

Emotional healing: Reduces cravings for the wrong kind of food and food binges or excess cigarettes, prescription drugs or alcohol; reduces anxiety caused by feelings of isolation or inadequacy; increases willpower and emotional stability to make health-improving regimes more likely to succeed.

Chakra: Root and Solar Plexus.

Tiger's Eye

Candle colour: Gold. **Fragrances:** Bay, carnation, copal, geranium, saffron, spearmint. **Practical uses:** Attracts the steady inflow of money to the home. Place a tiger's eye in a pot with a lid and add a coin every day. When full, spend the money on something fun or give to charity and start again. **Workplace:** Good for entrepreneurs and people setting out in business for the first time and for building up a skill and knowledge base for a major future career change or enterprise. **Magical significance:** Traditionally protective against the evil eye; carry a tiger's eye or wear one as jewellery if you suffer from the effects of jealousy, perhaps from a partner's ex, intensive sibling rivalry or envious colleagues. **Divinatory meaning:** Money-making ventures and new projects will succeed even better than anticipated if you persist and keep focused when you hit an obstacle. **Zodiac:** Leo **Empowerment:** I am filled with golden light and can reach out in the confidence that I will succeed.

Associated with the courageous and magical tiger, the king of beasts in Eastern mythology. Roman soldiers carried tiger's eye so that they would be brave in battle. To the Ancient Egyptians, tiger's eye offered the protection of the sun and earth combined, of Ra the sun god and Geb, god of the growing land.

The eye formation offers psychological and psychic protection to reflect back any malice or threats from others without your absorbing any of the negativity. To know whether a person or offer is reliable, hold a tiger's eye and trust your feelings. Traditionally it is said by the end of the day, any deception will be revealed or known.

If you seek to test an artistic or creative talent in a competition or public performance or to sell your gifts in the market place, tiger's eye will help you to overcome a fear of failure or competition and help you to shine. It also stops a pet trying to dominate the household or other animals.

Type: Silicate, microcrystalline quartz, often with mineral or organic inclusions.

Colours: Varying shades of yellow to golden to reddish brown; some brown jaspers with particular pattern formations are given names such as picture jasper though it also comes in a variety of colours.

Availability: Common.

Physical benefits: Seen to aid the bowels, anus, prostate, constant constipation, gastro-enteritis, IBS, coeliac disease, Crohn's disease, wheat and dairy allergies, feet, ankles, knees, joints, muscles, ligaments, fungus infections, warts, moles, verrucas, blisters, abscesses, rodent ulcers, genitals in both sexes, loss of libido, dry skin, kidney stones and kidney disease, tetanus, varicose veins.

Emotional healing: Brown jasper reduces insecurity in those who are constantly worried about losing their money, home or job, or who are filled with guilt about their past failings and inadequacies; breaks the self-defeating cycle and brings a sense of contentment.

Chakra: Root.

Brown Jasper

Candle colour: Brown. **Fragrances:** Anise, cinnamon, cloves, pine, thyme. **Practical uses:** Good for bringing yourself down to earth if you are panicking, angry or spooked at home or work or at a family event; wear brown jasper jewellery, touch it and press down hard with your feet, letting all the tension, fury or fear sink down so you relax. **Workplace:** Protective against electromagnetic energies, technological pollution, noise and hyperactivity; a piece of natural brown jasper acts slowly but its effects are long-lasting, so keep it as a fixture in your workspace or office; rest it monthly by placing it in the soil of a green plant overnight. **Magical significance:** Among Native North Americans brown was prized along with green jasper as a rain-bringer and was rubbed to call the rains; shake your jasper between cupped hands or shake it on the surface of a drum, reciting your need faster and faster and shaking or rattling till you end with a final call and rattle. **Divinatory meaning:** Stay calm and be realistic about possible problems and obstacles ahead; things will work out well, if slower than anticipated. **Zodiac:** Capricorn. **Empowerment:** I have no need to panic.

One of the traditionally used jaspers in Ancient Egypt, brown jasper was called Egyptian marble and used for amulets, ritual vessels and jewellery.

Brown jasper was also carved into arrow-heads in Native North America and other indigenous societies as a luck bringer and for protection. Use it as a charm for all property matters, buying and selling or renting a home, and for success in official meetings to do with finances and loans.

Wear brown jasper when trying to cut down or quit smoking and to stop a panic attack or rush of anxiety. Brown jasper makes an excellent worry stone to keep at work if you need to find a practical solution fast if you are being pressurized; gives stamina to old or sick animals and restores natural instincts to a pet that lives in a city apartment or only walks in urban streets.

Elephant Skin Jasper

Type: Silicate, microcrystalline quartz.

Colours: Brown, with brown and black lines running through.

Availability: Relatively common.

Physical benefits: Claimed to ease skin complaints, bowel and intestinal disorders, internal scar tissue, mobility problems, amnesia, long-term illnesses, scalp disorders and hair loss.

Emotional healing: A stone to overcome loneliness, learn to love your own company and gaining confidence.

Chakra: Root.

Candle colour: Brown. **Fragrances:** Almond, cedar, fennel, lavender, lemongrass. **Practical uses:** Tumblestones counteracts desire for instant gratification or excitement that may destabilize a happy relationship. **Workplace:** Use for long-term decision-making and forward planning; for apprenticeships and enterprise investment and those who cook traditional or organic food. **Magical significance:** Brings a deeper understanding of established religions or ancient forms of spirituality. **Divinatory meaning:** Ask the advice of an expert. **Zodiac:** Capricorn. **Empowerment:** Strength lies in wisdom.

As jewellery or tumblestones, these are an excellent counterbalance to the modern 24/7 society by bringing pleasure in nature and in older, slower ways of living. A potent travel amulet, particularly for driving long distances; also attracts prosperity on business trips and overseas deals made also by telephone or Internet. Protects old houses against subsidence and excessive deterioration; good for renovating older properties; a piece kept with tools will slow down haste that can lead to accidents. Bury behind a new wall, fireplace or radiator to bring luck and prosperity.

Leopardskin Jasper

Type: Silicate, microcrystalline quartz, sister to rhyolite.

Colours: Tan, yellow, pink, red or beige with spots and bands of darker colour, sometimes glassy inclusions.

Availability: Common.

Physical benefits: May improve glands, hormones, bites and stings, nervous system affecting coordination, eczema, rashes and skin allergies, viruses and infections, urinary tract, lower digestive organs, reproductive system, hair parasites.

Emotional healing: Attracts the right energies into your life to move beyond past traumas and scars caused by being forced into conformity by severe discipline in early life.

Chakra: Root.

Candle colour: Brown. **Fragrances:** Chrysanthemum, fennel, lavender, lime. **Practical uses:** Brings into our lives what we really need, restores sharpness and psychological hunting instincts. **Workplace:** A crystal for all who work with animals, also those who work with the skin; anyone in a physically dangerous job. **Magical significance:** Use to connect with your power animal and understand its purpose in your life; use with guided fantasy or drum music to travel astrally on the back of a magical animal to mystical realms. **Divinatory meaning:** It is cold outside but you have waited enough. **Zodiac:** Gemini and Scorpio **Empowerment:** I will not question what life brings.

Works slowly so needs to be used or worn for long periods, next to the skin, to benefit fully from its supportive energies. It can be particularly beneficial to wear as beads around your wrist or neck for a few months to re-harmonize your internal mechanisms whilst on the outside you will repel situations that are not good. At the same time you will be guided to new opportunities and to view existing situations in new ways; you may find your soul mate was close by. It is a powerful animal healer for adult pets, but too powerful for small or young animals or children.

Type: Wood that comes from fossilized trees in which the wood is replaced over many millions of years by a mineral, usually quartz or agate, that will assume the shape of the original tree.

Colours: Usually brown or grey-brown, grey, black, red, pink/orange, fawn, may be banded and include white (colour varies according to the impurities).

Availability: Common.

Physical benefits: Claimed to relieve back and hip pain, strengthens bones and skeletal alignment; help illness that is difficult to diagnose or treat, progressive or periodically recurring illnesses, mobility problems and those linked with the ageing process; be beneficial for bad backs, allergies, bone dislocation and broken limbs and hay fever.

Emotional healing: Heals relationships that cannot be put right on the earth plane because the person who hurt or neglected you has died; helps you to recall fond memories of deceased relations who perhaps were cold or found it hard to express emotions.

Chakra: Root and Sacral.

Petrified/Fossilized Wood

Candle colour: Brown. **Fragrances:** Basil, cedar, cypress, juniper, moss, vetivert. **Practical uses:** Petrified wood is helpful for those living in older buildings to keep the structure sound; put pieces in the attic near rafters and in basements and in any walls or fireplaces you renovate. **Workplace:** Petrified wood gives courage to begin in a new direction when a career change is needed or after redundancy or enforced early retirement; gives incentive for a new career or study after retirement. **Magical significance:** Brings positive contact with beloved deceased relations through dreams and unmistakable signs of their presence; connects you with family ancestors who act as your spirit guardians. **Divinatory meaning:** Time to let go of a friendship or activity that no longer brings pleasure and is starting to make you feel trapped. **Zodiac:** Virgo **Empowerment:** I welcome the wisdom that comes with age.

There are many legends worldwide about forests turned to stone or crystal by bad witches or evil magicians or buried under the sea that will one day be restored to living wood by a good magician or witch.

Petrified wood offers insight to access past lives through regression. A stone of transformation, to let go of what no longer works in our lives while preserving what is still of value.

During meditation or healing work, petrified wood provides protection from negative energies and afterwards grounds your energies; encourages a child to take an interest in their family origins. The crystal is beneficial to skin and hair as an elixir.

Turritella Agate

Type: Agate with a thick coating of fossilised sea shells.

Colours: Brown or black with coloured inclusions, mainly brown, black, white circular patterns.

Availability: Common.

Physical benefits: May relieve exhaustion, swellings of hands or feet, skin rashes and lesions, varicose veins, sexual dysfunction; alleviates problems of ageing, digestion, gastro-enteritis and gallstone pain; assist with the absorption of minerals.

Emotional healing: Helps overcome past grievances standing in the way of harmonious relationships: if healing others, turritella in a pocket or pouch unlocks deep-seated trauma being manifest as physical symptoms and phobias.

Chakra: Root.

Candle colour: Brown. **Fragrances:** Lavender, rose, sagebrush. **Practical uses:** A survival stone. Keep one in the centre of your home to unite the family or to give yourself roots. **Workplace:** If you travel a lot for work, it will protect you from danger, alleviate fears and keeps you connected with loved ones at home. **Magical significance:** Acts as record keeper crystal, so gives access to the wisdom of past worlds and past life recall or dreams. **Divinatory meaning:** Value what you are and where you have come from. **Zodiac:** Capricorn **Empowerment:** I acknowledge my roots and so I can grow strong in my own pattern.

Brings connections with your personal past: your ancestors, homeland and the country from which your ancestors came. Heals the earth if buried in land that has been neglected or polluted or placed on a map or photo of an endangered area. An excellent fertility crystal, also helpful for increasing chances of success with IVF, artificial insemination and other fertility treatments. Give to a person who always plays the victim. A stone for meditation, as gazing into one induces a trance state; also for allowing therapeutic hypnotism to work better if you find it hard to relax.

Pumice Stone

Type: Volcanic rock containing many bubbles.

Colours: Pale coloured, fawn to light grey or tan, occasionally black if it contains a lot of iron and magnesium.

Availability: Common.

Physical benefits: May ease pain, especially menstrual, painful muscles, locked joints, skin complaints and allergies, abrasions and bruises; traditionally said to ease labour pain; also useful for scars and scar tissue, lesions, ulcers; help any degenerative condition, particularly of the brain.

Emotional healing: Enables repressed anger to flow away; good for those who have accumulated heavy emotional luggage over years to gradually put them down.

Chakra: Solar Plexus.

Candle colour: Grey. **Fragrances:** Almond, bergamot, sweetgrass. **Practical uses:** Keep a small pile in a jar near a source of heat at home so that absent family and friends recall the warmth and keep in touch; also to draw good fortune and protect against fire and flood. **Workplace:** Pumice is traditionally kept in a workspace to absorb negativity and bad luck. When it feels heavy, throw it away in running water and use a new one. **Magical significance:** The holes in pumice can be used for whispering wishes and then floated away in running water. **Divinatory meaning:** Listen to your head and heart. **Zodiac:** Aries. **Empowerment:** I attract good luck and happiness.

Some of the lava that spews out of the volcanoes has bubbles of gas trapped in it. This form of lava is called pumice. Because of its dynamic creation, pumice is a stone of power; people who use it on their feet are filling their Root energy centre with stamina and earth power as a bonus. Massage the soles of your feet with pumice any time you know people or situations during the day ahead may unsettle you; this will fill you with courage and confidence. Because of the rough texture of pumice and its ability to float on water, it became associated with cleansing and beautifying.

Franklinite

Type: Oxide/zinc manganese iron oxide/spinel family.

Colours: Black, brown-black, metallic.

Availability: Relatively rare.

Physical benefits: Thought to assist with hair growth, vision, male reproductive system, resistance to colds and influenza, discovering new treatments and cures for stubborn illnesses.

Emotional healing: Brings sudden insight to emotional problems; teaches difference between truth and illusion and what should be preserved and what let go where these areas are blurred due to immaturity or psychological blockages.

Chakra: Root.

Candle colour: Dark purple or dark brown. **Fragrances:** Allspice, cinnamon, ginger, hibiscus, juniper. **Practical uses:** A talisman for rebuilding relationships; avoids wallowing in the past, but confronts issues that caused the problems. **Workplace:** Beneficial for work where imagination is important; enables you to step back and approach problems from a new angle. **Magical significance:** The weak magnetic charge makes this good for drawing what you want into your life; programme the crystal by holding it and stating what you need and picturing the outcome. **Divinatory meaning:** Be inventive and create opportunites. **Zodiac:** Gemini **Empowerment:** I can reinvent myself.

Mined at Franklin, New Jersey, franklinite has strong grounding energies that build up over time as practical results for all forms of healing work or spiritual development. Can trigger the subconscious to reveal hidden messages and act as a wakeup call for future problems. A mineral of diplomacy, franklinite is a welcome addition to a home or workplace where banter tips over into sarcasm; also helpful for detering an over-enthusiastic would-be lover. A survival crystal for hard financial times when money-making combines single-mindedness in economizing with ingenuity.

Desert/SandRos

Type: Gypsum, with brown sand inclusions, which forms clusters that resemble pale roses

Colours: Pale brown, dusty rose or reddish, rough texture with glints of silver, white or pearl from external drusy tiny crystals.

Availability: Common.

Physical benefits: May increase resistance to viral infections, skin growths and blemishes; help with prostate and testicular problems, travel sickness, stomach upsets, healing of animals.

Emotional healing: Eases panic attacks and claustrophobia; excellent if you have lost confidence in yourself because of an accident, illness, breakdown or loss.

Chakra: Root.

Candle colour: Brown. **Fragrances:** Almond, anise, cherry blossom, sandalwood. **Practical uses:** A good crystal if you feel life has passed you by to make changes, such as relocating to abroad or adopting a different lifestyle. **Workplace:** Encourages you to develop hidden talents; a perseverance crystal if you need to train, retrain or study. **Magical significance:** Because each desert rose is believed to contain its own guardian spirit, it is a good protective stone to keep with you if you feel vulnerable. **Divinatory meaning:** Make changes slowly as there are no short cuts. Giving up is not an option. **Zodiac:** Scorpio and Capricorn. **Empowerment:** I have immense inner resources.

As desert rose forms in desert areas, sand becomes trapped, making distinctive shapes. The overlapping blades of gypsum give it the characteristic petals. It should not be immersed in water or washed so is unsuitable for elixirs by direct methods. The stone encourages the development and expression of psychic powers and creativity. A useful crystal for making the best of things; good for children who are not conventionally good-looking, to learn to value themselves. Keep at home to draw in unexpected money and if you are fighting for what is yours.

Type: Clear quartz, bombarded with gold and iron or iron oxide or with vaporized gold and indium.

Colours: Soft but sparkling pale smoky gold, metallic, the colour of bubbling champagne.

Availability: Relatively rare and new on the market; quite expensive.

Physical benefits: Said to heal by calling down higher healing energies and reawakening the body's own immunity; assist all auto-immune problems, cellular disorders of the nervous system, complex conditions where causes of the body attacking itself are not clear; be good for encouraging remissions; thought to increase healing powers, help to resist and fight modern super-bugs.

Emotional healing: Brings unexpected joy to seemingly unpromising situations and a determination not to be a victim of fate; good for overcoming alcohol abuse and for keeping social drinking under control.

Chakra: Solar Plexus.

Champagne Aura Quartz

Candle colour: Cream. **Fragrances:** Bay, heather, hibiscus, musk, sage. **Practical uses:** A champagne aura cluster beautifies the home as a decoration and at the same time acts as a centre for spiritual harmony in the busiest of households; creates a sacred space on your crystal table and attracts a protective household guardian or domestic angel. **Workplace:** Keep a small cluster in your workspace if your job involves resolving complaints and conflicts with customers; if you have a confrontational colleague who is constantly stirring up trouble, champagne aura quartz will defuse the general situation and create an oasis of calm round you.
Magical significance: A protective crystal against negative spirit energies and essences; keep a cluster on the central table during a seance; hold when helping someone who has been dabbling with the darker side of magic out of curiosity and has frightened themselves or who has unintentionally encouraged a nasty spirit through a Ouija board. **Divinatory meaning:** A cause for celebration in your personal life as someone you were worrying about turns around their own life and relieves you of a burden. **Zodiac:** Gemini. **Empowerment:** Everyone has a good side and I will look for it.

Sometimes called smoky aura quartz, this is a worthwhile investment for those who have worked for several years in the spiritual world or healing profession, both conventional and alternative therapies; assists them particularly if they have encountered blocks to their progress or have lost enthusiasm and dedication because of stress at work or unhelpful management; also for those new to spiritual work or healing who doubt themselves and their gifts, to discover their personal healing guides and angels and to learn to trust their own instincts and innate clairvoyant and healing wisdom.

Keep champagne aura in your business to consolidate achievements or, if you work for someone else, to help you to meet targets and to increase your reputation for both reliability and vision; in any spiritually based or therapeutic company, champagne aura will attract clients and build up your reputation so that your business thrives; it is especially good for NLP and for life-coaching work.

Heulandite

Type: Silicate/inosilicate/zeolite.

Colours: Brown, green, peach, sometime so pale it appears white or colourless; also grey, yellow, pink, red; pearly lustre.

Availability: Relatively common.

Physical benefits: Thought to improve mobility of joints, especially knees, back and feet; help with the nervous system, liver, efficient processing of nutrients, food intolerances, breathlessness, complex illnesses where a virus or infection has side effects that are slow to clear.

Emotional healing: Reduces the power of addictions, particularly oral ones; for gradual weight-loss programmes based on healthy eating; every slimming club leader should take heulandite to meetings.

Chakra: Heart and Crown.

Candle colour: Brown or green. **Fragrances:** Cloves, hyssop, lavender, meadowsweet, sagebrush. **Practical uses:** Sends warmth and stabilizing energies throughout the home. **Workplace:** Beneficial during disruption at work, to embrace the situation with open-mindedness and positive negotiations, for resolving disagreements without litigation. **Magical significance:** Placed on the Third Eye it accesses visions and maybe memories of your distant root cultures; this can be very settling if you feel you do not belong. **Divinatory meaning:** Security is important; do not make hasty decisions. **Zodiac:** Libra and Sagittarius **Empowerment:** I am secure and rooted in my life.

Heulandite complex crystal structure, its variety of colours and worldwide locations make it an integrating crystal for any situation where many different people meet; keep pieces of different shades in a workplace that does worldwide business, or if you work or live with people of different cultures. It filters sarcasm, criticisms and those who drain energies with problems they refuse to tackle. A piece near the front door will deter neighbours who visit too regularly and stay too long. Hold when you want them to go as you ease them to the door and picture them leaving happily.

Brown Aragonite

Type: Dimorphous calcium carbonate, forms hexagonal shaped or stalactitic crystals

Colours: Golden brown; clear or colourless is its pure form.

Availability: Common.

Physical benefits: Said to assist with bone fractures, dislocation, spine, slipped disc, lumbago, bowel cancer; IBS, teeth, jaw, neuralgia, nervous system, hair loss, exhaustion, ME, cramps, diabetes, Vitamin A and D deficiencies, skin, eczema and psoriasis.

Emotional healing: Clears redundant anger lingering from old wrongs and prevents constantly returning to the past and fretting over loss or injustice that hinder emotional growth.

Chakra: Root.

Candle colour: Golden brown. **Fragrances:** Clary sage, neroli, pine, sagebrush, vanilla. **Practical uses:** Aragonite sputnik shaped hexagonal clusters with interpenetrating crystals or any aragonite clusters are natural integrators; keep where you and others sit to bring unity. **Workplace:** Encourages moderation, reasoned opinions; a dish of crystals makes workplace discussions practical, amicable and useful. **Magical significance:** Any cluster repels negativity and radiates a protective shield of golden light; keep one in your bedroom if you have bad dreams. **Divinatory meaning:** A time for honesty and putting aside old differences to resolve a problem. **Zodiac:** Capricorn. **Empowerment:** I can find common ground even with difficult people.

Brown aragonite has natural stabilising qualities and brings common sense and constructive suggestions to situations. All aragonite encourages collective enterprises and efforts. Brown aragonite clusters automatically ground and give protection to other crystals and so one is a good addition to your healing collection or your home crystals if you use your crystals a lot but are short of time. Use in the early stages of setting up a business or learning a new job to avoid feeling overwhelmed. Increases generosity, not only in money, but time, resources and sharing of ideas and praise.

Type: Fossilized sea creatures that first appeared about 435 million years ago and inhabited the sea in great numbers, living in the spiral shell now found as the ammonite fossil; the incredibly rare iridescent ammolite gem is formed from mineralized ammonites.

Colours: Brown, grey or fawn.

Availability: Relatively common.

Physical benefits: Can alleviate problems with genetically transmitted diseases, relieve chronic cramps and erectile dysfunction. Also a good-luck charm for pregnancy, believed to be beneficial for health in the over-eighties and in childbirth as a pain reliever.

Emotional healing: Protective against repeating old mistakes and from getting stuck in outmoded family roles with parents, partners and siblings; soothing near the cradle for babies after birth trauma such as prolonged or emergency deliveries and Caesareans.

Chakra: Root.

Ammonite/Snake/ Serpent Stones

Candle colour: Brown or grey. **Fragrances:** Cypress, lilac, patchouli, sweetgrass, vervain, vetivert. **Practical uses:** Ammonite brings lasting health, wealth and happiness to individuals and homes. Belief in the luck-bringing and protective powers of ammonites is found from the Australian Aboriginal culture to the Himalayas, Scandinavia and Native North America; in Feng Shui it is called *chi lin* after the scales of a mythical dragon-like creature. **Workplace:** Ammonites' incredibly grounding power is good for building a business from small beginnings; a lucky charm for family businesses. **Magical significance:** Place an ammonite next to your bed to bring dreams of past worlds, especially legendary lost sea lands such as Atlantis, Arthurian Lyonesse and Lemuria, and for prophetic dreams. **Divinatory meaning:** Do not repeat past mistakes, but use your experience to maximize a new opportunity. **Zodiac:** Cancer **Empowerment:** I do not fear ageing, but welcome wisdom that comes from experience.

Beloved by the Ancient Egyptians and Ancient Greeks and named after the Egyptian creator god Amun (Ammon to the Ancient Greeks), who was pictured as ram-headed with spiral horns; considered by the Romans to hold the power of prophecy.

Ammonites, sometimes embedded in jet were regarded in a myth of Whitby, northeast England, as fossilized snakes killed in AD 657 by the Celtic Christian St Hilda, who apparently turned all the snakes into stone on the land where she wanted to found her abbey, and threw them over the cliffs; a similar legend concerns St Keyna at Keynsham, not far from Bristol.

Holding an ammonite assists recall of the Akashic records, the spiritual collective store of wisdom past, present and future.

Sunstone

Type: Oligioclase feldspar.

Colours: Golden orange, red, red-brown, brown-orange and green with a sparkly iridescent sheen.

Availability: Clean red examples are very rare. Others are more common.

Physical benefits: May aid all lower-body ailments including the reproductive organs, digestion, stomach ulcers, prostate, feet, legs, Seasonal Affective Disorder, body odour.

Emotional healing: Excellent for easing phobias about the dark, enclosed places; also for any phobia sufferers, to become less fearful of the presence of their trigger.

Chakra: Root and Solar Plexus.

Candle colour: Red. **fragrances:** Benzoin, copal, cyphi, frankincense, honey. **Practical uses:** Wear to feel alive and enthusiastic; also when starting a new exercise regime to give you the impetus to persevere. **Workplace:** Increases your profile to get ahead; brings opportunities for leadership and promotion; keep by your computer if advertising your own business or services online. **Magical significance:** Carry with moonstone to integrate god and goddess powers, animus and anima, assertive and outward success and inner harmony within your life. **Divinatory meaning:** Enjoy the present without worrying if the good times will last. **Zodiac:** Leo. **Empowerment:** I am whole and happy.

Sunstone is formed within lava and, once it is released on to the Earth's surface, weathering of the lava reveals the crystals hidden within. It therefore attracts unexpected prosperity by uncovering your talents.

Attracts fame and good luck in competitions. Wear to lead you to the resources to travel and for happy holidays or relocation to the sun. It also protects you against those who drain your energies and finances and makes you tougher if people exploit you. An excellent crystal if you are dependent on others emotionally or have suffered sudden loss of a partner.

Brown Zircon

Type: Silicate/nesosilicate, zirconium.

Colours: Brown, golden brown.

Availability: Obtainable from specialist jewellery and crystal stores and online.

Physical benefits: Said to relieve problems with bowels, IBS, anus, prostate, constipation, food-and stress-related allergies and intolerances, coeliac disease, delayed, irregular menstruation; be good for animal healing; help the safe birth of second and subsequent children and aids older mothers in labour.

Emotional healing: Brings lasting stability to people who have suffered a long period of trauma.

Chakra: Root and Solar Plexus.

Candle colour: Brown. **Fragrances:** Carnation, chamomile, patchouli, wintergreen. **Practical uses:** Reduces the stresses of everyday travel; good on late-night journeys or dangerous urban areas. **Workplace:** Strengthens the wearer to make a supreme effort to meet a vital short-term goal, increases mental sharpness. **Magical significance:** A protective amulet against liars, thieves and attack; returns lost property, people or animals. Look into a clear gem and picture the item returning. Especially powerful in the autumn. **Divinatory meaning:** Do not deviate from your established pattern. **Zodiac:** Leo and Capricorn **Empowerment:** Life is an adventure.

Brown zircon is considered a shield against accidents and fires, as well as the effects of extreme weather.

A brown zircon becoming redder may indicate someone you have just met has a bad temper. Keep a natural piece or tumblestone under animal bedding or attach to an animal collar to deter parasites.

Brown zircon is said to bring a permanent home to those who do not have one and so can be worn if you are saving for a deposit or are experiencing housing difficulties. Hold to call to you a love you can trust or to increase contentment in love.

Type: Aluminium boron silicate .

Colours: Brown to dark brown or orange-brown.

Availability: Less common than other forms of tourmaline, but available at specialist crystal stores and online.

Physical benefits: Claimed to assist with the purification of the blood, hips and hip and joint replacements, legs, feet and ankles, pain relief; help to speed the healing of scars, ulcers and wounds, especially if they have become infected.

Emotional healing: Coming to terms with personal weaknesses and past failures to set us on our forward path to spiritual growth; for overcoming bad habits, self-abuse and addictions, especially coffee, chocolate, alcohol or painkillers.

Chakra: Root.

Dravite/Brown Tourmaline

Candle colour: Brown. **Fragrances:** Geranium, heather, honeysuckle, magnolia, patchouli. **Practical uses:** Reconciles long-standing family rivalries and disputes over inheritance or division of property; for happy retirement or for settling in a new home or area if you are leaving a well-loved house and lifestyle. **Workplace:** Helps you to feel relaxed and in control of yourself and the situation with a large group of people; for all who create beauty with their hands, professionally or for pleasure, and for putting on a successful exhibition of their creations. **Magical significance:** Sometimes called autumn tourmaline because, especially if banded, it resembles autumn leaves; associated with nature spirits, said to be the fallen leaves from fairyland/the elf kingdoms and offer fey visions. **Divinatory meaning:** Realign with nature for a day or two to avoid disappearing beneath the 24/7 demands of life. **Zodiac:** Virgo and Scorpio. **Empowerment:** People, not places, make a home.

Brown is a strong earth colour and this increases the already powerful grounding qualities of any tourmaline; should be worn or carried to keep a grasp on reality to know instinctively what needs fixing instantly and what can be safely left for a while.

Connected with the Root chakra, dravite spontaneously cleanses blocked energies in the lower body and energizes the aura when you cannot stop and meditate or do self-healing.

Beneficial for those who work with the land, whether through gardening, landscape conservation or with earth energies, by helping to commune with deva energies. Bury a small dravite into the soil or place it near a plant and watch it flourish. Carry or wear one at any time of the year as a charm to bring happiness or fulfillment of a dream or project within six months.

Type: Micro fossils.

Colours: Often golden brown and deep brown but they can include grey, tan and sandy; beautiful when polished.

Availability: Rare but obtainable online and in some specialist mineral stores.

Physical benefits: Viewed as assisting with memory, eye problems, throat, teeth, bones, headaches and nervous system; helping with maintaining health in people in their eighties onwards, building resistance to debilitating diseases, the release of harmonious flow of bodily fluids.

Emotional healing: Brings profound healing from deep within the earth, alleviating even overwhelming stress and triggering positive energies for an emotional turnaround.

Chakra: Crown and Brow.

Stromatolite

Candle colour: Any earth colour. **Fragrances:** Geranium, lilac, moss, patchouli, vervain. **Practical uses:** Hold stromatolite to your forehead to ground you if you are feeling spaced-out or if certain people are constantly questioning and correcting you and you feel insecure. Visualize energy flowing from the earth, materializing as roots that grow into the ground beneath your feet as certainty. **Workplace:** Use this stone to give perseverance if taking a project from conception to completion, particularly if it will involve personal investment in time and resources. **Magical significance:** Buy a polished stromatolite sphere or egg; sit outdoors on the ground when sun or moonlight shines on the surface. Read the patterns on the surface that will form images and suggest words in your mind to convey the wisdom of Mother Earth. **Divinatory meaning:** Advice and understanding from an older person you had dismissed as being out of touch will prove valuable in helping you to resolve a hidden worry. **Zodiac:** Capricorn. **Empowerment:** My roots are deep and draw on ancient wisdom.

Stromatolites are still currently being researched by geologists. They are actually fossils and are among the earliest forms of life. Some stromatolites are found with fossilized micro-organisms and some are not.

As with all fossils, stromatolite is a useful aid in past-life recall, past worlds, shamanic journeying and regression, especially before recorded historical times, as well as for contemplative meditation. Run your index finger repetitively and slowly over a

highly patterned large stromatolite palm or worry stone until you achieve an almost trance-like state.

A natural stromatolite in the home encourages love of family traditions and heritage, and can help adopted adults and children to discover and value their birth-roots while at the same time not rejecting their adoptive family; good for merging family cultural and religious values with those of the wider community or if you find that your loyalties are divided.

Type: Magnesium aluminium silicate.

Colours: Orange to deep red. Crystals can be pale yellow if nearly pure, but almost always are mixed with almandine garnet (p.74).

Availability: Gem quality is rare.

Physical benefits: Believed to be beneficial to both male and female reproductive systems, boosting fertility and sex drive; help kidneys, bladder, poor circulation, chilblains and Reynaud's disease; may improve food intolerances, particularly to wheat and dairy products, inability of body to effectively digest and process fat.

Emotional healing: For restoring the natural awareness of hunger and thirst and what is sufficient when physical sensations have been overridden by emotional factors and the need for comfort.

Chakra: Sacral.

Spessartine Garnet

Candle colour: Orange. **Fragrances**: Frankincense, ginger, orange, parsley, rosemary. **Practical uses**: Wear spessartine to attract happy, well-balanced, self-sufficient people to you, if you find yourself constantly acting as therapist, parent and counsellor to colleagues, friends and lovers. **Workplace**: A splash of colour in the world, spessartine inspires art, fashion and textile designers, jewellery makers, weavers and embroiderers, tapestry makers, interior decorators, architects, graphic designers, photographic artists and industrial-landscape artists. **Magical significance**: The garnet of the sun; wrap a small tumblestone with a holiday brochure of some sunny or more exotic location you would like to visit (or live in) in orange cloth tied with orange ribbon; leave the parcel in any available sunshine at least once a week. **Divinatory significance**: The problems do not lie with you but the company you keep, who are holding you back from new places and ventures. **Zodiac**: Sagittarius and Capricorn **Empowerment**: I make my own sunshine with laughter.

Spessartine is one of the lesser-known and rarer varieties of garnet. It takes its name from the Spessart district of Bavaria but is also found in Sweden, Brazil, the USA, Australia and Sri Lanka. Tape spessartine garnet over your navel or buy yourself a belly-button ring to rekindle fun and spontaneity in your life and to rid yourself of the old inner and maybe present voices who tell you life has to be hard.

Through activation of the Sacral chakra situated around this area, spessartine will awaken latent creative energies, not only those of procreation but also linked to artistic, physical and mental creativity, to make your world more colourful.

The energies emitted by spessartine evoke feelings of happiness from within, and in feeling happy you can make life step by step more fulfilling.

This crystal will assist all who have difficulty making themselves seen and/or heard within group situations, whether in work or leisure. Wear spessartine to become the life and soul of any party and to increase your sexual magnetism to attract someone you really like to whom you seem invisible.

Thunder Egg

Type: Spherical silaceous volcanic rock masses, generally about the size of a large ball.

Colours: Brown, black or grey exterior; the inner cavity filled with colourful patterned agate, chalcedony or jasper; some kinds may have inner crystalline forms.

Availability: Relatively rare.

Physical benefits: May help to improve pain release, growths and tumours, fertility and potency later in life, for reconstructive surgery.

Emotional healing: Gradually removes deep-seated needs for gratification; assists those who find it hard to express their personality or with negative self-body-image.

Chakra: Root.

Candle colour: Indigo. **Fragrances:** Anise, fern, moss, lavender, patchouli. **Practical uses:** Display in a dull or dark room to enliven the atmosphere and create a sense of beauty. **Workplace:** Encourages backroom staff or those who make others appear attractive or well-informed to maintain their own self-image. **Magical significance:** Excellent for guided fantasies, visualization or meditation, particularly group work to build up collective visions of other worlds. **Divinatory meaning:** Pursue an apparently mundane idea or get to know a person better as you may be uncovering hidden treasure. **Zodiac:** Scorpio and Capricorn **Empowerment:** I will not judge by appearances.

Thunder eggs' characteristic inner appearance is as if it has been torn or frozen, but until the stone is split in half there is no clue of its hidden treasure.

A thunder egg as one of nature's wonders is an investment as it lifts restrictions and makes anything more possible. A gift for a beloved relative who is going through a down period or is housebound. If you have always wanted to write, paint, act, sing or make music, look into your thunder egg and creative blocks will melt and ideas flow.

Siderite

Type: Iron carbonate.

Colours: Brown, pale yellow, brownish yellow, greenish brown, reddish brown, sometimes iridescent or pearly.

Availability: Relatively common, although good collectible specimens are rare.

Physical benefits: Seen as useful for strength and vitality' beneficial for skeletal system, chronic digestive and bowel disorders caused or made worse by food allergies, dizziness that does not have a specific physical cause, poor balance.

Emotional healing: Gives the courage to speak out against and act independently of controlling or super-critical relatives who try to rule adult life.

Chakra: Root.

Candle colour: Yellow or bronze. **Fragrances:** Allspice, basil, dragon's blood, galangal, tarragon. **Practical uses:** A comforting stone to display at home when relatives who disrupt your life visit. If you are alone at night, siderite calms fears. **Workplace:** Encourages fairer working conditions. If your job is insecure, keep a piece with you while renegotiating contracts or trying to improve employment rights. **Magical significance:** An amulet against bad luck, the carelessness of others, breakages, breakdown of vehicles or equipment and accidents. **Divinatory meaning:** Be careful not to be swept away by someone else's infatuation. **Zodiac:** Aries. **Empowerment:** I will not fail.

At times of weakness, hold siderite and allow its energies to recharge yourself. It is particularly potent if you are naturally shy. If you feel constantly unenthusiastic, it can trigger your inner passions.

Overuse of this crystal may cause a power struggle within an unsteady relationship as siderite has powerfully assertive energies. To counterbalance this, add copper or rose quartz for gentler feelings. Keep near stairs if you live with people who have a tendency to trip. Use to inspire loyalty. Keep in your car if you have an interfering passenger and to keep focused.

Type: Ilmenite, iron titanium oxide; quartz, silicon dioxide.

Colours: Ilmenite is brown to black and metallic and may be included within clear or, more rarely, smoky quartz, or on a quartz matrix or even occasionally vice versa, supporting the quartz.

Availability: Relatively rare.

Physical benefits: The combination of quartz and ilmenite is very dynamic, making it one of the most powerful quartz mixes. Both ilmenite and quartz are described as being good for healing for all aspects of the body and mind and especially effective for viruses that are new or are resistant to treatment, for auto-immune conditions and others that affect different areas of the body simultaneously.

Emotional healing: Gives a kick-start to new forms of therapy or medication for long-standing personality problems or severe recurring depression; brings self-awareness of personal responsibility for resisting seemingly uncontrollable impulses; for sex phone line and porn addictions.

Chakra: Root and Crown.

Ilmenite Quartz

Candle colour: Gold. **Fragrances:** Allspice, almond blossom, copal, eucalyptus, frankincense. **Practical uses:** Ilmenite reveals beauty in unexpected places; keep it close while you are working to convert a city backyard into an urban wildlife garden or making your room in a shared house a sanctuary of beauty and harmony; for all restorations and renovations where the object needs to be completely stripped down to bring back its former glory. **Workplace:** A stone that should be set as a talisman in a rundown business or workplace you have taken over and intend to bring back to life; for anyone who fixes and restores broken appliances, cars or computers, or works with people or animals society has rejected. **Magical significance:** A stone to use as a focus if you have a really difficult spell to cast or seemingly impossible healing to perform, to generate the energies to turn around the situation and bring light and hope. Burn gold candles round it for an hour or two before beginning, then hold it and picture the positive outcome you desire. **Divinatory meaning:** Try fixing a situation or relationship, as you may regret abandoning it without one last try. **Zodiac:** Capricorn. **Empowerment:** Any situation can be turned round with faith and effort.

A solid-looking quartz and one with a lot of stored power for those times when you need stamina to keep going when you cannot rest or an extra push to get a task finished that seems endless.

It is a good crystal if you have a very old pet that is no longer physically appealing and for rescue animals who have been scarred, to love their inner beauty and accept with patience their less appealing habits.

Ilmenite quartz puts a positive spin on any situation; good for anyone suffering from severe disabilities to persevere and prove their detractors wrong; a starting-again stone if you have hit rock-bottom.

Use small pieces and build yourself a pile as you take each new hard step towards success.

Type: Quartz (also called cairngorm).

Colours: Tinted smoky brown or dark grey by natural radiation.

Availability: Common.

Physical benefits: After a period of illness or depression this is said to be good for gently restoring physical energy, melting energy blocks or rigidity in limbs, the adrenal glands, kidneys (good for kidney stones) and the pancreas; also believed to help with the relief of chronic pain.

Emotional healing: Reduces anxiety, psychological sexual blocks, insomnia, self-harming and panic attacks.

Chakra: Root (opens the chakra gently).

Smoky Quartz

Candle colour: Indigo. **Fragrances:** Cedar, cypress, hibiscus, lily, mimosa, patchouli. **Practical uses:** Protects the home, vehicles and possessions against theft, damage and accidents caused by human error; keep one in a purse or bag in the glove box of a car or near valuables, especially if they are unattended for long periods. **Workplace:** Set on a desk or in a workspace, smoky quartz absorbs any negativity, whether intentional or free-floating; wash the stone weekly. **Magical significance:** Smoky quartz is said to create an astral pathway to past worlds or out-of-body travel if you shine candlelight into its centre and follow the pathway in your mind; this works especially well with smoky quartz spheres; protects against nasty spirits. **Divinatory meaning:** There is light at the end of the tunnel and you will slowly see improvements in a long-standing worry soon. **Zodiac:** Capricorn. **Empowerment:** I walk in hope towards the future, even if it seems uncertain right now.

A guardian against bad luck; in Switzerland, Germany and Austria, smoky quartz crucifixes were traditionally put on bedroom walls to keep away evil, human and paranormal, especially at night.

A very good driving crystal to protect you against road rage and when you are driving on motorways, on long journeys or in heavy traffic to reduce stress so you can concentrate; good also against any unexpected mechanical breakdown in vehicles and technical equipment or white goods;

helps very old animals and people of any age who are worn down with daily living to carry on.

Use smoky quartz to absorb misfortune, sorrows or seemingly impossible obstacles by standing with a pointed smoky quartz in each hand, point downwards towards the earth. Imagine whatever you need to shed pouring through your fingertips and the crystals into Mother Earth. If you can do this outdoors, afterwards plant some seeds or flowers, or indoors put a small herb into a pot.

Type: Magnetic space rock, alloyed with 90 percent iron content, 8 per cent nickel and smaller amounts of cobalt and phosphorus, plus even tinier quantities of carbon, sulphur, chromium and copper, and traces of zinc, gallium, germanium and iridium.

Colours: Brown or grey.

Availability: Obtainable now but there are problems over export, caused in part by the earlier illegal export of this Namibian treasure.

Physical benefits: Thought to help with blood purification, iron deficiency, relief of acute pain, wounds, wound or blood infections, anaemia, mineral deficiencies, epilepsy and chemical or electrical impulse malfunctioning in the brain, MRSA, C Difficile and other modern bugs resistant to antibiotics, CJD (Creutzfeldt-Jakob disease), bowel and colon blockages, and degenerative conditions in the elderly.

Emotional healing: Helpful for elderly people and the disabled after unsatisfactory treatment in hospital or a care home; brings back a sense of dignity and self-worth; for those who suffered abuse in residential or foster care as children or teenagers.

Chakra: Root and Crown.

Meteorite Gibeon

Candle colour: Brown. **Fragrances:** Allspice, cinnamon, ginger, patchouli, pine. **Practical uses:** Sold as watches and in jewellery to bring its power and protection into the everyday world; however, many collectors prefer an authentic small piece of natural gibeon meteorite to keep in a small soft pouch for stamina, courage and a sense of the wonder of life in the most mundane settings. **Workplace:** Excellent as charms to see projects through to completion, especially if there have been a lot of obstacles or opposition; wear or carry gibeon meteorite to bring a lifetime career dream to fruition, whether opening a boatyard on a tropical island or getting a best-seller or Number1 record. **Magical significance:** Traditionally protective against nature's hazards, particularly fire, storm, hurricane and flood, gibeon meteorites will open you to unexpected good fortune; have a piece to keep your home safe while another leads you on adventures that seem to come your way as if by magic. **Divinatory meaning:** Huge effort brings big rewards but first comes the hard part. **Zodiac:** All signs, especially Aquarius and Scorpio. **Empowerment:** Life is exciting because of its unpredictability.

Gibeon meteorites are characterized by particularly beautiful crystalline patterns, formed on their inner surfaces over millions of years of cooling.

Though it was discovered by Westerners until 1838 when small pieces were collected in southern Africa by Captain James Alexander, meteorite fragments had been polished and sharpened by indigenous people as arrow and spear heads for thousands of years.

Because of their beauty, gibeon meteorites

are wonderful centrepieces for the home and can be handed on as family treasures to younger generations.

Many have fine thumb-like indentations that make powerful meditation and worry stones to connect you to millennia of ancient wisdom and, some say, intergalactic energies. They have also absorbed the sunshine of their Earthly home and are excellent cold-climate and cold-winter energizers, protecting against Seasonal Affective symptoms.

Goldstone

Type: Glass with copper, smelted gypsum, feldspar and copper salts.

Colours: Bronzed red with gold sparkles.

Availability: Common.

Physical benefits: Said to help with circulation, arthritis, joint pain, skin complaints dresulting from food allergies, metabolism, bones, stomach disorders, especially stress-related, dizziness.

Emotional healing: Promotes a sense of self-worth and reduces chronic self-consciousness.

Chakra: Root, Sacral and Solar Plexus.

Candle colour: Orange or bronze. **Fragrances:** Elder, sage, thyme, valerian, vervain. **Practical uses:** Use as a lucky charm when entering competitions, financial speculation and the lottery; always use the same stone as its powers accumulate. **Workplace:** Carry when you need to create a good impression or to overcome your fears if you need to speak to a group or address a meeting. **Magical significance:** Amplifies healing directly through the hands and strengthens distant healing; keep with your other healing crystals and hold before you begin to give healing or transmit healing over distances. **Divinatory meaning:** A chance to prove your talent and gain recognition. **Zodiac:** Sagittarius. **Empowerment:** I am confident in my abilities.

Goldstone is potent both because glass is made from quartz sand and because of the power of added minerals, particularly copper, which combine in goldstone in a mix different from and greater than its separate components. Though goldstone appears reddish brown, its colour comes from the copper crystals and the glass is colourless. Hold goldstone to reorientate yourself if you get lost while driving or walking at night and at any time when life is dull or you feel sad, to remind you of the wonders of the world, both natural and those improved by human ingenuity.

Titanite in Quartz

Type: Silicate (calcium titanium silicate), found either growing on clear quartz or occasionally smoky quartz or as inclusions that can make the crystal golden brown.

Colours: Brown, green or yellow, sparkling.

Availability: Rare and expensive, but very beautiful.

Physical benefits: May bring powerful healing energies if rogue cells are multiplying, the auto-immune system is attacking the body or there is increasingly rapid brain-cell deterioration; be helpful for lupus, strokes and comas.

Emotional healing: Combines the best of the old and new, conventional medications and therapies and alternative remedies in dealing with long-standing psychological issues.

Chakra: Crown and Brow.

Candle colour: White. **Fragrances:** Almond, lavender, lime, rose. **Practical uses:** An integrating and order-maintaining crystal if a relative is moving in with you or you are buying a house with family members. **Workplace:** Excellent for anyone with conventional medical training who is drawn to spiritual healing to take the best of both. **Magical significance:** For anyone who needs proof about the psychic world, to succeed either professionally or informally in the field of parapsychology; brings discipline and objectivity to set up psychic experiments. **Divinatory meaning:** Find the point where it keeps going wrong and change the pattern. **Zodiac:** Pisces. **Empowerment:** I will create new patterns for happiness.

Though titanite is the official name of this mineral, it is often sold as sphene in quartz. It also grows on other minerals, such as albite or calcite. An excellent addition to any healing room if you have lost inspiration; or are training in divination or mediumship and feel blocked by the amount of information you need to learn.

Good if you are planning or need a new beginning, but are daunted by what needs to be resolved first. A house-moving crystal if you have clutter. Brings focus and accuracy for writing wills, planning applications or checking small print of insurance policies.

Cerusite

Type: Lead carbonate, white lead ore, beautiful twinned crystals and clusters or star shapes.

Colours: Brown, clear, misty white, sparkling.

Availability: Obtainable from specialist mineral stores and online. Occasionally found in jewellery.

Physical benefits: Believed to help balance the brain's hemispheres; assist with relief Alzheimer's, senile dementia, Parkinson's disease, prostate problems, bones, arthritis and rheumatism, any illness with an unpredictable pattern.

Emotional healing: Helps with addictions, fears of ageing, chronic depression or acute pessimism; sleep disorders.

Chakra: Root and Crown

Candle colour: Brown. Fragrances: Anise, fern, mimosa, myrrh, patchouli. **Practical uses:** Keep in the home or workplace in the weeks before any planned change to ease the transition. **Workplace:** Encourages communication involving really listening to and taking on board the opinions of others, so creating a sense of bonding and collective responsibility. **Magical significance:** Connects us with our spiritual side and the more evolved parts of the mind. This increases our intuitive and psychic powers; keep a cluster on the central table during collective spiritual activities. **Divinatory meaning:** A certainty suddenly becomes less so. **Zodiac:** Capricorn. **Empowerment:** I can adapt to any changes demanded of me.

Cerusite is good for practical matters, property and financial stability, and is associated with good luck in speculation. A crystal of increasing self-confidence through developing competence. Cerusite will help anyone involved in financial institutions, museums, teachers of history, religion and all who collect and communicate myths. Keep a small piece, well wrapped, with amazonite and green aventurine in a small bag with lottery numbers or any form of speculation where there is a random element. **WARNING**: It is toxic. Do not use in elixirs, ingest or keep near children or pets.

Staurolite

Type: Iron aluminium silicate; twinned crystals that form equal-armed crosses or cross shapes.

Colours: Red-brown, dark brown; black or yellowy brown, streaked with white; gradually weathers to grey,

Availability: Transparent or light translucent ones are rare. Opaque red-brown ones are more common.

Physical benefits: Seen as good for muscles, blood disorders, counteracting effects of ageing. Each person's staurolite adapts to their needs; puts the body, mind and spirit back into alignment.

Emotional healing: A stone of consolation for those suffering sickness or loss and to help those who comfort them.

Chakra: Root.

Candle colour: Brown. Fragrances: Bergamot, chamomile, copal resin, lemon. **Practical uses:** Carry if you are trying to give up smoking. Hold in the hand you hold a cigarette when you experience a craving until it passes. **Workplace:** Keep with you to reduce stress and gain respect by keeping to your beliefs. **Magical significance:** The cross formation represents the four elements that are believed to combine to create the fifth element called Aether or Akasha. Touch the four points of the cross whenever you need magical energies. **Divinatory meaning:** You will have a chance to take unfair advantage, but this may give someone unscrupulous power over you. **Zodiac:** Pisces and Scorpio **Empowerment:** This is the right course.

Staurolite, also known as fairy tears or fairy cross, has been prized since ancient times as a lucky charm and a protective talisman for travellers, including the Crusaders and US President Roosevelt. In myth, fairy crosses were the frozen tears of fairies or earth angels, who wept at the crucifixion of Jesus. Take staurolite outdoors to connect with nature essences. It provides a shield against negativity, helping to raise spirits. Gives strength and patience to all who carry the burdens of others, especially if you are a carer or cannot leave an unhappy home or workplace because of dependents.

Axinite

Type: Blade-like, a calcium, aluminium boro-silicate.

Colours: Usually brown to purple or brownish red.

Availability: Relatively rare but obtainable from specialist mineral stores and online.

Physical benefits: Said to help the adrenal glands, fractures, especially after an accident where there are multiple fractures or damage to organs, physical blockages, total breakdown of the body and mind.

Emotional healing: Helps loners, only children and anyone with psychological communication blocks to see the world as friendly and to reach out in. A good crystal for therapists to help uncommunicative clients open up.

Chakra: Root and Brow.

Candle colour: Brown. **Fragrances:** Cedar, juniper, musk, rosewood. **Practical uses:** Use to make the best of any life changes you have chosen. **Workplace:** Helps bring out potential in workers you have to train; excellent if you are promoted over co-workers to minimize resentment and to show your best qualities in a team; keep on a window ledge if people at work are bitchy or resentful of newcomers. **Magical significance:** Brings spirituality into the everyday world; keep in a room where you sit and visitors will lose their cynicism. **Divinatory meaning:** Make decisions based on what you feel as well as the facts. **Zodiac:** Capricorn **Empowerment:** I will make time for friendship.

Axinite is the stone of friendship, especially if you are older, retired or are living in a new area; a small piece in your bag or pocket will attract friends with similar viewpoints, deepen existing friendships and help love to grow from friendship if you have been hurt; good when kept by the computer for visiting Internet friendship sites and for rediscovering former friends online. Use to develop your psychic powers and explore other realms and dimensions; good for police and other security services such as the army to build up trust in hostile communities.

Lepidocrocite

Type: Iron hydroxide, found as a result of oxidation and a constituent in soil.

Colours: Brown, reddish brown to deep red to black.

Availability: Relatively rare, especially in the natural form not included in quartz.

Physical benefits: May relieve disorders with eyes, reproductive system, blood, bleeding from wounds, transfusions, appendix; help to assist with conventional cancer treatments, surgery, stomach ulcers, restoration and maintenance of health.

Emotional healing: Restores confidence after a serious illness, an accident or major trauma, to face life again.

Chakra: Root and Solar Plexus.

Candle colour: Brown. **Fragrances:** Anise, cloves, orange, sage. **Practical uses:** Carrying a lepidocrocite in quartz, or the mineral in a pouch, dissolves unfriendly behaviour in new places. **Workplace:** A wonderful crystal for staying alert; provides ongoing stamina and, if held, a burst of strength. **Magical significance:** Lepidocrocite in any quartz is easily programmed for strengths you need; hold and state what you need; to reprogramme, pass your hands over it, saying, "May all be as before", then add new qualities. **Divinatory meaning:** A time of growth when things may seem slower than hoped. **Zodiac:** Sagittarius. **Empowerment:** Each day brings potential for growth or stagnation.

Lepidocrocite, in its red form as dots, sometimes gives harlequin quartz its red inclusions and, when included in its scarlet form, becomes fire quartz. However, in clear quartz, amethyst or smoky quartz it is sold as a separate crystal, valued when included in clear quartz or amethyst as an elixir for hunger suppression. It is also one of the seven minerals in Super Seven. Often used by Reiki healers to transfer energies to areas proving resistant to healing. Also popular with rebirthing therapists. Brings a sense of security at times of transition, and is the basis and determination for growth.

Schalenblende

Type: Zinc iron sulphide.

Colours: Brown, yellow-brown, beige, silver-grey, blue, banded, undulating appearance.

Availability: Found in specialist crystal stores and online.

Physical benefits: Thought to assist with recovery of physical wounds, diabetes, immune system, cell regeneration, sense of smell, taste and vision, prostate gland, genitalia, preconception health and fertility.

Emotional healing: Helps recognize and safely release pent-up anxieties; for getting over a bad relationship.

Chakra: Root.

Candle colour: Cream or brown. **Fragrances**: Dragon's blood, galbanum, lemon verbena, mugwort, patchouli. **Practical uses**: Obtain a polished piece to guide you to what you need when you need it. **Workplace**: Protects against negative energies from modern technological communication aids; guards your computer against viruses and spam and your phone from nuisance callers; a good anti-stalker crystal for social websites. **Magical significance**: A fertility charm; also banishes undesirable influences from your life; bury a piece where nothing grows late at night on the waning moon. **Divinatory meaning**: An ongoing disagreement between yourself and a loved one will be resolved. **Zodiac**: Capricorn and Aquarius **Empowerment**: I replace negative with positive energies.

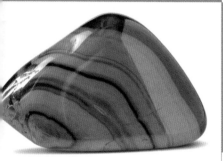

Schalenblende is an attractive stone of compacted layers of several minerals, usually sphalerite and wurtzite (both varieties of zinc iron sulphide), galena and/or pyrite. Traditionally it is a stone of protection during travel to spiritual realms. Helpful for all property matters and for changing bad luck into good. A powerful crystal for bringing together different people to create a team, whether to fix your home, get a project off the ground, form a social or healing group or for organizing a small party so everyone will mix; good for wedding planners and all who arrange events.

Dinosaur Bone

Type: Agatized dinosaur bone is fossilized bone from dinosaurs in which the cellular structure has been replaced with quartz, leaving the bone structure intact.

Colours: Brown, grey, white or black for natural; agatized as brown to black with splashes of red, blue and bright yellow; occasionally yellow-gold and red.

Availability: Becoming rarer as collection is restricted.

Physical benefits: Said to be good for bone strength and fracture healing, bone marrow, DNA and all hereditary conditions, relief of chronic pain, lifelong illnesses.

Emotional healing: Soothes grief after the death of a long-term mate, a child or the breakdown of a relationship.

Chakra: Root.

Candle colour: Grey. **Fragrances**: Cypress, lavender, musk, sage **Practical uses**: Good if you have older relatives living with you to help them feel part of the family. **Workplace**: Wear or keep in your workspace if working for a new company or in new impersonal premises to create a sense of permanence. **Magical significance**: Connects the wearer with the wisdom of many ages, bringing spontaneous recall of past lives and worlds. **Divinatory meaning**: Do not make the same mistake you have done before when dealing with a manipulative person; stand strong. **Zodiac**: Capricorn **Empowerment**: The past holds the key to the future.

Even the smallest piece of fossilized bone carries millions of years of the world's history within it; totally natural relics are even more magical than their more polished cousins. Hold when you are tired or others are taking your power away; draw strength from accumulated ancient Earth power, one of the most powerful and yet soothing energizers; bury a small natural dinosaur bone near the doorstep of a newly built house or in any wall, fireplace, new conservatory, extension or conversion. This will bring good fortune to the home and protect against teething problems.

Petoskey Stone

Type: Organic, fossilized coral, calcite.

Colours: Taupe, tan and shades of brown or greys with intricate hexagonal or eye patterns when polished.

Availability: Found in specialist crystal stores and online.

Physical benefits: Thought to help with infections, eyes, HIV and AIDS, chronic fatigue syndrome, lungs, fluid levels and balance within the body, polyps, growths and tumours, considered helpful for cancers of the blood, bladder, glands, bones or breasts, bone fractures, skin.

Emotional healing: For breaking free of constant interference and guilt-inducing pressures and overcoming prejudices about different lifestyle choices.

Chakra: Sacral, Brow and Crown.

Candle colour: Brown. **Fragrances:** Grapefruit, kelp, lavender, lemon, lime. **Practical uses:** A stone of creative expression andof travelling solo. **Workplace:** For all who work in restoration or renovation; also for writers of historical fiction or drama; for medical researchers. **Magical significance:** Protects against envy and malice; wear or set on table for all mediumship and when channelling spirit guides; prevents low-level spirits from pretending to be who they are not and causing trouble. **Divinatory meaning:** Ignore gossip as this is rooted in jealousy; you have an unexpected ally who will help you counteract the spite. **Zodiac:** Cancer. **Empowerment:** My spirit guardians are always with me.

With its fabulous eye patterns, petoskey is a stone of magic, with its ancient origins and watery energies, for the coral colony lived 350 million years ago when Michigan had a warm inland sea.

Wearing polished petoskey stone increases awareness of true feelings about situations and people, and assists in resolving unfinished business in past or present relationships; good for researching family origins and for finding branches of the family who are living overseas; place in the centre of the brow to increase psychic awareness.

Brown Topaz

Type: Silicate.

Colours: Red-brown (may fade in time id exposed to sun).

Availability: Common.

Physical benefits: Claimed to relieve problems concerning male reproductive organs and impotence, hips, legs, knees and lower back; be especially helpful for mobility after hip and joint replacements.

Emotional healing: Excellent as a gift for people who distrust life and other people to help them become more open and welcoming rather than hiding from life's challenges; relieves agoraphobia, excessive timidity and obsessive compulsive disorder.

Chakra: Root.

Candle colour: Brown or red-brown. **Fragrances:** Bluebell, geranium, honeysuckle, patchouli. **Practical uses:** Carry on long journeys to make the experience an adventure. **Workplace:** Motivates to push forward if there seems no immediate advantage; good for all who work on the land, with animals or in conservation. **Magical significance:** Sit in a quiet, natural place touching a brown topaz on one of the seasonal change points to see earth spirits and elf or fey energies. **Divinatory meaning:** An opportunity to sow the seeds for a new idea that will bear fruit in about six months. **Zodiac:** Scorpio and Sagittarius. **Empowerment:** The earth energies fill me with strength.

Often called the earth gem, brown topaz is not considered particularly valuable as a gemstone.

However, it is gaining popularity among earth and nature lovers; carry if you are starting a new practically based business, or are planning a family and need to create a stable environment; good also for making lasting friendships, especially if you have been uprooted. Increases faithfulness and brings a reminder of why you are together, if you are having relationship problems, good for attracting a partner you can trust. Easily mistaken for smoky quartz, but has more vitality.

Astrophyllite

Type: Titanium mineral, associated with feldspar, mica and titanite.

Colours: Golden yellow, red-brown, greenish brown or golden brown, with a metallic or pearly sheen.

Availability: Found in specialist crystal stores and online.

Physical benefits: Thought to help with cholesterol, reproductive organs, fertility, hormones, PMS, menopause, healthy cell regrowth, sensitivity to noise, light, chemical irritants or food.

Emotional healing: If you have been responsible for others from childhood, astrophyllite releases you from the feeling of needing to make others happy to follow your own path and desires.

Chakra: Crown

Candle colour: Gold or silver. **Fragrances:** Acacia, almond, anise, copal. **Practical uses:** Stroke when you feel anxious or irritable. It acts as an meditation tool and relaxant. **Workplace:** Excellent for anyone involved in massage, Reiki, acupuncture, acupressure, shiatsu and reflexology to help you tune in to the energies and needs of clients, good for anyone working in conventional medicine; also astrologers and diviners. **Magical significance:** A crystal for astral travel, connects with UFO energies. **Divinatory meaning:** You will get unexpected proof that your intuitions were accurate. **Zodiac:** Cancer, Scorpio, and Capricorn. **Empowerment:** I walk the path towards my true life's purpose.

Astrophyllite has become associated with astrology and star wisdom. It eases the transition from one life stage to another. Holding by candle or moonlight reveals light at the end of the tunnel and may attract an unexpected new opportunity or a lifeline soon afterwards. Meditating will reveal your destiny and you will coincidentally meet the right people and chances in the weeks you work with the crystal to lead you on the unfolding path to realizing dreams also to visiting places again apparently coincidentally where you need to be to fulfil this blueprint.

Holey Stones

Type: Any stone with a natural hole caused by water or weathering, usually in limestone; also crystals with artificial holes.

Colours: Brown, fawn, grey, white.

Availability: Common in commercial crystal form; relatively common in natural form near water. Can be bought online.

Physical benefits: Claimed to help draw out illness, absorb pain; protect against diseases, childhood ills and infections, lung infections and fevers, cramp, rheumatism, bone disorders, warts and verrucas.

Emotional healing: On a cord round the neck acts as a talisman during difficult times, touch the stone when experiencing doubts.

Chakra: Root.

Candle colour: Brown. **Fragrances:** Fennel, lavender, musk, wisteria. **Practical uses:** A stone of committed love. Keep a small natural stone on a red cord tied with three knots, together with a small bag of dried yarrow over the bed; replace the yarrow once a year. **Workplace:** A naturally found stone, particularly with three holes in the same stone, is a luck-bringer. Look through the stone, visualizing whatever you need in work. The resource will come. **Magical significance:** Look through a holed stone by candlelight to see an image in your mind that will answer a question. **Divinatory meaning:** A piece of unexpected luck will bring what is needed. **Zodiac:** Virgo and Capricorn. **Empowerment:** There is always an alternative.

Naturally holey (or holed) stones have a long magical history in many different cultures. They were considered a gateway to other dimensions and large ones were set near the entrance of Neolithic burial chambers to bring rebirth or easy passage to the Otherworld.

Natural and crystal holed stones protect against paranormal harm, ill-wishing and those who seek to control our minds; keep near the front door on a red knotted cord to guard the home or on the bedpost to repel nightmares and psychic attack while asleep. If you find a pointed one, use it on red cord as a pendulum.

Bronzite

Type: Silicate of magnesium and an iron-rich pyroxene.

Colours: Brown, dark black or greenish speckled and streaked with golden-bronze metallic patterns.

Availability: Relatively common.

Physical benefits: Believed to assist the absorption of minerals into the body; claimed to help anaemia and blood disorders, be good for restoring energy levels in physically tiring jobs or lifestyles.

Emotional healing: Assists indecisiveness and lack of self-belief, heals hurts and injustices from the past you may have buried, but use with rose quartz or sparingly if you are very vulnerable as they are very powerful.

Chakra: Root.

Candle colour: Golden-brown. **Fragrances:** Patchouli, any spices. **Practical uses:** Good for helping you to get through routine or duty with cheerfulness. **Workplace:** Excellent in any customer service or hospitality industries to maintain politeness and calm. **Magical significance:** Excellent for money magic: leave a pot of small crystals exposed to sunlight or light a golden-brown candle next to them once a week. **Divinatory meaning:** For now focus on small matters and details. The whole picture will emerge naturally. **Zodiac:** Capricorn **Empowerment:** I am strong enough to resist any who would diminish my self-esteem.

Bronzite is a good talisman to bring talents into the marketplace. In the less common chatoyant cat's eye form or indeed any particularly glinting bronzite, ask a question, gaze upon the surface and the right decision will emerge. It encourages consideration for others and so is excellent for family life. If your partner or children take an age to get ready, hold a bronzite and say "hurry up" nine times, or have one in your bag at work meetings that drag on forever. Do not use bronzite in the bedroom as its energies can disturb sleep, though it is good for meditation.

Lava

Type: Volcanic rock.

Colours: Brown, grey or blackish, also blue.

Availability: Common.

Physical benefits: It is believed that pointed, pock-marked lava can draw out pain and illness; move the crystal down the body, flicking it away regularly during treatment towards the flame of a red candle to symbolically cleanse the lava; may also relieve chronic skin conditions.

Emotional healing: Made from solidified volcanic material, it increases vitality in those sunk into lethargy; good for the long-term unemployed or dispossessed to make effort in the face of discouragement.

Chakra: Solar Plexus.

Candle colour: Red. **Fragrances:** Allspice, copal, frankincense, saffron. **Practical uses:** In the home or car it disarms troublemakers; protective also against fires, accidents and burglary. **Workplace:** Have a small display of pointed and rounded lava, hold pointed lava outwards to guard against bad-tempered employers and colleagues; touch rounded lava to activate your energies. **Magical significance:** Lava is very lucky because it involves the fusion of the four ancient magical elements. **Divinatory meaning:** Wait until feelings have cooled before tackling an emotive issue. **Zodiac:** Aries and Scorpio. **Empowerment:** I value nature's gifts.

Lava is sacred to Pele, the Hawaiian goddess of volcanoes, fire and magic. Sometimes smooth, rounded lava is regarded as female and is combined with the pointed pocked male lava in sex or fertility rituals or carried by a couple who want a baby. Wrap a piece of female lava in some greenery, tie it in with twine in three knots and set it on the earth facing west; ask that any misfortune may be taken away. Wear to shine in any situation and to attract passionate love; also good for earthing and containing irritability in anyone with a bad temper or who deliberately creates dramas.

Type: Complex silicate of boron and aluminium.

Colours: Clear and transparent, can be gem quality.

Availability: Relatively rare, but worth buying a small one.

Physical benefits: Said to bring body and mind back into balance after trauma or prolonged illness; may help clear chronic dull headaches, constrictions in the throat, physical blockages anywhere in the body.

Emotional healing: Lack of confidence, stuttering or incoherence, being over-trusting, feeling stuck in practical issues and burdens to which there seems no end or solution.

Chakra: Crown and Throat.

Achroite/Colourless Tourmaline

Candle colour: White or silver. **Fragrances:** Hyacinth, lily, lily of the valley, lotus, myrrh. **Practical uses:** Wear a small achroite if you have to speak in a meeting to make your words clear, concise and inspiring. **Workplace:** If you are in a workplace where you are constantly pressurized to achieve, keep your tourmaline where it catches the light to draw success to you by ethical means. **Magical significance:** Use achroite in automatic writing, written words dictated by your own inner wisdom, an angel, guardian spirit or ancestor that you write spontaneously. Hold the crystal in the hand you do not write with and let the other hand write freely. **Divinatory meaning:** Trust your instincts as someone may not be telling you the truth; a doorway of opportunity may open. **Zodiac:** Pisces. **Empowerment:** I can open the door that is closed to me.

Tourmaline is named from the Singhalese word *turamali*, which means coloured or mixed stone, because it is found in every colour of the rainbow.

The colourless variety represents the synthesis of all the rainbow colours and will connect you with other dimensions and especially angelic wisdom.

Achroite will amplify the effects of any other crystals, especially other tourmalines, and increases the luck-bringing properties of your zodiac or birth month stone. However, it is very powerful and

should only be worn for short periods.

Do not wear if you are driving or working with machinery as it can make you feel very spaced out.

If you are anxious or reticent around over-confident people or in a large group situation achroite will fill your aura with serenity so you speak and act confidently

Keep a tiny piece on or near the photograph or name of someone who is intolerant, dictatorial or unreasonable, whether a family member, employer or world leader, to encourage wise compassion.

Tourmalated Quartz

Type: Silicate/cyclosilicate within quartz. Needles of black tourmaline embedded in crystal quartz.

Colours: Clear or milky with sparkling black; occasionally green or pink tourmaline inclusions.

Availability: Relatively common.

Physical benefits: Believed to improve blocked arteries, strokes, veins, blocked heart valves, scars and lesions, growths.

Emotional healing: Reduces self-sabotage.

Chakra: Root and Crown.

Candle colour: Grey. Fragrances: Anise, cloves, dragon's blood, juniper, poppy. **Practical uses:** A natural lone traveller's crystal, moderating a spirit of discovery with caution; excellent for working holidays. **Workplace:** A protective stone to wear if you are temporarily working in an unfamiliar environment where you are uncertain of your reception. **Magical significance:** The best crystal for understanding intuitively the *I Ching* and for learning traditional Chinese medicine or acupuncture; use as pyramid for exploring mind travel and remote viewing. **Divinatory meaning:** Things are not black or white. **Zodiac:** Gemini. **Empowerment:** I can live with uncertainties.

Tourmalated quartz is a very powerful crystal, integrating yang and yin, male and female, darkness and light, active and receptive. Regarded as a symbol of great fortune, it is not carried as an ongoing charm but when specific good luck is needed. Some healers say it is too powerful for all but professional healers. Its integrating energies will benefit anyone who needs to restore harmony. Relieves shock after road accidents and injury where there has been emotional trauma.

Helps to rise above pettiness until you can speak out; a large natural crystal is a protective shield in a noisy

Girasol Quartz

Type: Silicon dioxide, a variety of quartz with a milky sheen.

Colours: Cloudy and colourless, with a translucent glow that may appear blue.

Availability: Common.

Physical benefits: Said to help blurred vision, headaches, dizziness, balance problems, pain relief, metabolism, diabetes, physical exhaustion, gynaecological problems, fertility, childbirth (particularly when a mother is fearful or has complications), lactation.

Emotional healing: Calms fears, phobias and acute sensitivity to stimuli; for city dwellers, two- and four-legged, to absorb excess noise, crowds and pollution.

Chakra: Sacral and Crown.

Candle colour: Silver. Fragrances: Almond, anise, cherry, musk. **Practical uses:** A large crystal or a dish of tumblestones filters out ongoing worries and resentments. Wear if you bring up past injustices, to speak softly but honestly from your heart; assists the other person to focus on now. **Workplace:** An egg or sphere calms a workplace that encourages stress; hold and centre yourself to avoid making rash decisions by being swept along. **Magical significance:** Hold a large natural chunk or sphere up to the last sunlight when the full or almost-full moon is in the sky and you know the information you need. **Divinatory meaning:** Not a time to rush in. **Zodiac:** Cancer. **Empowerment:** I create my own oasis of calm.

Use girasol quartz to express your innate creativity. At home it encourages family members to relax together rather than indulging in frantic activity or automatically turning on music or the television. Choose a girasol sphere or natural piece with markings inside and meditate spontaneously. Look within the crystal at the threads and pathways and allow your mind to let go of the everyday world and weave stories about magical worlds as you did when you were a child. A helpful crystal for teenagers who are confused by their sexuality, to talk about their worries.

Clear Quartz

Type: Silicon dioxide, clear quartz appears in many forms.

Colours: Colourless and glassy, sparkling in light.

Availability: Very common.

Physical benefits: Believed to heal and energize the body and anywhere it is directed for contact and absent healing; help with diabetes, exhaustion, memory, metabolism, weight loss; act as an amplifier or substitute for any other crystal in healing; can be used for pain relief and to remove a problem (anti-clockwise) and to restore health (clockwise).

Emotional healing: Hold a sphere to natural light every day and state the new beginning you will have; transmits prayers.

Chakra: Crown.

Candle colour: White or natural beeswax. **Fragrances:** Chamomile, orange, rosemary. **Practical uses:** Carry as tumblestone for ongoing energy; for an instant lift, touch it, absorbing the light so that it can circulate round your body. **Workplace:** Wear as a filter to transform critical words. You will become less affected by negativity. **Magical significance:** Absorbs energy from nature and draws down light from angels and the cosmos. This energy is then released as automatic ongoing cleansing and healing into your rainbow aura energy field and inner chakra power centres. **Divinatory meaning:** New beginnings, fresh energies and the need to move fast to catch up with life. **Zodiac:** Aries and Leo. **Empowerment:** Each day is a new beginning.

Clear quartz appears in traditions of almost every culture and age, and was believed to contain pure life force. Add quartz crystals to bathwater, or make clear crystal quartz water (crystal quartz left in water from first light to midday) to drink or splash on pulse points. Even the smallest quartz carries the properties of a master healer teacher because in its sparkling white light it contains the entire colour spectrum. If you have only one healing crystal it should be clear quartz. For an all-purpose charm to attract success, empower by breathing on it three times to endow it with your essence every week.

Metamorphosis Quartz

Type: Quartz, silicon dioxide, sometimes displays asterism (star shape) or intense patch of opalescent silvery light inside.

Colours: Milky white.

Availability: Relatively common.

Physical healing: Seen as useful for bringing a positive change to a resistant medical condition and any form of new growth of cells, tissues and bones, blurred vision, headaches, dizziness, balance, pain relief, metabolism, diabetes, exhaustion.

Emotional healing: Encourages anyone hesitating to make a transformation or doubting their abilities to start again.

Chakra: Sacral and Crown.

Candle colour: Silver. **Fragrances:** Apple blossom, cherry blossom, orange, passion flower, peach. **Practical uses:** Wear a pendant to make a positive difference to others. **Workplace:** Melting rigid attitudes and allows imaginative thinking; focus on the star or the silvery inner-light place as you put your hands round the quartz and let ideas flow. **Magical significance:** Strengthens the aura if you pass it over your head and shoulders a few centimetres above your hairline. Seals your aura against people who offload burdens. **Divinatory meaning:** Transformation brings freedom; keep going. **Zodiac:** Cancer. **Empowerment:** I have the potential for constant transformation.

If possible, buy your metamorphosis quartz directly from a supplier so you can hold it. It is often more opalescent and less regular in shape than tumbled girasol. Look for one with a star or patch of light. It is considered to have stronger energies than girasol, sensed as a stirring when you hold it and a burst of certainty and enthusiasm. It is considered to be a crystal with its own guardian spirit or angel who can be contacted through the crystal. This will ease changes and transitions and help you be yourself. Carry if you are starting again and feel uncertain.

Type: Calcium carbonate.

Colours: Clear, colourless.

Availability: Common.

Physical benefits: Labelled as an all-healer, it is said to cleanse organs connected with elimination and prevents calcification in bones; believed to be especially good as an elixir for intestines, skin, warts and ulcers and for detoxification; thought to assist healthy growth in children and growth disorders, improve eyesight, weight loss.

Emotional healing: Helpful for obsessive compulsive disorder, Tourette's syndrome, tics or any destructive or self-destructive behaviour.

Chakra: Crown .

Clear Calcite

Candle colour: White. **Fragrances:** Almond, jasmine, mimosa, peach, white rose. **Practical uses:** Helps you to find lost objects or papers; shine bright light on the surface and you will get a picture in your mind of where you left/ lost the item. **Workplace:** Excellent for starting at a new workplace or for effectively making necessary changes in your own or others' working practices or timetable gradually and with the minimum of disruption or conflict. **Magical significance:** A strong space clearer. Keep a small bowl of colourless calcite in the centre of any room where you meditate, practice therapies, do magic or divination, alternatively where you sense negative paranormal activity; useful if you move into a home where the previous owner suffered divorce, illness or misfortune or the house has been empty for a while. Wash the crystals weekly under running water. **Divinatory meaning:** A new beginning you seek may be taking longer than anticipated, but it will happen. **Zodiac:** Aquarius. **Empowerment:** I clear all clutter from my life.

Calcite is one of the world's most common and yet most diverse minerals: there are over three hundred calcite crystal forms recorded. It comes in many shapes and sizes; colourless or white is the purest form. In its most water-like transparent form, clear calcite is doubly refractive and called optical calcite or Iceland spar.

Colourless calcite is the best of the calcites for absent healing, better even than its more sparkling sister optic calcite.

A natural calcite or a cluster, sometimes attached to other minerals such as haematite or fluorite, is an excellent focus for transmitting light and healing from angels or healing guides via your fingers: hold the clear calcite and picture the person, animal or place to whom or which you are sending the healing.

A crystal for speaking the truth but with tact and compassion, especially if you are leaving a relationship or having to break bad news to someone.

Type: Beryllium with no chemical impurities.

Colours: Clear, colourless.

Availability: The rarest form of beryl but obtainable from specialist jewellery and crystal stores and online.

Physical benefits: Claimed to improve eyesight, detoxify, energize, reduce stress-related exhaustion, help leg and arm muscles, arm and leg fractures, dust-mite and pollen allergies, infections and viruses that damage the immune system; as a crystal of the moon, it is said to balance body fluids and hormones; take with you to help with medical tests or investigations for a clear diagnosis and effective treatment if necessary.

Emotional healing: One of the best anti-mood-swing crystals and so helpful for hormonally-related conditions such as acute PMS, post-natal depression and also for bi-polar disorder.

Chakra: Crown.

Goshenite/Colourless Beryl

Candle colour: White. **Fragrances:** Almond, apple blossom, bergamot, lemon balm, lemon verbena. **Practical uses:** The crystal of truth, natural goshenite spreads honesty if you live or work with people who find it hard to distinguish between reality and fantasy; also to deter gossiping neighbours. **Workplace:** Goshenite speeds up the tempo of colleagues who are always delaying completing tasks or following up queries, leaving you to compensate for their inadequacies; encourages honest dealings; keep goshenite hidden to deter a thief among staff and alert you to the culprit. **Magical significance:** Colourless beryl, whether as a cabochon or a natural one with pyramid faces, is worth seeking out to serve as a scrying crystal; look within and see images physically formed by the markings inside to answer questions that your conscious mind cannot solve. **Divinatory meaning:** The truth is important but it may hurt; speak what must be said gently and accept it may not be totally pain-free. **Zodiac:** Cancer. **Empowerment:** I will not hide behind illusion or false dreams.

Called the mother of crystals, goshenite is associated with motherhood and makes a wonderful Mothering Sunday gift, especially if your mother has struggled to bring up children, whether as a lone parent or because of health or financial hardships; also from a mother to a daughter when she becomes a mother herself.

Historically one of the earliest crystal balls or spheres; also used from antiquity for spectacles and traditionally placed on the eyelids at night to improve eyesight.

Wear goshenite if you fear a lover or partner is being unfaithful, as it encourages fidelity but also alerts you intuitively to the difference between unfounded insecurity and warning signs.

Wear or carry colourless beryl if you need to keep secrets and protect confidential information. Goshenite is an angel crystal, particularly for contacting moon or female angels.

Diamond

Type: Carbon, the hardest gem and mineral in the world.

Colours: Colourless with brilliant lustre, reflecting dazzling colour flashes known as fire; also yellow, brown, green, blue, pink, purple and black diamond – not black but with black inclusions.

Availability: Common.

Physical benefits: Diamond is a master healer because it is good for healing the mind and body; said to amplify the power of other crystals if arranged in a grid or pattern round a patient; may help detoxification, brain functioning, balance of brain hemispheres, female fertility, sexual dysfunction.

Emotional healing: Creates a sense of radiance and self-value, for anyone who has lost their identity and sense of worth.

Chakra: Crown.

Candle colour: White. **Fragrances:** Frankincense, lily, white lotus, white orchid, white rose. **Practical uses:** A symbol of fidelity; becomes cloudy if love is no longer true or when the wearer is unhappy about love; a sign to talk to your partner. **Workplace:** Attracts prosperity by increasing the positive profile of the wearer and by expanding the energy field to draw greater opportunities. **Magical significance:** A natural defence against jealousy. Wear diamond earrings or pendant to protect your Brow, Throat and Heart chakras. **Divinatory meaning:** Proof of your abilities will come from an unexpected source. **Zodiac:** Aries **Empowerment:** I attract light and love.

Because diamonds absorb thoughts and feelings, focus on remaining positive while wearing or holding them; the diamond will amplify positivity, projecting your thoughts outwards, so attracting a positive reaction from others. Rough diamond elixir counteracts exhaustion; put a few drops in your bath to energize you; add six drops of ylang ylang essential oil to the mix, shake well before adding to the bath to fill your aura with desirability before going on a date or lovemaking. Diamonds are traditionally a stone of courage, worn next to the skin by Roman soldiers to make them invincible to fear.

Herkimer Diamond

Type: Clear quartz, double terminated.

Colours: Colourless, sparkling; may contain rainbow inclusions, water, air bubbles or a black inclusion in centre.

Availability: Relatively common.

Physical benefits: Claimed to prevent physical exhaustion and burnout; stimulate immune defences; protect from radiation and toxins; assist with genetic problems.

Emotional healing: The unrestricted growth of Herkimers in mud makes them good for breaking restrictions.

Chakra: Crown.

Candle colour: White. **Fragrances:** Acacia, almond, pine. **Practical uses:** Hold it will vibrate if the person you are talking to is dishonest. Do not carry for prolonged periods, as it can cause disorientation. **Workplace:** Keep with you during study as it stores knowledge, good for teachers of spirituality and alternative therapies. **Magical significance:** Brings vivid dreams and dream recall; for out-of-body experiences, choose a Herkimer with a black inner seed and focus on the black **Divinatory meaning:** Be careful if making a purchase that you are getting value. **Zodiac:** Aries and Sagittarius. **Empowerment:** Beauty is more lasting than profit.

Herkimers are not a stone for children or animals as they have powerful otherworldly energies. For Reiki healing and attunements, or to bring yourself back together after a stressful event, place four small Herkimers around the body at regular intervals alternated with four rose quartz. Use four large Herkimers to make a grid formation around the four inner walls of your home. The crystals insulate against excessive electromagnetic pollution, negative earth energies and external stresses from neighbours; as an elixir room spray, it clears negativity after a quarrel.

Type: Calcium borosilicate produces crystals similar to topaz.

Colours: Colourless, white, sparkling when polished.

Availability: Relatively common; almost all danburite is colourless.

Physical benefits: Gentler than crystal quartz but thought to be equally clear for healing, danburite is believed to help to clear energy blockages throughout the whole body for sick children, old people, smaller animals or anyone who is weak or vulnerable if the sickness is acute; may also ease problems connected with liver, gall bladder, all organs or tissues or inoperable conditions.

Emotional healing: Injects positive feelings into ongoing negative situations and people we cannot walk away from, bringing the best possible outcome; helps us to see good in everyone, however difficult.

Chakra: Heart, Crown.

Clear Danburite

Candle colour: White. **Fragrances:** Lily, lily of the valley, lotus, musk, white rose. **Practical uses:** Called the celebration stone because it brings joy to any gathering or party (give a small tumblestone to everyone present as a gift), danburite jewellery is as perfect as the more expensive white sapphire or diamond for betrothals or any celebration to say "I offer you my love". **Workplace:** A stone of clear intellect, danburite brings instant recall of knowledge and directs it in the most effective way to impress others; a think-on-your-feet crystal, wear when you have to defend your position or appear expert when you have not had time or access to the relevant material to prepare. **Magical significance:** An angel crystal, especially as a perfectly clear cluster that in natural or candle light creates a powerful light energy to open visions of your guardian angel either within the danburite or around it. **Divinatory meaning:** You will see more clearly the good side of an uncommunicative older relative and will find you have a lot in common. **Zodiac:** Aquarius and Leo. **Empowerment:** I regard everyone as friends unless proved otherwise.

Clear danburite is a relatively recent discovery, named after Danbury, Connecticut, where it was first discovered in 1839. Clear danburite empowers inexperienced healers to send healing light from their eyes to a sick person or animal when they think of them or look on them with love or affection.

If you find clear crystal quartz too intense, clear danburite possesses all the energizing, clearing and light-bringing properties of crystal quartz.

However it is much more an empathic people-orientated crystal, encouraging progress through interconnections between individuals and groups.

It draws people who are in tune with you, so wear or carry one to singles or any social events if you are looking for a partner or while communicating via online socializing sites – it deters time-wasters, fantasists and less benign contacts who use the Internet.

Type: Zirconium silicate. Not to be confused with artificial cubic zirconia.

Colours: Clear, colourless or white, and sparkling like a diamond, usually brown zircon heat-treated but can be found occasionally as totally pure natural zircon.

Availability: Large, naturally clear specimens are quite rare but can be obtained from specialist crystal and jewellery stores and online.

Physical benefits: Believed to assist infertility, kidneys, liver, gallbladder and the immune system; promote efficient functioning of pituitary and pineal glands; energize and detoxify the whole system; if your system has been flooded with chemicals as part of a necessary treatment, may help restore natural balance.

Emotional healing: Brings deep restful sleep, overcomes trauma or loss and brings a sense of clarity in confusion. In sunlight clear zircon catches rainbows, offering a blast of the life force and spontaneous joy; cleanses the whole aura.

Chakra: Root and Sacral.

Zircon/Matura Diamond

Candle colour: White. **Fragrances:** Apple blossom, bluebell, cherry blossom, lily, lily of the valley. **Practical uses:** Clear zircon is the crystal of the carer; wear zircon if you are nursing someone you love, especially a long-term or degenerative illness; gives you the wisdom to do and say the right things. **Workplace:** Use clear zircon to assist with clarity of thought and protection against negative energies, also for fulfillment rather than success in material terms. **Magical significance:** Clear zircon is said to become dull if someone comes near who wishes you harm or who is incubating an infectious disease. **Divinatory meaning:** Have faith in the life path you have chosen and in your abilities to win through. **Zodiac:** Aries, Taurus and Sagittarius. **Empowerment:** I call upon my inner light to guide me.

Zircon has often been mistaken for diamond, even by professional jewellers – therefore it makes a very affordable alternative and is called matura diamond. Clear zircon was traditionally passed over food in the shape of a cross to remove all impurities or harmful influences from it.

Zircons are also key indicators in radiometric dating as they have the ability to survive through all forms of geological process.

They have been dated as the oldest minerals on planet Earth and so will amplify psychometry and psychic touch to provide hidden information about old places and artefacts. Associated with the planet and goddess Venus, this crystal empowers your emotions in love – and in this case no logic will be involved!

Petalite

Type: Silicate/phyllosilicate.

Colours: Clear, colourless, white, pink, grey.

Availability: Rare.

Physical benefits: Said to help with allergies, rashes, stomach upsets, muscle, neck and back pain, stress-related illnesses, eyelids and brows, dyspraxia, ADHD, ME, HIV and AIDS, respiratory system, intestines; has been considered helpful by some cancer patients with both primary and secondary tumours.

Emotional healing: Holding petalite creates a quiet space in your head in the midst of noise, rather than trying to sort out the chaos that will leave you more tense.

Chakra: Crown.

Candle colour: White. **Fragrances:** Almond, clary sage, rosewood, vanilla. **Practical uses:** Good at collecting scattered energies; stop and hold it for a minute and let life catch up with you. **Workplace:** Encourages the workaholic to take breaks. **Magical significance:** If you hold it to either ear petalite allows you to hear your guardian angel speak; carry it with your if you go on a vision quest or to a sacred site to shut out everyday thoughts. **Divinatory meaning:** Speak what is in your heart without fear as you need clarification of the feelings of someone. **Zodiac:** Aquarius. **Empowerment:** I will listen to my wise inner self.

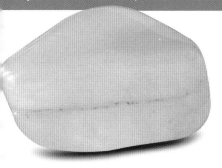

Clear Fluorite

Type: Halide, calcium fluoride. Pure fluorite is colourless but trace impurities result in various colours (p.95, p.210 and p.293).

Colours: Clear or colourless.

Availability: Relatively common.

Physical benefits: May improve the immune system, eyesight, bones, sinuses, spleen, skin, arthritis, teeth, fight debilitating viruses, colds or infections; assist infant and mother to recover from the shock of medical intervention during birth.

Emotional healing: Helps to bring order out of chaotic personal emotional turmoil or pressure from others and restores clear and positive thinking.

Chakra: Brow.

Candle colour: White or silver. **Fragrances:** Chamomile, elder, myrrh. **Practical uses:** Gives gentle energy to sick or recovering children and animals; keep a dish in the kitchen and dining area to encourage a balanced attitude to food. **Workplace:** Transforms work-related stress into clear strategies; counteracts excessive memos and unnecessary meetings. **Magical significance:** Acts as a pain absorber if you physically place the crystal on affected area; enhances the energies of other crystals so can be used in crystal healing combinations and layouts. **Divinatory meaning:** You are being offered the best possible deal that will get life moving. **Zodiac:** Pisces **Empowerment:** Gentle strength can move mountains.

Petalite is often called the stone of angels because of its delicate ethereal appearance, and looking into or through it in soft natural light helps you to see angelic light. It also connects you with natural energies and evolved nature essences in high places. Generally too soft to be made into jewellery, wrap petalite carefully and carry with you on journeys to seek the unexpected and the beautiful; good if you have a hectic travel schedule to appreciate the setting and stop and listen to natural sounds – and inner silence.

Clear fluorite cleanses impurities in the body and blockages in mind and spirit. Fluorite angels, spheres and eggs are gentle energizers and break down divisions between our world and angelic realms.

Meditation with this crystal can stimulate latent psychic abilities and enhance intuition that increases level and length of visionary experience. Clear fluorite brings balance during spiritual or psychic development work, and offers protection against malicious spirits and negative energies.

Clear Topaz

Type: Hydrous aluminium silicate, the purest form of topaz.

Colours: Clear and sparkling.

Availability: Common.

Physical benefits: Thought to speed recovery from illness or injury; relieve cystic fibrosis, emphysema, asthma, allergies to dust and pollution, colds, bronchitis, influenza, pleurisy and pneumonia; help clear eyesight.

Emotional healing: Though to energizes the spiritual essence of the self, cleanse and balance emotions to enable clear thought and insights when thoughts and feelings whirl round making it hard to function efficiently.

Chakra: Crown.

Candle colour: White. **Fragrances:** Benzoin, chamomile, heather, marigold. **Practical uses:** Wear to help you radiate confidence if you feel out of your depth with wealthy or sophisticated people. **Workplace:** Enables you to see information from several different perspectives. **Magical significance:** Though all topaz gets brighter as the moon waxes, clear topaz is most in tune with it. Hold one up to full moonlight to see images or symbols significant for you. Wear clear topaz when reading a crystal ball. **Divinatory meaning:** It is time to see the real truth. Listen to your inner voice to tell right from wrong. **Zodiac:** Aries and Sagittarius. **Empowerment:** There are no limits for the mind.

Set in a ring, clear topaz connects you with your power animals and increases your ability to communicate psychically with animals. Because topaz crystals have the ability to hold an electrical charge, clear topaz provides an extra mental and spiritual boost when you need it. Clear topaz with its clarity of spiritual vision pushes creative and spiritual endeavours to the limits, helping you to achieve levels you previously only dreamed of. A crystal of love that, because it is gentle and more lunar than a diamond, is excellent for a commitment ring for first love or one where trust has been rebuilt.

Grossular Garnet

Type: Silicate, calcium aluminium silicate.

Colours: Colourless, white, pink, cream, orange, red, honey, black or green.

Availability: Found in specialist stores and online.

Physical benefits: Said to be good for the immune system, heart, respiratory system, blood, vitamin deficiency, reproductive problems, deep vein thrombosis (carry green when on a long-haul trip); protect against highly infectious diseases.

Emotional healing: Reduces extremes of emotions; helpful if all your previous relationships have been a drama.

Chakra: Heart.

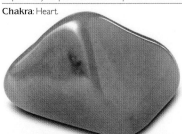

Candle colour: White or green. **Fragrances:** Juniper, rosemary, rue, sandalwood, vervain. **Practical uses:** Injects romance and fun into an over-practical life and boosts passion and fresh energies into a love weighed down by worry. **Workplace:** Carry colourless grossular garnet to increase chances of being recognized for your talents. **Magical significance:** Red or orange grossular is particularly protective against abusive neighbours or physical threats as it acts as an absorbing shield and reflects back nastiness. **Divinatory meaning:** Value yourself more highly. **Zodiac:** Capricorn and Aquarius. **Empowerment:** I do not need the praise of others to feel worthwhile.

A stone of strength, grossular garnet will benefit new business ventures. Have a display of small pieces in different colours: clear to boost the initial phase and keep new ideas and customers coming in; green for good luck, continuing growth and warm client contact; orange for ingenuity and creative ideas and advertising; red for stamina and determination.

Grossular garnet is particularly useful for companies offering spiritual products or services to maintain the right atmosphere and ethos but at the same time to make the necessary profit to be viable.

Candle Quartz

Type: Quartz that resembles a candle with melting wax.

Colours: Usually white and cloudy but can also be pink if iron oxide is present.

Availability: Common.

Physical benefits: Said to help with processing carbohydrates and fats, efficient production of insulin, thought to repair damage from neglect or unconscious damage to personal health, cell regeneration, temperature control of body, fevers or chills, burns and scalds; electric shocks.

Emotional healing: A "light in the darkness" crystal as a reminder that tomorrow is another day and step by step you will reach the light at the end of the current tunnel.

Chakra: Solar Plexus.

Candle colour: Beeswax. **Fragrances:** Acacia, anise, cinnamon, cloves, ginger. **Practical uses:** Folklore says it will bring abundance for your family and be a focal point for the household guardian. **Workplace:** Ideal for a small workshop or solo business, to help you gain contracts; keep in a car or lorry to light the way and make you feel safe at night. **Magical significance:** Surround it with small white candles; light them after sickness or sadness. **Divinatory meaning:** A time to socialize and regain enthusiasm for life. **Zodiac:** Leo. **Empowerment:** There is light in the darkness.

Candle quartz is a member of the elestial family, its surface covered by crystals and etchings. It has a central crystal point (the candle) and smaller downward-facing points along it (the wax), combining the intensity of a terminated point with the integrating energy of a cluster. A good crystal for independence, especially for women. Hold candle quartz against your solar plexus to absorb tension from body and mind and fill you with quiet energy; a charm for fame, fortune and a positive spotlight.

Snow/Milky Quartz

Type: Silicon dioxide, opaque quartz.

Colours: Polar white right through. Microscopic gas or water bubbles trapped in it cause the whiteness.

Availability: Common.

Physical benefits: Seen as good for bones, dislocation, bone marrow, breasts, teeth, absorption of calcium, lactation, infant feeding, blood disorders, fevers, menopausal symptoms, early-onset menopause, hysterectomy.

Emotional healing: After a family breach send snow-quartz carving or jewellery with a bridge-building note; in worst cases, circle a photo of the estranged person for a week with snow quartz before contact.

Chakra: Brow.

Candle colour: White. **Fragrances:** Almond, anise, magnolia, mimosa, neroli. **Practical uses:** Against winter hazards. Keep in a car for winter starting or driving in snow; in hot climates dip it in cold water for cooling. **Workplace:** Helps face unwelcome paperwork; put in a cash box or with accounts against temporary difficulty. **Magical significance:** Set three snow quartz in a bowl of ice; let it melt, stirring, to soften coldness in a love affair or get luck flowing. Tip the melted ice into water and crystals into a small bag. **Divinatory meaning:** Move forward with caution. **Zodiac:** Capricorn. **Empowerment:** Winter must come so spring will follow.

Snow quartz is the crystal of the snow moon, the January or February full moon that American Indians called Gnawing on Bones Moon. In Scandinavia it heralds deep snow. It is said Mother Holle or Hulda waved her icicle wand that the land might sleep and grow strong, and snow quartz fell from it. Often called the female or yin version of clear quartz, with slower but more lasting energies, it is essential in a frantic environment. A snow quartz sphere slows everything and everyone down to avoid accidents, and improves productivity.

Type: Sheet silicate, phylosillicate group.

Colours: Usually colourless/white, can contain rainbows or shine like mother-of-pearl where surface is fractured; also pale green, but can take on other colours such as pale pink from the presence of other minerals.

Availability: Obtainable from specialist crystal stores and online.

Physical benefits: Thought to help to ease asthma, cystic fibrosis, hay fever, emphysema and other respiratory problems; skin including eczema; called the Reiki crystal because its effects are said to be similar to a Reiki treatment (heal with an apophyllite point); may regularize heartbeat and pulse.

Emotional healing: Place a point or pointed apophyllite on your third eye/brow energy centre to make you feel whole and retrieve what you unwisely but in love have given away of your identity to others; green is best for emotional healing and spiritual work.

Chakra: Heart and Brow.

Apophyllite

Candle colour: White. **Fragrances:** Chamomile, lemon, lime, tea tree, violet. **Practical uses:** Keep an apophyllite cluster near the centre of the room where you relax as it will automatically cleanse the whole space, Feng Shui style. Pass incense smoke over the crystal monthly to keep it clear. **Workplace:** A crystal that encourages transparent honesty, efficiency and accuracy in detail; for all who work in the financial services or in the collection and processing of data and in historical research; also for writers of historical fiction. **Magical significance:** A crystal of connection with beings of other dimensions from power animals to spirit guides. Hold colourless apophyllite in sun, moon or candlelight to discover the identity of your personal guides and angels or increase communication. **Divinatory meaning:** Check and recheck plans and make sure you are up to date with paperwork and official forms. **Zodiac:** Gemini, Aquarius. **Empowerment:** I can take action rather than waiting for the cosmos to deliver.

Apophyllite, like amethyst especially as a cluster, draws negativity from other crystals used in healing or around the home or office, even quartz.

A crystal that as a cluster brings people together emotionally; for healing fractured love or family relationships, especially when outsiders are interfering or there are divided loyalties within or caused by step-family relationships; for action in

fulfilling major desired house or career moves or additions to the family; encourages saving and wise use of financial resources.

Apophyllite heals and calms horses and so should be used by horse whisperers as well as all who work with horses; helpful in learning languages, particularly later in life.

Snakeskin Agate

Type: Chalcedony, crypto-crystalline quartz.

Colours: White or cream with a wrinkled or cracked surface resembling snakeskin; also found in green.

Availability: One of the less common agates.

Physical benefits: Thought to assist skin disorders, dry skin, eczema, skin parasites, warts, verruccas, melanomas, bites or stings, hearing problems, intestines, stomach disorders, weight loss, cosmetic surgery, liposuction, breast reduction, reconstructive surgery; regrowth of cells and muscles.

Emotional healing: Protective against false friends and bad influences for those who are innocents, so easily led astray and hurt again and again by betrayal or trickery.

Chakra: Root and Brow.

Candle colour: Cream. **Fragrances:** Anise, basil, cloves, tarragon, sage. **Practical uses:** Good for leaving a place where you have been unhappy or a relationship going nowhere, and for quitting smoking. **Workplace:** Helps in an environment lacking trust or with fears of job losses, or to understand power structures. **Magical significance:** Said to make you less visible; hold agate and picture your energy field shrinking. **Divinatory meaning:** Time to shed old burdens and plan new strategies: things are changing for the better. **Zodiac:** Scorpio. **Empowerment:** I can travel light.

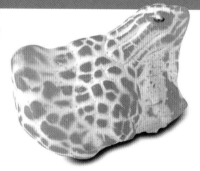

White snakeskin agate is sacred to the wise power serpent in the Native North American tradition.

Like other swirling agate dream stones, it aids meditation and relaxation. Follow the patterns with your eye, let your mind go blank. Good for stamina, and should be worn by all doing heavy physical work, especially in the construction industry, as it protects against accidents. Take it on country trips to connect with nature; helps awaken teenagers who find it hard to leave technology.

White Celestite

Type: Strontium ore/sulphate; also called celestine.

Colours: White, clear or like frosted ice; natural facets.

Availability: Relatively common.

Physical benefits: Seen as benefitting eyes, ears, thyroid, mineral absorption particularly potassium and magnesium, central nervous system, auto-immune diseases, bone marrow, transplants and transfusions, short-term memory loss, thrombosis, stress-related illness, an excellent Reiki crystal.

Emotional healing: For relieving hypochondria and fear of illness, pain or dying; brings a more realistic view of death and a focus on present health, not minor problems.

Chakra: Brow and Crown.

Candle colour: White. **Fragrances:** Bergamot, lemon balm, lemon verbena, magnolia, neroli. **Practical uses:** Clusters bring reconciliation to a gathering; encourage positive interactions; lighten the atmosphere for family discussions. **Workplace:** For peripatetic workers, to fit in while maintaining your own style and ethics. **Magical significance:** For angel communication; clear white celestite points make powerful healing or magic wands, with gentle energies; clear obstacles and initiate change. **Divinatory meaning:** Concentrate on the main task, halving both time and stress. **Zodiac:** Libra. **Empowerment:** I put aside what cannot for now be altered.

A light-giving crystal that brings intuition and clairvoyance so you can see the whole picture and hidden factors. Wear white celestite to achieve balance between acceptance and openness to new possibilities. A good anti-depression stone as it avoids the shock of clear quartz but keeps up a flow of positive thoughts. For healing or relief, apply to a place of discomfort for a few minutes; store near food to reduce toxicity from additives or pollution. Keep white celestite out of sunlight.

Type: Calcium magnesium carbonate.

Colours: Dazzling opaque white to milky white or greyish white; colourless transparent dolomite is occasionally found.

Availability: Relatively common.

Physical benefits: Viewed as being beneficial for teeth, bones, nails, gums, muscles, female reproductive system, PMS, lactation in nursing mothers, mastitis, breast lumps, breast implants and reconstruction after surgery, hormones, bone marrow; antiseptic for infected wounds, ulcers or lesions within the body and on the skin; eyesight, fractured skull, brain disorders and successful brain surgery.

Emotional healing: The purest form of dolomite, white brings clarity to a distorted self image and relieves guilt in those who have been made to feel responsible for their parents' unhappiness and so continue to accept blame from others in adulthood.

Chakra: Crown.

White Dolomite

Candle colour: White. **Fragrances:** Almond blossom, lily, lily of the valley, white orchid, vanilla. **Practical uses:** Keep polished, dazzling white dolomite sphere, eggs or tumblestones in different rooms where they will catch the light to spread health, harmony and happiness and to ensure generosity and altruism by all who live there or come to visit. **Workplace:** A stone that should be worn or carried by anyone who works for a charity, or undertakes voluntary work, to ensure efforts are focused to bring the best results for the intended recipients and efficient management of resources; for all who administer pension funds or budgets for hospitals or schools to spend wisely without sacrificing quality of care. **Magical significance:** Pure white dolomite angels make a wonderful gift for a newborn baby to keep them safe; hold a dazzling white sphere or egg up to sunlight, stare at the whiteness, blink and as you open your eyes you will see a flash of a future opportunity as an image in your mind or externally. **Divinatory meaning:** You can afford to be generous with your time and resources as you are entering a time when abundance will flow into your life. **Zodiac:** Taurus. **Empowerment:** I give freely only to good causes.

White dolomite is the more active version of its softer pink sister. It balances the gentle receptive and nurturing dolomite energies with a more abrasive quality that encourages giving only to those who really need and deserve it, and puts boundaries between self and others while giving or caring to avoid being drained of energy and resources.

A special kind of white dolomite is called sugar dolomite and has gold coloured inclusions of pyrites; use this to manifest in your life what would constitute for you happiness and fulfillment and to open up the realms of possibility.

A pure white dolomite worry stone absorbs anxiety, especially free floating worries and restlessness, and transforms it into creative inspirational and original thinking. White dolomite ornaments bring luck to newlyweds and to any new home.

White Moonstone

Type: Feldspar.

Colours: Cloudy white, shimmering like the moon; also yellow and brown and some with a bluish/grey tinge.

Availability: Common.

Physical benefits: Believed to improve digestion, epilepsy, gallstones, kidney stones, bladder, hormones, menstrual problems, ovaries, womb, pregnancy, breasts, hair, migraines, weight.

Emotional healing: Moonstone encourages calm, gentle but effective responses in fraught situations.

Chakra: Sacral.

Candle colour: Silver. **Fragrances:** Eucalyptus, jasmine, lemon, poppy. **Practical uses:** Wear travelling, especially overseas or at night; helps jet lag. **Workplace:** To combat tension with gentle lunar ebbs and flows; a stone for shift workers. **Magical significance:** At full moon, hold moonstone in each hand; turn anti-clockwise fast, focusing on the moon. Stop when you feel dizzy; you will 'bring down the moon' and feel empowered. **Divinatory meaning:** Now is the time to speak what is in your heart. **Zodiac:** Cancer. **Empowerment:** I recognize my ebbs and flows.

Moonstones have the same energies whether polished or natural. Especially beneficial to children; use to soothe those sleeping in unfamiliar beds, or for driving away nightmares or insomnia. The ultimate fertility crystal, a moonstone necklace worn while lovemaking at full moon harmonizes your body into the natural lunar cycle. Recharge moonstones overnight at full moon outdoors or on an indoor window ledge facing the moon.

Rainbow Moonstone

Type: Feldspar.

Colours: Milky white with rainbow sheen/flashes.

Availability: Rarer than ordinary moonstone, but relatively easily obtainable.

Physical benefits: Thought to assist with hormones, fertility, menstrual cycle, thyroid, pituitary gland, bowels, breasts, recovery after operations on breasts, womb, sterilization, anaphylactic shock.

Emotional healing: Combining gentle lunar energies with the optimism of the rainbow, reassures all who feel alone, lost or vulnerable; assists all emotional healing.

Chakra: Sacral, Brow, Crown.

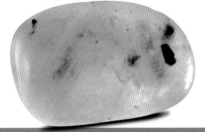

Candle colour: White or silver. **Fragrances:** Eucalyptus, jasmine, lemon balm, myrrh, neroli. **Practical uses:** Plant in the garden three days before full moon or when you see a rainbow for healthy growth in plants and attracting butterflies. **Workplace:** Wear when dealing with sensitive staff problems; helpful if you are having a relationship at work. **Magical significance:** The original mood stone, becomes brighter or duller in response to mood and energy levels; use in moon magic. **Divinatory meaning:** Nurture yourself and take time to relax. **Zodiac:** Cancer. **Empowerment:** I will collect moments of happiness.

This white labradorite variety of feldspar offers an intensified colour-spectrum sensation. Place under your pillow or where it catches the moon's rays to aid lucid dreaming and calm sleep, and find your dream lover. Rainbow moonstone is gentle and will offer ongoing strength against illness. A supportive stone for those who consider harming themselves. It may also improve learning difficulties in young children, and protects homes in remote areas.

Type: Hydrated silicon dioxide, generally common opal, though the name is sometimes applied to milky-white opalescent precious opal or opals with light backgrounds.

Colours: Milky white to light grey and translucent (cloudy).

Availability: Common.

Physical benefits: Said to assist with fertility and pregnancy, to act as an aid to labour and to soothe mother and child in the post-natal phase; help feeding difficulties particularly mastitis, all breast problems in women of any age, cell regeneration, mucous membranes, coughs, lung congestion, skin, fluid imbalances and hormones, Alzheimer's disease and senile dementia especially in women.

Emotional healing: For overcoming fears of childbirth that prevent a woman from trying for a baby; overwhelming fears during pregnancy and early months of a baby's life about infant mortality or disability, especially if there were problems with an earlier pregnancy.

Chakra: Sacral and Heart.

Milky Opal

Candle colour: Cream. **Fragrances:** Apple blossom, cherry blossom, lemon balm, lemon verbena, neroli. **Practical uses:** Milky opal creates a warm, safe environment if you care for foster children or your own or a partner's children are behaving badly to test your affection. **Workplace:** Wear milky opal if you are working with babies, children, mothers in distress or anyone who is vulnerable; also for assisting anyone whose memory is fading and their family carers; good for calming angry people if you work in customer complaints or on a helpdesk or helpline. **Magical significance:** Milky opals were once considered to have the power to confer invisibility in danger. In the modern world they can be used to maintain a low profile in potentially confrontational situations. Breathe gently on your opal and picture its milkiness enclosing you in a soft cloud until the difficult situation has passed. **Divinatory meaning:** A time for caring for a vulnerable friend or family member who may be too proud to ask for help but who is obviously struggling. **Zodiac:** Cancer. **Empowerment:** I can meet my own needs.

The word opal is derived from the Sanskrit world *upala*, which means precious stone. There is a Hindu legend that the first opal was created when the mother goddess changed the young virgin goddess of the rainbow into an opal, because the gods Brahma, Shiva and Vishnu were pursuing her.

Only occasionally does her rainbow self peep through the cloudy covering and that is why precious milky opals are so special.

Milk opals were called the milk drops of the mother goddess in a number of cultures. They are a popular gift for a new mother, with a new piece of jewellery being offered for the birth of each subsequent child. For best effect, milky opals, like all opals, should be worn close to the skin, avoiding direct heat and hydrating them occasionally by moistening them with a damp, soft cloth.

Milky opal eases a child into school or daycare; surround a photograph of the child with small milky opals while they are away to send loving and secure vibes to the child. Bury a tiny milky opal beneath a willow, the mother tree or any fruit tree at full moon to conceive a child.

Type: Silicate (zeolite group).

Colours: White, yellow or clear, colourless, often silky.

Availability: Quite rare, but obtainable from some specialist crystals stores and online.

Physical benefits: Believed to improve blood-related disorders, circulation, heart, adrenal glands, liver, spleen and the nervous system; thought to be excellent for a weight-loss programme and for increasing mobility.

Emotional healing: Brings about a sense of inner calmness that reflects on the outside with a relaxed attitude; hold a palm-sized polished scolecite beforehand if you dread social occasions or have panic attacks in crowded places.

Chakra: Brow and Crown.

Scolecite

Candle colour: White or silver. **Fragrances:** Eucalyptus, galbanum, lemon, lemongrass, myrrh. **Practical uses:** Natural scolecite is an integrating crystal for all team work and joint efforts at home or work; also for increased communication between different generations, both at home and work. Keep the home scolecite on display with family photographs. **Workplace:** If you are a manager, team leader or care professionally for a number of people and feel constantly pulled in different directions, scolecite will help you to resist trying to please everyone and delegate or offload without feeling guilty. **Magical significance:** Hold a scolecite polished wand or palm stone before sleep for vivid lucid dreaming, awareness during sleep of being in the dream and past-life dream recall; good for encountering a dream lover and calling him or her into your life. **Divinatory meaning:** A period of profound peace and happiness, in the form of a deep, harmonious love relationship or close friendship whether existing and improving or just around the corner. **Zodiac:** Capricorn. **Empowerment:** Each new experience, good or bad, holds the potential for growth.

Scolecite is a peaceful, tranquil crystal that instils its energies in all those that hold it. It also helps you to sleep deeply and peacefully – excellent for adult insomniacs as well as for children who have sleeping difficulties.

Make a sleep grid by placing a tumblestone scolecite in each of the four corners of the bedroom and a natural one in the centre beneath the bed. Scolecite offers safe communication with any spirit beings you encounter in dreams, astral travel or meditation, or with family presences

who return to the home from the afterlife with messages.

An excellent crystal to have in the centre of a healing table, especially if you are working with a group of healers, to combine your energies for absent healing.

Use a healing book, from which you read the names of people, animals and places in need of positive energies. A light-bringer to help people to move beyond their self-imposed restrictions and fears.

Type: Organic, salt or freshwater.

Colours: White, grey, pale cream, pink/peach and blue, black, iridescent.

Availability: Common.

Physical benefits: Viewed as being good for skin, nausea and biliousness, fluid imbalances, bloating, hormones and PMS, fertility, female reproductive problems and sexuality, childbirth, digestion, soft organs and tissues, growths and tumours of all kinds.

Emotional healing: Pearls form a connection between our body rhythms and those of the natural cycles of the moon and the seasons, and so are very helpful for work-related burnout or stress overload and to prevent it recurring.

Chakra: Sacral and Heart.

Pearl

Candle colour: Silver. **Fragrances:** Almond, apple blossom, magnolia, mimosa, peach. **Practical uses:** Though the traditional pearl necklace family heirloom is no longer common, collect a pearl a year for each child (your own or a niece or nephew). When the child is 18, the pearls can be made into a necklace for a young person or their future life partner, to hand on to the next generation. **Workplace:** Pearls are a symbol of prosperity grown from small beginnings and are good-luck charms for a sole trader or someone with big plans starting small. Start with a single pearl and each time you have a small success, add to your pearl collection, to build up the energies. **Magical significance:** Unthreading a string of broken pearls will loosen the psychological hold of a destructive or over-dominant person in your life; have the pearls restrung in a new way, perhaps adding new ones to strengthen your own identity. **Divinatory meaning:** You may have considered a lot of unpromising offers recently but keep looking, for the right opportunity is close. **Zodiac:** Cancer. **Empowerment:** Good fortune surrounds me.

Pearls are formed when an oyster swallows a foreign body such as grain of sand, and coats the irritant with calcium carbonate called nacre, which it secretes, deposited in concentric layers that build up the pearl. Pearls may be natural (saltwater or freshwater) or cultured, the latter grown by introducing the irritant into the oyster.

Healing and metaphysical energies are virtually the same for both forms. Natural pearls are rare and very precious. Pearls from the sea are valued more highly than freshwater ones. Some environmentalists prefer to avoid pearls since they come from a living source.

The Ancient Greeks claimed pearls brought happiness in marriage; borrow some from a happily married friend for your wedding to transfer it. Pearls represent integrity, especially if white or cream. In the home they encourage tradition, particularly if in the form of a necklace, an unbroken circle. Keep with family photographs or records such as birth certificates.

Lodalite

Type: Quartz family (silicate) with mineral inclusions.

Colours: Clear with mixed-colour inclusions; often brownish inside like tendrils under a clear quartz dome.

Availability: Relatively rare (only one source), but obtainable from some specialist crystal stores or online and well worth finding.

Physical benefits: Claimed to benefit all healing by balancing energies and calling down spiritual healing for any condition; be good for those near the end of their lives.

Emotional healing: Facilitates emotional healing by releasing old fears due to early memories or past-life trauma, and replacing them with loving, nurturing energies.

Chakra: Crown.

Candle colour: White or silver. **Fragrances:** Cherry blossom, copal, eucalyptus, myrrh, sandalwood. **Practical uses:** Keep lodalite in your special crystal place or relaxing area to let its otherworldly energies counteract television or computers and draw people together. **Workplace:** For inspiration, gaze into a dream stone. **Magical significance:** Look within lodalite and see forests, castles and landscapes. **Divinatory meaning:** Keep faith with a person or situation others tell you is no good. **Zodiac:** All signs, especially Scorpio, Aquarius. **Empowerment:** Maybe magic is true if I trust in it.

Each lodalite (also referred to as dream crystal) is unique so carefully choose to resonates with your energies. If buying online, ask to see clear photos from several angles. Used by shamans, it induces meditation visions and healing dreams, and can be used to connect with past-life issues, bringing gentle assistance from spirit guides; if you lost a relative recently, holding lodalite before sleep may bring a dream of them. Keep one in the garden to attract wildlife and nature spirits.

Satin Spar

Type: Gypsum, the fibrous version; satin spar in its polished form sometimes mistaken for its very close sister selenite, another form of gypsum.

Colours: White and always glowing translucent/opalescent with bands of moving white light that resemble satin; also less commonly brown, orange, pink, yellow, green.

Availability: Common.

Physical benefits: Considered to help regularize women's hormones and menstrual cycles, to ease migraines and visual disturbances caused by PMS; may help scar tissue, speedy recovery after operations, especially gynaecological ones and Caesareans, bones, particularly osteoporosis, skin health.

Emotional healing: A dual-purpose crystal to calm when life gets too stressed and hectic, and energize when you are feeling lethargic or uninspired; soothing for hyperactive adults and children.

Chakra: Sacral.

Candle colour: Silver. **Fragrances:** Jasmine, lemon, mimosa, myrrh, poppy. **Practical uses:** A good-luck crystal particularly for love, money, travel and fertility; recharge by leaving it in full moonlight. **Workplace:** A welcome antidote to a harsh open-plan office. **Magical significance:** Take satin spar into full or nearly full moonlight; do nothing, say nothing, but absorb the lunar energies and let peace flow through you. **Divinatory meaning:** Look for the hidden messages in what people say and signs around you to guide you to the truth you need. **Zodiac:** Cancer. **Empowerment:** There is time to spare if I do not squander it on worry.

In Ancient Greece satin spar was believed to have been part of the moon goddess's robe, discarded after she danced at full moon. In wand form, programme other crystals with it for specific healing purposes by moving clockwise over them, then anti-clockwise after use to clear and again clockwise to reprogramme. It will also cleanse and empower any spiritual artefacts. For gentle healing set satin spar on all seven chakra energy centres.

Amblygonite

Type: Phosphate includes other minerals such as lithium, aluminium and fluoride, often twinned.

Colours: White, creamy, clear, pastel green, lilac, pink, yellow.

Availability: Found in specialist mineral stores and online.

Physical benefits: Thought to assist with weakened immune system, stress-related or psychosomatic illness, reaction to pollution, auto-immune conditions and illnesses connected with addictions..

Emotional healing: As jewellery or polished stone, amblygonite soothes bad reactions to stress or noise; not good with children or animals, nor with everyone for long periods.

Chakra: Heart.

Candle colour: White or natural beeswax. **Fragrances:** Apple blossom, lily of the valley, magnolia, mimosa, vanilla. **Practical uses:** Helps you speak and act calmly but firmly in confrontational situations. **Workplace:** A calming, focusing stone for deadline pressure; also for students at exam time. **Magical significance:** Especially in clearer form, amblygonite enhances predictive powers; use or wear for any form of gambling. **Divinatory meaning:** Draw up a plan of action to deal decisively with a regular irritation in your life without overreacting. **Zodiac:** Taurus. **Empowerment:** I remain calm and efficient under stress.

Transparent amblygonite jewellery is an affordable love token though it is delicate and must be handled carefully. It is ideal for new love late in life, rekindling love after a difficult period or showing appreciation to a relative who has been ill or unhappy. A gentle energizer for when you are exhausted but unable to rest. Metaphysically amblygonite brings clarity of spiritual vision. Wear or carry it when you have to make a speech. Not suitable for making elixirs by a direct method.

Azezulite

Type: An unusual type of milky quartz, waxy with inclusions of microscopic bubbles of water.

Colours: White or colourless.

Availability: Relatively rare but similar stones are found from other sources.

Physical benefits: Said to promote whole-body healing, especially MS, Parkinson's or motor neurone disease; cell disorders and tumours; ease any physical blockages, tissue inflammation.

Emotional healing: Clears away deep emotional blockage and trauma; use with care, with therapeutic or emotional support. Can leave people feeling disorientated.

Chakra: Crown.

Candle colour: White. **Fragrances:** Chamomile, orange, rosemary, thyme. **Practical uses:** If you feel a very small cog, this enables you to make a difference, at home or in the wide world. **Workplace:** The person with everything against them from childhood has with this stone potential to be great. **Magical significance:** Offers contact with angels; can lead to trance and meditative states, so ground yourself afterwards and do not drive or operate machinery for an hour or so. **Divinatory meaning:** Even if odds are stacked against you, speak out and you will be heard. **Zodiac:** Leo. **Empowerment:** I accept there may be alternative realities.

Azezulite (also known as Azeztulite) is believed to have a high vibrational levels and so positively affect almost every illness, sorrow or imbalance, by bringing all chakra energy centres into harmony and awakening self-healing.

The healers' stone with the ability to project energies via higher spiritual sources to people and places over great distances, it can enable you to experience the energies of archangels and evolved teacher spirit guides from ancient civilisations. It is too powerful for animals or children.

Magnesite

Type: Magnesium carbonate resembles chewing gum or a cauliflower floret.

Colours: Usually white, also marbled with grey, brown or tan.

Availability: Common.

Physical benefits: Alleged to be good for the gall bladder, stomach acidity, cholesterol, slowing down blood clotting, migraines, headaches, body odour, regulating extremes of body temperature, cramps and spasms, strong bones and teeth (as bracelet or necklace).

Emotional healing: Reduces intolerance of others, chronic irritability and dislike of children and animals.

Chakra: Brow and Crown.

Candle colour: White. **Fragrances:** Cherry blossom, lemon balm, lemon verbena, neroli, vanilla. **Practical uses:** A very calming crystals; keep a small dish of white and /or dyed turquoise magnesite near food preparation and on the dining table. **Workplace:** To create a private oasis of calm if you multi-task or face conflicting demands. **Magical significance:** Hold white magnesite against your brow, close your eyes and relax into a meditative state. **Divinatory meaning:** Slow down, step back and what now seems insoluble will be manageable. **Zodiac:** Libra. **Empowerment:** All shall be well.

Magnesite has been used for centuries as currency by Native North Americans. An excellent crystal for exhausted mothers if they have sleepless nights, it is also used in jewellery, dyed turquoise, as it has a similar texture to turquoise. Since magnesite opens Brow and Crown chakras, it is possible by closing your hands around four or five magnesites and focusing on a white candle flame to perceive higher realms. It is easily scratched so is best kept separate from other crystals.

Banded Onyx

Type: Quartz, chalcedony, a variety of agate, the white banded kind tends not to be heat-treated.

Colours: White with streaks of black, grey or cream; also varieties of orange, brown or green; white banded onyx is often found as broad bands with black onyx.

Availability: Common.

Physical benefits: Thought to help cells, particularly white blood cells, bone marrow, Hodgkinson's disease, lymph glands, thrush, vaginal infections, breasts, teeth, jaw, bone disorders, pregnancy, after a gynaecological or breast operation.

Emotional healing: Restores faith in people.

Chakra: Heart and Crown.

Candle colour: White. **Fragrances:** Apple blossom, lily, lily of the valley, lotus, mimosa. **Practical uses:** For mending lovers' quarrels; exchange matching small white banded onyx ornaments on your wedding or betrothal day. **Workplace:** Put flowers in white onyx vases on window ledges for altruistic vibes. **Magical significance:** Use a white onyx mortar and pestle for mixing herbs to empower them; before use, put your hands round it and ask that it be filled with light. **Divinatory meaning:** Check with someone reliable what you have heard about your future. **Zodiac:** Libra. **Empowerment:** I seek highest motives in my words and actions.

Banded onyx has long been used for ornamental purposes, especially cameos. Now there is a huge array of banded onyx, some dyed or heat-enhanced, some natural, but all equally powerful in its protective energies. White banded bowls enhance and cleanse crystals kept in them, while white or pale banded candle holders increase the luck-attracting and protective powers of the lighted flame. Drink your crystal elixirs from a white onyx cup to increase their potency.

Type: Cryptocrystalline quartz.

Colours: Milky creamy white.

Availability: Relatively common.

Physical benefits: Thought to be good for breast problems; may assist flow of maternal milk, soothe a crying, colicky or teething baby; headaches, dairy-product allergies, healing wounds and open sores; health of milk teeth, healthy growth of second and wisdom teeth and the protection of teeth in pregnancy.

Emotional healing: Insomnia, especially in pregnant women, babies and children, nightmares and sleep disturbances; fears of dentists, childbirth and surgical procedures.

Chakra: Heart.

White Chalcedony

Candle colour: Silver or white. **Fragrances:** Almond blossom, apple blossom, lily, lily of the valley, lotus. **Practical uses:** Because of its associations with the moon and water, white chalcedony was traditionally carried by sailors to prevent drowning and shipwreck; a good stone therefore as jewellery or in a swimming bag for teaching children to swim with confidence or for adults to overcome a fear of water. **Workplace:** The stone of shift workers, especially those who work at night, to help them adjust to different sleep and waking patterns both at work and during leisure time. **Magical significance:** White chalcedony has from Roman times been considered protective against the evil eye and all forms of dark magic or curses. Wear or carry one over which you have drawn an eye in incense-stick smoke if you are suffering from malice or negative psychic experiences. **Divinatory meaning:** Allow yourself to relax and trust the cosmos, even though it is the last thing you feel like doing, as what you need will come to you quite naturally. **Zodiac:** Cancer. **Empowerment:** I will accept as well as show kindness.

The first white chalcedony was, it is said, formed from the spilled drops of the Virgin Mary's breast milk as she fed baby Jesus. The stones were worn by nuns who had taken the vow of chastity.

White chalcedony transforms sleep into a creative time whereby you can dream of solutions to questions or problems: write your question on a piece of white paper and wrap it round a white chalcedony tumblestone; place this under your pillow or near your bed, reciting the question softly as you drift into sleep – the answer will come in the dream or as you wake. Wear white chalcedony jewellery empowered by leaving it in full moonlight once a month as fertility symbol if you are undergoing medical tests or intervention.

Hold chalcedony before you say you "can manage" or refuse help you do need because you believe you should cope and it is weakness to rely on others.

Type: Organic, branching calcareous skeletons of sea creatures.

Colours: White, also found in red, orange, pink, blue and black.

Availability: Relatively common.

Physical benefits: Said to ease teething in infants, all children's illnesses, epilepsy, mobility; protect against falls in children and older people, female reproductive organs, scanty or absent menstruation, recovery from orthopaedic and microsurgery and for bone and cell regrowth, especially in older people; improve bone marrow, skin health, dry or inflamed skin, rashes, burns and scalds, acne, swollen scar tissue, digestion, stomach acidity, seasickness, arthritis in women; promote fertility,

Emotional healing: Overcomes intense fear of water and swimming in children and adults, and of travelling by sea; also for vertigo, particularly fears of falling from a great height.

Chakra: Sacral.

White Coral

Candle colour: White. **Fragrances:** Lavender, lemon, lily, lily of the valley, mimosa. **Practical uses:** White coral jewellery makes a wonderful gift for a new mother; traditionally a coral and silver teething ring or other coral and silver mementoes were given to the new child at the christening or naming ceremony since coral is so protective of the young and vulnerable. **Workplace:** Coral jewellery brings success and protection to all in beauty, hairdressing, chiropody, chiropractors, physiotherapists, sports-injury therapists; also sailors, fishermen, divers, snorkeling instructors and those concerned in marine conservation or research. **Magical significance:** White coral brings connections with all water essences and spirits, especially those of the sea; a rare off-white variety known as angel skin, because of its slight pink or peach tinge, is associated with angels of the waters such as Phul, angel of lakes and still waters, Rahab the angel of the ocean, Trsiel the river angel and Manakiel who protects dolphin, whales, seals and fish. **Divinatory meaning:** What or who has gone will come back when the time is right; do not waste time fretting what for now cannot be changed. **Zodiac:** Pisces. **Empowerment:** I accept loss and welcome gain as a two halves of the coin.

Coral has been valued for thousands of years in cultures from India and Ancient Egypt to Polynesia and Australia, as a gift from the sea mothers, and regarded as lucky, magical and protective, especially of children.

Associated in modern spirituality with Isis, the Ancient Egyptian mother goddess and mistress of magic and hidden mysteries, white coral is linked with female goddess rituals and sacred sex magic (red coral may represent the male).

The polished female white and a male natural red coral branch should be kept in a red bag beneath the bed when lovemaking, whether for a child or to increase passion. A woman should wear white coral to increase radiance and mystique, whether single and dating, seeking a life partner or in a committed relationship.

All coral is most powerful on a Tuesday and this is the day it is traditionally bought or ordered. If coral breaks, its powers are no longer strong and you should throw it back into the sea or any flowing water.

Milky Calcite

Type: Calcium carbonate.

Colours: Milky, cloudy white, softer and creamier than snow.

Availability: Common.

Physical benefits: Claimed to assist breast, tooth/gum problems, nursing mothers, osteoporosis/bone problems; pain; blood pressure, absorption of minerals especially calcium, negative energies; said to be antiseptic and gentle detoxifier.

Emotional healing: A mothering stone, for healing bad mothering experiences in adulthood, and helping new mothers to trust their instincts.

Chakra: Sacral and Heart.

Candle colour: White or natural beeswax. **Fragrances:** Apple blossom, lavender, lily, lily of the valley, neroli. **Practical uses:** Absorbs bad vibes from quarrels or criticism; wash or smudge regularly. **Workplace:** Place near noisy machinery to reduce stress. **Magical significance:** To soothe noisy neighbours, place near a wall or fence. Hold each piece and say, "I bind you from disturbance and disruption with peace and blessings". **Divinatory meaning:** Make peace with an old adversary but be vigilant. **Zodiac:** Cancer. **Empowerment:** I send healing to those in my life who are angry.

In London's British Museum is an ornamental calcite seal from Mesopotamia, 3200–3000 BC.

Milky white calcite was used widely in the ancient world – carved, as ritual bowls, and to keep food and drink pure. It is useful for past-life healing: sit by white candlelight or outdoors on a warm misty morning and let your mind drift. You may see images of why you have certain weaknesses; you can easily let them go. Even if you do not believe in past lives, this is a good healing exercise.

Optical Calcite

Type: Calcium carbonate, displays an optical illusion called double refraction:.

Colours: Pale and clear, sometimes with rainbows, usually colourless but can be pale yellow or pink, lavender or green.

Availability: Common.

Physical benefits: Believed to be good for eyesight, migraines, double the effect of other healing crystals or remedies. Said to energize the body and maintain good health, worth trying if nothing is working. Set above the head and lie down to clear blockages and activate self-healing.

Emotional healing: A stone of forgiveness, primarily self-forgiveness, letting go of old pain.

Chakra: Crown.

Candle colour: White. **Fragrances:** Frankincense, lily, lotus, orchid, violet. **Practical uses:** Cuts through jargon, hidden meanings and deception; good for contracts, accountancy, solicitors or detective work. **Workplace:** Excellent for multi-tasking, conflicting priorities or shift work. **Magical significance:** Can be used to double the power and speed of any magic spell, healing ritual or empowerment. **Divinatory meaning:** Assess what is realistic given your present circumstances and aim for that rather than waiting for the ideal. **Zodiac:** Leo. **Empowerment:** I am a very lucky person.

Optical calcite or Iceland spar is a naturally double-refractive crystal: if you look at a straight line through it, you see two wavy lines. If you look at a page of writing, the image you see will be doubled. This double image was believed to be a trick of the Icelandic fairy folk. Opens doors of opportunity and attracts good fortune to home and workplace, whereby results will be twice as good as anticipated. Good for prayer, especially for help in difficult situations.

Type: Hydrous sodium calcium borate.

Colours: White or colourless.

Availability: Common.

Physical benefits: Perceived as beneficial for eye problems, visual disturbances, wrinkles, headaches and difficulties with the nervous system, especially nerve endings, memory and concentration.

Emotional healing: Restores imagination, originality and creativity if these gifts were taken from you in childhood by unsympathetic teachers or parents; the best crystal for helping people recover from and resist brainwashing by cults or over-rigid political or religious regimes.

Chakra: Third Eye.

Ulexite

Candle colour: White. **Fragrances:** Benzoin, cedar, chrysanthemum, fennel, peppermint. **Practical uses:** Set ulexite on top of contracts, documents and letters you receive to become aware of any implications you may miss on first reading. **Workplace:** If you are studying or are in a job where your intellect is pushed to the limits, ulexite clarifies complicated concepts and helps to assimilate technical information; good if you have to master unfamiliar skills or a new language fast. **Magical significance:** Because even thin ulexite magnifies anything under it, put ulexite on top of tiny silver charms or symbols, for example a silver key for buying or selling a house, to attract what you want into your life as you name it aloud. **Divinatory meaning:** Something that has been eluding you becomes suddenly clear and you will instantly know what to do. **Zodiac:** Gemini. **Empowerment:** My mind is open to receive messages and insights from the divine realm.

Ulexite is also known as TV rock or the television stone. This is because when ulexite is about two or three centimetres (one inch) thick and polished on both sides, the fibres in the crystal act like optical fibres and transmit an image from one side of the crystal to the other.

Try placing ulexite on top of a book or newspaper and the writing will appear on top of the crystal without any distortion. It is also a crystal that increases psychic vision and insight.

Place ulexite on your Third Eye or Brow chakra, above and between the eyes, to stimulate clairvoyance and telepathy; use in meditations that require clear imagery and visualization.

Write down what you recall of a dream when you wake and leave ulexite on the writing, so that the meaning of the dream will become clear when you next read it.

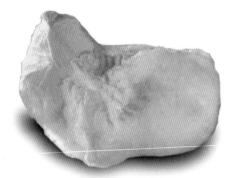

Type: Silicate. a hydrothermal mineral found lining the inside of cavities that protect okenite's delicate crystal fibres which resemble cotton-wool balls.

Colours: White or colourless.

Availability: Obtainable in specialist crystal stores and online.

Physical benefits: Thought to reduce fever, slow the ageing process and help with blood diseases, stomach problems including nervous stomach disorders and upper-body circulation, and to relieve the pain of acute strains or injuries, scalds, burns or inflammation.

Emotional healing: Self-forgiveness; heals the inner child and restores parts of ourselves others have taken from us; brings consolation in grief, loneliness or bewilderment.

Chakra: Crown.

Okenite

Candle colour: White. **Fragrances:** Chamomile, frankincense, lily, lily of the valley, sandalwood. **Practical uses:** In the living area of the home, okenite softens harsh words or unintended hurt to a sensitive child or vulnerable adult, perhaps by an unthinking visitor. **Workplace:** Overcomes disappointments, failure to pass examinations or gain promotion; helps with projects that require both intellect and inspiration. **Magical significance:** Okenite brings intuitive access to the wisdom of the planets and constellations, if conventional astrology is not for you by channelling planetary archangels and angels of the zodiac. **Divinatory meaning:** Listen to your dreams or meditations, the answer is within you to your new step. **Zodiac:** Sagittarius and Virgo. **Empowerment:** I know what is best for myself and my family.

Called the crystal snowball, because it resembles fuzzy mini snowballs, this is an Earth Mother stone that forms the bridge between earthly and cosmic energies. Because okenite is so delicate, buy within its geode outer shell so you can hold it without risk of damage.

Cleanse okenite using the smoke of an incense stick. Purifies and integrates the inner chakra energy system for self-healing: hold your geode in the hand you write with, passing it in spirals from your feet to the top of your head and down again.

An excellent stone if you suffer from interference from relatives who tell you how to live or bring up your family.

Helps overcome the frustration of temporary or more permanent immobility or restrictions caused by a long illness.

Muscovite/ Star Crystal

Type: Mica; when its twin yellow variety from Brazil forms a five-pointed star it is called star crystal.

Colours: White, silver, yellow, green (deep green as fuchsite) and brown, often white tinged with other colours; occasionally red or pink to purple.

Availability: Muscovite is common, star muscovite rare.

Physical benefits: Seen as helpful for pancreas, kidneys, allergies, insomnia, blood sugar levels and diabetes.

Emotional healing: Lessens self-doubt and insecurities. Promotes connections with a significant other.

Chakra: Heart.

Candle colour: White. **Fragrances**: Carnation, copal, galbanum, orange. **Practical uses**: Reveals lies or exaggeration; set near computers for Internet dating or in a pouch when shopping for goods or services. **Workplace**: Facilitates finding contacts, sources or workers. **Magical significance**: Use to enhance scrying visions (looking for images in a reflective surface such as crystal or water), held in the hand you do not write with. **Divinatory meaning**: You may be experiencing strong intuitive thoughts and feelings about a person. Trust these. **Zodiac**: Leo. **Empowerment**: I make bridges between people and cultures.

Muscovite, originally used for window glass, especially in sacred buildings, increases fast thinking and problem-solving skills; use as a good-luck charm for exams, interviews and quizzes. Keep muscovite with study material when learning foreign languages or mastering technical material with whose terms you are unfamiliar. Good for studying spirituality and healing, especially traditional wisdom from Native North America, India or China. Purple muscovite allows contact with higher spiritual planes.

White Selenite

Type: Fibre gypsum, hydrous calcium sulphate, glassy with pearl-like lustre, very similar to satin spar (see p.149).

Colours: Colourless or semi-transparent, but glows with luminescence; occasionally peach.

Availability: Common.

Physical benefits: Thought to be useful for blood cell regeneration, vitality, youthfulness, attention deficit disorder/ hyperactivity, fertility, pregnancy, fluid retention, bloating, PMS, menstrual and menopausal problems, spinal fluid, hormones, gallstone pain.

Emotional healing: Brings about inner peace if you live a lot in your head and constantly fear imagined disasters.

Chakra: Crown and Sacral.

Candle colour: White or silver. **Fragrances**: Eucalyptus, gardenia, jasmine, lemon, myrrh. **Practical uses**: Eggs or clusters protect from outside negativity, especially at night. Give children who fear the dark a sphere, explaining how moon rays captured their shine on them while they sleep. **Workplace**: Brings harmonious partnerships; aids recognition of potential profit. **Magical significance**: Wear selenite jewellery as a charm to attract love/fertility or maintain fidelity. Most powerful at and just before full moon. **Divinatory meaning**: A good chance of reconciliation, but you may have to make the first move. **Zodiac**: Cancer. **Empowerment**: I welcome dreams but not illusions.

Selenite, named after the Ancient Greek moon goddess Selene, glows with moonlight, bringing radiance and harmony. It is an angel crystal, linked with healing, fertility-bringing Gabriel. Keep a selenite angel where moonlight shines on her to spread calm, loving energies. It also brings chances of reconciliation: send a small crystal to someone you have been parted from.

Selenite jewellery induces calm through pregnancy and motherhood; also for a new grandmother. Not suitable for prolonged use outdoors.

Anhydrite

Type: Calcium sulphate.

Colours: White, grey or blue, lilac to pinkish, reddish or brownish; also colourless.

Availability: Found in specialist crystal stores and online.

Physical benefits: Viewed as an all-purpose healer that sends healing wherever needed, particularly useful if conventional treatment is not working; seen as easing all forms of incontinence in adults; thought to release energies for a healthier lifestyle.

Emotional healing: For moving on from the past and present, especially if you need to leave your long-term home or homeland after many years.

Chakra: Throat and Heart.

Candle colour: Blue. **Fragrances:** Apple, lavender, lilac, rosewood, vanilla, violet. **Practical uses:** A tracker crystal that draws to you the right people, opportunities and information. Keep it near your computer when surfing the Internet. **Workplace:** Useful if you multi-task or split your time, to keep all the balls in the air. **Magical significance:** Helps you discover how divinatory systems relate to one another; good if you like your New Age learning with structure and facts. **Divinatory meaning:** You may find yourself torn two ways, but in a week or two the right choice will be clear. **Zodiac:** Virgo. **Empowerment:** I can fit in if I cannot change the situation.

Anhydrite is formed by evaporation of water from gypsum; the best crystals come from rocky areas above salt domes that absorb underground water. Its lilac-blue nodular form, angelite, is usually polished. Store anhydrite in dry conditions. Because of its changeability, it is known as the mineral of double life, and can help those who need to keep part of their personality private, for example religious beliefs or a love relationship. Good also for adapting to climate change, whether temporary or permanent.

Cleavelandite

Type: Silicate, plagioclase feldspar.

Colours: Creamy white to white to clear.

Availability: Relatively rare.

Physical benefits: Believed to assist with strokes, seizures, haemorrhaging and sudden brain malfunctions, Parkinson's disease and other tremors of limbs, dyspraxia, epilepsy, helps restore everyday connections after unconsciousness, amnesia.

Emotional healing: Assists academically advanced people to connect with other people and the world; for all who have chosen a solitary religious path or who are alone from choice to avoid total disconnection from life.

Chakra: Crown.

Candle colour: White. **Fragrances:** Bergamot, lemongrass, neroli, thyme, vanilla. **Practical uses:** Bringing together two families on remarriage, particularly with twinned crystals. **Workplace:** To fulfil ambitions, especially those not shared, without losing touch with roots; place by applications for grants or scholarships. **Magical significance:** The best stone for anyone after a near-death encounter or religious experience to return to everyday life yet retain positive insights and changes. **Divinatory meaning:** Others may not share your dream but you may not have to leave them to fulfil it. **Zodiac:** Aquarius. **Empowerment:** I can walk seen and unseen worlds together.

Cleavelandite is a bladed form of albite with long plated crystals that can grow large; as clusters it can form snowflake patterns and act as a matrix for crystals such as tourmaline. Excellent for journeying, spiritual or physical, and for putting far-reaching ideas into practice. In the home it brings contentment, soothing mid-life crises and encouraging change within existing relationships. If you find crystal-gazing difficult, focus on the whiteness of a large opaque white cleavelandite until images superimpose.

Type: Hydrated silicon dioxide.

Colours: All precious opals with a light background are called white and have what is called a play of colours or inner fire of rainbow flashes in certain lights and when moved. Some white-coloured opals do not have opalescence (see milky opal, p.146).

Availability: Common.

Physical benefits: Claimed to be beneficial for balancing left and right hemispheres of the brain; ease eyesight and visual disturbances, lactation in new mothers and infant feeding difficulties; help hormonal levels to return gently to normal after birth; regularize biorhythms; nervous system, nausea, fluid imbalances; aid menstrual difficulties at puberty.

Emotional healing: Alleviates food-related disorders by allowing the causes of poor self- and body-image to surface and be resolved; assists post-natal depression or failure to bond with an infant after a bad birth or difficult home circumstances.

Chakra: Brow and Crown.

White Opal

Candle colour: White. **Fragrances:** Almond, fig, mimosa, neroli, peach. **Practical uses:** White opals are a symbol of lasting love on a very deep level and can be worn or given if an open permanent commitment is not possible between two lovers; traditionally exchanged between twin souls who have existing love responsibilities to fulfil. **Workplace:** White opals are the stone of all who write, dance, play music or sing, or who teach or organize creative and performing arts or art therapies; wear white opal if you one day hope to turn professional or work full-time in these fields, if for now bookings and contracts are intermittent. **Magical significance:** Wear white opal if learning yoga, Tai Chi and other gentle arts of spiritual movement, to merge with automatic subconscious levels of response so actions seem innate and natural rather than artificial and consciously learned. **Divinatory meaning:** Persevere if a new activity or form of learning seems difficult or alien to you as you will experience a breakthrough very soon. **Zodiac:** Cancer. **Empowerment:** I understand and respect my feelings.

Precious opals were considered a wonder. The Roman naturalist and historian Pliny the Elder (AD 23–79) said of opals, "There is in them a softer fire than in the carbuncle [ruby], there is the brilliant purple of the amethyst; there is the sea-green of the emerald – all shining together in incredible union." The rainbow colours in precious opals are made up of water and microscopic spheres of silica.

As light rays are scattered by spaces between the spheres, they reflect from different levels in the stone.

The different wavelengths of light produce the iridescent colours; some are enhanced while others

cancel each other out. White opals enhance beauty and inner radiance, and should be worn if you are returning to dating and have lost confidence in yourself.

Use white opal if you are trying to come to terms with life and find your true self; helpful to parents, particularly mothers experiencing empty-nest syndrome or women who have never worked outside the home who suddenly need or want to get a job. White opals are often cut into cabochons, semi-circular domed shapes, to show their full play of colours.

Type: Feldspar, sodium aluminium silicate, sometimes with the sodium partly replaced by potassium or calcium.

Colours: Usually white, but can be blue, yellow, orange or brown.

Availability: Relatively common.

Physical benefits: Thought to help with stomach upsets and disorders, heartburn and stomach ulcers, nausea during travel or pregnancy, eye problems, blockages in circulation or narrowing of veins or arteries, muscles and tendons, hormonal and fluid imbalances in both sexes, blood cleanser, menstrual difficulties and irregularities, fertility.

Emotional healing: Excellent for women who suffer from extreme PMS or post-natal depression; calms all mood swings and so also helpful for bi-polar conditions.

Chakra: Sacral and Solar Plexus.

Albite

Candle colour: Silver. **Fragrances:** Eucalyptus, jasmine, lemon, myrrh, poppy. **Practical Uses:** A travel crystal for happy, safe overseas trips or for buying a holiday home abroad; brings a sense of adventure, particularly for older travellers; good also for emigration or working abroad for a long period. **Workplace:** Albite is good for older workers, to counteract ageism in the workplace or find employment, and to remain enthusiastic about working and open to new ideas and technology; assists decisions where you have to follow your instincts and think fast without all the facts; for speculation, stocks and shares dealings and takeover negotiations. **Magical significance:** Associated with moonstones, albite was traditionally carried by women during their menstrual cycle, afterwards washing it under running water to bring fertility next month. Most powerful at full moon, hold albite in moonlight as a wish crystal, then keep it with symbols of the wish till the next full moon or the wish is fulfilled. **Divinatory meaning:** There is the right moment for everything, but at present there are no clear pointers; wait a day or two and you will know when to act or speak. **Zodiac:** Cancer. **Empowerment:** I trust my instincts as to when to wait and when to act.

Albite is a stone of balance, both emotionally and in lifestyle between work, home and leisure; carry or wear albite if one aspect of your life predominates or you feel you are on a constant 24/7 dash.

Albite helps to step back, reassess and flow with life rather than try to be constantly in control; good for those who work 24/7 or find it hard to relax; also for learning to listen to instincts as to

when to speak or remain silent and when to act or to wait. Albite brings back joy in life if things have become routine; also for accepting rather than fearing occasional unpredicted events.

Hold a piece of albite if you have mislaid something precious – close your eyes and its location should come clearly into your mind. Try this also for finding a missing pet, and you may recognize the location and so know where to concentrate your search.

Type: Silicate (calcium borosilicate hydroxide).

Colours: White with grey or black veins in a web-like pattern.

Availability: Common.

Physical benefits: Perceived as helpful for teeth and gums, nails, hair and bones, arthritis, rheumatism, bone and joint pains, dislocated and broken bones, back, spine, calcium absorption, pain relief, osteoporosis, lactation.

Emotional healing: An anti-frustration stone, white howlite calms adults or children who hit barriers due to physical limitations or circumstances, combining patience with persistence and ingenuity; good for those who expect others to put life right.

Chakra: Crown.

White Howlite

Candle colour: White. **Fragrances:** Chamomile, eucalyptus, sandalwood, tea tree, valerian. **Practical uses:** Encourages a desire for learning. Keep carved howliteww objects such as power animals around the home to foster a love of knowledge in children and young people, particularly if classmates are discouraging; good for completing home-work or school assignments. **Workplace:** Keep tumblestones in a pouch so when tensions rise you have immediate access to their calming properties. Place a few in small dishes along a meeting table. People will be drawn to touch them, tones will become softer and opinions expressed less forcibly. **Magical significance:** White howlite attracts blessings to the home, traditionally buried around the boundary edges and set over the front and back doors; keep a howlite angel on the meal table to attract abundance and make mealtimes pleasurable. **Divinatory meaning:** Familiar friends and places will give you a period of welcome stability to restore your energy and confidence in life. **Zodiac:** Gemini. **Empowerment:** I am secure and stable once more.

Howlite is a porous stone and often dyed to mimic other minerals, particularly as blue howlite.

White howlite calms from within and as jewellery is an ongoing stress dissolver and defuses irritability if you have to travel on crowded transport or commute on frequently gridlocked roads. In the home or at work, howlite ensures a gentle and positive energy flow, like a psychic fresh-air diffuser so that if you are visited by anyone who is highly strung or argumentative it will dispel their negative energies and calm them as well as you.

Attach a small piece of howlite to an animal collar or beneath the pet bed to encourage nomadic animals such as cats not to wander off, especially at night; bury howlite in the garden to deter hostile cats or, if you have no pets, to deter other people's cats and moles from digging up your garden. A stone that favours artists and all form of artistry.

Oligoclase

Type: Silicate/plagioclase feldspar, frequently twinned.

Colours: Colourless, white, cream, pale yellow, pink and brownish red, grey and occasionally green.

Availability: Relatively common.

Physical benefits: Said to relieve mumps and childhood diseases, especially in adulthood, shingles, herpes, glandular fever, inner-ear disorders, jaundice, illnesses carried by insects or vermin, hepatitis, auto-immune problems.

Emotional healing: Oligoclase restores trust in yourself after a breakdown or long illness to gradually go out again and return to your old life or start a better one.

Chakra: Solar Plexus and Crown.

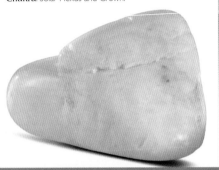

Candle colour: White. **Fragrances:** Apple blossom, chamomile, jasmine, marigold, poppy. **Practical uses:** Encourages people to be less territorial or possessive; good if families tend to disappear to their own rooms or you are trying to merge two families. **Workplace:** Oligoclase brings clarity and order to facts, figures, lists, schedules and agendas if you are tired or find detailed work hard or boring. **Magical significance:** Oligoclase is a channelling stone for spirit guides. **Divinatory meaning:** You may find yourself having to act as integrator or peacemaker at a function. **Zodiac:** Gemini. **Empowerment:** I can bring people together in harmony.

Oligoclase is very similar to and often mistaken for sunstone and moonstone, its close relatives. It has the same shimmer that is caused by light refracting back and forth between different crystal layers.

In fact, particularly in its clear or white form, oligoclase combines the solar and lunar aspects of opalescent moonstone and sparkling sunstone.

Therefore it is an integrating crystal that adjusts the balance in your daily life if you regularly carry a piece with you, combining outer success and inner harmony and logical clear thinking.

Bryozoan

Type: Micro-fossils within stones; fossilized portion of an animal colony.

Colours: Blue-grey, grey, brown, black with various markings.

Availability: Relatively rare as tumblestones or jewellery but these are best for healing.

Physical benefits: Recommended for helping with dehydration or balanced water levels in body, excess water retention.

Emotional healing: Sometimes worn in pendants to heal heartbreak, bryozoan is comforting for loss of parents at an early age.

Chakra: Root.

Candle Colour: Grey. **Fragrances:** Cypress, musk. **Practical uses:** Can be worn to resist emotional pressure. **Workplace:** Good for breaking into an established business profession. **Magical significance:** If you want to banish a bad habit, pass your hands anti-clockwise, a few centimetres above the crystal, saying, "May [name] move from my life with blessings, harming none." Light an incense stick. **Divinatory meaning:** You may be finding it hard to quit a bad habit that is damaging your health; persevere as relief will come soon. **Zodiac:** Capricorn. **Empowerment:** I will not be shaken from my core beliefs and standards.

Bryozoans are tiny organisms that grow permanently attached to stones or seaweed.

They feed on phytoplankton with tiny tentacles in the water and act like a filter to the marine environment. This fossil is a stimulus to creativity, especially for painting or sculpture based in traditional styles or methods and for writing historical fiction. Use as a focus for prayers or empowerments for clean water in parts of the world where there is drought or an unsanitary water supply.

Type: Plagioclase feldspar.

Colours: Grey-green, dark grey, black or grey-white with flashes of blue, red, gold, orange, purple and green.

Availability: Common.

Physical benefits: May help bronchitis, respiratory complaints, lungs, metabolism, colds, digestion, eyes, brain disorders, PMS, menstruation, warts, skin and hair parasites, gout, rheumatism, high blood pressure, pain relief.

Emotional healing: For reducing anti-social, reckless or impulsive behaviour in children, teenagers and adults who are easily led into trouble by others.

Chakra: Brow and Root.

Laboradite

Candle colour: Blue. **Fragrances:** Cedar, copal, dragon's blood, juniper, lemongrass. **Practical uses:** Wear laboradite to stay neutral and unflustered if you are caught in the centre of a family dispute or constant workplace disruption and are asked to take sides or pass judgment on other's actions. **Workplace:** Brings out the best in any person or situation; makes working life more congenial, whatever the circumstances; encourages willingness to show courtesy and full attention to customers; assists part-time and temporary staff to become fully involved in a company. **Magical significance:** Provides a powerful entry-point tool in developing clairvoyant vision; turn a laboradite sphere, egg or polished pebble round fast so it catches the light (like riding a fast carousel so the colours merge and separate into rainbow images). **Divinatory meaning:** You may have to temporarily make the best of a less-than-ideal situation, but soon you will be able to do things your way. **Zodiac:** Scorpio. **Empowerment:** I can be both independent and connected with others.

Labradorite was first discovered by Moravian missionaries to North America in 1770, although older Inuit peoples speak of a legend according to which a brave Inuit warrior struck the stone with his spear and created the Northern Lights.

Another version, one of several, tells that the first laboradite fell from the fire of the ancestors in the Aurora Borealis. Through the crystallization process two phases of layers are produced. When light hits the stone it is refracted on the different layers and produces labradorite's characteristic and iridescent colouring. Wearing laboradite brings the fun and spontaneity back into your life if you are stuck in routine or weighed down by responsibility; it awakens a sense of adventure, sometimes for the first time: do not be surprised if you find yourself on a long-haul flight, backpacking or trekking to Tibet.

A stone of independent thought and action, keep laboradite with papers or near computer files you are checking to avoid making errors or missing incorrect facts that have been inserted in a document.

Cloud Agate

Type: Chalcedony, crypto-crystalline quartz.

Colours: Grey, bluish grey or light grey, and off-white.

Availability: Rare.

Physical benefits: Said to aid recurring headaches or migraines, visual disturbances, dizziness, hearing difficulties, bone marrow, inflammation, fevers, reduce chronic pain.

Emotional healing: A restful crystal to wear as jewellery after burn-out or a period of intense work or pressure; the gentle cloudiness blurs the acuteness of circular thinking, worrying or trying to get back to full power too soon.

Chakra: Brow.

Candle colour: Grey. **Fragrances:** Clary sage, fern, musk. **Practical uses:** The stone of secret love; give one to your love and hide one with their picture wrapped in grey silk as a token of belief that one day you can be together openly. **Workplace:** A low-profile stone; breathe on it if you need to work undisturbed. **Magical significance:** Used to burst clouds by pointing the hand with the agate between thumb and finger directly upwards towards a cloud and picturing a hole appearing. **Divinatory meaning:** Be careful who you confide in. **Zodiac:** Gemini. **Empowerment:** I know when to remain silent.

This is an elusive agate, worn or carried by people who wish to keep work and home lives separate and are more comfortable with a few friends than partying. Agate was once believed to confer invisibility on the wearer. Wear cloud agate if you have many interruptions or curious people round you, if you have a high-profile job, or if you have inconsiderate neighbours or work anywhere with constant music or announcements, to insulate your senses against the constant noise.

Fulgurite

Type: Fulgurite is lightning-fused quartz sand.

Colours: Pale or smoky grey, also shiny black; can be fawn/brown or almost white.

Availability: Relatively rare, but obtainable from some specialist crystal stores and online.

Physical benefits: May improve ear, nose and throat problems, dizzy spells caused by inner-ear imbalance or stress, colon, alimentary tract, stomach lining.

Emotional healing: If a person is not responding to medical treatment or stimuli, fulgurite opens the channels for more conventional therapies.

Chakra: Root and Crown.

Candle colour: Grey. **Fragrances:** Fennel, lavender, sage, sagebrush, sweetgrass. **Practical uses:** Will get stubborn people to change their minds; if there is an obstacle in your way, hold fulgurite and picture a rock split open by lightning. **Workplace:** Keep fulgurite in your workspace to alert you to a person that can help fix a problem. **Magical significance:** Associated with visualization of life forms from other galaxies or dimensions. **Divinatory meaning:** Time for action, either to revive or, if not possible, to get out of a situation going nowhere. **Zodiac:** Aries. **Empowerment:** Any problem can be solved through creative thought.

Fulgurite is one of the most dynamic crystals, since it is instantly formed by intense temperatures whereas other crystals are created over millions of years. Therefore it is an all-or-nothing crystal to give you an instant infusion of whatever you need, whether power, courage, focus, creativity, health, passion or energy. It is considered a natural aphrodisiac. A crystal for inventors, for writers, for abstract artists and for anyone stuck in a career or personal rut who asks, "When will it all happen?"

Type: Citrine and smoky quartz combined in the same crystal.

Colours: Grey and translucent, sometimes with golden sparkles, especially in cut and polished forms.

Availability: Relatively rare but worth obtaining.

Physical benefits: Citrine smoky quartz is believed to heal on all levels, removing pain and deep-seated or chronic problems, at the same time energizing the body and triggering the self-healing system to recover and to resist future similar illness; seen as good where a condition affects several parts of the body or overall health, mobility and well-being; said to be useful if nothing seems to be working or a person is unwilling or unable to have or continue with intrusive conventional treatment.

Emotional healing: One of the best crystals for both relatively fast-acting and lasting improvements in depressive illnesses or conditions where a person has sunk into apathy or given up communicating; relieves fears of dark or enclosed places such as elevators.

Chakra: Root and Solar Plexus.

Citrine Smoky Quartz

Candle colour: Grey. **Fragrances:** Basil, bay, bergamot, lemongrass, mint. **Practical uses:** A crystal in its natural form to display in a home where three or more generations live together or adult children are sharing a house with parents, so no one feels restricted excluded or imposed upon. **Workplace:** Wear smoky citrine if you are involved professionally in speculation, making financial or business decisions with long-ranging effects or are uncertain about which option is best in your own career; combines logical and lateral thinking with wise caution; good for shift and night workers, to help the body clock readjust. **Magical significance:** A very protective crystal for mediumship or investigating ghosts to open the dimensions, while providing light to surround you; hold a citrine smoky quartz, point facing outwards, in the hand you do not write with while ghost hunting; set it on a table between you and a client, so the client can also feel and maybe see their deceased relative. **Divinatory meaning:** Life may seem gloomy but in fact there is light already if you push through uncertainty and clear what stands in the way of resolution. **Zodiac:** Gemini. **Empowerment:** There is always light in the darkness.

Citrine is clear quartz, heated naturally in the earth, and occurs in the same environments as smoky quartz: mostly in intrusive igneous rocks which contain traces of radioactive elements whose radiation causes coloration in both.

Sometimes there may be a citrine phantom (p.89) within the smoky quartz or the smoky quartz can form the inner phantom; one part of the crystal may be much yellower or light-coloured smoky quartz may merge with a dark-yellow-toned citrine. In all these cases, the energies of smoky quartz and citrine are powerfully combined.

Wear or carry citrine smoky quartz when you socialize in an unfamiliar place to open you to new friends and love while at the same time shielding you from predators or those who would deceive you for their own purposes. A gentle crystal if you have been ill or suffered a loss or betrayal, to open you up to new experiences while preventing you making old mistakes.

Type: Carbon, native element.

Colours: Silvery grey, black.

Availability: Common.

Physical benefits: May be helpful for feet, ankles, legs, spine, bowel and large intestine, for any physical blockages in the lower half of the body, constipation.

Emotional healing: Any form of post-traumatic stress, especially if resulting in disability or memory loss; for sudden uprooting of children from a familiar home or homeland.

Chakra: Root.

Graphite

Candle colour: Grey. **Fragrances:** Cedar, clary sage, vetivert. **Practical uses:** A Mother Earth crystal, graphite is a good addition to the home if money is short to get value for money in transactions; also to encourage thriftiness and creative alternatives to expensive outings and designer items. **Workplace:** Touch your soft graphite very carefully when you need to express an idea in writing, fill in an application or send an email if you know you need to talk up your expertise or if tact is vital; good for writer's block in any area. **Magical use:** If you wish to get rid of something harmful or destructive from your life, take a new pencil and write what you wish to lose very faintly on white or grey paper; rub a piece of graphite gently over the writing, then use an eraser to remove the writing. Burn the blank paper. **Divinatory meaning:** Sometimes what is useful is of more value than what is attractive, so make sure you are not being taken in by appearances. **Zodiac:** Capricorn **Empowerment:** I value quality and not cost.

Graphite and diamond both consist of the element carbon, yet are very different. Graphite is soft, shiny grey and is best known in pencils. Diamond, meanwhile, is a colourless sparkling gem, the hardest mineral.

The properties of graphite make the mineral itself increasingly valued metaphysically: as a focus for expressing knowledge and ideas clearly and creatively, and for removing resistance to gently let disappear what is no longer needed or is

destructive in a person's life. Keep graphite in quartz with your healthy-eating plan if you are dieting as a reminder of the beautiful person you are releasing; each time you lose half a kilo write your new weight on paper in pencil and rub the old weight out. Graphite is protective against electrical faults, fires and electrocution at home or work. Lie with a small piece on each knee to remove old sorrow and to balance your whole inner energy system.

Type: Fossil.

Colours: Grey and black.

Availability: Common.

Physical benefits: Seen as promoting long healthy life and helping to remove toxins from the body, place on a point of chronic pain for and it is said to be good for gradual relief; beliebed to help to align the spine and skeleton and so a natural addition to the consulting room of osteopaths and chiropractors, enhance the healing power of other crystals.

Emotional healing: Worn as a pendant or carried in a small bag, brings a sense of perspective and acceptance when everything seems o be going wrong.

Chakra: Crown and Root.

Orthoceras

Candle colour: White or grey. **Fragrances:** Carnation, geranium, patchouli. **Practical uses:** Helps to stay on track and within budget for any longer-term home-renovation projects and self-builds or major property conversions; set one in any new walls to protect the home. **Workplace:** Can be placed by or attached to your computer to balance negative radiation. Promotes pride in one's work and facilitates success in business; good for historians, history teachers and those in archaeology, restoration of old furniture or renovation work. **Magical significance:** Use two almost identical specimens, one each, to increase telepathic connections between you and a loved one when apart. **Divinatory meaning:** Long overdue and deserved advancement in your career path, but you may need to promote your cause more loudly. **Zodiac:** Virgo. **Empowerment:** I can wait a little longer, for my time is coming.

The orthoceras, an ancient mollusc, lived around 400 million years ago. The conical shell of this ancient ancestor of the modern-day squid is preserved in fossil form, usually in a black shale matrix. Presented as polished individual pieces or in sculptural group forms, they are a beautiful tool with which to work in past-life regression either alone in meditation or directing a session for someone else, using the fossil as the link between worlds; good for sensing and balancing earth energies in your home or identifying ley line energies

on a map (carry a small fossil with you in your map bag in the field). The smooth polished surface of individual fossils can be used as a worry stone, both to relieve fears about age and illness in self or loved ones and for finally letting go of an old hurt; good for counteracting ageism in the workplace and also minimizing intergenerational frictions when sharing a home; brings healing to the natural world if you bury one on New Year's morning in your favourite local natural place. Good for counteracting ageism in the workplace.

Type: Lead sulphide.

Colours: Silver-grey, shimmering.

Availability: Common.

Physical benefits: Said to be useful for respiration, nervous system, inflammation, boils, abscesses and ulcers on the skin, circulation, veins, hair, infections, radiation (both to assist necessary treatment and to filter harmful waves from the world), problems of ageing, absorption of minerals, particularly zinc.

Emotional healing: Assists the newly grieving to feel the love of deceased friends and family even though the physical presence is gone; overcomes fears of personal mortality.

Chakra: Root.

Galena/Galenite

Candle colour: Silver. **Fragrances:** Bistort, cypress, galbanum, mimosa, myrrh. **Practical uses:** A symbol of transformation of what is old or redundant, a piece of galena melts limits imposed by self and eases the transition from one stage to another; encourages the newly separated to explore single life rather than rushing straight into a new relationship. **Workplace:** A protector and empowering for those studying or practising the healing arts, medicine, herbalism, alternative health practices, for health and safety officers and all who research cures for disease; opens career doors previously closed. **Magical significance:** A piece of galena acts as a psychic shield if set where air flows all round, absorbing bad vibes, ill-wishing and free-floating negativity and transforming it into warmth, energy and optimism. **Divinatory meaning:** Do not give up on a lost opportunity or blocked resources; the door will open. **Zodiac:** Capricorn. **Empowerment:** I shield myself from unwelcome energies.

Galena was used as early as 3000 BC as a lead-containing ore and is still the most important lead-ore mineral today. Lead is sacred to Saturn, the planet and pre-Christian god of limitations and realism, property, financial stability and good luck in gambling.

Lead curse tablets were thrown by the Romans into sacred waters such as the Roman baths in Bath, southern England, to demand the return of stolen property. Because galena often contains other minerals, especially silver, zinc and cadmium,

and is found with beautiful crystals such as fluorite and marcasite, it has acquired the metaphysical power to reveal hidden treasures. This includes the return of what was lost, stolen or rightfully yours but has been withheld, and the unexpected gift or acquisition of something as valuable in its place; good for anyone who is involved in archaeological digs and trawling with metal detectors.

WARNING: Toxic due to lead content and other minerals. Do not use to make direct elixirs or let children or animals touch it.

Type: Sulphide, soft enough to leave a mark on paper and fingers.

Colours: Steel grey, bluish silver, metallic (looks similar to graphite but lighter and bluer).

Availability: Rare.

Physical benefits: Thought to promote strength and vitality by rebalancing the body in all its functions, circulation, teeth, jaw and face problems, assist if you have mercury fillings, with detoxification, immune system, soft tissues and ligaments.

Emotional healing: Used for retrieving buried memories to explain and release phobias or seemingly illogical fears; recovering or developing your true personality and potential if you have spent your life trying to please others.

Chakra: Brow.

Molybdenite

Candle colour: Silver. **Fragrances:** Galbanum, geranium, magnolia, mimosa, mugwort. **Practical uses:** Keep close when writing letters or emails when you have to disappoint someone or break some bad news about a change in plans. **Workplace:** Keep in the workspace to promote personal confidence and ambition; for a business, creates stability and improves organizational skills to increase profitability and bring expanding contacts. **Magical significance:** To get answers to questions in a dream, a practice beloved by the Ancient Egyptians and Greeks, write your question on paper, rub molybdenite on the paper over the writing, fold the paper and put near your bed, reciting the question softly till you fall asleep. **Divinatory meaning:** Listen to your dreams, especially recurring ones as they are warning you about a person or situation where you are shutting your mind to the truth. **Zodiac:** Aquarius. **Empowerment:** Dreams are for living.

Molybdenite contains one of the rarest elements in the Earth's crust, rhenium, a dense, highly expensive metal that is used mainly in the construction of jet engines. The crystal itself is often found attached to a quartz matrix, which amplifies the energies of the molybdenite.

As the dreamer's stone, it is beneficial with all forms of dream work including lucid dreaming, dream recall, receiving healing in dreams and past-life connection through dreams. Place this crystal near your bed for creative and peaceful sleep and to

overcome any sleep disorders, including sleepwalking.

In waking hours, it can be used in meditation to see ourselves from within and to identify imbalances in our lives or unhelpful influences.

Molybdenite will, if gently held close to the Heart chakra in the centre of the breast or chest, release healing for any physical or emotional problems. You can also visualize a person or animal in distress and send absent healing by rubbing the crystal gently over their written name. It is a soft crystal, so needs to be handled carefully and is not suitable for elixirs.

Molybdenite

Boji Stone

Type: Palladium (very rare). Smooth and round boji stones contain female energies; the slightly heavier male stone has a more angular shape with pointed, uneven, crystalline surfaces.

Colours: Dark grey, black or grey/brown.

Availability: From specialist crystal stores or online.

Physical benefits: Said to draw out pain if one is held over but not touching where the pain is most intense.

Emotional healing: Circle stones first anti-clockwise and then clockwise around the body, then above the hair still in alternating spirals to energize, calm and harmonize. Rainbow boji is good for restoring mental wellbeing.

Chakra: Root and Crown.

Candle colour: Indigo or burgundy. **Fragrances:** Cypress. **Practical use:** Stand in the centre of the room. Move stones towards each other, then apart until you feel an energy force. Rotate both stones, walking through the house. This is equivalent to using Feng Shui. **Workplace:** Increases concentration, enabling you to focus if you have to work from home. **Magical significance:** Place the female stone below your feet and the male above your head to activate spiritual powers. **Divinatory meaning:** Look for a small miracle if things are black. **Zodiac:** Scorpio and Capricorn. **Empowerment:** I am in tune with the heartbeat of the Earth.

Boji stones are found among fossils in an area of a former inland sea. When rain washes the soil away they appear to be on stems and are considered "living" stones. Boji stones need regular handling so that they retain their powers and do not crumble. They also need to be exposed to the light and, if possible, the sun once or twice a week. Boji stones encourage natural healing powers to develop. Not suitable for children or pets.

Trilobite

Type: Fossil.

Colours: Grey, also sometimes black or brown.

Availability: Common.

Physical benefits: Believed to assist with memory, eye problems, headaches and nervous system.

Emotional healing: Helps us to connect with our inner mind, releasing very early childhood memories; used by some rebirth therapists to overcome adult problems considered to be linked to traumatic pre-birth and birth experiences.

Chakra: Crown, Third Eye and Root.

Candle colour: White, black or grey. **Fragrances:** Fern, geranium moss. **Practical uses:** Carry or wear this stone to increase your perseverance in using tough love when a family member or close friend abuses trust. **Workplace:** Helps you to 'stay the course' on a long-term project, especially anything creative that requires sustained effort. **Magical significance:** Use for past-life work. It will provide protection as well as tuning you in to ancient energies to trigger past-life recall. **Divinatory meaning:** A fear of letting go is holding you back. **Zodiac:** Cancer and Pisces. **Empowerment:** I carry the best of the past within me.

Trilobites are known to have existed up to 540 million years ago. As one of the Earth's earliest complex life forms, metaphysically they represent joy and creativity, self-expression, generosity and inspiration, combined with ancient wisdom and traditions. This fossil can be used by all artists and writers to receive inspirational insight and the discipline to bring a creative project to successful fruition. Wearing a trilobite amulet can help to protect you from negative energies and to promote long-lasting relationships.

Type: Iron oxide, harder than iron.

Colours: Metallic grey, silver, black.
Availability: Common.

Physical benefits: Said to help with blood disorders, particularly of red cells, the absorption of iron and other minerals, blood clots, circulation, energy levels, fatigue, backache, travel sickness particularly by air, jet lag; function as a pain remover and reduce excessive bleeding, whether from a wound, during menstruation or in childbirth.

Emotional healing: Relieves fears of seeing blood, obsessions about contagious illnesses; over-sensitivity to bodily functions particularly using toilets not your own; fears of flying and of insects, especially spiders.

Chakra: Root.

Haematite

Candle colour: Silver. **Fragrances:** Allspice, basil, dragon's blood, poppy, thyme. **Practical uses:** Called the lawyer's stone. Carry haematite for the successful outcome of court cases; also for any DIY legal work such as drawing up or contesting a will or representing yourself in a divorce or tax dispute to ensure you are clear, concise and not swayed by pressure. **Workplace:** Wear haematite to boost your courage and confidence to resist bullying in an authoritarian or aggressive work situation; supportive if you are facing unfair accusations or pressure to quit. **Magical significance:** Polished haematite was used for magic mirrors to foresee the future in lands from Ancient Egypt to the pre-Columbian Americas. These mirrors were used both for divination and in magic spells to reflect back hostility to the sender. Gaze within a flat piece of polished haematite, a haematite sphere or egg by candlelight to see your guides. **Divinatory meaning:** Someone pressurizing to change your mind or make major concessions has no real authority or backing; ignore this petty bullying. **Zodiac:** Aries, **Empowerment:** I will not give way to unfair pressure.

All haematite has a rusty red streak that can be seen when it is powdered or when natural haematite is rubbed against a harder stone.

Its name in Ancient Greek means "blood" because it was believed the stone bled if scratched. Indeed, in Neolithic times, bones were interred with powdered haematite to represent the blood of Mother Earth. Haematite, as well as a Mother Earth symbol, represents the warlike planet Mars since it is very common on Mars, called the red planet. As a magnetic stone, haematite will draw success to you. If you are naturally modest and do not normally take credit for your achievements, wearing haematite jewellery will bring you praise and tangible rewards such as a rise in salary or promotion for what was previously overlooked. Matching haematite for Mars set in copper for Venus can be worn by a couple as a sign of commitment.

If you have a pacemaker, it is not advisable to wear or carry haematite.

Anthracite

Type: Carbon.

Colours: Dark grey, similar to jet in appearance but very shiny even in the natural state and silvery in tumbled version.

Availability: Common.

Physical benefits: A grounding crystal, thought to be good for righting chemical imbalances in the body.

Emotional healing: Heals the scars of an emotionally cold childhood or controlling relationship in older life; calms hyperventilation, phobias or crippling social shyness.

Chakra: Root.

Candle colour: Grey. **Fragrances:** Cinnamon, ginger, patchouli. **Practical uses:** Carry in a pocket when involved in physically dangerous activities to prevent accidents. **Workplace:** In a cliquey workplace, keep anthracite in a drawer to be accepted. **Magical significance:** Keep in a red bag near the hearth, so you will have enough, food, fuel and clothes through the year. Replace at midnight on New Year's Eve and bury the old piece. **Divinatory meaning:** Someone unwelcoming to you will display a softening of attitude. **Zodiac:** Scorpio and Capricorn. **Empowerment:** I attract and share abundance.

Keep with savings books when you are building up the deposit for a home, whether owned or rented accommodation. When you move in, transfer it to the place you pay your bills to continue to draw in money; anthracite guards against domestic accidents; good also to stop pets and children from being afraid of loud noises, fireworks and storms; store near a computer to find last-minute holidays and keep a piece near the photograph of an elderly relative or friend you worry about.

Chiastolite

Type: A form of andalusite.

Colours: Grey with black or brown equal-armed cross inclusion.

Availability: Obtainable from specialist crystal stores and online.

Physical benefits: May be beneficial for rheumatism and gout, nerve and muscle weakness and damage, mobility, strokes, paralysis.

Emotional healing: Can encourage slow but significant progress for people locked in destructive behaviour such as always choosing a faithless or abusive partner.

Chakra: Root.

Candle colour: Brown. **Fragrances:** Almond, anise, bay, benzoin, clary sage. **Practical uses:** Wear chiastolite jewellery or carry a stone with a clearly defined cross for international travel or if you work or live in any kind of trouble-spot. **Workplace:** A good crystal to decide whether to carry on or to try a new workplace. **Magical significance:** Protects against all forms of malice: traditionally worn to repel the evil eye and against all paranormal harm. **Divinatory meaning:** A time for choices and action, as doing nothing is not an option. **Zodiac:** Capricorn. **Empowerment:** I trust my judgement to make wise choices.

Chiastolite comes from China and is unique.

Associated in the modern world with Christianity, it is more anciently a symbol of the four cardinal points — north, east, south and west — and the central fusion of their energies. A chiastolite cross in the centre of your home will radiate life force in all directions and attract harmony and health. It is considered a bridge between dimensions, particularly in learning mediumship, practising spirit rescue or investigating a haunting, and it is also protective.

Type: Magnetic space rock, alloyed with nickel and iron.

Colours: Grey, black, brown-black or red-brown on outside, often silver-grey inside.

Availability: Some rare, some relatively common.

Physical benefits: May help with muscle spasms, muscular tension, stomach cramps, digestive system; illness difficult to diagnose or treatment slow to show results, head or brain disorder, injury or pain, eye problems such as squints or cataracts, facial disfigurement.

Emotional healing: Keeps feet firmly on the ground when caught up in heady emotional attachments or sudden temptations later regretted.

Chakra: Root and Solar Plexus.

Meteorite

Candle colour: Silver. **Fragrances:** Frankincense, grapefruit, lime, myrrh, sandalwood. **Practical uses:** Place meteorite around the home near entrances, to protect from fire or attack. Carry meteorite as an amulet against international terrorism, bombs, hijacking or violent crime, especially involving guns or knives. **Workplace:** Meteorite brings insight into others' perspective if they have fixed ideas, at the same time inspiring off-the-clock ideas to change the equation or workplaces practices. **Magical significance:** A stone for those involved in astrology or cryptozoology; helpful for any who have experienced alien encounters in dreams or more directly. **Divinatory meaning:** You may need to leave preconceptions behind when dealing with an unusual situation or person with a totally different life view. **Zodiac:** All signs, especially Aquarius and Scorpio. **Empowerment:** There is a whole universe of experience to be discovered.

Meteorites are classified into several categories, most originating in the asteroid belt between Mars and Jupiter where there are many rock fragments.

One of the most common small spherical meteorites, chondrite, is unchanged since the solar system was formed and unlike any rocks on Earth.

Meteorites have been used since ancient times: the Egyptians had a hieroglyph that translated as heavenly metal, and capped some of their pyramids with them. The Black Stone at Mecca is a meteorite, believed in Islamic tradition to have been sent from Heaven to show Adam and Eve where to build the first temple on Earth.

Meteorites help, whether we believe in extra-terrestrial life or not, to bring visions and messages from the cosmos to assist us to make the world a better place in small personal ways. Good for taking the first steps towards living a more fulfilling way of life, involving lifestyle change or even downsizing to attain a personal or family dream.

Type: Antimony sulphide.

Colours: Metallic silver-grey lustre.

Availability: Obtainable through specialist crystal stores and online.

Physical benefits: Assists with disorders of the stomach, digestion, the oesophagus, and eases muscle spasm or tension; for improving reflexes and building bodily defences against infectious diseases, including new strains.

Emotional healing: By giving us courage, support and protection, stibnite assists us in relationship issues, particularly involving those who seek to control or suffocate our individuality.

Chakra: Brow and Crown.

Stibnite

Candle colour: Grey. **Fragrances:** Honeysuckle, rosemary, thyme. **Practical uses:** Keep this crystal where natural light shines on it, even in winter, to draw in money from different sources and minimize demands on existing resources; a good anti-debt crystal, particularly if creditors are getting nasty. **Workplace:** Hold stibnite when you need to concentrate, to prevent getting sidetracked; useful on a room divider or desk in an open-plan workspace to deter gossips and time-wasters. **Magical significance:** Good for the return of lost, mislaid or stolen property or pets; set it on top of the name of items or photographs of a missing pet and picture the item or pet coming back. **Divinatory meaning:** You suddenly regain the confidence to remove the influence of someone who tries to control you. **Zodiac:** Scorpio and Capricorn. **Empowerment:** I am strong and so I am protected.

Stibnite offers concentrated focus during meditation if there is unavoidable background noise and your time is limited.

Healers should hold a healing pendulum or crystal above a stibnite cluster to direct the crystal or pendulum and your healing powers towards the root causes of physical or emotional problems if these are uncertain. If asking a pendulum yes/no questions where the truth is in question, again hold the pendulum above the stibnite for about a minute and then, with the pendulum still over the crystal, ask the question. Stibnite is a truth crystal. It also protects against mind games and intrusions into your personal space or privacy. One near your computer at home or work deters both Internet hackers and the over curious from trying to read private emails.

WARNING: Stibnite is toxic; wash hands after use, do not use in elixirs or ingest, and keep away from children and pets.

Arsenopyrite

Type: Iron, sulphur and arsenic, sometimes with quartz.

Colours: Metallic, from brassy white to metallic shiny grey.

Availability: Relatively rare but can be obtained from specialist crystal stores and online.

Physical benefits: Reported to help blood clotting and disorders, fungal infections, very energetic for overcoming blockages anywhere in the system, above all throwing all you can at any illness that is not responding to treatment.

Emotional healing: Enables us to overcome fears of illness, disability, ageing and mortality.

Chakra: Crown and Root.

Candle colour: Silver. **Fragrances:** Cypress, lily, vetivert. **Practical uses:** Put a piece near your computer or phone to resist the temptation of an extra-marital affair. **Workplace:** Keep a piece in a safe place in a company where emotions are highly charged. **Magical significance:** Use as a shield near the front door against against people who manipulate you or loved ones. **Divinatory meaning:** The price you have to pay for following your desires may be high, but it is your choice. **Zodiac:** Capricorn and Scorpio. **Empowerment:** I am not afraid to to speak my mind.

Represents beauty with danger, as its clusters or twin forms are beautiful and can produce crosses or stars yet it is a source of poison, a reminder that everything has a price and there is no such thing as perfect love, perfect happiness or a perfect home or job.

We must accept the consequences of decisions and moral dilemmas. This crystal helps to show the truth of what we are doing or planning so we can make balanced choices: good if you are too often cast in the villain role in relationship arguments.

WARNING: Toxic. Not for elixirs.

Silver Obsidian

Type: Natural volcanic glass.

Colours: Dark brown or black with silver-grey iridescent sheen over the surface.

Availability: Available through specialist crystal stores and online.

Physical benefits: May help pain relief, particularly of migraines or after surgery, acute conditions such as appendicitis or ruptures that need emergency intervention.

Emotional healing: A soothing stone for all who have issues with a possessive mother, whether she is still alive or remains in memory.

Chakra: Root, Sacral and Throat.

Candle colour: Silver. **Fragrances:** Bergamot, geranium, iris. **Practical uses:** A stone to have around on social occasions, especially parties in your home. **Workplace:** A silver obsidian sphere is a great ego buster for those who are quick to assign blame when things go wrong. **Magical significance:** One of the best scrying tools when moonlight reflects against the silver sheen to create a strong sense of knowing what you need to know. **Divinatory meaning:** Be sure you are not making a situation worse by the fact you do not like someone involved. **Zodiac:** Cancer and Scorpio. **Empowerment:** I will not waste energy.

A fascinating form of obsidian since it adds the mystery of lunar energies to the fiery obsidian; a perfect foil for anyone with a high-pressure career to minimize irritability at frustrations and so increase focus. Silver obsidian assists those who wish to pursue a path of spiritual development by dissolving conscious blocks to trusting inner wisdom. Silver obsidian assists in communication of information to others in an articulate fashion and to prevent personal likes and dislikes from affecting rational decision-making.

Braunite

Type: Manganese silicate.

Colours: Silver-grey, brownish black, metallic.

Availability: Obtainable from some specialist crystal stores and online.

Physical benefits: May help lungs, breathing difficulties, chest, breasts, heart and pulse, anaemia and blood-cell problems, healing of wounds or bruises; give strength to fight a debilitating condition; aid metabolism, healthy bone formation and healing of fractures; slow skin ageing.

Emotional healing: Brings courage to face an addiction and develop strategies, and perseverance to get past the first temptation.

Chakra: Root and Heart.

Candle colour: Silver. **Fragrances**: Anise, garlic, honey, patchouli, thyme. **Practical uses**: Overcoming obstacles in buying a home or raising finance for business or property; good for wise choices at auctions and seeing potential. **Workplace**: Brings stability in uncertainty; gives a sense of purpose to minor tasks; helps in raising standards. **Magical significance**: Unusually active focus for meditation, potent for life reviews when memories are let go; may bring insights from the past. **Divinatory meaning:** Hard work, the only way to push past an obstacle to improve your finances. **Zodiac:** Capricorn. **Empowerment**: I cannot be swayed from my purpose.

A crystal of strength and perseverance, slow but eventual victory. Keep a small piece with loose money in a lidded pot to symbolically build up financial stability. When the pot is full, put the money in a savings account, leaving a single coin and the braunite to start to refill the pot. If you feel stifled, braunite creates space to breathe; helpful for tough decisions.

Keep it near a chimney breast or in your living room to protect against storms, floods, earthquakes and subsidence. Carry a small piece of braunite in any uncertain situation to keep strong, assertive and calm.

Soapstone

Type: Concentrated form of talc, magnesium silicate; contains impurities of chloride, magnesite, dolomite and serpentine.

Colours: White, cream, green, grey, pink, green and brown.

Availability: Common.

Physical benefits: Said to aid rashes, wounds, skin ulcers, allergies affecting stomach or skin, excess fat and toxins, liver, gall bladder, digestion, hyperventilation and stress-related breathing difficulties; may balance chemical and electrical impulses, and protect against side-effects of radiotherapy.

Emotional healing: An anti-panic stone, soapstone calms those over-sensitive to atmosphere. Hold a tiny soapstone Buddha and breathe slowly till the panic subsides.

Chakra: Root.

Candle colour: Cream. **Fragrances:** Anise, chamomile, lavender, peach. **Practical uses:** A gentle antidote to harsh or inconsiderate behaviour, absorbing noise and hyperactivity. **Workplace**: Good for ideas people to apply schemes in practical form; helps with the reality of cost and time; also to adapt to necessary tedious routines. **Magical significance**: In India and Africa, soapstone is traditionally used for carving of people, animals and deities, empowered through chants and prayers; daily blessings over soapstone statues spread sacred energies. **Divinatory meaning:** Focus on how to achieve at least part of your plans here and now. **Zodiac:** Sagittarius. **Empowerment**: I adapt effortlessly to the needs of the day.

Wear soapstone (also known as steatite) jewellery to counteract radiation and electromagnetic energies at work or in the atmosphere; as earrings may be protective if you use a mobile phone a lot. Soapstone helps people with rigid ideas to adapt to a situation and acknowledge the validity of other lifestyles and beliefs.

Gentle soapstone animals and birds calm anxious or over-active children and act as guardians while they sleep. Buy a pair of soapstone animals or birds if you want a gentle, loving partner, and as many smaller creatures of the same species as you want children.

Type: Chalcedony.

Colours: Cream to silver, bluish grey to black, with silvery translucent swirls.

Availability: Obtainable from a specialist crystal store or via the Internet.

Physical benefits: Believed to be good for helping sleep disturbances and peaceful dreams, for migraines, especially those with visual disturbances, neurological conditions and illnesses such as MS and Parkinson's, also bipolar tendencies, autism and Asperger's syndrome.

Emotional healing: A crystal to overwrite bad memories, to overcome irrational fears of being persecuted or watched, dependency on prescription drugs, painkillers and over-reliance on clairvoyants and mediums for every decision.

Chakra: Sacral.

Silver Leaf Agate

Candle colour: Silver. **Fragrances:** Jasmine, lemon balm, lily, lotus, magnolia. **Practical uses:** Protective for people near water or those who sail, fish or swim; good also for overcoming fears of water and of travelling by boat. **Workplace:** The dual qualities of silver lace agate, grounding and opening oneself to abundance, are ideal for any business ventures when you have to take a chance or do not have all the facts when you have to make a decision. **Magical significance:** A moon crystal, especially powerful during the waxing moon: turn it over three times when the crescent moon appears in the sky and ask for any new projects to succeed, for new beginnings or for new love. **Divinatory meaning:** Beware illusions and following dreams to the exclusion of reality. **Zodiac:** Gemini. **Empowerment:** I accept that life will supply my needs if I open myself to opportunity.

Silver leaf agate is associated with the silver birch tree, a tree that in many cultures signifies new beginnings and that seeds itself.

The crystal therefore also represents new beginnings and a return to ourselves as we were before life diverted us or delayed our youthful enthusiasm and plans.

One of the gentler, dreamier agates; ideal for small children who are afraid of the night or ghosts,

set silver agate in their bedroom where a tiny night light will shine on it. Silver agate by the bedside helps you to recall dreams and to understand what they are saying at key moments in your life.

Good for helping children and teenagers to share attention and their property with siblings, as silver agate creates a sense of abundance in a very spiritual way.

Type: Metal.

Colours: Silver.

Availability: Common.

Physical benefits: Believed to help detoxification, digestion of essential elements, fertility, PMS , menstruation, pregnancy, hormones, migraines, speech and communication, fluid retention, circulation blockages, pineal and pituitary glands, wounds.

Emotional healing: Believed to assist women at every stage and age to value and care for their body; can be worn by men who have been forced into a macho role and all people who were inadequately mothered.

Chakra: Sacral.

Silver

Candle colour: White or silver. **Fragrances:** Eucalyptus, jasmine, lemon, myrrh, poppy. **Practical uses:** Wearing silver jewellery attracts love, fertility and prosperity; silver doubles the powers of any crystal jewellery. However, crystals are most powerful and harmonious if fastened in a silver wire cradle rather than being drilled with a hole for a chain. **Workplace:** Wear silver if your job demands patience, to persevere at your project or task; protects against free-floating negativity and energy-draining if you work with the public, particularly dealing with crises or complaints. **Magical significance:** Lucky charms are traditionally made of silver: a key for a new home, a silver heart for love, a tiny treasure chest for prosperity, a boat or plane for travel overseas. Build up a collection, wearing those charms representing current needs on a bracelet or in a bag. Empower by leaving them on an indoor window ledge all night at full moon. **Divinatory meaning:** Minor financial good luck is heading your way, but be careful the gain does not drain away in helping someone who really could manage. **Zodiac:** Cancer. **Empowerment:** I will trust my intuition and gut feelings.

Silver, the metal sacred to the moon and the pre-Christian moon goddesses, is energized by the power of the waxing and full moon. To pass on lunar energies to crystals, surround your crystals and any silver jewellery on the nights of the crescent and full moons with a circle of lighted silver candles; leave to burn through.

Traditionally silver is turned over three times facing the crescent moon when it first appears in the sky to attract success and abundance throughout the month ahead.

Silver is the crystal of love, especially new and young love or love after betrayal, and a powerful fertility symbol. Prick a moonstone or tiny rose quartz egg with a silver-coloured pin or paper knife on the night of the full moon before making love. Leave the egg and knife open on an indoor window ledge all night. Then wrap them in white silk to incubate till the next full moon.

Silver bullets, according to myth, will kill vampires and werewolves, and in the modern world silver St Christopher protects travellers from all harm.

Angel/Opal Aura

Type: Quartz crystal bonded with platinum and silver.

Colours: Rainbow, iridescent pearly opalescent white.

Availability: Common.

Physical benefits: An all-healer, but thought to be especially helpful for autism, Asperger's syndrome and nervous system.

Emotional healing: Anxiety, panic attacks, phobias and for Reiki healing, reflexology and shiatsu.

Chakra: Crown.

Candle colour: Silver or gold. **Fragrances:** Frankincense, sandalwood. **Practical uses:** Keep with you if you live or work in unlovely places to reveal beauty in the midst of ugliness. **Workplace:** Beneficial for all carers, whether professional or relatives, and all healers. **Magical significance:** The ultimate crystal for connection with angels. Each piece is said to contain its own angel. **Divinatory meaning:** Do not let a cynical person stop you believing in the ultimate fulfilment of your dreams. **Zodiac:** Cancer and Leo. **Empowerment:** I believe in angels.

In pregnancy, angel aura is protective and uplifting, especially if you are having a bad time with morning sickness or suffer from complications. Place opal aura on your womb to connect with the baby and buy the baby a piece to take into labour; supportive for single mothers, both in pregnancy and in the early years of the baby's life; use to channel messages from your angels and to recall and heal past lives, to see future possibilities in the Akashic records that hold all knowledge and potential in all times, and to glimpse visions of heavenly realms.

Bismuth

Type: Element, base metal.

Colours: Silver-white, with iridescent hues.

Availability: Rare in natural form.

Physical benefits: Said to ease fevers, assist finding and benefiting from new treatments for chronic conditions; help ME and muscle degenerative conditions; get patients back on their feet after major operations and accidents.

Emotional healing: Relieves emotional and spiritual isolation; helps people who have been institutionalized to settle back in the community.

Chakra: Root and Crown.

Candle colour: Gold. **Fragrances:** Acacia, copal, sandalwood. **Practical uses:** Provides stability in change situations; should be the last item out of an old home and the first in the new to transfer the luck and to keep everyone calm and organized. **Workplace:** Organizing social events at work; for all who lead people in groups. **Magical significance:** A crystal of transformation and so a focus for transforming life. **Divinatory meaning:** Change does not have to mean chaos. **Zodiac:** Leo and Aquarius. **Empowerment:** Life is exciting once I embrace rather than resist change.

In healing, bismuth simultaneously clears and opens the Root and Crown chakras and so is excellent for relieving exhaustion and a sense of being over-whelmed by responsibility: giving a rush of power from Mother Earth and the cosmos that meet around the heart, so creating a sense of release and sudden joy for life again. If people say "no way, it cannot be done" or "no chance", hold bismuth and silently wish for what you want or must have; ask the person again in 24 hours, when usually a solution or a good alternative will be offered.

Iron Pyrites

Type: Iron sulphide.

Colours: Metallic and silvery.

Availability: Common.

Physical benefits: May be useful for colds, flu and other viral attacks, digestion, healing diseased bones, blood disorders especially red cell, anaemia, lung disorders.

Emotional healing: Very protective against ongoing control, criticism and manipulation by a partner, parent or employer, giving the power to resist without becoming angry or upset and so change the balance of power.

Chakra: Solar Plexus.

Candle colour: Gold or silver. **Fragrances:** Copal, frankincense, ginger. **Practical uses:** At home and work iron pyrites deters the user from making unwise financial decisions. **Workplace:** Iron pyrites inspires leadership qualities and should be kept near if you are a manager or are working towards promotion. **Magical significance:** A large slab-like polished pyrite can be used as an excellent scrying mirror. **Divinatory significance:** A seeming bargain arrives at the time most needed. It could be the answer, but check carefully. **Zodiac:** Aries or Leo. **Empowerment:** I accept only what is positive into my life.

Iron pyrites contains hidden fire and the ability to generate wealth by one's own efforts. Iron pyrites has been given the name fool's gold, alluding to the fact that it has been mistaken for the more valuable material. However, real gold can sometimes be found adjacent to pyrite, so maybe the foolish person is one that does not follow the signs and omens life provides. Carry or wear pyrites as a protective amulet when you are away from home.

WARNING: Do not use in elixirs or ingest.

Silver Aura

Type: Actinolite, amphibole silicate, talc, hydrated magnesium silicate; actinolite is often found in talc deposits.

Colours: Silver.

Availability: Rare but growing popular in the esoteric world.

Physical benefits: May aid processing of nutrients and waste, kidneys, liver, intestines, bowels, rashes due to allergies, skin complaints especially eczema, acne and rosacea, digestion, mercury and lead poisoning, toxins, reactions to additives, parasites, fungus and skin growths.

Emotional healing: Increases self-worth and achievement if you have been denigrated all your life or put yourself down; helps those who cannot express emotion to be more open.

Chakra: Sacral and Heart.

Candle colour: Silver. **Fragrances:** Almond blossom, ap cranberry, mango, rosemary. **Practical uses:** If searching lasting love, to avoid falling in love with love and see a real person, not create impossible ideals and miss the pleasures flesh-and-blood partner with faults and strengths. **Workpl** Brings out the best in people, professionally and personally good for apprentices, disaffected teeagers or ex-prisoners. **Magical significance:** Expands the bounds of possibility helps those with blockages to increase psychic awareness. **Divinatory meaning:** Believe in small miracles and you be agreeably surprised. **Zodiac:** Taurus. **Empowerment** know everything will turn out for the best.

A stone of small miracles, worth searching out to restore faith in people and good fortune, perhaps because silver aura (also called actinolite in talc) harmonizes our own energies to flow with rather than struggle though life. A welcome addition to any healing room or situation, it opens energy fields to accept healing and unblocks frozen emotions; especially helpful for those with a poor self- or body-image, or who have a persecution complex not to see life in terms of victims and villains. Kept in the home, silver aura actinolite creates a sense o contentment and of being blessed.

Type: Element, metal, the most precious and rarest metal in the world.

Colours: Silver-grey to white-grey, white when highly polished.

Availability: More common as jewellery, rare as nuggets or flakes.

Physical benefits: Reported to help with testes, ovaries, endocrine system, DNA, all cell disorders, for twin or multiple births, lungs, for cleansing the body of toxins and impurities; to act as an energizer during invasive or prolonged treatments; to be helpful for all rare illnesses or conditions; amplifies absent healing and healing the environment.

Emotional healing: For relieving unusual but nevertheless debilitating phobias; for those who are resistant to counselling or talking therapies and hear only what they want.

Chakra: Crown.

Platinum

Candle colour: Silver. **Fragrances:** Cedar, copal, pine, mint, sandalwood. **Practical uses:** Because platinum in nature takes on the impression of a nearby crystal or rock matrix, wearing platinum acts as an antidote if you are easily persuaded to part with your heart or your money. **Workplace:** Wear platinum if you are studying for an unusual career where openings are few or you are competing for a job in any field where there is fierce competition. **Magical significance:** Platinum from any source is protective if you study UFOs or have had out-of-body or vivid dreams about alien abductions; guards also against paranormal sexual attack in dreams or half-sleep, traditionally called *incubi* attack. **Divinatory meaning:** Time to make a good impression on someone who can influence your career or open up new areas of opportunity; it will be easier than you think. **Zodiac:** Aquarius. **Empowerment:** I am open to new ideas and ways of thinking.

Platinum in nature always contains iron and a little copper, and may be found with other minerals such as gold.

The modern world uses platinum in surgery and laboratory instruments, and most recently as a pharmaceutical breakthrough in the treatment of certain kinds of cancer.

Platinum is a metal of truth, is long-lasting and, unlike silver, does not tarnish; a symbol of incorruptible love, often chosen by twin souls or lovers who have had to fight hard or wait a long time to be together.

A thin platinum ring or chain should be worn by dowsers, particularly those looking for archaeological treasures or underground water, to strengthen their natural intuition to guide the rods or pendulum more accurately.

Platinum also returns any ill will, curses or threats, however made, to the sender. Wear platinum if stress levels are consistently high, to deflect the negative aspects of the tension but be energized by the buzz of challenge.

Silver Aventurine

Type: Microcrystalline quartz.

Colours: Pale grey with silvery sparkles.

Availability: Relatively common, but less than other aventurine colours.

Physical benefits: May ease skin complaints, especially psoriasis and rosacea, hormonal imbalances, vertigo, glandular fever, squints and degenerative eye conditions.

Emotional healing: Healing for anyone at any stage. of life who has suffered sexual abuse or rape, to love and respect their own bodies again.

Chakra: Sacral and Brow.

Candle colour: Silver. **Fragrances:** Clary sage, poppy. **Practical uses:** Good to keep by computers when children are surfing the net as protection against online hazards. **Workplace:** For clairvoyants, to run a viable business while preserving their integrity. **Magical significance:** The most magical of the aventurines, especially in moonlight; hold under the crescent moon and turn over three times, but do not speak your secret wish; keep it wrapped in a silver cloth until the wish comes true. **Divinatory meaning:** Do not be tempted to share your secrets. **Zodiac:** Cancer. **Empowerment:** I believe dreams can come true.

Silver aventurine is the crystal of secret love and of lovers kept apart by circumstances, distance or existing relationships, who believe they are meant to be together: exchange matching silver aventurines and keep them hidden as a reminder that love can find a way. Silver aventurine jewellery is a lovely gift for a girl when she begins menstruating as a welcome to womanhood from her mother or grandmother; also a gift for the woman who has passed through the menopause as her wise woman symbol.

Marcasite

Type: Iron sulphide, called cockscomb marcasite when a twin marcasite crystal appears like a rooster's-head crest.

Colours: Metallic silver-grey to gold, sparkling.

Availability: Common, mostly as jewellery, relatively rare as tumblestone.

Physical benefits: Thought to calm overactive male hormones; assist memory function, spleen, safe childbirth.

Emotional healing: Increases feelings of self-worth without needing to prove it; overcomes a martyrdom complex; soothes those who are terrified of poverty even though they have enough money.

Chakra: Root.

Candle colour: Silver or gold. **Fragrances:** Anise, sweet pea, thyme. **Practical uses:** Carry in hand luggage to avoid jet lag and help you relax on flights. **Workplace:** Marcasite with air circulating round it gathers scattered thoughts to bring order to chaos. **Magical significance:** Endows the ability to become aware of dreaming, called lucid dreaming. This technique enables us to use sleep creatively to rehearse successes we can then achieve in our waking life. **Divinatory meaning:** You may be worried about your finances, but you will find an additional source of income. **Zodiac:** Aries. **Empowerment:** I am not ruled by the emotions of others.

Sometimes confused with pyrite, which has the same chemical composition but with differing crystal formation, marcasite is more fragile, crumbly and lighter in colour. It is sometimes called white pyrite. Marcasite was highly prized by the Incas, who wore it in jewellery and buried it as grave goods. They also created polished marcasite mirror-like plates, probably for sun worship and to tell the future. Indeed, in any form marcasite awakens natural psychic powers, especially clairvoyance and predictions.

Type: Combination of chlorite, serpentine, muscovite, pyroxene, hercynite, magnetite and white feldspar.

Colours: Black with flecks of white; resembles snowflake obsidian except the white is not in snowflake patterns in blizzard stone.

Availability: Relatively rare.

Physical benefits: Thought to help with menopausal symptoms, hot flushes, fevers, infections and swelling of cells, immune problems, bruises, sprains, epilepsy, chemical and electrical imbalances, migraines and visual disturbances, pain relief, bones; be good for animal healing especially larger animals; be protective against harmful radiation and the side-effects of radiotherapy.

Emotional healing: Helps people who are chronically antisocial to come out of their shell; good for anger and violence management.

Chakra: Root and Crown.

Blizzard Stone

Candle colour: White. **Fragrances**: Cherry blossom, lily, lily of the valley, mimosa, orchid, white rose.
Practical uses: Wear or carry blizzard stone if you daily deal with malicious or negative people to avoid them draining your energy and enthusiasm; keep in the home to unite family members who are very differently temperamentally and in their priorities. **Workplace**: Keep blizzard stones at the corners of your computer or near your work telephone if you use them frequently; wear if you are involved with radiation, x-rays, microwaves or making or servicing electronic and high technological equipment. **Magical significance**: As a magnetic crystal, keep blizzard stone near a photograph of a place you would like to live or visit on holiday, the kind of house, boat or car you would like to own or near the name of someone you wish to attract more closely into your life; light a candle to shine on crystal and picture on the night of the full moon; leave it to burn through. **Divinatory meaning**: You can obtain what you want but beware of being diverted or influenced in the wrong direction. **Zodiac**: Capricorn.
Empowerment: My desires are within reach.

Blizzard stone is also called gabbro, an igneous rock that cools slowly deep in the earth. As the name blizzard suggests, it is good for life's hard times, to promote endurance and cooperation even among people you would not normally consider as allies.

It is good for balancing a desire to stop those close to you from making mistakes with not taking over their lives or decisions, even for the best motives. It is a stone of tough love; give a piece to adult children who are reluctant to leave home or to any relative or friend who says they want employment but is not really trying.

Use blizzard stones to connect with past lives and avoid making the same mistakes now; protective against controlling partners and for helping people with obsessive compulsive disorders or obsessed about work or money to relax. Place blizzard stone on inside window ledges if you live near a mobile phone mast or electricity pylons.

Black Jasper/ Basanite

Type: Silicate, microcrystalline quartz; basanite is a flinty form.

Colours: Black.

Availability: One of the rarer forms of jasper.

Physical benefits: May be useful for pain relief, stomach disorders, hips and knees, joint-replacement operations, feet, deterioration of internal organs, sense of smell and taste, mineral balance; protective against side-effects of radiotherapy; to restore strength after illness or surgery.

Emotional healing: Brings discernment to those who are too trusting; sets personal boundaries to prevent over-identification with the lives and problems of others.

Chakra: Root and Solar Plexus.

Candle colour: Grey. **Fragrances:** Anise, cinnamon, cloves, ginger. **Practical uses:** Lucky in disputes; protects against lightning, fire or electrical accidents. **Workplace:** Wear if you work with electricity, gas, fossil fuels or nuclear energy, in the fire service, with metals, in security, the law, as a risk assessor or sell insurance; to deter bullies in the armed forces and security services. **Magical significance:** Wear against false friends and, if Internet dating, against those who are not what they claim; touch to know if a person is trustworthy. **Divinatory meaning:** A new friend has great plans for you both; check the details and be realistic. **Zodiac:** Aries and Scorpio. **Empowerment:** I will not be swayed by superficial factors.

Black jasper empowers the wearer to make a supreme physical and mental effort; helpful for those undecided whether to press on with a relationship or business that has hit a bad patch. In its polished form, cut as a cabochon dome or in a sphere, an excellent scrying stone.

An excellent scrying stone for discovering what is hidden about a situation or person; gaze into it by candlelight, extinguish the candle, sleep and you will dream of future pathways; wear it to shield against curses and threats.

Zebra Jasper

Type: Silicate, microcrystalline quartz, often with organic matter or other minerals as inclusions.

Colours: Black or brown with light stripes, resembles a zebra, also white and salmon pink with black inclusions that often form stripes.

Availability: Relatively common in brown or black forms.

Physical benefits: May help reduce stress and activate the fight-back mechanism; improve gall bladder, kidneys, skin, bone disorders, teeth, gums, muscle spasms, heart irregularities.

Emotional healing: Assists us to look at life in an optimistic way while also giving strength to deal with the causes of stress and to resist falling into apathy.

Chakra: Root.

Candle colour: Brown. **Fragrances:** Acacia, almond, anise sagebrush, sweetgrass. **Practical uses:** Carrying zebra jasper brings a sense of fun and the ability to experience life as it comes; helpful for trying new challenges; good if your life is in a rut. **Workplace:** Gives the ingenuity and persistence to bring ideas and projects to completion. **Magical significance:** Any carved zebra jasper power animal or large natural specimen acts as a personal or family amulet of protection. **Divinatory meaning:** Two sides of the same coin are revealed to you – you will be able to judge right from wrong. **Zodiac:** Virgo. **Empowerment:** I will not question life's experiences.

All jaspers are metamorphic, having undergone repeated actions of heat, movement and pressure over time that creates their underlying strength.

Zebra jasper energies are slow to materialize, but over time will stiffen resolve and initiative. It transforms creative energy into practical reality by banishing self-doubt and providing stamina and enthusiasm. Pink jasper is good for those seeking love who lack the courage to make the first move; a good love token for lasting love.

Type: Natural glass (shares some properties with the rarer green moldavite), usually measuring just a few centimetres in size, believed to have been created after meteoric impact with the earth's surface – tektites are only found in meteor-impact craters.

Colours: Black or very dark grey, smooth and shiny on the outside (some can appear dull).

Availability: Relatively common.

Physical benefits: Believed to assist in all physical healing. Said to speed up recovery from illness and injury, be good for skin disorders, problems with the auto-immune system and for illnesses that drain the body of strength such as ME or glandular fever; also for HIV/AIDS and conditions that defy diagnosis, malaria, typhoid.

Emotional healing: Tektite can be used for those who feel something is missing in their lives to fill an emotional gap by connecting with your inner fire; a reminder that only you can make yourself whole and complete, not other people.

Chakra: Crown.

Tektite

Candle colour: Very dark grey. **Fragrances:** Cedar, cloves, ginger, juniper, marigold. **Practical uses:** Place tektite near your front or back door to protect your property against fire, lightning strikes and storms, also protective for air travel. **Workplace:** Keep a tektite with you for prolonged periods to bring luck, increased sales and opportunities for travel and early advancement. **Magical significance:** This stone can be placed on the third eye or Brow chakra in the centre of your brow to enhance telepathic powers if you want to either connect with someone you love or regain contact with someone from the past. Only put it there for a few seconds as it is very powerful. **Divinatory meaning:** An amazing thought will strike you and, however unlikely, you have stumbled on the explanation for a loved one's behaviour. **Zodiac:** Aries and Sagittarius. **Empowerment:** I must meet my own needs to truly love others.

Due to its being created by the collision of heavenly descent and terrestrial origin, holding tektite brings out-of-body experiences when one's consciousness detaches itself from the actual body and travels in time or space; count upwards 1–30 slowly while focusing on a point of light on the ceiling (a sunbeam or spotlight is ideal).

Alternatively experience lucid dreaming when you are aware in a dream you are asleep and so can do anything, by putting tektite under your pillow.

As an otherworldly stone, tektite is associated with extra-terrestrial forces, carried by some people in areas of intense UFO activity to prevent unfriendly contact or bad dreams about abduction; good for past-life regression to prevent bad memories surfacing.

Type: Volcanic glass/magma, formed when lava hardens so fast that no crystalline structures are created.

Colours: Black and gleaming (see also the more transparent version called apache tear and green-tinted rainbow obsidian, pp.141 and 207).

Availability: Common.

Physical benefits: Claimed to assist with pain relief; improve circulation and artery health, also bowel problems. Thought to be useful to recover from physical shock, whether after an accident, an operation, trauma or domestic violence.

Emotional healing: Emotional healing after trauma of any kind. Good for victims of sexual assault. Assists in expressing grief that is blocked, especially in children. A small obsidian sphere in your workspace and at home absorbs free-floating irritability and restlessness.

Chakra: Root.

Black Obsidian

Candle colour: Bergundy **Fragrances:** Benzoin, gum arabic (acacia), mint, parsley, pine, pine resin (pinon or collophony), sandalwood. **Practical uses:** Protective when carried or worn as jewellery if others offload their problems on to you or make excessive demands on your time. **Workplace:** Ornamental small obsidian arrows in your workspace facing outwards protect you from gossip or spite. **Magical significance:** Gazing into an obsidian crystal is said to give you inner visions of the way through problems if you relax and let solutions come. **Divinatory meaning:** You have a great deal of power that you can use to improve a situation or relationship if you are not afraid to change the status quo and maybe tread on a few toes. **Zodiac:** Scorpio. **Empowerment:** I am filled with fire.

Called the wizard stone, obsidian has numerous magical associations. Highly polished obsidian oracle mirrors were used by the Mayans and Aztecs, and are still popular in modern Westernized magic. The seven obsidian arrow heads of the Ancient Egyptian lion-headed goddess Sekhmet were sent magically by her priests and priestesses against wrongdoers.

Seven-pointed obsidian arrow crystals are widely available and can be set in a semi-circle round your workspace or ringed round a burgundy candle, facing inwards, to draw power and health into yourself.

This is especially good to call employment or a better job to you. Obsidian beneath the pet bed will make a nervous pet less sensitive to traffic, being touched or sudden noises.

Obsidian tends to be a very personal stone and is generally bought, kept and worn by one person only.

Obsidian Arrows

Type: Volcanic glass; carved by hand from obsidian.

Colours: Black.

Availability: Relatively common.

Physical benefits: May benefit digestion, wounds, blockages, chest infections, chronic coughs, male illnesses, gastroenteritis, acute pain. Claimed to encourage safe, successful surgery.

Emotional healing: Obsidian arrows represent finding your true path; one as a pendant helps you to get on track.

Chakra: Root.

Candle colour: Black. **Fragrances:** Acacia, cinnamon, dragon's blood, saffron, sage. **Practical uses:** Obsidian arrows pointing outwards around your bed protect you from psychological attack and nightmares. **Workplace:** Keep a bag of obsidian arrows to set on any document where you are seeking a rapid return and say seven times, "Arrows fly swift and swift return". **Magical significance:** Point seven arrows outward round a written wish for three days, point inward for three days, and on the seventh alternate with four arrows outward, three inward. Burn wish on day eight. **Divinatory meaning:** Be active in seeking what you want. **Zodiac:** Sagittarius. **Empowerment:** I aim straight and true.

Snowflake Obsidian

Type: Volcanic silica glass containing small white, radially clustered christobalite nodules.

Colours: Black with white spots or small white snowflake patterns or black with grey.

Availability: Common.

Physical healing: Said to be good for strengthening bones, circulation, cells, tissue and bone marrow, influenza, sinus, eyesight, rhinitis, diarrhoea, processing of fat, pain remover.

Emotional healing: Strengthens determination to accept ourselves for who we are; recovery after sudden trauma.

Chakra: Root, Sacral and Solar Plexus.

Candle colour: White. **Fragrances:** Galbanum, hibiscus, mimosa, sage. **Practical uses:** Keep buried outside to prevent winter ills and misfortune and attract warmth and abundance. **Workplace:** A natural ongoing cleanser of stagnation, lack of enthusiasm and undercurrents of tension, drawing people with different viewpoints together. **Magical significance:** Excellent for healing magic where illness is persisting and in rituals to replace what is destructive or outworn with new growth. **Divinatory meaning:** Suddenly you really see someone new for who they are. Helps you make a wise decision. **Zodiac:** Capricorn, Virgo. **Empowerment:** For every ending there is a new beginning.

Obsidian has been used as a material for arrowheads since ancient times. Modern medicine has recently rediscovered obsidian blades for more healing purposes in delicate surgical techniques as the cut heals faster than other blades. However, obsidian is easily broken so keep your arrows separately from harder crystals.

Hide to deter thieves, pointing inwards as a shield and round your computer if you have private material stored on it. An anti-bullying crystal; wear a necklace and keep it with you until the bullying stops, whether it is you or a family member suffering.

The snowflake patterns on the surface combine fire and ice and the fusion of and unity of opposites. Good for bringing together different parts of your life, if necessary making tough decisions; and for balancing your personality. Associated with the Root, Sacral and Solar Plexus chakras, one should be placed while you are lying flat between your feet or thighs, a second on your navel and a third in the centre of your upper stomach, for 10 to 15 minutes. The stones will let pent-up resentment flow away, creating positive thought patterns. Melts frozen emotion so reduces feelings of isolation.

Type: Volcanic glass/magma, formed when lava hardens so fast that no crystalline structures are created (p.186 for general properties of obsidian).

Colours: Black and gleaming, often, as mirror, translucent black to smoky.

Availability: Relatively rare, look online.

Physical benefits: Said to be helpful as a natural pain remover; hold a small round obsidian mirror a few centimetres above a point of pain, to remove blockages in energy pass first the dark mirror over the body in spirals, followed by an ordinary small mirror, again in spirals, to energize. Obsidian mirrors are traditionally believed to call back health if the patient gazes in the mirror for a few minutes every day.

Emotional healing: An obsidian mirror held to the light reveals your shadow self, all the stored power and potential you have, locked in fears and doubts; each day increase the light source and let this shadow self out into the sunlight.

Chakra: Root.

Black Obsidian Mirror

Candle colour: Grey. **Fragrances:** Anise, cloves, hyssop, mint, pine. **Practical uses:** A very good energy clearer near the entrance of the home or any work premises to absorb negative vibes; polish the mirror with a soft cloth anti-clockwise weekly and wash the cloth; the mirror will radiate a sense of peace. **Workplace:** Keep a small dark mirror in your bag or desk; when you get stressed or need to clear your mind, focus on the black circle and let it fill your mind with peace; even five minutes a day will centre you and create an instant place of stillness and silence. **Magical significance:** Look into dark obsidian mirror by candlelight and ask to see your spirit guardian; close your eyes, open them slowly and you may see faintly in black and white your guardian over your shoulder; if this is too spooky, keep your eyes closed and picture the mirror in your mind as you stand in front of it. **Divinatory meaning:** If you look at the true situation, it is not half as bad as you feared; start sorting unfinished business in any area of your life. **Zodiac:** Scorpio. **Empowerment:** I am not afraid of my true nature.

A black obsidian mirror is the best scrying tool for answering questions and seeing future possibilities, and has inbuilt protection. In the Aztec world the sky god Tezcatlipoca, whose name means "smoking mirror", was said to see through his obsidian mirror all that occurred in the world and the heavens. It was also claimed that obsidian mirrors reflect an image of the person you can become, as well as giving visions of the future.

Buy a slightly concave mirror, as that will lead the eye in. You can use a dark mirror for connecting with your ancestors and answering questions about future possibilities, and also for seeing past lives, either in the mirror as grainy black-and-white images or in your mind if you prefer.

Even if you picture the images in your mind, face the mirror and focus on it as you ask the question before closing your eyes. A dark and light mirror on facing walls brings balance to the home and enables both calming and active energies to bounce throughout the home and all who enter or live there.

Type: Pyroxene, calcium magnesium silicate or calcium iron silicate (see also green diopside, p.292).

Colours: Dark brown to dark greenish black and black, with four-rayed star that can be seen when cut and polished in dome-shaped cabochons but lost in faceting; alternatively sometimes found as cat's eye (p.310).

Availability: Rare, but beautiful and worth obtaining.

Physical benefits: May help back, slipped discs, lumbago, spine, skeleton, back of the neck, muscle strains and spasms, ligaments, bowels, anus, large intestine, prostate, hernia, knees and feet, chronic constipation, kidneys, fluid blockages, chronic pain.

Emotional healing: Called the stone of healing tears, black diopside releases sorrows and grief that have become blocked, liberating for men who have been told it is unmanly to express softer emotions and cry.

Chakra: Root.

Black Star Diopside

Candle colour: Dark green. **Fragrances:** Cypress, lemon balm, mugwort, myrrh, tea tree. **Practical uses:** Black diopside in its natural form is a very calming crystal for hyperactive or aggressive pets if kept near a pet bed; also for rescue-centre pets or your existing pets after a home move or prolonged veterinarian treatment; for male animals that have not been neutered, to be more sociable with other pets. **Workplace:** Star diopside is a gem for attaining recognition in your field of expertise through a breakthrough after a period of intense effort; brings lucky breaks and opportunities to shortcut the slower, more conventional route to success. **Magical significance:** The star in black diopside acts a gateway to other dimensions; shine a narrow torch beam on the star or angle the diopside star so that candlelight illuminates it; in your mind travel inwards to a point of light that expands as a golden doorway in your inner vision; also for making wishes under a starry sky. **Divinatory meaning:** Express your feelings of frustration at the uncooperative attitude by someone who is thwarting your efforts, or the situation may continue indefinitely. **Zodiac:** Pisces. **Empowerment:** What I feel is valid and should not be denied.

Black star diopside is called the Black Star of India because that is where it is almost always found. It is the only crystal to produce a four- instead of a six-rayed white star and this distinguishes it from the visually similar black star sapphire (p.365 for star sapphires).

A dual-energy gem that enhances creativity but at the same time encourages logic and analysis so that your work or products fit what is required practically and can be marketed successfully. Black diopside in its natural form softens stubborn attitudes and is equally effective for toddlers who scream if they do not have their own way and temperamental adults; encourages over-conservative partners and older relatives to try new things.

Though it is not easy to obtain black diopside jewellery, wearing it will alleviate deep-seated fears, particularly of the dark, ghosts and phobias that began in childhood; a good gem for men.

Lodestone

Type: Naturally magnetized iron oxide, sometimes classed as a metal. The male stones are pointed, the female square or rounded. Buy a pair, one of each.

Colours: Black, dark grey, occasionally light brown.

Availability: Found in specialist crystal stores and online.

Physical benefits: Use male lodestones for men and female for women: believed to assist with arthritis, rheumatism, muscle aches, cramps, pain relief, circulation blockages, heartbeat, impotence, bowels, rectum, lower back, eyes, soles of feet.

Emotional healing: Hold your lodestone pair, one on each hand as seems right, each morning to feel long-standing burdens lift and helplessness be replaced by self-reliance.

Chakra: Root and Solar Plexus.

Candle colour: Red. **Fragrances:** Basil, bay, juniper, red rose, thyme. **Practical uses:** Keep a pair at home in a red bag to ensure balanced energies flowing in and out and reduce geopathic stress from negative earth energies; good to stop opposite-sex siblings from arguing. **Workplace:** A single pointed lodestone facing the door or a road-facing window draws prosperity; hold before an important phone call, sending a trawling email or trying to get your website higher on search engines. **Magical significance:** A male and female lodestone, or two the same for same-sex relationships, are traditionally kept in a red bag to maintain faithful love. **Divinatory meaning:** Follow your instincts. **Zodiac:** Virgo, Libra and Capricorn. **Empowerment:** I am tuned in to my radar.

Lodestones have been used to symbolically draw luck, money and love. In healing, a painful place or source of an illness would be stroked in downward movements and afterwards the stone placed in water and the water thrown away; rub a rounded stone in circles over the body if muscles are tense or for aches and pains. A pair beneath the mattress of a marital bed preserves passion and helps conceive a child; traditionally a male lodestone is anointed on the night of the full moon with a drop of patchouli to increase male potency (wash next morning).

Black Spinel

Type: Magnesium aluminium oxide or magnesium aluminate.

Colours: Black, glassy, dense colour, also gold to dark brown.

Availability: Obtainable from specialist jewellery and crystal stores and online; rare as tumblestone.

Physical benefits: Claimed to alleviate sources of illness, can help legs, female reproductive system, bladder problem, prostate, intestines, lymph nodes, the effects of toxins, septicaemia; some report it helpful in cancer treatments.

Emotional healing: Absorbs outbursts of anger and feelings of suppressed rage, assists controlled and more effective expression of negative feelings.

Chakra: Root.

Candle colour: White. **Fragrances:** Almond, anise, cherry blossom, magnolia, neroli. **Practical uses:** Wear to mend relationships and resolve issues when you still need to meet someone difficult, to absorb pettiness and behave with dignity. **Workplace:** Natural black spinel in a matrix is empowering if your workplace is losing money or threatened with redundancies; enables you to be supportive without sacrificing your future. **Magical significance:** A protective gem that repels negativity. **Divinatory meaning:** As one door closes, another opportunity opens. You must close the door you have been hesitating about. **Zodiac:** Taurus and Scorpio. **Empowerment:** I do not have to accept negative comments.

A good talisman if as an adult you need to temporarily move back to your parents' home, for creating a new mutually beneficial relationship and to avoid slipping back into the role of dependent child.

Wear if you are meeting a birth-parent for the first time or you are meeting an adult child from whom you were parted by circumstances. When you know them better you can give black spinel a "welcome back to my life" token. A good stone for rebuilding from the roots upwards.

Type: Silicon dioxide, often clear quartz, in which a phantom or shadow quartz crystal appears; the dark shadow inner may be smoky quartz, black shale, goethite or haematite.

Colours: The darkness of the crystal depends on the size of the inner black phantom and the smokiness or clarity of the outer quartz.

Availability: Obtainable from specialist mineral stores and online.

Physical benefits: Thought to improve the regrowth of bones after fractures, torn ligaments and muscles, tumours, transplants, implants and transfusions of all kinds, trigger self-healing and an awareness of lifestyle changes necessary to prevent illness or recurring problems caused by self-neglect or excesses.

Emotional healing: Brings understanding of the reasons behind personal addictions and obsessions and so breaks the cycle of reacting blindly to unconscious triggers; brings recall of the origin of fears and so reduces their hold.

Chakra: Brow and Root.

Black Phantom Quartz

Candle colour: Dark grey. **Fragrances:** Carnation, cranberry, lily, lily of the valley, saffron. **Practical uses:** A crystal for renovating your present home by redecorating or extending it rather than moving house if you want improvements but do not wish to uproot yourself; use it also in the centre of the home to absorb any negative earth energies beneath the home and to act as a welcoming focus for the luck-bringing house guardian. **Workplace:** Black phantom quartz is good for starting a business after bankruptcy or a period of unemployment using your existing talents, rebuilding slowly and avoiding past mistakes but basing the future on what was successful in the past. **Magical significance:** The black within the white makes black phantom quartz ideal for magical or spiritual work since it carries its own inbuilt grounding and protection; keep one with divinatory and magical tools and on your healing table to both empower and ensure you are not overwhelmed by the energy rush or spooked by anything negative. **Divinatory meaning:** Do not let shadows of past failures and disappointments hold you back from taking full advantage of the possibilities for present happiness; say yes. **Zodiac:** Scorpio. **Empowerment:** Within me are the seeds of the future.

The most spiritually focused of all the phantom quartzes, black phantom quartz banishes negative paranormal spirits and energies from your home while welcoming benign deceased relatives who will protect you. Use it for learning and understanding the *I Ching*, tai chi, yoga and any forms of Far Eastern spirituality and as a joint god/goddess symbol in magic.

Carry a small black phantom crystal point to attract people from your soul family: if you believe in past lives, those who have travelled through time with you; if not, people with whom you have a close spiritual affinity, a kind of spiritual family.

Black phantom quartz prevents people going over old grievances time and again or quarrelling over issues that should have long ago been forgotten; have one or two black phantom points facing the front door to deter bickering neighbours or relatives who visit to complain or cause trouble about past omissions or imagined injustices.

Type: Sodium iron silicate.

Colours: Black or dark green or brownish black.

Availability: Available from specialist crystal stores or online.

Physical benefits: Seen as useful to help boost immune system and trigger self-healing; good for general healing, to overcome insomnia and sleep disturbances, a natural energizer.

Emotional healing: Believed to assist in mending a broken heart after betrayal or loss; overcome a sense of being overwhelmed by life and responsibilities, relieve depression, self-consciousness and unnecessary shame over appearance and so good if a person has any disfigurement or body image problems.

Chakra: Root and Solar Plexus.

Aegerine

Candle colour: Dark green. **Fragrances:** Apple blossom, honeysuckle, rose, thyme, violet. **Practical uses:** Generates enthusiasm and a team spirit at home or work; encourages teenagers to get out of bed in the morning. **Workplace:** A very female-friendly crystal and so excellent for helping women to overcome hidden prejudice in the workplace and for emotional support for women returning to work after maternity leave. **Magical significance:** Powerfully protective if you are suffering jealousy, malice or psychological or psychic attack from others; once a week use the rod shape as a wand and thrust it away from you in all directions as you hold it in the hand you write with, saying, "May none penetrate this shield of protection." **Divinatory meaning:** Someone is trying to make you feel inadequate or guilty to offload their own insecurities and hang-ups, so do not accept blame or guilt. **Zodiac:** Pisces. **Empowerment:** I will remain true to my own principles whatever the pressures.

Named after the Norse sea deity, Aegir, since it was first found close to the sea in Norway.

A stone of particular benefit in Reiki or any other energy-transference healing systems using the power of touch. Aegerine helps acceptance of what cannot be changed and also acceptance of yourself and others as they are, not as you would like them to be. Use aegerine to defy outdated convention to follow your own path or to stand up for what you know is right.

Take aegerine on journeys of self-discovery, whether spiritual or travelling to see new far-off places; good for backpackers to protect them against negative energies and inhospitable places and people.

Colours: Organic, branching calcareous skeletons of sea creatures that can be highly polished and shine translucent as crystals or jewellery.

Availability: One of the rarer corals.

Physical benefits: Alleged to be a natural pain reliever, absorb energies from acute illnesses, fever and infections, improve functioning of bowels, spine and spinal fluid, bones; and to be good for blood-cell enrichment; absorption of iodine, the alimentary canal, thalamus, balance in older people, male potency.

Emotional healing: A soothing crystal to wear if a partner dies, particularly in the early years of marriage; also assists grieving parents who lose a child at any age.

Chakra: Root.

Black Coral

Candle colour: Dark grey or purple. **Fragrances:** Cypress, lemon balm, mugwort, myrrh, sweetgrass. **Practical uses:** Use in traditional fashion as a household protector and luck bringer. Touch every entrance door to the house and individual rooms, on each doorknob or handle on both sides of the door, with a branch of coral; then hang the coral inside over the front door to filter the energies of those entering. **Workplace:** A stone of diplomacy, black coral is good for behind-the-scenes negotiations and informal peacemaking in pay-and-conditions disputes and for resolving individual grievances without recourse to law; for all who work in the field of negotiations, especially those where human lives or freedom is at stake and where secrecy is of the essence. **Magical significance:** Called king's coral, in ancient times black coral could only be worn by kings who were believed to be divinely chosen and so had healing powers; for this reason black coral enhances wisdom and healing abilities in the wearer, woman or man. Wear if learning a spiritual tradition such as Buddhism, Druidry or Reiki, to tune into the innate energies. **Divinatory meaning:** Keep a low profile and listen rather than speak until you are sure what the intentions of others are. **Zodiac:** Pisces. **Empowerment:** I will use my gifts for the right reasons.

Though mainly associated with Hawaii, where black coral is the official US state gemstone, in Ancient Egypt coral was ground and mixed with seeds and scattered on the ground after the Nile flood receded to bring fertility to the land.

Black coral found in the Middle East was sacred to Osiris, the corn and vegetation god, who was believed to cause the plants to grow. Black was considered not a colour of death in Egypt but of fertility. Its name in Arabic means ease or

well-being, and black coral is said to bring serenity to the wearer, while at the same time absorbing any negativity. For this reason black coral needs cleaning with incense regularly. Black coral is not so suitable for children.

Some ecologists only use coral that has naturally broken off and been taken from the shore as a gift from a sea deity, and has not been cut or harvested. Black coral protects against bad weather, particularly hurricanes, typhoons, high winds, floods and tsunamis.

Apache Tear

Type: Volcanic glass/magma; a form of obsidian that is sufficiently translucent you can see light through it.

Colours: Black in the hand, dark grey-brown when held to light.

Availability: Common.

Physical benefits: Believed to relieve muscle spasms, pain and blockages in the lower parts of the body; remove toxins from the body; help the body absorb Vitamins C and D; relieve bites, boils, abscesses and stings.

Emotional healing: Releases blocked or unresolved feelings when held; grief will pour into the stone which may get darker. Wash it and hold it to the light to see the way forward.

Chakra: Root.

Candle colour: Grey. **Fragrances:** Cypress, lemon balm, magnolia, musk, myrrh. **Practical uses:** A good-luck crystal, a wonderful present for someone setting out in the world; helps you say no to unreasonable demands. **Workplace:** Place a dish in your workspace and wash weekly to remove absorbed bad vibes; good for preventing business opportunities slipping away. **Magical significance:** A stone of psychic invisibility, when travelling at night, hold crystal and breathe in the darkness. As you exhale your aura becomes hidden and lowers your profile. **Divinatory meaning:** Do not dwell on what is wrong, you can put it right. **Zodiac:** Capricorn. **Empowerment:** Tomorrow is another day.

Apache tears are named after an incident in Arizona in the 1870s, when the US cavalry attacked 75 Pinal Apaches. The women of the lost warriors wept for a whole month and the Great Spirit pressed their tears within the rock to form the crystals. Owning one will protect from sorrow, as the stone absorbs it, for the Apache women cried your tears as well. Carry one if you are finding it hard to forgive, yet know bitterness is holding you back. Protects you against human snakes.

Also place between your feet to slow you down.

Chrysanthemum /Flower Stone

Type: Black metamorphic rock with flashes of pale andalusite crystals.

Colours: Black and white or very pale colour.

Availability: Rare, especially in a perfectly formed flower design.

Physical benefits: Assists with maturation of child to adult, especially puberty, so an ideal gift for pregnancy/birth; claimed to help with tumours, growths, absorption of nutrients, skin, eyes, bones, removal of toxins, good for severely disabled people so they may reach their full potential.

Emotional healing: When emotional growth has been stunted because of abuse or neglect, it brings light flooding to open up channels to trusting connections with others.

Chakra: Root and Sacral.

Candle colour: White. **Fragrances:** Chrysanthemum, geranium, hyacinth, lilac, lily of the valley. **Practical uses:** For anyone about to make a change to be open to future possibilities; for people to find a relationship later in life after devoting their lives caring for others. **Workplace:** Carry a natural or polished stone if you are working abroad in a land where you are not welcome or have a job where people are hostile. **Magical significance:** Tracing the pattern by candlelight will induce a trance whereby you travel inwards in your mind through the stone. **Divinatory meaning:** An unexpected opportunity; do not hesitate. **Zodiac:** Aquarius. **Empowerment:** I expect the unexpected.

A stone that reminds you that you can follow some of your dreams and that life is not a dress rehearsal: gives you the courage to make decisions and to leave the comfort zone. Attracts good fortune to the workplace if kept next to either a growing pot of any colour chrysanthemums or a vase of any multi-petal flowers (replace as soon as they wilt). Light a white candle once a week, hold the stone in your hands and say, "I open myself to the abundance and good fortune of the universe". Leave candle to burn. Opportunities will flow.

Black Kyanite

Type: Aluminium silicate.

Colours: Steel grey or black.

Availability: Rarer than blue kyanite, but available from some specialist crystal stores or online.

Physical benefits: Alleged to be useful for adrenal glands, reducing blood pressure, pain relief, vocal cords, bone marrow, sickle cell, neurological disorders, visual disturbances.

Emotional healing: Absorbs panic and inability to switch off negative cycles of thoughts; helps us to forget what we cannot resolve, whether a bitter divorce or someone who was unkind to us dying without reconciliation.

Chakra: Root.

Candle colour: Silver. **Fragrances:** Anise, galbanum, mugwort, myrrh, thyme. **Practical uses:** Keep blades pointing outwards on indoor window ledges to deflect incoming tensions and disperse emotions. **Workplace:** Keep as a shield against personalities who find it impossible to distinguish between private and professional life. **Magical significance:** Point individual blades away from you to deflect harm and towards you while naming what you need. **Divinatory meaning:** Something thought wrong for you is returning and is now right. **Zodiac:** Aquarius and Pisces. **Empowerment:** The stars fill me with inspiration.

Favoured by energy healers for cleansing the aura energy field and the energies of a room after healing; pass diagonally up and down the body to clear the inner chakra power system. Circle over the hairline and round head and shoulders to mend tears in the aura.

Stimulates psychic energies, but protects beginners from frightening psychic phenomena. Move vertically down the body to close your psychic energies after a session or still yourself. A dream crystal that will enable you to travel safely in sleep to other dimensions.

Merlinite

Type: Silicate, black form of psilomelane.

Colours: Black with white inclusions, white with black inclusions, black and dark grey or dark blue with white.

Availability: Rare.

Physical benefits: Claimed to energize the body, removing and healing energy blockage; help with deep-seated healing and major surgical procedures, brain hemisphere balance, brain stem.

Emotional healing: Heals old deep wounds and encourages self-forgiveness.

Chakra: Brow.

Candle colour: White or grey. **Fragrances:** Acacia, copal, cyphi, frankincense, sweetgrass. **Practical uses:** Carry if you are hunting for accommodation in an area where it is very scarce or expensive. **Workplace:** As tumblestones, drives away confusion; gives the courage and stamina to stay at an unpleasant workplace and turn the situation around. **Magical significance:** Can form an offering in ceremonial magic and Earth healing rituals. **Divinatory meaning:** Lucky breaks do occasionally come along as if by magic and you are about to get such a chance. **Zodiac:** Scorpio. **Empowerment:** I make my own magic.

Merlinite enhances all forms of psychic development. It is, linked with alchemy and wizardry, assisting us to learn from the knowledge from other worlds and to understand what to do with that knowledge. Many magical practitioners acquire merlinite jewellery to wear in rituals connecting them with the roots of magic. Rounded nodular pieces are sometimes called goddess merlinite and will help break the hold of a cult or those who use magic, religion or psychic powers to manipulate others.

Type: Chalcedony.

Colours: Black.

Availability: Common.

Physical benefits: Thought to be beneficial for relieving bone and joint problems, shoulder and neck pain, also mobility difficulties; like all agates it is supposed to help to balance the body and so is very good for maintaining balance as people get older; also helpful for the menopause and breast problems.

Emotional healing: Heals sorrow and shields against ongoing abuse, especially self-abuse or self-harming; a kind stone immediately after bereavement when anger, self-doubt and pain are most acute; relieves claustrophobia.

Chakra: Root.

Black Agate

Candle colour: Grey. **Fragrances:** Apple blossom, cedar, cypress, myrrh, oakmoss, patchouli, vetivert. **Practical uses:** Brings physical and emotional stability to a frantic household where everyone is constantly rushing. **Workplace:** An anti-stress stone that, especially worn as jewellery, will neutralize any angst or hyped-up energies coming your way and radiate calm. **Magical significance:** Traditionally removes jinxes or a run of bad luck if you toss a black agate nine times saying "Bad luck away". Wash thoroughly under running water afterwards and repeat daily till your luck turns. **Divinatory meaning:** Let past bitterness go to move freely to the future. **Zodiac:** Capricorn. **Empowerment:** I stand my ground with calmness and assurance that I am right.

Black agates, especially those with a white circle or eye shape in the centre, are considered protective against the evil eye in a number of societies: guards against paranormal evil, fears of the dark, human spite and traditionally against lightning and snake bites.

Sometimes black agate was engraved with the image of a snake to signify protection against all harm. You can draw either a snake or an eye formation with the smoke of a lighted incense stick over your black agate to make a protective amulet if you are facing difficulties.

Wear or carry black agate when working with or fixing electrical goods or anything potentially dangerous. Good for winning competitions. Black agate will steady you if you have to make a difficult decision or show tough love.

Type: Calcium iron silicate, andradite variety of garnet.

Colours: Black, glossy and shiny.

Availability: Relatively rare.

Physical benefits: Believed to assist with pain relief, bones, rheumatism, arthritis, bowels, colon, constipation, anus, testes, male sexual dysfunction, prostate, hernia, absorption of medication while minimizing side-effects, blood particularly red cells and iron deficiency, strokes, heart attacks, considered helpful for cancers of lower half of body, liver, infections, immune system, moles and melanomas anywhere on the body.

Emotional healing: Often called the male-focus garnet, good for men whose feelings are locked, maybe due to stern fathering or a strict single-sex school, and who find it hard to express love or enjoy spontaneous pleasure.

Chakra: Root.

Melanite Garnet

Candle colour: Grey. **Fragrances:** Anise, dragon's blood, musk, mugwort, sage. **Practical uses:** A dual-focus crystal for resolving relationship issues in a practical way with the minimum of hurt and blame; wearing one will either lead you to reconciliation or, if this is not possible, assist you in gentle parting; it also absorbs unnecessary guilt and grounds you in the real situation if a partner is trying to offload their bad behaviour as your fault. **Workplace:** Melanite's strongly male energies concentrate power, stamina and perseverance; ideal for men and women facing an uphill struggle because of high unemployment in their area of expertise; to push towards the top in an overcrowded market or where there is resistance to progress from the establishment. **Magical significance:** One of the best protective crystals to wear against black magic, curses, hexes or a sense of menace when you meet someone; if psychic manipulation is acute, use natural melanite to absorb negative vibes and ground them in Mother Earth, and wear the gem to reflect back deliberate malice. **Divinatory meaning:** Stay in the here-and-now and defeat immediate problems rather than jumping ahead to future hazards or triumphs not yet in sight. **Zodiac:** Capricorn. **Empowerment:** I am totally rooted in reality.

Melanite is the most earth-related garnet and is worn by men and women to draw strength from the earth for all practical endeavours and starting any venture from the roots upwards; ensures any creation is based on firm foundations, is realistically valued or priced, and above all is useful.

Natural black garnet on a matrix (rock or crystal base) should be worn if you live with head-in-the-clouds people; give melanite to a partner who forgets to pay household bills or fill in necessary forms and then wonders why there are problems.

An excellent domestic room cleanser, melanite absorbs anything that is not fresh and pure; also a welcome addition to a healing room or clairvoyant's table at a psychic fair, both to protect from residual unhappiness and sickness from clients and to give stamina on a long day or weekend of work.

Type: Organic: fossilized wood that has been turned into a dense form of coal called lignite.

Colours: Black, very dark brown, glassy.

Availability: Common.

Physical benefits: Considered helpful for headache, migraines, epilepsy, swollen glands, colds, labour pains, menstrual cramps, toothache, neuralgia, stomach pains caused by irritations of the colon or bowel and colds.

Emotional healing: Overcomes grief and depression after bereavement, especially after the death of a partner, and conquers negative thought patterns or fears of others doing harm or sending bad luck even if unfounded.

Chakra: Root.

Jet

Candle colour: Black, natural beeswax or dark brown. **Fragrances:** Cypress, galbanum, mimosa, myrrh, patchouli. **Practical uses:** For those that live with relatives who suffer depression or psychological illness, place pieces of jet around the home, especially in the area where they spend most of their time, to absorb negative energies. Smudge the jet weekly with the smoke of jet-fragrance incense. **Workplace:** An ideal gift to someone setting up a new business venture or taking over premises, particularly placed in the cash till of shops; for starting a new job to bring good luck, success and a steadily rising income as well as protection from jealous rivals. **Magical significance:** Worn around the neck, jet acts as a shield against envy, jealousy, ill wishing, spiteful words and psychic attack, whether from human or paranormal source. **Divinatory meaning:** Financial stability will come unexpectedly as a result of earlier hard work and input you thought had been unsuccessful. **Zodiac:** Capricorn. **Empowerment:** I can let go of the past with gentleness.

Jet has been used since ancient times in association with death and protection against evil entities, having been discovered in prehistoric burial chambers.

Used by Viking women in spindles to sew with magical chants protection to their husbands' garments. Jet was also carried by sailors' wives in Europe as an amulet to keep their husbands safe at sea – and faithful. Carved ornate jet jewellery was made popular in mourning by Queen Victoria,

while jet crosses were worn around the neck to repel evil witches and the powers of darkness. Traditionally, jet should be buried with its owner and not resold or inherited. If it is handed on, wash weekly for three weeks and dry outdoors.

Use a piece wrapped in a towel to allow a very sick or old animal to let go of life gently. Jet kept with bills and bank statements is a powerful anti-debt stone and reduces outflow of money through mishaps or items needing replacement.

Ferberite

Type: Sulphate, iron tungstate with high iron content, slightly magnetic, minor ore of tungsten.

Colours: Black, reddish brown, blackish brown.

Availability: Common.

Physical benefits: Believed to help with physical strength and recovery after illness, blood disorders, sickle-cell disease, arthritis and all muscle and joint pains and stiffness, free circulation of blood and bodily fluids, boils, abscesses, ulcers, bladder weakness and stress incontinence.

Emotional healing: Relieves over-controlling behaviour and obsessive-compulsive disorder.

Chakra: Root and Sacral.

Candle colour: Grey. **Fragrances:** Acacia, juniper, manuka, plum, vanilla. **Practical uses:** Good for recognizing alternative viewpoints; allows detachment; keep at home if you want adult children to leave the nest. **Workplace:** Makes living with uncertainty easier if you work for yourself and income is irregular; brings adaptability to changing demands; good for market traders and for getting new commissions. **Magical significance:** Use when working with a pendulum to determine the correct option. Hold pendulum above crystal and focus on question. **Divinatory meaning:** Take time to make a decision. **Zodiac:** Capricorn. **Empowerment:** I let go of the need to control everything.

Good for understanding motives where these are confused or hidden; distinguishes a good friend from a false one if you focus on the stone while visualizing the person.

An amulet for those who work in rescue services, particularly fire personnel, paramedics and those in hospital accident and emergency departments to act decisively without panicking. Gradually reduces emotional baggage and unwise old attachments. Place a piece with a photo of a love best forgotten, wrapped in a cloth in a drawer; after seven days transfer all to an attic or memory box. Not suitable as a direct elixir or for children.

Black Onyx

Type: Quartz, chalcedony, a variety of agate.

Colours: Either naturally black though iron and carbon being present in its formation or heat-treated to change grey to black; also naturally as brown, grey and black and white.

Availability: Common.

Physical benefits: Seen as improving cell regeneration, bone marrow, fingernails, skin, hair, stamina, vitality, animal bites and insect stings, ear infections, earache, balance, sensory and motor mechanisms, soft tissue, nausea.

Emotional healing: Good for those suffering addictions.

Chakra: Root.

Candle colour: Grey. **Fragrances:** Bergamot, chamomile, copal, mimosa, musk. **Practical uses:** Use when it is time to let go of people who are troublesome in a non-destructive way; wear if you have a lot of people who depend too much on you. **Workplace:** Focuses those who are easily distracted; wear for defending yourself effectively but calmly in an argument. **Magical significance:** Holds magical empowerment for a long time for ongoing needs. Breathe on a tumble- or worry stone three times and fill it with your wishes. **Divinatory meaning:** Happiness and good fortune are around the corner. **Zodiac:** Leo. **Empowerment:** I can resist unwise temptation.

Wear an onyx necklace or bead bracelet to calm nerves. Great powers of protection and grounding energies if worn as jewellery as an antidote to the fast pace of modern life. Hide a tumblestone in a teenager's bedroom to deter undesirable influences. Keep one by computers. Onyx jewellery also protects against people who play mind games. Care should be taken while cleansing it and it is better to use incense or smudge smoke. Wearing or using onyx regularly will assist you in achieving a positive outlook, increasing energy levels and having the determination to succeed.

Dendritic Limestone

Type: Limestone with iron and manganese oxide inclusions.

Colours: Black dendrites or fern-like inclusions in white or creamy limestone.

Availability: Relatively rare but worth obtaining.

Physical benefits: Believed to be good for veins and arteries, circulation of blood and body fluids, hands and fingers, growths, skin tags, excess hair in women, digestion, heartburn, internal parasites, fungi and skin-burrowing parasites, diseases carried by vermin, speedy wound healing.

Emotional healing: Releases inaccurate deep-seated beliefs about self; restores confidence.

Chakra: Root and Crown.

Candle colour: White. **Fragrances:** Anise, juniper, lavender, patchouli. **Practical uses:** Give a polished sphere or slab to children to stimulate imagination. **Workplace:** Keep a polished piece of in your workspace as a worry stone; look into the inner landscape and let your mind wander for five minutes. **Magical significance:** Buy for a meditation focus; look into the dendritic forms but do not consciously visualize anything; connects you with your inner self if you analyse spiritual experience rather than flowing with it. **Divinatory meaning:** A good time for networking and making contact with people with whom you have lost touch. **Zodiac:** Capricorn. **Empowerment:** I do not need to force spiritual insights.

One of Mother Nature's wonders, every specimen is unique. Some people collect different polished pieces as art forms and to bring natural harmony; keep one if you live or work alone and do not socialize very often to draw positive emotional connections to your life; an excellent focus for setting up an Internet blog or on-line interest group, and for finding genuine like-minded people online. A good logo for business collectives or cooperatives, for forming music or singing groups or starting an amateur or professional theatre company.

Nuumite

Type: Metamorphosed igneous rock composed of anthophyllite and gedrite.

Colours: Black and white, and grey and white, with bronze or flashes of other colours.

Availability: Rare and quite expensive, but worth obtaining.

Physical benefits: Claimed to be good for all-purpose healing, infections that are slow to clear or recur, blood, kidneys, insulin regulation, diabetes, low blood sugar and low blood pressure, fainting and dizziness, eyes, ears, tinnitus, central nervous system, heart valves and arteries.

Emotional healing: Defends against subtle but persistent undermining.

Chakra: Solar Plexus.

Candle colour: White. **Fragrances:** Allspice, cinnamon, cyphi, ginger, saffron. **Practical uses:** Brings stability to a new place; good for issues with your father or grandfather, and for fatherhood in general especially single fathers. **Workplace:** Carrying a tumblestone encourages fast intuitive reactions without sacrificing logic; if you are often ignored because others are more knowledgeable, it will make you be taken seriously. **Magical significance:** Good for drum healing through sound and drum divination where nuumite is placed on a drum and the drum gently shaken; the sounds will form as words in your mind. **Divinatory meaning:** Listen to your inner self. **Zodiac:** Scorpio. **Empowerment:** I trust the rightness of my opinions.

Nuumite has very strong wild-nature energies, which give it its fiercely protective powers and strong direct access to nature in the raw. It is a perfect antidote to modern urban living that blunts the instincts and can bring over-reliance on technology. A tumblestone near a source of heat shields the home from natural disasters.

Wear if there is a major initiative or you feel exhausted but need to get through the day. Hold in the centre of your forehead to send a blast of nature energy down towards your feet, and it will bounce up again.

Sphalerite

Type: Zinc sulphide in crystalline form, the chief ore of zinc, and almost always containing some iron.

Colours: Black, dark grey, red, brown and yellow.

Availability: Obtainable from specialist crystal stores or online; clear is rarer.

Physical benefits: Thought to assist with problems with women's reproductive system, male genitals and sperm count, increased libido, vitality, immune system, infections, extremities of temperature, fevers or hypothermia.

Emotional healing: A grounding stone if someone loves too much or mistakes indiscriminate sex for affection; resolving gender and same-sex-partnership issues; bi-polar disorder.

Chakra: Solar Plexus, Sacral and Root.

Cuprite

Type: Copper oxide, one of the highest-yielding copper ores.

Colours: Black and red within, dark brownish red, red or a deep red that can appear almost black.

Availability: Relatively common, rarer as jewellery or polished cabochons.

Physical benefits: May act as a natural energizer; may help with bladder, kidneys, cystitis, haemorrhoids, thymus, heart, hernia, blood, vertigo, altitude sickness, menstrual problems, cramps, arthritis, rheumatism, veins, feet, hands, mobility.

Emotional healing: Prevents chronic worrying; helps mothers let adult children make their own mistakes.

Chakra: Heart.

As well as its grounding properties, sphalerite can act as a wake-up call, usually if we have rooted ourselves in a situation that is not as stable as it appears. The black variety, known as black jack, has a higher iron content than the other colours and is very grounding.

In contrast, the red crystals, known as ruby jack, have very little or no iron content and will bring change, inventiveness and independence. A crystal of truth; meditate or hold sphalerite to tell reality from illusion or deception; protects against treachery.

Minimizes conflict between sexes at work in professions where women are discouraged from promotion; also if you are a woman in a traditional community. Encourages harmony if men find it hard to work for a female employer or are uncomfortable with a successful female partner. Wear if you are discriminated against because of your accent, education or social status. A stone for overcoming fears of mortality in later life. If you are facing difficulties in love, matching cuprite cabochons or tumblestones is a reminder that love usually finds a way.

Type: Corundum; can display six-ray star effect (p.365).

Colours: Black or brownish black; translucent (cloudy) to opaque; sometimes dark green, dark, brown or blue rather than black.

Availability: Relatively rare.

Physical benefits: Believed to be useful for powerful pain relief, severe bowel disorders, gangrene, serious illness when the body is attacking itself, boils, ulcers, IBS, backache, internal haemorrhages, blood clots, deep vein thrombosis, bruising and dislocation of bones; recovery from accident or trauma, male sexual potency.

Emotional healing: An excellent crystal for men experiencing a major mid-life crisis or ageing issues on retirement; for profound grief at the loss of a lifetime partner by either sex.

Chakra: Root.

Black Sapphire

Candle colour: Dark brown. **Fragrances:** Anise, cloves, cyphi, dragon's blood, juniper. **Practical uses:** Black sapphire shields against unreasonable anger from partners or employers and prevents you absorbing it or becoming fearful or intimidated; reflects calm strength to establish boundaries with bullies or gives the courage to walk away. **Workplace:** Wear black sapphire if you have a very stressful or demanding career or you have to deal with human tragedy, whether as part of the armed forces or rescue services; absorbs and reflects away (especially as the star sapphire) negativity, sorrow, shock and horror, and helps you to deal with difficult matters in a practical, compassionate way. **Magical significance:** A stone that should be kept or worn by healers who work with very sick or terminally ill patients or who over-empathize with patients and take on their sorrows or symptoms. Wear it over your heart/throat to relate to patients but not agonize over their problems and so render yourself ineffective. **Divinatory meaning:** Now is not the time, while things seem black, to make any decisions; nurture yourself and temporarily withdraw from conflict and others' battles. **Zodiac:** Capricorn. **Empowerment:** I accept and honour sad as well as happy feelings.

Black sapphire keeps your feet on the ground in chaotic situations or with chaotic people; helps determine what is your responsibility and what must be done to avoid meltdown, without allowing others to avoid responsibility for problems of their making; an anti-panic crystal if you are over-sensitive to other people's quarrels or to situations where everything goes wrong and you do not have the means to put things right.

Use natural black sapphire for working with nocturnal power animals; during the three days when the moon is not visible in the sky at the end of the moon cycle before the crescent appears, use black sapphire to remove from your mind and life anything that you do not wish to carry forward to the next moon month; good for meditation in total darkness and to overcome fears of the dark as an adult; not a crystal for children but loved by cats – rub it on their paws to stop them straying at night. The black star sapphire is especially powerful for contacting ghosts and for safe mediumship as it is also highly protective.

Type: Iron hydroxide.

Colours: Black-brown or brownish red, orangey or yellowish brown.

Availability: Common though its crystals are rarer.

Physical benefits: Claimed to assist with the digestive system, veins and circulation, blood disorders particularly anaemia, oxygenation of blood, bone marrow, absent or scant menstruation and convulsions, ears, nose, throat and the connective passages and oesophagus.

Emotional healing: A Mother Earth nurturing power for adults who care for others personally and professionally and feel no one cares for them.

Chakra: Root, Sacral and Solar Plexus.

Goethite

Candle colour: Gold. **Fragrances:** Coriander, cypress, fern, pine, sagebrush. **Practical uses:** On dark rainy days or those times when you feel dispirited, goethite will bring optimism and enthusiasm to work your way out of the gloom; for concentration and to avoid being distracted by others, particularly if you have a home-based business. **Workplace:** Goethite brings openness to new opportunities, new skills and the flexibility to take on a new role if your company has been radically modernized, automated and jobs replaced by overseas operators or computers. **Magical significance:** Keep a small piece of goethite with dowsing rods or your pendulum to attune your energies with the dowsing tool and amplify information passed through it; channels clairaudient or spoken messages from angels and spirit guides, usually through your own inner voice. **Divinatory meaning:** Trust a recent prediction or premonition and act accordingly. **Zodiac:** Aries. **Empowerment:** I can easily learn new skills.

Goethite is the second-most-important ore of iron and source of colour for ochre, a pigment that has been used since prehistoric times and has been found in the cave paintings at Lascaux in France.

Goethite can be found inside some quartz specimens and also the *Super Seven* crystal (p.307).

Often used in artists' materials or cosmetics, goethite is sometimes called the fairy paint box, because it can sometimes appear quite unexpectedly sparkling within another mineral as though the mineral had been painted.

Goethite encourages everyone to create for pleasure rather than worrying about whether creations are good enough for public scrutiny; a gift for anyone graduating, entering a profession, completing an apprenticeship or long course of study and training; buy yourself a piece if you dedicate yourself to a spiritual path such as

Druidry, mediumship, Reiki or Wicca as a reminder of your determination to learn more when time is short or other activities and responsibilities intrude.

Goethite

Type: Silicate (semi-precious).

Colours: Black.

Availability: The most common tourmaline, especially as tumblestones and natural.

Physical benefits: Said to help with arthritis, bowels, constipation, IBS and coeliac disease, immune system, heart problems, lower back, legs, ankles, feet, aching or torn muscles, absorb pain, realigning of the skeleton, scar tissue.

Emotional healing: Anxiety, stress, suicidal thoughts, self-harming, drug abuse; soothes panic attacks, especially those caused by confined spaces and fears of dentists or doctors.

Chakra: Root.

Schorl/Black Tourmaline

Candle colour: Black. **Fragrances:** Almond, anise, hyssop, lavender, lemongrass. **Practical uses:** Wear to protect you against moaners, whingers, complaining neighbours or emotional vampires who burden you with their problems but will take no action to remedy them. **Workplace:** To repel electromagnetic negative energy this stone should be worn or kept close when using computers or other electronic equipment. Also hold for a few minutes when you need to use all your concentration, or when you need to wake up your mind, such as first thing in the morning. **Magical significance:** For all purification and protection rituals: create a ring of eight small natural schorls to place on an altar to mark a circle of protection. **Divinatory meaning:** A confusing or clouded issue will be made clear and you will receive an insight to overcome the problem. **Zodiac:** Libra and Scorpio. **Empowerment:** I empty my mind of all clutter and worry.

A stone associated with the Roman god Saturn, god of time and also the planet Saturn. Schorl was once used by magicians to offer them protection against earth demons when they were casting spells; in the modern world, iron-rich schorl deflects, dispels and shields the wearer or carrier from external negative energies and internal conflicts.

Schorl will stop you feeling spooked in dark places or those where the atmosphere is frightening; returns bad wishes to the sender.

Black tourmaline is a powerful crystal when working with chakras. It can realign the chakras, balancing the body from crown to root. Its strong grounding energies facilitate a connection between the earth and the human spirit creating the ability to receive insights from higher realms; also good to hold if you are feeling spaced out after a healing session or meditation. This stone will bring you back to earth.

Type: Quartz embedded in crocidolite with little of the hydrated oxide that gives tiger's eye its customary golden colour; very dark form of hawk's or falcon's eye (blue).

Colours: Black or very dark blue, also includes darker greys, sometimes dyed.

Availability: Rarest form of tiger's eye.

Physical benefits: Believed to provide help for all slow-moving degenerative conditions, to trigger the body's natural resistance, deep-seated tumours or growths anywhere, particularly in men, prostate, hernia, bowels, large intestine and anus in both sexes, internal bleeding for example from an ulcer, deep vein thrombosis, mental and physical blackouts whatever the cause.

Emotional healing: A stone for men who have suffered a severe emotional or psychological setback, such as the loss of a lifetime partner through death or desertion, redundancy in later life and no prospect of re-employment or a financial disaster, to work through grief and anger and rebuild their lives step by step in a new way.

Chakra: Root.

Black Tiger's Eye

Associated candle colour: Dark grey. **Associated fragrances**: Anise, cloves, grapefruit, lime, tea tree. **Practical uses**: The toughest of the tiger's eyes, wear black tiger's-eye jewellery at the most difficult of times to give you the sheer doggedness and stubbornness not to give in to adversity or bullying; touch the jewellery in the darkest hours to push towards the light at the end of the tunnel. **Workplace**: Use or wear black tiger's eye if your business is about to go under or your job is under severe threat, to put 110 percent effort into salvaging the situation or, if impossible, to get the very best outcome for yourself. **Magical significance**: The ultimate defensive shield to reflect back hostility and to protect you against emotional or psychic vampires. If you know you will be meeting a draining or nasty person, touch your brow, your throat and your heat with the stone to seal your main chakra or psychic-energy centre weak-points. **Divinatory meaning**: If the odds seem stacked against you, keep pushing, as a week or two will see you through the other side. **Zodiac**: Scorpio. **Empowerment**: I overcome adversity with courage.

This very unusual tiger's eye is much heavier in its energies than its brother the hawk's or falcon's eye. Even if dyed, it maintains its gleaming exterior and is sometimes called the impenetrable fortress stone; the best stone for allowing anything that is not helpful to bounce back with triple the force it was sent with and for galvanizing the body and mind's defences.

Black tiger's eye is both empowering and protective for anyone in the armed forces serving on the front line of conflict, to focus on their strengths and loyalties to one another, even in the midst of tragic and frightening events.

Give black tiger's eye to any woman who has to walk home alone at night or lives alone in an area where there is a lot of gang warfare or trouble with local young people, to remain calm and exude personal power.

Cassiterite

Type: Tin oxide/tin ore, often found on matrix or as nuggets.

Colours: Black, brown and very shiny or silvery and metallic; less frequently red, yellow or grey.

Availability: Found in specialist crystal stores and online.

Physical benefits: Claimed to assist with problems with reproductive organs, wounds, cuts, bruises, sprains, hormonal imbalances, perimenopause and menopause, obesity.

Emotional healing: Brings contentment to those who are envious and so miss enjoyment in their own lives; overcomes fears of illness, pain and mortality.

Chakra: Root.

Candle colour: Silver or deep blue. **Fragrances:** Fennel, honeysuckle, sage, sandalwood. **Practical uses:** Creates the energies to get things done; place near the toolbox of someone who is always promising to fix things, or by the most urgent DIY job. **Workplace:** Increases productivity and gets results noticed by management and customers. Brings success to advertising strategies. **Magical significance:** Place in the centre of a chart or close to your computer when casting or interpreting horoscopes. **Divinatory meaning:** Weigh up the odds of success in any new opportunity; check your facts and figures before committing. **Zodiac:** Sagittarius. **Empowerment:** I have many options.

Larvakite

Type: Black feldspar.

Colours: Black-grey, blue-grey, grey, all with sheen or iridescent colour flashes, often of silvery blue.

Availability: Found in specialist crystal stores and online.

Physical benefits: Said to help high blood pressure, brain functioning, recovery after strokes and thrombosis, brain stem, intellect, congested lungs, PMS, menopausal hot flushes, skin.

Emotional healing: Encourages rationality; ideal for hormonal teenagers, pregnancy, perimenopausal mood swings and passionate new lovers.

Chakra: Base, Throat, Brow, Crown.

Candle colour: Blue or silver. **Fragrances:** Myrrh, poppy, rosemary, sage, sweetgrass. **Practical uses:** Carry if you are learning new skills; you have to combine learning with work or caring for a family, if you are under financial pressure or face opposition to your studies. **Workplace:** For managers in any business to avoid allowing emotions to intrude on decisions; wear if you teach children with learning or behavioural difficulties. **Magical significance:** Reverses spells; wear to neutralize nasty wishes and consign them to the cosmos for transformation. **Divinatory meaning:** Do not part with money unless you are sure the person asking has a genuine need and will pay you back. **Zodiac:** Leo and Sagittarius. **Empowerment:** I open my heart wisely.

Cassiterite protects against physical danger. Keep it close to travel documents and luggage in the days before air travel or visiting somewhere dangerous; carry a nugget if you drive fast or on hazardous roads, for extreme sports, if you work in construction, operating machinery or in hazardous occupations; good for working with calculations and for filling in forms. Stabilizes anyone betrayed or rejected, to try again; for adopted children whose birth-mothers refuse contact; brings couples closer or attracts someone whose lifestyle reflect yours.

Larvikite, or Norwegian moonstone, is an igneous rock that is mined in Norway, named after the local town of Larvik. It is useful for activating those with grand dreams who are going to start tomorrow. Larvikite has grounding energies to connect with nature and counteract over-exposure to artificial stimulants, over-bright lighting and constant background noise. It brings psychic dreams, connecting with ancestors, spirit guides and past lives, and aids recall and understanding of dream messages. Brings healing during sleep.

Type: Phyllo or sheet silicate from the mica family, sometimes in the shape of lenses.

Colours: Black, brown, grey or dark green.

Availability: Obtainable from specialist crystal stores and online.

Physical benefits: Believed to act as a detoxifier; relieve constipation, kidney stones, acidity in the digestive tract and bile duct; help with problems with eyes, cells, growths, rheumatism and sciatica; wear or keep close to the body.

Emotional healing: Helps to connect you with your inner child who may have been wounded or disappeared beneath burdens.

Chakra: Sacral and Crown.

Biotite/Birthing Stone

Candle colour: White or cream. **Fragrances:** Apple blossom, lemon balm, lemon verbena, peach. **Practical uses:** Brings order out of chaos; put a piece of biotite near the centre of your home a day or two before spring cleaning, clearing clutter or Feng Shui, to help hoarders let go and to fill the home with a sense of order. **Workplace:** Good to introduce to the office in the days before an audit, tax returns are due in or you have to balance the books; keep a piece by your cash register to avoid careless mistakes. **Magical significance:** Used in rebirthing in adulthood to remove pre-birth and birth trauma; good in past-life work for discovering the cause of present-life phobias, disabilities or inexplicable scars. **Divinatory meaning:** You may have to wait longer than expected for results from an investment or outlay of time or resources. Do not give up for you will see those benefits soon. **Zodiac:** Capricorn. **Empowerment:** Transform ideas into reality.

Produced when the mountains of northern Portugal were formed: when the summer heat causes the rocks to expand, the biotic lenses swell up in a lens shape and burst forth quite spontaneously from the rocks, hence they are associated with childbirth.

Used by pregnant women when their baby is due as a charm to hasten labour and during labour to ease birth pains.

Excellent for all birth situations, from a natural or home birth to a hi-tech hospital delivery.

When the mother and child return home the biotite can remain in the child's nursery to help the little one settle in the world and may help establish a sleep pattern. If the baby is premature or has to remain in hospital, the mother can take the biotite home as a reminder the baby is coming home.

Biotite assists effective acupuncture, acupressure, shiatsu, reflexology and other energy touch therapies.

Type: Jadeite (p.268), also nephrite jade (p.266), which have different chemical compositions but look similar. Though nephrite is softer than jadeite it is actually tougher because of the way the tiny crystals and fibres are packed together within the stone.

Colours: Black, sometimes coloured with graphite and/or iron oxide.

Availability: Black jadeite, for example black Burmese jade, is much rarer than black nephrite.

Physical benefits: Thought to assist with the reproductive system in both sexes, bowels, constipation, IBS, illnesses in older people, feet, legs, knees, hips and hip or knee replacement operations, kidney stones, bile duct, gallstones, restricted blood flow; believed to be beneficial for deep vein thrombosis.

Emotional healing: A water stone, black jade helps very old people eager for active living not to give up on dreams because they physically take longer to manifest; the stone of independent living in spite of physical limitations.

Chakra: Root.

Black Jade

Candle colour: Indigo. **Fragrances:** Lemongrass, mugwort, myrrh, poppy, vetivert. **Practical uses:** A small bowl of black jade tumblestones, one for each person, smudged regularly with a black jade fragrance incense stick, ensures everyone in the home gains respect and a voice, from the youngest to the oldest; balancing if certain members are dominant, clever with words or manipulative. **Workplace:** Wear or carry black jade if you work with or for a control freak to avoid being swept along by their unreasonable demands; protective also against those greedy for power who will use any means to succeed. **Magical significance:** Choose a natural piece of either kind of black jade as a guardian stone for your home. Set it near your hearth, in the north of the home or inside the front door; unlike other dark guardian stones, protective black jade does not need to be replaced after a year and a day, but remains as a cumulative power guardian of abundance and material security. **Divinatory meaning:** You may need to be firm to avoid being disregarded or pressurized into a decision you rightly know will be a disaster. **Zodiac:** Scorpio and Capricorn. **Empowerment:** I welcome darkness as the other half of light.

It does not matter which of the jade types your black jade is, as the properties are remarkably similar. Jadeite feels grainier but takes a more mirror-like polish than nephrite, and black jadeite in particular makes fabulous protective jewellery.

The Mayans treasured black jade as magical. It has never had negative connotations, but rather has been regarded as guardian against the powers of paranormal evil and human malice in various cultures. Being jade, it is one of the most healing of black stones, absorbing and transforming fears, sorrow and anything negative.

Wear black jade if you have reasons to feel insecure or afraid, and leave it just once a month on an indoor window ledge on full-moon night.

Type: Magnesium aluminium oxide. Some spinels are made artificially, but are not so good for healing or empowerment.

Colours: Purple from light to dark violet, including lavender.

Availability: Relatively common.

Physical benefits: Said to be a whole-body healer if placed in the centre of the brow; remove deep-seated pain; relieve epilepsy, migraines, hardening of arteries in brain, hydrocephalus, Parkinson's disease, motor neurone disease, paralysis of lower body, circulatory problems in legs, skin and hair health; detoxify blood.

Emotional healing: Reduces a sense of feeling isolated from any social group, whether colleagues, family or the community; wear if you are disabled to find the resources and support to overcome practical difficulties and ignorance in others

Chakra: Brow.

Purple Spinel

Candle colour: Purple. **Fragrances:** Acacia, copal, hydrangea, juniper, sage. **Practical uses:** A wonderful inter-generational harmony stone; give one to older relations to encourage independence, but as a reassurance you are there if necessary; keep natural spinel in your home to create a sense of space and personal boundaries if your living space is crowded because family members have temporarily returned. **Workplace:** A spiritual form of this energetic crystal whose name means little thorn or little fire; wear darker purple spinel if people take advantage of your good nature to offload extra work and responsibilities on you; helps you to discriminate between real need and times when you should say no to avoid overload. **Magical significance:** Draws to you and at the same time guides you to like-minded people who share your spiritual outlook and interests; good for setting up mediumship circles, ghost investigation societies and for working on high-quality paranormal media projects. **Divinatory meaning:** You have the interests of others at heart; since your current decision does involve them, consider their needs, but do not forget your own first. **Zodiac:** Scorpio and Pisces. **Empowerment:** I can find the best in any situation.

Purple spinel combines spirituality with the dynamic regenerative powers of spinel; good therefore for launching a spiritual business as a second career so that it provides a living. It is fiercely protective against both everyday nastiness and paranormal harm, by acting as a shield to reflect back any ill wishes sent deliberately or unconsciously, without amplifying them or sending anything harmful in return.

Use purple spinel in natural form or wear as jewellery to maintain your own ethics and beliefs if you have to work or live among cynical, materialistic people or if you are trying to fit in with people with whom you have to socialize who have very different lifestyles and beliefs. Purple spinel is very reassuring for much older people who find the modern world hard to understand or who get confused easily.

Purple Spinel

Purple Fluorite

Type: Halide/calcium fluoride.

Colours: Purple, violet or lilac.

Availability: Relatively common.

Physical benefits: Assists with problems concerning bone tissue and bone marrow, ear infections, fluid retention, sinus, sore throats; building up resistance against colds and infections; headaches, all stress-related illnesses and childhood illnesses caught in later years.

Emotional healing: Deeply calming, purple fluorite assists with obsessions that are based in an inability to face reality.

Chakra: Brow.

Candle colour: Purple or lavender. **Fragrances:** Cherry blossom, sage, honeysuckle, lavender, sweet pea. **Practical uses:** Purple fluorite focuses thoughts on everyday responsibilities. **Workplace:** Useful for New Age practitioners to combine spirituality with practicality and realize they need to earn money. **Magical significance:** Good for helping young people who are not at home in the world to learn to work within its limitations. **Divinatory meaning:** What you want may not be practical, but you should not compromise your principles. **Zodiac:** Pisces. **Empowerment:** I seek the best in others.

In Ancient China, it was believed that purple fluorite would offer protection from evil spirits.

Purple fluorite crystal is said to become more protective the longer it is used and relieves stress, spiritual discomfort and physical blockages; therapeutic for those who hate being touched or examined. Take or wear purple fluorite for medical tests to enable you to keep calm and consider the options. The most peace-giving of the fluorites.

Lilac Kunzite

Type: Silicate/spodumene.

Colours: Lavender, violet and purple.

Availability: Less common than pink, but available from specialist crystal stores and online.

Physical benefits: Believed to help relieve menopausal symptoms of all kinds and for older women to resolve gynaecological problems that reduce libido; protect against chemical pollutants, also memory loss.

Emotional healing: Prompts acceptance that a former partner does not want to be with you, the need to constantly have company, also schizophrenia.

Chakra: Brow.

Candle colour: Lilac. **Fragrances:** Lavender, lilac, magnolia, violet. **Practical uses:** Keep kunzite in the car to ease tension of driving, also to counteract road rage. **Workplace:** A protective stone worn as jewellery, set near a computer or mobile phone to filter electromagnetic energies and being constantly on call. **Magical significance:** Increases intuitive powers; a good channel through which to increase awareness of spiritual guardians. **Divinatory meaning:** Think carefully before an expensive purchase. **Zodiac:** Pisces and Taurus. **Empowerment:** I do not need to spend money to be happy.

Keep all kunzite out of sunlight, as it fades. Because kunzite does splinter and because of the nature of the stone, you will rarely find flawless gems, but kunzite jewellery has a healing power that more expensive gems sometimes lack.

Wear lilac kunzite to attract a partner who is open to life's adventures. Lilac kunzite protects against harmful spirits. Carry lilac kunzite if you are visiting a house where an unhappy event has occurred.

Type: Silicate, microcrystalline quartz, often with organic matter or other minerals as inclusions.

Colours: Imperial jasper is swirling rich purple, with brown and beige; royal plume jasper has shades of purple with plume-like markings; other purple jaspers share the same properties.

Availability: Obtainable from specialist crystal stores or online.

Physical benefits: Claimed to assist with the relief of migraines, headaches, sinus, ongoing minor illnesses that contribute to a sense of malaise, epilepsy, the central nervous system, Parkinson's disease, brain-cell health, particularly in ageing, visual disturbances, pituitary problems, Type-2 diabetes.

Emotional healing: Reduces conflicting and contradictory feelings that make decision-making or clear action hard; helpful for personality disorders and fragile personalities.

Chakra: Brow and Crown.

Royal Plume Jasper

Candle colour: Purple. **Fragrances:** Acacia, cyphi, lotus, orchid, sandalwood. **Practical uses:** An excellent stone for single-parent households, to create cohesion and help the parent maintain authority during the teenage years without losing the counterbalancing affection. **Workplace:** Wear purple jasper for authority or if you are deputizing in an unfamiliar position or role where you have to supervise others; keep close when interviewing employees, to make the right decision. **Magical significance:** The noble jasper of spiritual wisdom; use when working with archangels or deity figures from different cultures; adopt as your power stone if you are studying a formal spiritual path such as druidry, Wicca or Astaru, or undergoing training in mediumship or any healing tradition. **Divinatory meaning:** You may be ask to choose between two people or situations, but you should not be pressurized into commitments you are not ready for. **Zodiac:** Scorpio and Sagittarius. **Empowerment:** I can disagree without being disloyal.

Royal plume jasper has slow-acting energies that build up over time; wear for long periods, especially on the ears or round the neck, to create an aura of wisdom and authority that can be helpful if you have a high-profile position and are still relatively young or inexperienced; also for older people whose experience is disregarded professionally or personallly.

Wear Royal plume jasper (also called purple jasper) or keep around the home if you are encouraging children to be more honest and unselfish or if you work with young people; helpful also if you are trying to give up habits that are bad for your health but you experience strong cravings.

Holding a purple palm or tumblestone improves memory if you are constantly rushing and forgetting names or simple facts, to slow the tempo of your mind and filter out irrelevancies.

Type: Purple form of crystallized quartz; the colour comes from the presence of manganese during its formation.

Colours: Pale lilac and lavender to deep purple, also purple and white (as chevron, see separate entry).

Availability: Common.

Physical benefits: Called the all-healer of people, animals and plants; this is believed to benefit migraines and headaches if you rub the forehead anti-clockwise, having dipped the amethyst in running water.

Emotional healing: Amethystos meant not to be intoxicated in Ancient Greek, and amethyst reduces addiction, obsessive compulsive disorder, hyperactivity in children and animals; called nature's tranquillizer.

Chakra: Brow.

Amethyst

Candle colour: Any shade of purple. **Fragrances:** Acacia, almond, lavender, fern, lily. **Practical uses:** Amethyst counteracts negative earth energies beneath a building; place amethyst near where plants will not grow or animals refuse to sit; use natural unpolished amethysts or geodes. **Workplace:** Make an amethyst elixir, from water in which a washed amethyst is soaked for a few hours; use in drinks and on pulse points for calm in a pressurized workplace. **Magical significance:** Protects against paranormal harm or ill-wishing and attracts good luck. Draw a sun image and the crescent moon over an amethyst in lavender incense smoke for both powers. **Divinatory meaning:** I do not need to reward myself any excesses of any kind to feel good. **Zodiac:** Aquarius. **Empowerment:** I can control my cravings.

Amethyst was worn by the first Christians and later bishops. It is the stone of St Valentine and of faithful lovers, because St Valentine is believed to have worn an amethyst ring engraved with an image of Cupid.

Wear as an engagement or eternity ring for fidelity or as a locket to call back lost love.

However, it was once believed that a person could call any love by speaking his or her name in an amethyst, even if that person was committed to another. An unpolished amethyst in the bedroom guards against nightmares and insomnia: rub anti-clockwise in the centre of the forehead, just above and between the eyes, the seat of the Third Eye; especially effective for children's night terrors or fears of the dark. It helps to protect against homesickness; enhances Reiki treatments.

Placed in the centre of the brow, it aids meditation and visualization; keep unpolished amethyst near other crystals to recharge them.

Charoite

Type: Phyllo or sheet silicate.

Colours: Purple, lilac and violet in swirling patterns.

Availability: Rare. The only place in the world it can be found is in the Chary River in Russia.

Physical benefits: Thought to improve cramps, high blood pressure, migraines, sleep problems including sleepwalking and sleep-talking, autism and Asperger's syndrome, ADHD.

Emotional healing: Fear of ill-health, pain and dying; acute loneliness and alienation from life and other people.

Chakra: Crown.

Candle colour: Lilac. **Fragrances:** Lavender, lilac and musk. **Practical uses:** For people who work away from home to maintain connection with their home, and for those who live alone and have little contact with others. **Workplace:** Assists adapting to new working practices. **Magical significance:** Strengthens telepathic bonds. Hold a tumblestone, close your eyes, picture the person you wish to contact and speak to them. **Divinatory meaning:** News of an old friend or love and a chance to make a positive connection. **Zodiac:** Pisces. **Empowerment:** I can feel at home anywhere.

Because charoite comes from an area of Siberia once associated with political prisoners, it has become a symbol of endurance and comfort in adversity; gives the courage to start over after repossession, for job loss in an area of high unemployment, for anyone in prison or in residential care; from boarding school to hospital.

A carers' crystal when nursing the sick or elderly and for adoptive parents to bond with children with behavioural difficulties. Wear charoite to prevent premonitions of disasters you cannot prevent, and to channel these powers into positive intuition.

Purple Tourmaline

Type: Silicate, sometimes called siberite. All tourmalines can appear transparent when viewed from the side and almost opaque from either end.

Colours: Purple from pale to deep violet.

Availability: Relatively rare.

Physical benefits: Believed to help to relieve chronic fatigue syndrome, Alzheimer's disease, epilepsy, migraines, pineal gland, thyroid, dyslexia and dyspraxia in children, neurological dysfunctions.

Emotional healing: Reduces compulsive behaviour and an inability to relax or socialize.

Chakra: Heart and Brow.

Candle colour: Violet. **Fragrances:** Cherry blossom, lavender, lilac, peach, violet. **Practical uses:** Wear to live in a more imaginative way. **Workplace:** For all writers, musicians, dream analysts, and life coaches. **Magical significance:** Hold purple tourmaline to connect with higher nature essences, particularly those connected with fragrances and flowers. **Divinatory meaning:** Use your imagination to plan a social event or party, as that will be far more effective than throwing money at it to make it truly memorable. **Zodiac:** Pisces. **Empowerment:** I see my future happiness clearly and so bring it nearer.

Purple tourmaline increases the power to visualize and so bring closer what is desired. Also helps you to tell children stories and to stimulate them to weave their own stories.

Give purple tourmaline as an expression of devotion to your partner and, before giving, picture the hopes you have for your future together. An anti-depressant, it is believed to enhance anti-depressant medication and talking therapies Wear purple tourmaline if you find it hard to trust your intuition.

Amesite

Type: Silicate, kaolinite-serpentine.

Colours: Lavender to more intense purple, also colourless, pink or green.

Availability: Rare

Physical benefits: Believed to improve skin conditions, including rosacea, acne, eczema, moles, warts, sun damage, stomach disorders, including nausea.

Emotional healing: Absorbs anger, also curbs swearing, whether deliberate or caused by Tourette's.

Chakra: Root and Brow.

Candle colour: Purple. **Fragrances:** Cherry blossom, hibiscus, juniper, lilac, violet. **Practical uses:** Speeds recuperation, whether from illness or bereavement. **Workplace:** Keep it in the workplace if you work through the night, then take it home and put it by your bed to allow you to rest. **Magical significance:** Amesite should be kept on a shelf; take it down weekly, and talk about the good fortune you need; then blow three times on it to endow it with your essence. **Divinatory meaning:** Trust your intuition to know when to take a chance. **Zodiac:** Capricorn. **Empowerment:** Good fortune surrounds me.

Amesite is a crystal that increases sensitivity to what is going on around you, so that you instinctively know the right time to act. It is one of the best charms for turning around your fortunes. Hold and say "My luck is changing for the better" every morning. Amesite is a natural energizer and blocks emotional vampires who drain you of energy or vulnerable people in your life who constantly demand your time and attention but whom you cannot abandon. Hold before choosing lottery numbers or any other random form of gaming.

Violan

Type: Purple/blue form of diopside, coloured by manganese.

Colours: Violet to pale blue, streaked with white and silver rutiles, also lavender to pink-purple.

Availability: Rare.

Physical benefits: Said to be an all-healer that works on the whole body; supposed to be especially good for muscles, reproductive system, communication difficulties including autism and Asperger's syndrome, to boost the immune system.

Emotional healing: Hold a large, flat palm to talk about a loss or abuse; good for opening up about subjects where silence maintains their power.

Chakra: Brow.

Candle colour: Lilac. **Fragrances:** Lavender, lilac, mimosa, peach, poppy. **Practical uses:** An anti-worry stone, especially in pale blue. Sit in candlelight after a stressful day stroking violan and let worries slip away. **Workplace:** A stone for all who work to alleviate poverty. **Magical significance:** The stone of dolphins. Put blue candles round your bath, hold your violan and play dolphin music; has a magical effect on children with Down's Syndrome. **Divinatory meaning:** A peaceful time when you have time to enjoy your own company or that of loved ones. **Zodiac:** Libra. **Empowerment:** I will value my quiet times more.

The stress-reducing energies of Violan make it popular with people who need an antidote to urban living. It is protective by radiating light to shield the home from undesirable influences.

Violan can also create an oasis of tranquillity in which you will not float away, but cope more efficiently with daily demands. Place violan in the bedroom if you suspect your partner is contemplating an affair, as a psychic reminder of the love you once shared and could share again.

Type: Silicate, quartz, treated with gold, niobium and indium at exceedingly high temperatures, giving it a permanent metallic sheen.

Colours: Indigo. It is slightly paler than its sky-blue cousin aqua aura.

Availability: Relatively rare, but so beautiful it is worth seeking out.

Physical benefits: Assists all problems of the head and neck, including thyroid glands, vision, memory, mental faculties; good for memory loss and for halting age-related effects on the mind, dysfunctional neural functions, epilepsy, helpful for brain damage after strokes, accident or viral infections.

Emotional healing: Good for releasing negativity that has built up over many years in a mentally abusive relationship; good for kidnap victims, hostages after their release, for dealing with near-death experiences and for anyone who has suffered violent crime.

Chakra: Crown, Brow, Throat and Heart.

Tanzanite Aura

Candle colour: Purple. **Fragrances:** Cherry blossom, lavender, lily, Solomon's seal, thyme. **Practical uses:** Helps adults and children who have learning difficulties or multiple disabilities and for anyone with Down's Syndrome to achieve their full potential. **Workplace:** Carry or wear this crystal if you are feeling challenged at work or surrounded by negative people; use also for finding an inspired solution for a situation that potentially has dire consequences for individuals or the workforce. **Magical significance:** A relatively new angel crystal that brings connection with Raziel the Archangel of mysteries and all esoteric knowledge. Hold tanzine aura and ask Raziel to remove bad karma holding you back from happiness. **Divinatory meaning:** Time is running short, but you will be offered what you have asked or applied for, or something as good. **Zodiac:** Sagittarius and Capricorn. **Empowerment:** There is always a way to fix things.

A crystal of many names, (such as tanzanite aura, tanzan aura or indigo aura) tanzine aura helps us to connect to our inner source of knowledge and the Akashic wisdom of humankind everywhere; improves intuition and sense of knowing the right answer in the everyday world as well as spiritually; brings the earthly and spiritual worlds closer to recognize and express our true qualities for success with integrity.

A valuable crystal for mediums, especially trance mediums, clairvoyants, psychic investigators and paranormal researchers looking for evidence acceptable to the scientific community of psychic powers and life after death; also for beginners in the psychic world to feel safe and for anyone leading a group meditation or guided visualization.

Type: Manganese phosphate.

Colours: Violet, pink-purple.

Availability: Obtainable from specialist crystal stores and online.

Physical benefits: Helps to alleviate problems with wounds, cuts, bruises, excessive bleeding, pulse rate, high blood pressure and other blood circulation and oxygenation, heart palpitations, adverse effects of radiation from any source, sunburn, acidity in stomach or urine, increase absorption of nutrients; improve brain functioning

Emotional healing: Encourages those that have self-imposed limitations or self-effacing tendencies to become more proactive; reduces victim and martyr complexes; also calms panic attacks.

Chakra: Crown and Brow.

Purpurite/Purperite

Candle colour: Purple or violet. **Fragrances:** Bergamot, bistort, iris, myrrh, sandalwood. **Practical uses:** Provides confidence when faced with speaking in public, whether the local school parents' meetings, a community group or professionally as a politician, lecturer or teacher, taking the lead at works' meetings or acting on the stage in an amateur or professional capacity. **Workplace:** Boosts leadership skills, financial matters and prosperity in general; guides the self-employed to know instinctively what is realistic and what will overstretch resources; use purpurite as a touchstone to tune in to your entrepreneurial abilities. **Magical significance:** Enhances the healing abilities of new and experienced healers, particularly with crystals. Hold purpurite before beginning healing to attune your fingers to crystalline vibrations and link healing via your Heart energy chakra and your Crown to your angels and guides; you will intuitively find the source of the problem once you begin healing. **Divinatory meaning:** Plan financially in advance if you can take advantage of what is a very good offer, but do not overstretch yourself. **Zodiac:** Virgo. **Empowerment:** I need not be over-modest.

Purpurite is formed by the alteration of the mineral lithiophylite. Purpurite is a pseudomorph, a mineral that has the shape of one mineral but has a different chemistry and/or structure.

This makes purpurite a powerful psychological and psychic tool for adapting to change in a very positive way: encourages leaving behind bad memories, particularly in openness to love.

It is a mineral that naturally attracts prosperity or its return after a reversal due to bad luck or illness; leads to a reinventing of the self and the adaptation of old skills to a new career at any age.

Purpurite opens natural psychic powers, notably clairvoyance and mediumship, bringing natural control of random psychic powers that may otherwise cause disturbing spirit energies.

Type: Copper carbonate with high copper content, occasionally with a copper sheen.

Colours: Bright azure blue usually mixed with dark blue.

Availability: Common.

Physical benefits: Useful for spine and rib-cage disorders, circulation, oxygenating the blood, brain-cell repair and so good for Alzheimer's, dementia and other degenerative brain-related disorders and for easing conditions related to ageing; detoxifying the system.

Emotional healing: Excellent for overcoming an inferiority complex, living only to please others and domestic bullying, whether by your children, partners, parents or friends who always know best.

Chakra: Throat and Brow.

Azurite

Candle colour: Bright blue. **Fragrances:** Clary sage, lotus, orchid, sagebrush, sandalwood. **Practical uses:** At home azurite lessens tensions between different generations, especially when sharing a home with three or more generations; for harmoniously bringing together different sets of grandparents and relations in the lives of families involved in step-parenting. **Workplace:** For long-term career plans, especially within a large or very structured organization and for succeeding in passing internal interviews or examinations; for careers in all government departments, museums, libraries and universities. **Magical significance:** A stone for connecting with sacred powers through religious music, for example Gregorian or Buddhist chants, choral music and hymns; also for healing using sound, especially drums, the didgeridoo, pipes and the voice. **Divinatory meaning:** Look to the long-term advantages and not immediate gain or results. **Zodiac:** Sagittarius. **Empowerment:** I can be noble in victory and defeat.

The Ancient Chinese called azurite the stone of heaven because they believed it opened celestial gateways. The Ancient Egyptians used the pigment to paint the protective eye of Horus, the young sky god, on their foreheads.

Azurite is a good crystal for older people living alone or in sheltered accommodation to maintain their independence, mental alertness and physical health.

A stone to encourage study, concentration and memory for older school children and university or college students; especially helpful for mature students to fit in study with other commitments; encourages study during retirement and also travel and relocating abroad for the over-fifties. A natural long-term prosperity bringer.

Crush azurite which is relatively soft in a mortar and pestle and roll nine copper coins in it. Tip the coins and mix into a pot with a sealed lid and replace every summer solstice, burying the old mix beneath a fruit- or nut-bearing tree.

Azurite

Type: Beryl, ring silicate.

Colours: Clear light blue, blue-green or aqua. The deeper and purer the blue, the more valuable the aquamarine.

Availability: Common.

Physical benefits: Believed to be useful for throat infections and voice loss, teeth and gum problems, bladder, kidneys, cystitis, lymph glands and fluid retention, colds, bronchitis and other upper respiratory difficulties, body and mouth odour, sunburn; helpful in hot climates to keep cool.

Emotional healing: Calms perpetually angry or bad-tempered people, mood swings and excessive toddler and teenage tantrums, heals the effects of over-judgemental parents who set impossible standards and panic attacks that linger as guilt and inadequacy in adulthood.

Chakra: Throat and Heart.

Aquamarine

Candle colour: Aquamarine. **Fragrances:** Lavender, lemongrass, musk, mimosa. **Practical uses:** Since aquamarine's power is enhanced by water, aquamarine elixir – water in which tumbled aquamarine has been soaked for a few hours – is a good gargle for sore throats; will help prevent all motion sickness and can be used in drinks to bring calm and prompt kind words by individuals or a group. **Workplace:** Keep or wear aquamarine that has been soaked weekly overnight in water collected during the waning moon period, to act as a problem solver at work to diminish obstacles or delays imposed by other people's inefficiency and to deflect unfair criticism and pettiness. **Magical significance:** Attracts and keeps good luck and love with you if worn or carried; leave aquamarine in moonlight on the night of the full moon and sprinkle it the next morning with water also left overnight in moonlight, to recharge its talismanic powers. **Divinatory meaning:** Go with what is on offer rather than waiting for the ideal opportunity or time. **Zodiac:** Pisces. **Empowerment:** I open my heart to forgiveness.

Its name from the Latin aqua marinus, 'water of the sea', refers to its sparkling ocean-like colour.

The stone of mermaids, aquamarine protects sailors and all who travel by or over water and minimizes travel delays; given as an eternity ring or other love token; prevents love quarrels, increases commitment and preserves fidelity so long as the waters of the earth flow.

A stone of natural justice through compromise and negotiations, pass aquamarine over any written complaints you receive or before you send them; wear or carry aquamarine if you have to visit your child's school because of a complaint against or by them or if resolving a neighbourhood dispute especially over boundaries or car parking. Touch the stone and say, "May wise justice prevail."

Aquamarine will give you quiet courage and clear reasoned words if you normally back away from confrontations; good for learning to swim at any age.

Blue Holley Agate

Type: Chalcedony, crypto-crystalline quartz.

Colours: Blue, blue-lavender to rich violet, may be banded.

Availability: Found in specialist crystal stores and online.

Physical benefits: Believed to assist with the relief of headaches, ear problems and deafness, nausea and muscles, especially in the neck, made stiff by tension, fevers, high blood pressure, skin allergies, eczema, acne, sore throats, voice loss, coughs, dementia, dizziness, degenerative eye conditions, recurring mouth ulcers (use elixir).

Emotional healing: Brings acceptance of what is lost.

Chakra: Throat.

Candle colour: Blue. **Fragrances:** Bergamot, lavender, lilac. **Practical uses:** If you are a worrier, hold it over your navel, analyse the worry and if it cannot be fixed, put it aside, either to be resolved when you can or dismissed. **Workplace:** Helps focus if you get distracted by emails, your phone or surfing the net. **Magical significance:** Hold at the base of your throat to release your clairaudient powers. **Divinatory meaning:** You will be relieved from old worries; do not replace them with new ones. **Zodiac:** Virgo. **Empowerment:** I am at peace within myself and the world.

Blue Lace Agate

Type: Oxide, cryptocrystalline quartz.

Colours: Pale blue, sometimes brighter blue with white or even brown threads of colour.

Availability: Common.

Physical benefits Thought to relieve sore throats and aching or swollen glands in the neck by soaking a crystal in water for eight hours, removing crystal and gargling (p.20); also to be good for thyroid problems, high blood pressure and soothing skin allergies and tension-related headaches.

Emotional healing: Calms stress-related conditions and communication difficulties.

Chakra: Throat.

Candle colour: Pale blue. **Fragrances:** Fern, lavender, star anise, vervain, vetivert, yarrow. **Practical uses:** Protects those who help others or who act as carers for the disabled, sick or very old; also for parents of small children, to give them patience. **Workplace:** Set in a bowl on the table for any workplace meeting. **Magical significance:** Assists you to hear the words of your guardian angel by activating your psychic hearing abilities. **Divinatory meaning:** Express the feelings that are in your heart honestly and you will receive a favourable response. **Zodiac:** Aquarius. **Empowerment:** I speak the truth with kindness.

Though holley agate is similar to its sister, blue lace agate, each piece has its own unique angelic connections to heal you and those you love by allowing healing to pass through the crystal, even if you have never healed before. Natural blue holley agate in the centre of a table encourages conciliation in workplace or domestic disputes since it enables all present to understand the viewpoints of others; ask each person to hold it as they speak. Keep a tumblestone by your bed to improve dream recall and bring peaceful sleep.

In pre-Christian times in Scandinavia and Denmark, blue lace agate was dedicated to Nerthus the earth mother. Carry or wear blue lace agate to improve your communicative abilities, if you struggle to express your emotions without getting upset. Will also lower the volume of communication, so keep a bowl of crystals in the home if you have noisy children, a howling dog or screeching cat. Put blue lace agate on pictures of armed forces personnel you know to keep them safe.

Type: Silicate/pyroxene, jadeite with mineral inclusions.

Colours: Pale to mid blue.

Availability: Relatively common.

Physical benefits: Claimed to assist with children's eye and ear problems, adenoids, tonsils, chronic headaches, all stress-related conditions and those made worse by stress, tinnitus in adults, methods of sound healing and laser treatment; healing birds and marine life.

Emotional healing: For anyone overwhelmed by burdens, wearing a blue jade pendant or necklace breaks down problems to more manageable steps; for breaking the cycle of serious sleep deprivation and chronic insomnia.

Chakra: Brow and Throat.

Blue Jade

Candle colour: Blue. **Fragrances:** Bergamot, bluebell, lavender, lotus, rosemary. **Practical uses:** If you, a partner or any family members are stressed or angry, each person should in turn hold a communal large blue jade worry palm stone for five minutes and speak; everyone else must remain silent and listen; calming for inter-generational conflicts and for family conferences. **Workplace:** Hold a blue jade tumblestone in the centre of your brow for a minute to create your private oasis of calm; enables your mind to escape from a noisy environment to prioritize and plan; ideal if you work from home with small children. **Magical significance:** Buy a blue jade statue, a religious icon, an angel, a deity figure from another or older culture such as Kwan Yin the Chinese mother of blessings or a healing dolphin or dove; keep it in your special crystal place or your bedroom to bring you instant peace by holding it in times of stress. **Divinatory meaning:** An unresolved injustice or misuse of power against you will at last be resolved in your favour. **Zodiac:** Libra. **Empowerment:** I value others' opinions, but do not have to accept them.

A stone of wisdom, loved by healers who use sounds such as drum, bell, rattle or voice healing; for those who are struggling with the earlier stages of Reiki or another touch therapy, blue jade brings a breakthrough in understanding. Wear blue jade if you are seeking justice against a corrupt official or in personal litigation such as a divorce or custody battle where the other person is lying.

A helpful stone for Indigo children or those who are at odds with the educational or social system to accept life can sometimes be unfair, while not losing their idealism and innocence.

If a person embroiled in a long-running dispute with you is too bitter to accept reconciliation, surround a photo or their last correspondence with blue jade stones; burn a blue candle next to the stones monthly to isolate the issue from spoiling your life.

Blue jade on an outdoor window ledge encourages wild birds.

Type: Variety of zoisite, epidote (calcium aluminium silicate).

Colours: Blue to blue-violet.

Availability: Becoming rarer and more valuable, as supply is expected to dry up in around 15 years.

Physical benefits: Said to strengthen the immune system; detoxify the body and improve vitality; promote the regeneration of cells, skin and hair; preserve youthfulness; protect against the side-effects of medical or surgical intervention.

Emotional healing: Calming and soothing, even a tiny piece of tanzanite is good for adults to overcome communication difficulties.

Chakra: Third Eye or Brow Chakra, Crown and Throat.

Tanzanite

Candle colour: Blue or purple. **Fragrances:** Lemon verbena, lilac, mimosa, vanilla, violet. **Practical uses** Helps bring out the other side of your personality; if, for example, you are normally serious, you will discover quite spontaneously your fun side emerging. **Workplace:** If there seems no solution to a problem, tanzanite will help to reveal one; good for career changes. **Magical significance:** Meditate while holding this crystal to make contact with your spirit guides and to connect with deceased loved ones, especially in the early days after the bereavement. **Divinatory meaning:** Trust your intuition – it is guiding you in the right direction, even though others may be blinding you with facts and figures to the contrary. **Zodiac:** Gemini, Libra and Sagittarius. **Empowerment:** My hidden abilities unfold in unexpected ways.

Tanzanite was originally discovered in 1967 at the foot of Tanzania's (hence the name) Mount Kilimanjaro. Popular legend regards tanzanite as a gift from the gods, since its discovery is attributed to Masai cattle herders who first saw the blue stones after brown zoisite crystals on the ground were burned in a bush fire caused by lightning.

Indeed, some tanzanite on sale is heat-treated brown zoisite. Tanzanite is an excellent crystal to wear if you are beginning to explore your psychic powers, as it is very protective and enables your clairvoyant Brow chakra to open gradually so you are not overwhelmed by psychic impressions before you are more experienced.

Circle your tanzanite clockwise in the centre of your brow to open your third eye and psychic powers, and against the clock to close it so you can relax.

Blue Andean Opal

Type: Hydrated Silicon Dioxide, common opal, displaying no iridescence.

Colours: Blue, softly coloured with a pearl like sheen.

Availability: Relatively rare as true Andean opal (some are dyed substitutes).

Physical benefits: Thought to be beneficial for exhaustion, ME, metabolic imbalance, absorption of minerals, assists weight loss, childbirth and the days afterwards and childhood illnesses.

Emotional healing: Releases creativity for those forced into conformity at any early age by family, community or religion.

Chakra: Throat

Candle Colour: Blue **Fragrances:** Cedar, copal, lavender, lilac. **Practical uses:** Give or wear blue opal to move towards commitment and to overcome fear of loss of freedom. **Workplace:** Wear and have around a workplace where the exchange of ideas is discouraged. **Magical significance:** Where it seems a present problem is linked to a past world or experience, whether actually or symbolically, blue opal will heal the problem. **Divinatory meaning:** Believe in your own abilities or you cannot expect others to believe in them. **Zodiac:** Libra **Empowerment:** I know where I am on my life path.

Blue opal is the negotiators' stone, used to express sticking points clearly, whether in a relationship or in the workplace.

A stone of courage if you seem to be facing injustice from faceless officialdom to find a more amenable source of support and not to be overwhelmed. Buy as a gift for young women who are teased by peers about their appearance.

Blue Coral

Type: Organic, branching calcareous skeletons of sea creatures.

Colours: Light to mid blue with white spots or smudges.

Availability: Relatively common.

Physical benefits: Said to promote the speedy healing of fractured bones; relieve rashes, acne, burns, high blood pressure, recurring seasonal illnesses such as hay fever, sunburn, sunstroke; help balance minerals in body.

Emotional healing: Helpful for women during or after the menopause to overcome fears of lack of desirability and to welcome the serenity of growing older.

Chakra: Throat.

Candle colour: Blue. **Fragrances:** Kelp, lavender, lemon, lotus. **Practical uses:** Protects travellers, especially those who travel by boat. **Workplace:** The stone of communication for anyone in industries where tact is essential. **Magical significance:** Light blue candles in the bathroom, play dolphin sounds and lie in your bath holding blue coral, to relax totally. **Divinatory meaning:** You may disagree strongly with someone's opinion, but now is not the time to speak out; wait and the opportunity will come to turn matters your way. **Zodiac:** Pisces. **Empowerment:** I do not fear being carried by the tides of life.

Blue coral is sacred to Diwata ng Dagat, the goddess of the sea in the Philippines, one of the main areas from which blue coral comes. When worn as jewellery, many women find it gives them a calm strength in daily life and that it counteracts PMS.

Men also relate well to blue coral as it brings out an ability to let go of irritations. Keep as blue tumblestones in your home if you have small children, to protect them from water-related hazards.

Lapis Lazuli

Type: Rock, formed by multiple minerals including lazurite, sodalite, calcite and pyrite.

Colours: Rich medium to royal blue, purple-blue, green-blue with gold flecks (pyrites).

Availability: Relatively common.

Physical benefits: May help with the endocrine and nervous systems, headaches, migraines, lymph glands, bone marrow, ears and nasal passages; reduce pain and inflammation; believed to be good for autism or Asperger's syndrome.

Emotional healing: Helps take responsibility for self, rather than blaming others for missed opportunities.

Chakra: Throat and Brow.

Colour: Blue or gold. **Fragrances**: Cyphi, geranium, lotus, magnolia, orchid. **Practical uses**: If you want fame, wear or carry lapis lazuli to auditions. **Workplace**: A career stone, lapis attracts promotion. **Magical significance**: Place lapis in the centre of your brow to open your Third Eye. **Divinatory meaning**: It is the right time to get yourself noticed in a positive way: a high-profile presentation of your talents is the key. **Zodiac**: Virgo and Libra **Empowerment**: I reach for the stars.

Covellite

Type: Copper sulphide, minor ore of copper.

Colours: Almost black, indigo blue or midnight blue, with a blue metallic iridescence.

Availability: Rare but obtainable from some specialist crystal stores and online.

Physical benefits: Considered good for ears, eyes, throat, sinuses, mouth, cellular disorders; helpful in cancer treatment; helpful when diagnosis or prognosis is uncertain or treatment is causing bad side effects.

Emotional healing: For anyone with or living with a person with an inflated ego, to get in touch with reality.

Chakra: Throat and Brow.

Candle colour: Dark blue. **Fragrances**: Cedar, cyphi, sandalwood, ylang ylang. **Practical uses**: Good for any physical activity where strength and stamina are needed; for mental endurance when one is overloaded with responsibilities. **Workplace**: Brings constructive and creative solutions to problems. **Magical significance**: The best stone to hold during rebirthing, where a therapist guides you back through your own birth process to overcome blind spots. **Divinatory meaning**: One of those times when the greater good has to take priority over personal desires; in the longer term this will benefit you. **Zodiac**: Libra and Sagittarius. **Empowerment**: I can wait a little longer for fulfilment.

Lapis lazuli has been mined in the mountains of Afghanistan for 6,000 years, and was amongst the first gemstones to be used as jewellery. Lapis Lazuli is a stone of truth, encouraging truth in the spoken and written word and honesty in the spirit.

Wear it for all forms of deep communication, for example when you have a heart-to-heart with a loved one. Lapis lazuli is also considered a stone of friendship and can help bring about harmony in any relationship and make it long-lasting.

Covellite, sometimes called covelline, is regarded as a crystal of small miracles to turn dreams into reality and bring hope where there is none, combining Earthly effort with what is sometimes called divine intervention.

Wear it as you remind yourself of the success that is coming, and to overcome a period of despondency or acute anxiety. Use also in healing or psychic work if there are blocks, or if knowledge is getting in the way of spiritual insight and messages.

Ajoite Quartz

Type: Copper silicate mineral, often found as an inclusion in white quartz.

Colours: Blue, blue-green and turquoise.

Availability: Extremely rare, but worth searching for.

Physical benefits: Deemed effective for the relief of rheumatoid arthritis, muscular dystrophy, hormone imbalances related to PMS, post-natal depression and menopausal mood swings. Use at beginning and end of life as a general healer for body, mind and soul.

Emotional healing: Brings to the surface emotional wounds; helpful on victim support programmes, intensive psychotherapy and when confronting perpetrators of abuse in a controlled setting.

Chakra: Heart, Throat, Brow and Crown.

Candle colour: Turquoise. **Fragrances:** Acacia, benzoin, copal, sandalwood. **Practical uses:** Powerful against jealousy and bitterness. **Workplace:** A crystal that encourages the highest standards; good for journalism and lawyers. **Magical significance:** A stone for connecting with kindred spirits by sending out telepathic signals. **Divinatory meaning:** Someone is being unfair; concentrate on getting the best outcome for you. **Zodiac:** Virgo. **Empowerment:** I have my feet in the earth as I journey upwards.

Considered to be one of the most effective healing crystals for emotional as well as physical illnesses.

Ajoite quartz enhances the properties of plant medicines, especially herbs you grow yourself. Set ajoite quartz in the centre of a layout of copper and quartz-based crystals to increase peace and harmony within and beyond your home; put a map of your immediate locality beneath the cloth on which you make your layout.

Blue Quartz

Type: Silicon dioxide, clear quartz that contains various inclusions which give the blue colour.

Colours: Pale to mid blue, or as bright cobalt blue in artificially grown Siberian quartz.

Availability: Depends on type of blue quartz.

Physical benefits: Blue quartz is maintained to strengthen the immune system, thyroid, throat, glands, spleen, hay fever, absorption of minerals, heat stroke, sunburn and burns.

Emotional healing: Assists those who absorb hurtful behaviour by others into themselves rather than speaking out, so creating stress that manifests as physical symptoms.

Chakra: Throat.

Candle colour: Blue **Fragrances:** Eucalyptus, lavender, lilac, tea tree. **Practical uses:** Soothes excitable adults and children. **Workplace:** Blue quartz makes us strive for excellence, whether raising a family or studying. **Magical significance:** Helps develop mediumship abilities. **Divinatory meaning:** You may feel overwhelmed by work, but this will pass if you take time for yourself. **Zodiac:** Libra. **Empowerment:** I find fulfilment in doing things well.

All blue quartz brings harmony and order to chaotic situations and people and clarity to muddled thinking; excellent therefore for sorting accounts or creating organized and focused reports or proposals. It is very lucky for anyone trying to make a career in music and is a power stone for music lovers, from rock to opera.

Blue quartz enhances the effect of reciting prayer beads, chanting mantras, singing sacred songs or listening to religious music.

Type: Aluminium silicate.

Colours: Blue to blue-green, striated, sometimes streaked with black; can be shiny, almost pearly, sometimes with white.

Availability: Rare in transparent gem quality, but more common in other forms.

Physical benefits: Said to promote mobility, cells, tissues, bone marrow, throat, voice, neurological system; assist with strokes particularly with improvement in speech and mobility, blockages and constrictions anywhere in the body.

Emotional healing: Brings tranquillity as a result of breaking free from emotional blackmail, possessiveness and self-imposed guilt.

Chakra: Throat and Brow.

Blue Kyanite

Candle colour: Blue. **Fragrances:** Bergamot, cedar, iris, juniper, peppermint. **Practical uses:** If your child does not get asked to parties or is ignored in play parks, keep bladed kyanite near their outdoor or school clothes at home to make them more popular; helpful if your child is physically different in any way or has difficulty in integrating. **Workplace:** Hold or wear blue kyanite when addressing a group or leading a seminar or team meeting; sharpens in situ communication skills, particularly in answering questions and improvising when needed. **Magical significance:** Hold blue kyanite and ask aloud for your heart's desire, from the first day of the month till the next first of the month. On the second, leave your kyanite where someone else can find it to pass on luck. **Divinatory meaning:** You will have cause to speak your mind. But do not waste words on those who will not listen. **Zodiac:** Pisces. **Empowerment:** I understand my life's purpose.

If you have lost your way in life or are doing totally the wrong thing, create an empowerment grid by laying out rows of small kyanite blades on a table radiating from a central kyanite in six different directions.

Each night, touch and walk in your mind a different kyanite path from the centre, letting images and ideas appear spontaneously; start with the first row you set. After six days, wait a day and begin again, repeating the row sequence until you are back on track and no longer need the grid.

Touch the centre of your brow with a kyanite blade to access forgotten childhood memories or to recall a word or name that eludes you. Blue kyanite, like black, does not accumulate or store negative energies and, along with citrine, these are the only crystals that do not require cleansing.

Blue kyanite has all the aura- and chakra-cleansing properties of black kyanite, but is much more active in energizing (p.195). Blue kyanite can also assist in cleansing and clearing other crystals.

Type: Silicate/nesosilicate, zircon, usually free of inclusions.

Colours: Light pastel to deep intense blue with subtle greenish undertones; sometimes heat-treated.

Availability: Relatively common.

Physical benefits: Said to help relieve allergies, particularly connected with breathing, due to air-borne pollen, spores, dust mites or fur; long-term memory loss resulting from trauma or accident, blood clots, strokes; improve eyesight, optical nerve, cataracts, voice loss especially due to stress; be good for healing women over 50 of all problems.

Emotional healing: Blue zircon brings peace of mind where faith has been shaken by betrayal from someone who was deeply trusted; restores self-esteem if the guilty party tried to offload all the blame.

Chakra: Throat.

Blue Zircon

Candle colour: Blue. **Fragrances:** Honey, honeysuckle, hyacinth, lavender, lilac. **Practical uses:** A traveller's crystal on long journeys, especially to countries where there has been unrest or terrorism incidents; good for discovering the real place and culture; also for successful long-term contracts abroad and emigration or naturalization in a new land. **Workplace:** Deeper blue brings understanding to those who study history, old languages, archaeology and traditional forms of medicine; helpful for mature students and for learning or retraining while holding down a job or caring for family, for tracking down missing beneficiaries, for custodians and guides at old sites and buildings. **Magical significance:** Blue zircon is said to lose colour just before a potential crisis, not to predict the inevitable but to advise wise caution in current projects or dealings with people you do not know very well; check the small print and information given and all will be fine. The zircon is reflecting uncertainties in your own inner radar. **Divinatory meaning:** Look to tried-and-tested forms of information and consult experts in area of potential dispute or uncertainty. **Zodiac:** Sagittarius. **Empowerment:** I draw strength from my ancestors.

The Roman historian and naturalist Pliny the Elder, who lived between AD 23 and 79, compared blue zircon's colour to hyacinth flowers; this name is occasionally applied to blue zircon though it is more usually now called starlite in the gem trade. Blue zircon has been prized in jewellery for hundreds of years and was beloved by Victorians as large ornate stones in rings and brooches, notably around the 1880s.

An excellent crystal for connecting with your ancestors, researching family origins and visiting ancestral areas or homelands. Blue zircon is a wise-woman stone, worn by older women following a spiritual path or those who choose to remain alone after a separation or bereavement; a lovely gift for a woman on the birth of her first grandchild or great-grandchild, especially if she is, for whatever reason, the oldest surviving woman in a family, to mark her role as matriarch. Blue zircon is a symbol of wise justice; set it on papers for planning permission for extensions or new homes, for all legal matters and for resolving official disputes.

Shattuckite

Type: Copper silicate.

Colours: Deep blue, turquoise-blue, sometimes with azure or brown streaks.

Availability: Relatively rare, but obtainable from specialist crystal stores and online.

Physical benefits: Thought to help with ear, nose and throat, particularly infections and inflammations such as swollen glands, tonsillitis, mouth, tooth and gum disorders, coagulation of blood, arthritic and rheumatic conditions.

Emotional healing: Releases within you the need to hold on to the past – especially useful in getting over a relationship breakdown or waiting for someone who will never commit.

Chakra: Throat and Brow.

Candle colour: Blue. **Fragrances:** Cherry blossom, copal. **Practical uses:** Enables those in love to reveal their feelings. **Workplace:** Wear this crystal when you need to communicate clearly. **Magical significance:** To improve your automatic writing, hold shattuckite in the hand you do not write with and a green-ink pen in the other. Words will flow on to the paper from your angels. **Divinatory meaning:** Time to say goodbye to the past rather than waiting for what you know will never happen. **Zodiac:** Aquarius. **Empowerment:** I can share my deepest feelings with those I love.

Shattuckite was a traditional magical healing and love charm among indigenous people in Arizona and parts of Africa. Use shattuckite to enable you to interpret information and wisdom you receive and to protect you from feeling threatened by entities from other dimensions during channelling or mediumship. Shattuckite can resolve past-life issues that prevent you from moving forward in present-life spiritual development and help you to bring back strengths and strategies from past worlds to assist in present-day dilemmas.

Falcon/Hawk's Eye

Type: Quartz embedded in crocidolite with a little of the hydrated oxide that gives tiger's eye its golden colour.

Colours: Blues, gleaming, also green-greys (stones like green tiger's eye are sometimes called cat's eye).

Availability: Relatively common.

Physical benefits: Considered beneficial for circulation, cholesterol, long-distance sight, sore throat, pharynx, laryngitis, sinuses, nasal congestion, motion sickness especially by air, medical tests, chemotherapy.

Emotional healing: Hypochondria and excessive terror of harm to or death of healthy loved ones; self-limiting behaviour.

Chakra: Throat.

Candle colour: Blue. **Fragrances:** Agrimony, anise, honeysuckle. **Practical uses:** Safe travel, especially when backpacking and by air. **Workplace:** Hawk's or falcon's eye should be taken to gain promotion or new job interviews to inspire success. **Magical significance:** Hawk or falcon's eye is a charm against ill-wishing, especially from people we may not know are feeling malicious towards us, such as a jealous ex-lover. **Divinatory meaning:** A sudden intuitive insight into a situation will overcome a problem where logic has failed. **Zodiac:** Sagittarius. **Empowerment:** I can travel in my mind to where I most wish to be.

Use when meditating in sunlight outdoors to reach a tranquil state of mind and guide you into spiritual realms for visions and insights of a personal or even global nature. A crystal that tells you instantly by its feel if someone is lying.

Place hawk's eye on your Brow chakra and relax for a few minutes to bring a new state of calm, when you are feeling stressed. Good for remote viewing, i.e. seeing people and places beyond the range of the physical eye, for clairvoyance and for out-of-body or mind travel.

Type: Silicate, microcrystalline quartz, often with organic matter or other minerals as inclusions.

Colours: Various shades of blue, often swirls of blue with darker patches or veins; can be artificially treated to accentuate the blue.

Availability: One of the rarer jaspers.

Physical benefits: Thought to encourage recovery from trauma, severe accident or a major illness where a person has to learn to live again; recovery of speech faculties and relearning language after a stroke or accident; the relief of post-traumatic stress syndrome, especially for those returning from war; recovery from brain and eye surgery; assist with problems of ageing.

Emotional healing: Called the warrior stone, jasper in its blue shades strengthens self-determination in a fight against an addiction that has proved resistant to therapy and rehabilitation.

Chakra: Throat and Brow.

Blue Jasper

Candle colour: Dark blue. **Fragrances:** Benzoin, bergamot, lemon, lemongrass, myrrh. **Practical uses:** A stone for studying any subject where there are a lot of facts, particularly if you have to combine study with work; benefits older people taking evening or weekend courses or examinations for a later-in-life qualification or career change, to concentrate when they have other responsibilities. Workplace: The perfect anti-stress crystal for anyone who has a lot of responsibility for the well-being of others or whose decisions affect the lives of others; for magistrates, judges, solicitors and barristers, examination adjudicators, anyone responsible for administering funds for charities or grants, for priests and for counsellors. **Magical significance:** Hold a piece of blue jasper jewellery if you would like to discover a wise teacher spirit-guide to help you in your career, studies or spiritual learning path; close your eyes and ask that your guide will appear in your dreams and meditations; wear the jewellery during sleep, quiet contemplation and while learning or studying, and you will feel supported. **Divinatory meaning:** You may need to decide how far you can help someone close who is in trouble without making things too hard for yourself. **Zodiac:** Sagittarius. **Empowerment:** I speak the truth without fear.

Blue jasper brings the courage of one's convictions to speak out against injustice or prejudice and to risk unpopularity to protect the vulnerable; a stone for making a difference through effectively and practically supporting charitable ventures and working towards a fairer society; let older children and teenagers carry or wear blue jasper to resist being led into unwise behaviour or risky situations in order to gain popularity.

A tiny blue jasper on an animal collar prevents smaller animals being bullied and deters aggressors without the smaller animals showing aggression themselves.

Blue jasper is a stone linked with nobility of spirit and purpose, and was once worn by royalty and clergy to indicate their possession of wisdom and higher ideals; wear it if you work in a situation where others are less than honest, to stand by your principles. Keep a dish of tumblestones at home to teach children how to tell the truth without being hurtful, for blue jasper represents honesty but with kindness.

Cavansite

Type: Hydrous calcium vanadium phylosillicate, in clusters or balls.

Colours: Bright or aqua blue.

Availability: Rare, but available in some specialist crystal stores and online.

Physical benefits: Considered good for pain relief through the release of endorphins, for athletes to give stamina and a sense of well-being; to regularize pulse and metabolism; an all-healer that acts to prevent diseases returning.

Emotional healing: A crystal that replaces anxiety with calm, sorrow with joy, and bad memories with hope and plans for the future.

Chakra: Throat and Brow.

Candle colour: Bright blue. **Fragrances:** Bergamot, lemongrass, mugwort, musk, vanilla. **Practical uses:** Cavansite will act as a spiritual filter in your home, absorbing tension. **Workplace:** Keep cavansite in your workspace; ideal if you have to motivate a team. **Magical significance:** An excellent crystal for more advanced clairvoyants, healers and mediums who feel blocked. **Divinatory meaning:** Rather than dealing with an obstructive person, find an alternative method. **Zodiac:** Libra. **Empowerment:** I will reach my goal one way or the other.

A relatively recently discovered crystal, cavansite is another stone offered by Mother Earth as an antidote to the fast pace of modern life.

If you heal, counsel or conduct one-to-one sessions in any capacity, from giving mortgage advice to social care, keep cavansite on your desk or in your consulting room to transform negative feelings from the client into cooperation.

A good crystal for all who speak first and think afterwards, to prompt reflection and an awareness of consequences.

Lazulite

Type: Phosphate; also found as inclusions in quartz.

Colours: Blue, from azure or dark to pale blue to bluish green.

Availability: Rare.

Physical benefits: Thought to help to relieve burns, scalds, sunburn, bruises, problems with teeth and gums especially wisdom teeth, liver, pineal gland, spleen; promote healthy growth in children; counteract communication disorders, Tourette's syndrome, Asperger's syndrome, hyperactivity and ADHD.

Emotional healing: A crystal of purity for all who were robbed of their innocence at a young age, to believe again in the innate goodness of most people.

Chakra: Brow.

Candle colour: Dark blue. **Fragrances:** Anise, bay, benzoin, cherry blossom, honey. **Practical uses:** Lazulite should be carried or worn at any legal disputes, pay rise or work-condition discussions. **Workplace:** Wearing lazulite brings serenity if you are constantly undermined by someone with less ability but a big ego. **Magical significance:** Set lazulite on pictures of world leaders to send peaceful feelings, and light blue candles round the pictures. **Divinatory meaning:** Say no once and for all, unless you really mean yes maybe. **Zodiac:** Libra **Empowerment:** I respect the opinions of others, even when I do not agree.

Lazulite should not be confused with blue and gold lapis lazuli, nor with lazurite, one of the main constituents of lapis, though they are all similar colours. Lazurite is a silicate, whereas lazulite is much rarer and a hydrous magnesium aluminium phosphate. Lazulite is a good stone for men who find it hard to settle into a relationship or family life. Keep lazulite in quartz at home if you have rebellious teenagers and do not wish to enter constant disputes. One of the best crystals to work through a mid-life crisis in either sex.

Blue Apatite

Type: Phosphate that is present in teeth and bones.

Colours: Blue, light to bright to dark, sometimes within the same crystal, colourless grey, brown, pink and violet, occasionally with white veins, also green (p.251).

Availability: Common.

Physical benefits: Said to strengthen teeth, gums and bones; aid broken bones and damaged cartilages; soothe teething babies if placed by crib; ease chronic illnesses; improve appetite, but also to control cravings.

Emotional healing: Reduces irritability; encourages a healthy attitude to eating, helping to attain and maintain a healthy weight; overcomes fears of dental treatment.

Chakra: Throat and Root.

Candle colour: Blue. **Fragrances:** Cedar, rose-wood, sandalwood, vanilla, vetivert. **Practical uses:** Keep blue apatite with credit card bills or near the phone when negotiating with debt counselling agencies. **Workplace:** Helpful in times of unemployment, forced early retirement or a reduction in working hours to seek alternative work. **Magical significance:** Owning a blue apatite increases synchronicity. **Divinatory meaning:** A period of slow improvement rather than feast or famine will follow. **Zodiac:** Gemini and Libra. **Empowerment:** I do not need to over-indulge to be satisfied.

Apatite is a mineral that forms the tusks of large wild animals such as elephants; a stone associated with animal conservation. It improves memory and concentration and so is believed to be good for study; helps to establish a realistic timetable for any projects.

Good for business consultants, account or investment managers. Apatite often tells us what we know deep down, but have not acknowledged.

Euclase

Type: Beryllium aluminium hydroxide silicate.

Colours: Blue, blue-green, light green, yellowish, colourless.

Availability: Rare.

Physical benefits: Considered helpful for arthritic pain, muscle tension, muscle pain and cramps, pain and tension anywhere in the body, cuts, scratches, bruises, inflammation and swellings, blood-vessel constrictions, hardening of arteries, headaches caused by sinus problems, difficulties in swallowing, anti-spasmodic, anti-bacterial and antiseptic.

Emotional healing: Reduces unhealthy lifestyle patterns.

Chakra: Throat.

Candle colour: Blue. **Fragrances:** Cinnamon, copal, saffron, sage, thyme. **Practical uses:** Associated with happiness and good health, attracts sociable people; excellent for workaholics; for spontaneous getting together with people. **Workplace:** For all logical matters; for architects, creators of sacred buildings, designers, town planners, marketing, physicists and all who teach sciences or maths. **Magical significance:** Excellent for healers, if held near the base of the throat of a nervous patient; opens the channels to healing by allowing light and hope to enter the mind and flow into the body. **Divinatory meaning:** Be precise as careless mistakes could be costly. **Zodiac:** Libra and Sagittarius. **Empowerment:** Happiness is there for the making.

A crystal of infinite possibility; give a euclase crystal to young people embarking on further education or first job to welcome what life brings and overcome obstacles; eases communication to persuade defensive or emotionally closed people to accept new ideas and changes. Carry euclase for exploring sacred sites; to understand the minds of the original creators and appreciate the sacred geometry.

Type: Hydrated copper silicate. Gem silica is chrysocolla agatized in chalcedony quartz (p.152).

Colours: Mixed blues and bluish greens; occasionally turquoise.

Availability: Common.

Physical benefits: Maintained to be beneficial for digestion, hip joints and hip replacement, arthritis, rheumatism, metabolism, PMS, painful menstruation, foetal health, labour pains, thyroid, high blood pressure, blood sugar levels, diabetes particularly Type 2, blood disorders, lungs.

Emotional healing: Helps men to show their vulnerable feelings and recovery from violence by partners of either sex.

Chakra: Heart and Throat.

Chrysocolla

Candle colour: Turquoise. **Fragrances:** Lily, lotus, orchid, vanilla, violet. **Practical uses:** A protective stone against obstructive neighbours, malice via the computer or mobile phone, or spiteful remarks about age or physical appearance by creating a reverse energy force field that makes attackers feel the shamefulness of their words. **Workplace:** Chrysocolla helps older women to cope with dignity and resilience with the societal emphasis on youthful beauty and the trend of replacing older women in the media or publicity-related areas of life with younger, less experienced women. **Magical significance:** For world peace, create a chrysocolla grid: set a circle of very small chrysocolla round a picture of world leaders meeting together, with four rows of chrysocolla radiating from a larger chrysocolla in the middle of the picture, touching the circle at the four compass points. **Divinatory meaning:** You may need to be generous to someone you dislike to avoid hurting their feelings. **Zodiac:** Taurus **Empowerment:** I can use my life experiences to guide others.

Chrysocolla is the stone of wise women everywhere, worn or carried in a charm bag to help older women express their knowledge and experience through writing, painting, music, crafts or acting; give chrysocolla to first-time grandmothers and great-grandmothers to help them balance their new caring role with their own need for freedom and independence; good for all older people who may feel nervous at home at night if living alone.

Chrysocolla is the symbol of musicians; use as a charm to learn new musical instruments at any age or to join a choir, orchestra or theatre group and to have the confidence to perform in public;. Chrysocolla is excellent for people of any age who act childishly, throw tantrums or refuse to accept responsibility, to bring maturity without losing a sense of spontaneity; hide the stone in the luggage or glove box of the car of a partner who is undergoing a mid-life crisis and has a roaming eye.

Aqua Aura

Type: Clear crystal quartz bonded with molten gold.

Colours: Electric or sky blue.

Availability: Relatively common.

Physical benefits: Thought to activate a sluggish immune system; relieve diseases of the immune system and genetic disorders, asbestosis, autism, Asperger conditions, cerebral palsy, diseases and malfunctioning of the brain; detoxify the body; resist new strains of influenza; reduce swellings and growths.

Emotional healing: For clearing away secrecy, helpful for adopted children to find out about their birth; use in crystal healing layouts to bring the body, mind and spirit into harmony.

Chakra: Throat.

Candle colour: Bright blue. **Fragrances:** Lavender, sage, sagebrush, thyme, violet. **Practical uses:** Use to shield against the negative effects of the modern world. Keep with credit cards and when going online for financial transactions to protect against identity theft. **Workplace:** Supportive for working all hours to make your dream happen; good the travel industry; for those responsible for pharmaceutical research and development. **Magical significance:** Use as a pendulum to channel automatic writing from angels and guides by holding the pendulum in the hand you do not write with and allowing words to flow on to paper. **Divinatory meaning:** It may be better to be honest about doubts now. **Zodiac:** Aquarius. **Empowerment:** My positive thoughts can affect events.

Aqua aura expands the boundaries of possibility and lateral thinking, and transforms restrictions to reaching out into opportunities: wear to break through factions, closed doors, glass ceilings and written rules. Wear to enable your true self to shine through and to attract a lifestyle and people who value you for your unique qualities; for spiritual and emotional rather than material gold and to make that once-in-a-lifetime leap. A cluster will encourage openness and the expression of affection and appreciation of others among an emotionally constipated family.

Blue Calcite

Type: Calcium carbonate.

Colours: From pale to mid blue, sometimes with white veins; resembles blue ice in natural form.

Availability: Common.

Physical benefits: Believed to assist with neuralgia, sore throats, hormonal headaches, the menopause and hot flushes, skin rashes, high blood pressure, burns and scalds, toothache and mouth abscesses and ulcers, sunburn; increase the speed of wound healing.

Emotional healing: Creates awareness of when you are overdoing things and need to rest or pace yourself.

Chakra: Throat.

Candle colour: Pale blue. **Fragrances:** Bluebell, magnolia, rosemary, violet. **Practical uses:** A natural soother, set by the crib of teething or colicky babies and small crystals beneath the four corners of the bed of a sensitive pet. **Workplace:** The crystal of clear, calm communication; keep a dish of tumblestones in a workplace where colleagues are over-hyped. **Magical significance:** Hold a polished sphere or rough-cut calcite in your hands as you gaze into water. You may see images in the water or in your mind about what you need to know. **Divinatory meaning:** Do not be provoked to reveal confidential information. **Zodiac:** Pisces **Empowerment:** I will not over-react to stressful situations.

Blue calcite protects the home and business premises against intruders; set unpolished pieces on road-facing indoor window ledges and put a small tumblestone in your bag or pocket or in a pouch with your mobile phone or laptop, to deter thieves. Good for calming nerves in the days before a special event. Assists memory and encourages clear and inspiring words. Have blue calcite on a negotiating table or at a public meeting to soften opposing views and hostile comments; good for defusing tensions over racial or religious differences.

Type: Silicate (calcium borosilicate hydroxide).

Colours: Bright sky blue, sometimes with veins.

Availability: Common.

Physical benefits: Believed to help with disorders concerning back, spine, neck, teeth and gums, sore throat and tonsilitis (good for recurring infections), balance and mobility, gives stamina and strength to recover from a long illness, exhaustion or depression.

Emotional healing: Gives determination to succeed in those who have given up on life because of long-term unemployment, bad housing or difficulties in education.

Chakra: Throat and Root.

Blue Howlite

Candle colour: Blue. **Fragrances:** Acacia, cedar, copal, sage, sandalwood. **Practical uses:** For selling a house, place small pieces of howlite on inner window ledges to attract buyers and create favourable first impressions; carry with you or wear when viewing a new home to buy or rent, to convince landlords and vendors of your seriousness and reliability. **Workplace:** An empowering stone for young people who leave school without clear idea of a future career; for adventurers and long-haul travellers of any age; helps career advisers, trainers and assessors to maintain enthusiasm and focus, and anyone trying to improve qualifications. **Magical significance:** A key dream crystal that adapts to the needs of the user; brings peaceful sleep, happy dreams, lucid dreaming (awareness of being in a dream), astral travel; contact with spirit guides, angels, deceased relatives, power animals or shamanic worlds. Hold it before sleep and picture the sleep or dream experience you need. **Divinatory meaning:** Do not feel you are accepting second-best if you are not offered what you want; you will uncover unexpected benefits. **Zodiac:** Sagittarius. **Empowerment:** There is hidden treasure in unexpected people and places.

Howlite, dyed or stained blue, unusually for an artificially coloured stone, adds to the strength of white howlite the rich blue qualities of the stone it most resembles, turquoise. It is particularly effective for empowering women and young people, as it is gentler and more gradual in its energy build-up than turquoise; especially helpful for a mother of twins, triplets, a premature infant or a sick child who needs constant care.

A good stone for improving whatever you already possess through the mixture of perseverance and

vision, whether imaginatively extending or renovating your home or living space, taking evening classes to increase your qualifications, or upgrading and restoring equipment, furniture or vehicles; wear or carry blue howlite if you have a career or keen amateur interest in antiques or restoring old buildings.

Blue howlite encourages clear speech in children or adults who mumble or are self-conscious about asking or answering questions, particularly in a formal or test situation.

Type: Silicate, a copper mineral, often found in clusters, attached to or encrusted with other minerals such as apophyllite or dioptase (p.142 and p.292).

Colours: Light blue to deeper blue, always as a pure colour.

Availability: Rare.

Physical benefits: Thought to cleanse wounds; fight infections; relieve bruises, bones and muscles, skin tags, moles, warts, growths and cysts, problems with the vocal cords, larynx, tonsillitis, adenoids, sinuses, HIV and AIDS.

Emotional healing: Overcomes self-limiting attitude and narrow horizons of possibility due to restrictive upbringing and negative life experiences that prevent or hinder efforts to attain full potential.

Chakra: Throat.

Kinoite

Candle colour: Light blue. **Fragrances:** Bay, geranium, sagebrush, thyme, vervain. **Practical uses:** Helps you to maximize your strengths and recognize your weaknesses; coming to terms with what you can and cannot do physically if you are not as mobile as you were or have a disability, a progressive illness or temporary physical restrictions on your life. **Workplace:** Kinoite provides insight as to the right path of action to take during any policy-making decisions where you are responsible for the future well-being and work practices of others; good for all negotiators, company lawyers, policy administrators or civil rights workers. **Magical significance:** Improves your ability to connect with and enhance your own spirituality; during meditation or angel channelling, opens clear contact with higher realms to receive clairaudient messages as words in your mind. **Divinatory meaning:** A chance to improve your economy but the potential rewards will involve incredibly hard work in the months ahead. **Zodiac:** Pisces **Empowerment:** I strive for excellence.

This very rare crystal is named after the Jesuit explorer Eusebio Francisco Kino (1645–1711). It is a minor ore of copper found in only a few locations, one of which is the famous Christmas Mine in Arizona. A stone of love goddesses in many cultures, it represents both slow-growing and longer-lasting love and the love of humanity that may guide users towards voluntary charity work or lawful and peaceful campaigns for the rights of the downtrodden and mistreated. It

raises your spirituality to higher levels, bringing about feelings of love and compassion for yourself and those around you, and gives the impetus to translate compassion into practical action. Its calming qualities overcome problems with sleep: place kinoite crystals at the head and foot of your bed to achieve deep and healing sleep. It will also assist in the everyday physical world to assimilate ideas and to be able to communicate honestly and decisively.

Kinoite

Blue Aventurine

Type: Microcrystalline quartz.

Colours: Pale to medium blue, also dark blue.

Availability: Common.

Physical benefits: Considered to relieve sinus problems, nasal congestion, eyesight, migraines and headaches, allergies, colds, coughs, congestion, insomnia; release toxins from the body; good for any degenerative disease.

Emotional healing: To bring peace to a troubled soul, speak your fears into a small blue aventurine. Breathe on it three times and cast it in water from a hilltop or bury it.

Chakra: Throat.

Candle colour: Blue. **Fragrances:** Coconut, lavender, lime, vanilla. **Practical uses:** Makes desired travel plans happen. Put one in your luggage so a journey goes smoothly. **Workplace:** Blue aventurine is a crystal of leadership and helps to win respect. **Magical significance:** Blue aventurine helps you to become aware of your spiritual guardians. **Divinatory meaning:** A chance to travel comes unexpectedly; you may regret it if you turn it down. **Zodiac:** Libra and Sagittarius. **Empowerment:** I open myself to infinite possibility.

The gentlest of aventurine colours, blue aventurine is sacred to Raphael. Hold a flat aventurine palm or worry stone, wear as jewellery or drink as an elixir before any sports competition for a calm, focused performance; also before any public speaking or musical event.

Blue aventurine brings or restores a desire for adventure at any age; a natural room atmosphere cleanser: spray blue aventurine-infused water as an environmentally friendly room spray.

Benitoite

Type: Cyclosilicate/barium titanium silicate.

Colours: Blue, purplish blue, some with white bands, sometimes colourless or yellowish, fluorescent.

Availability: Relatively rare, but very beautiful.

Physical benefits: May assist with mobility, joints, muscles, ligaments, throat problems, eyesight, glaucoma, insomnia, nightmares, cosmetic or plastic surgery, liposuction, Botox, any beautifying surgery or treatment, burns, scalds, high blood pressure, fevers, skin inflammation, scarring.

Emotional healing: Brings love of self, self-belief and improved body image; for all who have been rejected because of their physical appearance or a disfigurement, to know their true value.

Chakra: Throat.

Candle colour: Blue. **Fragrances:** Lilac, lotus, orchid, poppy, sandalwood. **Practical uses:** A great joy-bringer that encourages the user to make the most of every moment; wear benitoite jewllery when you attend any social event. **Workplace:** For all who work as fitness instructors, and who practise energy therapies. **Magical significance:** Benitoite, especially when used with moldavite, enhances astral travel. **Divinatory meaning:** A time for inspired ideas and the means to put them into practice. **Zodiac:** Sagittarius. **Empowerment:** I enjoy every new day and experience.

Benetoite was originally thought to be a form of blue sapphire because of its intense blue colour when it was discovered in 1906. However, the crystals are small, and are in fact a rare mineral associated with the equally rare neptunite and natrolite. Wear benetoite for launching plans and for activity holidays such as rock-climbing or pot-holing. Benitoite inspires natural courage but not foolhardiness; helps overcome the fears of pushing yourself to the limits.

Blue Spinel

Type: Magnesium aluminum oxide, coloured by iron or cobalt; artificial spinels are not as good for power or healing.

Colours: From mid to dark blue.

Availability: Rare in natural cobalt blue, obtainable from specialist jewellery and crystal stores and online.

Physical benefits: Thought to assist with high blood pressure, skin, hair, spine, whole-body healing; detoxify blood; claimed by some to be helpful for cancers of upper body, weight loss, eyesight, fevers, burns, throat constrictions, teeth, gums, memory, energy and stamina; long life, health in old age.

Emotional healing: Rejuvenates and restores joy; good if previous attempts to kick bad habits failed; claustrophobia.

Chakra: Throat.

Candle colour: Sky blue. **Fragrances:** Bergamot, carnation, cedar, lemongrass, lilac. **Practical uses:** Wear on first day of the week, month, season or year to give new resolutions a boost. **Workplace:** Wear for success in work-related study and for moving up a career path. **Magical significance:** Traditionally used in magic in healing spells for strength and a long, healthy life and to attract money and success in learning; wear or choose a special tumblestone as your personal luck-bringer; have it with you always close to your skin to amplify its powers. **Divinatory meaning:** A health worry is unfounded, but you should start a healthier lifestyle. **Zodiac:** Sagittarius. **Empowerment:** I will not panic over trivialities.

A very positive stone, reawakening new enthusiasm and revives sexual desire with your partner. A blue spinel ring offers reassurance that the giver will never break your heart or desert you for another; if alone, buy one for yourself to attract a lifelong considerate partner. Blue spinel tumblestones focus the mind for study in the build-up to an examination and revive impetus for an assignment; use for safe and pleasurable air travel or air-related activities. A crystal for anyone who is 60-plus to plan new activities.

Blue Wernerite

Type: Silicate; wernerite is the old name used for the mineral.

Colours: Pale to rich blue, sometimes with pyrite specks.

Availability: Found in specialist mineral stores and online.

Physical benefits: Believed to help with veins and arteries, high blood pressure, circulation overload, nervous breakdown, stiff neck or swollen neck glands, glandular fever, Hodgkin's lymphoma, headaches caused by tension, toothache and gum health, persistent ear infections.

Emotional healing: Prevents us sabotaging our own efforts to break free of bad habits and then blaming others or circumstances; assists in taking responsibility..

Chakra: Throat.

Candle colour: Sky blue. **Fragrances:** Eucalyptus, lavender, lily, rosemary, vanilla. **Practical uses:** A stone to encourage children to persevere in learning new skills; give to those leaving the nest to encourage self-reliance. **Workplace:** The crystal of setting your heart and mind on a goal and persisting until it is attained. **Magical significance:** A crystal for connecting with angels and spirit guides through written messages; place on a bible, book of poetry or sacred writings, hold in one hand and open the book anywhere with the other; run crystal down page until you feel you have reached the message and read. **Divinatory meaning:** You know more than you realize. **Zodiac:** Libra. **Empowerment:** I know the answer.

Blue wernerite (also called scapolite) brings a calm response to any challenge; removes irritability and encourages a balanced reaction to apparent injustice. Use if you are building up expertise. Wear if you are applying for a leadership position or want to start your own enterprise to get resources; good also for expansion into a business partnership with someone whose skills complement your own or for developing two separate but parallel careers which eventually you can merge into a larger venture. Helps all shared ventures.

Blue Moonstone

Type: Feldspar.

Colours: Shimmering pale blue.

Availability: Rarest of the moonstones.

Physical benefits: Claimed to benefit the lymphatic system, sinuses and sinus-related headaches, stomach, pancreas and pituitary gland; relieve bladder weakness and bedwetting in older children, insomnia, snoring, travel sickness.

Emotional healing: Blue moonstone should be worn to bring peace when you have been working hard for a prolonged period and cannot switch off.

Chakra: Sacral.

Candle colour: Blue. **Fragrances:** Eucalyptus, jasmine, lavender, magnolia, mimosa. **Practical uses:** A blue moonstone ring makes a wonderful gift for a love where there have been many uncertainties. **Workplace:** For anyone involved in health-service provision. **Magical significance:** According to myth in Asia, the best blue moonstones are washed up by the tides once every 21 years. **Divinatory meaning:** A lucky opportunity, so say yes even if the timing is not ideal. **Zodiac:** Cancer. **Empowerment:** I have moments of pure joy.

The stone of the traveller. A sphere with bluish tints should traditionally be set on a yellow cloth on the night of the full moon and used for divination. Hold the moonstone, best in moonlight or, if not, silver candlelight, and let the light play on the surface.

You may see images, mainly in your mind, and hear words to explain the significance of the image, generally referring to events within three moon months. Give to to any drama kings or queens in your life, to take them and life less seriously and to react calmly to minor crises or upsets.

Vivianite

Type: Hydrated iron phosphate.

Colours: Blue, green and colourless, darkens on exposure to light to deeper blue or even purple.

Availability: Relatively rare.

Physical benefits: Said to benefit teeth, bones, osteoporosis, brittle bones, pain relief, memory loss owing to accident or trauma, senile dementia, balance and mobility, pigmentation problems, melanomas.

Emotional healing: Transformative for those who feel ill at ease in their own bodies and are excessively self-conscious; makes growing older a welcome and not a frightening experience.

Chakra: Throat and Sacral.

Candle colour: Turquoise. **Fragrances:** Fuchsia, hibiscus, lavender, juniper, rosemary. **Practical uses:** The stone of patience; for all carers of the sick or disabled and elderly relatives. **Workplace:** Keep wrapped in a dark cloth to make gradual but significant changes in what seems like an intractable situation. **Magical significance:** A natural piece of vivianite will connect with ancient worlds through visualization and meditation. **Divinatory meaning:** An older person may be causing you problems, but this will ease if you can keep your sense of humour. **Zodiac:** Cancer and Capricorn. **Empowerment:** I take treasure from my ancestry to build my future.

Vivianite is not a mineral to be kept on display as exposure to light, especially sunlight, will darken it to almost blackness. So use vivianite for healing or empowerment and then keep it in a dark place or wrapped in dark silk to ensure its vibrant colours are not lost. Vivianite strengthens the healing power of any fossil such as ammonite or the brown, green or yellow earthy agates or jaspers, when a problem is very deep-seated and resistant to treatment.

Type: Silicate. All tourmalines can appear transparent when viewed from the side and almost opaque by looking down the long axis from either end. This phenomenon is called pleochroic.

Colours: Blue, medium to dark and more rarely turquoise.

Availability: Relatively rare, but obtainable from specialist jewellers, crystal stores or online.

Physical benefits: Deemed to relieve problems with the pulmonary and immune system, neck, thyroid, pituitary, adrenal and all major glands, throat, eyes and ears, kidneys, bladder, regulation of the fluid balance in the body.

Emotional healing: Insomnia and nightmares; heals childhood trauma, injury or abuse; coming to terms with buried emotions and memories from the past when you cannot have justice.

Chakra: Throat and Third Eye.

Indicolite/Blue Tourmaline

Candle colour: Blue. **Fragrances:** Dill, lavender, lemon verbena, lilac, neroli. **Practical uses:** Encourages an open, broad-minded attitude and tolerance of the differences and weaknesses of others; a good counter-balance to organizations or families who demand conformity and to inflexible individuals who try to change you. **Workplace:** Use to increase commitment to and passion for your work or to change your career to one that is close to your heart; if a manager or employer helps you to motivate workers; good for charity and aid workers. **Magical significance:** Makes spells more powerful and improves psychic vision; associated with the blue ray that is one of the main spiritual energies sent from angelic realms. **Divinatory meaning:** You will receive good advice from an unexpected source. **Zodiac:** Libra and Scorpio. **Empowerment:** I open my mind to guidance from higher realms.

A gemstone coveted by collectors and jewellers due to its beauty. It also provides increased energies of protection, which are extremely useful when carrying out any spiritual or healing work.

Healers use blue tourmaline because of its ability to open the channels to higher realms, assisting the healer to find and understand the cause and facilitate its healing.

Place this gem under your pillow to help you sleep well, have insightful dreams and vivid dream recall. A stone of fidelity that makes a wonderful wedding or wedding anniversary gift.

Above all it gives the ability for clear and honest communication, with the courage to speak from the heart about things that we are passionate about.

Type: Phosphate with traces of copper and iron.

Colours: Blue-green, sometimes mottled.

Availability: Quite rare and highly prized if natural and untreated; otherwise widely obtainable and often found as jewellery.

Physical benefits: Assists in dealing with problems of the brain, eyes, ears, neck and throat, respiratory and lung disorders, viral infections, migraines and headaches, allergies such as hay fever, arthritis, rheumatism and problems with balance.

Emotional healing: Calms the mind and eases depression; for jet lag and fears of flying; good for empowering yourself if you feel a victim or suffer prejudice or bullying.

Chakra: Throat.

Turquoise

Candle colour: Blue or green. **Fragrances:** Cedar, honeysuckle, pine, sage, sandalwood. **Practical uses:** Overcomes writer's block, attached to a collar, bridle or cage; turquoise prevents animals straying or being stolen and makes horses sure-footed and obedient to their riders. **Workplace:** A stone of clear communication when you are giving information, whether verbally or in writing; a stone for all who seek promotion or leadership positions or work in the law or for local or central government. **Magical significance:** A stone of wisdom, to access knowledge from your unconscious mind and what has been called by the 20th-century psychotherapist Jung the collective unconscious of humanity in all times and places. **Divinatory meaning:** A need for honesty and clearing up misunderstandings to set you free. **Zodiac:** Sagittarius and Capricorn **Empowerment:** I will not fail or fall.

Turquoise has been prized for thousands of years as a symbol of wisdom, nobility and the power of immortality, among the Ancient Egyptians, Aztecs, the Native North Americans and the Ancient Chinese; the death mask of Tutankhamun was studded with turquoise.

Turquoise adorned the mosaic masks dedicated to the gods, the fabulous inlaid skulls, shields and power statues of Moctezuma, the last ruler of the Aztecs in the early 16th century, as a symbol of his power and

wealth and to acknowledge his position as an immortal deity. Though often considered a symbol of male power, Hathor, the Ancient Egyptian mother goddess, was called Lady of Turquoise; turquoise empowers men and women equally. Worn as jewellery or carried in a pouch, turquoise is a talisman for immense good luck, success, money, fame, ambition and creativity.

Above all a crystal of justice, both for obtaining it through the legal system and for fair and equal treatment in every area of life.

Turquoise

Type: Silicate.

Colours: Blue, from pale to deep blue.

Availability: Quite rare if natural, usually the paler shades, but obtainable from quality sources.

Physical benefits: Said to be a body-vitalizing gem, blue topaz is believed to aid whole-body regeneration and delay the ageing process; disperse effects of negative energy, from whatever source, that may weaken resistance to illness; good for metabolism, thyroid, throat, eyes, ears, nasal passages and menopausal symptoms.

Emotional healing: Controls feelings of anger by bringing hidden emotions to the surface in a calm way so that they can be dealt with; good for speech and communication problems, especially in younger people and for emotional balance.

Chakra: Throat and Third Eye.

Blue Topaz

Candle colour: Blue. **Fragrances:** Bergamot, chamomile, eucalyptus, lavender, sandalwood. **Practical uses:** Put blue topaz under your pillow to prevent nightmares and psychic attack, also touch one when you need people to reveal secrets or correct misinformation. **Workplace:** Blue topaz, when worn or carried, inspires leadership skills, facilitating clear communication and natural authority whatever your current position. **Magical significance:** Blue topaz is a good luck charm if kept in a small blue bag. Hold the crystal to the crescent moon and say, "May my fortunes be changed for the better by the time the moon is full." Repeat every night and on the night of the full moon, catch the moonlight in the blue topaz if possible and say "Good fortune be mine." Do the same, changing the words, for a matter on which you need justice. **Divinatory meaning:** Speak the truth with confidence and you can take control of the situation and turn matters to your advantage. **Zodiac:** Sagittarius and Libra, **Empowerment:** I will receive the justice I deserve.

Golden or imperial topaz is the stone of the sun and blue signifies the moon; the two together in a small pouch or one in each hand balance logic and intuition, power and gentleness, and the creative side of your mind with the analytical.

Blue topaz is a stone that helps you to be honest but with gentleness and so to end relationships or friendships going nowhere with the minimum of hurt.

A tiny blue topaz on a chain or in a pouch helps sensitive children and teenagers to cope with teasing with good humour.

Good for bird conservation.

Larimar

Type: Pectolite, chain silicate of volcanic origin.

Colours: Blues, light blue, sky blue, green-blue and deep blue, occasionally turquoise, streaked with white and sometimes red spots.

Availability: Relatively rare.

Physical benefits: Believed to be helpful for thyroid and thymus glands, chest, throat and head pains, infections and fevers; to enhance alternative treatments particularly those involving heat, light and water.

Emotional healing: Overcomes fear of doctors, hospitals, injections and surgery, and encourages clear and confident communication with health personnel.

Chakra: Throat.

Candle colour: Blue or silver. **Fragrances:** Balm of Gilead, cherry blossom, clary sage, eucalyptus, sandalwood. **Practical uses:** The best stone if you are having problems getting together with your soul mate because of other relationships, fears or unresolved issues. **Workplace:** Use a larimar worry stone if you are anxious about job losses. **Magical significance:** A crystal associated with earth, sea, sky and dolphins; wearing the stone brings out innate healing powers. **Divinatory meaning:** A peaceful but not dull time ahead. **Zodiac:** Pisces **Empowerment:** I can heal myself and the situation.

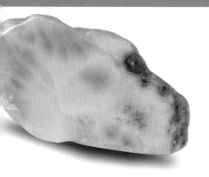

Larimar (also known as blue pectolite) is believed to channel ancient wisdom from Atlantis during meditation or sleep; hold as you sit on the seashore anywhere to reconnect with the ebbs and flows of your inner tides. Use to remove stress by connecting with the healing power of dolphins, through visualization and dolphin call music as you sit in the bath surrounded by blue candles; add water in which larimar has been soaked; sprinkle elixir at home to bring calm and heal disagreements or over items you buy that have belonged to someone else to make them your own.

Blue Selenite

Type: Fibre gypsum, hydrous calcium sulphate, with pearl-like lustre, very similar to its sister satin spar (p.149).

Colours: Blue and glowing.

Availability: Relatively rare.

Physical benefits: Deemed to be good for fevers, inflammation, burns, spine, extreme hormonal swings, Attention Deficit Disorder, hyperactivity, communication disorders, bi-polar condition; an excellent balancing crystal.

Emotional healing: Assists anyone who speaks before they think and so gives offence; gives a sense of objectivity and detachment from self, mixed with heightened empathy in those who misread social signals.

Chakra: Throat and Brow.

Candle colour: Blue. **Fragrances:** Cornflower, eucalyptus, jasmine, mimosa, myrrh. **Practical uses:** Blue selenite is very good for seeing through illusion, as it combines assessment with the intuitive awareness of this stone. **Workplace:** The blue form of selenite quietens a racing mind. **Magical significance:** Like blue moonstones, blue selenite is especially lucky in a month where there are two full moons, called a blue moon month. **Divinatory meaning:** A time to get back in touch with your feelings and instincts. **Zodiac:** Cancer. **Empowerment:** I reach for what is possible to attain.

Blue selenite is a stone that has the full intuitive and imaginative power of a moon crystal, but combines with it connection with intellectual knowledge. It is an excellent business crystal for balancing integrity and people-skills with financial acumen; ideal for anyone setting up or trying to improve the turnover of a therapy or a new New Age business. The best crystal for producing or making meditation or New Age music CDs.

Angelite

Type: Anhydrite/sulphate, a form of celestine that has been compressed for millions of years.

Colours: Pale or mid to celestial blue, lilac or violet; also white or grey violet; occasionally flecked with red.

Availability: Common.

Physical benefits: Said to help with infections, healing using sound, relief from throat inflammations, balancing the thyroid, indigestion and stomach acidity, nervous rashes, intestinal and abdominal problems, internal parasites.

Emotional healing: Use for channelling healing from angels via your hands and voice; good for any communication difficulties; weight-related problems.

Chakra: Throat.

Hold Angelite to connect with your guardian angel and when praying for guidance from your personal deity form. Acts as a psychic shield against ill-wishing, but will not harm the sender, so can be used if a nasty person is psychologically ill or deeply unhappy. A crystal that helps you speak the right words in any situation; keep with you if you are finding it hard not to say what you really think, but know you cannot. Give to anyone moving home to connect with their home guardian and bring blessings.

Blue Barite

Type: Sulphate, very soft.

Colours: Pale blue crystals.

Availability: Found in specialist crystal stores and online.

Physical benefits: Believed to assist with lowering blood pressure; soothing fevers, stress-related throat disorders; pain relief; protect against effects of radiotherapy and prolonged chemotherapy; good for physical shock; for mother and baby after a prolonged birth or one where there was surgical intervention.

Emotional healing: Releases blocked feelings and words that prevent you from sharing your deeper emotions.

Chakra: Throat.

Blue barite is a stone for healing the earth and the skies; helpful for global warming and the ozone layer; a crystal of self-sufficiency, it motivates you to live in a more ecologically sound way. A good stone for anyone in a war zone. Will give you confidence to live life your own way and to teach your children ethics so they can make wise decisions. Blue barite in a home can help a couple to make reasoned decisions. Each person should hold the crystal and be allowed to speak while the other must listen without comment for their turn.

Cobalt Aura

Type: Molecules of pure cobalt bonded by a natural electric charge to clear quartz.

Colours: Brilliant shades of metallic blue, violet and gold mixed.

Availability: Found in specialist crystal stores and online.

Physical benefits: Believed to help combine the body's own self-healing powers with higher healing; help if illness is unresponsive to treatment or a patient is exhausted by prolonged medical intervention, absorption of vitamins and minerals, functioning of enzymes, kidneys, pancreas, liver, spleen, myelin sheath; processing of glucose.

Emotional healing: Even a small piece of opens doors and both calms and inspires agoraphobics.

Chakra: Throat.

Candle colour: Sky blue. **Fragrances:** Almond, cedarwood, lemon, lime. **Practical uses:** Makes every day seem special; even a small cluster in the home removes restlessness and discontentment. **Workplace:** Cobalt aura removes the constraints that may hold us back from expressing ourselves through work. **Magical significance:** Like other combined aura crystals, cobalt aura brings special moments of joy. **Divinatory meaning:** A good time for redecorating your home. **Zodiac:** Sagittarius. **Empowerment:** I will bring more colour into my daily world.

Cobalt aura is one of the generations of New Age crystals, created from natural minerals using the best of modern techniques, to join the old and new worlds in harmony. They contain natural minerals and elements, and so can be used for healing as well as empowerment and protection; indeed, they gain powers the separate components do not possess.

Cobalt aura increases natural clairvoyance and healing powers; a cluster held regularly will ease the transition between personal spiritual work and formal training or turning professional. Aids creative cooking.

Blue Fluorite

Type: Halide, calcium fluoride.

Colours: Blue, either single colour or banded or as Blue John typically dark-blue/blue-purple and yellow banded.

Availability: Relatively rare.

Physical benefits: Seen as good for the immune system, inflammation and infection of the throat, bedwetting, earache and infections, improved speech after an accident, brain trauma or illness, Alzheimer's and senile dementia.

Emotional healing: The best stone for those who find it hard to accept everyday reality, to open up channels of communication.

Chakra: Throat and Brow.

Candle colour: Blue or purple. **Fragrances:** Hyacinth, honeysuckle, lavender, lilac, wisteria. **Practical uses:** Blue fluorite is a stone of gentle honesty in all dealings; carry with you to soften dealings with those who are brutally frank. **Workplace:** Blue fluorite brings logical thought to cut through waffle and move meetings on where people argue in circles. **Magical Significance:** Hold single colour blue fluorite while cloud scrying. **Divinatory meaning:** You are right to question the motives of someone unduly secretive. Be cautious **Zodiac:** Pisces **Empowerment:** I will speak honestly without giving hurt.

The most famous blue fluorite, Blue John, a zoned or banded fluorite, is found only near Castleton in Derbyshire, England, and has at least 14 different banded or veined varieties. The Blue John colouring, a variety of banded blue-purples, greys and yellows, was created naturally by exposure to oily films millions of years ago. Good for resolving official or legal matters that have been slow-moving or delayed; helps children to distinguish between fantasy and truth. Place on base of your throat and on your brow to encourage clairaudience and clairvoyance.

Blue Azulicite

Type: Feldspar, a variety of sandine.

Colours: Transparent blue to grey-green, iridescent.

Availability: Found in specialist crystal stores and online.

Physical benefits: Considered to benefit eyesight, optical nerves, digestive disorders, liver, dizzy spells, malfunctioning brain waves, epilepsy, ear infections and problems, sore throat, laryngitis and tonsillitis, adenoids, facial muscles, Bell's palsy, wisdom teeth, gums and jawbone.

Emotional healing: For anyone with a learning, speech, hearing or communication disability, to overcome fears and blocks as well as prejudices and obstacles created by the indifference or lack of understanding of others.

Chakra: Throat and Brow.

Candle colour: Sky blue. **Fragrances:** Fuchsia, lilac, moss, musk. **Practical uses:** Encourages letting go of things that are outworn or which hold sad memories. **Workplace:** Keep azulicite near computers for re-trieving missing data. **Magical significance:** Powerful in establishing connection with essences and spirits from other dimensions; use if you wish to contact a deceased relative but feel blocked. **Divinatory meaning:** A time to preserve what is of beauty and worth in your life and possessions and let the rest go. **Zodiac:** Libra. **Empowerment:** I need quality not quantity in my life.

A crystal of clarity of ideas, and so brings new input and directions at work, socially and in rela-tionships; use azulicite at work for professionalism and avoiding personal emotions getting in the way of fairness; deters factions among groups of people or organizations; encourages positive words and praise as motivation rather than criticism and so is a good family crystal with teenagers who may try to provoke confrontation, to avoid heavy-handed parenting.

Blue Chalcedony

Type: Cryptocrystalline quartz.

Colours: Shades of soft blues; can be banded.

Availability: Relatively common.

Physical benefits: Thought to encourage fluid flow within the body to avoid the building up of pressure; relieve fluid retention, hay fever and other plant allergies that cause respiratory problems, Alzheimer's and dementia, childhood illnesses, gallstones, inflammation.

Emotional healing: May help with obsessive compulsive disorder, Tourette's syndrome, autism- and Asperger's-related obsessions, bi-polar disorder.

Chakra: Throat.

Candle colour: Pale blue. **Fragrances:** Almond blossom, valerian. **Practical uses:** Blue chalcedony is a calming travel crystal. **Workplace:** Assists learn-ing foreign languages. **Magical significance:** In the thirteenth and fourteenth centuries, blue chalcedony was sometimes engraved with the image of a man with his hand lifted to bring good luck in legal matters. Draw the image with your finger in the air over a blue tumblestone and keep with documents to protect against misfortune. **Divinatory meaning:** A legal dispute will be settled in your favour. **Zodiac:** Libra, Cancer **Empowerment:** I accept that justice will be done.

Called the deep-blue pool crystal, blue chalcedony assists meditation if your mind is naturally over-active: gaze into the depths of your crystal and listen to your wise inner voice speaking in your mind. A stone of peace and peacemaking; a blue chalcedony in the home will encourage stillness and calm if you have a family who are each fighting for their place in the pecking order. Wear blue chalcedony if you have a daily stressful journey to work, have to take small children shopping or have to shop in your lunch hour.

Celestite

Type: Strontium ore/sulphate.

Colours: Pale to mid blue, also white, occasionally green, looks like ice crystals:

Availability: Common.

Physical benefits: Believed to assist with the relief of problems with thyroid, eye, ear, throat, mouth, headaches, speech, digestive disorders caused or made worse by stress; protect against intestinal parasites and infections and fevers.

Emotional healing: Acute anxiety states, fear of travel, agoraphobia; fear of crowds, speaking in public; even in front of a few people, eating in front of others; excessive blushing, nervous tics.

Chakra: Throat and Brow.

Candle colour: Pale blue **Fragrances:** Lemongrass, mugwort, myrrh, neroli, sweetgrass. **Practical uses:** The perfect antidote to modern life, celestite slows us down. **Workplace:** Carry or wear in any situation where you fear intimidation. **Magical significance:** Natural celestite often contains caves, and pathways within the crystal: looking through them provides a route into past worlds **Divinatory meaning:** Today is the tomorrow you worried about yesterday and you have survived. **Zodiac:** Libra **Empowerment:** I will make time to be still and silent.

Celestine is the approved name for the mineral celestite. A stone associated with angels and used as a focus for communication with guardian angels. Blue celestite prevents us worrying away our lives: keep by the bed if you wake in the night panicking or hold before sleep and let your mind wander freely within its pathways if your mind is whirling with seemingly insoluble problems. A tiny piece in a child's pocket or bag will fill their aura energy field with protective energies to deter those who would bully them.

Blue Halite

Type: Halide/sodium chloride.

Colours: Blue and indigo.

Availability: Obtainable from specialist crystal stores and online.

Physical benefits: Thought to help with thyroid, thalamus, absorption of minerals by the body especially iodine, exhaustion in hot weather, heat and sunstroke; good for any cleansing or detoxing programme.

Emotional healing: Removes self-defeating attitudes that prevent you from improving your health, particularly if you have a tendency to give up after a few days.

Chakra: Throat and Brow.

Candle colour: Blue. **Fragrances:** Juniper, lavender, rosemary, sandalwood. **Practical uses:** Attracts unexpected gifts; finding a fossil on a walk or receiving a small but valued inheritance from a distant relative or an old friend. **Workplace:** Blue halite will absorb workplace stress, releasing calm. **Magical significance:** Halite makes spiritual connections with the past, whether you are visiting an ancient site or trying to feel close to your own ancestors. **Divinatory meaning:** You need to step back from life and let matters settle round you. **Zodiac:** Libra and Pisces **Empowerment:** I can detach myself without being uncaring.

Blue or indigo halite should be kept near other crystals or spiritual artefacts to continuously cleanse and empower them, for halite traditionally represents purity and incorruptibility. If you can obtain indigo halite, it makes any place or space feel sacred and helps sleep patterns in your bedroom if you have to work late and cannot go to sleep because your mind is racing. Blue halite in the living area draws adults, children and even animals into a quieter mode.

Dumortierite

Type: Borosilicate.

Colours: Deep blue to violet, sometimes with black inclusions, can be pinkish brown..

Availability: Relatively rare.

Physical benefits: Believed to help with ligaments, tendons, finding and alleviating root causes of illnesses, Tourette's syndrome, fevers, thyroid, spleen, endocrine system, blood.

Emotional healing: Gently releases pent-up emotions that would otherwise be expressed as uncontrolled fury; good with anger-management therapy.

Chakra: Throat and Brow.

Candle colour: Violet. **Fragrances:** Almond blossom, lavender, orchid, violet. **Practical uses:** Brings improvement in circumstances when you have given up hope. **Workplace:** A piece in your workspace encourages tidiness. **Magical significance:** Surround natural dumortierite or jewellery with violet candles; raise it over the centre of the lighted candle circle, calling your soul mate to find you, wherever they are. **Divinatory meaning:** Speak your mind. It is better to ruffle a few feathers than for injustice to pass unchallenged. **Zodiac:** Leo and Aquarius **Empowerment:** I find the sacred in my daily life.

Not discovered until the end of the 1800s and named after its discoverer, the French palaeontologist Eugene Dumortier, dumortierite has become associated with the planet Uranus because both planet and crystal seem to bring about change in unexpected ways. It is effective in calming over-excitable dogs that jump up and bark at visitors or on walks: attach a small tumblestone on a wire cradle to a collar and keep one or two in their sleeping place.

Sodalite

Type: Tectosilicate.

Colours: Dark indigo blue with white streaks, sometimes with purplish to grey markings; the amount of white can vary from a little to a lot.

Availability: Common.

Physical benefits: Seen as useful or relieving menopausal symptoms, racing pulse or heart, high blood pressure, burns, inflammation.

Emotional healing: Women should wear this crystal to come to terms with ageing issues such as loss of fertility and the empty nest syndrome.

Chakra: Brow and throat.

Candle colour: Dark blue or indigo. **Fragrances:** Bergamot, gardenia, juniper, lavender, pine. **Practical uses:** Sodalite is the ultimate calming crystal. Hold a sodalite when flying during take-off and landing. **Workplace:** Helps people facing retirement or redundancy; useful for those who need confidence at a presentation or interview. **Magical significance:** Sodalite is the crystal of the wise woman and with rituals and empowerments for post-menopausal women to enter a new phase of life. **Divinatory meaning:** There is something that needs to be said, but you will have to use the right words. **Zodiac:** Cancer and Sagittarius **Empowerment:** I welcome the growth of wisdom in my life.

Associated with the balance between mind and the emotions, sodalite will assist anyone impulsive to gain an old head on young shoulders. Carry or wear sodalite if you have aspirations to be a writer. Sodalite will help anyone who has to move home frequently, or lives out of a suitcase, to establish a welcoming home base.

Finally: if you are having trouble with sleeping, place a sodalite crystal under your pillow to encourage restful sleep.

Type: Corundum (aluminium oxide).

Colours: Pale to midnight blue.

Availability: High quality is rare, but lower and non-gem quality more common.

Physical benefits: Reported to help thyroid, nervous system, blood disorders, dementia, degenerative diseases, ear infections, hearing, eyesight and eye infections, fevers, swollen glands, nausea, speech and communication.

Emotional healing: Helps to release spiritual and emotional blockages, allowing you to express your true self and needs and open to love.

Chakra: Throat.

Blue Sapphire

Candle colour: Blue. **Fragrances:** Lemon balm, lemon verbena, lily, lotus, orchid. **Practical uses:** Sapphire is a stone of love, commitment and fidelity and has become popular in betrothal rings. Twin matching sapphire tumblestones can be given to a couple moving in together or marrying; collect one for each year you are together with your own partner. **Workplace:** Since blue sapphire was traditionally worn when treaties were signed, wear or carry even a tumblestone if signing a new contract or entering into pay negotiations for yourself or on behalf of others. **Magical significance:** Blue sapphire is considered effective for channelling healing powers from an angelic or higher source into the healer and is popular with Reiki healers. Sapphire amplifies healing through the voice. **Divinatory meaning:** You are wondering whether to trust someone you have recently met. Take your time as you do not know the whole story yet. **Zodiac:** Virgo and Libra. **Empowerment:** Truth is the key to trust and trust the key to truth.

King Solomon's fabulous magical ring was said to have been a blue sapphire and so a symbol of wisdom. The Ancient Greeks called the sapphire the jewel of the sun god Apollo. The blue stone was worn when consulting Apollo's oracle at Delphi in order that the questioner might have the wisdom to understand the answer given.

Blue sapphire, especially the velvety blue cornflower, also known as Kashmir, is the most desired of sapphires and hence commands more value. This precious gemstone offers calming and healing energies to all who wear or hold it. It will also bring good luck. Sapphire will helps during times of change to maintain clear vision of where it is you want go and how to get there.

Sapphires are a symbol of integrity and, at home and work, are a good counterbalance to cynicism and less desirable aspects of modern culture; effective for the speedy and positive resolution of all legal matters and all issues concerning justice.

Type: Gem-quality chrysocolla agatized in chalcedony quartz/aggregate quartz.

Colours: Bright blue, bluish green, clearer and more translucent than ordinary chrysocolla.

Availability: Relatively rare in high quality.

Physical benefits: Respiratory system, vocal chords, laryngitis, thyroid, vision, women in childbirth and the weeks afterwards, fevers, hot flushes and menopausal problems or after hysterectomy; balancing HRT and any hormonally based therapies; Tourette's syndrome, particularly girls and young women, heart, blood-sugar levels, diabetes.

Emotional healing: For people who do not speak or communicate, for whatever reason, to open up channels of direct communication; helpful for learning sign language.

Chakra: Heart, Throat and Brow.

Gem Silica

Candle colour: Bright blue. **Fragrances:** Hyacinth, lavender, lilac, rose, rosemary. **Practical uses:** A natural prosperity-bringer, even a single gem silica tumblestone helps restore fortunes after loss or setbacks; excellent for rebuilding credit rating, restarting a business or obtaining a new home after a financial reversal. **Workplace:** A clear and harmonious communication gem for dealing with anyone who deliberately uses words to confuse, misinform or cause discomfort; wear if your words are twisted or used against you, to get your true opinions across to those who matter. **Magical significance:** Gem silica jewellery worn around the heart area or on wrist or fingers that link with the Heart energy chakra protects you against future heartbreak; if you always choose the wrong person out of kindness and the belief that anyone can change, gem silica will attract someone less emotionally dependent. **Divinatory meaning:** Go slowly with a new friendship or relationship rather than offering everything too soon. **Zodiac:** Taurus and Sagittarius **Empowerment:** I communicate only what is positive.

Gem silica is harder than ordinary chrysocolla because of the quartz in it, and so it can be made into jewellery or carved more easily. Sometimes other copper minerals (as well as chrysocolla) are embedded in it, such as malachite, and a very rare form called quattro silica has shattuckite, malachite and dioptase as inclusions.

If you can obtain a gem silica cabochon or a beautiful large tumblestone, it makes a wonderful centrepiece for a layout for healing someone who is not present (surround it with a circle of appropriate healing crystals). The powerfully peace- and reconciliation-bringing gem silica fills your home and all who enter with a sense of harmony and well-being.

Gem silica is a natural home or workplace filter; wear one if you travel through traffic-filled streets or work or live in a place with air pollution.

Type: Glass with copper inclusions, also cobalt, manganese or chromium combined.

Colours: Creates the appearance of a blue or green stone with golden sparkles (in fact the glass is colourless). Blue goldstone resembles a starry night sky.

Availability: Common.

Physical benefits: Thought to assist with the relief of migraines, headaches, epilepsy and visual disturbances particularly night and tunnel vision or glaucoma; be helpful after surgery or intensive chemical therapies, for allergies resulting from chemical irritants and pet hair or dust mites.

Emotional healing: For those whose dreams were shattered by the insensitivity of parents or teachers at an early age, a reminder of what has been and can still be achieved.

Chakra: Throat, Brow and Crown.

Blue Goldstone

Candle colour: Gold. **Fragrances:** Lily, lotus, magnolia, orchid, vanilla. **Practical uses:** To help children and adults to overcome fears of the dark, hold a goldstone angel, egg or tumblestone as symbol of the night sky and keep by the bedside; take with you when you stay in unfamiliar hotels and on long-haul flights to relax into a natural sleep-and-waking pattern. **Workplace:** The stone of actors, actresses, of all performers and any involved in the theatre or media for getting a break or good contract. Touch your goldstone and visualize your big chance materializing; take it along to every audition or interview. **Magical significance:** In modern magic blue goldstone is associated with Nut, the Ancient Egyptian sky goddess, whose body arched over the whole world covered with stars, and so is a crystal of female empowerment; man or woman, wear as a talisman and gaze into a goldstone egg for visions of old worlds by starlight. **Divinatory meaning:** When you find yourself suddenly centre stage in life, you will know what to do and say; do not hesitate. **Zodiac:** Sagittarius. **Empowerment:** I am moving beyond my former expectations.

The crystal of all who are interested in or practice astrology or astronomy, blue goldstone worn or carried for a few months helps you to understand underlying patterns in your life and how to avoid repeating old mistakes and the kind of relationships that make you unhappy.

Gradually, you will become luckier in small but significant ways. Keep a blue goldstone with your CV, job references or qualification certificates to meet people who will open doors of opportunity,

particularly connected with travel, a better-paid career or fast track to the top. Above all, blue goldstone is a wish stone.

Breathe into a goldstone or goldstone jewellery on a starry night and whisper your wish into it. Carry it with you at all times and re-empower whenever the stars are particularly bright.

Surround yourself with blue goldstones for ten minutes to energize your body and clear your thoughts.

Blue Goldstone

Emerald

Type: Beryl.

Colours: Bright green.

Availability: Common.

Physical benefits: May be useful for angina, eyesight, bleeding, epilepsy, fevers, fertility and childbirth, asthma, bronchitis and respiratory complaints, heart, thyroid, lungs, plant allergies, glands, teeth, kidneys and bladder, insect bites.

Emotional healing: In tumblestone form emerald restores the confidence of young girls and teenagers who have been teased about their weight or any young person who is made to feel inferior because parents cannot afford the latest designer goods.

Chakra: Heart.

Candle colour: Green. **Fragrances:** Hyssop, peach, rose. **Practical uses:** Revives passion, whether for an interest, person or job. **Workplace:** Natural emerald or tumblestone held for five minutes a day brings rapid recall of facts. **Magical significance:** To receive psychic information, place an emerald for five minutes on a Bible, then open the book at any page. The first sentences of the first page will offer the answer. **Divinatory meaning:** You will be able to silence the sniping of someone who tries to make you feel inferior through your success. **Zodiac:** Taurus. **Empowerment:** I am proud of my achievements.

Emeralds were considered a symbol of eternal life in Ancient Egypt. Emerald mines existed near the Red Sea coast as early as 1300 BC and were later called Cleopatra's mines because of her love of the stone. Wear or carry an emerald out of sight near your heart for attracting love, especially in later life. To call back an estranged love, speak the words you wish to say as you hold the emerald close to your lips; then seal it in an envelope and, if appropriate, send it to your love with a message.

Emerald Gem

Type: Green gem variety of beryl; minute flaws are an indication of authenticity.

Colours: Sparkling deep green, caused by traces of chromium.

Availability: Relatively common.

Physical benefits: Believed to be the best for eyesight and eye infections; may also help heart, lungs, gallstones and gall-bladder problems, pancreas, eczema or rashes and skin allergies, viruses and infections.

Emotional healing: Assists with fears of ageing.

Chakra: Heart.

Candle colour: Green. **Fragrances:** Carnation, lotus. **Practical uses:** Believed to protect women against abuse. **Workplace:** A bringer of success for older women. **Magical significance:** For lasting love, surround an emerald ring with a circle of rose petals. Light two green candles; pass the ring over both candles saying "Round and round the ring of truth, love in age and love in youth, love in sickness and in health". Blow out the candles. **Divinatory meaning:** You may have doubted the loyalty of someone recently, but you don't need to worry. **Zodiac:** Taurus. **Empowerment:** I offer and expect fidelity in all relationships.

As well as a symbol of eternal life and beauty, emeralds were linked with wisdom by the Ancient Egyptians who considered them a gift from Thoth, the god of wisdom. Indeed, the first-century Egyptian magician Hermes Trismegistos was said to carve on a pure emerald tablet the words that held the key to magic, "As above, so below". Emeralds have always, for this reason, been considered a magical stone for a connection between cosmic and Earthly realms and for bringing thoughts and desires into reality.

Type: Apatite is the most common phosphate. Beautiful green apatite comes from the Printzskiold Mine in Malmberget, Sweden.

Colours: Green, yellow-green, yellow, also blue (p.230).

Availability: Obtainable through specialist jewellery and crystal stores and online, but rare in yellow.

Physical benefits: May aid brittle bones, growth problems in children, hypertension, heart valves, jaw, metabolism, the absorption of calcium, glands, fluid imbalances, gallbladder and spleen in more yellow shades; autism, Attention Deficit Hyperactivity Disorder and hyperactivity, especially where diet may be implicated.

Emotional healing: Assists with aloofness and alienation, heartbreak in love and inability to move on from love that did not last or develop; yo-yo dieting where bingeing is followed by fasting, bulimia.

Chakra: Heart and Root.

Green Apatite

Candle colour: Green. **Fragrances:** Basil, bay, fern, moss, rosemary. **Practical uses:** Plant natural green apatite for success in organic gardening, whether growing flowers, fruit or vegetables, and for relocating realistically from town to country living. **Workplace:** A single stone or circle of apatite set round a green plant will awaken or reawaken enthusiasm for a personal long-term project or refocus co-workers or employees who spend too much time on non-work emailing or phone calls during the working day. **Magical significance:** Good for increasing psychic and telepathic communication with animals and birds, especially pets and local wildlife, and for animal healing. **Divinatory meaning:** Open yourself to new friendships and connections to regain your old love of life. **Zodiac:** Virgo and Libra. **Empowerment:** The rhythm of life has a powerful pulse.

The name apatite is derived from the Greek word meaning "to deceive" because varieties of the gem were often confused with other minerals. Called the "bones of the Earth" and so one of the best crystals for healing the Earth and for receiving healing through natural essential oils, herbs and flower essences.

The stone of the crystal healer, green apatite increases receptivity to its healing properties and enhances the effects of any other crystals used;

excellent as a central stone in a healing crystal layout placed round a patient or as the Heart chakra crystal in a full chakra crystal healing. It also encourages children to gain good hand–eye coordination and, if carried or worn, especially as earrings, makes adults less clumsy.

Keep green apatite near a computer or printer if you are sending out invitations or inviting neighbours or local people either for a social event or to join together over an environmental issue.

Type: Phosphate, arsenate.

Colours: Vivid grass green to light green, yellowish.

Availability: Relatively rare.

Physical benefits: Said to be useful for skin problems, particularly psoriasis, herpes, kidney, bladder, removing toxins from the body; helping the body and mind to adapt to medical or surgical intervention, hormone therapies or fertility treatment, accident or serious injury.

Emotional healing: A stone for any talking therapies as it opens up meaningful communication and assists self-knowledge and patient-led initiative.

Chakra: Heart.

Conichalcite

Candle colour: Green. **Fragrances:** Cedar, clary sage, eucalyptus, juniper, pine. **Practical uses:** A copper-based crystal and therefore associated with love, here the love that knows when to hold on and when to let go; an excellent empty-nest syndrome or relationship-ending crystal to open the way to new freer emotional connections. **Workplace:** Conichalcite brings adaptability to current changing needs and encourages the use of imagination to come up with fast solutions; ideal therefore for crisis-solving by personal assistants, conference or event organizers and those who work in psychology or psychotherapy to avoid getting stuck in standard responses. **Magical significance:** A colourful piece encrusted with yellow or red limonite makes the perfect focus for meditation or guided visualizations based in nature and connection with nature essences. **Divinatory meaning:** You will get a reminder of how much more fun life used to be and can be again with just a little imagination. **Zodiac:** Taurus and Virgo. **Empowerment:** I will improve my quality of life.

Conichalcite forms in the oxidation zone of copper ore, an area where oxygen-rich waters react with copper sulphide and/or copper oxide minerals to produce colourful copper-based minerals such as malachite and azurite. This oxidation gives conichalcite the power to open up boundaries; it stimulates the imagination to create the thought, "Maybe I could give it a try".

A stone for adding fun and colour to your life; encourages the mind-set not to "make the best of what you have" but to "make what you have more colourful and richer", whether repainting your home in bright colours or buying a tent for weekends away.

WARNING: Like other copper-based crystals, conichalcite is not suitable for direct elixirs, especially as it contains arsenic and should be handled with care; not suitable for children.

Type: Clear or milky white quartz that has inclusions of manganese or iron.

Colours: Either delicate green inclusions have grown into fine patterns very similar to moss or lichen or the crystal looks dark green with bluish inclusions that give the stone a look similar to blue cheese.

Availability: Common.

Physical benefits: May relieve colds, flu and other viral illnesses and boosts immune system; improve bone marrow; assist in childbirth to reduce pain and speed delivery; speed recovery from illness; protect against low blood sugar and dehydration, pulse and heartbeat irregularities, circulation; treat fungal and skin infections; act as an anti-inflammatory.

Emotional healing: A crystal of new beginnings and the growth or regrowth of trust, releasing old fears, creating a new purpose for life and reconnecting with the world after a period of withdrawal or disillusion.

Chakra: Heart.

Moss Agate

Candle colour: Dark green. **Fragrances:** Cedarwood, juniper, moss, rosewood, rosemary, sage. **Practical uses:** Set a moss agate beneath a pet bed or energize their water with one to help city or indoor pets to maintain connection with the natural world. **Workplace:** Moss agate will draw new business and encourage gradual expansion and growing prosperity over a period of 12 months, so excellent for the self-employed or small businesses to thrive; also for any who work in financial institutions or horticulture. **Magical significance:** Good for connecting with fairy energies and other nature essences and for increasing the power of herbal treatments. **Divinatory meaning:** A very lucky omen for the gradual growth of what you currently most need in your life, whether money, promotion, health or love. **Zodiac:** Virgo. **Empowerment:** I draw strength and harmony from the natural world.

Throughout history and in all cultures, moss agate is the crystal of gardening and gardeners, because planting one in a flower bed or plant pot does seem to increase growth and health of the plant.

A helpful crystal to have near if you are struggling with tax returns, spread sheets or figures that will not add up. Keep one with bank papers to encourage savings and reverse the outflow of money.

Moss agate brings new friendships with like-minded people and, especially if worn as jewellery or placed on the heart each night before sleep, will attract new love or the regrowth of former love that has died or has experienced a period of turbulence. Twin moss agates kept in a small green bag with a sprinkling of dried rosemary near the bed will encourage faithful love that grows steadily through the years.

Tree Agate

Type: Chalcedony with dendrite inclusions; quite coarse and knobbly even when tumbled.

Colours: White with feathery green tree-like inclusions or veins or, less commonly, green with white tree-like markings.

Availability: Common.

Physical benefits: May clear energy blockages and fluid retention, and absorb pain, especially if placed on a point of pain; said to help vein and capillary problems, neuralgia.

Emotional healing: Brings peace to a troubled mind; heals the pain of unhappy childhood or effects of divorce.

Chakra: Heart.

Green Agate

Type: Chalcedony, crypto-crystalline quartz, may be infused with iron and aluminium.

Colours: Green and translucent, often banded with different greens, from mid- to darker green.

Availability: Relatively rare agate.

Physical benefits: May help with eyesight, food allergies that cause hyperactivity in children and aggressiveness in adults, and people bordering on Type 2 diabetes.

Emotional healing: An excellent stone for balancing excesses; keep tumblestones near hyperactive children and adults to deter impulsiveness.

Chakra: Heart.

Candle colour: Green. **Fragrances:** Basil, bay, cedar, fern, moss. **Practical uses:** A bowl of green agate tumblestones will restore the balance in any place or situation. **Workplace:** Brings good luck, encourages fairness; wear it if you are attending unfair dismissal tribunals, not to be vengeful, but to attain fair compensation. **Magical significance:** Buy a green agate frog if you would like twins or triplets. **Divinatory meaning:** There are many blessings in your life and these you gladly share; make sure others are equally generous. **Zodiac:** Virgo. **Empowerment:** All is right in my world.

Candle colour: Pale green. **Fragrances:** Cedar, cypress, pine, tea tree. **Practical uses:** A crystal of abundance if planted with a small tree. **Workplace:** If you work in an air-conditioned environment, a dish of dendritic or tree agates brings a breath of fresh air to a stagnant indoor atmosphere. **Magical significance:** Place one on a picture of rainforests to protect them and trees everywhere. Light a green candle and visualize new shoots emerging. **Divinatory meaning:** Not a time to be alone; seek support and, if in doubt, go back to your spiritual roots for the answer. **Zodiac:** Virgo. **Empowerment:** I constantly seek new connections.

Tree Agate, proper name Dendritic Agate, is named after Dendrite – the old Greek name for a tree and is associated with the Ancient Greek dryads, woodland and tree spirits. Dendritic or tree agate was buried in the fields by the Ancient Greeks at the time of sowing to ensure a good harvest.

Strengthens family connections; use dendritic or tree agate to call estranged family members home by keeping a crystal next to a photograph of the person who has gone away. Protective for travel by air or car.

Though much rarer than moss agate (p.253), green agate is a faithful love stone, carved into a heart shape or if twin green agates are surrounded by a heart shape made out of dried rose petals. It calls slow-growing but lasting love, particularly in its darker shades; ideal to restore trust if you have been hurt previously or to bring reconciliation in an existing relationship if outsiders or family members caused a rift. Beloved by the Ancient Egyptians for seals, amulets, rings and for adorning vessels.

Type: Epidote (calcium aluminium silicate).

Colours: Green.

Availability: Common.

Physical benefits: Believed to assist problems with reproductive organs, the heart, migraines, colds, hay fever and pollen allergies, lung and arm problems; may be helpful for repetitive strain injuries caused by using computers: keep zoisite taped to the most painful part; also for wrist strains and sprains and arthritic or damaged fingers, hyperventilation.

Emotional healing: Helps release any deep-rooted fears that have caused an apparently irrational phobia, for example a phobia of dogs caused unknowingly by being bitten by a dog as a very young child.

Chakra: Heart.

Green Zoisite

Candle colour: Green. **Fragrances:** Cedar, mint, pine, rosemary, rosewood. **Practical uses:** Hold or wear green zoisite to dispel lethargy and boost your get up and go when all you want to do is to stay in bed, especially in winter. **Workplace:** A welcome stone if you are constantly being interrupted at work, especially if you work from home, to get you back on track after the interruption; keep near the phone to prevent time-wasting callers. **Magical significance:** A wonderful stone for young children who have an invisible friend or talk about seeing fairies if other children laugh at them. **Divinatory meaning:** You may have temporarily lost your way, but you will be drawn back by a helpful unmistakable sign in the next week or two. **Zodiac:** Virgo. **Empowerment:** I give myself permission to do the things I want to do.

Zoisite, named after the mineral collector Sigmund Zois, was first found in the Sau-Alp Mountains in Karnten, Austria, in 1804. A stone sacred to the mountain spirits whose powers are believed to be contained within the zoisite crystal.

This crystal is a teller of truth about yourself. If you have something to hide, it may not be the crystal for you. Zoisite encourages you to spend time in the natural world and to stop rushing round doing things, taking time to be still and

quiet even in a local park. Excellent for urban children and animals and to help your children to value a simpler, slower lifestyle and rely less on consumer goods and simulated entertainment.

Zoisite is good for camping, caravanning, trekking or outdoor pursuits, acting as protection and also connecting with the joys and challenges of nature. Makes you more alert and observant; use to improve your success in competitions, quizzes and games of all kinds.

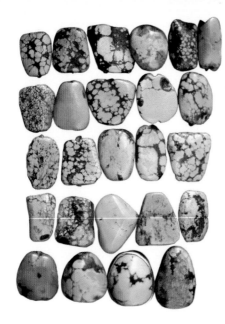

Type: Hydrous aluminium phosphate coloured by copper (blue) and iron (green).

Colours: From light to deep blue (the most valuable) or greenish blue or apple green, often with spider-web black, dark grey or brown veins and streaks.

Availability: Common.

Physical benefits: May help problems with liver, anaemia and blood health, nerve endings, physical strength, mobility, ear and inner ear, eyesight, throat, bladder weakness, stomach acidity and problems, rheumatism, gout, viral infections, muscles, pain relief, cramps and as an anti-inflammatory.

Emotional healing: An excellent anti-hysteria stone, worn to calm people who over-react to situations; helpful for the narcissus syndrome whereby someone is unable to see the world except for their own needs and from their point of view.

Chakra: Solar Plexus, Throat.

Tibetan Turquoise

Candle colour: Turquoise. **Fragrances:** Acacia, copal, frankincense, galbanum, sandalwood. **Practical uses:** The ultimate prosperity and luck bringer, keep turquoise in the centre of a layout of a pattern of blue and green crystals to attract good fortune and money and also the happiness and health to enjoy it. **Workplace:** A stone of wise leadership and also of speaking and acting honestly. Wear Tibetan turquoise if you want to gain promotion or set up your own company; hold it if you know you must speak out against dishonest practices; good for selling what you believe in. **Magical significance:** Tibetan turquoise is a personal stone, said to absorb the essence of the owner; expresses by colour changes the moods and state of health of the owner, becoming greener or paler if the owner is sad or unwell; also transmits health and happiness, automatically stored within it by wearing and touching your turquoise in more joyous moods. **Divinatory meaning:** Consider if you want to go for a leadership position or promotion, as this is possible, or whether you are happier fulfilling your life in other ways. **Zodiac:** Sagittarius. **Empowerment:** I am in good health and will remain so.

In Tibet, turquoise is worn by men and women as jewellery and in sacred prayer beads, and is sometimes associated with the creator and star goddess Dolma or Tara, who is often depicted with a bluish-green complexion.

Turquoise also adorns musical instruments, prayer wheels and bells, and a turquoise rosary is said to help prayer to whatever deity is being invoked. Tibetan turquoise is traditionally received as a gift, rather than bought, to pass on its natural fortune-bringing powers;

however, if you buy your own, you can make it a gift to yourself, a special purchase, even a tumblestone; hold it for a few minutes to transfer its good luck into your life.

Turquoise jewellery is a promise of fidelity and protectiveness to a lover or partner. Considered a master healing crystal that will empower other crystals, turquoise is enhanced in healing powers if set in copper or silver. Place on the Solar Plexus in the upper centre of the stomach to empower the whole body.

Serpentine

Type: Hydrated magnesium silicate.

Colours: Green in a variety of shades, sometimes with spots or veins of darker colours, and can be distinguished by its oily feel.

Availability: Common.

Physical benefits: May ease Alzheimer's and senile dementia, bites and stings, low blood sugar, diabetes, muscle weakness, skin inflammation, eczema or rashes, varicose veins, warts and skin or hair parasites.

Emotional healing: For overcoming bingeing, bulimia and emotionally related obesity.

Chakra: Heart, Crown and Root.

Candle colour: Green. **Fragrances:** Acacia, galbanum, juniper, pine, thyme. **Practical uses:** Wear serpentine when you use social networking or dating websites to avoid fraudsters. **Workplace:** Representing the snake shedding its skin, serpentine is excellent for starting over. **Magical significance:** Wonderful for working through guided trance work. **Divinatory meaning:** A new chance to show the hidden side of yourself will enable you to reinvent your image in a very positive way. **Zodiac:** Scorpio. **Empowerment:** I do not need to carry emotional luggage.

Named after its serpent-like colouring, serpentine has been mined since Palaeolithic times and considered a protective amulet against snake bites, disease and the dark arts. It was used in medieval days to increase the healing powers of medicines. It is still one of the most all-purpose protective stones, especially as jewellery. Serpentine increases self-confidence and helps you trust your judgment in situations where there is conflicting information. I err on the side of caution and do not use any form of serpentine in elixirs.

Verdite

Type: Silicate; fuchsite mica, often found close to deposits of gold.

Colours: Usually deep rich green, also shades of green including emerald, golden brown; may be mottled with white, red, or yellow and lighter green.

Availability: Relatively common.

Physical benefits: Traditionally used to increase potency and fertility; may relieve sexual dysfunction, especially caused by anxiety, genito-urinary problems, dizziness.

Emotional healing: Relieves unspoken fears about hereditary illnesses.

Chakra: Heart.

Candle colour: Green. **Fragrances:** Benzoin, lotus, sage. **Practical uses:** The bargain hunter's stone; take a piece of verdite along to car boot sales or auction rooms. **Workplace:** Wear verdite where there are issues of trust, hold your verdite close to your heart and you will know the truth. **Magical significance:** Use to make connection with deceased relatives; wear in a green bag with olive leaves over your womb for three days before ovulation as a fertility charm. **Divinatory meaning:** Ask a friend to answer your question. **Zodiac:** Virgo. **Empowerment:** There is no such thing as a new problem, but there are new solutions.

Verdite, which comes from South Africa and Zimbabwe, is the oldest form of exposed rock, dating back more than three and a half million years. From time immemorial, local craftspeople have created ancestral statues from verdite.

Keep small, beautiful verdite statues around the home if you do not have living older family or they are far away; this will create a sense of tradition and family roots, even in a newly built house or apartment.

Type: Silicate (calcium titanium silicate); gem quality can be brittle.

Colours: Green, yellow, brown, black and white, also sometimes orange and very occasionally red or with red and orange tinge (red and orange may be heat-treated).

Availability: Relatively rare, particularly high-quality crystals, but available from some specialist mineral stores and online.

Physical benefits: Said to help with blood and bone disorders, immune system, inner ear, balance and mobility, illnesses in older people or anyone who suffers a chronic medical condition.

Emotional healing: Aligns the emotional and spiritual elements of self to create balance and harmony and therefore strengthens the effects of ancient healing systems that have enjoyed a revival in the modern world

Chakra: Crown and Brow.

Sphene/Titanite

Candle colour: Green or yellow. **Fragrances:** Peppermint, pine, rosemary, rosewood, vanilla. **Practical uses:** Use sphene as a get-up-and-go energy booster by holding it to the centre of your brow for a few minutes. Relax with it and let its energies flow into yours. **Workplace:** Particularly useful in assisting with problem-solving, logistics, research and other intellectual activities: good also for retraining or learning new skills in later life and for bringing order to workplaces that lack structure or clear leadership. **Magical significance:** This crystal combines the ability to understand underlying patterns and to access ancient wisdom spontaneously, aiding learning of structured divination systems such as numerology, runes and tarot. **Divinatory meaning:** You will need your wits about you as you may have to juggle a number of priorities to restore order to a chaotic situation. **Zodiac:** Virgo and Libra. **Empowerment:** I am surrounded by light.

Sphene is also named titanite due to its titanium content and has been for many years a source of titanium dioxide, used as a pigment in artists' oil paints. Called the stone of ancient wisdom, sphene is linked with the legendary Lemurian peoples of the Far East who were believed to store their wisdom in crystals (see also Lemurian seed crystals, p.380).

The crystals were, according to the stories, carried to lands worldwide where indigenous spiritualities grew up, for example the Native North Americans. Sphene in the home helps younger people to value their cultural and ancestral heritage. Wear sphene jewellery while meditating, to access images and maybe memories of past worlds that relate to present questions and dilemma.

A light-bringer that will flood every aspect of your being and life with optimism and joy; good as a Reiki grounding crystal and in the centre of a healing layout to balance energies.

Chlorite Phantom

Type: Quartz crystal with chlorite phantom or faint crystal outline within, or occasionally clear quartz phantom enclosed by chlorite, both formed when the inner crystal stopped growing.

Colours: Pale green, watery clear white with pale green inner ghost.

Availability: One of the more common phantoms.

Physical benefits: May help bladder infections, return to health after surgery, relief of side-effects of illness or treatment; protect against toxins.

Emotional healing: Unblocks an emotionally frozen heart or long-term anger expressed in self-destructive behaviour.

Chakra: Green.

Candle colour: Green. **Fragrances:** Cedarwood, moss. **Practical uses:** Helps parents as children seek more independence. **Workplace:** Chlorite phantom quartz brings freshness to workplaces, encouraging the acceptance of new ideas. **Magical significance:** Reveals nature creatures that live under the earth. Go to a hillside as the light is fading; sit with your phantom chlorite to connect with energies that are sensed by children and some adults as tree spirits. **Divinatory meaning:** Let go of old hurts and take a chance on friendship. **Zodiac:** Virgo. **Empowerment:** I let worn-out anger go.

Chlorite phantoms are formed within clear quartz when green chlorite attaches itself as a coating round a quartz crystal during its early development. If the crystal later grows larger and outwards to enclose the chlorite coating, a green phantom is created. Chlorite phantoms are beloved of healers, who hold the stone above the patient to see psychically the source of the problem within the body and to gently stimulate healing from within the person's own self-healing system.

Seriphos Quartz

Type: Silicon dioxide.

Colours: From pale to darker green, colouring often caused by presence of inclusions of the mineral hedenbergite.

Availability: Rare but worth searching for.

Physical benefits: Believed to be useful for eyes, speech and communication difficulties, pollen allergies; strengthening healing with herbs, crystal healing, flower remedies and hydrotherapy.

Emotional healing: A calming stone for all who are afraid of ghosts or have dabbled in dark arts and scared themselves; helpful for dark nights of the soul.

Chakra: Heart and Brow.

Candle colour: Green. **Fragrances:** Almond blossom, lemon, neroli, thyme. **Practical uses:** Wear or carry if you want to live in a remote area, also for all outdoor activities; good for those who want to be self-sufficient. **Workplace:** An empowering crystal for anyone working outdoors. **Magical significance:** Hold seriphos quartz outdoors, in a green place or near water, especially the sea; induces an instant connection **Divinatory meaning:** You may be thinking about moving to a desert island; find a compromise so you can relax more. **Zodiac:** Taurus and Virgo. **Empowerment:** I find spiritual satisfaction in nature.

Mined only on the Greek island of Seriphos in a cave at low tide, seriphos quartz is associated with enchanted underwater worlds. Seriphos is a crystal that guides you towards a better quality of life, whether downsizing or working from home in the countryside; often, a few months after acquiring this crystal, opportunities do open for a more spiritually fulfilling lifestyle. Seriphos quartz is a valuable healing crystal for any angel-inspired healing therapies such as Angel Reiki.

Type: Clear quartz with epidote inclusions, either as a green phantom (p.259) or shadowy inner crystal, or with epidote filling the quartz.

Colours: Light green to bluish green, sometimes with darker markings in the tumblestone.

Availability: Obtainable from specialist mineral stores and online, rarer as tumblestones.

Physical benefits: May help with obesity, glandular fever, Hodgkinson's disease, mumps, fluid retention, kidney stones, recurring viruses and infections, internal parasites; recovery after illness or surgery.

Emotional healing: Brings back hopes after a major setback; good for people whose long-term relationship ends either in unwanted separation or through death.

Chakra: Brow.

Epidote Quartz/Dream Quartz

Candle colour: Green. **Fragrances:** Cedarwood, lemongrass, moss. **Practical uses:** Use dream quartz to take small steps to fulfilment if life is frustrating major plans, such as redecorating if you cannot afford to move, having a self-catering holiday if you cannot afford your usual hotel break; giving the impetus to explore money-spinning ventures or cost-cutting to bring dreams closer. **Workplace:** Epidote in quartz brings nearer the attainment of an earlier ambition after many years of effort and/or study, assists career changes after redundancy or retirement to fulfil an old creative talent or desired business venture. **Magical significance:** A natural protector against negative energies, human and paranormal, especially at night or in dreams; encourages beautiful dreams and astral travel in sleep to past worlds and to connect with deceased loved ones and guardian angels. Dream quartz will bring the dreams you most need and want and assist clear dream recall. **Divinatory meaning:** Do not let past failure or present restrictions deter you from future plans, it may just take a little longer to happen. **Zodiac:** Pisces. **Empowerment:** I can manifest abundance.

Dream quartz, with its blend of the action-bringing quartz with the potential-offering epidote, brings closer the realms of possibility and actuality. Carry dream quartz in the daytime to protect you from energy vampires and over-critical or sarcastic people who are jealous of your potential.

At night, write down the answers to any questions that are troubling you just before sleep and set them under your pillow or on a bedside table with your dream quartz on top of the paper. Repeat the questions like a mantra,

softer and softer and slower and slower, until you drift into sleep. The answers will come either in your dreams or as unmistakeable signs in the everyday world. This technique is called dream incubation and has been practised from Ancient Egyptian times (see also lodalite, another excellent dream stone that can be used in conjunction).

Wearing or carrying dream quartz makes you more intuitive and alert to the right opportunities and people, acting as a radar to steer you away from harmful influences and dead ends.

Type: Amphibole silicate, may be found in quartz.

Colours: Light to rich and dark green, greyish green to black.

Availability: Relatively common.

Physical benefits: Thought to assist the building up of cells and tissues and the regeneration of the body; clear and remove toxins and so assist the healthy functioning of liver and kidneys.

Emotional healing: A "light in the darkness" crystal that counteracts a sense of having lost the way from goals and dreams; helps to prevent loneliness and alienation by opening our heart to others and so creating correspondingly friendly vibes in social encounters (especially lighter and brighter green actinolite).

Chakra: Heart in its green form, Root in black.

Actinolite

Candle colour: Bright green. **Fragrances:** Fennel, fern, grapefruit, lavender, lime, orange. **Practical uses:** Keep actinolite in any colour shade in a window if you live in a neighbourhood where there is intolerance or trouble with gangs to shield your household from threat or harm. **Workplace:** Use darker shades or black in your workspace to shield you from any negativity and especially from divisive energies, troublemakers and gossips. **Magical significance:** Actinolite in black or dark green is an anti-worry stone. At any time you are worried, sad or feel unnecessarily guilty, touch your actinolite with your index fingers, name the worry and say, "May this worry/burden be taken from me". Once a month pass a lighted incense stick in any tree fragrance such as cedar or pine over the actinolite to cleanse it. **Divinatory meaning:** Look for new contacts, groups and networks who will give you the openings you need both professionally and in meeting like-minded people. **Zodiac:** Scorpio. **Empowerment:** I open myself to the love of humankind.

Often called the ray stone because of its physical structure and the way its energies radiate light throughout the aura, so expanding positive connection with others and with the cosmos. In the modern world it is said to promote the unity of all humankind by spreading goodwill and accentuating understanding and tolerance between people of different faiths and political systems.

An ideal crystal, especially actinolite in quartz or green actinolite, when travelling to different countries to help you to tune in to the lifestyle and customs of the locals and the energies of the place; helpful also if you are the new boy or girl in any situation to blend in and understand any underlying power structure.

After trauma or unwelcome change, actinolite offers a personal sense of security to reach out for new opportunities.

Type: Silicate with iron, magnesium and aluminium; often the name given to a group of minerals, but here referring to the green kind.

Colours: Green, occasionally white, yellow, red, lavender or black.

Availability: Rare as separate crystal; more common as inclusions in other crystals.

Physical benefits: Believed to be a whole-body healer, may help with skin surface growths, blemishes, skin tags, assimilation of vitamins and minerals especially A and E, iron, magnesium and calcium, pain relief, deep-seated growths or illnesses that attack or mutate the body's cells or immune system.

Emotional healing: Releases secret sorrows; allows the acutely sensitive and easily wounded to become more emotionally robust.

Chakra: Heart.

Chlorite

Candle colour: Green. **Fragrances:** Apple blossom clary sage, cedarwood, rosewood, thyme. **Practical uses:** Clears away dissension, disharmony, dissolves anger and irritability at home or work; defuses the easily offended, supercritical, sarcastic and tactless who are unaware or uncaring of the effects they have on others. **Workplace:** Chlorite in quartz alerts you to false friends, hidden enemies, plots, lies and malicious gossip; good for investigators in any field, but particularly medical research, detective work and espionage. **Magical significance:** Chlorite is regarded as a very magical stone, showing an inner green land where tiny beings live; use for visualization or guided fantasy shamanic journeys into worlds of magical animals and forests to rediscover your lost inner self. **Divinatory meaning:** Do not listen to gossip nor pass scandal on as you may become implicated in a secretly growing conflict. **Zodiac:** Virgo. **Empowerment:** I seek wisdom within myself.

Chlorites are most frequently found as strong green inclusions in or coatings on quartz, danburite, topaz, calcite and other minerals. This is the most useful form for healing and everyday purposes.

The more rare chlorite phantom quartz is formed when chlorite coating around a quartz crystal is enclosed by further growth by the quartz so the chlorite appears ghost-like within; an excellent other-dimensional exploration tool.

A crystal of vegetarians and vegetarianism and

organic food; keep a bowl of chlorite in quartz on the dining table to encourage healthy eating or if you wish to open a wholefood business, store or restaurant.

Keep any form of chlorite on your healing table or in your healing room to make people more receptive to absent healing if they are naturally nervous or sceptical. Place in the four corners of your home or sprinkle the elixir if you are troubled by a ghost or negative earth energies that make a home seem dark or cold.

Type: Mixture of chrysocolla (p.231), malachite (p.283), turquoise (p.239), sometimes with azurite (p.217), silver (p.178) and copper (p.81) included.

Colours: Green-blue, turquoise, swirling deep green with blue running through it, precise colour depending on proportion of different minerals.

Availability: Obtainable from specialist crystal stores and online, but it no longer all comes from Israel, its land of origin.

Physical benefits: May aid pain relief, massaged or held close to source of pain (best as natural unpolished and dipped in warm water beforehand), sinuses, lung, throat and mouth infections and blockages, fevers, inflammation, bone and tissue regeneration, arthritis, wrists, knees and elbows.

Emotional healing: Gives the wisdom to become complete within the self, the best basis for any relationship; detachment from placating immature adults who are never satisfied.

Chakra: Solar Plexus, Heart and Throat.

Eilat Stone

Candle colour: Turquoise. **Fragrances:** Benzoin, copal, frankincense, galbanum, sandalwood. **Practical uses:** As a powerful energy conductor and stone of loving connections, Eilat stone, worn round the neck or carried in a pouch, gives older people the confidence to use their wisdom and experience to advance or shine professionally in a youth-orientated world, to command respect, to live happily alone or attract a partner of similar emotional maturity. **Workplace:** Keep natural Eilat stone in a workplace where there are a number of immature people, practical jokers and those who treat the workplace like a playground and social club; gradually introduces wisdom, consideration, restraint and thought before speaking or acting. **Magical significance:** As Solomon's magical stone, Eilat stone is valued as a crystal of more formal magic since King Solomon is credited in mystical tradition with the creation of ceremonial magic, planetary and colour associations; in colour therapy and healing a central stone to integrate the hot and cool colours and to assist absorption of colour energies. **Divinatory meaning:** Someone is behaving very childishly but you should not descend to their level in retaliation; stand back until tantrums end and then have your say. **Zodiac:** Sagittarius. **Empowerment:** Wise thoughts precede my words and deeds.

The national stone of Israel, associated with the biblical wise King Solomon and his base near the Red Sea, Eilat is highly prized as a stone of wisdom and of authority; it brings success to singers and all who work with words or teach media or communication skills, for judges and legal professionals, academics, archaeologists, historians, head teachers or educational administrators, for ministers of all religions and for embassy positions.

Wear Eilat stone for safe travel and for journeys along established trails or to reconstruct pilgrimage routes of the past and to cities or lands steeped in history, especially those to which you feel strong spiritual affinity. Eilat stones bring deeper understanding of literature and sacred texts from ancient cultures, learning extinct or difficult languages and, most of all, *in situ* exploration of the context and background of ancient languages.

Eilat Stone

Type: Very hard antigorite form of serpentine (p.257).

Colours: Pale to mid-green.

Availability: Common.

Physical benefits: Said to help with blood sugar, diabetes especially Type 2 levels, hormonal swings especially in pregnancy, flow of milk in mothers who are having problems breast-feeding. Also believed to be good for alopecia in women and hair thinning in men, nails, heart, cholesterol levels, DNA issues, fertility if medical intervention is necessary.

Emotional healing: Overcomes crippling fears of perceived physical danger, such as heights, darkness, elevators and unfamiliar places; helps to make a total break whether from a destructive person or giving up a habit that is damaging health.

Chakra: Heart.

Bowenite/New Jade

Candle colour: Pale green. **Fragrances:** Basil, bay, eucalyptus, lemon, lemongrass. **Practical uses:** Gives confidence to try new activities and so especially good for nervous children to socialize, to answer questions in class and also to stand up to bullying or teasing. Keep a piece with a picture of your child having a good time. **Workplace:** Bowenite is the perfect crystal to wear or have in your workspace if your desk is piled high with work that never seems to diminish or if you take on more than your share because you do not trust the competence of others; a good anti-workaholic crystal. **Magical significance:** Use as a protective love amulet if people interfere in your relationships or a love rival is trying to tempt your partner away. **Divinatory meaning:** Because you are naturally eager to help, someone close is asking for one too many favours and so not learning to stand on their own feet. **Zodiac:** Cancer and Aquarius. **Empowerment:** I can be assertive without being aggressive.

Before the Russian Revolution, bowenite was greatly prized in the Russian imperial court as a crystal that combines strength with beauty. It diminishes the power of a controlling partner or bullying boss or relation, and is the crystal of the warrior in love and life, to show tough love for friends, family or neighbours to help you to say no and leave people to fix their own problems;

a good house-buying or -selling crystal, especially if kept with official papers to minimize legal delays.

Hold bowenite before sleep and immediately on waking for clear dream recall and insight into the meaning of dreams. Rub bowenite anti-clockwise on your brow to remove any free-floating anxiety that may be distracting you from the day.

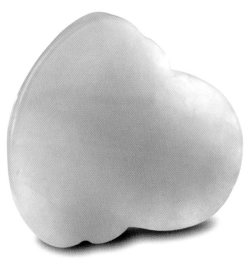

Type: Silicate/inosilicate/pyroxene, colour given by chromium.

Colours: Emerald green and translucent.

Availability: A rare and expensive jade.

Physical benefits: The richness of imperial jade makes it a very powerful healer; may help with kidneys, bedwetting, hips, legs, knees and ankles, heart, blood purification, nervous system, immune system, blood sugar and diabetes, high cholesterol, illnesses caused or made worse by over-indulgence, bad habits or self-neglect, hair, skin, plastic surgery, reconstructive surgery after a disfiguring illness or accident, head injuries, memory loss in old age.

Emotional healing: Restores dignity to anyone who has been mocked for looking different; gives very overweight people who are stuck in self-loathing the courage to seek help to resolve the problem and persevere with treatment.

Chakra: Heart.

Imperial Jade

Candle colour: Green. **Fragrances:** Cedar, lily, orchid, pine, sandalwood. **Practical uses:** As the richest colour, imperial jade is the luckiest of the jades for drawing love of all kinds, for peace and for abundance; even a small piece in your home makes people think you have redecorated or come into money, for it spreads beauty, harmony and a sense of plenty. **Workplace:** Imperial jade encourages leadership bids and success in senior positions, mixing determination and perseverance with high ethics; especially lucky if you can find a charm or dragon statue (jade is known as the stone of the dragon) etched with the five traditional virtues of jade, charity, modesty, courage, justice and wisdom, associated with the sage Confucius. **Magical significance:** Imperial jade is the most powerful of the jades as a manifestation or dream stone; use a small piece to call into your life what you most need and bring not only material manifestation but treasure on the spiritual level, which may prove even more valuable. **Divinatory meaning:** Not a time for easy rides, free lunches and offers too good to be true; honesty and hard work are the only safe options. **Zodiac:** Virgo. **Empowerment:** I will not be diverted by easy temptations.

Beloved by the emperors of the later Chinese dynasties since the late 1700s, when jadeite became better known in China; a particularly fabulous piece was, according to legend, exchanged by an emperor for 15 cities. It is found in Upper Myanmar (Burma) near Tawmaw and Hpakon.

Keep or wear imperial jade if you run a family business or have a large family, particularly where there is close contact between different generations, to encourage family unity; increases your personal confidence and sense of authority if a member of the older generation criticizes your childcare or marriage.

The ultimate symbol of immortality and health, give imperial jade to anyone who has been unwell or who worries about their health. A tiny imperial jade green dragon symbolizes the Chinese element of wood and the springtime, and is often placed in the east of the home to bring new beginnings, gentle growth, health and opportunity. Imperial jade frogs and fish are also luck- and prosperity-bringers.

Type: Calcium magnesium iron silicate (variety of actinolite-tremolite).

Colours: Mid- to dark green when iron-rich, creamy-coloured when there is more magnesium, also white and sometimes black.

Availability: Common.

Physical benefits: May improve acne, skin and hair conditions (elixir is helpful), asthma, lymphatic system, bones and joints, particularly hips, bacterial and viral infections, bladder, kidneys, cystitis and genito-urinary infections, bedwetting, balance and inner-ear problems.

Emotional healing: Nephrite insulates the shock for the very young and the very old in hospital or being cared for away from their home or family, temporarily or permanently.

Chakra: Heart and Root.

Nephrite Jade

Candle colour: Green. **Fragrances:** Carnation, crocus, rose, sweet pea, vanilla. **Practical uses:** Green jade is the ultimate good-luck crystal in all its forms, and at the same time traditionally protects against sickness. Jade is gentle enough to be a child's first jewellery, perhaps a tiny bracelet that protects a child against tumbles, illness and harmful people. **Workplace:** A natural increaser of prosperity if kept in the cash register or near an accounts computer in a business and near a source of heat such as a radiator. Nephrite will also attract new business to a company; helpful for all professional gardeners. **Magical significance:** An earth healing stone, nephrite jade is often made into power animals. Choose an animal whose qualities you feel close to and the nephrite (or indeed the other form of jade, jadeite) will add both strength and protection to the creature. A nephrite Buddha brings good fortune, prosperity and peace to any home or workplace. **Divinatory meaning:** Now is a time to think about your longer-term future and consider making a commitment or investment you have been avoiding. **Zodiac:** Taurus and Pisces. **Empowerment:** I am healthy and will remain so.

Jade is the generic term for two different gems, nephrite and jadeite. The term nephrite was applied to jade because of its beneficial effects on the kidneys, and one name for jade is *lapis nephriticus*. In fact it was only in the 1800s that experts differentiated between the two kinds of jade, since both are very similar in appearance, if not chemically, and much pre-1800 jade in China was in fact nephrite. Jade was called the royal gem or *yu* in Ancient China as early as 3000 BC, and was believed to contain *chi* or the life essence.

Jade burial suits were made for royalty during the Han dynasty (206 BC–AD 220), both to preserve the physical body and to grant eternal life to the spirit, and jade is still regarded as a symbol of health and long life. Drink a glass of jade-infused water every morning and put jade in the water you give your pets for an hour or two, to both energize and calm them.

Type: Nephrite, calcium magnesium iron silicate (variety of actinolite-tremolite).

Colours: Olive green, from light to dark olive.

Availability: Relatively common.

Physical benefits: Said to help with acne, skin and hair conditions, asthma, bones and joints particularly hips, bacterial and viral infections, bladder, kidneys, cystitis and genito-urinary infections, childbirth, travel sickness, hyperactivity in children, childhood ear infections, perforated ear drums.

Emotional healing: The most peace-bringing of the jades; wear during emotional meltdown until you feel normality return; soothes panic attacks and phobias when the phobia focus unexpectedly appears.

Chakra: Heart.

Olive Jade

Candle colour: Pale green. **Fragrances:** Cherry blossom, honey, lemon balm, neroli, olive blossom. **Practical uses:** An olive jade Buddha statue or Kwan Yin, mother of compassion, kept with fragrant white flowers, brings peace to the home and soothes aggressive children and temperamental people of any age. **Workplace:** Dark olive green is considered very lucky as an "improve your fortunes" charm if you are earning a minimal wage or cannot get full-time work. Wear or have olive jade nearby when you apply online for jobs, visit recruitment agencies or scan the newspaper, for a firmer foothold on the employment ladder. **Magical significance:** For meditation, finger the beads one by one on an olive jade necklace and for each one recite a rhythmic slow four- or five-word phrase or mantra, such as "May all be at peace"; go round and round the beads until you are in a state of deep relaxation. **Divinatory meaning:** Make peace with someone who has offended, as it is not worth wasting any more time fretting about their insensitivity. **Zodiac:** Virgo. **Empowerment:** Peace is more powerful than aggression.

Olive jade is the jade of generosity and sharing; jade tumblestones around the home help mean people to be more open with time and money, and help children to share toys with siblings and friends. Wear olive jade to encourage generous and willing giving if you are collecting for charity or you are responsible for organizing social events at work or buying presents for members of staff who leave or have babies.

A travel stone for exchange student holidays or exchanging homes with someone in another country.

Traditionally, olive jade is the stone of reconciliation after a quarrel with a friend, particularly if you lost touch because of the disagreement; good also for calling back a former love or someone you would have liked as a love earlier in your life. Place an olive jade necklace or bracelet in front of a photo of you and the person you want to bring back into your life; keep olive jade by the computer when surfing old friends' sites, to make telepathic connections and to find someone who could make you happy again.

Olive Jade

Type: Silicate/inosilicate/pyroxene, rarer than nephrite jade, which is silkier (p.266).

Colours: Green, white (pure form), lilac, pink, brown, red, black, orange and yellow. Emerald jade is called imperial jade.

Availability: Relatively common.

Physical benefits: May help with kidney, bladder, bedwetting, cystitis, fluid retention, hip and arm socket disorders and arthritis particularly of the hip and knees, blood-sugar imbalances, bronchitis, cystic fibrosis, burns and scalds, menstrual difficulties (endometriosis), PMS, eye problems and preserving youthfulness of body and mind, pregnancy, childbirth, babies (colic and fretfulness), children and small animals.

Emotional healing: For violent children and teenagers, especially those who attack their parents; also for domestic abuse against men.

Chakra: Root and Heart.

Jadeite/Jade

Candle colour: Green. **Fragrances:** Bay, clary sage, fern, moss, rosewood. **Practical uses:** Give or wear jade jewellery for young or new love, love in old age or after loss or recovery from abuse. It carries within it the power of immortality and so promises lasting love. **Workplace:** Since jadeite was traditionally fashioned into weapons as well as tools, jadeite signifies peace through strength; helpful if you have to deal with bullying or intimidation as a teacher, social or youth worker, a workplace human resources officer or in the prison service; for security or armed-service peacekeepers in areas of conflict. **Magical significance:** Jade in all its forms has always represented nobility, not only of rank but of ideals; wear jade to assist you in creating magic for the highest good and in spirit work to protect you from harmful or deceitful entities. **Divinatory meaning:** By acting unselfishly now you are storing goodwill for yourself in future; any personal inconvenience will almost immediately be more than compensated for. **Zodiac:** Libra and Pisces. **Empowerment:** I am rich in spirit.

Jadeite was highly prized among the indigenous people of Mexico, Central and South America, carved into deity masks (as early as 800 BC) and ritual artefacts, and cast into wells as an offering to the water spirits for fresh and plentiful water.

Jadeite was polished and cut to sharpness because it was tough and dense, and was used as axe heads in the British Isles up to 6,000 years ago. An example was found at La Trinité St Helier in Jersey. Jade pendants and necklaces

protect against those who deceive or abuse authority for financial or sexual gain. Jade bowls once used to transfer the life force to food, and jade ornaments on a table bring blessings to mealtimes. Jade is also the gardener's crystal.

Plant it in the corners of your garden, in pots of indoor plants or in vases of cut flowers for prolonged life. Keep three or four jadeite in a bowl of water to permeate fresh living energies through the home or workplace.

Type: Silicate; a chromium-rich variety of muscovite (p.157).

Colours: Emerald green, in some high-quality pieces solidified green glitter with golden highlights.

Availability: Relatively common.

Physical benefits: Thought to maintain healthy red and white blood cells; may help carpel tunnel syndrome, spinal alignment, muscles, immune system, throat, larynx, arteries, inflammation, eczema, rashes, skin allergies, snoring and sleep disturbances.

Emotional healing: Restores equilibrium, emotional stability and encourages fight-back after a major setback or long or serious illness in self or someone close; reduces dependency on stimulants or placebos.

Chakra: Heart and Throat.

Fuchsite

Candle colour: Green. **Fragrances:** Agrimony, anise, lavender, rosemary, sage. **Practical uses:** Fuchsite in the home brings more coordinated domestic schedules such as child care, school runs, visiting elderly or sick relations and outside work commitments, especially if you have to rely on other people for the smooth running of your life. **Workplace:** The crystal of gardeners, landscapers, conservationists, farmers; also for law-enforcement agents and anyone who has to organize and implement schedules or timetables, such as transport workers, receptionists and personal assistants. **Magical significance:** Brings positive and joyful energies into nature magic rituals; for herbalism, flower and tree essences and work with essential oils to connect with plant-energy healing. **Divinatory meaning:** Irritating problems will at last disperse, leaving you with enthusiasm for new people and places. **Zodiac:** Libra and Aquarius. **Empowerment:** I attract good fortune by my thoughts.

Fuchsite increases the energies of other crystals and so is an excellent crystal for healing layouts or those created to bring harmony to the home. It is the crystal that reminds us of our inner child and need for fun, relaxation and joyfulness in life, which may have been forgotten if we work long hours or have to struggle financially. Called the fairy crystal because it scatters green shimmers and flecks of gold if rubbed, fuchsite carried in a small cloth drawstring bag adds sparkle to family outings and is a wish crystal when asking for small miracles. Fuchsite in the home encourages children who are naturally solemn and afraid of life to laugh, socialize and become light-hearted.

Fuchsite is a soft mineral, therefore not well suited for jewellery. In its natural form, however, it can be used in meditation outdoors to increase awareness of Earth energies in old sites or beautiful places; a tiny piece buried in an unlovely place helps Earth healing.

Type: Calcium magnesium carbonate with zinc that colours it green.

Colours: Olive, variety of greens.

Availability: Rarer form of dolomite.

Physical benefits: May be good for eyesight, colds and influenza, bronchitis and pneumonia, wound healing, general immunity, memory, hair, skin, nails, pregnancy, teeth, nails, bones, breasts, cramps, genito-urinary system, bedwetting, blood sugar and temperature balance.

Emotional healing: Assists recovery from alcohol abuse and addictions; reduces tendencies to self-harm or starving because of obsession with obtaining a celebrity-thin figure.

Chakra: Heart.

Green Dolomite

Candle colour: Green. **Fragrances:** Chamomile, clary sage, honeysuckle, manuka, sweetgrass. **Practical uses:** The dolomite of lasting faithful love, wear green dolomite jewellery or keep a dish of tumblestones in your home if your partner works away a lot or has a job where they frequently socialize or entertain business clients; acts as a strengthener of natural loving bonds and reminder to both of you that nothing can split two people who want to be together. **Workplace:** An excellent workplace stone for encouraging friendly but professional relationships and to deter inappropriate levels of flirting or sexual innuendos; good if you have a senior who oversteps normal bounds of friendliness or harasses you sexually. **Magical significance:** Green dolomite is sometimes called the crystal herb because it works especially well with any plant medicines or remedies; keep a piece with your medicinal herbs, potions, plant oils and essences to empower them and keep their energies fresh; good for attracting nature spirits into your garden. **Divinatory meaning:** If you are anxious about a partner straying, ask gently without accusing, as you may be reflecting your own fears about your desirability. **Zodiac:** Virgo. **Empowerment:** I am worthy of consideration.

Green dolomite has steady energies like a healthy heart or pulse beat, and radiates both calm and focused energy. Carry or wear it to attract like-minded friends if you have moved to a new job or area or you feel isolated in your neighbourhood or community.

Green dolomite is a stone for encouraging a friendly or friendlier atmosphere among neighbours; put a piece on your front-facing window ledges to encourage community spirit in the immediate area; wear it for establishing any community activities or neighbourhood groups and for campaigning for better local facilities for children.

Green dolomite makes mean people more generous; wear or carry green dolomite if you socialize with people who never take their turn at paying; a good crystal for voluntary or charity workers for successful fund-raising; place it on or near applications if you are hoping to gain a work-experience placement or internship with a charity or international organization.

Uvarovite Garnet

Type: Calcium chromium silicate, tiny lustrous crystals.

Colours: Emerald green, the only consistently green garnet, though rare in gem form.

Availability: Very rare garnet.

Physical benefits: May aid cell regeneration, heart, lung weakness and diseases, emphysema, plant allergies such as hay fever, liver, pancreas, bladder weakness, sexual dysfunction and libido in both sexes.

Emotional healing: For someone who feels inadequate this brings a sense of self-worth.

Chakra: Heart.

Candle colour: Green. **Fragrances:** Cedar, rosewood, thyme. **Practical uses:** Keep or wear uvarovite if you live alone to prevent loneliness. **Workplace:** A prosperity crystal for where you have perfected a skill, but are not getting adequate financial reward. **Magical significance:** The drusy (covered by many minute crystals) kind of uvarovite calls spiritual love into your life. **Divinatory meaning:** Unexpected good luck will bring the growth of prosperity in an area in which you were missing out. **Zodiac:** Taurus and Capricorn. **Empowerment:** I have come so far and can go so much further.

It is sometimes hard to distinguish uvarovite from green grossular tsavorite (p.272), though their chemical composition is different. Uvarovite has consistently small crystals and is often found in its drusy form; where there is a natural surface coating of tiny sparkling crystals covering a rock, sometimes made into beautiful jewellery. If a crystal is faceted or tumbled, it is almost certainly tsavorite. Because uvarovite is so rare, it is a very special crystal to give to a loved one as it symbolizes what is precious and lasting.

Demantoid Garnet

Type: Andradite garnet, calcium iron silicate. Russian demantoid has golden-brown crystal thread inclusions of chrysotile, called horsetail.

Colours: Deep emerald green (most precious and rarest colour), various shades of green from light green.

Availability: Very rare garnet, highly valuable.

Physical benefits: May help eyesight (second only to emerald in effectiveness), recurring colds, bronchitis, pneumonia, septicaemia, secondary tumours, blocked arteries.

Emotional healing: Reduces loneliness and isolation, especially only children or those away from parents in care.

Chakra: Heart.

Candle Colour: Green. **Fragrances:** Cedar, lily, lotus. **Practical uses:** Wear if you know your insecurities or those of your partner put a strain on relationships. **Workplace:** Good for working with a love partner. **Magical significance:** Demantoid garnet removes obstacles in the way of love. Light a green candle and hold your demantoid. Wait until the wax begins to melt and say, "May his/her heart be softened and turn to me." **Divinatory meaning:** A stubborn person will come round to your viewpoint if you ask again and then leave it. **Zodiac:** Aquarius. **Empowerment:** I do not need to intervene to make things happen.

This fabulous garnet can be difficult to buy and the most expensive. However, you can obtain rough-cut gems online or pick up demantoid garnets set as antique jewellery. Smudge over an old demantoid with an incense stick in a tree fragrance to make it your own. Often called the star of the garnets, its name means diamond-like because of its brilliance; a stone to pledge that nothing will come between your love. Buy yourself one if alone as a reminder to value yourself highly and demand consideration from others.

Type: Silicate/calcium aluminium silicate, transparent green variety of grossular garnet.

Colours: Pale to emerald green.

Availability: Obtainable through specialist jewellery and crystal stores and online.

Physical benefits: May help with immune system, heart and lungs, pituitary and thyroid glands, plant, animal and pollen allergies, blood-sugar disorders, skin irritation, boils, swollen scar tissue or wounds, detoxifying kidneys and blood, influenza and repeated colds, restoring libido in women; an anti-inflammatory.

Emotional healing: If people have played favourites with you since childhood or you are the family scapegoat, wearing tsavorite releases the cycle and stops you accepting the blame in every situation.

Chakra: Heart.

Tsavorovite/Tsavarolite Garnet

Candle colour: Green. **Fragrances:** Bluebell, galbanum, geranium, honeysuckle, mimosa. **Practical uses:** Wear tsavorite to boost feelings of joy and positive thinking that attract abundance, not necessarily in a materialistic sense but as improved quality of life and openness in getting to know people on the fringes of your life. **Workplace:** Natural or tumbled tsavorite in the workplace reduces the "mother hen" complex if you or anyone else feels responsible for the welfare, nutrition and happiness of the people around you. **Magical significance:** If you are unattached, every Friday, the day of Venus and love, put two small pieces of matching tsavorite, for example earrings or tumblestones, in front of a lighted green candle to call or call back lost love. Leave the candle to burn for about 20 minutes. **Divinatory meaning:** You may face disapproval from someone close over a new interest or activity, but this will lessen if you persist. **Zodiac:** Virgo. **Empowerment:** I will please myself this time.

Tsavorite is the name used most frequently in the USA, tsavolite in Europe. Meditate with tsavorite to facilitate communication with higher spiritual realms. Regular meditative use of this crystal increases psychic awareness and latent psychic abilities, particularly intuition.

At the same time it releases old emotional trauma or feelings of inadequacy, assisting you to trust people and life more and to socialize for its own sake, not just to meet the right person or for business reasons.

Green garnets reduce the power of factions and rivalries at work and prevent over-fierce competition between brothers and sisters in the home.

Keep tsavorite or any natural green garnet near entrances to protect rural homes. If you feel threatened by the success of others or envious of their apparently idyllic lifestyle, tsavorite worn as a necklace or ring or carried near the heart helps you to recognize your own blessings and to work to attain whatever is missing.

Type: Silicate/inosilicate, spodumene.

Colours: Pale green to yellow-green, emerald green when coloured with chromium.

Availability: Rare.

Physical benefits: May assist with healing on all levels; boosts the power of herbs, essential oils, homeopathic remedies and hydrotherapy; balance the hemispheres of the brain; may help with hyperventilation, fluid imbalances, fertility, sick animals and children for whom conventional treatment is traumatic or not working.

Emotional healing: Eases the heart of emotionally distressed children or panicky animals; relieves self-neglect or active self-harming tendencies and excesses of all kinds in adults.

Chakra: Heart.

Hiddenite/Green Kunzite

Candle colour: Pale green. **Fragrances:** Geranium, hyacinth, magnolia, rose, vervain. **Practical uses:** Hiddenite soothes you when you have lost someone dear to you, whether through bereavement, moving far away or because of estrangement; also if you have lost something central to your life such as your home, your job or an essential vehicle you cannot afford to replace, hiddenite assists with coping strategies. **Workplace:** Hiddenite helps you determine if you are in the right place doing the right job. It reveals choices from the heart, not the head, while at the same time being realistic as to how and when you can make changes; uncovers buried hopes and dreams forgotten due to pressures of daily life. **Magical significance:** A wonderful healing stone when treating members of the family, a lover, close friends or pets, because its powers are amplified by the connection of love. Focus on how much you love the sick or sad person; pass the crystal close to a place of pain or over a photograph. **Divinatory meaning:** Acknowledge what you really want as it may not be as impossible as you think to attain it. **Zodiac:** Taurus. **Empowerment:** I evolve daily.

Hiddenite, one of the gem varieties of spodumene, was first discovered in 1879 by William Hidden in North Carolina. Found usually as tiny green crystals growing with its pink or lilac sister kunzite (p.57 and p.210), hiddenite is sometimes called the evolution crystal.

This is because it assists individuals to grow more spiritual and aware of their collective responsibility for the care of the Earth. It can be occasionally be made into jewellery, though it is quite soft. Carrying hiddenite awakens and attracts true love in the

earthly sense as well as spiritual twin soul love. For hiddenite fuses the spiritual with nature; if you have a deep relationship with someone on the Internet, hiddenite next to the computer will either assist moving the relationship into the everyday world or connect you with someone who does want more than cyber romance.

Hiddenite helps you and those around you to focus on the present situation without being distracted by injustices from the past and worries about the future.

Green Jasper

Type: Silicate, microcrystalline quartz, often with organic matter or other minerals as inclusions.

Colours: Green, single colour from pale spring green to a deeper tea or olive green.

Availability: Rare as single colour and often of high quality, relatively common with other colours included.

Physical benefits: May help with bladder and kidneys, cystitis, travel sickness, body odour, digestion(bloating), fluid retention, bronchitis, colds, coughs, influenza.

Emotional healing: Good for overcoming phobias about germs, controls fears of small crawling things, obsessive compulsive disorder.

Chakra: Heart.

Candle colour: Green. **Fragrances:** Cedar, geranium, vervain. **Practical uses:** The ultimate sleep crystal, green jasper helps young children to establish proper sleep rhythms. For adults, add the crystal to a bath or elixir. **Workplace:** Green jasper prevents social workers becoming drained of energy. **Magical significance:** Green jasper has been used in fertility ceremonies in cultures from Eastern Europe to Africa. Wear one in a pouch around your waist if you wish to conceive. **Divinatory meaning:** A good time for fertility, the time when a dream will start to grow. **Zodiac:** Virgo and Pisces. **Empowerment:** I acknowledge my emotions.

Green Jasper has been used since ancient times. It has been found in one of the most important archaeological sites, at Mehrgarh in Pakistan, where it had been used as a bow drill for semi-precious stones, dating from the fourth to fifth millennium BC. A dark green jasper seal-stone engraved with the Minoan "hieroglyphic" script from Crete, dating from 1700–1550 BC, is in the British Museum. Single-coloured green jasper has been prized for carvings and fine jewellery in many ages and cultures.

Arizona Lizard Jasper

Type: Silicate, microcrystalline quartz, often with organic matter or other minerals as inclusions.

Colours: Light to dark green, patterned to resemble lizard skin.

Availability: Common.

Physical benefits: May ease sunburn, burns and scalds, headaches, circulation, assist body to throw off disease and build up immunity to common infections.

Emotional healing: Gives the determination to start again or to salvage what is possible from a bad situation rather than rejecting it because of hurt feelings.

Chakra: Root.

Candle colour: Green. **Fragrances:** Cedar, pine, sage. **Practical uses:** A good-luck charm for successful lifestyle changes, particularly for returning to an area where you lived in childhood. **Workplace:** Wear or carry for recouping lost business and for branching out into new areas of expertise; good if you are involved in setting up a new branch of your company. **Magical significance:** The lizard brings clairvoyant recall of ancient worlds if held in sunlight. **Divinatory meaning:** Beware of people whose self-interest predominates, who may offer to help you at a price. **Zodiac:** Scorpio. **Empowerment:** I can regain what I have lost.

As with all the jaspers named after creatures, Arizona lizard jasper carries the strengths of its namesake, the ability to enjoy quiet moments of leisure and to wait till the right moment to leap in or run; good for stressed executives to avoid burnout by pacing themselves to make rapid decisions when needed, but to avoid a constant state of over-alertness. Because of the ability of the lizard to regrow its tail, lizard jasper has taken on the power to regenerate, rebuild and transform life; keeps backpackers safe.

Variscite

Type: Hydrated aluminium phosphate.

Colours: Light green to apple to bright green, bluish green or turquoise, often with patterned light and darker brown veins across the surface.

Availability: Obtainable through specialist crystal stores and online.

Physical benefits: Said to help strengthen male reproductive system, a crystalline Viagra; improve and maintain health, arteries, veins, blood vessels, nerves.

Emotional healing: Thought to ease fear and worry, relieve stress and depression and increase awareness of the cause of problems; attract new friends.

Chakra: Solar Plexus and Heart.

Candle colour: Green. **Fragrances:** Anise, basil, geranium, jasmine, thyme. **Practical uses:** Acts as a filter of irritations and outside worries disturbing domestic peace. **Workplace:** Particularly useful for carers as it gives patience when treating the sick or elderly. **Magical significance:** Pass round a group for focusing healing powers. **Divinatory meaning:** You may need to draw on your inner resources rather than outside help. **Zodiac:** Taurus and Gemini. **Empowerment:** I release my fears and welcome harmony in my mind, my body and my spirit.

Variscite is named after the Latin name for Vogtland in Saxony, where its colour matched the costumes of the dancers at the traditional spring festivals that may still be seen today. Flat, polished varieties make excellent worry stones. By holding and stroking them, your anxieties will be reduced. Whenever in a difficult situation, hold the stone, reciting a comforting empowerment in your mind, such as "I feel calm and happy". Variscite will help you settle in a new area or career; good for any pets who are far from their native habitat or natural climate.

Wavellite

Type: Hydrated aluminium phosphate; fibrous.

Colours: Usually green, but also white, colourless, yellow or brown.

Availability: Obtainable from specialist crystal stores and online.

Physical benefits: Believed to stimulate antibodies to resist infection and disease; said to be a good detoxifier and to ease illnesses brought on or made worse by shock or trauma.

Emotional healing: Aids bonding and healing of rifts between parents, step-parents, adoptive and foster children.

Chakra: Heart and Solar Plexus.

Candle colour: Green. **Fragrances:** Apple, rose, violet. **Practical uses:** Use as a study aid to help you understand all aspects of a subject. **Workplace:** Wavellite aids decision-making by enabling us to understand the overall situation, not just from our own perspective. **Magical significance:** Carry wavellite during the new moon and crescent moon periods improves intuition; when held in full moonlight, it allows us to glimpse opportunities ahead. **Divinatory meaning:** You have a decision to make that may affect your longer-term future. **Zodiac:** Aquarius. **Empowerment:** I will not be pressurized to make decisions before I am ready.

Wavellite is considered a magical gift from the earth spirits. Radial (wheel-like) clusters of wavellite are often found embedded in limestone or chert, reflecting light to produce a sparkling pinwheel star effect – in Native American lore stars that fell to earth that were enclosed in rock to keep them safe. Wavellite increases lucid and psychic dreams and aids dream recall. Use it in past-life healing therapy to reduce past-life trauma.

Type: Quartzite (a rock rather than a mineral) with green actinolite needles embedded in it; often pointed and elongated so it resembles the onion-like vegetable leek or thin leaves; also in modern mineralogy applied as a general name for pale green quartzes or leek-green jasper (see also the unique seriphos quartz, p.259).

Colours: Pale dull green.

Availability: Obtainable from specialist crystal stores and online.

Physical benefits: May improve fevers, high temperatures in children, swellings and bruises (warm it slightly for these), psycho-sexual problems, particularly premature ejaculation or impotence in men, high blood pressure.

Emotional healing: Calms irritability and temper tantrums, whether in adults or children.

Chakra: Heart.

Prase

First referred to by the Roman historian Pliny, who called it *prasius* for its wonderful spring-like energies, prase was sacred in Germany to the Anglo-Saxon goddess Oestre, after whom Easter is named. She opened the gates of spring at the spring equinox (around 21 March in the northern hemisphere).

The first eggs of the year were decorated and set on her altar, along with prase crystals and the first greenery.

It is an earth mother stone, with tiny pieces often buried in gardens to encourage rich growth or in rituals to heal polluted or waste land spoiled by industry and now abandoned. Prase encourages children to play in a friendly non-aggressive way, to share their toys and take turns; soothes female animals on heat that cannot mate.

Mariposite

Type: Mica (chromium-rich), with white quartz veins, and spots of gold or pyrite.

Colours: Bright green, with white, white sometimes with purple.

Availability: Rare as a polished crystal and jewellery, but obtainable from specialist crystal stores and online.

Physical benefits: May prove helpful after transplant operations, brain damage or strokes to assist other parts of the brain taking over from damaged areas.

Emotional healing: Helps to alleviate fears and anxiety that magnify normal stress out of proportion, causing inaction or panic reactions to everyday situations.

Chakra: Heart.

Candle colour: Green. **Fragrances:** Acacia, almond cedar. **Practical uses:** Brings profit to any venture, whether in monetary terms or satisfaction. **Workplace:** Keep mariposite near you at work to be tolerant with co-workers or employees. **Magical significance:** Obtain a polished mariposite sphere to use for shadow scrying. Shine candles and pick out shadow patterns to answer questions. **Divinatory meaning:** Keep going on a venture for you will see results, as you have invested so much time already. **Zodiac:** Aquarius. **Empowerment:** I trust the way will become clear.

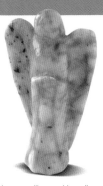

Nebula Stone

Type: Green quartz, igneous: quartz, aegirine, riebeckite, anorthoclase, acmite, arfvedsonite and zircon.

Colours: Deep dark green, almost black.

Availability: Rare, only one occurrence on Earth, available from some specialist crystal stores and online.

Physical benefits: Believed to be useful for whole-body healing and malfunctions of nervous and neurone systems.

Emotional healing: Nebula offers grounding to stand firm when others are pulling in different directions.

Chakra: Crown.

Candle colour: Green. **Fragrances:** Cedarwood, mugwort, musk, myrrh, valerian. **Practical uses:** Nebula brings settled energies if you feel ill at ease in your home. **Workplace:** A stone when injustice cannot be ignored to take measured but effective action. **Magical significance:** Hold nebula and focus on a star. Plot the star on a sky map, connecting with the star when it is visible, holding your nebula to merge with cosmic energies. **Divinatory meaning:** Do not take anything for granted; you may have found what you were looking for. **Zodiac:** Scorpio. **Empowerment:** I am part of the bigger picture of creation.

As well as its crystalline and jewellery use, natural mariposite is more commonly used as a landscaping stone. If you have some in your garden, the stone will release harmonious energies; acts as a filter if you live in a town or near a busy road for not only physical pollutants but the stress and noise of modern urban living. Keep a small ornamental piece of the stone near the front door or on the balcony of an apartment to mark out your stress-free zone if you have noisy or intrusive neighbours.

The nebula stone has patterns and depths reminiscent of the night sky and an otherworldly quality that makes it a powerful healer for all stuck in what feels like a dead end, whether in a career, a relationship or in a place you have lived all your life that now seems too small and restrictive.

The stone was discovered by Karen and Ron Nurnberg in the mid-1990s in a remote area of Mexico and they describe the place as wondrous and magical, rather like the stone itself.

Type: Silicate/nesosilicate, zircon.

Colours: Brilliant green, yellowish green, brownish green; can sometimes be cloudy.

Availability: Relatively common.

Physical benefits: May help with lungs, cystic fibrosis; allergies due to pollen and plants, wheat and other grain allergies, heart, heart pacemaker surgery; assist all forms of natural healing especially using herbs and tree essences; good for connective tissue, nerve connectivity, regrowth and restoration of normal body functioning after invasive treatment, transplants and transfusions.

Emotional healing: Reduces emotional dependency on others that can stifle relationships and friendships and over-possessiveness or over-concern with the lives and problems of others.

Chakra: Heart.

Green Zircon

Candle colour: Green. **Fragrances:** Basil, clary sage, pine, rosemary, thyme. **Practical uses:** Encourages development of new friendships and the revival of those that have ceased through physical distance, a new partner or pressures of work; good for forming social groups based on mutual needs and interest, such as for single parents and children or neighbourhood improvement schemes; for networking with national organizations. **Workplace:** Green zircon enhances beauty; an ideal workplace support if you have less than ideal conditions, if you spend a lot of time dealing with complaints about malfunctioning or broken equipment or with crime or extreme social deprivation; helps you to avoid being dragged down and to find positive solutions to restore or create order. **Magical significance:** One of the most powerful zircon anti-theft and -loss crystals; wear green zircon when travelling to keep your possessions safe; keep your zircon out of sight when in crowded places (a pendant is ideal). **Divinatory meaning:** Buy something small and beautiful or make a small improvement to beautify yourself or your home to kick-start your feel-good factor. **Zodiac:** Virgo and Libra. **Empowerment:** I make beauty out of ugliness.

Green zircon is the zircon of abundance and growth in every area of life and of creating beauty and harmony even in unpromising situations; good for all personal, home or work makeovers and for creating a good social life if you have got out of the habit.

Wear green zircon to feel prosperous and in doing so to attract prosperity through the growth of income; traditionally worn by those who want a wealthy or beautiful partner, in the modern world wear it to find someone who shares your dreams and will work with you to fulfil them.

Green zircon is helpful for those who want to combine conventional medicine and surgery with spiritual knowledge within their existing workplace or disciplines; wear green zircon if you are a patient of an unsympathetic or overbearing medical practitioner or consultant, to create awareness of your feelings and not just clinical needs.

Type: Silicate with corundum inclusions.

Colours: Green with red inclusions.

Availability: Relatively common.

Physical benefits: Recommended by some for carpal tunnel syndrome, repetitive strain injury, immune system, infections, energizing the body, spinal column, red and white blood cell imbalances, heart and restoration of health after a period of feeling unwell.

Emotional healing: Helps to bounce back after emotional upset or tension and deal with situations as they really are, without over-reacting or internalizing the problem and fretting endlessly over it.

Chakra: Heart.

Ruby in Fuchsite

Candle colour: Green or pink. **Fragrances:** Basil, bay, cherry blossom, lavender, rose. **Practical uses:** A stone for adapting to unexpected new circumstances in a long-term relationship, such as a baby when you thought your family was complete; good for the partners of service personnel to adjust to frequent location changes. **Workplace:** Wear this crystal if you are in conflict with those you work with to deflect an all-out confrontation and steer a compromise without losing face or giving up essential principles. **Magical significance:** Use a ruby in fuchsite massage wand as a magic wand to bring lasting love into or back into your life; spiral it in different directions as you call a lover known by name or love as yet unknown, faster and faster as you move the wand faster and faster to release the power. **Divinatory meaning:** You may be passionate about a new person or plan but let matters develop slowly so you can be sure of your feelings. **Zodiac:** Aquarius. **Empowerment:** Each day I grow in a new way.

Fuchsite is the green chromium-rich variety of the muscovite family of crystals (p.157); when it contains inclusions of ruby (p.279) it becomes a very dynamic stone, even more active than the similar-looking ruby in zoisite. Fuchsite is a stone of nature spirits, earth and air; ruby of love, passion and fire.

These energies together rejuvenate your mind, body and spirit, and ruby empowers you to reach out to your heart's desire – giving you motivation and strength to succeed in any and every area of

your life. As a massage wand you can smooth away tension and resentment from your mind and body, and replace them with harmony and enthusiasm.

Wear ruby in fuchsite when you are coming out of a difficult life change or emotional trauma to regenerate your passion for life and replace what did not work with new, attainable goals and dreams. Take a ruby in fuchsite angel or sphere with you if you are emigrating or you are going to live in your partner's home country or adopt your partner's religion.

Type: An amalgamation of epidote, feldspar and quartz.

Colours: Pinks and greens.

Availability: Relatively common.

Physical benefits: May aid heart function, circulation, balance bodily fluids and metabolism; said to be good for hyperventilation and breathing irregularities, in labour particularly to ease the transition; useful for nutrition and maintenance, so helps fussy eaters.

Emotional healing: Helps to release deep-seated emotions in a slow and gentle way, easing long-standing addictions and phobias; carry to help give up smoking; good for dreamy children and anyone who finds it hard to remain in the reality of the here and now.

Chakra: Solar Plexus and Heart.

Unakite

Candle colour: Pink or green. **Fragrances:** Bluebell, geranium, magnolia, rose, vervain. **Practical uses:** Hold unakite whenever you are feeling a little lost or do not know where to start with a mountain of jobs or to meet simultaneous demands. It will focus you in the here and now, overcoming freezing in panic and suggesting novel solutions. **Workplace:** Unakite encourages harmonious partnerships, both in love and in business; especially helpful if you are working with a relation or friend or in a very small workplace where happy personal interactions are vital. **Magical significance:** If you have trouble finding things, keep this crystal with you; a good luck charm when you must take a risk. **Divinatory meaning:** You may feel uncertain about life, but to go backwards would be a mistake and old problems recur. **Zodiac:** Scorpio. **Empowerment:** I focus on the promises of tomorrow, not the mistakes of yesterday.

The crystal of happy, lasting relationships, unakite is traditionally sprinkled with dried yarrow and placed in a sealed bag as a marriage or commitment symbol; replace on anniversaries and throw the old crystal and yarrow into running water.

When you hope two will become three, place unakite under your pillow to aid conception. In pregnancy regularly set a piece of unakite on the womb so that the parents-to-be can make spiritual connection with the unborn baby. Take the unakite to the delivery room.

Unakite sends relief to the root of a health problem, whether the cause is known to the healer or patient or not, by pulling towards the source, not the symptom area.

Type: Silicate/nesosilicate, olivine is the name for a group of minerals; in crystal work, olivine is known as the more opaque, greasier and usually smaller sister of the bottle-green gemstone form peridot (p.282).

Colours: From its characteristic olive green to pale, yellowish or brownish green, according to iron content, the green owing to nickel.

Availability: Common, one of the most abundant mineral constituents of the planet.

Physical benefits: Thought to help with asthma, pollen, plant or fur allergies, bites, stings, breasts, eyesight, infections and viruses especially connected with the respiratory system, nausea, gallstones, bile duct, liver and liver transplants, Crohn's disease, jaundice, hepatitis, swellings and growths.

Emotional healing: In its yellower forms, olivine protects against subtle bitching and mental bullying for teenagers who frequently receive nasty text messages from peers or are teased and undermined on social-networking sites.

Chakra: Heart.

Olivine

Candle colour: Green. **Fragrances**: Almond, anise, basil, fennel, thyme. **Practical uses**: If your partner will be absent, the night before departure leave four olivine crystals, one at each corner of a suitcase, overnight to encourage loving contact and fidelity while s/he is away. If you are the one going away, conceal a bag of olivines behind the bed. **Workplace**: A bowl of olivines in your workspace prevents paperwork being mislaid or items and tools being borrowed by colleagues and not returned; hold an item you are lending over the olivines to imprint it with home base. **Magical significance**: Because olivines are tiny and cheaper than peridot, they can be used in ongoing long-term money magic, as can green olivine sand; add a pinch of green olivine sand each morning or a tiny olivine to a pot. When the pot is full, scatter the sand to the winds or drop one or two of the olivines into a river or stream and start again with the rest or new sand. **Divinatory meaning**: Money will come in small amounts that will build up, but be careful it does not drain out the same way. **Zodiac**: Taurus. **Empowerment**: Each small step is a step nearer success.

Olivine, also called chrysolite in its yellower form, is found in stony and stony iron meteorites, in some lunar rock, also in deep rock that is brought to the surface in volcanic activity. Because olivine crystals are often tiny and relatively cheap, they tend to be used in larger quantities in healing and ritual than the gem form peridot.

Olivine crystals are said to be the tears of the Hawaiian volcano goddess Pele, and green olivine sand is found naturally at South Point, Hawaii, but can be bought on the Internet. Put olivine sand inside a glass candle-holder and burn a green candle set in the sand every Friday so your luck will increase weekly. Olivine helps children and teenagers to resist pressure from their friends to do wrong or take unnecessary risks; sew one into the lining of a pocket or hem to bring them safely home at night.

Olivine

Type: Silicate/nesosilicate, gemstone variety of olivine.

Colours: Usually bright green, due to its iron content.

Availability: Relatively common.

Physical benefits: Claimed to Increase effectiveness of other medications and treatment; may help with ulcers, stings and bites that cause an allergic reaction, asthma, digestive disorders, colon, pancreas, gall bladder; eyesight, gastroenteritis, IBS, Crohn's disease, breasts; assist weight gain; believed to stimulate overdue labour; relieve swellings and growths of all kind.

Emotional healing: Guards against destructive jealousy caused by betrayal in past relationships and personal fears that we are unlovable, rather than relating to the present relationship.

Chakra: Solar Plexus and Heart.

Peridot

Candle colour: Olive green. **Fragrances**: Bay, cedar, juniper, lemon balm, lemon verbena. **Practical uses**: A wise money crystal, keep with credit cards to spend sensibly. Wear a peridot ring when you go shopping with shopaholic friends or family. Good also for getting bargains on eBay and other auction sites, especially of nearly-new items. **Workplace**: Wear or carry peridot for bartering, whether for supplies or a good price for your products and services; good for auctioneers, valuers, insurance assessors and underwriters, risk assessors in any area, bookmakers and anyone who makes a regular income from buying and selling or profits from exchanges. **Magical significance**: Peridot is a magical stone for finding love via the Internet if it is difficult for you to get out and socialize. Hold your peridot jewellery just before opening a friendship or dating site and say, "Wise gem, guide me to good love and protect me from those who would deceive me." Put on the jewellery and follow your instincts. **Divinatory meaning**: Rely on luck and take a chance on a new offer or opportunity rather than holding back. **Zodiac**: Taurus and Libra. **Empowerment**: People respond positively towards me.

Peridot was used in Ancient Egypt as early as 1580 BC for jewellery; here and in many other locations it was considered a stone of the sun and so very lucky in drawing money, health, success and love.

Peridot is naturally protective against envy, gossip behind your back and people who deceive you. In modern healing, it is considered very effective in amplifying Reiki energies. Hold peridot immediately after therapies using heat or warmth, such as sweat lodges, hot rocks or sauna treatment, to continue the beneficial effects.

The Romans wore peridot in gold rings to bring peaceful sleep, and it is very effective if you suffer from recurring nightmares about evil spirits, murders or sexual attacks. Peridot, especially set in gold, evokes a positive, helpful response from normally unhelpful people; wear or carry peridot when approaching faceless officialdom, especially concerning financial or legal matters.

Malachite

Type: Copper carbonate.

Colours: Emerald to grass green with black or pale green stripes, bands, swirls or marbling effect.

Availability: Common.

Physical benefits: May help with immune system, arthritis, tumours, torn muscles, broken bones. toothache, gum infections, sinus blockages. Use only externally and work with polished tumbled stones as the dust can be slightly toxic.

Emotional healing: Gives resistance to emotional blackmail and heals emotional abuse, especially from childhood; encourages healthy relationships based on love and not need.

Chakra: Heart.

Candle colour: Bright green. **Fragrances:** Cedar, copal, pine, sage. **Practical uses:** Keep near microwaves in the kitchen and by televisions in living areas. **Workplace:** Malachite protects against noise, over-bright fluorescent lighting and harmful rays from technological equipment, negative phonecalls and emails. **Magical significance:** Overcomes fears of flying if you empower the crystal before a trip by holding it and picturing yourself in the wings of Raphael, the archangel. **Divinatory meaning:** Let go of the past and move forward to what you most desire. **Zodiac:** Scorpio. **Empowerment:** I will follow my heart.

A stone of the most powerful love goddesses, for example our Lady of the Mountains in Central Russia or Freyja the Viking goddess of love and beauty.

Malachite will help you battle against depression or anxiety by encouraging you to uncover the reasons for your distress and then helping you to break negative patterns of behaviour. Speak your fears and sorrows daily aloud as you hold the crystal and then leave your malachite in a sheltered place outdoors overnight to carry away the fears on the winds.

Vesuvianite

Type: Silicates. Its appearance can be similar to jade.

Colours: Usually green or olive, but colours include yellow, brown, red, blue and purple as idocrase, blue as cyprine and green gem quality as californite (found in California).

Availability: Obtainable in specialist crystal stores and online. Rare in transparent form, used in jewellery.

Physical benefits: Alleged to helps digestion and the intake of nutrients from food; may relieve stress-based illnesses, racing heart and pulse.

Emotional healing: Disperses feelings of anger and irritability, lifts fear, depression and unwarranted guilt.

Chakra: Heart.

Candle colour: Green or any earth colour. **Fragrances:** Cedar, valerian. **Practical uses:** Promotes loyalty to family and patriotic feelings. **Workplace:** Use vesuvianite to encourage team effort; reduces confrontations. **Magical significance:** Cleanses and energizes the aura, assists anyone to see auras more clearly; keeps contact with your spiritual nature even when earthly matters demand attention. **Divinatory meaning:** Your true path in life is revealed. Follow your convictions. **Zodiac:** Sagittarius and Capricorn. **Empowerment:** There is always room for compromise.

The name vesuvianite was given to the mineral because it was originally found on the volcano Vesuvius in southern Italy. Renowned for its qualities in releasing anger and dispelling negativity, vesuvianite relieves feelings of claustrophobia, especially in relationships. This crystal breaks the chains by which you feel bound and helps you to escape repetitive negative thoughts and actions that strengthen them. It also speeds healthy weight loss where overeating has emotional roots.

Adamite

Type: Phosphate, arsonate.

Colours: Most commonly lime or yellow-green or yellow.

Availability: Readily obtainable from specialist crystal and mineral stores and online.

Physical benefits: Said to be beneficial for heart, lungs, throat, Seasonal Affective Disorder, menstrual and hormonal problems.

Emotional healing: Good for freeing blocked communication, helps resist emotional manipulation especially by those who play on weakness or guilt.

Chakra: Heart and Throat.

Candle colour: Green. **Fragrances:** Lemon, lemongrass, lime, pine, wintergreen, witch hazel. **Practical uses:** Adamite will discourage interruptions from neighbours, colleagues and distracting chatter; keep on a shelf above the phone to discourage cold callers. **Workplace:** Use adamite for brainstorming. **Magical significance:** Adamite is excellent when using a pendulum, tarot cards or runes to decide between options. **Divinatory meaning:** Speak what is in your heart rather than suffering in silence. **Zodiac:** Cancer. **Empowerment:** I have the right to my opinions and my beliefs.

Though adamite is named after the 19th-century French mineralogist Gilbert Joseph Adam, it has become associated with the quest for knowledge and the desire to regain Paradise after the fall of Adam because of its transformative fluorescent properties. For this reason, adamite will bring wealth and success through the expression of existing talents and give quiet people deserved recognition.

WARNING: Handle with care as toxic; do not ingest, and wash your hands after handling.

Moldavite

Type: Silica-based tektite, with impurities of magnesium, iron and other elements, from only one location in the world.

Colours: Usually deep bottle green, glassy.

Availability: Rare and becoming rarer.

Physical benefits: May help asthma, allergies or rashes caused by modern chemicals or pollution; disturbances in the electrical impulses in the brain, hard-to-treat progressive illnesses.

Emotional healing: When you are troubled but do not know the source, moldavite eases away doubts.

Chakra: Heart, Brow and Crown.

Candle colour: Green. **Fragrances:** Cinnamon, frankincense. **Practical uses:** Make moldavite massage oil for chakras, soles of the feet, elbows and knees (not the face or near eyes). Place in a jar; fill with almond oil, plus six drops of rose oil. Leave in a light place for two weeks. **Workplace:** Good for counteracting cynicism. **Magical significance:** Connects even the most world-weary adult with the wonders of the universe. **Divinatory meaning:** Dramatic change in your life for the better. **Zodiac:** Aquarius. **Empowerment:** I seek inspiration from the skies.

Moldavite was formed by the union of cosmic fire and Mother Earth. It possesses a fusion of earthly and spiritual qualities that enables its wearer to experience both spiritual development and earthly progress on their own unique path. It calms worries about money by providing solutions not considered. Moldavite is associated with the legendary Holy Grail and was throughout the Middle Ages so highly prized only nobility or royalty were allowed to wear it.

Alexandrite

Type: Rare form of chrysoberyl.

Colours: Rich transparent green.

Availability: Obtainable from specialist crystal stores, high-quality jewellers and online.

Physical benefits: May help spleen, pancreas, testicles, swollen lymph node, Parkinson's disease, Alzheimer's and senile dementia; preserve youthfulness.

Emotional healing: Alexandrite alleviates grief for people lost through death, estrangement, time and distance and for lost opportunities; keep one in the bedroom of bereaved children.

Chakra: Sacral or Heart.

Candle colour: Green and red bands, or use two candles, one green and one red. **Fragrances:** Almond blossom, benzoin, bergamot, marigold, sweet marjoram. **Practical uses:** Keep one in the car to reduce motion sickness. **Workplace:** Reduces stress and anger in the workplace; encourages initiative, lessens excessive workaholic tendencies. **Magical significance:** Develops clairvoyant powers. Keep with tarot cards or runes while you are learning the meanings and wear or set on a table while giving readings. **Divinatory meaning:** Unexpected good luck; enjoy it and do not waste time worrying if it will last. **Zodiac:** Scorpio or Gemini. **Empowerment:** I open myself to infinite possibility.

Alexandrite was first discovered in the Ural Mountains in Russia on the day Tsar Alexander II came of age in 1830. A luck stone, because alexandrite is personal to the owner; dedicate your alexandrite at noon on the day of the full moon and then monthly. Say as you hold it, "Be for me power and protection." Alexandrite is at its most powerful and luck-bringing when the sun shines on it. It protects against jealousy if you or your partner have a jealous ex-lover who causes trouble.

Green Aventurine

Type: Microcrystalline quartz, sometimes containing mica that gives aventurine a metallic, iridescent glint.

Colours: Light to dark green.

Availability: Common.

Physical benefits: May benefit irregular heart rhythms, fertility, genito-urinary problems, eyesight especially long-sightedness and astigmatism, dyslexia, dyspraxia, cerebral palsy, hay fever.

Emotional healing: Leave one in the soil of a green plant overnight and hold it in the morning to let Mother Earth replace depression and anxiety with wellbeing and hope.

Chakra: Heart.

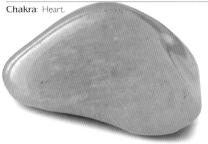

Candle colour: Green. **Fragrances:** Cedarwood, rosewood, wintergreen. **Practical uses:** The luckiest of all crystals. Keep one with you in a green bag and a four-leafed clover if you can get one, for all games of chance. Green amazonite in the same bag will increase the luck. **Workplace:** A money-spinner crystal if you are prepared to take a chance. **Magical significance:** Green aventurine is called fairy treasure. Place three in a dish in front of your garden gnome to attract good luck to your home. **Divinatory meaning:** Speculate to accumulate. **Zodiac:** Virgo and Taurus. **Empowerment:** I attract good fortune into my life.

Green aventurine helps children and adults with written work, typing and computer skills, and reduces clumsiness. One of the best crystals for conceiving a baby: when you are close to ovulation, dig a small hole in earth, break an egg in the hole, place the green aventurine in the broken egg shell in the earth and fill the hole. Green aventurine increases the power of homeopathic remedies. Have green aventurine in your office or home if you live or work in a city centre.

Type: Feldspar.

Colours: Blue-green or turquoise to darker greens with white lines, opaque.

Availability: Common.

Physical benefits: Said to help with breast problems, passages of the throat, thyroid gland, nerve and neurological connections, upper spine, recovery after illness and to maintain health and a healthy lifestyle.

Emotional healing: Increases self-respect especially in women, reduces tendencies to self-neglect, directs free-floating anger and irritability into positive action.

Chakra: Throat and Heart.

Amazonite

Candle colour: Turquoise. **Fragrances:** Basil, bergamot, fennel, hyacinth, mint, patchouli. **Practical uses:** Giving stamina to multi-task with a minimum of stress (good for working women especially). **Workplace:** Helps you to be in the right place at the right time for new opportunities. **Magical significance:** A lucky charm for winning competitions, lotteries and all matters where a sudden burst of luck is needed. **Divinatory meaning:** You are in a strong position so stand up for what you think is important, especially in fighting prejudice or injustice. **Zodiac:** Virgo. **Empowerment:** I expect fair treatment and consideration from others.

Called the stone of courage, amazonite is named after the semi-mythical 10th-century-BC Amazon women warriors, because it was said to adorn their shields. Keep a dish of amazonites on the kitchen table to persuade others to help more with chores.

Hide one in children's and teenage bedrooms to encourage tidiness. Make a lucky-charm bag with three amazonites, a little dried basil and mint. Leave the bag in front of a turquoise candle until the candle burns down.

Keep the bag where you fill in competition entries or near the computer for online lottery or contest applications. Nine small amazonites placed in a circle in your workspace will attract new business and prosperity to a company, and will also help women to overcome any hidden prejudice in the workplace. Hold the nine crystals in your closed hands and shake them nine times to bring strength or new orders, and to increase your concentration.

Atlantisite

Type: Combination of stitchtite and serpentine.

Colours: Green serpentine with inclusions of pink to purple stichtite.

Availability: Relatively rare, obtainable through specialist mineral stores and online.

Physical benefits: May help with heart, lungs, stomach, kidneys, cramp, menstrual pain and excess or absent flow, hernias, skin complaints and wrinkles, digestion, stomach acidity, diabetes, hypoglycaemia.

Emotional healing: Overcomes insecurity; for overcoming a victim mentality.

Chakra: Solar Plexus.

Candle colour: Purple. Fragrances: Bayberry, hibiscus. **Practical uses:** Set in the place where you and the family relax with purple candles to create a sanctuary of calm. **Workplace:** Put one in your pocket for meetings to prevent you saying what you might later regret. **Magical significance:** Associated with Atlantis, atlantisite is an ancient wisdom stone that offers access to knowledge of different times to make learning ancient forms of healing easier. **Divinatory meaning:** Someone from the past will return to your life and connect you with people who can enrich your present world. **Zodiac:** Leo. **Empowerment:** I take pleasure in childhood spontaneity.

A crystal for those who live alone, to create a happy welcoming home environment and to enjoy your own time and space. It is called the crystal of inner fire, for atlantisite placed on your solar plexus centre, located in the middle of your upper stomach, draws upwards your Kundalini energy.

This is the power in the base of your spine that activates your sun solar plexus centre for action and success in the world. Do this for a major business surge or for any time you need an instant power boost to succeed or shine.

Brochantite

Type: Sulphate formed in oxidation zone of copper deposits; closely linked with other copper minerals such as azurite and malachite.

Colours: Emerald green, black-green.

Availability: From specialist crystal stores and online.

Physical benefits: May act against fluid retention, environmental pollutants and illnesses made worse by stressful lifestyle, junk food, additives, excessive stimulants; may help spleen, pancreas, prostate, blood, asthma, emphysema and other chronic lung conditions.

Emotional healing: Helps mean people to be more generous with money and love.

Chakra: Heart.

Candle colour: Green. Fragrances: Cedar, juniper, rosewood. **Practical uses:** Helps with day-to-day practical functioning of relationships rather than romance; a piece in the home encourages friendship between family members and a willingness to share attention as well as necessary chores. **Workplace:** A crystal to have for any public service career to maintain high standards. **Magical significance:** A bringing-together crystal of the spiritual and material, thoughts and emotions. **Divinatory meaning:** If someone close is being irritating, let them fix their own problems. **Zodiac:** Libra. **Empowerment:** I will let life come to me.

Brochantite was named in 1824 after the eminent French mineralogist Brochant de Villiers, who is most famous for his involvement in the creation of the geological map of France. A hard-working crystal that builds up goodwill in relationships and the expression of love in deeds. In the workplace it represents fulfilling promises; an energizing crystal at home or work for those who are always saying what they will do but never act. Frequently found as twinned crystals, brochantite attracts people who are like you so you do not feel alone.

Pyromorphite

Type: Lead chloro-phosphate, small crystals in clusters.

Colours: Bright green, yellow or brown.

Availability: Relatively common.

Physical benefits: Said to increase personal energy levels, help coeliac disease, IBS and all stomach disorders, chills, cleanse blood; assist assimilation of vitamins and minerals, especially B vitamins; regrowth of health after a long illness; can stimulate resistance to disease.

Emotional healing: Clears the mind of negative energy blocks that prevents participation in life and relationships and experiencing feelings of joy.

Chakra: Heart and Solar Plexus.

Candle colour: Green. **Fragrances:** Cedarwood, vervain. **Practical uses:** Draws money through good luck. **Workplace:** Called the victory stone, because possessing one helps us achieve dreams. **Magical significance:** A crystal of Mother Earth, gives the ability to connect with nature essences. Keep one in a safe place (as it is toxic if ingested), to attract the blessings of the guardians of the land on which your home is built. **Divinatory meaning:** Rely on logic not emotion. **Zodiac:** Aries. **Empowerment:** I can move forward.

This crystal will increase the effectiveness of other crystals – therefore it is often used in conjunction with one or more other crystals for healing work. If you work with nature in any way, such as gardening, farming or conservation, pyromorphite will assist you to make the best use of available resources and provide stamina needed for the physical aspect of your work.

WARNING: Toxic, do not use pyromorphite in elixirs, wash hands well after handling and keep out of reach of children and pets.

Verdelite/Green Tourmaline

Type: Silicate.

Colours: Green, green-blue, green-yellow.

Availability: The darker the green, the more rare and valuable the verdelite.

Physical benefits: May benefit blood sugar disorders, rashes, eczema, scars and birthmarks, irritable bowel syndrome and other chronic bowel diseases.

Emotional healing: Balances male and female energies within both men and women; good for overcoming jealousy and envy in self and others.

Chakra: Heart.

Candle colour: Green. **Fragrances:** Apple blossom, peppermint, rosemary. **Practical uses:** Sportspersons can use this crystal to promote stamina. **Workplace:** Keep this stone in your workplace or near where you deal with your financial matters to attract success in your business ventures. **Magical significance:** A stone of protection. **Divinatory meaning:** Now is the time to be tolerant, particularly relating to a situation involving a man who may be causing difficulties. **Zodiac:** Libra and Scorpio. **Empowerment:** I value myself for who I am.

Verdelite (green tourmaline) was traditionally regarded as a magical stone, because if you apply friction, the crystal polarizes and one end becomes magnetic and will attract small light objects. The other end repels them. For this reason, tourmaline may have become the first magic wand, especially as it forms naturally into wand shapes. Green is the colour of good luck and abundance in all things.

Green tourmaline increases opportunities to earn a second income by turning an interest into a money-spinner.

Infinite Stone

Type: Silicate/phyllosilicate, form of serpentine, associated partly with the chrysotile variety.

Colours: Pale and opaque to dark and translucent green, with variety of greens between, some including grey, brown or black.

Availability: Found in specialist crystal stores and online.

Physical benefits: As a massage stone, it is believed to draw out pain in the body; though to be good for skin complaints, acne, boils and ulcers, and after facial or jaw surgery; said to help to ease a patient unconsciously fighting recovery.

Emotional healing: A dissolver of doubt, fear and negativity in people stuck in a seemingly pointless existence; offers courage to take a step towards finding quality of life; supportive if you care for a terminally ill or disabled relative.

Chakra: Brow and Root.

Candle colour: Pale green. **Fragrances:** Almond, anise, basil, lemongrass, tarragon. **Practical uses:** Carry in a pouch as a worry stone to let go of fears; hold if you are scared of enclosed places. **Workplace:** A protective stone if you work at night to help you feel less alone. **Magical significance:** Hold outdoors and you will for a minute become part of the unity of life and creation. **Divinatory meaning:** For once let the world manage without you; remember your small plans; make a date as soon as practical to fulfil at least one. **Zodiac:** Aries and Pisces. **Empowerment:** I reach towards what is infinite.

The name was chosen its discoverer Steven Roseley, because of its powerful healing, spiritual and angelic connections. A larger piece of infinite stone in Reiki encourages deeper relaxation and meditation in nervous patients; a wonderful attunement gift from a Reiki teacher to student. If you work irregular hours and have to sleep during the day, you travel between time zones, or young children mean you have a disturbed sleep pattern, look at the surface of your stone and allow the colour to fill your mind until you feel your eyes closing and relax into sleep.

Prehnite

Type: Silicate; broken surfaces shine like mother-of-pearl.

Colours: Pale green to yellow-green, also grey, white and colourless.

Availability: Common.

Physical benefits: Believed to increase energy at the same time as calming so aids regeneration after fatigue and for stamina when you cannot rest.

Emotional healing: A crystal of unconditional love: helps during relationship crises not to give up. It also eases worries, especially about health.

Chakra: Solar Plexus and Heart.

Candle colour: Green or white. **Fragrances:** Lemon valerian, vanilla, vervain. **Practical uses:** Prehnite should be carried by anyone who finds it difficult to refuse the requests of others. **Workplace:** Relieves tension in the office (and home). **Magical significance:** A stone of prediction, especially with other divinatory practices such as reading the tarot or pendulum. **Divinatory meaning:** It is time to let go of painful memories that may be holding you back. **Zodiac:** Virgo. **Empowerment:** I can say no to unreasonable demands.

Named for the 18th-century Dutchman Hendrik von Prehn, who discovered it in South Africa, prehnite was regarded as a stone of prophecy and shamanism by indigenous *sangomas*, medicine men and women.

Prehnite can be used in meditation to provide protection and stop thoughts wandering. It is a dream crystal: placed under a pillow, it will encourage lucid dreaming. Good, too, for remembering early childhood. Calms hyperactive children or animals and assists children with communication difficulties. Place prehnite in your laptop bag to prevent theft.

Type: A jasper form of chalcedony.

Colours: Dark green with red or orange spots and sometimes white markings.

Availability: Common.

Physical benefits: May be good for lower back pain, nosebleeds, blood disorders such as anaemia, diabetes, high blood pressure and circulation problems, healthy bone marrow and intestines, PMS, menstrual problems and the menopause, and for women who are giving birth to keep up their strength in labour.

Emotional healing: The long-term effects of bullying, mental as well as physical in adults as well as children; helping human and animal mothers to bond after a traumatic birth or one where mother and baby were separated for a time because the baby was early.

Chakra: Root and Sacral and Heart.

Bloodstone/Heliotrope

Candle colour: Red. **Fragrances:** Copal, cinnamon, cumin, dragon's blood, ginger. **Practical uses:** For all sports and exercise, whether you are a beginner or a professional athlete, **Workplace:** Protective in an over-competitive workplace or if you are pressurized to achieve unrealistic targets. **Magical significance:** For helping you tune in to the power of the weather, for example winds to bring change or rain to wash away sorrow; also for recalling past lives. **Divinatory meaning:** You can get what you want with politeness if you stand your ground and repeat your words until you are heard. **Zodiac:** Aries. **Empowerment:** I welcome challenges.

"Heliotrope" means turning with the sun. A stone of the sun, heliotrope dipped in water was believed in a number of cultures to transfer the power of the sun to cure any wound or blood disorder.

Another legend tells that bloodstone or heliotrope was once green jasper, but at the crucifixion the blood of Christ fell on to it. Bloodstone is helpful as a mother goddess stone for easing misunderstandings or difficulties with mothers or mothering issues. Keep a crystal by

family photographs of your mother. It also assists diets and detoxes by taking away underlying emotional issues. Sew a tiny bloodstone into the lining of the coat of a child or teenager who is being bullied.

Keep a bloodstone in a glass pot of loose change where natural light shines on it to attract money to your home or business. Lucky for any sports competitions or matches, kept in a sports bag or taped inside the programme if you are a spectator.

Green Obsidian

Type: Volcanic glass.

Colours: From transparent bottle green to creamy opaque green.

Availability: Rare as genuine green obsidian.

Physical benefits: Natural obsidian is seen as a valuable Reiki stone, particularly for working around the heart to clear blocked energies; thought to heal other crystals that have lost their power, enabling them to heal as though whole.

Emotional healing: Helps those who are fixated on counselling to tackle their own problems and become self-reliant on their own coping abilities for future life.

Chakra: Solar Plexus and Heart.

Candle colour: Green. **Fragrances:** Cedarwood, clary sage. **Practical uses:** Protective against people who try to drag you into their personal crises and problems. **Workplace:** All green obsidian promotes international business. **Magical significance:** Though black obsidian has always been considered the most spiritually powerful, green obsidian is Gaia and softens the fiery energies of obsidian with a calming power. **Divinatory meaning:** You may need to prioritize your own needs for a time, if you are caught up nurturing those close to you. **Zodiac:** Scorpio. **Empowerment:** I draw healing from plants and by being outdoors.

Green obsidian is also found as green-sheen obsidian, with a greenish lustre over the surface, and as green perlite obsidian, a hydrated derivative of obsidian. Obsidian is said never to allow itself to be used for evil, and so green obsidian is an excellent shield against negative earth energies in a building. Wear green obsidian if you work with people, particularly troubled ones, to keep your own energies light and positive.

Prasiolite

Type: Quartz: naturally found prasiolite is green quartz.

Colours: Olive green or pale yellow-green.

Availability: Rare in natural form, though obtainable from specialist crystal stores and online.

Physical benefits: Thought to trigger the immune system and balance the endocrine glands; may relieve burns, scalds and abrasions of all kinds, eczema and allergic rashes.

Emotional healing: For replacing extreme dieting or excessive exercise regimes with more moderate healthy lifestyle; helpful for obese children and pets who need gradual weight reduction.

Chakra: Heart.

Candle colour: Green. **Fragrances:** Benzoin, bergamot, chamomile, cinnamon, orange, peppermint. **Practical uses:** A prosperity crystal; reversing bad luck, overcoming job loss or finding means to pay a mass of bills by an inflow of money. **Workplace:** Encourages high standards of work. **Magical significance:** Absorbs negativity: keep a tumblestone in your home to shield you from malice. **Divinatory meaning:** Do not give up hope, for small miracles do happen. **Zodiac:** Though often not assigned one, prasiolite works well with Virgo. **Empowerment:** Expressing love and gratitude costs nothing but is of immense value.

Prasiolite has all the inherent healing and balancing qualities of amethyst, with the additional regeneration, fertility, health-giving and rebirth properties of the colour green. Use prasiolite therefore for small miracles, fertility later in life, love when you had given up hope, employment when there are few jobs around and the odds are stacked against you, and healing when the prognosis is not good. Prasiolite is the bridge between the physical body and the mind and spirit.

Dioptase

Type: Hydrated copper silicate, usually too soft for a gemstone.

Colours: Emerald to deep rich green, often shiny.

Availability: Common.

Physical benefits: May assist angina, inner ear, Ménière's disease, dizzy spells, bowel disorders, constipation, irritable bowel syndrome, nausea, ulcers, heart, cardiovascular and central nervous system, stabilizes blood pressure, varicose veins, HIV and AIDS.

Emotional healing: Overcomes neglect or disregard of body and personal needs: eating wrong foods, excessive smoking or alcohol, overwork, lack of sleep or exercise.

Chakra: Heart.

Candle colour: Turquoise or deep pink. **Fragrances:** Pink rose, vanilla. **Practical uses:** An ideal gift for someone who saves their best things for the future. **Workplace:** Eases returning to work after illness or a long period of unemployment. **Magical significance:** Dioptase is a crystal of love. Surround a photograph of your estranged love with small pieces of dioptase in a heart shape; write over the picture with the hand you normally do not write with, "Come back to me in love without reproach". **Divinatory meaning:** Take better care of yourself. **Zodiac:** Taurus. **Empowerment:** I will nurture myself as well as others.

A crystal of realistic love that encourages acceptance of ourselves and others with strengths and weaknesses; good to carry wrapped in a small, soft bag if you are constantly searching for perfect love and never find it or are always disappointed when someone you set on a pedestal proves all too human. Dioptase is the crystal of living for now, enjoying each day without harking back to what went wrong in the past or fretting over possible disasters in the future.

Enstatite in Diopside

Type: Silicate/pyroxene, magnesium silicate.

Colours: Green, yellowish, colourless.

Availability: Obtainable from specialist crystal stores and online.

Physical benefits: Said to help anaemia and blood disorders, bruising, damaged tendons or muscles, short-term memory loss after concussion.

Emotional healing: A stone for those who are afraid of being alone who go from one relationship to the next, constantly seeking someone to fill the inner void, to learn to value themselves and their own company.

Chakra: Heart and Crown.

Candle colour: Dark green. **Fragrances:** Cloves, juniper, tea tree. **Practical uses:** The winner's crystal; place enstatite on top of a competition entry or lottery numbers. **Workplace:** Called the stone of chivalry because it represents courage. **Magical significance:** Enstatite in diopside can be worn or carried as a symbol of intention if you follow a particular spiritual path. **Divinatory meaning:** Justice matters more to you than winning, but you can have both, so strive for justice. **Zodiac:** Aries. **Empowerment:** I walk in faith and trust, most of all in myself.

If you cannot find enstatite with diopside, pure enstatite properties are very similar and tend to predominate even in the combined specimen. Pure enstatite can sometimes be of facet quality or cut into dome-shaped cabochons, which may display a cat's-eye effect. Therefore it is very protective and empowering to wear, particularly if you are fighting any legal matters or dealing with unhelpful officialdom. For healing and empowerment, carry a small piece of natural enstatite in diopside in a pouch, to release harmonizing energies that ensure a constant energy flow.

Green Calcite

Type: Calcium carbonate.

Colours: Green from pale to mid green, occasionally emerald or apple green.

Availability: Common.

Physical benefits: May act on infections especially colds, flu and chest infections, heart irregularities, heart bypass surgery and transplants, tumours and growths anywhere in the body but especially lungs, breasts and lymph glands.

Emotional healing: Counters hyperactivity and ADHD in children, obsessive behaviour in adults and an inability to give to others, whether love, time or resources.

Chakra: Heart.

Candle colour: Pale green. **Fragrances:** Eucalyptus. **Practical uses:** Green calcite is a natural relaxant, add to bathwater. **Workplace:** Good for outdoor jobs. **Magical significance:** To attract money, surround with a circle of coins; surround the coins with seven green candles. On night one, light the first candle and say, "May light shine on my endeavours." Blow out the candle. On night two, repeat, each night lighting an extra candle. On night seven leave them to burn. **Divinatory meaning:** Money will come in soon. **Zodiac:** Virgo. **Empowerment:** I give freely.

Green calcite is sacred to earth spirits and earth healers from Native North America to Scandinavia; a good addition to any healing crystal layouts to give stability to higher spiritual energies and direct them into the patient's body gently so healing is gradual and not too intense; good therefore for Reiki healing with nervous patients, those with psychological problems and when treating teenagers, children and small animals. Keep an unpolished green calcite where you prepare food to ensure that the goodness remains.

Green Fluorite

Type: Halide, calcium fluoride.

Colours: Green.

Availability: Common.

Physical benefits: May help heals infections by boosting the immune system, regeneration of cells, energy and vitality, absorption of minerals, especially for teeth and bones, blood vessels, lungs and spleen.

Emotional healing: Green fluorite releases blocked grief from an unresolved bereavement, sometimes years earlier or in childhood, healing the freed emotions and bringing new growth; also helps with eating disorders.

Chakra: Heart.

Candle colour: Green. **Cragrances:** Balm of Gilead, eucalyptus. **Practical uses:** Keep green fluorite in a room where children play to minimize conflict. **Workplace:** Green fluorite disperses negative energies caused by electrical equipment. **Magical significance:** Use a green fluorite wand to programme other crystals for healing purposes. Touch with the wand and state the name of the person to be healed. **Divinatory meaning:** Beware of mistaking sentiment and extravagant expression of devotion for true caring **Zodiac:** Pisces **Empowerment:** I will not be swayed by false sentiment.

Green as well as other coloured fluorites was carved into vessels in China more than 500 years ago and used as substitute for jade. Green fluorite offers the same beneficial energies as pure fluorite (p.293) but adds growth and nature energies to bring a breath of fresh air to the most polluted setting. Give a piece to children who travel through fume-filled streets to school or have to play in urban areas. If you love butterflies, keep a piece of green fluorite in your garden to attract them.

Buddstone

Type: Called African or Transvaal jade, in fact a form of grossular garnet but resembles jade.

Colours: Rich deep green or sometimes lighter and mottled.

Availability: From specialist mineral stores and online.

Physical benefits: Said to help headaches, migraines, pain relief, toxicity, menstruation, muscles, kidneys, bladder, stress incontinence, genital diseases/infections, diabetes, hypoglycaemia, dizziness, Alzheimer's disease, senile dementia.

Emotional healing: For those caring for small children, disabled family members, terminally ill or elderly confused relatives to develop patience and stamina.

Chakra: Heart.

Candle colour: Deep rich green. **Fragrances:** Fennel, hyacinth, lavender, lilac, rosemary. **Practical uses:** Place at the four outermost compass points downstairs in the home and a fifth in the centre to harmonize and energize. **Workplace:** Good for business deals based on trust and efficiency rather than hard sell; to pace yourself if your work/pay is target-driven. **Magical significance:** A talisman to draw the beauty, strength and courage of African creatures into your life. **Divinatory meaning:** A chance to put right past resentment and talk amicably with a former rival or enemy. **Zodiac:** Virgo. **Empowerment:** I can free myself from the inner voices of doubt.

Buddstone (also known as Transvaal Jade) comes from Zimbabwe and Transvaal in South Africa, and is opaque like jade but has more active energies. It encourages step-by-step growth and is good for foot complaints; helps to make non-confrontational, determined progress against corruption or tough odds while inducing a sense of wellbeing and certainty that all will be well. Buddstone in the bedroom reduces sleep disturbances and nightmares. Pass over and round the body regularly to remove negativity and create a shield. It also encourages self-sufficiency of all kinds.

Gaspeite

Type: Nickel magnesium iron carbonate.

Colours: Light to apple or bright or lime green, may contain brown host rock.

Availability: Relatively rare.

Physical benefits: May help heart, gall bladder, lungs, breathing difficulties such as asthma or bronchitis, cystic fibrosis, allergies to plants and pollen, oxygenation of blood, speech and sensory organs, sense of taste and smell; strengthen crystal and herbal healing and homeopathy; increase the healing powers even of those new to healing.

Emotional healing: Brings serenity and acceptance of what cannot be changed in the middle of turmoil; take gaspeite with you if you have to move residence suddenly or leave friends and family behind for work commitments, to ease the transition and maintain loving links.

Chakra: Heart.

Candle colour: Green. **Fragrances:** Cedar, cypress, lemon, lime, wintergreen. **Practical uses:** Hold to relieve stress during delayed journeys; also soothing if waiting for news of someone undergoing an operation or in difficulty. **Workplace:** Balances commercial demands and ethics, particularly if you run your own company; for employees, aids balancing work and personal time. **Magical significance:** Creates a balance between everyday success and following a spiritual path; helps a busy person develop psychic awareness. **Divinatory meaning:** Your life may be out of balance; take a day or two away from work to return refreshed. **Zodiac:** Taurus. **Empowerment:** My spiritual life is important to me.

A crystal used by Australian Aboriginal people as a charm to bring good fortune and visions of the Dreamtime, although it is named after the Gaspé Peninsula in Quebec, Canada, where it was identified in 1966. In Western Australia, where it is also found, it is sometimes called allura. Gaspeite is a "one foot in both worlds" crystal. Wear gaspeite jewellery to attract success at work, lasting friendships and love, while at the same time valuing quiet moments and connection with the unseen world, particularly of nature spirits.

Epidote

Type: Calcium aluminosilicate; occasionally found as gem.

Colours: Olive green or pale to dark green.

Availability: Relatively common.

Physical benefits: May help with liver, gall bladder, digestion, recovery after prolonged illness or surgery, dehydration and fluid imbalances, Parkinson's disease, brain disorders and haemorrhage, nervous system, cystic fibrosis, thyroid; considered helpful for most cancers.

Emotional healing: Changes thought patterns from "I cannot" to "I can and I will"; encourages actions rather than words; carry an epidote tumblestone to overcome agoraphobia or fears of travel.

Chakra: Heart.

Candle colour: Green. **Fragrances:** Basil andcedar. **Practical uses:** A piece of epidote in the home brings energy. **Workplace:** Opens the eyes to what is really happening. **Magical significance:** Surround a photograph of what you want to come into your life with a circle of epidote, and encircle it with eight green candles. Light the candles and leave them to burn. **Divinatory meaning:** You have choices, but you have to stop defeating yourself with doubts before you put your plans into action. **Zodiac:** Gemini. **Empowerment:** I increase my opportunities daily.

Discovered in the early 1800s, epidote has gained a reputation as the stone that awakens users both to their own potential and to the wonders of the world.

According to crystal folklore, one special epidote crystal, not yet discovered, will make the invisible world of nature spirits visible to all humans with good hearts. Create a health and abundance layout in your home, with a piece of natural epidote in the centre and a cross of green crystals, including epidote. Keep the layout on a table in a hallway with green plants or somewhere fresh air can circulate.

Greenstone

Type: Mainly nephrite (pounami) (p.266), but some is bowenite or serpentine (tangiwai) (p.264).

Colours: Lightish green with lighter cloud-like streaks, very translucent strong green (kahurangi) and semi-translucent pearly whitish (kawakawa).

Availability: Getting rarer, but obtainable as traditional Maori jewellery and carvings on the Internet.

Physical benefits: Claimed to be Maori universal healer, held against feet, troubled areas or as massage stone.

Emotional healing: Any greenstone pendant is regarded as part of its owner and a sacred treasure.

Chakra: Heart.

Candle colour: Green. **Fragrances:** Cedar, kiwi fruit, lavender. **Practical uses:** Pounamu is worn on a leather thong, level with the cavity where the two collarbones meet above the chest; brings luck, love or health, depending on the design. **Workplace:** Wear hei-matau, a traditional fish-hook pendant, to attract opportunities. **Magical significance:** To turn your luck around, obtain a Hei-tiki carving. **Divinatory meaning:** You have control over your future, take time to decide what you want rather than drifting. **Zodiac:** Virgo and Capricorn. **Empowerment:** There is much beauty in my life.

Greenstone, found only in the South Island of New Zealand, has been used by the Maoris for tools, weapons and ornaments since their arrival in Aotearoa (New Zealand). There are various legends of the origin of greenstone, one telling it was brought to New Zealand by a chief, Ngahue, driven out of the legendary Maori homeland, Hawaiki, by a jealous chieftainess. Keep your greenstone when not in use in a leather pouch and apply oil to it regularly to keep it moist; hold and touch it to strengthen its connection with you.

Chrysoprase

Type: Gemstone variety of chalcedony.

Colours: Apple or mint green, occasionally lighter green. The colouration is due to trace amounts of nickel.

Availability: Common.

Physical benefits: May help with ears, eyes, stomach ulcers, liver, gout, skin perforations and infections, heart; powerful detoxifier especially of pollutants in the atmosphere; can relieve side-effects of necessary prolonged medication.

Emotional healing: Green chrysoprase worn as jewellery breathes life into a relationship after a betrayal.

Chakra: Heart.

Candle colour: Mint green. **Fragrances:** Cedarwood, clary sage. **Practical uses:** To bring spring into your home at any time of the year; open windows and sprinkle water in which green chrysoprase has been soaked. **Workplace:** A luck charm: rub one over the envelope of any letters you send out relating to employment. **Magical significance:** Keep a piece with tarot cards, runes or other divinatory tools to help you see the unexpected in a reading. **Divinatory meaning:** A new opportunity could move you out of an impasse. **Zodiac:** Taurus. **Empowerment:** I open myself to new beginnings.

Keep green chrysoprase out of direct sunlight for prolonged periods to avoid fading, and rehydrate occasionally with wet cotton wool. Excellent for problem-solving and finding new approaches and angles, for anyone in the media, publicity or advertising and for writers of fiction to give both originality and realism. In Eastern Europe, possessing a chrysoprase was traditionally believed to help communication with lizards and other reptiles – it certainly brings a closeness and understanding of nature.

Green Diopside

Type: Calcium-magnesium silicate or calcium-iron silicate.

Colours: Light to greenish brown to very dark green with a glassy or pearly lustre, also white.

Availability: Obtainable from specialist crystal stores and online.

Physical benefits: Said to help with headaches, high blood pressure, tremors of hands, recovery after surgery, menopause, heart problems and heart attack recovery.

Emotional healing: Drug addiction; helps to resolve the reasons for any addiction or obsession.

Chakra: Heart.

Candle colour: Green. **Fragrances:** Cedar, tea tree. **Practical uses:** Good for coping with relatives with physical and mental disabilities. **Workplace:** A crystal to ease the shock of redundancy; makes it easier to learn new skills and sell yourself. **Magical significance:** Diopside is a natural information dowser. Take diopside with you to a library or museum when you are seeking specific knowledge. **Divinatory meaning:** Go through the places you have already looked to find a missing item as it *is* there. **Zodiac:** Gemini and Virgo. **Empowerment:** I look at the world with new eyes and see its wonders.

Often called the mystery stone, diopside is said to be a stone that holds many secrets of the universe, especially within its rarer star or cat's eye crystals. According to myth, these universal secrets are slowly revealed in dreams to an owner of a stone, who should keep it for many years and not hand it on. Green cat's eye diopside has tiny rutile (needle-like) inclusions and is protective for travel after dark, particularly if you live in the countryside.

Type: Compacted sandstone in a shell of iron compounds, ranging in size from a small marble to a baseball.

Colours: Brownish black, tan or lighter reddish brown.

Availability: Obtainable from specialist crystal stores and online, but becoming less common.

Physical benefits: Used as pair, one large and one small, or one rounded – considered female – and one more disk-like male: it is believed that you can hold the rounded one in the left hand and the disk shape in the right to balance body energies; alternatively place the larger or disk-shaped one beneath the feet and the other above the head while lying down; leave for ten minutes to realign energies or may also help to relieve pain.

Emotional healing: Moqui marbles create a sense of belonging to the earth and to society where there is a sense of alienation or disconnection as a result of trauma or psychological illness.

Chakra: Root.

Moqui/Mochi Marbles

Candle colour: Brown. **Fragrances:** Chamomile, fern, moss, musk, sage. **Practical uses:** A moqui marble, set on either side of the front door just inside, is believed to protect the home both from natural disasters, especially fire, flood and lightning, and from unfriendly spirits as well as more earthly nuisances, troublemakers and burglars. **Workplace:** Keep a pair on your desk and hold to know who you can trust; set one either side of the computer when buying goods via the Internet or making new contacts, and you will, if you touch them, instinctively feel a warning vibration, slightly cold and tingling if you need to proceed with caution. **Magical significance:** Used as shamanic visionary, healing and magical stones in Native North America and thrown into a ritual fire to create an explosion (not recommended for safety reasons); hold your stones during meditation to enter a deep but gentle trance state where worries flow away and are replaced by peace and a sense of being part of the earth and nature. **Divinatory meaning:** Do not be afraid of being misled; as long as you are cautious you can get satisfaction from a less trustworthy source you need to use. **Zodiac:** Capricorn. **Empowerment:** I am connected to other people but not stifled by them.

Native North American Hopi myth says moqui marbles were the gaming stones of the departed ancestors, who would return to Earth to play with them at sunset.

Smaller ones are still used as gaming stones. Similar rocks have been found on Mars; the earthly forms are considered helpful for astronomers, astrologers and anyone interested in UFOs or crypto-zoology (the study of animals that do not fit into any earthly species). If you are left-handed you may prefer to hold the female or smaller stone in your right hand; good for night and shift workers to restore patterns of sleep and for anyone who has insomnia.

Hold them for a few minutes before sleep and let your mind flow into a sand sea of brown and yellow.

Picture Jasper

Type: Silicate, microcrystalline quartz (see also Picasso jasper p.299).

Colours: Creamy sand, tan or brown.

Availability: Relatively common.

Physical benefits: Said to help to heal skin disorders and allergies, especially if caused by chemicals, chronic lung conditions, immune system; might aid IBS, chronic constipation, hernia, prostate anus, hips, knees, feet, obesity.

Emotional healing: Should be worn for a period of weeks or even months to unlock hidden fears that may go back as far as early childhood and to gradually dissolve them.

Chakra: Root and Brow.

Candle colour: Brown. **Fragrances:** Almond, basil, sage. **Practical uses:** A stone for travel abroad, especially for backpacking or living in other countries; exchange picture jasper with your partner if you are from different lands and/or cultures to help you fit into each other's worlds. **Workplace:** An ecological stone, for those who work in alternative forms of energy and all in conservation. **Magical significance:** An excellent stone for encouraging psychic artists who paint spirit guides. **Divinatory meaning:** Focus on the bigger picture. **Zodiac:** Leo and Capricorn. **Empowerment:** I will focus on the end result.

Picture jasper is a remarkable mix of banding, flow patterns, created by petrified or silicate mud and sometimes dendritic (vegetation-like) inclusions.

It is one of the best stones for encouraging initiative; wear or carry it to give you the confidence, creative vision and practical application to set up your own business. If you are trying to give up smoking, hold picture jasper whenever you get a craving and focus on the patterns to relax you as you gently breathe in its healing strength.

Spider Jasper

Type: Silicate, microcrystalline quartz, often with organic matter or other minerals as inclusions.

Colours: Earthy browns with white or dark spider-web markings.

Availability: One of the rarer jaspers.

Physical benefits: May help veins and arteries, blood vessels, brain haemorrhages, nerve connections. Could help chronic fatigue syndrome.

Emotional healing: Frees a person from the manipulation of others and from webs of lies or secrecy surrounding birth or early life; good for escaping from emotional abusers and those who use love as a weapon.

Chakra: Root.

Candle colour: Brown. **Fragrances:** Anise, basil, bay, dragon's blood, mugwort, musk. **Practical uses:** Dishes of spider jasper tumblestones encourage people to mix at parties or family gatherings. **Workplace:** The ultimate stone for networking, for bartering and for making money from selling antiques. **Magical significance:** One of the best crystals for keeping away bad dreams; attach one to a dreamcatcher and hang it over your bed. **Divinatory meaning:** Avoid getting caught up in a web of gossip, though this will be hard. **Zodiac:** Scorpio. **Empowerment:** We are all part of the same universal family.

As its name suggests, spider jasper contains the power of the wise spider, represented by the Native North American goddess, Grandmother Spider, who created people from four different-coloured clays as the nations of the earth and led them from the underworld into the open, where Grandfather Sun breathed life into them. Wear or keep spider jasper with you to overcome a fear of spiders or other crawling insects; for uncovering secrets concerning family members or partners being hidden, for whatever reason.

Ocean Jasper

Type: Orbicular jasper describes several jaspers displaying perfect circles throughout the crystals.

Colours: Multiple colours of green, red, orange, yellow, cream, pink, white and brown with orb-like inclusions.

Availability: Ocean jasper is quite rare but obtainable from some specialist mineral stores and online.

Physical benefits: Claimed to be good for the digestive system; remove toxins that cause body odour and flatulence; help to ease problems with the thyroid, seasickness and inner-ear disturbances.

Emotional healing: Gentle and gradual release of pent-up anger or emotional blockages.

Chakra: Heart.

Ocean jasper is occasionally called orbicular jasper in reference to the orb or bull's-eye patterns that can occur which are also seen in leopardskin and poppy jaspers. The name ocean jasper was given to those orbicular jaspers that can be collected on a remote shore of Madagascar only at low tide as the rest of the time the ocean conceals them.

Ocean jasper is full of positive gentle nurturing energy that helps anyone who wears or holds it regularly to develop self-love and empathy for others.

Picasso Jasper

Type: Silicate, microcrystalline quartz.

Colours: Mixture of black, brown, grey, rust and cream, in abstract patterns.

Availability: Relatively common.

Physical healing: Thought to help arteries, bowels, constipation, colon and intestines, feet, legs, whole-body healing by boosting immune system, nerve connections, Parkinson's disease and MS.

Emotional healing: A joy-bringer if worn regularly, bringing awareness of the beauty in others as well as surroundings; for all who have given up on people and life.

Chakra: Root.

A metamorphic rock that undergoes many changes created by heat and pressure during its formation. Picasso jasper is a reminder it is never too late to enjoy life to the full. Hold a Picasso jasper polished palm or worry stone when you are about to turn down an invitation or feel guilty about taking some self time. A Picasso worry stone can be used to great effect to enter a light trance state, whether for mediumship, out-of-body travel, contacting angels and guides or to enter a deep meditative state.

Type: Silicate, microcrystalline quartz, often with organic matter or other minerals as inclusions.

Colours: Pale grey, cream or beige-brown with dark spots, resembling the coat of the dog with the same name.

Availability: Common.

Physical healing: Thought to boost the immune system and remove toxins, muscles, tendons and cartilage (also help prevent strains and muscle spasms), bowel disorders particularly IBS, constipation, skin problems and allergic rashes.

Emotional healing: If life has become a burden and you have lost all sense of joy, wearing or carrying Dalmatian jasper reawakens a sense of fun and humour from within; an anti-smoking crystal.

Chakra: Root.

Dalmatian Jasper

Associated candle colour: Brown. **Associated fragrances:** Bluebell, geranium, honeysuckle, patchouli, sweet marjoram. **Practical uses:** Place as large a piece of Dalmatian jasper as you can find in your home where you relax (in the relationship area of your home if you practice Feng Shui) to encourage loyalty among family members and happiness in your sanctuary if you live alone. **Workplace:** One of the jaspers whose properties reflect its appearance, Dalmatian jasper is remarkably successful for calming, training and healing pets, especially dogs; if you would like to turn your love of dogs into a profession this is your crystal: for dog breeders, trainers, dog handlers in any field and those who rescue injured or abandoned animals. **Magical significance:** Increases telepathic communication with all animals, but especially dogs; also for working with canine-like power animals such as the wolf and if carried for improving your dowsing abilities to find lost items and pets. **Divinatory meaning:** A fun relationship may be turning into something more permanent. To succeed, remember to keep the fun side active. **Zodiac:** Virgo. **Empowerment:** I value my true friends.

Dalmatian jasper is a protective and healing stone on many levels. It should be used long-term as its energies are slow but effective. It counteracts disillusion, cynicism and scepticism and is a good gift for bad-tempered relatives or colleagues; keep a small dish of tumblestones in the office and use a few drops of the elixir in making hot drinks.

The crystal protects from nightmares, particularly childhood dreams of monsters, and will help adults and children overcome an irrational fear of dogs. Dalmatian jasper strengthens family bonds and long-term friendships, especially with people known from childhood; encourages team effort and co-operation at work.

The determination within the crystal assists in translating ideas into actuality and so is an excellent talisman in the early stages of setting up a new business or solo venture.

Type: Sulphate, lead chromate; usually on matrix (rock base).

Colour: Orange-red, often bright, sometimes orange, red or yellow.

Availability: Rare.

Physical benefits: Said to help reproductive system, particularly in women, endometriosis, fertility, fibroid and hysterectomy operations and after-effects, internal parasites, speedy healing of fractures, liver damage, absorption of minerals and vitamins A, B and E; be protective against gastro-enteritis and stomach bugs; assist food intolerances, particularly wheat.

Emotional healing: A laughter crystal for restoring joy, fun and optimism in over-serious people or those where life has taken away their major source of happiness.

Chakra: Sacral and Solar Plexus.

Crocoite

Candle colour: Gold. Fragrances: Anise, frankincense, honey, marigold, sunflower. Practical uses: Traditionally carried by uncommitted women to attract the right mate, especially if she wants children and so seeks a man who will be a good father as well as life partner; helps you to enjoy socializing for its own sake while waiting for the right person. Workplace: A crystal for changing your image, having a complete makeover or reappraisal, to succeed in an image-conscious industry; also for upgrading skills and learning new technological methods; speeds basic language learning when it is necessary to communicate with overseas business connections. Magical significance: A crystal for active forms of spirituality such as Sufi whirling, shamanic dance or drumming; carry a tiny piece of crocoite in a bag when walking if you find meditation sitting still hard or unproductive. Divinatory meaning: If you think your ideas are going to meet with resistance, go slowly as a head-on approach will damage chances of acceptance. Zodiac: Aries. Empowerment: I am open to sources of new happiness.

Crocoite is a feel-good crystal, enhancing inner radiance and charisma; ideal if you have returned to the dating scene after a relationship breakup or you are naturally shy but have to socialize as part of your job.

It encourages sexual pleasure without guilt or fear, especially after a period of celibacy, after an operation that adversely affects fertility and after the menopause; helpful also for alleviating male virility crises, such as the mid-life crisis, becoming a grandfather or retiring.

Place a piece of crocoite on your navel if you wake up feeling lethargic and out of sorts, to seize the day with enthusiasm. Place on your solar plexus if you are distressed after a quarrel or an emotional crisis and have to go to work and act normally.

This is a good crystal if you have food issues, to accept and value yourself as you are now and to develop a positive realistic body image where food is fuel and pleasurable and not an enemy or obsession.

WARNING: Not suitable in direct elixirs.

Crocoite

Agate Slice

Type: Most agates form as geodes or cavities in volcanic rock. Agate slices are segments of these and are often found with a crystallized (frequently quartz) centre.

Colours: All the natural colours of banded agate, but also injection-dyed in a variety of bright colours.

Availability: Common.

Physical benefits: Agate slices with holes or indentations are said to be good for eyesight, for encouraging the flow of oxygen round the body, for improving balance in older people.

Emotional healing: Allows light and hope to creep into a hopeless situation and offers a rock of stability.

Chakra: Root and Brow.

Candle colour: Yellow **Fragrances:** Heather, valerian, vanilla. **Practical uses:** For minimizing accidents, especially falls, if set in the centre of the home. **Workplace:** Have agate slice coasters in your workspace to give protection from malice and a burst of energy when needed. **Magical significance:** A dark coloured, highly polished agate slice, held up to candlelight, forms a mirror in which it is said you can see your spirit guardians. **Divinatory meaning:** Look through the superficial promises before saying yes. **Zodiac:** Gemini. **Empowerment:** I take a step into the unknown, in the certainty I am protected.

An agate slice with a tiny crystalline hole in the centre is believed to give you access to other dimensions; good therefore for astral travel or glimpsing the future: look through the hole with one eye in a darkened room so only the slice is illuminated by candlelight. Those with crystal indentations but no hole in the centre can, also by candlelight in a dark room, create a perfect focus for meditation world and, it is said, channel wisdom from the Akashic records or collective well of wisdom in answer to specific questions.

Agatized Coral

Type: Formed when ancient lime-based coral is gradually replaced by agate (chalcedony).

Colours: From white and pink to golden yellow, with small flower-like patterns in the agate.

Availability: Obtainable from specialized crystal stores or online.

Physical benefits: May assist breathing difficulties, also diseases such as bone weakness, such as brittle bone disease or osteoporosis; believed to be protective against falls and bone fractures, especially in children and older people.

Emotional healing: Eases personality disorders, outbursts of temper, gambling, drinking addiction to sex or clairvoyant phone lines.

Chakra: Sacral and Root.

Candle colour: Cream. **Fragrances:** Eucalyptus, sweetgrass. **Practical uses:** Reduces over-sensitivity to the environment when taking small children into noisy places. **Workplace:** Encourages cooperation,. **Magical significance:** Empower a piece to bring you ease in difficult social situations: hold between your hands while saying nine times, "Make me shine like the sun and flow like the waters." Repeat. **Divinatory meaning:** A gentle response towards a difficult person will produce good results within a short time. **Zodiac:** Cancer. **Empowerment:** I can transform my life and still preserve what I value.

Agatized fossil corals occur in many parts of the world and may be up to 395 million years old. One kept in a teenager's bedroom or given as ear-rings will help to filter over-loud music, especially through headphones, that can damage hearing.

Agatized coral increases imagination and is the stone of fiction writers, transmitting ideas while preserving integrity. If you belong to a dysfunctional family, agatized coral replaces obsession or old wounds with harmony and the ability to mend the spirit and move forward.

Type: Iron sulphide.

Colours: Metallic, darker grey/black with a drusy covering of miniature minerals on the surface, which shimmers with rainbow colours including gold, green, rose pink and blue.

Availability: Relatively rare but very beautiful and so worth obtaining.

Physical benefits: Believed to hellp with migraines with visual disturbances, brain disorders that cause degeneration of the whole body, auto-immune diseases, Huntington's chorea and genetic conditions, colds, influenza and other viral attacks, digestion.

Emotional healing: A very potent stone for adults who have communication difficulties and miss social signals, and so find it hard to make relationships or keep friends; good for adults with Asperger's syndrome.

Chakra: Solar Plexus.

Russian Rainbow Pyrites

Candle colour: Silver. **Fragrances:** Basil, dragon's blood, garlic, ginger. **Practical uses:** Rainbow iron pyrites brings positive recognition in talent contests, televised quizzes or game shows; should be placed with applications for a few hours before sending to win a place in a reality-TV production. **Workplace:** Wear or carry a small piece of rainbow pyrites to make a living in the creative or performing arts; opens doorways to unusual careers that involve movement and action, and for success in the sporting world in individual fields or in extreme sports that require stamina and courage; good for circus performers and dancing, acrobatic or juggling troupes. **Magical significance:** Rainbow pyrites is a welcome addition to ghost-investigation equipment, especially in polished form; set one on a table or the floor in a haunted house or bedroom you are staying in to attract the spirits to manifest and to offer protection from any that are not friendly. **Divinatory meaning:** Try a new interest or activity that may seem difficult or even a little risky; you will really enjoy it and are braver than you realize. **Zodiac:** Aries. **Empowerment:** I will enjoy new activities.

Like many rainbow crystals, rainbow pyrites, though discovered relatively recently near Ulianovsk, on the Volga River in Russia, is acquiring folk myths about being treasure left by earth or water spirits or having fallen from the rainbow. It is therefore considered a good-luck stone and most potent for making wishes when there is a rainbow or, even better, a double rainbow in the sky; use rainbow pyrites to generate enthusiasm at a potentially dull social gathering or one where the hosts and most of the guests are very cliquey and you know your presence is necessary but not welcome. Give a piece to young travellers on their first holiday alone, particularly if they are camping or participating in water sports such as white water rafting that involve potential hazards; keep them safe and ensure they enjoy every moment.

WARNING: Do not use in elixirs or ingest.

Type: Hydrated silicon dioxide, precious opal.

Colours: Rainbow.

Availability: Obtainable from specialist crystal stores and online.

Physical benefits: Believed to improve eyesight and visual disturbances, neurological disorders, metabolism; be good for helping mothers and infants who have experienced a traumatic birth, communication disorders, Down's syndrome.

Emotional healing: Rainbow opal is the most uplifting of the opals and will ease distress of any kind, particularly if this has been suppressed; gently dissolves hopelessness and helplessness, and gets anyone back on their feet emotionally fast.

Chakra: Brow.

Rainbow Opal

Candle colour: Silver or blue. **Fragrances:** Hyacinth, lavender, neroli, peach, vanilla. **Practical uses:** The happiest of the happy opals, a piece of natural rainbow opal radiates optimism and good humour, and gently energizes anyone who comes into regular contact with its energies to try new experiences; good for children and adults who hold back socially. **Workplace:** Wear or carry rainbow opal if your job is routine or dull to inject enthusiasm into it and find ways of improving your working life; protective if you deal with other people's problems or sorrows, not to become drained or cynical. **Magical significance:** Like all rainbow gems, rainbow opal is a wish stone and is uplifting if you have suffered many disappointments and have almost given up on life; wear even a small one to reverse a run of bad luck; particularly lucky to wish on your opal if there is a rainbow in the sky. **Divinatory meaning:** Just when you had given up, good luck makes a return appearance; maximize opportunities to ensure it lasts. **Zodiac:** Cancer. **Empowerment:** I can make my own wishes come true.

Over 90 percent of precious opals come from Australia and opal is Australia's national gemstone. Australian Aboriginal legend tells that where the creator god or goddess first stepped on to the earth, the rocks turned rainbow colours and became opals: this is especially seen in the rainbow opal. The rainbow effect can occur in opals with both a light background (called white opals) and those with a darker background (black opals).

Rainbow opal is the stone of happy dreams and is especially soothing if you or a child have always slept badly or suffer from recurring and nasty dreams without any apparent external source.

A stone that naturally opens psychic pathways last experienced in childhood, particularly for mind travel and for making predictions; a small rainbow opal relieves any problems a child has with an invisible/imaginary friend and can be held before sleep if the child wants the friend to go away at bedtime.

Banded Agate

Type: Chalcedony.

Colours: Banded agate contains a variety of natural earth colours, characterized by concentric bands of colour, predominantly grey, black or brown with different coloured bands such as cream or orange/red within.

Availability: Common.

Physical benefits: Brown banded agate is claimed to be useful for bone problems, IBS, intestines, liver and pancreatic problems; and grey is thought to be useful for ME.

Emotional healing: If life has been interrupted by illness, any banded agate helps people to feel whole again.

Chakra: Root.

Candle colour: Brown. **Fragrances:** Mimosa, moss. **Practical uses:** Good for all physical feats of endurance. **Workplace:** Shields the workplace from the side effects of electrical impulses of office equipment. **Magical significance:** If you cannot let go of an injustice, bury a piece of agate where nothing grows, on a night when the moon is waning. Before filling in the hole, sprinkle seeds on top of your agate. **Divinatory meaning:** Consider both sides before making a decision. **Zodiac:** Capricorn. **Empowerment:** I walk through life at my own pace to my chosen destination.

Called the earth rainbow, banded agates are among the most ancient of stones, used for bowls in many ages and cultures to protect the eater and aid digestion.

Good for anyone with two jobs or who juggles commitments; aids writers to express ideas in a marketable form.

Banded agate stops the burning desires for what we do not need, a good counter to consumerism. Banded agates help young children to learn to walk and not fall over as they get older.

Crazy Lace Agate

Type: Chalcedony.

Colours: Mixed rust red, orange, grey, brown, yellow ochre, cream or opaque white.

Availability: Relatively common.

Physical benefits: Claimed to assist skin disorders, eyesight, problems with the colon and the heart, varicose veins, arteries, blood circulation.

Emotional healing: Overcomes fear of spiders and other crawling insects; increases self-esteem, absorbs emotional pain, especially when worn as jewellery over the heart or throat.

Chakra: Throat/Brow or Third Eye.

Candle colour: Multi-coloured. **Fragrances:** Copal, dragon's blood, saffron. **Practical uses:** Have a dish of crazy lace agates on the table to spread laughter and fun at a party. **Workplace:** Good for uniting an office where people tend to sit in their own areas and do not communicate directly. **Magical significance:** Place a crazy lace agate under an old spider's web monthly for 24 hours to attract happy experiences in love. **Divinatory meaning:** Take time to relax, invite a few people round for an impromptu party. **Zodiac:** Aquarius. **Empowerment:** I open myself to joy and laughter, even if life is gloomy.

Called the laughter stone, both because it is associated with sunny Mexican fiestas and dancing and because it brings joy to those who wear it.

If you suffer from sudden energy dips, crazy lace agate will regularize your daily energy flow. Associated with the web of fate, use this crystal if you go ghost hunting or when visiting very old places to stop you being spooked and to protect you from negative vibes, but enable you to see past worlds and spirits.

Rainbow Quartz

Type: Silicate/tectosilicate, clear quartz with prismatic fractures within the crystal.

Colours: Light refracted by the prismatic effect of the inclusion.

Availability: Relatively common.

Physical benefits: Thought to be good for bladder, cystitis, kidneys, bowel disorders, constipation, exhaustion, menstrual difficulties, metabolism, Seasonal Affective Disorder.

Emotional healing: Rainbow quartz overcomes deep disappointments and disillusion over the way love, career, family or life turned out: brings the optimism to try again

Chakra: Brow and Crown.

Candle colour: White. **Fragrances:** Copal, frankincense, lemon, orange, sandalwood. **Practical uses:** One of the best crystals if you are shy or lacking confidence at social occasions. **Workplace:** Keep in the workplace where it catches the light to reduce a bad atmosphere and lack of commitment. **Magical significance:** Rainbow quartz spheres are the perfect divinatory tool for the beginner to see images within. **Divinatory meaning:** This is a time when lady luck smiles on you. **Zodiac:** Cancer and Leo. **Empowerment:** I am optimistic about the future.

Rainbow quartz combines the dynamic power of clear quartz with the mystical rainbow energies associated with reconciliation and the promises of a better tomorrow. The rainbow amplifies the power of white light into different forms to offer courage and confidence in red, creativity in orange, logic and entrepreneurial qualities in yellow, love and luck in green, career and justice in blue, spiritual powers and imagination in indigo and the ability to make a huge life leap in violet.

Dendritic Quartz

Type: Quartz, containing manganese oxide as fern or plant-like black inclusions.

Colours: Clarity varies according to the amount of the inclusion; some quartz can be yellowish or smoky.

Availability: Found in specialist crystal stores and online.

Physical benefits: Said to assist veins, arteries, small capillaries and orifices in the body, nerve connections and endings.

Emotional healing: A crystal for reducing over-dependency on others; for freeing up a co-dependent relationship.

Chakra: Root.

Candle colour: White. **Fragrances:** Clematis, ivy, vetivert. **Practical uses:** Take along to community events or activities at your children's school to find like-minded people. **Workplace:** Good for mergers. **Magical significance:** A crystal associated with seasonal celebrations; hold dendritic quartz up to moonlight, press your quartz against the nearest trunk and you will hear psychic messages. **Divinatory meaning:** You may be feeling claustrophobic in a situation; take a few steps back and gently create your own space rather than walking away. **Zodiac:** Pisces. **Empowerment:** I do not need constant company.

Dendritic quartz is a natural choice to wear or carry if you want to move into the countryside or live by the sea, to open up all kinds of ideas and attract unexpected opportunities. A back-to-nature crystal, hold it in soft sunlight to reconnect with the energies of the natural world and to fill yourself with the life force in its purest form.

Dendritic quartz opens up children's powers of communication and increases sociability, particularly if they are shy with strangers or do not like being left at nursery or going to school.

Super Seven

Type: Contains the fusion of seven minerals.

Colours: Dark purple transparent with gold and misty grey within.

Availability: Relatively rare.

Physical benefits: May help illnesses for which there is not yet a conventional cure or where prognosis is poor; to help bring the best quality of life for the sick person.

Emotional healing: Super seven gives confidence to be ourselves, rather than constantly trying to please others; healing for children who have been made to feel evil or dirty.

Chakra: Crown but harmonizes all seven main chakras.

Candle colour: White or gold. **Fragrances:** Cedar, myrrh. **Practical uses:** Set four crystals in the centre of your dining table so the four crystals touch, to act as a home blessing. **Workplace:** Reminds you why you are working. Take it out of your drawer each morning as you define what you hope to achieve. Magical significance: Amplifies psychokinesis to draw what we want into our lives. **Divinatory meaning:** Focus on life as it is, not as it ought to be, and then see if the two can become the same. **Zodiac:** Aquarius. **Empowerment:** I will not hurry too fast along my life path.

Super seven was introduced to the healing community by Melody, the US crystal healer and expert, and is found only in Brazil. Like the seven legendary good fairies of myth, its seven separate minerals combine to form an eighth cumulative energy; it is this rather than the separate components that gives the Super Seven crystal the healing energies that have made it increasingly popular in therapy and everyday life. Children love super seven, especially those who find the world a hard place.

Creedite

Type: Sulfosalt, hydrated calcium aluminium sulphate.

Colours: Colourless, violet, orange-red.

Availability: Rare.

Physical benefits: May help blood detoxification, nerve endings and illnesses involving nerve malfunctioning or degeneration, Bell's palsy, strengthens immune system.

Emotional healing: A fast-acting crystal for relieving chronic depression or an inability to take any responsibility for or any initiative in life; for strengthening parents struggling with responsibility.

Chakra: Throat and Crown.

Candle colour: White. **Fragrances:** Cherry blossom, vanilla, white rose. **Practical uses:** Creedite helps you get over a lover you know logically could never be right or cannot be revived. **Workplace:** A creedite cluster ensures things get done and encourages high standards. **Magical significance:** Place sparkling white or violet creedite high in a room, illuminated by a lamp, to create a psychic entry point for astral travel. **Divinatory meaning:** Just one major push and you will be free of someone who interferes with your happiness. **Zodiac:** Virgo. **Empowerment:** I can live life my way without hurting anyone else.

Not only a beautiful crystal, especially as a cluster, but one that helps you carry through plans and decisions you have been postponing until the right moment; creedite makes *any* moment the right one. Orange creedite brings successful results in a career or relocation, particularly where independence is an issue. Violet creedite gives the confidence and determination to make time for your personal and spiritual development. Colourless creedite makes easier necessary if not desired changes e.g. starting a long-overdue fitness regime.

Watermelon Tourmaline

Type: Aluminium boron silicate.

Colours: Green outer core melts into inner red-pink.

Availability: Less common than other tourmalines, but obtainable from specialist crystal shops and online.

Physical benefits: May alleviate immune-system disorders, heart problems, mobility or co-ordination difficulties; balance metabolism and endocrine system; harmonize energies.

Emotional healing: Balances and cleanses the chakras; believed to assist personality disorders.

Chakra: Heart.

Candle colour: Pink or green. **fragrances:** Apple blossom, cherry blossom, geranium, rose, thyme. **Practical uses:** For young animals and children; sew a piece in the lining of the coat of a child who goes to nursery to avoid them becoming overwhelmed. **Workplace:** A bringer of peace and workplace sociability; especially for works outings to avoid behaving in a way you may regret. **Magical significance:** Used in wand formation as a wish crystal; direct energy into the cosmos through the pointed end to attract what you want. **Divinatory meaning:** Take the time to enjoy the beauty in the world. **Zodiac:** Libra and Scorpio. **Empowerment:** I sow the seeds of happiness and joy within me.

Watermelon tourmaline increases feelings of self-worth, healing the wounds of unrequited love; good for people who dream constantly of ideal love or put a lover on a pedestal and become disappointed. The gentleness of pink and the growth energies of green are the yin and yang of nature, bringing joy and spontaneity into your life after a period of domestic upheaval, illness or being overburdened by trying to do too much; increases fertility, not just physically but to live in a more fulfilling way.

Healer's Gold

Type: Pyrite and magnetite combined.

Colours: Black with gold (sometimes white inclusions) or black and silver.

Availability: Relatively rare but worth obtaining.

Physical benefits: Allows healers to work with patients without becoming depleted; believed to assist with blood conditions, circulation, bowels, intestines, excessive bleeding, blood clots, pain relief, exhaustion from illness or treatment.

Emotional healing: Protects against all who drain energy and from emotionally draining situations.

Chakra: Solar Plexus.

Candle colour: Gold. **Fragrances:** Chamomile, copal, cyphi, myrrh. **Practical uses:** A stabilizing crystal that attracts good fortune; a natural piece restores normality after a crisis, eases grief and assists in rebuilding. **Workplace:** Wear if you work with computers or electronic equipment or use a mobile phone; hold when you cannot rest. **Magical significance:** Enhances spiritual healing, also for practitioners of conventional medicine to channel energy from the earth to act as a conductor of healing and to shield patients from harmful effects of equipment or drugs. **Divinatory meaning:** A creative period to attract the necessary resources through hard work and by making tough decisions to shed what is working against you. **Zodiac:** Leo. **Empowerment:** I have the strength to resist pressure.

Attracts what is needed and keeps away unhelpful energies. Light white candles round a natural piece in your central downstairs room; ask blessings on all departed spirits and request that they either remain in peace and love or depart. Leave candles burning and when they are burned down, open the nearest window. A stone of fidelity and love. Hang a pendant over the bed with sprigs of dried rosemary in a drawstring bag; replace the herbs monthly and scatter them. Smudge monthly with a frankincense or myrrh incense stick spiralled over it, asking that you remain together in fidelity and love.

Type: Calcium carbonate.

Colours: Pure as white; also black, green, orange, red, yellow in many colour combinations.

Availability: Common.

Physical benefits: Said to be good for abscesses, conjunctivitis and other eye problems, headaches, hormonal imbalances, acute pain or fever; slowing down progressive illness; assimilation of calcium for strong bones and teeth.

Emotional healing: Restores clarity and focus to those suffering from emotional stress and mental fatigue, while at the same time reducing hyperactivity and restlessness of mind.

Chakra: Brow and Crown.

Marble

Candle colour: White. **Fragrances:** Anise, cedarwood, lavender, lemongrass, thyme. **Practical uses:** Let hyperactive children play with marble tumble stones (under supervision) to calm and balance their energies; have a bowl of the stones as worry stones for fidgety adults in an area where you sit; discourages mindless flicking through satellite channels or random Internet surfing. **Workplace:** Improves self-discipline and single-mindedness, if your concentration tends to wander; encourages creative people to channel energies and pay attention to detail. **Magical significance:** Marble ritual bowls and cups have been set on altars for thousands of years in many cultures; use marble objects around the home to bring sanctity to your everyday world. **Divinatory meaning:** An emotional issue or conflict will be solved through the use of common sense once you disregard preconceived viewpoints. **Zodiac:** Gemini and Cancer. **Empowerment:** I put my preconceptions aside to see the truth.

Marble is an organic metamorphic rock that forms over millions of years. It starts life usually as limestone that undergoes many geological changes.

White marble has been used by many cultures and ages for temples, sculpture and carvings as a symbol of purity and incorruptibility over time, notably statues of deities in Ancient Greece and Rome and angels in churches, particularly in Victorian times. Its use in funerary statues and crosses has strengthened marble's connections with immortality and the heavenly realms.

Used as massage stones or wands, white marble is increasingly popular with alternative health therapists to realign the chakras ; at the same time it connects the healer with higher spiritual energies such as angels and healing guides.

Marble slabs are still used for altars, as touching marble seems to free the spirit to pray or express innate but often buried connection with higher sources of wisdom. Small spheres can be carried to bring protection to an individual who must walk physically or spiritually alone along a hazardous or unknown path.

Marble

Amethyst Chevron

Type: Mixture of purple and white quartz.

Colours: Darker purple and white; pointed chevrons where the white is at the top are often called dogstooth amethyst.

Availability: Common.

Physical benefits: Claimed to be excellent for righting any imbalances, and for alleviating symptoms of degenerative conditions; may be helpful for multiple sclerosis.

Emotional healing: Relieves extremes of mood or behaviour.

Chakra: Brow and Crown.

Candle colour: Purple. **Fragrances:** Acacia, lemon, lotus, meadowsweet, papyrus. **Practical uses:** Keep a dish in a room where you are having a party to encourage tolerance and good spirits. **Workplace:** Keep some different ones in a drawer; if things are fraught get out the one with more purple; if you feel lethargic use the crystal with more white. **Magical significance:** Hold one each hand for powerful but safe out-of-body travel, shamanic journeying or pathworking, and between your hands while praying or reciting mantras. **Divinatory meaning:** Find peace within yourself by withdrawing from a stressful situation and then act. **Zodiac:** Aquarius. **Empowerment:** I see beauty everywhere.

The life force is filtered from the cosmos via the crown, represented by the white, through into the brow. Here it opens up spiritual and psychic channels through the purple, as well as energizing and harmonizing body and mind. For learning any form of spiritual healing, it enables you to channel healing powers by using its dual-focus energy; remove, pain, tension and blockages, by passing the purple end anti-clockwise over any problem areas or slowly up the back of the body and down the front for whole-body healing; use the white end to energize in the reverse order clockwise. A pointed chevron is best.

Cat's Eye

Type: Varies according to the crystal or gem; officially only chrysoberyl is referred to as cat's eye, others are called, for example, ruby cat's eye in the jewellery trade.

Colours: Varies according to the crystal or gem but always displays the effect of a moving cat's eye.

Availability: Relatively common as the less valuable or occidental cat's eye quartz. More exotic chrysoberyl is often called oriental cat's eye.

Physical benefits: Tought to be helpful for eyesight, coughs, haemorrhoids, hair and skin health, mobility, nausea, cholesterol, blood sugar fluctuations.

Emotional healing: Use if you are easily influenced by others

Chakra: Heart.

Candle colour: Green. **Fragrances:** Apple blossom, catmint, cedar, lilac, sandalwood. **Practical uses:** Cat's eye helps you to remember where you left things; also good for all forms of speculation where you assess odds. **Workplace:** A stone of independence; detects opportunities and problems before they develop; can act as a mood stone to highlight your own feelings and the motives of others. **Magical significance:** Considered in India as a lucky charm against sorrow, poverty, diseases and hidden enemies. **Divinatory meaning:** Distinguish between loyal friends and superficial ones. **Zodiac:** Pisces. **Empowerment:** I do not need to accept unpleasant behaviour in others.

As light hits tiny tube-like cavities or needle-like fibres within the gem or crystal, if the cavities or fibre bundles lie in the same direction, a single band of light bounces off at right angles creating the cat's eye effect.

Cat's eyes in the Near and Middle East are considered protective against the evil eye, to make the wearer invisible and to attract wealth. Any jewellery therefore is incredibly lucky financially, as well as protective against malice and envy. People often wear the same cat's eye for years so it grows in strength and good fortune; traditionally bought on Wednesday, Thursday or Friday.

Amethyst, Chevron & Cats Eye

Type: Quartz that contains both amethyst and citrine naturally within the same crystal.

Colours: Sparkling yellow and gentle purple mixed.

Availability: Obtainable through specialist crystal stores and online, but is becoming rarer.

Physical benefits: Claimed to be beneficial for minimizing side effects of necessary prolonged invasive treatments, for helping a treatment to be effective if the body is weak or not responding; for any transplant or transfusions, for ME and any chronic fatigue syndrome.

Emotional healing: Reduces cravings while quitting smoking or keeping to a health plan or diet: hold ametrine on your navel for a minute or two when a craving becomes too strong; acts against panic attacks.

Chakra: Solar Plexus and Brow.

Ametrine

Candle colour: Yellow. **Fragrances:** Bergamot, lavender, lemongrass, lemon verbena, mint. **Practical uses:** Encourages equality between the sexes, racial and religious tolerance; for peacefully overcoming opposition because of your lifestyle and family prejudice over same-sex relationships. **Workplace:** Excellent for self-employed people or anyone working from home to prevent work taking over your life; also for people balancing caring for family with a career. **Magical significance:** Hold ametrine, name what is bad in your life; wash the crystal, then hold it up to sunlight or natural light and name what you want to bring into your life. **Divinatory meaning:** You can win without resorting to tactics you are not ethically comfortable with. **Zodiac:** Gemini. **Empowerment:** I make my own choices and am not at the mercy of my desires.

A crystal that combines the power of the sun with the gentleness of the moon to maintain enthusiasm and impetus without becoming stressed; very healing since amethyst removes pain or tension while citrine brings energy and a sense of wellbeing to mind and body; gentler than purple and white chevron amethyst for energizing; a gateway crystal for opening angelic or spirit guide contact: a natural money bringer: leave ametrine in natural light from noon on the day of the full moon and then all night to catch lunar rays, then put in a purse when you buy a lottery ticket or try some money-spinning venture; increases immunity against cold, flu and winter ills; protects against emotional and psychic vampires.

Uvite

Type: Silicate (tourmaline group).

Colours: Yellow-brown, light to dark brown, dark green to black.

Availability: Once rare, but now more common.

Physical benefits: May help with immune system, digestive disorders; be helpful after a colostomy or ileostomy, stomach stapling or gastric-band surgery, useful for fertility and male potency.

Emotional healing: Boosts self-confidence where a person has been undermined over a number of years, perhaps as the youngest child in a family.

Chakra: Heart, Root and Solar Plexus.

Candle colour: Any earthy colour. **Fragrances:** Coriander, dragon's blood. **Practical uses:** The ultimate environmental crystal; assists any form of green activity. **Workplace:** Wear uvite to increase your tolerance of others who have inflated egos, at the same time developing your objectivity and maintaining your values and work ethics. **Magical significance:** Used in earth healing rituals and those to awaken personal responsibility for global warming. **Divinatory meaning:** Do not allow someone with a lot of money to intimidate you. **Zodiac:** Aries and Scorpio. **Empowerment:** I am content with what I have.

Uvite is a member of the tourmaline group of minerals named after the Uva district in Sri Lanka and is magnesium- and iron-rich. The difference between the other tourmalines, such as dravite (p.117), schorl (p.204) or elbaite (p.327), and uvite is that one of the aluminium elements has been replaced by magnesium. It has stubby crystals rather than the normal longer prismatic typical tourmaline crystals. Uvite offers grounding energies to make you feel secure within yourself.

Hyalite Opal

Type: Hydrated silicon dioxide, common opal.

Colours: Colourless and glassy.

Availability: Obtainable from specialist crystal stores and online.

Physical benefits: May help with laser surgery and all light therapies, facial and jaw problems and surgery, fevers, particularly recurring ones, low blood sugar, sunburn, burns and scalds, migraines, recurring colds.

Emotional healing: A good stone for slowly clearing a distorted body image or acute self-consciousness about a minor physical defect that prevents social interaction.

Chakra: Sacral and Heart.

Candle colour: Silver. **Fragrances:** Clary sage, rosewood, sweetgrass. **Practical uses:** A piece of hyalite is a natural magnet for accumulating anything you need, whether resources, money or friends. **Workplace:** Helpful for valuing people for their personality and performance. **Magical significance:** Natural hyalite drives away dark energies caused by unhappiness in a home you buy. Light a silver candle in the evenings to illuminate the hyalite, and leave the candle burning. After a week or two the energies will be clear. **Divinatory meaning:** Be yourself. **Zodiac:** Cancer. **Empowerment:** I am comfortable in my own skin.

Hyalite usually forms botryoidal masses (covered in opal grape-like forms) as well as strange and unusual shapes; contains less water than other opals. It is fluorescent under UV light and forms in small globes. It is therefore the most unusual opal and so represents all the magical qualities of the opal, yet encourages the individuality of the wearer to shine through. Its own beauty in natural form is not conventional but, if worn, hyalite brings out the wearer's inner radiance.

Pietersite

Type: Member of quartz family (silicon dioxide).

Colours: Combination of blue-black, blue, gold, golden brown tiger's eye and quartz.

Availability: Becoming increasingly rare and gaining in value.

Physical benefits: Thought to help to balance the endocrine system; stimulate the pituitary gland, metabolism and body temperature; ease eye infections, said by some users to improve long-distance-focus eyesight and night vision.

Emotional healing: For those who have tried and failed many times to beat an addiction, by strengthening willpower to stick to a programme.

Chakra: Third Eye and Crown.

Candle colour: Dark blue. **Fragrances**: Basil, cedar, orange, sandalwood, sage. **Practical uses**: Pietersite is called the storm or tempest stone because it is believed to carry the power of the storm within; a bowl of pietersite in the home brings order out of chaos. **Workplace**: Have a large polished egg in your workspace between you and the direction people bother you from to minimize constant interruptions. **Magical significance**: Brings spontaneous visionary experience and precognitive knowledge. **Divinatory meaning**: You will see something in a new light. **Zodiac**: Sagittarius. **Empowerment**: Spirituality is a 24/7 experience.

Pietersite is protective when driving in bad weather conditions and calms nervous people and animals during storms; guards homes and business against storm damage; acts as a shield against the adverse effects of technology, particularly if you work long hours with a computer or live near a mobile phone mast.

Pietersite boosts the self-esteem of creative people who lack confidence in their abilities and so do not earn money from their gifts; gives confidence if worn constantly for several weeks.

Sardonyx

Type: Chalcedony layered with sard

Colours: Varied range of patterns and colours.

Availability: Common.

Physical benefits: May help with impotence, sterility, lungs, spine, chronic back pain, bowel, prostate and bladder problems, kidney and urinary-tract infections, cleanses the whole system of blockages and impurities, parasites of all kinds, septicaemia, HIV and AIDS, feet and legs.

Emotional healing: Removes a sense of helplessness and victim mentality, lifts depression and encourages action to make overdue changes.

Chakra: Root.

Candle colour: Brown. **Fragrances**: Fennel, musk, thyme. **Practical uses**: Mends quarrels in a marriage and also divisions between parents and children. **Workplace**: Sardonyx aids study. **Magical significance**: Greeks and Romans wore amulets of sardonyx carved with gods such as Ares/Mars, the god of war, to protect them in battle. Hold a tumblestone and say aloud the courage or power you need; repeat every time you need strength. **Divinatory meaning**: You will make an unexpected new friend that could lead to a lasting happiness. **Zodiac**: Aries, Virgo, and Capricorn. **Empowerment**: I can easily attain my goal.

Sardonyx symbolizes good fortune and happiness, particularly in relationships, marriage and love. If you are given sardonyx and you are unattached romantically it is foretold you will be married within the year.

A lucky talisman for legal matters and for obtaining justice, especially over money or property. If you find yourself hesitating over speaking out or acting over an issue that is unfair, hold sardonyx to give you courage without aggressiveness. Sardonyx rings are the ultimate fidelity token.

Type: Crypto-crystalline quartz.

Colours: Variety of earth hues.

Availability: Becoming scarcer, but still available from specialist crystal stores and online.

Physical benefits: Believed to be useful for increasing fertility; relieving impotence and other male sexual dysfunction and premature ejaculation; increasing libido in both sexes; easing childbirth.

Emotional healing: Unites and balances the male and female energies within to create a harmonious whole; good for resolving gender-related issues and for overcoming personal doubts about entering a same-sex relationship.

Chakra: Brow.

Shiva Lingham

Candle colour: Indigo. **Fragrances:** Almond, apple, bluebell, orange, rose. **Practical uses:** If you are still looking for your twin soul, cast a Shiva lingham into a deep lake or on the outgoing tide on New Year's Day or the first day of any month, having breathed on it three times and said, "call my other half to make me complete." **Workplace:** Keep a Shiva lingham in your workplace if there is unwelcome sexual tension or resentment over gender between you and a boss or colleague. **Magical significance:** Good for sacred or Tantric spiritual sex; for full-moon fertility rituals; leave your Shiva lingham outdoors, if possible in moonlight on the three nights before the full moon. Place it by the bed on the night of the full moon during lovemaking. **Divinatory meaning:** A turbulent time will pass and new unexpected positive input bring calm to troubled waters. **Zodiac:** Scorpio, the Scorpion. **Empowerment:** I welcome my twin soul into my life.

In Onkar Mandhata, a sacred site of India, the holy river Narmada flows. It is here that once a year in dry season, a few select locals wade into the shallow waters to gather the stones named Shiva lingham from the river bed.

They are carefully selected in a wide variety of sizes and are then skilfully polished by hand to the correct and balanced proportions to create a very potent spiritual talisman or healing stone that is now sold all over the world. This traditional limited collection method is now under threat.

Shiva lingham is used in the practice of Feng Shui to direct the flow of energies around the home, presumably related to the stones being subjected to centuries of the energy flow of the sacred river prior to extraction.

Use it to strengthen sexual and loving relationships by placing one or more of these stones in the relationship area of your home (if you are familiar with Feng Shui) or keep a large one in the bedroom and add a smaller on next to it to conceive a child.

Type: Epidote (calcium aluminium silicate) with ruby (corundum) inclusions.

Colours: Green, dark pink to red and black.

Availability: Relatively common as tumblestones.

Physical benefits: Claimed to assist with reproductive disorders, especially fibroids and fertility problems; bring healing after a miscarriage or termination, a hysterectomy or early menopause; slow down racing pulse and heartbeat; protect against viruses and infections, especially bacterial ones.

Emotional healing: Good for worries over sexual dilemmas; helps young people to accept if they want a single-sex partnership and to resolve worries about trans- or bisexuality.

Chakra: Crown, Heart and Solar Plexus.

Ruby in Zoisite/Anyolite

Candle colour: Green or red. **Fragrances:** Apple and apple blossom, ginger, jasmine, magnolia. **Practical uses:** Keep this crystal near your bed to restore passion and heal relationship issues if one partner is having sexual difficulties or is contemplating infidelity. **Workplace:** Wear this crystal or keep it near your work area to achieve targets and deadlines; also for sexual equality and harmonious male and female relationships, especially if one sex is very under-represented or women are in traditionally male roles such as fire services or in the front line in the armed services. **Magical significance:** Use ruby in zoisite in Mars and Venus sacred sex rituals or Tantric sex where lovemaking becomes a spiritual expression of unity. **Divinatory meaning:** A time for balancing your desire for immediate action with the safer but duller path of waiting and seeing. **Zodiac:** Aries and Taurus. **Empowerment:** I acknowledge the need to balance passion with practicality.

Ruby in zoisite or anyolite is a beautiful combination of red ruby crystals in green zoisite, merging the energies of fire and earth, passion and patience, immediacy and allowing life to unfold. It gives us the strength of mind to pursue our dreams while still keeping us connected with the real world and balancing our own needs to fulfil our own unique blueprint with those of others around us.

Good for helping children and teenagers to understand that they have to keep necessary rules and laws without feeling over-controlled or resentful. This crystal calms swings of mood and over-reaction; good for cooling the emotional and sexual temperature at work and in social situations where a liaison would be unwise or inappropriate.

Take ruby in zoisite on foreign holidays to instinctively follow local customs and avoid giving unintentional offence to locals.

Type: Hydrated silicon dioxide, precious opal formed in veins and patches within brown ironstone boulders.

Colours: Opalescent colours with brown.

Availability: Relatively common.

Physical benefits: Argued to be helpful for dealing with deep skin lesions, wounds and second- or third-degree burns, eyesight, bone weakness or calcification, veins and arteries, all problems associated with ageing, Parkinson's disease, Alzheimer's disease and senile dementia, bowels, constipation and IBS, wheat and dairy intolerance.

Emotional healing: This practical earthed opal stirs those who prefer to live in a dream world and a golden tomorrow because they are afraid to face the realities of today.

Chakra: Root and brow.

Boulder Opal

Candle colour: Rainbow colours in one candle. **Fragrances:** Cedar, eucalyptus, patchouli, pine, vetivert. **Practical uses:** If you or a partner find it hard to put down roots, but need to, because of career demands or you want to start a family, boulder opal offers energies for a stable home environment without sacrificing a spirit of adventure; wear boulder opal also to prevent homesickness when you leave home for the first time or for long periods. **Workplace:** A strong enduring opal form, boulder opal encourages vision and perseverance when the going gets tough or tedious; wear during a long course of study or training, or if temporary restrictions on salary or progress last longer than expected. **Magical significance:** A stone associated with indigenous rites of passage among the Australian Aboriginals and, with modern ease of export, adopted by several Native North American peoples as a power stone; give boulder opal jewellery on key birthdays or milestones; hold also in an earthy place to connect with earth and plant spirits. **Divinatory meaning:** You may need to be more practical and work within current restrictions if you are to get a plan off the ground. **Zodiac:** Cancer and Capricorn. **Empowerment:** I can turn restrictions into the foundations for success.

Boulder is a remarkable opal since it combines precious opal from Australia with ironstone or sandstone, so blending beauty and ethereal qualities with firm foundations. When the opal is mixed through the ironstone it is called matrix opal.

Opal can partly take the place of wood and form fossils, still growing the trees' original growth rings. This is also called boulder opal. These close-to-nature opals are excellent as charms, for practical people who would like to develop their spiritual

sides but find it hard to let go of logical blocks to possibilities beyond the material; boulder opal can also assist spiritually minded people to succeed in the everyday world, particularly in practising alternative therapies or clairvoyance or running New Age stores or centres and surviving financially. A gift for a partner going through a hard time at work or during a down patch in a relationship, to say "hang on in there"; good for past-life work.

Paua Shell

Type: Sea opal shell (*haliotus iris*), a member of the abalone family

Colours: Deep blue, green or purple.

Availability: Common in New Zealand, obtainable online.

Physical benefits: May aid fertility, womb and ovaries, skin rashes and blemishes, spine weakness and slipped discs, breasts, heart valves.

Emotional healing: Give paua-shell jewellery to a new mother who is suffering post-natal depression.

Chakra: Sacral.

Candle colour: Green. **Fragrances:** Honey, kelp, manuka, vanilla. **Practical uses:** Wear to give confidence in social situations to be yourself and let your natural charisma shine through. **Workplace:** Obtain a wooden carving containing paua shell or a polished half-shell to act as a cohesive force if you are responsible for coordinating people. **Magical significance:** Paua shell, particularly if combined with New Zealand greenstone, is a lucky charm for love, health and prosperity. **Divinatory meaning:** You will experience a moment of pleasure as a sign it is all worthwhile. **Zodiac:** Cancer. **Empowerment:** There is beauty in unexpected places and people if I look.

Mookaite

Type: Silicate; contains chert, sometimes with fossilized inclusions.

Colours: Mottled.

Availability: Increasingly common.

Physical benefits: Thought to boost immune system, calms digestive system by reducing stress, bladder, cystitis, blood sugar disorders (high), cuts, wounds, fluid retention, bloating, hernia, thyroid.

Emotional healing: Makes it easier to accept change and to allow ourselves to take a chance now and then, without worrying about the future.

Chakra: Root, Sacral and Solar Plexus.

Candle colour: Pink. **Fragrances:** Basil, bay, patchouli, sage, vetivert. **Practical uses:** Use mookaite when you need to make a decision and there are conflicting factors to consider – hold it close to receive a gut answer and go with it, even if external circumstances suggest otherwise. **Workplace:** Provides enthusiasm for work. **Magical significance:** As a Mother Earth stone, mookaite connects you with earth power; press a palm stone against your upper stomach. **Divinatory meaning:** An adventurous and challenging time ahead. **Zodiac:** Virgo and Scorpio. **Empowerment:** Beauty is everywhere if I stop and look.

Paua shell, said to be the most colourful shell in the world, is used by the Maori people as adornment and in religious ceremonies. The eyes of Maori carvings are inlaid with paua shell.

These eyes are considered all-seeing, the eyes of the owl or associated with the stars in the night sky. Paua shell isa powerful symbol of wisdom and far-reaching vision whereby you automatically know the right path by a sense of inner certainty.

Mookaite is a form of jasper found in Western Australia, and is named after the district where it is mined. An Australian Aboriginal Mother Earth stone that is becoming increasingly popular throughout the world for healing and connecting with positive earth energies, even in cities.

A very protective and grounding stone, whilst at the same time providing a motivational energy boost. For those who feel a bit stuck in either their personal life or at work, this gem can bring about the courage to seek adventure.

Type: Corundum (ruby) and aluminium silicate (kyanite).

Colours: Deep red and blue, sometimes teal as well as darker blue in varying proportions that seem to melt together.

Availability: Rare but definitely a stone to seek out.

Physical healing: A totally balancing stone with the warming red of ruby combining with the cooling blue of kyanite, so seen as beneficial for heart, muscles, throat and throat constrictions, cell disorders, circulation, hormones and blood pressure, pressure within eyes, once balance and health is restored, ruby in kyanite is belibeved to help maintain it.

Emotional healing: The best crystal for bi-polar disorder, for anyone who works away for long periods, for example the armed services or on oil rigs.

Chakra: Root, Heart, Throat and Brow.

Ruby in Kyanite

Candle colour: Blue. **Fragrances:** Almond, geranium, hibiscus, poppy, red rose. **Practical uses:** Keep a statue or sphere in the home to balance a relationship where there are issues of commitment or fears of losing freedom and identity by living as a couple; good for resolving issues where one of the couple is afraid or unwilling to have children. **Workplace:** A crystal for all who care for others professionally, to maintain the balance between warmth and detachment, support and encouragement of independence in clients; in counselling prevents a therapist from getting too emotionally involved with clients. **Magical significance:** A ruby in kyanite massage wand guides a new therapist who blocks their natural awareness of a client's needs because of anxieties about getting it right; ensures the client receives precisely the healing needed and the ensuing success builds up a novice therapist's confidence to make more active treatment decisions in future. **Divinatory meaning:** You need to offer wise advice but not take responsibility for what is someone else's problem. **Zodiac:** Sagittarius, Cancer and Pisces. **Empowerment:** I can love without losing myself.

One of the most beautiful, healing and spiritual combinations, polished ruby in kyanite is usually found as massage wands, spheres, eggs or as statues, particularly deities representing good fortune and protection.

Wear ruby in kyanite jewellery if you have to spend time or stay overnight with people you do not know well, for example relatives of a new prospective partner or a dinner party at the home of your employer; good for people who misread social signals, especially with conditions such as Asperger's syndrome, to communicate more effectively

A very protective stone from over-emotional people and social vampires who at first acquaintance try to move into your life. Wearing ruby in kyanite makes the learning of boring but necessary information more personally relevant and turns duty social events into fun.

Amegreen

Type: Amethyst and chlorite or prasiolite (natural green amethyst)

Colours: Mauve/purple and green.

Availability: Obtainable from specialist crystal stores and online, but becoming rarer.

Physical benefits: May help hearing difficulties and ear infections, sleep disturbances and disorders such as narcolepsy, snoring and apnoea, heart disease and recovery from injury, accident or trauma.

Emotional healing: A crystal for those who love too much or give too much to others, to draw boundaries and to ask for and accept support from others.

Chakra: Heart, Brow and Crown.

Candle colour: Purple or green. **Fragrances:** Benzoin, peppermint. **Practical uses:** A natural money maker, whether in business or through personal ventures, amegreen can act as a money magnet, but make sure air can circulate all round it. **Workplace:** For those who work or seek to work professionally in the spiritual arts. **Magical significance:** Very powerful against psychic or psychological attack. **Divinatory meaning:** Your spiritual powers are developing fast and you will soon have a chance to use them in the way that is right for you. **Zodiac:** Pisces. **Empowerment:** I trust my spiritual abilities to guide me on the right path.

A very spiritual crystal that offers instant links with your guardian angel, especially outdoors; if worn or carried, automatically cleanses the aura psychic energy field and the chakra inner psychic energy centres. Use for spiritual healing of self and others, held in the hand you do not write with and circle anti-clockwise close to the skin near a site of pain or close to the heart to draw out illness or sorrow; a crystal of small miracles when nothing seems to be working health-wise or in life.

Dragon's Egg

Type: Usually clear quartz.

Colours: Depends on the mineral but characterized by a polished glass-like window revealing the crystalline interior.

Availability: Obtainable from specialist crystal stores and online, worthwhile obtaining several in different minerals.

Physical benefits: May aid ovaries and female reproductive system, fertility, communication difficulties in children, particularly Asperger's syndrome, Tourette's and autism.

Emotional healing: Helps children in care.

Chakra: Root and Solar Plexus.

Candle colour: Purple or pink. **Fragrances:** Almond blossom, lime, tea tree. **Practical uses:** A bowl of assorted polished pebbles act as worry stones when you are trying to get to the bottom of a matter. **Workplace:** Hold a clear quartz pebble when you are seeking clarity. **Magical significance:** Once believed to be the eggs of dragons after the baby dragon had hatched. Gaze into one and allow the markings to create images, a very portable crystal ball. **Divinatory meaning:** A secret will be revealed if you ask the right question. **Zodiac:** Cancer. **Empowerment:** I look beyond the immediate to the hidden meaning.

Many dragon's egg pebbles sold have a natural frosted finish on the outside from being in streams, while others are abraded to give a rough powdery exterior. One side is cut and polished to create a crystalline window revealing the inclusions in the centre of the pebble. Ideal as a child's first crystal, particularly in the softer shades of purple amethyst and pink rose quartz; will stimulate all kinds of stories about the world within the egg; an amulet for a very sensitive child, teenager or one who has had to grow up quickly.

Type: Outer casing of chalcedony within which is sealed a quantity of water. You can hear the water moving if you shake the stone and the water can be seen, if the crystal is held to the light.

Colours: Cloudy white, also in other coloured agates, such as red, grey, dark brown or black or blue.

Availability: Obtainable from a specialist crystals store or online

Physical benefits: Enhydros are a woman's stone; the waters within the crystal will reflect her own monthly ebbs and flows, so are believed to benefit hormones and energies; be good for relieving PMS, menstrual pain or absence of menstruation.

Emotional healing: One of the most effective stones for healing emotional traumas.

Chakra: Sacral.

Enhydro/Water Agate

Candle colour: Silver. **Fragrances:** Jasmine, lemon, lemon balm, lemon verbena, poppy. **Practical uses:** Helpful around the home for teenagers and pre-pubescent children, especially girls, and for pregnant women and new mothers, to stabilize and positively channel powerful emotions. **Workplace:** Good for anyone in counseling, psychology or social care to understand instinctively the unspoken needs and feelings of others; also in negotiations to pick up the hidden agenda and underlying tempo. **Magical significance:** Enhydros make men and women more intuitive, telepathic and clairvoyant; use also to connect with your spirit guides and family ancestors. **Divinatory meaning:** You may be suddenly flooded by the emotions of another person but do not allow this to override your common sense and logic. **Zodiac:** Cancer. **Empowerment:** I open myself to my true feelings and desires, and trust my instincts to guide me.

Representing the waters of the womb of the earth mother, enhydro agate is the stone of Iemanjá, the Yoruba sea goddess, and so a stone both of fertility and abundance.

The water within the agate may be millions of years old. When the water is in the stable earthy agate as opposed to the more changeable pure quartz, this gives access through meditation to what are called the Akashic records or collective well of wisdom. These record the experiences of all people in all places and ages, past, present and the future yet to be made. Use enhydro or water agate for preserving relationships and situations in the midst of wanted or unwanted change, turbulence and crisis, to enable people to adapt to the new while maintaining and valuing the best of the old: good for seances or astral travel to keep feet on the ground while the head is in the stars.

Type: Silicate, microcrystalline quartz, often with organic matter or other minerals as inclusions.

Colours: Deep green with black can sometimes be mistaken for nebula stone because of external physical similarities.

Availability: Obtainable from specialist stores.

Physical benefits: Thought to boost the immune system, cellular growth, DNA, the ability to cope with hereditary conditions, digestive system, dietary stabilization, assimilation of vitamins and minerals; cleanse the body of toxins; improve internal, skin and hair parasites, nails, skin lesions, jaw, teeth, wisdom teeth, all dental work, neck and skull.

Emotional healing: Brings peace and tranquillity to troubled minds.

Chakra: Heart and Root.

Stromatolite/Kambaba Jasper

Candle colour: Green. **Fragrances:** Basil, galbanum, mimosa, patchouli, sweetgrass. **Practical uses:** If you have a stressful life and find it hard to concentrate on the task in hand or enjoy relaxation because your mind is always racing ahead, keep a handful of tumbled kambaba in your pocket or a small bag; use them as worry stones to ease your state of mind. **Workplace:** Kambaba improves an established career or business interests in tried-and-tested areas and jobs in family firms; wear as jewellery or have a piece of natural kambaba to resist unnecessary changes or colleagues who paint a falsely dark picture of prospects to destabilize you. **Magical significance:** A very grounding stone in ancient places, both natural and created by humans, to tune into the people who once lived there; protective if you sense past evil practices in a building or realize at any time you are in the wrong place and are in psychic danger. **Divinatory meaning:** Ask if the changes being planned are necessary to bring improvement or are just for their own sake. **Zodiac:** Cancer and Capricorn. **Empowerment:** Nothing needs changing right now.

Green stromatolite jasper is the modern name for kambaba jasper. It is a sedimentary stone, containing the earliest records of life on earth, fossilized algae and other primaeval microorganisms. It is found in Madagascar and South Africa.

One of the more exotic jaspers, keep kambaba jasper with any salt-water or tropical fish, exotic pets or those that need a lot of heat such as lizards; use for getting back to basics in any area of your life, whether downsizing, reassessing priorities or reworking your budget; brings happiness and protects on any back-to-nature holidays or deep-sea diving. Keep kambaba in bedrooms to induce a deep and peaceful sleep.

Kambaba jasper strengthens those whose hearts have been deeply hurt by sudden rejection or abandonment in love, to see ways out of the darkness emotionally and to deal logically with what must be resolved.

Septarian

Type: Bentonite clay or marl concretions, cemented together by silica, carbonates or iron oxide; veins and concentric cracks of aragonite and/or calcite forming a circular web pattern.

Colours: Mainly browns, pale to rich.

Availability: Relatively common.

Physical benefits: Believed to be useful for the immune system, blood, kidneys, muscle spasms and pains, skin lesions, eczema or cracked skin, hair.

Emotional healing: Offer a nurturing energy; fosters independent living among those in care.

Chakra: Root.

Candle colour: Yellow. **Fragrances:** Benzoin, bergamot, orange, rosemary, sweet pea. **Practical uses:** A good stone for getting to know neighbours. **Workplace:** Keep near you for focus on your current activity rather than trying to do too many things at once. **Magical significance:** Septarians, carved and polished into spheres, are an exceptional tool for meditation, divination and scrying. **Divinatory meaning:** Not a time to go it alone or disregard other people's opinions. **Zodiac:** Taurus. **Empowerment:** I offer and accept the hand of friendship.

Septarians (also called Dragon Stone) formed around 60 million years ago as a result of dead organic matter being covered in sedimentary material. As the ocean receded, the mud balls dried and cracked. Minerals formed from the organic matter to fill the cracks, creating the often yellow centres. This formation gives septarian its ability to harmonize our inner and outer selves, to integrate past with future via the present and to walk the line between connection with others and individuality. Absorbs and amplifies your essence if you hold it regularly, so it can transmit stored strength.

Titanium Aura

Type: Quartz fused with a fine layer of titanium and niobium.

Colours: Multicoloured iridescent.

Availability: Relatively common.

Physical benefits: Thought of as a healer of many ailments, and to be especially good for water retention, bone diseases and growths, multiple sclerosis, any degenerative conditions.

Emotional healing: Hold titanium aura when life is dark, if you are facing bankruptcy, repossession, unemployment, serious illness

Chakra: Crown.

Candle colour: Rainbow or gold. **Fragrances:** Acacia, anise, dragon's blood. **Practical uses:** Take titanium aura with you if you are staying in an impersonal hotel to bring the beauty of the rainbow into your life. **Workplace:** Brighten up your workspace with a cluster to enhance positivity. **Magical significance:** Illuminate a titanium aura sphere, like a crystal ball, with one or two candles for scrying by candlelight, reading the images created on the surface in darkness. **Divination Meaning:** You cannot put the clock back, but you can start again. **Zodiac:** Pisces. **Empowerment:** I can transform without losing my true self

Titanium aura quartz is a powerful aid to seeing auras. Look at the colours in a titanium aura and then at the space around the head and shoulders of the person you are with. The colours round the head will transmit themselves as accurate impressions about the character of other people, useful when you are unsure of someone. A titanium aura shaped as a point will energize and empower your own aura when you feel tired, fragmented or dispirited. Pass the point through and above your hair in spirals until you feel the power flow.

Septarian & Titanium Aura

322

Rubellite in Lepidolite

Type: Rubellite, lithium-rich crystalline silicate; lepidolite, a type of mica, contains varying amounts of lithium.

Colours: Red and lilac-grey, rose and purple, mixed together.

Availability: Found in specialist crystal stores and online.

Physical benefits: The combination of the two minerals means this is viewed as a powerful healing crystal.

Emotional healing: The presence of lithium in both minerals makes rubellite in lepidolite a potent for calming mood swings; relieves bi-polar symptoms.

Chakra: Brow, Heart and Root.

Candle colour: Lavender. **Fragrances:** Lavender, lilac, thyme. **Practical uses:** Keep a rubellite-in-lepidolite sphere or a natural piece of rubellite on a matrix of sparkly lepidolite in your crystal place to bring and keep love in your home and to create a welcoming atmosphere for visitors. **Workplace:** Protects against harmful energies from computers; creates an oasis of calm. **Magical significance:** Keep rubellite in lepidolite in your healing area for healing sessions. **Divinatory meaning:** Make space for yourself away from the demands of the world. **Zodiac:** Libra and Capricorn. **Empowerment:** I can create my own inner space.

A "two for the price of one" crystal in which each mineral enhances and complements the properties of the other. It is especially helpful for reducing physical stress reactions and symptoms, and the automatic fight-or-flight mechanism; creates in the most confrontational situation a private bubble of peace to enable us to take that essential one step back and then respond with quiet confidence and authority; a good crystal if you teach children or control large numbers of people as a security officer or member of the armed forces.

Rhyolite

Type: Igneous rock crystal rich in silica; a mixture of mainly quartz with feldspar.

Colours: Greens, browns, grey, tan, pink, often speckled, patchy or with web-like markings, but also in plain and banded forms.

Availability: Common.

Physical benefits: Seen as assisting with stamina and muscle efficiency, immune system, colds, winter chills, flu, vein and artery healing, rashes and skin allergies.

Emotional healing: Called the stone of rejuvenation, for those who are made to feel old and useless.

Chakra: Heart.

Candle colour: Green. **Fragrances:** Cedarwood, lemon. **Practical uses:** Use if you are at a point of change in career or relationships. This crystal will give you the strength to make the right decision. **Workplace:** Wear or carry to attract good luck if your business plans are slow to bear fruit. **Magical significance:** Obtain a sphere; let your finger travel its surface pathways. One path will become very clear and reveal answers. **Divinatory meaning:** Do not postpone an inevitable confrontation; you will know the right things to say and do. **Zodiac:** Gemini and Sagittarius. **Empowerment:** I live today for today.

Rhyolite is said to be the container of hidden treasure as sometimes it forms the outer casing for Oregon blue opal. It represents therefore our hidden talents, which can now be developed. As the stone of youthfulness, rhyolite empowers retired people to develop creative gifts, embark on travel or study. It brings a change of perspective, so that problems that were draining enthusiasm suddenly become resolvable; opens us to love and to forgiving ourselves and others. Helps us to live in the present and enjoy every moment; good for fitness plans and a healthier lifestyle.

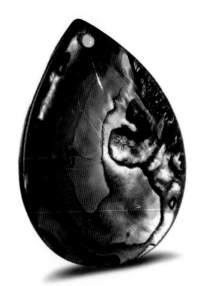

Type: Shell, mollusc.

Colours: Iridescent green-blue pearl contained within the convex oval brown or greyish shell.

Availability: Farmed abalone is common, natural sources are decreasing rapidly.

Physical benefits: Thought to help with high blood pressure, palpitations, dizziness, vertigo, headaches and eye problems, psychosomatic conditions, digestion, liver.

Emotional healing: Especially calming for hyperactive children; encourage them to stop regularly and hold the shell or give them a small piece of abalone jewellery or a charm on a chain to wear. Calms panic attacks in people of all ages.

Chakra: Brow.

Abalone Shell

Candle colour: White. **Fragrances:** Acacia, eucalyptus, gardenia, jasmine, valerian. **Practical uses:** Abalone shells around the home calm angry moods. Wear abalone-shell jewellery if you are a mother to cope with daily dramas, from young children's tantrums to a partner's mid-life crisis. **Workplace:** Helps you to keep your head in a tense or agitated situation and to defuse ongoing office tension; since abalone aids digestion, keep one on your work desk if you have to eat hurried snack meals on the run. **Magical significance:** Follow Native North American tradition and burn dried sagebrush and cedar leaves in the shell for smudging; also for holding small lighted smudge sticks and sweetgrass braids as you walk round cleansing a room or artefacts. **Divinatory meaning:** Unexpected visitors may outstay their welcome; do not be taken advantage of through your natural desire to be hospitable. **Zodiac:** Cancer. **Empowerment:** Every day is sacred and a gift to be used wisely.

Inside the abalone shell is a thick layer of resilient iridescent material, known as mother-of-pearl, created as a result of a substance getting inside the shell and causing irritation. The shell has been used in healing since ancient times and is still used today in herbal remedies. As a meditation tool, abalone can focus our mind and allow it to open up to the natural world and receive its insights. Hold the shell between your hands by candlelight and look into the pearly centre.

Abalone is a symbol of protection – the mother-of-pearl interior was created by nature to form a protective barrier shielding the mollusc from intrusion. This protective energy is passed on to those that hold or wear this shell. It can also assist its wearer to shine from within, helping their inner goodness come to the fore and radiate into their persona.

Gaze at the iridescent colours and allow abalone to trigger your imagination and inspiration for all forms of creative activity.

Chrysoltile/ Chrysotile

Type: A variety of serpentine, chrysotile contains asbestos so best used as a tumblestone

Colours: Grey and white, brown and white, creamy yellow.

Availability: Found in specialist crystal stores and online.

Physical benefits: Believed to relieve chronic fatigue, throat, lung problems, inflammation within body, multiple sclerosis, veins and arteries, assist blood thinning, skin, tissue regrowth.

Emotional healing: For issues of co-dependency and of problematic control issues with and by loved ones.

Chakra: Root and Throat.

Candle colour: Grey **Associated fragrances:** Lemongrass, lime, mugwort, musk, vetivert **Practical uses:** Carry in a grey or brown drawstring bag when going out with somone who is mean with money or time or at sharing. **Workplace:** Encourages resourcefulness and self-reliance; use when looking for a partner. **Magical significance:** Aids psychometry, receiving unknown information about a person or object via psychic touch. Hold a tumblestone in the hand you write with and touch an object belonging to the person or their family with the other hand, asking the questions. **Divinatory meaning:** Resist pressures to change your mind. **Zodiac:** Gemini and Capricorn. **Empowerment:** I control my own life..

A very earthing stone for times when you are being manipulated towards changes you may not want or you feel others have control over your life; gives you the strength and resourcefulness to make your own plans; good for the period after a separation; hold nightly if you need to move on from a person or situation but are afraid of being alone. Promotes telepathic bonds with people far away; helpful for tracing birth-parents or children given up early in life. **WARNING:** Contains asbestos so do not use in elixirs; do not ingest or breathe in the natural form; keep away from children and pets.

Amphibole Quartz

Type: Quartz containing fibrous amphibole minerals, usually has phantoms or shadow crystals.

Colours: Milky white, inclusions of amber, red-brown, white, yellow, occasionally pink that can colour the quartz.

Availability: Rare.

Physical benefits: Claimed to help with glands, tear ducts and eye problems that cause blurring of sight, arteries, veins, scar tissue, burns, blisters and inflamed skin, sunburn, for reducing build-up of excess fatty deposits, cholesterol.

Emotional healing: Insulates those who have been verbally abused from internalizing the comments.

Chakra: Brow.

Candle colour: White. **Fragrances:** Almond blossom, apple blossom, rose, violet, ylang ylang. **Practical uses:** A bringer of light that will benefit others in a household. Not a crystal for communal use but best for self-healing and self-empowerment. **Workplace:** Blurs the edges of unhelpful undercurrents. Use its intense light to bring out gifts and experiences that bring your unique perspective; good for one-off ventures and for patenting your own brand. **Magical significance:** Gives direct access to a spirit guide who will send strength, healing and wisdom through the crystal. **Divinatory meaning:** Be yourself. **Zodiac:** Aquarius and Pisces. **Empowerment:** I value my uniqueness.

Amphibole (or angel) quartz is called angel quartz because the inclusions have a wispy angel-like appearance. The mixing of the active quartz and the fibrous amphibole minerals makes this a powerful crystal for bringing the spiritual and mysterious into the everyday sphere, both in healing and in enriching daily life. Keep near to your phone or computer to deterring gossip and pointless emails. A protective crystal, surround with angel crystals such as angelite, celestite, opal aura and seraphinite to create a place of beauty and connect with angelic energies.

Type: Copper iron sulphide.

Colours: Coppery red, or bronze, metallic tarnishing to iridescent blue, purple and red in air, hence its folk name.

Availability: Common.

Physical benefits: Said to assist with the renewal of cells, convulsions, adrenaline flow, healthy metabolism, fevers; be good in illness where cellular structure is altered or for any kind of growths, lumps or blemishes, protect against infectious diseases.

Emotional healing: Reduces the flight-or-fight tendency in inappropriate situations and so encourages reactions that are related to actual external situations and not perceived dangers or threats.

Chakra: Brow.

Bornite/Peacock Ore

Candle colour: Purple. **Fragrances:** Anise, bayberry, cherry, geranium, narcissus. **Practical uses:** A mood lifter and bringer of happiness. Keep a piece in the car or your bag on family outings or visits to relatives to keep everyone in a good mood. **Workplace:** Hold bornite to identify potential adversaries. Your innate protective radar will alert you by a cold tingling sensation in your fingers. Keep in your workspace to shield yourself from their negativity. **Magical significance:** Good to reconnect with the intuitive awareness and possibilities we saw in childhood; carry if you would like to see ghosts in old houses or family spirits; keep some on the fireplace or in the kitchen to welcome the home guardian. **Divinatory meaning:** You may be given or acquire something old that is of more value than it first appears. **Zodiac:** Aquarius. **Empowerment:** I value natural beauty rather than artificial substitutes.

Said to have been formed in alchemy in the search to create the philosophers' stone that would transform other metals into gold and give immortality, bornite was described as a beautiful magical metallic peacock; also called peacock copper, bornite can be artificially enhanced to make it more shimmering. Set near you while getting ready to go out socially to brighten your aura and make you confident and relaxed if meeting someone new for the first time; if going

for an audition or interview carry bornite to get you noticed and remembered.

Naturally moves energy blockages and so is helpful used in Reiki, acupressure, shiatsu, reflexology and any therapies where energy is moved around the body; helps you to trust your own judgement and not seek the approval of others; good for keeping exotic birds such as parrots or wildfowl.

Type: Aluminium boron silicate.

Colours: Combinations of two or more shades of pink, green, clear, purple, blue, pinkish oranges and red or yellow, generally in bands, within the same crystal. In the paler watermelon crystals, the red and green merge (p.308).

Availability: Relatively rare but found in specialist crystal stores and online.

Physical benefits: An integrator crystal, it is believed to be helpful for mending any malfunctioning connections in the mind or body and for any illness where the brain causes problems in the body and for all whole-body problems or those where psychological problems affect physical health and vice versa.

Emotional healing: For acute psychological problems, psychosis, hallucinations or troubles that flare up intermittently; for any personality disorders with teenagers and children; for anyone who has become institutionalized; assists hypnosis and hypnotherapy.

Chakra: Heart.

Elbaite/
Multi-coloured Tourmaline

Candle colour: Any shade of pink or green or multi-coloured. **Fragrances:** Apple blossom, cherry blossom, geranium, rose, thyme. **Practical uses:** Keep a bicoloured piece at home and obtain two more tourmalines, one in each of the colours of the bicoloured tourmaline; carry or wear one and give the other to your lover if you live or work in different towns or countries or travel separately a lot, to maintain the unity between you. **Workplace:** For multi-tasking, bringing together people from different departments or skill bases in a single project, or for combining two skills or part-time jobs into a new career or business. **Magical significance:** A bringer of visions and insights through visiting ancient sites or places of worship, for vision quests and shamanic journeys. **Divinatory meaning:** Let life flow and be prepared for the unexpected that will make sense of something that is puzzling you. **Zodiac:** Libra and Scorpio, the Scorpion. **Empowerment:** I am at peace with myself and the world around me.

The most colourful member of the tourmaline group of crystals. Some may have subtly different shades of the same colour but others have a variety of two or even three colours within the same crystal, hence the traditional belief in different cultures that tourmalines fell from the rainbow.

Elbaite brings harmony between the mind, body, spirit and soul, balancing all aspects of the self. This in turn assists all forms of spiritual, emotional and physical healing.

Use elbaite to improve lucid dreaming and sleep in general. Inspiring dreams are likely so it is a good idea to have a notebook handy by the bed if you are searching for a creative solution to a problem.

By helping you to access the inner self and the higher realms this gem stimulates the creative imagination. This is particularly useful for anyone working in the visual arts or any creative activity that requires that little bit of extra vision; helps children to love art and crafts.

Type: Banded ironstone (a combination of black haematite, red jasper and tiger's eye).

Colours: Banded colours of black, gold and red.

Availability: Common.

Physical benefits: Claimed to promote the production of red blood cells and the efficient oxygenation of the blood; relieve fatigue and increases stamina; also be beneficial for the liver and nervous system. Wear next to the skin or hold against your solar plexus centre in the middle of your upper stomach for a sudden burst of energy.

Emotional healing: Strengthens willpower when fighting illness, depression or addictions; provides stability during times of emotional change and mental fatigue. Tiger iron is a potent grounding stone to minimize panic attacks and virtually all phobias and obsessive compulsive disorder.

Chakra: Root, Sacral, Solar Plexus.

Tiger Iron/Mugglestone

Candle colour: Red. **Fragrances:** Frankincense, myrrh, orange, sandalwood, sage. **Practical uses:** Carry as an amulet to help protect you from physical danger; essential protection tied in a pouch round your waist or neck or as jewellery if you participate in extreme sports. **Workplace:** Provides practical dexterity and creative inspiration for artists, sculptors, potters, craftspersons and for all who create with their hands. The stone of reality, in planning offices and government departments, ensures ideas take practical workable forms. **Magical significance:** Creates a protective shield against vicious people, curses and malevolent ghosts and poltergeists. **Divinatory meaning:** A huge effort is needed to overcome a stumbling block, but the chance to be free may not come again for a while. **Zodiac:** Aries and Leo. **Empowerment:** I fear nothing for I am strong.

A "three for the price of one" crystal. Haematite brings inner fire, mixed with emotional balance and clarity of thought. Jasper promotes power, strength and stability.

Tiger's eye enhances passion and creativity, gives courage and promises your needs will be met. For spiritual or conventional healing, tiger iron stops you taking on the problems or ailments of your patients or becoming physically or mentally drained during your healing sessions.

Wonderful for reassuring over-imaginative adults and children who magnify fears of every noise especially at night, and for over-sensitive pets, especially cats. Keep one in the car or the horsebox or attached to the bridle to prevent over-reaction to noise or other animals.

Type: Calcite, a minor ore of zinc, forming in parts of oxidized copper zinc deposits. The crystals form in small round shapes similar to a bunch of grapes.

Colours: Shades of pink, mauve and lavender. Purple considered most desirable, also white, blue, yellow or brown. Each colour has slightly different properties.

Availability: Relatively common in natural form in apple green or aqua and really beautiful.

Physical benefits: Viewed as beneficial for skin disorders and immune system. Placed on your brow, especially pink, aqua or mauve, smithsonite helps to balance the body in whatever way is necessary, removing excesses and boosting deficiencies. Pink smithsonite is said to speed recovery, especially when convalescing if you place it near your bed or under the pillow to boost immunity.

Emotional healing: Smithsonite offers gentle nurturing, in pink or purple or green; close to the heart it comforts us in time of emotional distress, when we feel unloved or are not loved.

Chakra: Brow and Heart.

Smithsonite/Zinc Spar

Candle colour: Any pastel shade. **Fragrances:** Bergamot, fennel, lavender, lily of the valley, peppermint. **Practical uses:** Smithsonite in aqua, green, pink or lavender safely high up in any nursery helps babies to settle; for children who have been hospitalized or had uncomfortable prolonged medical treatment **Workplace:** Blue or aqua smithsonite enhances leadership skills, bringing quiet confidence and authority if you are new to a position and are challenged by existing staff who think they should have your position. **Magical significance:** The silky pearly lustre of smithsonite has been described as the glow of a melting candle. Use smithsonite in wish candle magic: light a candle the same colour as the crystal, hold it up to the candlelight and make a wish; blow out the candle; repeat nightly till the wish is granted. **Divinatory meaning:** Right now you need to care for yourself so step back and take a day or two away from life's frantic dash. **Zodiac:** Virgo and Pisces. **Empowerment:** I will be kinder to myself.

Smithsonite was named after the British mineralogist James Smithson (1764–1829) who founded the Smithsonian Institute in Washington, DC. However the Romans used the mineral centuries earlier to make brass. Aqua smithsonite brings peaceful healing energies to a home shaken by divorce or separation to reduce bitterness if there are children involved and make arrangements as amicable as possible, especially if a third party caused the split.

Purple smithsonite increases psychic abilities and intuition; yellow smithsonite, less common in healing, opens previously closed doors and prevents misunderstandings in communication; alsohelps settle conflicts by taking the heat out of any situation.

Type: Crystal angels – polished crystals carved into angel shapes, some as pendants – come in many crystal kinds and sizes; read the separate crystal entries to choose the one that is right for you.

Colours: Varies according to crystal kind.

Availability: Common from gift shops, crystal stores and online.

Physical healing: Crystal angels amplify the power of the crystal type; they are said to help when the cause of an illness cannot be discovered or the patient is resistant to treatment, for major surgery or when treatment is prolonged.

Emotional healing: Use for channelling healing from the angels; also for pregnant women, newborn babies, children or teenagers who feel vulnerable or afraid for whatever reason.

Chakra: Brow and Crown.

Crystal Angels

Candle colour: White. Fragrances: Lavender, lotus, rose or any floral fragrance. **Practical uses**: Buy a birthstone or zodiac angel for a newborn baby or as a birthday gift to bring good fortune, health and happiness. **Workplace**: Either wear a crystal angel pendant or have a small angel in a pouch or your workspace near your computer or phone to protect you against malicious or confrontational phone calls or emails. **Magical significance**: Set four crystal angels in the four main directions in a room: red jasper for Uriel who stands in the north, citrine or amethyst for Raphael in the east, clear quartz or carnelian for Michael in the south and moonstone in the west for Gabriel. Each night, touch each angel in turn to invoke archangel protection. **Divinatory meaning**: Unexpected help is at hand in a current crisis or uncertainty. **Zodiac**: Cancer and Leo for lunar moon and solar energies combined. **Empowerment**: I connect with my inner angel.

Buy a variety of tiny crystal angels as the form amplifies the healing, protective and spiritual properties of any crystal. If you have a challenge at work, at home or in love, choose an angel by passing your hand or a pendulum over each of the angels in turn and you will feel the one who is most helpful.

Make an angel place in your home by purchasing a medium-sized clear crystal angel and setting it on a small table in the centre of your home.

Add fresh flowers and a regularly light a white candle and floral incense. You will notice how harmonious and peaceful your home feels even if you have a hectic life or a large family.

Type: Depends on kind of crystal.

Colours: Depends on kind of crystal.

Availability: Obtainable very widely.

Physical benefits: Dolphins are believed to help heal all illnesses; fierce creatures are seen as being good for bites, stings, wounds, active healing of acute conditions; gentler creatures are thought to remove pain and are better for chronic conditions; a crystal replica of your pet is seen as act as a healing amulet; birds are claimed to be good for mobility and viruses; and fish or sea creatures are said to be beneficial for all hormonal and fluid-based problems.

Emotional healing: Each person is said to have a shadow animal whose qualities we dislike or fear, for example a territorial bear if you always share everything with everyone. Wearing or carrying a crystal image of an animal you dislike or fear releases the hidden part you have been suppressing and brings you strength.

Chakra: Root.

Power Animal Crystals

Candle colour: Red for fierce animals, blue for gentler creatures, birds or fish. **Fragrances:** Cedar, copal, pine, sagebrush, sweetgrass. **Practical uses:** Let the family choose a power creature each to represent what they regard as their greatest strength; choose another for what they would like to become, for example an eagle for a teenager who wants to fly high. Keep these where the family relaxes; you can choose animals for absent family. If alone, buy yourself large beautiful creatures. **Workplace:** Whatever quality you need in the workplace, there is a crystal power animal or bird to represent that strength. Keep a selection in your drawer; if the atmosphere gets confrontational take out your dove of peace, your wise authoritative elephant or your fierce, sleek obsidian jaguar, according to your instinctive response. **Magical significance:** Either wear a Navajo animal or bird fetish necklace with a number of different power creatures, or have a number of very small crystal animals and birds. Pick one each morning without looking, to act as your power creature of the day. This will invariably have the qualities you need in the day ahead. **Divinatory meaning:** Right now trust your instincts; act swiftly and stealthily to make sure you are not left out of the action or share of rewards. **Zodiac:** Aries. **Empowerment:** I trust my instincts and not my ego.

The concept that individuals and groups of people have a particular animal or bird with whom they identify, whose idealized qualities they try to emulate, for example the courage of a lion or the loyalty and protectiveness of a dog towards its owner, is a very ancient one and may go back to cave dwellers. In the modern world, too, we may need a spiritual animal icon to give us instinctive strengths in the urban jungle.

Have a pair of matching domesticated or faithful crystal creatures who mate for life – swans, ducks, dogs, or your favourite animal – and set them facing each other to attract your soul mate; put side by side facing the same way for lasting happiness; add a miniature animal or bird for each child you have or hope to have.

Rutilated Quartz

Type: Silicate/nesosilicate, rutiles or oxide crystal needles within quartz.

Colours: Gold, silver, can be reddish to deep red.

Availability: Common.

Physical benefits: Reported as useful for bronchitis and asthma, regenerating brain cells improving the condition of blood vessels and veins, transplants and transfusions.

Emotional healing: For anyone who has dabbled unwisely in black magic.

Chakra: Root and Crown.

Various names have been given in different traditions to describe what appears to be golden hair within this crystal, for example angel hair, and rutilated quartz is an excellent angel communication crystal. It is also called the golden hair of the Roman love goddess Venus or the Viking goddess of beauty Freya; the goddesses' golden hair was preserved by the earth spirits when it was cut, because they could not bear to see it thrown away.

Enhydro Quartz

Type: Quartz with moving bubbles of water

Colours: Takes the colour of the quartz, but is transparent so you can see the water bubbles.

Availability: Relatively rare.

Physical benefits: Said to help fluid imbalances, hormones, safe removal of foreign objects in the body (whether bullets or shrapnel in war or fish bones in throat), stomach acidity, chronic flatulence, purifying the blood.

Emotional healing: Enhydro quartz washes away old destructive emotional patterns that can cause us to repeat mistakes again and again.

Chakra: Heart.

The fluidity, antiquity and reaching-inward energies of the enhydro combined with the active outward-seeking quartz are the perfect combination of building on the roots of the past to move forward to the future; good for researching your family history and for teaching children about the family roots, especially if you are living in another area of the country from the family birth area or another land. Carry if you have a difficult person in your life you must maintain amicable contact with, whether a relative, neighbour or colleague.

Clusters

Type: Crystals that have grown together on a matrix

Colours: Varies with the kind of crystal.

Availability: Common.

Physical benefits: While this varies according to the properties of the crystals, all clusters are thought to have an integrating energy that will bring the body back into harmony with itself and right any imbalances.

Emotional healing: Restores a sense of being complete in yourself if you have suffered problems with unrequited love or have loved too much and been hurt.

Chakra: Crown and Heart.

Candle colour: Natural beeswax. **Fragrances:** Cedarwood, clary sage. **Practical uses:** Attracts health, wealth and happiness to the home. Set a cluster in the middle of the home (downstairs) and four, six or eight smaller clusters in different rooms downstairs to make the outer points of the grid. **Workplace:** Crystal clusters draw people together; keep one in your workspace and/or main meeting room. **Magical significance:** A crystal cluster energizes other crystals. **Divinatory meaning:** You may get the chance to join a group that will bring advantages. **Zodiac:** Libra. **Empowerment:** I reach out to others.

For absent healing, use an apophyllite, celestite, clear quartz, citrine, fluorite, amethyst or aragonite cluster; surround it with small white candles to radiate healing in all directions to a number of people, animals or places at the same time.

A crystal cluster in a room where you practice Reiki, healing or divination absorbs negative vibes away from healer and patient.

Use as a collective focus while teaching Reiki or any form of psychic development to a group.

Window Quartz

Type: Quartz, usually clear, with a diamond window as an extra seventh face.

Colours: Most usually in clear quartz .

Availability: Relatively rare.

Physical benefits: May help with eyesight, finding new treatments for existing conditions via the Internet; send concentrated healing energy by holding the window on a painful spot.

Emotional healing: A crystal for accepting imperfections in self and others; helpful for anyone suddenly disabled through an accident, injury or illness, to cope psychologically.

Chakra: Brow.

Candle colour: White. **Fragrances:** Juniper, pine. **Practical uses:** Keep by your computer for safe communication with people abroad. **Workplace:** Keep the window towards you when problem-solving; point the window face outwards to find out if there is intrigue. **Magical significance:** Use to locate missing people by remote viewing; look through the window in sunlight or moonlight and you will see an image of what you are seeking and the background may give you a clue. **Divinatory meaning:** Good news will clear up something that has been worrying you. **Zodiac:** Leo. **Empowerment:** The future is clear.

Window quartz, particularly in its clear, sparkling quartz form, is a master crystal, assisting with natural acquisition of spiritual wisdom for beginner and expert alike. Hold the diamond to the centre of your brow to connect with angels, guides and your wise family ancestors.

Window quartz is helpful if you are trying to gain insight into the motives of others, for example why someone has an apparently irrational dislike of you, why a lover will not commit, and also into your own seemingly self-destructive actions.

RecordKeeper Quartz

Type: Usually quartz crystal, but occasionally found in rubies, indicated by a perfect raised triangle or several trianles on one or more sloping faces of the crystal (usually the largest).

Colours: Depends on crystal.

Availability: Rare.

Physical benefits: Record keepers are best for healing the person who buys them. They send the healing we need, which may not be the healing we asked for.

Emotional healing: Eases acute worries about future illness.

Chakra: Crown and Brow.

Candle colour: White. **Fragrances:** Acacia, galbanum. **Practical uses:** One day, maybe years after acquiring it, you may sense your record-keeper is ready to move on: give it to a beloved child or dear friend. You will know when and who. **Workplace:** Keep on your desk to keep work in perspective; essential to pay the bills, fulfilling, but only part of life. **Magical significance:** Record-keepers offer access to the collective wisdom of humankind, called the Akashic records. **Divinatory meaning:** Value your family and traditions. **Zodiac:** Aries and Aquarius. **Empowerment:** I carry the seeds of my ancestors within me.

Though it is sometimes claimed that only the person for whom the crystal is intended will feel or psychically see the indentation of the triangle on the crystal face, it *should* be physically visible to the naked eye in a good light and clearly felt.

Since record keepers are expensive, you want to be sure it is genuine. You can programme your record keeper with memories and experiences of your life, a kind of family memory chest. In this way it becomes a living repository of harmony and strength in sad times.

Twin/Gemini Quartz

Type: Two very similar clear quartz crystals, usually growing from the same base .

Colours: Most common in clear quartz.

Availability: Found in specialist crystal stores and online.

Physical benefits: Said to help twin and multiple pregnancies, births and after-birth care; back, spine, rib cage.

Emotional healing: Consoling if you cannot be with your true love because of other commitments, to build a good life without totally giving up hope of being together one day.

Chakra: Crown and Brow.

Candle colour: White. **Fragrances:** Almond, anise, bay, lavender, lemon verbena. **Practical uses:** Twin crystals are a good-luck charm for all partnerships. **Workplace:** Helpful for working with family members, especially siblings. **Magical significance:** For calling your twin soul in sleep or in rituals, light matching candles, one either side of the twin crystal and place your hands round each twin crystal, asking that you will find your twin soul. Leave the candles to burn. **Divinatory meaning:** You will encounter someone like-minded who will improve the quality of your life. **Zodiac:** Gemini. **Empowerment:** My twin soul is waiting for me.

Tantric twin crystals are crystals approximately the same size growing from a common base. Twin soul or soulmate do not grow from the same base but are equal length and size growing side-by-side. They may join on onbe side during formation and end in separate terminations. They bring peace to couples, families, workplaces and communities. All twin crystals encourage more openness if twins make another sibling feel left out in a family.

334

Type: Quartz crystal with a five-sided face (normally as the front or main face).

Colours: Clear and colourless in crystal quartz; varies in other quartzes.

Availability: Relatively rare.

Physical benefits: Said to help female reproductive system, conception, fertility, pregnancy, childbirth, post-natal depression, PMS, menstrual disorders, early-onset menopause, for HRT treatment, breast problems, hormonal imbalance in either sex; a gentle healer for anyone with a weakened immune system or who is allergic to antibiotics and other conventional medication.

Emotional healing: Helps people of either sex to heal past abuse of any kind; teaches love and respect for the body and reduces self-neglect; a spiritually nurturing crystal for anyone who has lost their mother at any age or was badly mothered.

Chakra: Sacral and Heart.

Isis Quartz

Candle colour: White. **Fragrances:** Apple blossom, lily, lily of the valley, lotus, meadowsweet. **Practical uses:** Isis crystals are very powerful when a parent is bringing up children alone, whether from choice or necessity: Isis, the Ancient Egyptian mother goddess after whom the crystal was named, was the first single-parent deity. **Workplace:** An Isis crystal strengthens men and women to rediscover their power, drive and confidence if sidelined, passed over for promotion or made redundant; for speaking out calmly but assertively if you always get the tedious or unpleasant jobs because of favouritism or discrimination against you for whatever reason. **Magical significance:** Often adopted by all female Wiccan, goddess or spiritual groups as their central altar focus; however, men and women can use an Isis crystal to explore the divine feminine and in earth healing rituals. **Divinatory meaning:** It is time to give up a bad habit or an attachment that is making you unhappy and holding you back from new connections. **Zodiac:** Cancer. **Empowerment:** I do not need to be constantly mothered.

The gentlest of the master or teaching crystals, Isis crystals are associated with Mother Isis because five was a number that was sacred to her and they have five faces.

In addition, they have magical, healing and nurturing energies, and both solar and lunar powers attributed to Isis herself. Isis is still a focus in modern goddess worship and also as a power icon for modern multi-tasking mothers, and the crystal forms a tangible symbol of the powerful but loving female.

In Christianity, the Isis crystal has become associated with Mary the Mother. An Isis crystal helps men to get in touch with their gentler nature and to show them how to be an affectionate partner and father if they experienced coldness in their own childhood; good for men who are uncomfortable around women if they grew up in an all-male environment.

An Isis crystal makes a wonderful gift for a woman on her wedding day or a first-time mother whose own mother is estranged, far away or who has died.

Type: A natural quartz point in which six equally sized sides join sharply to form a terminating point.

Colours: Depends on quartz but usually clear quartz.

Availability: Relatively rare.

Physical benefits: Reported as benefiting all surgery, laser treatment and light therapies, radiotherapy, dentistry, conditions requiring regular injections, successful childhood and adult inoculations, relief of acute pain and acute conditions, appendicitis and peritonitis; as the name suggests, the crystal powerfully generates, focuses and transmits via the point concentrated energy on every level.

Emotional healing: An awakener for anyone who has lost enthusiasm, passion or the ability to take action; briefly touch the tip to the navel to awaken physical desire and emotional needs, the centre of the upper stomach to restore enthusiasm, and the heart to reconnect with people and trust.

Chakra: Crown.

Generator Quartz

Candle colour: White. **Fragrances:** Anise, benzoin, bergamot, lemon, lemongrass. **Practical uses:** Use your generator to bring joy to an outing or holiday. Touch a packed picnic basket or luggage before a trip, any event-entrance, travel or theatre tickets; picture yourself and anyone accompanying you having a good time. **Workplace:** An excellent crystal for rush jobs or meeting deadlines and for regular infusions of focus and energy if you constantly work under pressure; place the tip on order forms, advertising or publicity material or point the tip towards your computer screen or telephone to give impetus to applications or requests for business. **Magical significance:** A ready-made magic wand: to create a powerful protective circle of light turn round clockwise, tip pointing outwards, before you go into a potentially confrontational situation or before travelling; for wishes touch a written wish with the tip as you say it aloud, then raise the crystal vertically and bring down vertically to retouch the words. **Divinatory meaning:** Health, enthusiasm and energy are returning or increasing and any plans will go well. **Zodiac:** Sagittarius, the Archer. **Empowerment:** I generate the power to attain what I desire.

A generator crystal is a valuable healing tool and can be used like a laser wand in empowering healing grids or layouts.

Touch each of the crystals set round a patient to join the crystals with visualized lines of light to amplify the power of the layout.

You can also use it for absent healing by touching a central crystal sphere or pyramid representing a sick person or animal with the tip;

then in turn touch a layout of six smaller crystals or crystal points, set round the pyramid or sphere, to create a power grid.

Finally, draw visualized light lines from each of the six small crystals to connect each to the central pyramid or sphere, in order to make a star of healing light.

Except in absent healing, generator crystals are too powerful for healing children or animals.

Type: Quartz crystal, usually clear, with an eight-sided face.

Colours: Depends on colour of quartz.

Availability: Rare.

Physical benefits: Thought to help healing by whatever method to reach the place that needs the healing without unduly damaging other cells or organs or weakening the immune system excessively; may also aid chemotherapy, radiotherapy, prolonged steroid treatment or other necessary prolonged treatment with potential side-effects, all transplants and transfusions.

Emotional healing: An earthing crystal for people addicted to the Internet who spend every free moment surfing and have relationships only online; also for those addicted to sex or clairvoyant phone lines.

Chakra: Crown and Root.

Grounding Quartz

Candle colour: White. **Fragrances:** Carnation, hyacinth, lilac, narcissus, patchouli. **Practical uses:** A crystal for dreamers and their partners to keep alive dreams and fulfil them, but at the same to cope with the realities of daily living, necessary timetables and schedules; good for people who begin every sentence with, "One day I will…." **Workplace:** For any workplace with an excess of ideas people but few who can apply those ideas to what is actually wanted or needed; keep in the premises of esoteric businesses or stores to avoid becoming a free drop-in centre and not making enough money to survive. **Magical significance:** A grounding crystal is a perfect tool if you or a client can easily connect with spirit realms but get very spaced-out or find it hard to apply wisdom to the everyday world; good for students who can walk with angels but find learning necessary spiritual information hard or irrelevant. **Divinatory meaning:** Be practical, cost and plan major travel or relocation, as it is more possible than it immediately seems. **Zodiac:** Taurus and Virgo. **Empowerment:** I can be both visionary and practical.

A valuable crystal for any spiritual and healing work, to combine inspiration with knowledge and practical skills and to protect both healer and patient and clairvoyant and client; protective also when learning mediumship or if you have a ghost in your home, which may not be unfriendly but spooks you or the family, to make the atmosphere lighter.

On a practical level, hold grounding quartz to focus on the task in hand if you have a mountain of pressing jobs and do not know where to start.

Conversely, grounding quartz lifts people who get wrapped up in routine or trivial details, to see wider possibilities and make practical changes.

A sensible crystal to deter rash investments, impulse purchases and spending beyond your means if kept with existing debit- and credit-card statements or cards.

Barnacle Quartz

Type: A crystal covered with smaller crystals.

Colours: Clear and colourless in crystal quartz.

Availability: Relatively common.

Physical benefits: Said to protect against highly contagious diseases or virus epidemics, head lice, impetigo, shingles, scabies.

Emotional healing: Comforting after any bereavement, especially a late miscarriage.

Chakra: Heart

Candle colour: White. **Fragrances:** Chamomile, orange, white rose. **Practical uses:** Helps resolve family problems through actions rather than words. **Workplace:** The crystal for all who work in service industries. **Magical significance:** Because the mother crystal is metaphysically regarded as the old soul around whom younger crystals cluster for advice, look at a clear quartz barnacle crystal sparkling in candlelight; allow your mind to drift and answers will come. **Divinatory meaning:** Ask advice on a matter where you are not certain. **Zodiac:** Gemini. **Empowerment:** I value those close to me.

Barnacle quartz is a good prioritizing crystal if you are considering relocating, downsizing or becoming independent of family, workplace or a relationship that is not working. Its dual energies assist in getting rid of clutter, both actual and emotional, and in conserving what is of value.

Good for helping large or extended families to get on well together if kept with family photographs or mementoes; in times of bereavement, clear barnacle quartz encourages family loyalty and the highest motives, particularly if there are disputes over a will.

Lithium Quartz

Type: Clear quartz with inclusions of lithium ions.

Colours: Magenta, pink and lavender-grey.

Availability: Rare.

Physical benefits: May help balance brain and emotions, particularly in relation to serotonin levels, epilepsy, motor neurone disease, heart attacks, hardening of the arteries, repetitive strain injury (RSI), muscle and tendon tears and strains, infections of blood or body fluids, healing pets and plants.

Emotional healing: Counters extreme mood swings.

Chakra: Heart

Candle colour: Grey. **Fragrances:** Anise, musk, moss. **Practical uses:** A restoring-order-out-of-chaos crystal. **Workplace:** Clears a poisonous atmosphere; helpful if you feel excluded from cliques. **Magical significance:** A crystal that increases love between lovers, especially if one person seems to be withdrawing; set two matching lithium quartz so they touch. Each day, hold one in each hand and say, "May we grow closer together." **Divinatory meaning:** No point in getting irritable about other people's shortcomings. **Zodiac:** Libra. **Empowerment:** I can channel my restlessness into positive change.

Lithium does not need cleansing and will store any empowerments you make while holding it, to be gradually released into your life. The crystal restores balance and channels free-floating restlessness into positive projects, whether travel, relocation, change of career, a new love or new stage in a relationship, or the release of a creative gift.

An excellent crystal as a gift if your partner has little patience co-parenting infants or teenagers. Carry if you tend to panic when travelling long distances or on holiday in an unfamiliar place.

Channelling Quartz

Type: Quartz with seven edges surrounding the largest sloping face. The facet directly at the back of this side forms a triangle.

Colours: Usually found as colourless clear quartz.

Availability: Rare, particularly in non-clear quartz.

Physical benefits: Said to amplify the power of other crystals and direct healing to where the energy is most needed.

Emotional healing: Breaks the circuit of self-destructive actions; holding the seven-edged face to the brow daily for a week opens the possibility alternative actions.

Chakra: Brow and Crown.

Candle colour: White. **Fragrances:** Cedarwood. **Practical uses:** Brings harmony to the home. **Workplace:** Write down any problem and set your crystal on top. Write on the paper without thinking. When you read the answer, your unconscious wisdom will have offered a solution. **Magical significance:** Hold by candlelight; trace over first the seven sides of the main face, then the three sides of the triane with your index finger. This accesses your unconscious wisdom. **Divinatory meaning:** Your angels are warning you to be careful about a plan you have not thought through. **Zodiac:** Aquarius. **Empowerment:** I can move between worlds.

Channelling quartz is considered a teaching crystal that will help the owner to evolve spiritually.

Channelling crystals are powerful receivers of wisdom from higher sources. But they also direct healing light from the cosmos. Holding a channelling crystal before healing will set the fingers and palms tingling.

Place your fingertips above your head or that of the person you are treating, pointing downwards or directed towards area of pain or disease; you will feel the healing light transmitted like a warm glow.

Transmitter Quartz

Type: Quartz. Most usually clear quartz with a large triangular main front face and a symmetrical seven-sided face on either side of the main face.

Colours: Depends on the kind of quartz.

Availability: Rare.

Physical benefits: Transmits healing energy from angels or higher sources of light; said to help with any treatment involving heat, laser; for surgery to widen arteries or replace heart valves.

Emotional healing: For therapists, to show they care if a patient is resistant.

Chakra: Crown.

Candle colour: White or natural beeswax. **Fragrances:** Anise, bay, bergamot. **Practical uses:** The crystal for saying whatever is important clearly to avoid misunderstandings; whether "I love you", or "I must have help". **Workplace:** For all who make a living through communicating information in any form. **Magical significance:** Potent for telepathic communication with loved ones (you can have a transmitter crystal each). **Divinatory meaning:** Giving and receiving should be equal most of the **time**. **Zodiac:** Gemini. **Empowerment:** I make each word of value.

All crystals, especially quartz crystals, are natural transmitters and receivers of energy, healing and wisdom. You can sometimes find a transmitter formation in a single quartz point and so they need not be hugely expensive.

A transmitter quartz adds sanctity to the most frantic home, if held by anyone feeling uncertain of the point of life or a temporary feeling of not being able to go on, the transmitter restores calm.

Crystal Points

Type: Clear crystal with a single six-sided or six-faced point at one end, also in amethyst, smokey quartz and citrine

Colours: Varies according to the kind and purity of the quartz, often milkier or cloudier near base.

Availability: Common.

Physical benefits: Claimed to direct healing energy into self or patient. The clearer the crystal, the faster the action.

Emotional healing: Hold an amethyst point to your brow to relieve panic, then a clear quartz point to your stomach for focus.

Chakra: Brow and Crown.

Candle colour: White. **Fragrances:** Almond. **Practical uses:** Create a crystal point grid in your home with 12 crystal points in any quartz, pointing alternatively in and outwards. Name for each month something you want to achieve and hold that point when you waver. **Workplace:** Arrange a semi-circle of clear and smoky quartz points, smoky quartz to deflect negativity and clear ones to energize. **Magical significance:** Makes an excellent pendulum. Ask a question; assess the way it feels as you hold it in your hand: if warm, it's positive; if jarring, you should be cautious. **Divinatory meaning:** A time to be single-minded. **Zodiac:** Sagittarius. **Empowerment:** I can be single-minded.

Crystal quartz points are a multi-purpose tool and are very reasonably priced. Have several different ones.

Choose a highly polished clear point for spreading light around the home; every week lift it to any source of light and turn round and round, pointing it outwards and picturing the light pouring into every corner; ideal if there has been a lot of illness, bad luck or unhappiness, or everyone is extra lethargic; use citrine for empowering any materials you have to learn, or have one pointing towards your computer if you have to work late.

Gateway Quartz

Type: Quartz, often clear, distinguished by an aperture or opening from the side of the crystal into the interior.

Colours: Depends on quartz.

Availability: Relatively rare.

Physical benefits: Said to be helpful for breakthroughs in unresponsive illnesses, finding new practitioners and treatments, regrowth and regeneration of cells, bones and tissues.

Emotional healing: Learning to trust again.

Chakra: Brow.

Candle colour: White. **Fragrances:** Basil, bay, tarragon. **Practical uses:** A crystal for rites of passage, from single to committed, the birth of children, significant birthdays and anniversaries, children leaving home, bereavement. **Workplace:** For all who work in medical research. **Magical significance:** If the crystal has a cup like indentation, pour a little flower essence into an opening; focus on that by candlelight for meditation; use the water as an elixir afterwards. **Divinatory meaning:** Do not regret a natural transition point in your life or hold back from it. **Zodiac:** Aquarius. **Empowerment:** I welcome the change points on my life journey.

Gateway quartz is a very powerful spiritual tool and is sometimes regarded as a master or teaching crystal. The portal that will be very clearly indented in the side or face of the crystal is considered an entrance to other dimensions, both angelic and to what are called the Akashic records.

We are believed to be able to see in our minds a page in these books of destiny describing the aspects of our life we most want to know about, whether a past world or future possibilities.

Bridge Crystal

Type: A large quartz crystal with a smaller crystal or crystals which is located partially in and partially out of the larger crystal.

Colours: Depends on the quartz.

Availability: Obtainable from specialist crystal stores and online.

Physical benefits: Said to help connections between brain and the body, when another part of the brain takes over from a damaged part, for example after a stroke.

Emotional healing: For a person who has been rejected at an early age and so distrusts relationships.

Chakra: Heart.

Candle colour: Green. **Fragrances:** Lavender, lilac. **Practical uses:** A bridge crystal is the ultimate communication crystal if you live in a multi-cultural area where cultural differences make friendships difficult; take a small bridge with you if you work overseas. **Workplace:** For working in an organization where you meet people from different cultural backgrounds. **Magical significance:** Creates mind connections with past worlds and angels. **Divinatory meaning:** A chance for reconciliation with someone from the past. **Zodiac:** Gemini. **Empowerment:** I am open to new ideas.

A bridge crystal usually has the smaller crystal or crystals at almost a right angle, with the base of the smaller crystal(s) inside the host. Some crystal practitioners regard this as a master or teaching crystal and call it an inner child crystal, particularly if the tip of the small crystal is embedded in the host. Inner-child crystals help undeveloped gifts to emerge, and in rediscovering spontaneity if childhood was traumatic.

Empower other crystals for healing by placing them next to or resting on the bridge crystal.

Himalayan Quartz

Type: Silicon dioxide/quartz from the Himalayas that at its finest can be unusually clear, described as "water clear".

Colours: Clear, sometimes with natural rainbows.

Availability: Relatively rare.

Physical benefits: A gentler energizer than ordinary clear quartz, it is thought to help illnesses with painful, emotionally distressing or embarrassing symptoms or side-effects, auto-immune problems, brain dysfunction, rabies; be good for sick mothers and babies.

Emotional healing: Soothes those racked with guilt over past misdeeds.

Chakra: Crown and Sacral.

Candle colour: Silver. **Fragrances:** Clary sage, lavender, neroli. **Practical uses:** The perfect antidote to modern living; keep a piece in the bedroom to relax into sleep. **Workplace:** A cluster creates ongoing harmony in a large room if you teach yoga, tai chi, dance therapies. **Magical significance:** Hold to attain a trance-like level of meditations. **Divinatory meaning:** Seek some time to recharge your batteries. **Zodiac:** Pisces. **Empowerment:** I can learn from silence.

Himalayan quartz is considered sacred because of the many associations with the Himalayas as a place of great spirituality.

Himalayan quartz wands can be used for all kinds of healing where ordinary quartz is too powerful and amethyst not sufficiently active, to kick-start the immune system of the vulnerable or very ill; especially effective for Far Eastern healing arts such as Reiki, shiatsu and Indian head massage and to empower herbs used in traditional Chinese medicine.

Type: A quartz crystal, often clear, in which a phantom or shadow crystal appears. Often the inner phantom quartz forms a pyramid shape. Phantoms grow in other quartzes such as amethyst and may contain a phantom of another crystal kind such as chlorite (p.259).

Colours: Depends on the inner crystal, which may be white, green, blue, red or purple.

Availability: Relatively common.

Physical benefits: Believed to help with shadows on lungs, successful scans, radiation treatment, micro-surgery, illnesses for which the cause is not fully understood by medical science, psychosomatic conditions, tissue and organs deep within the body, deep vein thrombosis, old illnesses that suddenly flare up.

Emotional healing: Relieves shadows from the past that still cause sorrow; for forgiving yourself if a loved one died with bitterness between you; overcomes fears of death and the spirit world.

Chakra: Brow.

Phantom Quartz

Candle colour: Grey. **Fragrances:** Lavender, mugwort, musk, myrrh, thyme. **Practical uses:** A phantom quartz, either white or amethyst, is a wonderful crystal for a pregnant woman. Place the phantom on the womb to transmit love and to connect emotionally with the unborn child. Take along to scans and the birth, and afterwards place in the nursery so the angels said to live in phantom quartz will protect the child. **Workplace:** A red or blue phantom brings confidence for a first job or for returning to the workplace after illness, maternity leave or a period of unemployment; white phantoms with an inner white or grey veil help maintain a low profile and discreet silence while a tense situation disperses. **Magical significance:** Phantom quartz is traditionally used by ghost investigators or anyone who wishes to see a presence in old places. Look through the crystal and the inner phantom if you sense a ghost; you may see in your mind the spirit and the background of their lifetime or an apparition may build up externally. **Divinatory meaning:** Something at the back of your mind is troubling you, a reminder that you need to clear unfinished business that still bothers you. **Zodiac:** Aquarius. **Empowerment:** I do not fear shadows from the past.

A phantom is caused by a pause in a crystal's growth, leaving a partial or complete phantom within the crystal after it continued to grow, a pause that could last for thousands of years.

Sometimes quartz encloses another phantom crystal, not necessarily quartz, or another crystal grows around quartz that stopped growing.

Red phantoms release old anger and repressed power; purple phantoms or those in amethyst help a person with blocked emotions or undeveloped spiritual potential; blue phantoms allow natural wisdom and knowledge to be expressed and remove a sense of injustice from the past. The white or true ghost phantom is a talisman for any makeover or transformation after a setback, or progress after everything stopped when either you ran out of energy or circumstances restricted you.

A silver phantom where tiny sparkling crystals become embedded around the phantom is one of the most magical crystals available and in your crystal place or living area attracts good fortune, health and wealth to your home.

Quartz Double Terminated

Type: Double-terminated crystals have points at both ends.

Colours: Varies according to the quartz.

Availability: Common.

Physical benefits: Hold both ends to create a circuit of power before beginning healing. Belived to remove pain and energize if placed on the chakra energy centres.

Emotional healing: Opens connections if you cannot get through to someone who has switched off emotionally.

Chakra: Heart.

Candle colour: White. **Fragrances:** Fennel, grapefruit. **Practical uses:** Make a circle of five double terminators end-to-end to create a centre of power. Within this circle you can put anything you wish to empower. **Workplace:** One of the best networking crystals; keep one beside your computer. **Magical significance:** Double-terminated crystals grow freely in clay pockets so their energies are fluid. Point one upwards to link you and the other-worldly power you wish to contact. **Divinatory meaning:** Beware misunderstandings with someone close. **Zodiac:** Pisces. **Empowerment:** I form a circuit of energy and protection.

Double-terminated crystals, particularly in clear quartz or amethyst, are very effective set round a person to energize the chakra system in a stressed but healthy person.

Have one above the head and one below the feet as you or the patient lie down, and arrange another four or six at regular intervals, a few centimetres from the body; relax for 10 or 15 minutes and let the crystals do the work.

Double terminators can send love or strength to a loved one who is not with you.

Master Crystal

Type: Most often clear crystal quartz, with unusual markings that have been identified as especially powerful; can be other kinds of quartz or even gems such as ruby.

Colours: Varies according to the crystal or gem.

Availability: Becoming more common.

Physical benefits: Seen as being a powerful healer, alone or as part of a crystal layout set round a patient to amplify the power of individual crystals.

Emotional healing: All master crystals have the power of light bringers to heal as well as bring insight into past sorrows, trauma and deep fears.

Chakra: Crown.

Candle colour: White. **Fragrances:** Frankincense, lily. **Practical uses:** Purifies the atmosphere; tempers improve. **Workplace:** Keep a small master crystal to raise the level of courtesy without sacrificing efficiency; empowering if you work for a faceless corporation. **Magical significance:** You may find that one master crystal works for you. **Divinatory meaning:** Say what you need in order to feel fulfilled. **Zodiac:** Leo. Individual masters may have their own star signs as listed in separate entries. **Empowerment:** I know there is so much more to life than our material existence.

The master crystals I find particularly helpful are: channelling crystal with one seven-sided face and one three-sided face on the opposing side (p.339); transmitter crystal with two seven-sided faces either side of a three-sided face (p.339); isis crystal with one large five-sided face (p.335); record keeper with one or more triangle shapes etched or indented on one or more of the faces (p.334); manifestation crystal, a crystal with a small crystal totally enclosed within (p.345) and bridge crystal that has a smaller crystal(s) protruding (p.341).

Laser Quartz

Type: A long, slender quartz wand-like crystal, with small faces at the tip, wider at the base than at the tip; may have three-sided points at the top or a rounded finger-like point.

Colours: Usually clear quartz.

Availability: Rare

Physical benefits: May help with laser or radiotherapy treatment, pain relief. Hold the point of the wand over the pain, then pull the wand away and hold the tip near a flame to cleanse.

Emotional healing: For cutting ties with destructive habits; bring the wand downwards in the air in a slashing movement and say, "I cut the ties with —."

Chakra: Solar Plexus.

Candle colour: Gold. **Fragrances:** Acacia. **Practical uses:** Protect items if going away by pointing the laser in a circle over them. Point it towards your door from outside, to act as a light shield round your home. **Workplace:** Hold the laser gently against the centre of your stomach; empowering if you feel anxious. **Magical significance:** Place six crystals round a crystal sphere. Touch each one with your laser, naming the healing you wish to send. **Divinatory meaning:** Let go of doubts and aim for your goal. **odiac:** Aries. **Empowerment:** I will not keep changing my mind.

A laser wand, often regarded as master crystal, is a natural wand that can be used for personal empowerment as well as healing. It is the best kind of healing wand; many Reiki practitioners and other psychic-energy therapists use one to direct energy and to remove emotional knots, tangles and blockages.

You can also use a laser wand to draw a visualized circle of light around yourself in the morning to protect you during the day and at night round your bed for peaceful sleep.

Self-healed Quartz

Type: Quartz crystal, often clear quartz, where the crystal broke off from its matrix or cluster during its formation but continued to grow with new terminations

Colours: Depends on kind of quartz.

Availability: Relatively common.

Physical benefits: Said to be usefuor bone fractures and splintering, growth problems, spine, wounds, all transplants, implants and transfusions, IVF.

Emotional healing: Taking responsibility for decisions; for those who have assumed a new identity; helps in beating addictions.

Chakra: Root and Crown.

Candle colour: White. **Fragrances:** Apple blossom, lily of the valley. **Practical uses:** A starting-over-again crystal, from home repossession to major illness or bereavement; restores courage to recreate a good, if different, quality of life. **Workplace:** For self-employment, particularly in an entrepreneurial capacity, whether selling products on the Internet or running a market stall. **Magical significance:** Essential crystal for all who practise self-healing. **Divinatory meaning:** Sort out your own issues and then you can deal with the rest of the world. **Zodiac:** Virgo and Capricorn. **Empowerment:** I can heal myself.

Self-healed crystals continue to form in new ways after a major earth movement. The self-healing crystal could have been part of a crystal, a cracked crystal or a complete crystal that broke off from the matrix or cluster. In all cases, a new crystal structure grew over the severed place, and in double-terminated crystals which are often self-healed this join can be clearly seen in the shaft.

Hold the crystal if you feel you cannot face another day of problems, to give you the strength and perseverance to carry on.

Manifestation Quartz

Type: Crystal, usually but not always one or more quartz crystals enclosed within another quartz crystal.

Colours: Varies according to the crystals but often clear.

Availability: Rare.

Physical benefits: Reported to be helpful for clear diagnosis and effective treatment, treatment for fertility problems, safe pregnancy and childbirth, for quality of life in terminal conditions.

Emotional healing: Balancing for bi-polar or schizophrenic conditions.

Chakra: Crown.

Candle colour: White. **Fragrances:** Frankincense, lily, lotus, orchid, violet. **Practical uses:** For fulfilling dreams that may involve lifestyle changes. **Workplace:** Keep one to launch a long-awaited personal project. **Magical significance:** The crystal is the magic. Decide what you want to manifest in your life and formulate aloud what you wish to bring into the world, anything from a baby to a talent. **Divinatory meaning:** The dress rehearsal is over. **Zodiac:** Leo. **Empowerment:** My inner and outer worlds move closer together.

This rare crystal, that may contain one or several smaller crystals, is regarded as shamanic. It offers the ability to connect with angels by focusing on the inner crystal.

Formed when a quartz completely encloses another crystal or crystals, the outer crystal is of course younger: the inner crystal is associated with the accumulated wisdom of ancient worlds we may carry in our genes, and also with bringing out in the second part of life undeveloped dreams and plans that have been set aside.

Chandelier Quartz

Type: Usually clear quartz with tiny diamond shape faces around the termination of the crystal; also found in rose, smokey and rainbow quartz.

Colours: As clear quartz with flickers of light, sometimes with cloudiness near the centre.

Availability: Relatively rare.

Physical benefits: Said to aid depression, ME and other chronic fatigue syndromes, wounds, eyesight.

Emotional healing: Soothes those eaten up with envy

Chakra: Crown.

Candle colour: White. **Fragrances:** Apple blossom. **Practical uses:** Chandelier quartz brings awareness of the limitations of present circumstances in order to not waste time dreaming about what we cannot do right now (we may some day). **Workplace:** Make the most of a dead-end job and, until it can be changed, to study to improve future career. **Magical significance:** Hold the crystal in moonlight to see images of past and future worlds that may explain present feelings. **Divinatory meaning:** You may feel frustrated at not getting a chance you deserved. **Zodiac:** Leo. **Empowerment:** I value the blessings I have.

Though this formation is quite rare, chandelier quartz is called a light a bringer, with the tiny faces representing as-yet-unfulfilled possibilities and the indentations learning experiences from life that can make us unique and wise.

Chandelier quartz is, however, also supportive to the individual to follow your own inner light and calling; valuable to anyone who wishes to follow a vocation or mission that may involve giving up material comfort to help others and make a difference in life.

Type: Quartz that forms multiple-terminated points emerging from a main crystal body, in clear quartz, citrine or amethyst.

Colours: Clear/white called fairy spirit quartz, shades of purple as amethyst, rich orange or yellow as citrine.

Availability: Relatively rare but available from some specialist crystal stores and online.

Physical benefits: May help skin problems especially resulting from allergic reactions, melanomas, scars, cysts, ulcers, scar tissue, growths, swellings and tumours on internal organs, problems with fallopian tubes and ovaries, testes, fertility, pregnancy, cleft palate and congenital deformities that need surgery.

Emotional healing: Cactus quartz relieves acute loneliness or a sense of being different from other members of the family; assists to find common ground with others in your life.

Chakra: Heart.

Spirit/Cactus Quartz

Candle colour: Purple. **Fragrances:** Apple blossom, cherry blossom, lemon verbena, neroli, sweetgrass. **Practical uses:** An excellent home crystal if there are fierce sibling rivalries or a relative who visits frequently encourages rivalry and jealousy between adult family members; helps an unsociable partner to be more open when people visit or you go out together; also if you build a house extension. **Workplace:** Cactus quartz encourages team building, whether within a department or a works or professional sports team; for cooperation among a group of people who all want to be leaders and planners; keep on the table for staff meetings so one person does not dominate, and to keep to the agenda. **Magical significance:** Set cactus quartz in the centre of a room where a group of you are sending healing to people who are not present or in a mediumship development circle to unite the energies of those present, both as a form of protection and to generate collective energies. **Divinatory meaning:** You may find people more cooperative than usual; use the friendliness to subtly introduce some new ideas. **Zodiac:** Libra. **Empowerment:** I welcome good company.

Cactus quartz is a crystal that promotes any collective activity, whether socially, at work, in the community or for sporting or charity ventures.

A bonding crystal if a new member joins the family, whether a foster or adopted child or a young relative; for helping step-families to merge with the minimum of resentment and for older family members who give up their home to live with you.

A small piece of cactus quartz should be carried in a bag if you work in a public-service industry

such as health care or teaching, particularly if the organization is administration-heavy; helps to focus on the people needing teaching or care and not be worn down by budget or target pressures.

The more crystals growing on a piece of quartz, the more powerful its energies will be; even a relatively small piece is very effective if it has many tiny points or crystals covering it. Cactus quartz with distinctive baby crystals growing from it is a powerful fertility charm.

Type: Complex anhydrous borate, containing potassium, cesium, beryllium, aluminium, boron and oxygen.

Colours: Tiny, pale yellow, white or colourless, grey or green ten-sided glassy crystals.

Availability: Rare.

Physical benefits: Believed to assist with tissue inflammation, cellular disorders, brain malfunctioning, strokes and tumours; considered helpful for all cancers (particularly breast, liver and ovarian), eyes, headaches; thought to assist the healer to direct healing power to the right place and with the right intensity; often used in sevens, rhodizite is a master crystal, able to empower other crystals.

Emotional healing: Even a tiny crystal carried or worn in jewellery overcomes a crippling lack of confidence in adults who are afraid to leave their parents or the family home and so lock themselves and their family in the past.

Chakra: Solar Plexus, Brow and Crown.

Rhodizite

Associated candle colour: Yellow. **Associated fragrances**: Chamomile, copal, frankincense, lavender, rosemary. **Practical uses**: A very sensitive crystal to thoughts, so you can visualize what you need and draw it closer by mind power; however, do not use rhodizite when you are angry or anxious as it will also amplify negative thoughts, not to do harm but will make you feel worse. **Workplace**: Three rhodizites worn in a small bag around your waist or round your neck gives the power and self-confidence to go as far as you want in your career; wear to interviews if you have been unemployed for a while or face stiff competition, to impress whoever is interviewing you with your competence, charisma and drive. **Magical significance**: Rhodizite is most powerful at noon on the midsummer solstice, around June 21 in the northern hemisphere and six months earlier in the southern, for any healing purpose; a sun crystal, it increases clairvoyant vision, both for making accurate predictions and for accessing past lives and ancient worlds. **Divinatory meaning**: Believe in yourself and go for what you want now as there will never be a better time. **Zodiac**: Leo. **Empowerment**: I can and I will.

A powerful healing energy, so even tiny crystals or broken pieces held in the hand you write with open up the body's own self-healing system and will clear emotional or mental blockages.

Rhodizite heals people and places and then re-empowers itself. Some crystal healers say it needs no cleansing; others consider it benefits from cleansing by being smudged with one of its own incense fragrances, especially frankincense.

A crystal that draws power from the sun and can be left to catch natural light for a few hours, then held above the crown of the head to fill the aura with health, energy and focus.

It is very comforting to anyone who is terminally ill to help them make peace with themselves and others and to connect with their inner spiritual self to overcome fears of dying. Rhodizite is associated with Michael, the archangel of the sun.

Rhodizite

Type: Usually quartz, though other materials are used such as citrine, amethyst or smoky quartz.

Colours: Usually clear quartz, though other crystals are used, such as citrine, amethyst or smokey quartrz.

Availability: Relatively easy to obtain.

Physical benefits: While not used in healing therapies, as a personal power tool a skull is believed to help to focus light and power for whole-body healing; assist with easing migraines, headaches, brain disorders, auto-immune problems, neck and skeletal pain; skulls, even new ones, are said to be powerful healers for adults, but are too intense for children and animals.

Emotional healing: In mediaeval times, a memento mori, a death's head, a tiny jewelled skull was carried as a reminder that earthly life is finite so the bearer should make the most of every chance; a skull therefore is not gloomy but a power icon to seize life with enthusiasm.

Chakra: Crown.

Crystal Skulls

Candle colour: White, silver. **Fragrances:** Cypress, mugwort, myrrh, pine, vanilla. **Practical uses:** Crystal skulls are not for everyone: keep yours wrapped in silk and when alone or with friends set it on a table; allow its protective and restorative energies to flow through you and clear your head of trivialities so you can put life up a notch; good to explain to children who have lost a relative about immortality and the enduring spirit. **Workplace:** The Celts considered the head contained the soul and intelligence so they decapitated dead heroes and buried the heads in places of tribal power. Keep a small skull in your desk or in your workspace to touch when times are hard as a reminder that with logic and determination you can overcome anything. **Magical significance:** Ancient crystal skulls have been considered to hold the keys to ancient wisdom and the future of humankind for hundreds of years, maybe much longer; modern crystal skulls, if held, can also give answers not just for everyday issues but questions about existence and mortality; wait and the answers will come into your mind. **Divinatory meaning:** Think clearly and coolly, and decide what is of lasting value and what is just a passing phase or fancy. **Zodiac:** Scorpio. **Empowerment:** I am a spiritual being in a physical body.

There are a number of apparently ancient crystal skulls in existence that have caused much dispute as to their authenticity as ancient relics. The most famous was in the possession of the Mitchell-Hedges family until recently, referred to as the Skull of Doom and believed to be old Mayan.

After intense scientific investigation, no evidence has been found as to how it was carved or with what tools; there are no tooling marks, ancient or modern, to date it.

Though most archaeologists believe that almost all existing life-sized crystal skulls are 19th-century fakes, there is a legend that in Ancient Mayan culture there were 13 sacred crystal skulls, hidden in different places, which must be found before 21 December 2012, the end of the current Mayan calendar cycle which has lasted 5,126 years.

On that date, the myth says the Earth will be knocked off its axis unless the 13 skulls are brought together and aligned to save the planet.

Type: Silicate/aluminosilicate.

Colours: Golden and clear.

Availability: Relatively common.

Physical benefits: Said to help to build and regenerate cells, tissues and organs, particularly relating to liver damage; before and immediately after any surgical procedures; ease Seasonal Affective Disorder, melanomas and sun damage to body or skin.

Emotional healing: A cheerful crystal for natural pessimists, for people who are chronically depressed and for children who have become withdrawn because of bullying or abuse.

Chakra: Solar Plexus.

Feldspar

Candle colour: Gold. **Fragrances:** Copal, frankincense, marigold, sagebrush, sunflower. **Practical uses:** The holiday crystal, for attracting and enjoying time away from work and chores, whether a weekend outdoors, a week or two in the sun or more ambitious travel plans. **Workplace:** If you work in a career where you have to be very serious most of the time or if you are working with colleagues or an employer who rarely smiles, small pieces of golden feldspar will bring warmth and lighter moments to the most solemn day. **Magical significance:** Golden feldspar is most magical at those times of the month and year when the sun and the moon are in the sky at the same time. Hold a piece of gold feldspar in each open hand or one gold for the sun and one clear and milky for the moon and allow the heavenly bodies to empower the feldspars as a lucky charm for the month ahead. **Divinatory meaning:** Things are nowhere as bad as they seem; do not defeat yourself in advance by worrying excessively about what may not happen. **Zodiac:** Leo. **Empowerment:** The sun will shine again tomorrow.

Feldspars are the one of the most common rock-forming minerals on Earth and are a major component of most igneous rocks, molten rock from deep under the earth that has cooled

They are also found in moon rock; any feldspar has earth, fire and cosmic energies, while golden or clear feldspar also has the power of the sun, and is naturally luck- and prosperity-bringing. Golden feldspar, unlike most feldspar, has not been given a specific name though it is sometimes sold as

a cheaper form of rich orangey sunstone. Clear feldspar can resemble quartz but it is softer.

If you are a natural worrier or find it hard to focus on the here and now carry a small piece of golden feldspar in a gold purse; take out the crystal whenever you start to feel anxious or defeat yourself in advance. Gold feldspar is ideal around the home in the winter or during periods when everything seems to be going wrong or breaking down to restore optimism and good fortune.

Type: Sodium aluminium phosphate, short prismatic sometimes striated crystals.

Colours: Green, yellow, yellow-green, colourless.

Availability: Relatively rare, even rarer as gemstone quality, but worth obtaining.

Physical benefits: Said to help fevers, sunstroke, heatstroke, sunburn, skin rashes and sensitivity (sometimes made into elixir for skin but indirect method must be used), glands, bladder, kidneys, cystitis and bedwetting, bile duct, spleen, nausea, travel sickness, heart irregularities and slow heartbeat, endocrine system, hormone regulation; reduces harmful effects of mercury and other metals on body.

Emotional healing: Breaks over-reliance on the judgement and approval of others and so reduces the co-dependency of manipulation/control by oppressor and martyrdom by the oppressed.

Chakra: Solar Plexus and Heart.

Brazilianite

Candle colour: Green. **Fragrances:** Grapefruit, lemon, lime, pine, vetivert. **Practical uses:** A crystal that encourages setting and keeping boundaries; a natural piece in the home improves parent/child and parent/teenager interactions; helpful for gentle parents who find it hard to say no or impose rules on strong-willed offspring. **Workplace:** A crystal to encourage self-expression and development of unique talents; good for aspiring writers, artists and others involved in creative ventures or performing arts to test their work publicly; allows you to be yourself in any situation and not be over-impressed or intimidated by those with big egos. **Magical significance:** Brazilianite is believed to give access to the wisdom of ancient worlds and particularly to lost civilisations such as Atlantis and Lemuria that may have inspired later cultures with their wisdom; take to sacred places, especially open or mountainous areas, to connect with evolved nature spirits and essences. **Divinatory meaning:** What you are and where you are is on track; stop practising and give the performance of your life. **Zodiac:** Capricorn. **Empowerment:** I do not need constant guidance from others.

A stone of healthy relationships in love, with family, friends and the workplace, to balance the needs of the other person with your own; good if you find it hard to listen and not prejudge or alternatively need constant reassurance you are loved; a crystal that helps relationships to breathe and so grow.

If you can obtain a small piece of gemstone brazilianite, wear it near your heart to take risks to attain your dreams; also to take chances on love rather than waiting to be asked out or defeating yourself before you start by considering yourself unlovable or unattractive. A good crystal to have around constantly irritable or angry people and to express your disapproval firmly in situations you consider unjust without completely losing your temper or backing down at the first opposition.

A small piece in children's bedrooms discourages complaining and tale-telling among siblings and will change the energy field of an older child or teenager who seems always to be blamed for everything that goes wrong at home and school.

Cancrinite

Type: Felspathoid, sodium calcium aluminium silicate carbonate.

Colours: Yellow, orange, pink, white or blue.

Availability: Obtainable from specialist crystal stores and online.

Physical benefits: Said to help muscles, ligaments, congestion of lungs, pneumonia, bronchitis and chronic breathing difficulties, neck and throat (place directly on/above affected area).

Emotional healing: Reconnects fractured relationships.

Chakra: Solar Plexus and Throat.

Cancrinite connects earth and cosmos and draws energies from both, so making it a potent home-blessing stone in all its colours, but especially orange and yellow; makes any social or family occasion harmonious and encourages stimulating communication at mealtimes with a minimum of dramas.

A supportive stone to carry if asking for support or favours and if the outcome of a meeting or application is uncertain, to swing positive energies in your favour.

Flint

Type: Quartz/chalcedony.

Colours: Black, brown, grey.

Availability: Common, rare as arrowheads, but available via some specialist mineral stores, museum shops and online.

Physical benefits: Believed to help liver, kidney stones, digestion, lungs, skin disorders, lesions, tags and growths.

Emotional healing: Helps let go of old emotional ties and destructive relationships with parents or elderly relatives that cause pain to a new generation.

Chakra: Root.

For thousands of years flint was used to create sparks to light fires and so became regarded by people as magical. In parts of Scandinavia, larger pieces of flint were kept in the home as they were believed to contain protective spirits and the stones were regularly anointed with beer and butter.

It can be polished to a high gloss and is popular as jewellery, the best way to absorb its ongoing protective and abundance attracting powers built up over many thousands of years.

Type: Silicate/nesosilicate, beryl.

Colours: Milky to clear white, also tinted yellow, pink or brown.

Availability: Rare, but worth obtaining.

Physical benefits: Could assist nerve damage and brain imbalances, whole-body healing, helps illnesses where conventional treatment is not working or where the body has been weakened by chemotherapy or radiotherapy, genetic disorders, auto-immune diseases, HIV and AIDS.

Emotional healing: A light-in-the-darkness crystal, but as it is very powerful and buzzes with energy, phenacite should be combined with counselling and other therapies to support sudden painful insights.

Chakra: Crown.

Phenacite/Phenakite

Candle colour: White. **Fragrances:** Lily, lily of the valley, lotus, neroli, orchid. **Practical uses:** Phenacite aids any life changes or transition periods, both tangible ones such as leaving home, getting married or retiring and for a decision to live in a more fulfilling way; good for remarriage after retirement. **Workplace:** Wear or carry phenacite to develop any talents that may have receded into the background and to turn an interest or gift into the basis for a second career or new direction in retirement; the best stone for taking up healing, clairvoyance or mediumship professionally; take to festivals to attract clients and protect you from negativity. **Magical significance:** Considered by many healers to have the highest vibration of any crystal, phenacite is a powerful connector with guardian angels, archangels and healing angels; stimulates clairvoyance if you hold a phenacite wand or tumblestone between your hands; direct connection with the brow is generally too powerful. **Divinatory meaning:** Reconsider the possibilities you have if you are feeling restless or dissatisfied, as you can make changes without quitting. **Zodiac:** Aquarius. **Empowerment:** I do not need to keep life as it is.

A stone traditionally associated with rituals that has become very popular as a symbol in hand-fasting or pagan weddings as well as more traditional marriage ceremonies; also as a gift at special milestones in life.

A small piece of phenacite is sometimes presented to a new Reiki master by their teacher after final attunement.

Particularly if faceted, phenacite lives up to its name, which comes from the Ancient Greek for 'false diamond', just as beautiful but with more spiritually rooted properties than the conventional diamond.

Use phenacite in white or pale yellow for whole-body healing by filling the body with transformative white/gold light from the head downwards. Move the crystal in spirals, down the body. Allow your hand to guide a natural path anti-clockwise as it removes blockages or tension and clockwise to gently energize.

Flash Opal

Type: Hydrated silicon dioxide.

Colours: In a flash opal, colours which could be just one or several rainbow colours appear as sudden brilliant flashes.

Availability: Relatively common.

Physical benefits: Thought to be beneficial for illnesses that have no regular pattern and can suddenly recur and then go into remission or disappear as rapidly.

Emotional healing: For unpredictable psychological illnesses or personality disorders.

Chakra: Sacral and Brow.

Candle colour: Silver. **Fragrances:** Copal, hibiscus. **Practical uses:** Wear so it flashes to attract attention; good at parties if you are normally shy. **Workplace:** For all who work with their imagination or with colour in any form; hold the opal and rotate it while brainstorming to trigger inspiration. **Magical significance:** The most vibrant of the opals, rotate the opal so it flashes as you recite an empowerment, and keep doing so until you feel the power. **Divinatory meaning:** A flash of insight seems to clear up indecision; do not doubt yourself. **Zodiac:** Cancer and Sagittarius. **Empowerment:** I am inspired and motivated.

Though flash opal is a distinctive variety of opal, the flash phenomenon can appear in other kinds of opal, for example as green flashes in the precious Mexican orange fire opal or as multi-coloured flashes in colourless satin flash opal, which is a form of hyalite opal (p.159).

Flash opals are very sensitive to mood, but can also be moved to the light to give energy.

Opalite/Tiffany Stone

Type: Silica and/or calcium carbonate base.

Colours: Bright to royal dark purple with pink, orange, red, white, black, clear and green.

Availability: Common as manufactured opalite, rare as tiffany stone or natural opalite.

Physical benefits: Said to help hormones, childbirth, blood thinning, kidneys, also migraine related nausea, serotonin deficiency, tinnitus.

Emotional healing: Natural and manufactured opalite helps the expression of natural feelings, positive and negative.

Chakra: Sacral and Brow.

Candle colour: Cream. **Fragrances:** Acacia, mint, musk. **Practical uses:** Has an inbuilt feel-good factor. Have dishes of tumblestone opalite around party rooms. **Workplace:** Tiffany stone encourages success in youth enterprise. **Magical significance:** Glass opalite with its soft opalescent colours and blue glow is made into beautiful angels, Buddhas, animals and statues that will act as a focus in a quiet corner. **Divinatory meaning:** A change does not have to be for the better; be sure what or who is new will be lasting. **Zodiac:** Cancer. **Empowerment:** I will not resist the inevitable.

Because opalite has two distinctive forms, one natural, one manufactured, there can be some confusion. Natural opalite is not in fact opalescent, though it can be highly polished and gleaming as cabochons.

Manufactured opalite does look like glass, but in fabulous opalescent colours. It has been found to have very calming, balancing properties. Some healing practitioners have discovered manufactured opalite also helps with hormonal problems, particularly in young people.

Type: Magnesium aluminum iron boro-silicate hydroxide.

Colours: Emerald green, greenish brown, pink, yellow, brown, colourless, blue.

Availability: Rare.

Physical benefits: Seen as a total health restorer to mind and body, particularly by discouraging bad habits or an unhealthy lifestyle that is harming health; thought to be good for connective-tissue disorders, infections and bacteria that can poison the body and bloodstream, modern bugs such as MRSA and C difficile that are resistant to treatment; may help tropical diseases or those carried by insects or vermin.

Emotional healing: A very soothing crystal for those who self-harm or who frequently contemplate suicide to bring self-love and an awareness that what matters is living the present and future as positively as possible and not giving in to despair or self-hatred.

Chakra: Heart and Throat.

Kornerupine

Candle colour: Green. **Fragrances:** Basil, lemongrass, juniper, orange, pine. **Practical uses:** The reality-principle crystal for all who daydream or regret their life away; wear or carry it to break out of a rut and to take control of your life direction; good for alleviating a mid-life crisis in both sexes and for feeling desperate because the right love partner has not yet come along. **Workplace:** The crystal of all who teach or lecture at every level of expertise and for every age; wear kornerupine jewellery if you teach children or adults with special needs or you work in a school where there is a lot of unruliness and bad behaviour, to give yourself an aura of authority and quiet confidence even if you do not feel it inside. **Magical significance:** For people who hand over their destiny to fortune tellers or who are addicted to clairvoyant readings or messages from the departed to make decisions; encourages them to develop and trust their own intuitive awareness and to predict possibilities they can then follow or consciously change by future actions. **Divinatory meaning:** You are putting off tasks that need clearing and are using vital energy avoiding them; they are far easier than you fear. **Zodiac:** Gemini. **Empowerment:** I will live today for today.

Sometimes mistaken for emerald, kornerupine in all its colours displays pleochroism, where different colours can be seen from different viewing angles.

A crystal of eloquence, kornerupine can be worn or carried to successfully challenge unfair legal or official claims, decisions or accusations; excellent if you frequently become tongue-tied or anxious in the presence of authority or someone with a big ego who is sarcastic or critical.

Kornerupine is also helpful if you are a compulsive worrier or hoarder, to live in the present and let go of what you no longer need.

Take kornerupine with you if you are holidaying alone or travelling to somewhere distant, to embrace new experiences and cultures wholeheartedly; domestically it broadens the taste of fussy eaters or partners and children who are reluctant to try new dishes.

Type: Phosphates.

Colours: White, colourless, pale yellow-tan, rose, pale green or blue.

Availability: Rare.

Physical benefits: Reported as being helpful for headaches, migraine, pancreas and spleen, illnesses that may lead to erratic behaviour patterns such a bipolar disorder or schizophrenia; beneficial for brain reactivation and re-learning after brain injury or trauma; bringing a swift blast of healing energy when and where needed, but not for children or animals.

Emotional healing: To modify antisocial behaviour of adult family members, perhaps who have left home but whose actions still affect family happiness and peace; also for adults with behavioural or learning difficulties to reach their potential.

Chakra: Crown and Brow.

Herderite

Candle colour: White. **Fragrances:** Balm of Gilead, copal, myrrh, sandalwood, sagebrush. **Practical uses:** Herderite in the home enriches family life and encourages individual members to develop and change creatively over the years; avoids keeping roles we have outgrown or repeating old mistakes through different generations. **Workplace:** Brings out leadership qualities even in timid people who need to take charge of a situation or group of people; combines tact, diplomacy and understanding of others' needs in group or team situations with the ability to speak and act decisively. **Magical significance:** For a long time herderite was a secret among professional healers because it was considered too powerful for novices. However it guides not only those who teach or wish to teach healing to others but for anyone to develop the innate healing powers we all possess by connecting with wise spirit guardians. **Divinatory meaning:** A time for swift decisive action and no doubts or regrets to clear the air and the way for fast progress. **Zodiac:** Aries. **Empowerment:** I know where I am going.

Herderite is a very spiritual stone that connects spontaneously to the higher realms and healing energies from angels or guides; however, when meditating or healing with herderite, you may need other crystals close by such as banded agate, jet or gentle amethyst to keep you grounded both during and after your explorations.

During meditation you may encounter wise healing guides from old cultures who will accelerate any formal psychic study or healing.

Herderite stimulates brain and memory functions to assist us with all forms of learning, from the esoteric to the most scientific or technological.

Wear a small herderite gem or carry a small natural crystal in a soft pouch for a quick blast of power when people are being stubborn, a piece of equipment keeps jamming or you are trying in vain to get through a series of automated messages to speak to someone at a call centre.

Herderite

Type: Cavities in rocks which contains numerous well-developed tiny or sometimes larger crystals, such as clear quartz, amethyst or citrine, calcite or needle-like goethite.

Colours: Varies according to the crystal content, but usually grey, brown or black outside.

Availability: Relatively common, particularly as amethyst geodes.

Physical benefits: Varies according to the inner crystal; may help migraines, malfunctioning or injuries to the brain, skull, head and neck, assist with deep-organ or -tissue surgery, calcification of bones and osteoporosis; geode pairs are said to balance health and bring fertility.

Emotional healing: For deep-seated problems where the person is in denial; for those who feel bound to secrecy, such as victims of sexual abuse, incest or whose families are involved in crime.

Chakra: Root.

Geodes

Candle colour: White. **Fragrances:** Almond, anise, cloves, rosewood, tea tree. **Practical uses:** A geode pair is a good love crystal whereby the two halves are kept together even when the couple must spend time apart; a symbol for secret love or where one or both of the lovers has an existing love commitment they must honour. **Workplace:** An amethyst geode, even a small one, facing the door absorbs anger, resentment, pressure and anxiety and replaces them with gentleness, kind words and deeds; protective against hostile visitors and a good anti-theft device in a shop or workshop. **Magical significance:** Surround a cave-like geode with tiny candles and travel in your mind within its pathways; a good entry point for other lands and worlds, even for those inexperienced in psychic exploration to experience beautiful visions. **Divinatory meaning:** A new, seemingly dull person may prove a lively companion and a great source of knowledge once you get to know them. **Zodiac:** Cancer **Empowerment:** I look for what is hidden, not obvious.

Geodes are hollow, crystal-lined globe-like cavities found in sedimentary rocks such as limestone, dolomite or volcanic rocks. In legend, geode eggs were laid by magical birds, for example the North American Indian thunderbird, whose flashing eyes and huge wings brought the rain and storms.

They were also called dragon treasures in Eastern Europe, because when split open they revealed sparkling crystals. Keep a small geode in a garden or on a balcony to see nocturnal creatures,

especially those normally too shy to reveal themselves.

Geodes bring out whatever is hidden, whether a person's true nature, good or bad, hidden talents, secret motives and for recovering what is missing.

Place both index fingers inside a geode, ask what you want to know or to be revealed, and the answer will come like a flash in your mind.

A geode is a wonderful gift for a child to stimulate the imagination and act as a fairy castle.

Type: Silicate; cyclosilicate.

Colours: Pink-red, yellowish brown to brownish red or red, red-violet, pink, blue, yellow or brown; can have black and white inclusions.

Availability: Rare.

Physical benefits: Said to help nervous system, skin, heart problems, inability to tolerate certain foods or chemicals, energy, eyes especially the optic nerve, pancreas, thyroid, blood, cell and organ regeneration, trigger body's self-healing system.

Emotional healing: Reduces compulsions such as obsessive compulsive disorder and opens up anyone who is driven to achieve success or to build up material security to the exclusion of everything else.

Chakra: Root and Heart.

Eudialyte

Candle colour: Pink. **Fragrances:** Almond, anise, cherry blossom, hibiscus, juniper. **Practical uses:** An excellent stone if you are having problems of jealousy in your relationship, whether the jealousy of a partner or an ex-partner or you are constantly afraid of being betrayed because of past hurts. **Workplace:** A stone of personal power and the ability to trust your own decision-making, particularly if these are questioned by power-hungry colleagues; wear a piece of eudialyte jewellery or carry a polished stone and hold it to centre your thoughts before making a choice. **Magical significance:** Eudialyte is a fine-tuner and amplifier of ESP; develops clairaudience (the ability to hear words and messages from other dimensions), whether from wise ancestors, angels or spirit guides. Hold a polished sphere, usually eudialyte in a rock matrix, to each ear for a minute or two and let the words flow through your mind. **Divinatory meaning:** Rely on your own judgment and refuse to be pressed for a decision until you are ready. **Zodiac:** Taurus. **Empowerment:** I will not question my decisions, but go along with them.

Eudialyte is occasionally used as a gemstone, but needs handling with care as it can easily break. It is also known as almandine spar and associated with a form of pink garnet.

Eudialyte is a complex mineral that does not often form good crystals and sometimes none at all. It is usually embedded in its host rock and may be polished in that form.

It often contains zirconium, cerium and yttrium in its structure, as well as being sodium-rich, and

can have as many as 46 different chemical elements. Its main use metaphysically is as a stone of self-love and self-acceptance, carried or worn to diminish the need to put the world's troubles right and to live through other people's happiness and needs.

It is also a good stone to have around the home if a family member has behaved badly and partly destroyed the family structure, to rebuild and, if not forgive, to try to come to some reconciliation with the betraying member.

Type: Large often flat and oval smooth crystal, usually with a central indentation for the thumb in a wide variety of materials.

Colours: According to the crystal; many palm stones are opaque and a number richly patterned.

Availability: Common.

Physical benefits: Held between the thumb and forefinger, the palm stone if gently rubbed is thought to reduce stress levels dramatically and releases natural endorphins or painkillers; said to be good for all stress-related conditions or those such as high blood pressure and breathing difficulties made worse by stress.

Emotional healing: Use a worry stone before a dental or medical appointment, an examination, test, court case or stressful meeting to ease away fears and panic that can cause adverse reactions; one particular stone will become your psychic security blanket and gain in speed and intensity of effect the more you use it.

Chakra: Heart and Sacral.

Palm/Worry Stones

Candle colour: Green. **Fragrances:** Chamomile, clary sage, lavender, lemon balm, lemon verbena. **Practical uses:** Have a basket of different worry stones, some softly coloured, others brightly patterned, some semi-transparent. When you feel restless or troubled without knowing why, take one without looking and hold it until you feel better. Your choice dictated by your intuition is invariably right. **Workplace:** If you are trying to stop snacking at your desk or having to go outside for cigarette breaks, use an earthy agate or soothing jade; hold it in one hand, if necessary typing with the other until the craving subsides. **Magical significance:** Choose a highly patterned palm stone such as a picasso, orbicular or kambaba jasper; trace the pattern with your index finger over and over in faint candlelight until you enter a light trance and can travel along the pathways to other worlds. The Druids used stones with mini labyrinths drawn on them to become entranced. **Divinatory meaning:** Stop worrying about what will not happen as you are wasting energy you need to make sure you do stay on top. **Zodiac:** Libra. **Empowerment:** I will not worry needlessly.

People have for thousands of years found a particular stone they have held in times of crisis or uncertainty and pushed their worries into it. You may find a naturally smoothed stone with an indentation on the sea shore or a hillside and that can be even more magical than buying a worry stone.

It is important you do cleanse your worry stones at least weekly. If the stone is hard and not porous you can wash it under running water. However,

incense-stick smoke is just as effective in a cleansing fragrance such as pine or juniper.

If you experience hostility from neighbours or live in a dangerous area, bury a black worry stone upright in the front and back garden or a plant pot outside the front and back doors. The earth cleanses it.

At work prop a black worry stone upright facing outwards to absorb any negativity; cleanse it weekly. Hold it in your hands every week after cleansing it to fill it with your own inner defensive power.

Type: Zeolite, hydrated sodium calcium aluminum silicate, radiating needle- or hair-like tufts as sprays or balls.

Colours: Clear, white, grey, yellow, terracotta, occasionally pink.

Availability: Relatively rare.

Physical benefits: Claimed to reduce toxins caused by environmental pollution and effects of harmful metals; be good for animal healing and for conditions with multiple causes and symptoms; may help allergies to antibiotics and other modern prescription drugs, pH balance (degree of acidity or alkalinity), antioxidant, premature ageing, degenerative diseases.

Emotional healing: Assists all talking therapies by creating warmth and empathy so that a reluctant or emotionally closed client can trust the therapist enough to share feelings perhaps never before expressed.

Chakra: Heart.

Mesolite

Candle colour: White. **Fragrances:** Lavender, lily, lily of the valley, lotus, white rose. **Practical uses:** Mesolite improves and deepens relationships, encouraging heart-to-heart communication and the ability to accept love as well as give it; brings recognition of a twin soul; good for spiritual and profound emotional sexual experiences beyond the physical connection. **Workplace:** A mesolite crystal cluster resolves personality clashes, personal prejudices and dislikes that get in the way of positive professional relationships; good for gently discouraging unwanted attention from a colleague who wants to intrude on your private life or begin a romantic relationship that is inappropriate or where feelings are not returned. **Magical significance:** A crystal for connecting with other dimensions, especially deceased relatives or family ancestors. Set mesolite on a west-facing indoor window-sill with a clove of garlic for protection; light a candle in the window to welcome the spirit; when you feel the presence, transfer the candle and crystal to a table and accept any telepathic messages or signs. **Divinatory meaning:** A time to put differences aside and to build bridges with a colleague or acquaintance, for it is better to have them on your side in the days ahead. **Zodiac:** Taurus. **Empowerment:** I welcome my ancestors into my heart and life.

Mesolite is an excellent crystal for overcoming a strong, seemingly irrational dislike of or by someone you work with or must meet regularly; brings acceptance that what you most object to in them may be characteristics you share but deny in yourself.

Keep a mesolite cluster in your home for entertaining colleagues or your partner's relatives whom you may not know very well, to create a warm, welcoming atmosphere. It also softens

over-judgmental people, if you have a partner who is constantly criticizing you or the children or an employer with impossibly rigid expectations.

At work, mesolite encourages team-work and diminishes destructive rivalries and bickering that are harming productivity and harmony. A crystal to develop telepathic communication between two people and to give knowledge of shared past lives with close friends and family.

WARNING: Not suitable for making direct elixirs.

Mesolite

Type: Feldspar, microcline labradorite.

Colours: Dark green or grey to grey-green with milky inclusions that, when held to the light, flash and appear opalescent, resembling the galaxy, planets and stars.

Availability: Relatively rare but a wonderful addition to any collection.

Physical benefits: Claimed to be helpful for stress-induced or related illnesses, brain, visual disorders and disturbances, migraines, travel sickness on high-speed trains and long-distance journeys especially by bus and on planes, nerve damage and degeneration, radiation sickness, adverse effects of radiation or laser treatment, dizziness, disorientation and problems with digestion.

Emotional healing: Assists anyone who is physically immobile or restricted or totally isolated to explore ways of expanding physical and mental horizons, particularly if you as the sufferer or carer are coming up against unhelpfulness by local service providers.

Chakra: Crown.

Galaxite/Galaxyite

Candle colour: Dark green. **Fragrances:** Acacia, mugwort, myrrh, orchid, poppy. **Practical uses:** Give galaxyite tumblestones to children in their imaginative years to keep wonder alive in a materialistic, consumer world; hold one under a starry sky to become aware of self-imposed limitations on your life or those you have allowed others to impose on you; carry it in the days ahead to remove a few of those blocks. **Workplace:** For astronomers, space scientists, astronauts, pilots and air crew, science fiction and fantasy writers, computer software and games designers, all involved in hi-technology or inventing new products and approaches; stunts people and those who teach or organize extreme sports; parapsychologists researching UFOS or alien animals. **Magical significance:** Galaxyite is a stone for astrologers, amateur and professional; set a tumblestone in the centre of a birth chart for an enhanced intuitive understanding; also for those who seek inter-galactic communication or have out-of-body dreams of different galaxies and communicate telepathically in these dreams with alien life forms. **Divinatory meaning:** A sense of restlessness and expectation that something good is coming; it is, but why not peep round the corner to hasten it? **Zodiac:** Sagittarius. **Empowerment:** I believe we are not alone in the universe.

Galaxyite is often called galaxite, but in fact galaxite is the name of a black mineral from the spinel family that is a magnesium aluminium oxide, so check a picture if buying online. A myth surrounding galaxyite is that it was given by the angels to help humans cope with modern life and its stresses; galaxyite was not discovered until 1995 in Quebec, Canada.

Galaxyite is considered one of the best aura cleansers and energizers; held over the crown of the head, it heals gaps in your aura where you are leaking energy, perhaps giving too much to a person who is taking advantage or fretting unnecessarily about what might never happen.

It is a very protective stone against all forms of negativity and from nasty psychic dreams, and is good to keep children safe when you cannot be with them.

Andalusite

Type: Aluminium silicate.

Colours: Pleochroic, showing different colours in different directions; colours include orange-brown, pale yellowish brown, yellowish green, bottle green, golden or dark brown, also pink, white, grey, violet, blue.

Availability: Relatively common.

Physical benefits: May help bone fractures, connective tissue, psychosomatic and stress-related conditions; set against a painful place or the source of a problem directly on the skin.

Emotional healing: Releasing unresolved childhood sorrows.

Chakra: Root and Heart.

Andalusite is best known in its grey with black or brown opaque variety with a cross, called chiastolite or fairy stone, often sold as a tumblestone. But the polished faceted form with its changing colours, if worn, overcomes depression and self-doubts and it is a popular gem with men as well as women.

Andalusite eases the return to your former home area to live or work, particularly if the past has troubled memories, to overwrite on the present new positive experiences.

Brucite

Type: Magnesium hydroxide.

Colours: White, pale green, grey or blue.

Availability: Common as industrial mineral, but rarer in the healing and esoteric world.

Physical benefits: Brucite reaches any blocked or out-of-balance areas of the body, wherever it is held near (the throat or brow are good entry points for whole-body healing); may help cholesterol, migraines and confusion, digestive system, gall bladder, heartburn.

Emotional healing: For anyone disappointed with life, to bring optimism that it is not too late to start living.

Chakra: Throat and Crown.

Brucite is slowly growing in popularity, as more healers and those interested in crystals metaphysically realize that its energies are actually enhanced by the fact that it is part of daily life; as a bonus, brucite is relatively inexpensive.

Brucite is a light-bringing crystal which draws power from the cosmos and higher spiritual sources and spontaneously clears the aura energy field and chakras if held in the morning light for a minute or two; energizes you for the day ahead.

Type: Sorosilicate, calcium aluminium silicate, melilite group.

Colours: Yellow-brown, green-grey, colourless.

Availability: Obtainable from some specialist mineral stores and online.

Physical benefits: Said to help with bones, healing of fractures and bone diseases and tumours, brain connections and chemical and electrical imbalances, cardiovascular system, coccyx, spleen, pancreas, liver and efficient fat and toxin processing, jaw, teeth and especially bruxism or teeth-grinding in adults and children.

Emotional healing: Self-preservation and self-rescue, finding the real person for those who adopt the interests and values of those around them and never develop their own identity.

Chakra: Solar Plexus.

Gehlenite

Candle colour: Yellow. **Fragrances:** Chamomile, cedarwood, lavender, rosewood, sweetgrass. **Practical uses:** Gehlenite awakens practical skills and coping strategies if you are an ideas and theory person; good for fixing and mending, and for all outdoors activities and living such as camping, cycling or walking holidays; for people who have spent too much time in the city or who are naturally clumsy to develop dexterity. **Workplace:** The crystal of craftspeople, especially those who work with wood, metal or natural fabrics; for gardeners and horticulturists, farmers, plumbers and all in the building trade; a crystal to give to apprentices learning practical trades and to anyone starting up or running their own business where they use their hands as well as their minds. **Magical significance:** A crystal associated with earth energies and with our instinctual side; keep on display when chanting, circle dancing, drumming, to link with the rhythms of the earth and to awaken your intuitive inner radar to know the right direction and action. **Divinatory meaning:** Do not be swayed by the opinions and preferences of others; what you want and feel should take priority if you are to express your true personality freely. **Zodiac:** Gemini. **Empowerment:** I am myself and no one else.

Gehlenite is a Mother Earth crystal that makes any home feel welcoming and safe, especially homes in tall apartment blocks or in the centre of a city where there is little greenery. It helps those who are not naturally nurturing, maternal or paternal to develop empathy and good parenting skills if they have a new baby and little experience of infants; brings out caring and nursing skills as well as patience if suddenly coping with a sick relative.

A natural reducer of stress and hyperactivity in the home or workplace and for helping immature people to grow up and welcome commitment and responsibility for others.

One of the best strengtheners if, for whatever reason, you are thrown back on your own resources, whether on a wilderness holiday or working with an aid agency in a place where there are not even basic facilities to depend on; good for assessing at any life stage who you really are and what and who are your priorities.

Augelite

Type: Aluminum phosphate hydroxide.

Colours: Colourless, white or pale shades of yellow, pink.

Availability: Rare.

Physical benefits: Thought to balance red and white blood-cell count; may help all blood-cell disorders, circulation problems, obesity, food intolerances, restore health to and increase efficient functioning of digestive and elimination organs and processes in the body.

Emotional healing: Harmonizes people who are deliberately difficult or cause trouble at family gatherings.

Chakra: Solar Plexus and Heart.

Candle colour: Yellow. **Fragrances:** Bay, basil, chamomile, lilac. **Practical uses:** Excellent for helping relationships go smoothly; good to win round new family members. **Workplace:** Keep a cluster in your workspace if you work in the law, the legal department of a company, with contracts, estate agency or property development. **Magical significance:** A sleep crystal, keep a bag of tiny colourless or pink augelites by your bed close to your head; brings peaceful sleep and drives away nightmares. **Divinatory meaning:** A difficult person at work will suddenly get easier to deal with; build on this. **Zodiac:** Virgo. **Empowerment:** I can overcome divisions and dissension.

Augelite, though hard to obtain, is much loved by healers and spiritual or magic practitioners because it ensures all work is done for the highest good; it makes an easy and powerful connection with higher sources of help and healing, especially angelic; keep it between you and a negative or psychologically troubled patient or client and, if you are a medium, in a channelling circle, to exclude mischievous spirits set on disruption.

Amethyst Sage Agate

Type: Chalcedony, crypto-crystalline quartz, mixed with manganese and iron.

Colours: Deep lavender/purple or light blue, with tan or gold and black dendritic fern-like inclusions.

Availability: Rare but well worth obtaining.

Physical benefits: Said to help growths and tumours, cysts, blockages in veins, arteries and connective passage.

Emotional healing: A stone for overcoming vulnerability to the indifference of the world.

Chakra: Throat, Brow and Crown.

Candle colour: Purple. **Fragrances:** Bergamot, neroli, sage. **Practical uses:** Use it to focus on what needs to be developed if you have a lot of distractions. If you are doubting the point of what you are doing, helps to finish it anyway and then understand. **Workplace:** A crystal of perfection; wear or carry if you create intricate artefacts, fine-tune systems, work with very detailed facts or figures where precision is essential. **Magical significance:** A very magical agate with surreal landscapes, especially when carved into a domed cabochon shape. **Divinatory meaning:** You will make beneficial connections through friends of friends, family or colleagues. **Zodiac:** Aquarius. **Empowerment:** I welcome connection with new people and experiences.

Amethyst sage agate with its beautiful colours and dendritic tree inclusions is a stone of great beauty; in natural form it is a harmonious addition to a crystal collection or table in your home as it encourages unity and warm connections with others without being stifling or over-possessive.

Wear amethyst sage agate or give to someone you care for if you or they find the balance hard between 24/7 togetherness and total withdrawal.

Type: Solid narrow pieces of crystal, shaped into a wand, rounded at one end and more pointed at the other; alternatively wood, crystal or metal in which a pointed crystal is inserted in one end; occasionally natural blades of crystal such as kyanite or naturally shaped quartz terminations (p. 195).

Colours: Varies with the materials used.

Availability: Common.

Physical benefits: Wands of all kinds are used for directing energy through the body and the aura; the rounded end of massage wands is applied with different degrees of pressure on the body in massage therapies and Reiki.

Emotional healing: A chakra wand on which seven crystals – red, orange, yellow, green, blue, indigo, violet (or purple and white) – are set should be directed towards the brow to bring harmony to a racing mind at night and towards the navel in the morning to give confidence to face the world.

Chakra: Brow and Sacral.

Crystal Wands

Candle colour: Silver or gold. **Fragrances:** Apple blossom, jasmine, lavender, neroli, peach. **Practical uses:** Collect different massage wands in your favourite crystals. Keep them on a table in a star formation, points alternately outwards and inwards to create a balanced energy grid. **Workplace:** Put a small copper wand with a pointed quartz on one end in your desk drawer to direct positive opportunity inwards to you and conduct negativity away. **Magical significance:** Any wand can be used in the age-old tradition to attract good fortune: circle the wand clockwise nine times while visualizing the successful outcome; buy small clear quartz wands for embryo Harry Potters. **Divinatory meaning:** No harm in wishing for the moon as long as you can work on improving the here-and-now as well. **Zodiac:** Sagittarius. **Empowerment:** Wishes can come true in unexpected ways.

Crystal wands are multi-purpose tools for crystal work. Use the pointed end of a wand to empower other crystals for healing, luck or protection by passing the wand through incense smoke or over a candle flame and touching each crystal in turn.

Once a week de-stress and re-empower your energy system. Pass the wand up the front of your body slowly, the point towards the body a few centimetres away. Let your hand, not your conscious mind, guide its path.

Sometimes it will move clockwise to energize a particular place. It may stop at an energy blockage and spiral in both directions alternately until you feel the energy freeing. The wand may stop at your major chakra energy centres and, if the energies are too fast or intense, make a sideways movement to smooth.

At other times it may untangle an energy knot or turn in circles to infuse the chakras with extra energy.

Type: Corundum, aluminium oxide.

Colours: The star effect is most prized in deep blue sapphires and is also found in darker-coloured sapphires; the star is most distinctive in light silver-grey, blue-grey, greyish white, blue-white or yellowy white sapphires.

Availability: Rare.

Physical benefits: The star amplifies the healing properties of sapphire; said to help to purify the blood, blood cells and bone marrow, protect against infections and rarer viruses, glands, glandular fever; help to ease Alzheimer's disease and senile dementia, degenerative conditions, ear infection and ear ache, eyesight and eye infections, fevers and menopausal hot flushes, nausea and vomiting, speech problems.

Emotional healing: Wear even a small star sapphire if you were always told you were useless at everything and as a result have an inferiority complex and are afraid of socializing or speaking out.

Chakra: Crown.

Star Sapphire

Candle colour: White. **Fragrances:** Almond, carnation, orange, rosemary, sage. **Practical uses:** White star sapphire is a token of pure and lasting love without conditions, sometimes given or exchanged by first lovers who have had to give up everything for each others; for marriage in later years, especially following the loss of a partner, to avoid the sense of feeling second-best; discourages jealousy of earlier partners in remarriages. **Workplace:** A star sapphire, especially in the paler shades, is a symbol of wise and honest leadership; worn also by businesswomen or female entrepreneurs who succeed but never compromise their integrity or deliver less than the best to their clients and employees; use for following a childhood dream or ambition that seems almost impossible. **Magical significance:** The three cross bars in the six-ray sapphire represent faith, hope and destiny, sometimes associated with three angels who offer protection to star sapphire wearers. The moving star brings ongoing safety to travellers and guides their way home. **Divinatory meaning:** Because you are so honest, dishonesty in others hurts you; stick by your principles and shame them into making reparation. **Zodiac:** Gemini. **Empowerment:** I can fulfil small ambitions while striving for bigger ones.

The star effect occurs when the gem fibres lie in more than one direction and several bands reflect light as a moving star with six rays, rarely 12. The most famous star sapphire is the blue Star of India or, as it should correctly be called, the Star of Sri Lanka, since it was discovered in Sri Lanka about 300 years ago.

It has been in the American Museum of Natural History gem collection in New York City since 1900 and is flawless, the size of a golf ball, and has stars on both sides.

Black star sapphires are a powerful success-with-integrity symbol for men. They also protect from narrow-mindedness men with everyday jobs who are developing mediumistic or clairvoyant gifts with a view to turning professional. Black star sapphires are translucent (cloudy) to opaque and may be dark green, dark brown or blue rather than black.

Colour Changing Sapphire

Type: Corundum

Colours: Generally blue in natural light, changing to light purple or violet in artificial light or candlelight.

Availability: Rare

Physical benefits: Said to help epilepsy, ear infections, degenerative conditions, severe communication difficulties, gender issues and sex change operations.

Emotional healing: An unlocking gem if someone is unresponsive or reacts badly to psychological intervention.

Chakra: Crown

Candle Colour: Rainbow or white. **Fragrances:** Apple blossom, benzoin, ylang ylang. **Practical uses:** Wear to change your image; good if you have just come out of a restrictive situation. **Workplace:** Wear if you have two part-time jobs or are in transition between careers but still have to manage both. **Magical significance:** A transformation crystal if you practice magic or mediumship in the evenings and a conventional lifestyle during the day; light candles in a dark room and, as the gem changes colour, assume your spiritual persona. **Divinatory meaning:** There is a side to you that is emerging and needs expression. **Zodiac:** Sagittarius. **Empowerment:** Life just got more exciting.

A very exciting gem to wear during any periods of transition or transformation; good if you want to break out of a conventional lifestyle and live in a freer way; for long-distance or long-term travelling and downsizing to attain a better quality of life.

An excellent gem as matching rings or other jewellery as a love token in same sex marriages or formal commitments.

Rainbow Obsidian

Type: Volcanic glass.

Colours: Black with a blue sheen or green-black with flashes of purple, red and blue, always characterized by the rainbow shimmer of light.

Availability: Relatively common.

Physical benefits: Reported to help with pain relief, digestion, detoxification, rheumatism, arthritis, slipped discs, chronic back pain, IBS, chronic conditions.

Emotional healing: Offers a glimmer of light at the end of the tunnel – beneficial for those suffering from deep despair, depression or paralysing fears.

Chakra: Root and Solar Plexus.

Candle colour: Silver. **Fagrances:** Dragon's blood, vervain. **Practical uses:** Acts as a reminder after betrayal that you can start over and should let bitterness go. **Workplace:** Turns around bad fortune; hold five tumblestones in your hands, shake five times, then toss and catch them, saying, "Bad fortune be gone." **Magical significance:** When viewed by candlelight, a large polished piece forms a magic mirror in which you can see your wise guides. **Divinatory meaning:** Time to cut ties with the past that are occupying too much time. **Zodiac:** Cancer and Libra. **Empowerment:** There is light at the end of the tunnel.

According to myth, rainbow obsidian can be found after the sky turns black with rain and then the rainbow appears as the rain clears away.

Rainbow obsidian looks the same as ordinary obsidian until you hold it to the light, when it reveals its beautiful multicoloured iridescence.

If you find black obsidian too intense to work with on a daily basis, rainbow obsidian worn as jewellery combines the creative proactive obsidian fire with the gentler optimism of the rainbow. A crystal for cutting ties with the past.

Type: Depends on the crystal. Very clear spheres without inner markings may be glass and do not have the same healing properties.

Colours: Depends on the crystal.

Availability: Common.

Physical benefits: All spheres are claimed to be healing for all purposes; the more sparkling the crystal the more instant and intense the energies; clear quartz is most dynamic. Hold the sphere and transmit visualized light via your fingertips, amplified through the sphere, towards a person who is present and can also hold the ball, or as absent healing to a person, animal or place.

Emotional healing: Gentle amethyst, selenite or rose quartz spheres in a bedroom transmit healing protective light while you sleep to relieve ongoing or long-standing anxieties, doubts and fears; bring restorative sleep so you wake more able to cope.

Chakra: Crown.

Crystal Spheres

Candle colour: White, silver or gold. **Associated fragrances:** Acacia, cedar, frankincense, myrrh, sandalwood. **Practical uses:** Set a clear crystal sphere near the centre of your home to draw in continuing good health, abundance, the life force and happiness, and cleanse the home of stagnation like an open window on a sunny day. **Workplace:** A clear sphere will attract personal success, money and new orders to a business. Place it where natural light falls into the ball; hold the ball if you need a sudden infusion of energy or inspiration and before communicating with anyone to resolve a misunderstanding or to maximize a major opportunity. **Magical significance:** Crystal balls are the best tool for gazing within and seeing images in the lines and markings of a transparent sphere; for a translucent ball or one with a gleaming opaque pattern, use candlelight to cast shadow images on the surface. **Divinatory meaning:** Let the future unfold for the next month or two; do not be pressurized into choices before you are ready. **Zodiac:** Cancer for translucent or shimmering spheres, Leo for clear sparkling spheres, Scorpio for dark or opaque spheres. **Empowerment:** The answers to my questions lie within me.

Spheres, the perfect shape to amplify crystalline energies, are considered an essential tool in all forms of spiritual healing, both for holding near a painful spot or source of illness and for keeping a therapy room constantly pure.

From Ancient China has come the tradition of the sphere reflecting power from the sun to spread good luck, health and success throughout home and workplace; it has been adopted by Westernized practitioners of Feng Shui as an ongoing energy balancer. However, crystal spheres still remain mainly associated with clairvoyance.

In the modern world as for hundreds of years, crystal spheres reveal answers to questions, through images and impressions invoked from their inner markings, and show scenes far beyond the physical eye range and of past worlds; also for communicating with angels, spirit guides and wise ancestors.

Shark Tooth

Type: Organic, fossil varies in age, but some can be between 50 million and 100 million years old.

Colours: Variety of colours.

Availability: Relatively common, but purchase from a reliable fossil, crystal or mineral store or museum; many will offer a certificate of authentication.

Physical benefits: Reported to help with teeth, jaw, bones, cartilage.

Emotional healing: Prevents the repetition of old mistakes.

Chakra: Root and Sacral.

Candle colour: Cream. **Fragrances:** Anise, thyme. **Practical uses:** Made into jewellery, shark's tooth guards against postal, telephone and Internet scams and identity theft. **Workplace:** Attracts business in a field of fierce competition. **Magical significance:** The ultimate lucky charm, give one to teenagers on school trips for protection. **Divinatory meaning:** Some money you did not get, though rightfully yours, may become an issue again, but may involve more trouble than it is worth. **Zodiac:** Capricorn. **Empowerment:** I will not be haunted by the past.

Wearing or carrying animal parts dates back more than 15,000 years and was believed to endow the wearer with the power of the creature.

Fossils have always been prized as they add the power of millions of years to the charm and are symbols of long life and health in old age. Sharks' teeth give added protection to all who travel by or earn a living from the sea. Fossilized sharks' teeth in a bowl attract abundance into the home and are a good anti-debt symbol.

Williamsite

Type: Phyllosilicates, variety of serpentine, oily feel.

Colours: Translucent light green with irregular black inclusions, also bluish green.

Availability: Relatively common.

Physical benefits: May act against internal and external parasites, inflammation, lung problems and plant allergies, multiple sclerosis, kidney stones, stomach cramps, PMS, bites and stings, wounds, diabetes, heart irregularities, toxicity from environment and food.

Emotional healing: Clears chaotic energies and feelings after major shock, trauma or setbacks.

Chakra: Heart.

Candle colour: Green. **Fragrances:** Cedar, grapefruit, patchouli. **Practical uses:** Hold when the world gets too much;. **Workplace:** Brings achievement of goals through hard work rather than good luck or opportunism. **Magical significance:** Protective against psychological and psychic attack and against those who deliberately lead others into taking bunnecessary risks or temptation. **Divinatory meaning:** Other people feel able to tell you what they do and do not want from you; now it is your turn, so choose your moment. **Zodiac:** Virgo and Scorpio. **Empowerment:** I can make order out of chaos.

There are two main types of serpentine used in gemstone jewellery, the harder green bowenite (p.264) and the softer and less common williamsite. Although this is a gem used in jewellery, it is relatively soft, so keep it separate from other jewellery and hard objects that could scratch it.

Best protected by storing separately in a cloth bag, and it should only be cleaned using a soft cloth.

Williamsite is often used for sacred objects such as rosaries or prayer beads, or in adorning beautiful artefacts.

Type: Most commonly clear quartz, but can be any carvable material or metal.

Colours: Varies.

Availability: Common.

Physical benefits: The pendulum is itself seen as an all-purpose healing tool. Pass a clear quartz pendulum over the front of your body (front and back for othe people) slowly head to foot in spirals: moving it first anti-clockwise is said to remove stress and energy blockages and then clockwise is thought to energize and harmonize the whole body. It is believed that if you you can hold it near a painful spot to remove pain.

Emotional healing: Hold an amethyst or rose quartz pendulum in the hand you write with and fold your other hand round the pendulum body so it nearly touches. This will instantly calm you in any situation where you cannot cope.

Chakra: Brow.

Crystal Pendulums

Candle colour: White. **Fragrances:** Lemon, mugwort, musk, myrrh, orange. **Practical uses:** If you have lost something, go to where you last had it and start walking. The pendulum will swing clockwise if you are on track and continue to swing faster the closer it gets to the missing item. If it swings anti-clockwise you are off track. **Workplace:** To decide between options, write them all down and hold the pendulum over each option in turn. The pendulum will vibrate and pull down over the best option, often unexpected as your intuition unconsciously directs the physical pendulum response. **Magical significance:** To discover the source of food intolerance, hold the pendulum in turn over suspect substances. You will experience coldness in your fingers or the pendulum may spiral anti-clockwise or in different directions over a problem substance. Hold it next over different herbs and oil bottles and it will vibrate and pull down over the best remedy. **Divinatory meaning:** Some information you need is maybe deliberately being hidden; continue to probe till you discover the truth. **Zodiac: Empowerment:** My inner world is full of meaning.

A pendulum, a small heavy symmetrical pointed crystal on a chain or cord, is the most portable and valuable of psychic tools.

Indeed pendulums can help us to tune into what has not yet happened by allowing us to sense and see or hear knowledge not yet accessible to the logical mind, and by amplifying our innate but often unrecognized gift to see what is just over the horizon.

But the pendulum has many practical uses in the everyday world to alert you to the unconscious signals that your inner radar has picked up.

Use your pendulum to trace an electrical fault, a blockage in a pipe from above ground, the presence of a ghost, the right direction back to the car if you are lost on a walk, or by holding the pendulum over a map to discover the best location for a holiday or a new home or where a lost pet might be.

Type: Clear quartz infused with gold and platinum.

Colours: Bright yellow and, like all the aura quartzes, with an unmistakable iridescent gleam.

Availability: Relatively rare and quite expensive but worth obtaining even a small piece.

Physical benefits: Crystalline sunshine, this form of aura quartz is seen as powerfully positive for removing toxins; helpful for any digestive problems and especially healing for pancreas, liver, spleen, and gall bladder; useful for constipation, the nervous system, for Seasonal Affective Disorder and for absorption of Vitamins A, D and E.

Emotional healing: One of the best anti-depression crystals; give a sunshine aura pendant to anyone who is naturally pessimistic or over-serious; releases the inner child and gives permission to have fun.

Chakra: Solar Plexus.

Sunshine Aura Quartz

Candle colour: Gold. **Fragrances**: Copal, frankincense, marigold, orange, rosemary. **Practical uses**: Place sunshine aura quartz in any naturally dark or gloomy rooms and also in your home crystal centre or in a layout, to fill your home and all who enter with sunshine and joy, even in winter; excellent if you live in a land where the winters are long and the days dark for several months. **Workplace**: A small golden sunshine aura cluster in your workspace or the centre of a home work area attracts success and fulfillment in the way you most want and need; hold when you feel exhausted or have received a setback or an unenthusiastic response to a proposal; place it on any proposals, submissions or study essays or projects to make your work stand out. **Magical significance**: An uplifting crystal in the centre of any healing crystal layout; set on a patient's or your own Solar Plexus in the centre of your upper stomach; surround the body with sparkling citrine or sunstone to clear any blockages or fears and to infuse the whole system with health and energy. **Divinatory meaning**: Look on the positive, bright side of any situation as there are improvements coming into your life soon; trust all will be well, for it will be. **Zodiac**: Leo. **Empowerment**: I am filled with the light of hope.

Though sunshine aura quartz usually refers to the golden-yellow kind, there are variants that are also called sunshine aura, all of which are characterized by a light glow as if illuminated by sunlight.

Aurora quartz is a lighter, more rainbow version of titanium aura and is created when titanium particles bombard the quartz in a particular way.

An orange-gold variety, sometimes called imperial gold sunshine aura, is created from bonding of titanium and silver on to clear quartz.

Purple sunshine aura quartz is made from gold, platinum and magnesium bonded on quartz. But whatever its colour or composition, sunshine aura lights up a room and brings natural joy and spontaneity, as well as healing old hurts and traumas and overcoming a sense of disappointment with life or bitterness at lack of opportunities; keep a cluster on the buffet table at social gatherings to encourage laughter and positive fun and diminish the desire to be clever at the expense of others.

Type: Varies according to the crystal composition, but always polished.

Colours: Many colours, transparent or semi-transparent such as amethyst or clear quartz with inclusions, translucent and gleaming such as selenite or tiger's eye and opaque patterned ones like jasper.

Availability: Common.

Physical benefits: Could help fertility, both totally natural and medical intervention such as IVF, womb, cervix and ovaries, breasts, hormones, PMS and menstrual cycles, pregnancy and birth, growth issues at any age.

Emotional healing: Any crystal egg, particularly rose quartz or jade, relieves intense anxiety about conceiving a baby; encourages single people or couples planning to adopt or foster to work through any doubts.

Chakra: Sacral.

Crystal Eggs

Candle colour: Silver. **Fragrances:** Almond, apple blossom, lavender, neroli, rose. **Practical uses:** Give miniature eggs as party, birthday or Christmas gifts or to say thank you; choose a larger egg every year as a birthday gift for a godchild, friend or relative's child whose life you share. **Workplace:** A clear quartz egg or a gleaming one draws opportunities and success in ventures that need time and input to reach fruition; if you are frustrated, hold the egg and remind yourself of your goal and that you have the power to win through. **Magical significance:** Buy nine miniature eggs of different kinds that seem right for you; keep them in a small bag. Each morning pick an egg by touch to act as luck-bringer for the day. If you keep picking the same egg, hold it in your hands, close your eyes and the reason for the choice will become clear. **Divinatory meaning:** A period of gradual growth, but there are no short cuts; you may need to put in extra effort temporarily. **Zodiac:** Cancer. **Empowerment:** I have the seeds of success within.

All crystal eggs are symbols and attracters of abundance, good luck, creativity and fertility. Build up a collection as the egg formation releases individual crystal energies steadily and over a long period of time.

Keep smaller eggs in an ornamental basket, one for each existing family member; when someone moves away give them their egg to transfer family love to the new home.

However, the main use of crystal eggs is in healing: the pointed end draws pain from the body; use the flat surfaces for gentle massage. Eggs have been adopted in Reiki, acupressure, shiatsu and reflexology practice.

Hold the egg between thumb and fingers in either hand; let the hand move as it wants a few centimetres away, all over the head and body, to clear any blockages in your energy field. We all have the innate ability to heal the self and loved ones in this way.

Crystal Eggs

Augite

Type: Silicate, pyroxene, contains calcium, magnesium, iron, titanium and aluminium.

Colours: Greenish black to black, dark green, brownish green, occasionally purplish brown.

Availability: Relatively rare in polished crystals.

Physical benefits: Reported to help calcium deficiency, teeth, bones, brittle bones, osteoporosis, mending fractures.

Emotional healing: For anyone afraid of change to routine or of going to different places and meeting new people.

Chakra: Root.

Candle colour: Dark green. **Fragrances:** Basil, tarragon. **Practical uses:** Eases all transitions, whether career changes or a new relationship. **Workplace:** A crystal to be in the right place at the right time. **Magical significance:** If you have struggled with any form of spiritual work, augite eases the transition from the everyday world. **Divinatory meaning:** Only you can decide whether to stay where you are or take a leap. **Zodiac:** Capricorn. **Empowerment:** I do not need to be stuck in this situation.

Augite is a useful addition to any crystal collection at a time when you feel ready for changes or know they are inevitable but are clinging to the old. Buy as brown if others are causing complications because of their desire to keep you or a situation safe for them and predictable. Black is dynamic and removes redundant guilt or responsibility and encourages translating plans into action. Green emphasizaes the growth element in change and brings enthusiasm for the future. Purple is for spiritual awakening and may offer unexpected proof of the psychic world in everyday life.

Cordierite

Type: Cyclosilicate, magnesium aluminium silicate; gemstone variety called iolite (p.377).

Colours: Blue, greenish, yellowish, grey or brown, colourless, purplish blue in gemstone form.

Availability: Less common in natural form than as iolite.

Physical benefits: May help with cholesterol, effective processing of fats within body, liver regeneration, liver transplants, reduce the effects of alcohol on body.

Emotional healing: Eases obsessive-compulsive disorder, over-obsession with cleanliness and terror of germs or contamination of food or clothing.

Chakra: Sacral and Throat.

Candle colour: Blue. **Fragrances:** Acacia, lavender. **Practical uses:** A living within your means and anti-debt mineral; keep a chunk of natural cordierite where you deal with your finances. **Workplace:** Steadies those who have to make fast decisions. **Magical significance:** Slows emerging psychic awareness in adults new to spirituality who are afraid of their spontaneous premonitions. **Divinatory meaning:** Balance what is known with your own gut feelings and intuitions, and you should get the right answer as to whether to trust a person. **Zodiac:** Libra. **Empowerment:** I can balance reason and intuition.

Cordierite in its natural form encourages independence within close relationships; relaxes an over-possessive or controlling partner. Good in the home for children who are over-reliant on siblings for companionship, and for only children to make friends outside the home. Use to make changes slowly to your career or home circumstances if you have responsibilities or expectations you need to fulfil; helpful if you want to end a long-term relationship with the minimum of hurt. When you do finally leave, do not take your cordierite with you but bury it.

Fluoroapatite

Type: Fluorinated calcium phosphate, most common source of fluoride in the environment and a major component of apatite.

Colours: Green, blue, purple, pink, yellow, brown, colourless, quite glassy.

Availability: Relatively rare in this form.

Physical benefits: Said to help with teeth, gums, bones, brittle bones, fluid and blood sugar imbalances, nausea, stomach acidity and ulcers, IBS, removal of toxins.

Emotional healing: Reduces personal excessive irritability and inappropriate anger, and insulates others from the effects of living with a volatile person situation.

Chakra: Sacral and Solar Plexus.

Candle colour: Yellow green. **Fragrances:** Moss. **Practical uses:** A natural room cleanser that ensures a gentle circulation of *ch'i* life force. **Workplace:** Fluoroapatite eases changes such as management changes. **Magical significance:** Moves situations on that are holding you back. Hold fluoroapatite each morning in the open air and say, "May the winds of change blow gently into my life." at least once weekly. **Divinatory meaning:** Do not be pressurized into agreeing to changes if the time is not right for you. **Zodiac:** Pisces. **Empowerment:** I do not resist what must necessarily move forward.

Gyrolite

Type: Phyllosilicate, hydrated calcium silicate hydroxide.

Colours: White, colourless, green and brown.

Availability: Obtainable from specialist mineral stores and online.

Physical benefits: Gyrolite is claimed to bring balance to the body, especially the spine and the skeletal system.

Emotional healing: Reduces excessive introspection and introversion where people shut themselves away from company; removes the secrecy from addictions and so makes them more amenable to treatment.

Chakra: Root.

Candle colour: Brown. **Fragrances:** Fennel, fern, lavender, lemon verbena, neroli. **Practical uses:** An excellent crystal for people who are shy. **Workplace:** Gyrolite brings personal stability and self-confidence when dealing with unpredictable people; good for medical staff working with patients with personality disorders. **Magical significance:** Empowers other crystals; keep some with your healing crystal set. **Divinatory meaning:** Avoid allowing others to involve you in a crisis they have exaggerated out of all proportion. **Zodiac:** Virgo. **Empowerment:** There is nothing to worry about.

Though most often found as part of the apatite mineral, fluoroapatite is a worthwhile mineral to acquire for healing and enabling your life to find its natural rhythms and direction.

If you are someone who either likes to do everything by the clock and the rules or conversely Have fluoroapatite if you are a new parent or are living with a new partner and are anxious to get everything right; helps you to trust your own instincts as to what matters in terms of routine and boundaries.

Gyrolite is a balancing mineral in every aspect of life as well as within the body and mind; keep a small piece in a cloth bag with you if you have a hectic day ahead. As a meditation crystal, it connects with ancient wisdom; whatever your field of expertise you may afterwards find you know new information without consciously learning it. A crystal of quiet strength, have it near when you need to say no; good for the willpower to stick to rules you established; if teenagers are pressurizing you to go to places you are uncertain about, touch your gyrolite, take a deep breath and refuse to be moved.

Type: Lithium aluminium silicate, yellow kind called triphane, pink or lilac gemstone variety kunzite (p.57), green gemstone variety hiddenite (p.273).

Colours: Colourless, white, grey or pink (non-gemstone).

Availability: More common as kunzite.

Physical benefits: Reported to help epilepsy, sensory-organ problems particularly with hearing and blurred vision; sciatica, neuralgia, trapped nerves, joint problems, bones, spinal cord; good to carry or wear during the weeks before any fertility investigations or treatment, especially if low sperm count is a problem; thrush, chlamydia, herpes and any sexually-related conditions.

Emotional healing: Clear, grey or white spodumene reduces the power of addictions, particularly gambling, shopaholic tendencies and running up debt for social reasons rather than out of need, also alcohol abuse.

Chakra: Crown.

Spodumene

Candle colour: Grey. **Fragrances:** Frankincense, lavender, musk, mimosa, vetivert. **Practical uses:** In any form, spodumene assists house clearing, whether for a spring or clutter clear, home moving or to remove memories of someone who has moved out; brings an air of freshness and purity and new optimism. **Workplace:** A bowl of ice-clear or white spodumene crystal chips in your workspace raises the level of honesty and integrity and clears away secrecy and uncertainty; good for new positive beginnings after someone has left suddenly under unpleasant circumstances or there have been redundancies and there are worries about the new structure. **Magical significance:** The grey form, particularly found as crystals, can be carried or worn to aid any form of spirituality where there are hidden aspects that become better understood with deeper study; particularly helpful for the study of the Kabbalah or Qabala and for learning trance mediumship. **Divinatory meaning:** There is something eluding you but you may have to wait a few weeks until the missing link appears spontaneously. **Zodiac:** Aquarius. **Empowerment:** I understand my weaknesses as well as strengths.

Spodumene is the mineral name. Spodumene in its natural opaque form is a major source of lithium and it is better known in jewellery and healing as the more colourful kunzite or hiddenite. However, clear, white or grey spodumene crystals are regarded by many healers and crystal practitioners as of an even higher spiritual vibrational level than kunzite.

Passed in spirals over the body and the aura energy field, clear spodumene removes lingering sad memories, anxieties about past mistakes or failures and any negative input from others, to restore energy, optimism and a sense of purpose.

Spodumene is good for seeing a task through when enthusiasm wanes, particularly for people who are constantly starting projects as or taking up new interests and abandoning them when difficulties or boredom set in. Wear or carry grey spodumene to set up protection round yourself if someone tries to dominate or control you, whether through manipulation or bullying.

Wear spodumene for giving yourself emotional space if you are constantly in the company of others.

Type: Varies according to crystal: some pyramids are naturally formed, for example apophyllite, clear quartz or amethyst.

Colours: Vary from clear to totally opaque pyramids, sometimes engraved with Egyptian hieroglyphs.

Availability: Common.

Physical benefits: Said to be an all-healer, particularly in the squat shape of the ancient pyramid of King Cheops at Giza near Cairo, built around 2500 BC. It is believed that holding a mini one will energize or regenerate any aspect of health; using amethyst elixir may assist with bites, stings, headaches, allergies and the womb to relieve menstrual pain or cramps; send absent healing through a natural pyramid.

Emotional healing: An amethyst pyramid in the bedroom of an adult or child will reduce nightmares and night terrors; heals during sleep traumas, daytime phobias or obsessions. The shape amplifies the natural soothing powers of amethyst.

Chakra: Brow and Crown.

Crystal Pyramids

Candle colour: Purple. **Fragrances:** Copal, cyphi, frankincense, myrrh, sandalwood. **Practical uses:** A crystal pyramid in the home, whether natural as part of a cluster or cut and polished, continuously diffuses health, healing and tranquillity through the home; calms over-active children and teenagers and inter-generational squabbling; works wonders for wilting plants. **Workplace:** You need three small squat pyramids, clear quartz to energize, a citrine or red jasper to attract success and a rose quartz or amethyst to calm. Place them in a triangle and hold the one whose powers you need most at any moment. **Magical significance:** The Cheops pyramid was discovered to have strong psychic energies that exist even in miniature versions; hold or meditate with a pyramid to increase clairvoyance, telepathy, out-of-body travel, prophecy and lucid dreaming. **Divinatory meaning:** Do not be too sceptical about a series of seeming coincidences as they are signs you should be more aware of what is going on around you. **Zodiac:** Scorpio and Aquarius. **Empowerment:** I do not dismiss what I cannot explain.

The geometry of the pyramid has from its early creation been recognized as generating healing powers that can be adapted for everyday living.

Instead of having a power nap, hold a small pyramid between your hands and slowly relax so that your rigid personal boundaries begin to melt and your aura joins that of the pyramid.

Keep a small squat pyramid with your fruit and vegetables and next to milk in the fridge for extra freshness and longer shelf-life.

Add clear quartz pyramid elixir to fish tanks for healthier fish and to your own bath water for energy (use rose quartz to relax).

Place a pyramid directly beneath a bed or chair pointing towards a source of a pain for rapid and ongoing relief; give a jade or rose quartz pyramid to hyperactive children and a lapis or sodalite pyramid to children with communication difficulties.

Anglesite

Type: Sulphate/barite, lead sulphate.

Colours: Yellow, colourless, white, pale grey, blue and green; darker grey if impure.

Availability: Found in some specialist crystal stores and online, very beautiful but must be handled with care.

Physical healing: Said to be good for circulation, nerve endings and nervous system, infections, skin conditions, digestion, fevers and joint inflammation, detoxifying the body, speeding wound healing, problems of ageing; use only indirectly as lead and sulphur are toxic.

Emotional healing: Transforms anger and grief over bereavement, abuse or injustice into a desire to help others.

Chakra: Root and Heart.

Candle colour: Yellow. **Fragrances:** Chamomile, copal, lavender, sweetgrass, vervain. **Practical uses:** Place with any tangible symbol of any dreams; leave overnight to give you the determination to fulfil your dreams and to fill the symbols or creations with good fortune. **Workplace:** Can act as a focus for moving your workplace; good for home-based industries and for using technology to work from home. **Magical significance:** For connecting in a gentle, loving way with deceased relatives; brings contact through healing dreams or signs in the everyday world. **Divinatory meaning:** Now is the time for doing and not dreaming. **Zodiac:** Aries. **Empowerment:** Dreams do come true.

Anglesite is a very spiritual crystal which opens up channels of mediumship for beginners and enables more advanced mediums to work with deeper trance techniques; helpful for spirit rescue when a ghost is stuck in a house. Light a white candle to shine on the anglesite, sprinkle three circles of salt round it, ask that the spirit departs to the light where loved ones are waiting and blow out the candle. **WARNING:** Do not ingest or use in direct elixir, and wash your hands after use. Keep away from dogs and pets.

Datolite

Type: Calcium boron silicate hydroxide.

Colours: White, colourless sometimes with green tinge, yellowish, pink-red, reddish, grey, brown and green.

Availability: Relatively rare.

Physical benefits: Rumoured to help diabetes, hypoglycaemia, memory loss after accidents, strokes or degenerative brain conditions such as Alzheimer's and senile dementia, especially early-onset, brain damage at any age.

Emotional healing: Datolite builds up personal power and initiative to counteract excessive dependency on others for company.

Chakra: Solar Plexus.

Candle colour: White and yellow. **Fragrances:** Orange, peach. **Practical uses:** Hold when things are chaotic to recall where you left things like car keys and to focus your mind so you deal with priorities; buy a piece for forgetful people who are constantly missing appointments and losing things. **Workplace:** Datolite brings more rapid and efficient learning of complicated data. **Magical significance:** Hold by candlelight to retrieve ancient wisdom from the collective treasury of human knowledge. **Divinatory meaning:** Be clear about what is being asked of you. **Zodiac:** Gemini. **Empowerment:** I know what I am capable of.

A crystal that reduces free-floating worry and anxiety to specific manageable proportions; good for problem-solving in a logical, hands-on way, cutting through unnecessary words and agenda in business meetings. Keep it with any divinatory tools to avoid over-reliance on specific techniques and tools that may block natural intuition. Encourages a sense of adventure; enables us to think outside the box and avoid self-defeating limitations on what is possible. Take yellow or white to competitions where fast, logical thinking is required or for mind-eye coordination.

Enstatite

Type: Silicate/pyroxene, magnesium silicate.

Colours: Green, some green gem quality called chrome enstatite, pale green, yellowish brown, orangey brown, light and dark brown, pale yellow, white, colourless, grey.

Availability: Relatively rare.

Physical benefits: May be helpful after broken or bruised limbs, an accident or car crash where there are multiple internal and external injuries, short-term memory loss after concussion, head injury, brain operation or stroke, heart conditions, and transplants involving more than one organ.

Emotional healing: Brings the courage to say what must be said; especially good of silence is causing long-term trauma.

Chakra: Heart.

Candle colour: Green. **Fragrances:** Cloves, juniper, tea tree. **Practical uses:** Enstatite will break a run of bad luck if worn or carried daily in a small bag; within a week or two lucky coincidences and opportunities will start to occur that will continue to increase. **Workplace:** The public speaker's crystal. **Magical significance:** Wear as protection against hexes, ill wishing, envy and jealousy; leave overnight if you have a nasty ghost or poltergeist in your home. **Divinatory meaning:** You may feel alone and unable to share your worries; contact an old friend or family member and you will discover they are still there for you. **Zodiac:** Aries. **Empowerment:** I feel lucky.

This crystal entry concentrates on unique properties to enstatite that are not found so strongly in enstatite with diopside (p.189), especially its function as a gem. Enstatite is often called the stone of chivalry and associated with high standards of ethics and an awareness of the need to protect the vulnerable; wear or carry it if you are fighting a local environmental threat or a cut to public services. It is both soothing and empowering if you are facing an uphill struggle or a fight for the custody of children or property after divorce; gives you the courage to fight – and triumph.

Iolite/Water Sapphire

Type: Silicate/cyclosilicate, gem version of cordierite.

Colours: Pale blue/purple/purplish blue.

Availability: Found in specialist crystal stores and online.

Physical benefits: Could assist eyesight, migraines and headaches, disorientation and dizziness, Meniere's disease; prevents insomnia, nightmares or sleep disturbances.

Emotional healing: Restores a sense of perspective to those who feel they are jinxed; for anyone with chaotic lives to start to bring order in small practical ways.

Chakra: Throat and Brow.

Candle colour: Violet. **Fragrances:** Hyacinth, lavender, lilac, magnolia, violet. **Practical uses:** Place in living area if sibling rivalry or the presence of a new step-parent is causing a child to feel excluded. **Workplace:** Wear to learn the unspoken rules and underlying factions in a new workplace and to make a role for yourself. **Magical significance:** Is helpful if you are exploring goddess energies. **Divinatory meaning:** An alternative viewpoint you have always rejected suddenly makes sense. **Zodiac:** Cancer. **Empowerment:** I am on track again.

Iolite is used as an amulet to guide travellers safely home; a piece of iolite jewellery or a tumblestone in a pouch is an ideal farewell gift for gap-year students or emigrating family members. Wear to lessen alcohol misuse.

A good crystal if family members have over-high expectations of you or you are in a career you were expected to adopt because of family connections; assists you to see clearly what *you* want, which may be what you have or that you need to express your gifts and lifestyle in a more independent way.

Stichtite

Type: Carbonate.

Colours: Green, greenish-yellow, purple to pink shades.

Availability: Rare, but available from Internet stores.

Physical benefits: May assist with physical problems that may have manifested themselves because of emotional issue such as eating disorders, high blood pressure and headaches.

Emotional healing: Stichtite is a beautiful calming and gentle stone. It will ease your worries and heal you gently from within.

Chakra: Heart.

Candle colour: Purple. **Fragrances:** Basil, Chamomile, Cherry Blossom, Lavender, Rose. **Practical uses:** Place stichtite crystals around your home to improve tranquility. **Workplace:** Hold and focus with it before making presentations as it will assist with clear thinking. **Magical significance:** Use this stone to improve bonds between friends. **Divinatory meaning:** Stichtite says that it is the time to be truthful, not only with oneself but with someone close to us, to help create a more loving and caring relationship. **Zodiac:** Virgo. **Empowerment:** The calmness of my spirit heals my loving energies.

Stichtite is a rare crystal and even rarer in large crystal form, more usually attached in small clusters to other crystals. It is a very feminine stone and teaches about being kind and gentle, to ourselves and to others. Keep near you if you have a tendency to be self-critical. Stichtite also has calming qualities and is excellent when placed throughout the home or office to negative energies. In a family environment, it calms excitable children and promotes loving behaviour towards family members. Use to release blocked energies in the Heart chakra and assist in all emotional issues.

Lepidolite

Type: Silicate, a type of mica, contains varying amounts of lithium.

Colours: Lilac-grey, rose and purple colour range; can be confused with pink mica when pale in colour.

Availability: Becoming more common.

Physical benefits: Believed to assist with nerve-related disorders, joint pain; strengthen immune system.

Emotional healing: Detoxifies emotions, bringing calm and reducing dependency on others for emotional wellbeing; soothing for personality disorders, psychosomatic and psychological illnesses.

Chakra: Heart, Throat, Brow and Crown.

Candle colour: Lilac or Pink. **Fragrances:** Bergamot, lemon verbena. **Practical uses:** Overcomes fears that restrict us from doing what we really want. **Workplace:** Place near electrical equipment around the office or loud equipment to clear electromagnetic pollution. **Magical significance:** Each lepidolite crystal is, according to tradition, believed to have a keeper who offers protection to the owner of the stone. **Divinatory meaning:** Take a leap of faith. There are no certainties but you gain nothing by waiting. **Zodiac:** Capricorn and Aquarius **Empowerment:** I do not need reassurance from others.

Lepidolite has soft nurturing energies that connect us to our inner being and helps us love ourselves. Meditating daily with it helps to resolve long-standing weight issues, alcohol dependency, smoking or drugs where these act to mask unhappiness; wearing it encourages independence from all forms of neediness. Assists older people not to live in the past. A good crystal if you obsess about trivialities, worry excessively about cleanliness in the home and germs and hate staying away from home. Hold a lepidolite sphere or egg regularly if you are anxious about death or childbirth.

Type: Quartz, most usually in clear quartz, identified by a three-sided or six-sided indented shape located on the crystal surface.

Colours: Depends on the kind of quartz crystal but clear enough for you to see, as well as feel, the indentation markings.

Availability: Rare.

Physical benefits: Hold before any healing to open your healing powers, especially if you want help from the angels or your healing guides; said to be beneficial for any blockages or narrowing of arteries, veins or passages within the body; for hard-to-diagnose or -treat illnesses, especially if you are searching for a new treatment or specialist.

Emotional healing: Good for children or young people locked in their minds, whether because of a major communication disorder or trauma; putting their fingers on the key will slowly open pathways.

Chakra: Crown.

Key Quartz Crystal

Candle colour: White or natural beeswax. **Fragrances:** Bergamot, lily, lotus, sagebrush. **Practical uses:** The most powerful and harmonizing of all worry stones. Place both index fingers on the indentation, close your eyes and start worrying consciously; before long you will run out of worries and feel totally relaxed; smudge the crystal after intense use with an incense stick in your favourite fragrance by wafting it in circles over the key crystal. **Workplace:** A missing-link crystal which can be used for answering any questions that puzzle you. Touch the indentation before surfing on the Internet for hard-to-find information or telephoning or mailing the elusive person. **Magical significance:** The key to missing links, whether locating an item or animal that is missing or a person you need to contact but for whom you have no address; use for establishing other-worldly links, particularly as a gateway to past lives; in each case touch the indentation with closed eyes; picture a crystal door opening to wherever you want to be or whoever you want to see. **Divinatory meaning:** The key to your future is available but it may take a lot of seeking an effort to find, so persevere. **Zodiac:** Sagittarius. **Empowerment:** I hold the key within myself.

Key crystals are one of the most magical of all the teaching quartz crystals and are sometimes counted as a master crystal.

The ideal is when the indentation, which can be anywhere on the crystal, narrows as it goes within the crystal and may end as a point within the crystal, looking like a key. But even if yours is less defined, it will work as well. If you can afford only one of the special quartz crystals, this is a

good choice as it opens all kinds of doors to both spiritual knowledge and everyday opportunities.

The crystal will teach you, so just relax and let the crystal open those doors safely and pleasurably.

A truth-seeker; place the indentation face-down on any correspondence you receive that you feel may not be entirely honest or may have a hidden agenda; use also on obscure material you need to learn or explain to others.

Type: Unusual form of crystal quartz, matt, frosted with distinctive horizontal striations running up at least one side.

Colours: Usually colourless but may be pink, have a reddish glow or be smoky.

Availability: Rare.

Physical benefits: Lemurian seed crystals are believed to be useful for whole-body healing and bringing relief or improving quality of life with serious or terminal illnesses, soothing for all chronic conditions, reducing pain and strengthening the body's immune system to fight back; a crystal associated with small miracles, it is often used with coma patients; a popular Reiki tool.

Emotional healing: When there is not much to hope for, a lemurian wand brings light to penetrate deepest spiritual darkness; soothes those who have witnessed murder, terrorism, war or violent crimes; good for post-traumatic stress syndrome.

Chakra: Crown.

Lemurian Seed Crystal

Candle colour: White. **Fragrances:** Copal, frankincense, lily, lotus, sandalwood. **Practical uses:** Because of their deeply spiritual nature, lemurian seed crystals, if held when things are bad, strengthen anyone struggling to care for a sick or disabled relative who must carry on; also to fight against personal chronic illness or disability. **Workplace:** Lemurian crystals are associated with charity and peace initiatives; each crystal is said to be connected with other lemurian crystals, wherever they are in the world. Keep one with you if you work for a charity in the field or in fundraising or administration or for any peace-keeping organizations, to spread the influence and practical effects of your work. **Magical significance:** Place a striated side in the centre of your brow just above your eyes to experience images of ancient lost worlds and receive wise words in your mind from indigenous spiritual traditions such as the Native North Americans. Alternatively, stroke striations with the index finger of the hand you do not write with to enter into a light trance. **Divinatory meaning:** There is more to life than work and chores; explore your own spirituality in a way that appeals to you to enrich your daily world. **Zodiac:** Aquarius. **Empowerment:** I reach out to others in my spiritual searching.

Lemurian crystal quartz points come from Brazil and grow in beds of sand; unusually for quartz points, they are not attached to any cluster.

As the name suggests, lemurian seed crystals are associated with the legendary lost land of Lemuria in the southern Pacific, between America and Asia/Australia, which is believed to have existed 14,000 years ago. Lemuria was said to be the source of the wisdom of indigenous peoples, for example the cultures of Native North America and that of the Australian Aboriginal people.

Legend has it that the holy people or the prophets of the Lemurian culture had foreknowledge of the Flood and began to store information in crystals.

These crystals were taken deep within the earth. Lemurian crystals were planted as seeds in the earth at this time. For this reason, any user is believed to draw power from ancient healing wisdom.

Pass a lemurian wand around you in a circle to enclose yourself in protective light. Place one in the centre of a healing grid to connect in a web with other earth healers.

Columbite-Tantalite

Type: Iron manganese tantalum niobium oxide.

Colours: Dark black, iron black to dark brown or reddish brown, metallic to resinous. Manganese rich tantalite can be brown and translucent.

Availability: Rare.

Physical benefits: Said to help if a method of healing is no longer working effectively. Hold your medication or your hands close to the crystal for a minute or two everyday.

Emotional healing: Prevents becoming or remaining a victim of past or present abuse.

Chakra: Solar Plexus.

Candle colour: Grey. **Fragrances**: Clary sage, grapefruit, lemon, lemongrass, lime. **Practical uses:** Put near suitcases and travel documents to prevent loss while travelling. **Workplace:** A positive workplace mineral in your workspace to overcome lethargy if a task seems endless. **Magical significance:** Very protective against energy vampires who suck out your energies; place the mineral under the table. **Divinatory meaning:** You may need to change your tactics if one particular person is taking up too much of your time with their needs and problems. **Zodiac:** Aries. **Empowerment:** I will not take on unnecessary burdens.

Tantalite and columbite are separate minerals within the same series, containing the same elements but with varying proportions. .

Some crystal practitioners keep their columbite-tantalite with them while they exercise and get ready for the day, to allow the balancing energies to flow in and round the body as it is physically awakened. Do not ingest the stone.

Hemimorphite

Type: Silicate/sorosilicate (zinc silicate).

Colours: Electric blue, green-blue, grey, brown, white, colourless.

Availability: Found in specialist crystal stores and online.

Physical benefits: Reported to be good for blood disorders, cells, ulcers, headaches, hormonal imbalances, pain relief.

Emotional healing: Reduces unwise or obsessional attachments whether to an impossible love, risk-taking or the inability to give others space for independent thought and action.

Chakra: Crown, Brow and Throat.

Candle colour: Blue or white. **Fragrances**: Almond, anise, pine, poppy, sandalwood. **Practical uses:** For regaining health after a long illness. **Workplace:** Assists with self-expression and creativity, so beneficial to anyone wishing to communicate creatively. **Magical significance:** A very lucky charm for you to be in the right place at the right time and to say the right things to the right people. **Divinatory meaning:** You could sell ice cream at the North Pole right now; capitalize on your entrepreneurial qualities and ask for what you want. **Zodiac:** Libra. **Empowerment:** I have what I need.

Hemimorphite (or Buddha stone) crystallizes in two forms, one as a glassy clear or white bladed crystal, the other forming a blue-green botryoidal (grape-like) cluster. This name is due to the crystals creating different terminations at either end. The more this crystal is handled and worked with, the more potent its energies become. As a small cluster, hemimorphite provides a central focus for a group healing circle, particularly for healing people or animals that are not present. Use the stone if you need to charm someone who has taken an irrational dislike to you.

Type: Quartz-based, one or more of smoky or clear quartz (p.122 and p.132), citrine (p.89) or less commonly amethyst or ametrine (p.212 and p.311); looks like many smaller crystals randomly stuck together; also called skeletal quartz.

Colours: Depends on the composition but crystals can be mixed; a characteristically smoked effect.

Availability: Obtainable from specialist crystal stores and online.

Physical benefits: Said to assist with problems concerning the pineal gland, pituitary gland, brain disorders (particularly after a stroke or other brain malfunction), skeleton, bones, neurons and all connective major nerves and tissues; believed to help with whole-body healing, illnesses where treatment has been delayed because of fear.

Emotional healing: Releases the ability to make a big leap and take a chance on life; allows you to try what you have been told *people like you* could not achieve; for schizophrenia and for gradually reducing harmful drugs.

Chakra: Crown.

Elestial Quartz Crystals

Candle colour: White. **Fragrances:** Copal, frankincense, lily, lotus, myrrh. **Practical uses:** A crystal to form a centrepiece, elestial crystals release healing and empowering energies that give any home, from bedsit to palace, a sense of sanctity, harmony and light. **Workplace:** A small elestial makes people kinder, more willing to cooperate; reduces complaints inside the workplace and from customers; for very commercially and target driven workplaces, elestials put the people factor back. **Magical significance:** A master crystal with particularly powerful geometric formations, even a small elestial crystal empowers other crystals and healing or divinatory tools; connects with archangel energies, even if you are new to spirituality. **Divinatory meaning:** A magical time even for cynics when people react with unusual friendliness and you can relax your guard. **Zodiac:** Leo. **Empowerment:** Life can be good and people kind.

Make an elestial elixir to sprinkle around your home or workplace and to splash on your chakras to spread happiness and healing within yourself and where you live and work; put six small elestials round the body and relax for ten minutes to remove toxins and infuse a sense of well-being and sunshine.

Elestial crystals often have etchings on the faces that are believed to hold the key to ancient wisdom; run your fingers along them and allow words to come (keep a notebook handy): good in Reiki or any form of crystal healing, but only with clients seeking change and not for the very emotionally unstable without prior healing work.

For soul-to-soul connection with your partner both should touch the crystal with one hand and put the other on their own heart, and talk from the heart.

Type: Iron pyrites/marcasite with quartz (pp.180, 182).

Colours: Golden.

Availability: Rare but worth searching out.

Physical benefits: Thought to be beneficial for male genito-urinary system, impotence, low sperm count, hernia, prostate, energizer for men and women, scanty or irregular menstruation; it is believed that this is a stone that, if held in the hand you write with for men and the opposite for women, rebalances the whole system, removing impurities and toxins if you move it slowly up the body, feet to crown, a few centimetres away.

Emotional healing: Brings a sense of certainty of your own worth if you have always been told you are wrong or stupid; fills the whole self with a sense of abundance and self-containment if you worry about being left alone and so stay in an unsatisfactory relationship.

Chakra: Root and Solar Plexus.

Keyiapo Stone

Candle colour: Gold. **Fragrances:** Copal, dragon's blood, frankincense, galbanum. **Practical uses:** Keyiapo is one of the most protective stones against internal fears and free-floating anxieties that can spoil moments of leisure and disturb sleep. Hold your stone day or night if you wake and start fretting; allow the golden sparkling energies to transform doubts and fears into positive thoughts and happy memories. **Workplace:** The stone of gold that attracts natural abundance, fulfilment and golden opportunities so you can make your own fortune; good for independent enterprises and for making money from hobbies or by speculation; place your golden stone on your lottery form or a competition entry to inspire you before choosing the numbers or answering the questions. **Magical significance:** Hold your keyiapo stone in open cupped hands so gold candlelight shines on it; focus on it until your eyes are tired, then close them; picture the golden Akashic records, the books that are said to contain all knowledge of past, present and future; ask a question and you will see in your mind the book open at the answer and the way to attain what you desire. **Divinatory meaning:** A golden opportunity seems just out of reach; if you go all-out to reach it there is a good chance, though not certainty, you will succeed. **Zodiac:** Aries. **Empowerment:** I have more than enough for my needs.

Keyiapo stones have returned to the marketplace after they appeared and reappeared during the early 1990s, but are still quite elusive. They are a very powerful healing stone if no other remedy seems to be working, and on a daily level they bring energy and a sense of well-being.

Keep one in your bedroom if you are disturbed by nasty paranormal dreams and any unfriendly energy will entirely melt away from the whole house.

Unlike other stones such as boji, keyiapo stones work with just one stone that resembles a golden cluster. However, some practitioners do use a boji stone or another of the metaphysical concretion stones with their keyiapo stone for an extra boost of power or healing.

Women who wish to conceive an infant should hold the golden stone for a few minutes every night before lovemaking.

Hackmanite

Type: Tectosilicate, rare form of sodalite (p. 246).

Colours: From colourless, light pink, red, green, blue or purple to intense blue or deep purple.

Availability: Relatively rare.

Physical benefits: Claimed to be good for temporary rapid relief of menopausal hot flushes, racing pulse or heart.

Emotional healing: Called the chameleon crystal, excellent for people who are constantly getting into trouble through over-exuberance or inability to read social signals, to adapt to the reality of daily living.

Chakra: Brow.

Candle colour: Pink. **Fragrances:** Almond blossom, anise, ylang ylang. **Practical uses:** Wear to ease any personality clashes in communal living, whether at a conference or if you share a house. **Workplace:** Wear if you work irregular shift patterns or travel frequently between time zones, to rebalance your inner clock a. **Magical significance:** Enables you to see ghosts and family ancestors. **Divinatory meaning:** You may not know where you are with a person constantly changing their mind; talk privately to reveal true intentions. **Zodiac:** Gemini. **Empowerment:** I can easily adapt to different life challenges.

Hackmanite is a wonder of nature and its tenebrescence was first noticed in 1896 in Greenland by L.C. Boergstroem, when the pink colour of some newly exposed sodalite from Greenland rapidly became colourless when exposed to sunlight. Then, when it was left in the dark, the vibrant colour slowly returned.

This chameleon effect makes hackmanite a perfect charm for all short-term changes. It also relaxes you if you tend to stay in the background at work.

Haematite Botryoidal

Type: Iron oxide, grape-like masses; in rarer kind called kidney ore, red and looks like animal kidneys.

Colours: Silver, metallic grey, black, bluish, red, reddish brown; iridescent as specular rainbow haematite.

Availability: Relatively common.

Physical benefits: Thought to help with blood, circulation and absorption of iron, internal organs, major surgery, transplants and transfusions, haemorrhoids, hernia, male genitalia, muscle weakness, fractures, sunburn, spine, MS.

Emotional healing: Dissolves negative thinking and fears about future; assists men who hate their body.

Chakra: Root.

Candle colour: Silver. **Fragrances:** Allspice, basil, dragon's blood, geranium, hibiscus. **Practical uses:** Attracts loyal, likeminded friends. **Workplace:** Draws customers from overseas particularly to manufacturing or craft-based businesses, helps the newly self-employed to be proactive and visible without being aggressive. **Magical significance:** Very small clusters of botryoidal haematite passed through a red candle flame, then buried near entrances and boundaries, create a protective invisible wall. **Divinatory meaning:** You might not have chosen your present allies but cooperation will benefit everyone. **Zodiac:** Aries. **Empowerment:** I attract loyal friends.

Haematite, sometimes spelt hematite, is a magnetic stone with powerful healing and grounding properties. It feels heavier than many other crystals owing to the compact metallic composition. Any haematite clusters stimulate courage; helpful for boys or teenagers in an all-female environment to get in touch with their positive masculine qualities without becoming aggressive. It protects metalworkers, welders and those working with heavy machinery against accidents. Being magnetic, it should not be worn by anyone with a pacemaker or any other implant.

Cumberlandite

Type: Ferrogubbro, a porphyritic igneous rock.

Colours: Brownish black, grey-black with white crystals.

Availability: Rare.

Physical benefits: Could help over-active thyroid, parathyroid glands, restless limbs, excess fidgeting, brain disorders, sympathetic nervous system.

Emotional healing: Gives purpose and structure to the lives of people who cannot focus on a task without being distracted; excellent for counteracting attention-deficit conditions and guiding people who never finish anything.

Chakra: Throat and brow.

Candle colour: White **Fragrances:** Cedar, pine, sagebrush, sweetgrass, vervain. **Practical uses:** Assists dyslexia and anyone with literacy or numeracy problems; good for sorting chaotic financial affairs; encourages tidiness. **Workplace:** For those who teach or communicate ideas and information; encourages honest journalism, programme and film making. **Magical significance:** Calms restless spirits and poltergeist activity; Take a small piece with you to a haunted building to avoid unpleasant surprises. **Divinatory meaning:** You will find a piece of information in an unexpected place in the next few days that will solve a question **Zodiac:** Virgo. **Empowerment:** I will learn something new every day.

Cumberlandite has a unique history and was formed more than 1.5 billion years ago by the force of a small volcanic eruption. In the process, 24 different minerals were combined with molten rock, to become, on cooling, a slightly magnetic iron- and titanium-rich rock. It is the official state rock of Rhode Island, which is the only place in the world where it is found. Cumberlandite, being magnetic, is a good business stone, particularly for opening a new store in an area where there is a lot of competition.

Edenite

Type: Amphibole, sodium calcium magnesium iron aluminium silicate hydroxide.

Colours: Green and translucent to black, dull grey or brown when it resembles petrified wood.

Availability: Rare in healing and metaphysical world, but slowly growing in popularity.

Physical benefits: May help muscle weakness, muscle spasms, heart irregularities, recovery after heart attack.

Emotional healing: Balancing at crisis times when a person discovers they have been living a lie.

Chakra: Heart.

Candle colour: Green. **Fragrances:** Basil, bay, fig, honey, peony. **Practical uses:** Edenite in the home prevents irritability over minor issues and absorbs daily tensions that can escalate into quarrels. **Workplace:** Edenite brings peaceful negotiation of conflicts in one-to-one resolution; e.g. where there are hostages or kidnap victims. **Magical significance:** Use as a focus for calling your own or the deceased relatives of others. **Divinatory meaning:** If you ask for honesty, do not be surprised if you get it. **Zodiac:** Pisces. **Empowerment:** Truth brings freedom from uncertainty.

Like other amphiboles (see amphibole quartz p.325), edenite connects the everyday and spiritual worlds, and is a good family crystal to link together the family ancestors and the living, set with old photographs and mementoes.

Although edenite has not received the hype of many other New Age healing minerals, it is quietly prized by collectors for its ability to keep open channels of honest communication with those people who tend to keep their intentions and feelings to themselves.

Hypersthene

Type: Silicate/inosilicate/pyroxene.

Colours: Brownish green, grey or black, sometimes with silvery brown streaks or swirling bands.

Availability: Relatively common.

Physical benefits: May assist blood disorders particularly leukaemia and anaemia, Hodgkinson's disease, gland and rogue-cell conditions, absorption of minerals and nutrients into the body, gut, large intestines, prostate and ovaries, ME and all forms of chronic exhaustion, muscle weakness, growth problems.

Emotional healing: Overcomes shyness and social awkwardness; express affection and emotions more freely.

Chakra: Root and Solar Plexus.

Candle colour: Silver. **Fragrances:** Almond, basil. **Practical uses:** Hypersthene assists relationships to grow. **Workplace:** Keep a worry stone to combat your own irritability at the inefficiency of others. **Magical significance:** Will enable you to make small but testable predictions in the realms of clairaudience oto hear the exact phrase of deceased loved ones in ways that cannot be imagination. **Divinatory meaning:** You may need to stand up for your rights. **Zodiac:** Sagittarius and Capricorn. **Empowerment:** I respect myself for what I am and not my achievements.

A member of the bronzite family (p.130), this iron-rich mineral (about 50 per cent is iron) is found in igneous and metamorphic rocks as well as in stony and iron meteorites; therefore is considered a transformative mineral, giving the courage, confidence and all important determination to push open doors or opportunities; it encourages a proactive approach to sell your own talents and good qualities, both in the workplace and personally, and not accept second-best.

Neptunite

Type: Potassium, sodium, lithium, iron, manganese, titanium silicate.

Colours: Black to reddish black.

Availability: Relatively rare.

Physical benefits: Said to help eeth, bones, gums, pH balance of acidity and alkalinity in body, absorption of essential minerals, including potassium, speedier wound healing.

Emotional healing: Helpful for those over-involved in the lives of others, who find it difficult to let an adult child grow up or to allow people to sort their own problems.

Chakra: Root and Sacral.

Candle colour: Green. **Fragrances:** Kelp, lemon, lime. **Practical uses:** For all communal and community activities, especially voluntary work. **Workplace:** Neptunite is excellent for a workplace with a rigid hierarchy as it opens up more equal relationships. **Magical significance:** Keep neptunite in the centre of a healing, psychic development or mediumistic training circle to establish and maintain cohesion. **Divinatory meaning:** Join an association or group, as this will give you support on a matter you cannot deal with alone. **Zodiac:** Pisces. **Empowerment:** I welcome the support of others.

Neptunite is named after Neptune, the Roman god of the sea, and, like its namesake, has become a special stone for those born under Pisces; also associated with developing in users the planet's qualities of sensitivity, intuition and hidden potential, and with evolving psychic gifts to explore the unknown and mysterious; a good stone for reducing the hold of any addiction or bad habit that may be adversely affecting your lifestyle or that of a loved one, particularly alcohol abuse groups such as Alcoholics Anonymous.

Flower Jasper

Type: Silicate, microcrystalline quartz, often with organic matter or other minerals as inclusions.

Colours: Cream with varying shades of grey, mauve, pink, red, white, green and yellow swirls, resembling petals or a flower bouquet.

Availability: Obtainable from specialist crystal stores and online, especially as jewellery.

Physical benefits: May be useful to help kidneys and fluid balance in body, glandular disorders, hair, face, bones of skull, white blood cell count.

Emotional healing: A joy-bringer for those who find it hard to let down their guard and have fun.

Chakra: Heart.

Candle colour: Pink. **Fragrances:** Geranium, hyacinth, rose. **Practical uses:** Makes a wonderful betrothal or wedding gift to endow happiness and lasting blessings on a bride. **Workplace:** Brings joy to any over-serious workplace or if working with people with an inflated sense of their own importance. **Magical significance:** Use for practising flower psychometry; hold it to establish a psychic link in order to answer questions clairvoyantly. **Divinatory meaning:** Indulge yourself with something that makes you feel good as a reminder of what you are working for. **Zodiac:** Virgo. **Empowerment:** I welcome the joy of simple pleasures.

Flower jasper is a feel-good crystal that is instantly uplifting and continues to fill you with happiness and serenity even where people are unenthusiastic or cynical; good for assisting people with dyslexia and dyspraxia or excessive clumsiness to overcome their difficulties.

A stone that helps mend a broken heart by increasing self-love and self-worth and that enables a person to become complete in themselves to avoid rushing into another relationship straight after a break-up for the wrong reasons.

Novaculite

Type: Quartzite, rock composed of microcrystalline quartz.

Colours: White to greyish black, cream and black.

Availability: Relatively common.

Physical healing: Reported as helping cuts and wounds, feet, callouses, bunions, nails, skin, fingers, all operations, healing scar tissue.

Emotional healing: A stone for overcoming obsessions, whether obsessive compulsive disorder or lesser compulsions.

Chakra: Root and Solar Plexus.

Candle colour: Grey. **Fragrances:** Lavender, moss. **Practical uses:** Shields you from friends, colleagues and family who drain you. **Workplace:** For cutting through obstacles; touch it when you need to be sharp. **Magical significance:** Use to cut ties with a destructive relationship; cut a piece of thread in which you have tied three knots and slice through them with a sharp piece of novaculite; say, "I cut the ties that bind me from happiness." **Divinatory meaning:** You need to let go of a bad habit that is stopping you from moving on. **Zodiac:** Scorpion and Capricorn. **Empowerment:** I can break free of what holds me back.

The name novaculite comes from the Latin word for razor stone, because of its potential to be sharpened. Indeed, prehistoric Native Americans created weapons and tools from sharpened novaculite.

Many centuries later, French fur trappers who were the first European inhabitants of Arkansas, one of the places where novaculite is found, used novaculite as a whetstone to sharpen knives needed for preparing animal hides.

In healing, novaculite is good for gently lifting depression or conditions resistant to healing.

Type: Silicates, phyllosilicates (sheet silicates), very soft.

Colours: Various, very delicate with shimmer, pink to violet, grey to black, brown, green, purple, red, white, yellow.

Availability: Common.

Physical benefits: Said to assist liver, insomnia, dehydration, digestion, intestines, colds, blood sugar levels; benefit skin by the renewal and hydration of cells; increase strength and stamina; improve memory and concentration.

Emotional healing: An anti-anger and anti-hysteria mineral for people whose life is one constant drama; reduces tendency to binge-eat and the ongoing cycle of feast and famine.

Chakra: Brow.

Mica

Candle colour: Silver. **Fragrances:** Cedarwood, lily, musk, orchid, vanilla. **Practical uses:** Mica balances the earth energies beneath your home if it is hard to relax or conversely you always feel tired in certain rooms; set mica near the centre of your home on a small rock; protective if you live in an earthquake zone. **Workplace:** A piece of mica helps to leave personal problems at home, particularly if you are going through a turbulent emotional time; deters colleagues from over-curiosity about your private life if you wish it to remain private. **Magical significance:** A natural shield against anger, spite and violence, mica keeps nastiness away from your home; bury a piece in the front garden or in a pot by the front door if your area is plagued by noisy or potentially threatening gangs of young people or is near a busy city street. **Divinatory meaning:** Life is out of balance, but matters will naturally right themselves and action now will only make things worse. **Zodiac:** Aquarius. **Empowerment:** I can restore balance to my life.

Mica was known in Ancient Egypt, Greece, Rome and the Aztec world and is in fact a generic name for a group of 37 complex hydrous potassium-aluminum silicate minerals that differ in chemical composition.

Some have strong individual characteristics and distinctive crystal names, for example biotite (p.207), lepidolite (p.378), fuchsite (p.269) and muscovite (p.157), which is the most common form of mica.

However, other less-well-known forms of mica or those which combine more than one mica form,

for example the rare and prized purple lepidolite with pink mica, are sold as natural specimens under the name of mica; all share common properties and often the sparkly finish of the better-known micas.

Mica is a hard-working crystal and very protective against excess energy from phone masts, pylons and the array of electrical appliances in most homes and workplaces; if it seems duller than usual, rest your mica on soil near greenery. It also relieves sleep disturbances and nightmares, especially in children or teenagers who are afraid of ghosts.

Type: Organic, the lining mainly of pearl oysters shells, formed from the nacre or calcium carbonate that forms the shell lining.

Colours: White, cream or brown, black or deep purple, iridescent. The multi-coloured variety is called abalone (p.324).

Availability: Common.

Physical healing: Thought to be useful for skin complaints, allergies or rashes and for relieving fluid retention, preconception health, pregnancy, birth and post-birth recovery, for infantile problems, particularly feeding difficulties, sinuses, colds, influenza, visual disturbances, migraines, epilepsy.

Emotional healing: A consoling but powerful crystal for adults who constantly seek a mother or father figure in personal and professional life and in love, to learn to parent themselves.

Chakra: Sacral.

Mother-of-Pearl

Candle colour: Silver. **Fragrances:** Apple blossom, kelp, lavender, peach, rose. **Practical uses:** Place a small tumblestone on a newborn infant's stomach to help the baby feel protected even when alone in the crib and to cope with maternal separation anxiety. A mother-of-pearl shell or ceiling mobile also protects an infant or small child from occasional inevitable parental irritability. **Workplace:** Wear or carry mother-of-pearl if you work with infants or small children in any capacity; helps a mother to leave her child more easily with a carer, relative or childcare and return to work, especially if the child took a long time to conceive or was very ill in infancy. **Magical significance:** Mother-of-pearl is a natural attracter of prosperity, love, health, good luck and opportunity; cast a small piece of mother-of-pearl on to an incoming tide to bring what you need and on the outgoing to call back love, health or good luck; also works on a tidal river or if necessary in any flowing water if you specify your need. **Divinatory meaning:** A lot of people to take care of, a lot of claims on your attention; are you making it harder for yourself, always saying yes? **Zodiac:** Cancer. **Empowerment:** I accept my need for nurturing.

Mother-of-pearl is sacred to the sea mothers in a number of cultures, for example in Peru, as Mama Cocha or Mother Sea. Wear mother-of-pearl jewellery if you have tried to diet and failed many times, to restore natural rhythms of appetite and pleasure in food and to avoid the feast-and-famine syndrome.

Hold tumbled mother-of-pearl if you have to make difficult medical decisions about a child and give the child a small piece of mother-of-pearl jewellery or a beautiful piece of mother-of-pearl to keep during treatment or in hospital.

Keep a large mother-of-pearl half-shell in the home; on the crescent and full moon, fill it with symbols of abundance such as gold and silver jewellery, wealth-bringing crystals such as tiger eye, citrine or turquoise, and small bottles of abundance-bringing essential oils like cinnamon, frankincense and patchouli. Light silver candles round it to call abundance and happiness into your home.

Carry mother-of-pearl especially if travelling alone overseas or after dark.

Type: Zeolite, hydrated sodium aluminum silicate.

Colours: Clear or white, can be brilliant white; also tinted reddish, yellow and brown.

Availability: Relatively rare.

Physical benefits: Reported to ease fluid imbalances, bloating, oedema, detoxification, soil-borne diseases, goitre, mineral absorption especially iodine and zinc, sudden blood pressure rises or falls, pre-eclampsia in pregnancy, irregular pulse, eyesight particularly night vision and degeneration of vision with age.

Emotional healing: Natrolite relieves excesses, whether over-eating, drinking, smoking too much, gambling or over-spending, over-reliance on painkillers or prescription drugs, or being over-emotional or obsessed with cleanliness and germs.

Chakra: Sacral.

Natrolite

Candle colour: White. **Fragrances:** Lily, lily of the valley, mimosa, neroli, white rose. **Practical uses:** A crystal of natural growth: bury tiny pieces in the garden or in the soil of a precious exotic indoor plant or tree to bring healthy growth; kept in a crystal layout in the home, natrolite is a light-bringer and fills the other crystals and the room with natural outdoor spring energies, regardless of the location or time of year. **Workplace:** For sudden breakthroughs in career after a period of inaction or stagnation, for unexpected promotion or being offered the job you really want; keep a polished sphere for inspiration if you work with ideas and need to solve problems fast or to come up with a stream of original and workable concepts without time to recharge in between. **Magical significance:** Natrolite is often used in rebirthing, where people relive in therapy their birth and in-the-womb experiences, to make the experience gentle and releasing; a powerful meditation stone to fill yourself with light and happiness and to feel connected with cosmic energies and with other people; especially effective when used with herkimer diamond (p.136). **Divinatory meaning:** Light at the end of the tunnel is closer than you think; a breakthrough is coming and you will feel so much happier soon. **Zodiac:** Sagittarius. **Empowerment:** I open myself to cosmic light and experience.

Natrolite is a stone of immense positive power, associated with victory and overcoming challenges, and so it is helpful to the high-flier in the everyday world and to those seeking to take their spiritual development to higher levels.

As a light-bringing crystal, natrolite dissolves rather than banishes or absorbs negativity; a polished white natrolite sphere or egg in your workspace or at home not only protects against free-floating tension or actual malice, but empowers the user with the confidence and untouchability to rise above pettiness. It overcomes a fear of water, whether travelling by sea, for swimming or in water sports, particularly in adults.

Hold natroilte when you need to come up with a solution fast or are trying to recall a name or source of information.

Index

Ailments list

Each of the 500 crystals listed in the book has its own healing properties that are described under the individual crystals. The crystals in this chart are ones that are very common and easily obtainable almost everywhere in the world or from a wide variety of online sources. Should you want to find crystals not on this list for a specific illness, colour is generally a good guide. Therefore if, for example, you wanted to read about alternative crystals that are believed to be helpful for arthritis to those given here, you would look firstly in the crystals of similar colour to those suggested in this chart. You may also find it helpful to consult the chakra crystal lists on pages 21–23.

AILMENT	HEALING CRYSTAL
Abuse of any kind	Chrysocolla (p.231), desert rose (p.112), jade (pp.98, 208, 220, 264–8), mangano or pink calcite (p.56), orange calcite (p.80), rose quartz (p.50)
Addictions, smoking, overeating, alcohol etc	Angelite/celestite (p.242), amethyst (pp.212, 291), carnelian (pp.72, 84, said to be good for all food-related disorders), lepidolite (p.378), kunzite (p.57, good for women), labradorite (p.102), rhodochrosite (p.63) and smoky quartz (p.122), ruby in zoisite (p.315) or fuchsite (p.279), golden tiger's eye (p.107), unakite (p.280)
Ageing	Emerald (p.250, especially for older women), all chalcedony (pp.61, 152, 244) fossilized or petrified wood (p.110), iron pyrites (p.180), lepidolite (p.378), rutilated quartz (p.332, thought to be good for older men), pearl (p.148), sodalite (p.246, for older women)
Allergies, food- and environment-related	Amber (p.82), citrine (p.89), petrified wood (p.110), topaz (p.104), turquoise (p.239), zircon (pp.75, 105, 116, 138, 226, 278)
Alzheimer's and senile dementia	Blue chalcedony (p.244), fossils (pp.167, 368), flint (p.351), fluorite (pp.95, 139, 210, 243, 293), serpentine (p.257), sapphire (p.247), tree agate (p.254)
Anaemia, blood and blood cell disorders Anger, irritability	Red agate (p.69), bronzite (p.130), chrysocolla (p.231), red and orange jasper (pp.66, 67), heliotrope (p.290), haematite (p.171), milky/snow quartz (p.141), meteorite (p.173), ox eye or red tiger's eye (p.70), tiger iron (p.328)
Anger, irritability	Amazonite (p.286), amethyst (pp.212, 291), black tourmaline (p.204), blue topaz (p.240), chrysocolla (p.231), orange aragonite (p.84), rose quartz (p.50), peridot/olivine (p.282), ruby (p.71), sodalite (p.246)
Angina	Bornite (p.326), dioptase (p.292), emerald (p.250)
Anxiety, panic attacks, phobias	Angelite/celestite (p.242), ametrine (p.311), aquamarine (p.218), amethyst (pp.212, 291), aventurine (p.235), desert rose (p.112), kunzite (p.57), kyanite (pp.195, 225), rose quartz (p.50), opal (p.179), sodalite (p.246), garnet (pp.74, 119, 197, 271, 272), sunstone (p.116)
Appetite, loss of	Amber (p.82), apatite (pp.230, 251), carnelian (pp.72, 84)
Arteries	Blue lace agate (p.219), brecciated jasper (p.67), picture jasper (p.298), tourmalinated quartz (p.132), tree agate (p.254)
Arthritis, rheumatism, bone and joint pains	Carnelian (pp.72, 84), chalcopyrite (p.99), red and orange jasper (pp.66, 67), jet (p.198), garnet (pp.74, 119, 197, 271, 272), green fluorite (p.293), green calcite (p.293), jade (pp.98, 208, 220, 264–8), turquoise (p.239), any crystals with holes, white howlite (p.161)
Asthma	Morganite (p.55), pietersite (p.313), sodalite (p.246), rhodochrosite (p.63), tektite (p.185)
Attention deficit disorder/ hyperactivity	Azurite (p.217), blue quartz (p.224), red calcite (p.73), prehnite (p.289), selenite (pp.83, 157, 241), sodalite (p.246)
Autism, Asperger conditions	Tourmalinated quartz (p.132), aqua or cobalt aura (p.232), chrysocolla (p.231), lapis lazuli (p.223), sodalite (p.246), tektite (p.185)
Baby and childhood illness and problems	Crystals with holes in, jade (pp.98, 208, 220, 264–8, good for colic and fretfulness), mangano calcite (p.56), mother-of-pearl (p.389, soothes a baby or child when the mother is not there), blue and pink opals (pp.59 245), pink, white and blue chalcedony (pp.61, 152, 244)
Back, spine	Amazonite (p.286), citrine (p.89), blue and white howlite (pp.161, 233), double terminated quartz (p.343), green tourmaline (p.288), jet (p.198), fossilized wood (p.110), yellow calcite (p.87)
Balance, inner ear, also unsteadiness walking	Coral (pp.78, 128, 153, 193, 222), dioptase (p.292), jade (pp.98, 208, 220, 264–8), onyx (pp.151, 199), turquoise (p.239)
Bedwetting	Citrine (p.89), jade (pp.98, 208, 220, 264–8), any fluorite (pp.95, 139, 210, 243, 293)
Bipolar condition	Apache tear (p.194), kunzite (p.57), rutilated quartz (p.332)
Bites and stings	Serpentine (p.257), brecciated jasper (p.67), jet (p.198), snakeskin and leopardskin agate (p.143, 109)
Bladder/cystitis	Aquamarine (p.218), aventurine (p.235, good for genito-urinary problems), jade (pp.98, 208, 220, 264–8), mookaite (p.317), prehnite (p.289), rainbow quartz (p.306)

Blessings for home and people or places	Angelite (p.242), aventurine (p.235), blue celestite (p.245), chrysoprase (p.296), chrysocolla (p.231), jade (pp.98, 208, 220, 264–8, animals, babies, children, new homes and lovers), ruby (p.71), rose quartz (p.50), any banded agate (p.305), especially pink Botswana agate (p.54)
Blockages, emotional and physical	Ametrine (p.311), kyanite (pp.195, 225), mahogany obsidian (p.79)
Blood sugar disorders	Amethyst (pp. 212, 291), chrysocolla (p.231), garnet (pp.74, 119, 271–2), jade (pp.98, 208, 220, 264–8), mookaite (p.317), pink opal (p.59, low), serpentine (p.257), green tourmaline (p.288)
Blood pressure	Blue lace agate (p.219, high), chrysocolla (p.213, high), pietersite (p.313, high or low), haematite (p.171, high), sodalite (p.246, high), carnelian (pp.72, 84, low), ruby (p.71, low)
Body odour	Aquamarine (p.218), blue calcite (p.232), green jasper (p.274), sunstone (p.116)
Bones, including dislocation and broken	Apatite (pp.230, 251), aragonite (pp.84, 114), coral (pp. 78, 128, 153, 193, 222, 302), fossils (pp.167, 368), snow or milky quartz (p.141), white howlite (p.161), mother-of-pearl (p.389)
Bowel disorders and constipation	Amber (p.82), banded agate (p.305), dioptase (p.292, may be good for IBS), dalmatian jasper (p.300, also seen as good for IBS), rainbow quartz (p.306), rainbow moonstone (p.145)
Brain	Aqua aura (p.232), amazonite (p.286), opal aura (p.179), lapis lazuli (p.223), rutilated quartz (p.332) and turquoise (p.239). Herkimer diamond (p.136) is seen as slowing brain waves to slower, deeper patterns and so may help to avoid burnout, physically or emotionally
Breasts	Amazonite (p.286), mangano or pink calcite (p.56), olivine/peridot (p.282), rainbow moonstone (p.99), milky or snow quartz (p.141), moonstone (pp.99, 145, 237)
Bronchitis and respiratory complaints, lungs	Aquamarine (p.218), emerald (p.250), jade (pp.98, 208, 220, 264–8), lapis lazuli (p.223), green jasper (p.274), pietersite (p.313), orange aragonite (p.84), rhodonite (p.58)
Bruises	Amethyst (pp. 212, 291), rose quartz (p.50), smoky quartz (p.122)
Burns and scalds	Red agate (p.69), jade (pp.98, 208, 220, 264–8), rose quartz (p.50), sodalite (p.246)
Calm and to bring a sense of perspective to any situation that threatens to escalate	Amethyst (pp. 212, 291), ametrine (p.311), bronzite (p.130), green fluorite (p.293), flint (p.351), jade (pp.98, 208, 220, 264–8), sardonyx (p.313), rose quartz (p.50), white (p.152), pink (p.61) and blue (p.244) chalcedony, strawberry quartz (p.52)
Cells, tissue and bone marrow	Amber (p.82), boji stone (p.170), kyanite (pp.195, 225), coral (pp.78, 128, 153, 193, 222), iron pyrites (p.180), moss agate (p.253), rutilated quartz (p.332), snowflake obsidian (p.187), sugilite (p.55)
Childbirth and post-natal	Fossils (pp.128, 167, 368), heliotrope (p.290, believed to be good after Caesarean and any surgical intervention), jet (p.198, may ease birth), pink chalcedony (p.61, seen as good for first-time mothers, those who have had surgical intervention and post-natal problems); kunzite (pp.51, 210, 273, may help post-natal depression), mangano calcite (p.56, thought to help mother to bond with babies and for post-natal depression), malachite (p.283, believed to ease birth and strengthen the mother in a long labour), pink (p.59) and blue (p.222) opals for seen as useful in the early days after birth and to assist bonding, Shiva lingam (p.314) may ease birth
Cholesterol	Chrysoberyl (p.93), cat's eye (p.310), yellow fluorite (p.95)
Circulation	Carnelian (pp.72, 84), garnet (pp.74, 119, 271–2), ruby (p.71), tree (p.254) and moss (p.253) agates
Colds and coughs	Aquamarine (p.218), green (p.274) and ocean (p.299) jasper, green fluorite (p.293), jet (p.198), moss agate (p.253), turquoise (p.239), orange aragonite (p.84), golden topaz (p.104)
Colon and intestines	Red agate (p.69), banded agate (p.305), all brown and sandy jaspers (pp.108, 109), jet (p.198), rose quartz (p.50), yellow jasper (p.97), yellow calcite (p.87)
Cramps and spasms	Aragonite in all colours (pp.84, 114), crystals with holes, turquoise (p.239)
Confidence, charisma and courage	Amber (p.82), bronzite (p.130), carnelian (pp.72, 84), red jasper (p.66), turquoise (p.239)
Cuts, wounds, grazes	Carnelian (pp.72, 84), copper or chalcopyrite (p.99), if wound infected haematite (p.171), heliotrope (p.290), mookaite (p.317), rhodonite (p.58) are believed to help
Decision-making	Chiastolite (p.172), phantom quartz (pp.191, 259, 342), pink banded agates (p.305)
Degenerative conditions of all kinds	Azurite (p.217), lapis lazuli (p.223), lepidolite (p.378), malachite (p.283), rhodochrosite (p.63), sapphire (pp.202, 247, 365, 366), sugilite (p.55)
Depression	Apache tear (p.194), aqua aura (p.232), citrine (p.89), clear quartz crystal (p.133), jet (p.198), ox eye (p.70), sunstone (p.116), rainbow quartz (p.306), smoky quartz (p.122)
Detoxifying of system	Abalone shell (p.324), aqua (p.232) and cobalt (p.243) aura, green fluorite (p.293), heliotrope (p.290), herkimer diamond (p.136), moss agate (p.253), rhodochrosite (p.63), ocean jasper (p.299), ulexite (p.155)

Diabetes	Clear quartz (p.133), chrysocolla (p.231), orange aragonite (p.84), pink opal (p.59), sodalite (p.246)
Ear infections and ear ache	Amber (p.82), blue fluorite (p.243), lapis lazuli (p.223), onyx (pp.151, 199), purple fluorite (p.210), sapphire (pp.202, 247, 365, 366), turquoise (p.239)
Emotional stability	Amethyst (pp. 212, 291), blue quartz (p.224), blue topaz (p.240), jade (pp.98, 208, 220, 264–8)
Epilepsy	Bornite (p.326), coral (pp.78, 128, 153, 193, 222), emerald (p.250), golden topaz (p.104)
Exhaustion, lack of energy	Amber (p.82), carnelian (pp.72, 84), citrine (p.89), clear quartz (p.133), red agate (p.69), red jasper (p.66), golden tiger's eye (p.107), ox eye (p.70), golden topaz (p.104), rainbow quartz (p.306), ruby (p.71), smoky quartz (p.122), sunstone (p.116), tourmalinated quartz (p.132)
Eyesight, eye infections and night vision	Amethyst (pp. 212, 291), blue sapphire (p.247), cat's eye (p.310), emerald (p.250), labradorite (p.102), ox eye (p.70), pietersite (p.313), lapis lazuli (p.223), gold tiger's eye (p.107), ulexite (p.155)
Feet, legs	Jet (p.198), any of the sandy yellow or brown patterned jaspers (pp.97, 108, 109), sunstone (p.116)
Fertility problems or to restore cycles of ovulation after artificial contraception	Amber (p.82), carnelian (pp.72, 84), coral (pp.78, 128, 153, 193, 222), moonstone (pp.99, 145), red jasper (p.66), rhodochrosite (p.63, believed to be good for IVF and artificial insemination), rose quartz (p.50), selenite (p.83), unakite (p.280), any crystal eggs
Fevers	Blue sapphire (p.247), blue lace agate (p.219), chrysocolla (p.231), clear fluorite (p.139)
Fibromyalgia	Amethyst (pp. 212, 291), aventurine (p.235), citrine (p.89), rose quartz (p.50), ruby (p.71)
Fluid retention, bloating	Blue chalcedony (p.244), blue and green calcite (pp.232, 293), fluorite (pp.95, 139, 210, 243, 293), mookaite (p.317), moonstone (pp.99, 145, 237), selenite (p.83), titanium aura (p.322)
Gallstones and gallbladder problems	Amethyst (pp. 212, 291), carnelian (pp.72, 84), citrine (p.89), blue chalcedony (p.244), emerald (p.250), garnet (pp.74, 119), imperial topaz (p.104), olivine/peridot (p.282), orange calcite (p.80), gold tiger's eye (p.107)
Glands, swollen and glandular disorders	Blue lace agate (p.219), blue quartz (p.224), emerald (p.250), jet (p.198), lapis lazuli (p.223), moonstone (pp.99, 145, 237), sapphire (pp.202, 247, 365, 366, for glandular fever), selenite (p.83), sodalite (p.246), sugilite (55)
Grief/bereavement/painful or bitter divorce	Angelite (p.242), celestine/celestite (p.245), Apache tear (p.194), smoky quartz (p.122), jet (p.198), kyanite (pp.195, 225)
Hair	Chalcopyrite (p.99), jade (pp.98, 208, 220, 264–8), moonstone (pp.99, 145, 237), larimar (p.241), rose quartz (p.50)
Hay fever and plant-related or airborne allergies	Blue chalcedony (p.244), blue quartz (p.224), carnelian (pp.72, 84), petrified wood (p.110), turquoise (p.239)
Heart	Amazonite (p.286), aventurine (p.235), chrysoprase (p.296), dioptase (p.292), emerald (p.250), red jasper (p.66), sodalite (p.246)
Health, for promoting and maintaining	Citrine (p.89), clear quartz crystal (p.133), herkimer diamond (p.136), red jasper (p.66), ocean or orbicular jasper (p.299), sapphire (pp.202, 247, 365, 366), turquoise (p.239)
Hernia	Aventurine (p.235), lapis lazuli (p.223), mookaite (p.317)
Hormones	Chrysocolla (p.231), imperial topaz p.104), moonstone (pp.99, 145, 237), pearl (p.148), opal (pp.159, 31), pietersite (p.313, especially growth hormones), selenite (p.83)
Jet lag	Haematite (p.171), turquoise (p.239)
Inflammation anywhere in the body	Clear fluorite (p.139), lapis lazuli (p.223), blue chalcedony (p.244), ruby in zoisite (p.315) or in fuchsite (p.279)
Influenza	Garnet (pp.74, 119), green garnet (pp.271, 272), green jasper (p.274), obsidian (p.186) and snowflake obsidian (p.187), aqua aura (p.232), moss agate (p.253)
Indigestion, digestive disorders and stomach acidity	Amber (p.82), amethyst (pp. 212, 291), angelite/celestite (pp.242, 245), any chrysoprase (p.296), ruby in zoisite (p.315) or in fuchsite (p.279), lepidolite (p.378), yellow jasper (p.97)
Insomnia and nightmares	Amethyst (pp. 212, 291), charoite (p. 213 seen as good for sleepwalking and sleep disturbances), labradorite (p.102, if worries or fears are keeping you awake), moonstone (pp.99, 145, 237), smoky quartz (p.122), rainbow obsidian (p. 366), rose quartz (p.50)
Intestinal and abdominal problems, also internal parasites	Angelite (p.242), banded agate (p. 305)
Iron deficiency	Heliotrope (p.290), iron pyrites (p.180), tiger iron (p.328)

Kidneys	Aquamarine (p.218) carnelian (pp.72, 84), white, green and blue calcite, jade (pp.98, 208, 220, 264–8), moonstone (pp.99, 145, 237), green fluorite (p.293), flint (p.351) or heliotrope (p.290)(thought to be good for kidney stones), smoky quartz (p.122), yellow calcite (p.87)
Lactation, nursing mothers	Blue (p.244), pink (p.61) or white (p.152) chalcedony, blue howlite (p.233), clear fluorite (p.139)(believed to be good after Caesareans), milky or snow quartz (p.141)
Lack of motivation/ enthusiasm	Golden tiger's eye (p.107), topaz (p.64, 104, 128, 140, 240), herkimer diamond (p.136), natural (unsmoked) citrine (p.89), turquoise (p.239)
Libido to increase	Garnet (p.74, 86, 94, 119140, 197, 271, 272), red jasper (p.66), haematite (p.171), lodestone (p.190), ox eye (p.70), ruby (p.71), jet especially when if with amber (pp. 198 and 82)
Liver	Amethyst (pp. 212, 291), azurite (p.217), banded agate (p.205), citrine (p.89), flint (p.351), heliotrope (p.290), malachite (p.283), olivine/peridot (p.282), orange calcite (p.80), gold tiger's eye (p.107), yellow calcite (p.87), yellow jasper (p.97)
Love, to feel loved, to love yourself as you are and to improve relationships	Amber (p.82), carnelian (pp.72, 84), chrysocolla (p.231), diamond and herkimer diamond (p.136), emerald (p.250), jade (pp.98, 208, 220, 264–8), mookaite, ruby (p.71), sapphire (pp.202, 247, 365, 366), sardonyx (p.313), green, purple or watermelon tourmaline (pp.288, 213, 308)
Memory and concentration	Clear fluorite, (p.134), carnelian (pp.72, 84), citrine (p.89), lapis lazuli (p.223), sodalite (p.246)
Menstrual difficulties	Chrysocolla (p.231), coral (pp.78, 128, 153, 193, 222), moonstone (pp.99, 145, 237), jade (pp.98, 208, 220, 264–8), red jasper (p.66), opal (pp. 54, 83, 95, 146, 154, 179, 222, 304, 312, 352, 353), selenite (pp. 83, 156, 241), pearl (p.148), rainbow quartz (p.306), ox eye (p.70)
Metabolism	Clear quartz (p.133), citrine (p.89), rainbow quartz (p.306), titanium aura (p.322), unakite (p.280)
Migraines and headaches	Amethyst (pp. 212, 291), charoite (p.213), lapis lazuli (p.223), malachite (p.283), moonstone (pp.99, 145, 237, especially when hormonal or stress-related), rose quartz (p.50), sodalite (p.246), turquoise (p.239), titanium aura (p.322), lemon chrysoprase (p.296) (if food-related)
Muscle weakness	Haematite (p.171), lemon chrysoprase (p.296), serpentine (p.257)
Nausea and vomiting	Citrine (p.89), desert rose (p.112), green fluorite (p.293), lemon chrysoprase (p.296), sapphire (pp.202, 247, 365, 366), sodalite (p.246)
Neck	Amazonite (p.286), blue howlite (p.233)
Neurological system	Kyanite (pp.195, 225)
Nervous system	Amazonite (p.286), orange aragonite (p.84), lapis lazuli (p.223), leopardskin jasper (p.109)
Nosebleeds	Heliotrope (p.290), red jasper (p.66), garnet (pp.74, 119)
Obsessive compulsive disorder	Red calcite (p.73), all chalcedony (p.61, 152, 244)
Ovaries, womb	Orange or brown aragonite (pp.84, 114), moonstone (pp.99, 145, 237), opal aura (p.179)
Pain, chronic	Boji stone (p.170), chrysocolla (p.231), celestite (p.245), jet (p.198), lapis lazuli (p.223)
Panic attacks	Ametrine (p.311), red calcite (p.73), green calcite (p.293)
Pancreas and spleen	Banded agate (p.305), citrine (p.89), emerald (p.250), green fluorite (p.293),
Peace and reconciliation, good for creating a happy atmosphere and attracting good fortune	Aventurine (p.235), amethyst (pp. 212, 291), ametrine (p.311), apache tear (p.194), blue lace agate (p.219) or blue quartz (p.224) chalcopyrite (p.99), jade (pp.98, 208, 220, 264–8), rose quartz (p.50), rutilated quartz (p.332), smoky quartz (p.122), sodalite (p.246)
PMS and menopausal disorders	Chrysocolla (p.231), emerald (p.250), green fluorite (p.293), selenite (p.83, 157, 241), kunzite (pp.51, 210, 273), red jasper (p.66), heliotrope (p.290), jade (pp.98, 208, 220, 264–8), moonstone (pp.99, 145, 237), all crystal eggs, rose quartz (p.50)
Pregnancy	Angelite (p.245), white and pink chalcedony (p.152, 61), jade (pp.98, 208, 220, 264–8), kunzite (pp.51, 210, 273), moonstone (pp.99, 145, 237), pink and blue opals (pp. 59, 222), opal aura (p.179), rose quartz (p.50), ruby (p.71), selenite (p.83, 157, 241)
Prolonged medical, chemical or surgical treatment	Aqua aura (p.232), banded agate (p. 305), chalcopyrite (p.99), herkimer diamond (p.136), malachite (p.283), rainbow moonstone (pp.99, 145, 237, believed to be good for women after operations), titanium aura (p.322)
Prosperity and success	Ox eye (p.70), carnelian (pp.72, 84), citrine (p.89), clear crystal (p.133), falcon or hawk's eye (p.227), heliotrope (p.290), lapis lazuli (p.223), golden tiger's eye (p.107), turquoise (p.239)
Protection against adverse effects of technology	Ametrine (p.311), malachite (p.283), pietersite (p.313), smoky quartz (p.122)
Protection from malice, bullying or attack of any kind	Amazonite (p.286), black tourmaline (p.204), obsidian (p.79, 106, 175, 186–8, 291, 266) hawk or falcon's eye (p.227), haematite (p.171), lapis lazuli (p.223), red jasper (p.66) smoky quartz (p.122), turquoise (p.239)

Protection against theft, fire, storm, loss or accident	Aventurine (p.235), carnelian (pp.72, 84), fire or blood agate (p.69), blue calcite (p.232), heliotrope (p.290), kunzite (pp.51, 210, 273), meteorite (p123, 173), turquoise (p.239)
Protection against ghosts and negative earth energies	Amethyst (pp. 212, 291), clear crystal (p.133), rutilated quartz (p.332)
Protection from emotional vampires	Any grey agate (p.164, 177), ametrine (p.311), aventurine (p.235), blue celestite (p.245), prehnite (p.289), iolite (p.377), smoky quartz (p.122), ulexite (p.155)
Prostate	Orange and brown aragonite (p.84, 114), aventurine (p.235), desert rose (p.112)
Psychosomatic conditions	Kunzite (pp.51, 210, 273), ox eye (p.70), sugilite (p.55), lepidolite (p.378)
Pulse and heartbeat irregularities	Aventurine (p.235), banded agate (p.305(, moss agate (p.253), ruby in zoisite (p.315) or in fuchsite (p.279)
Quitting smoking	Kunzite (pp.51, 210, 273), staurolite (p.125), chiastolite (p.172)
Rashes of all kinds	Angelite (p.242), aquamarine (p.218), blue calcite (p. 232), larimar (p.241), rose quartz (p.50)
Recovery after illness or surgery	Amber (p.82), ametrine (p.311), carnelian (pp.72, 84), red agate (p.69), red jasper (p.66), any chrysoprase (p.296), ox eye (p.70), ruby (p.71)
Scars and birth marks	Green fluorite (p.293), rhodonite (p.58), rose quartz (p.50), tourmalinated quartz (p.132)
Self-esteem	Carnelian (pp.72, 84), citrine (p.89), kunzite (pp.51, 210, 273), Isis quartz crystal (p.335)
Sexual dysfunction in men, male genital disorders	Ox eye (p.70), carnelian (pp.72, 84), orange aragonite (84), ruby (p.71), iron pyrites (p.180) or haematite (p. 171), Shiva lingam (p.314)
Shyness	Bornite (p.326), yellow (p.87) and orange (p.80) calcite (pp.56, 73, 87, 101, 134, 154, 232, 293,) flint (p.351), garnet (pp.74, 86, 94, 119, 140, 197, 271, 272), pearl (p.148)
Skin inflammation, eczema or rashes and skin allergies	Emerald (p.250), red agate (69), blue coral (p.222), blue lace agate (p.219), fuchsite (p.269), lapis lazuli (p.223), leopardskin jasper (p.109), moss agate (p.253), serpentine (p.257), snakeskin agate (p.143), titanium aura (p.322), turitella agate (p.111)
Sinus	Clear and purple fluorite (p.139, 210), snowflake obsidian (p.187), sodalite (p.246), tourmalinated quartz (p.132)
Speech and communication problems	Angelite (p.242), blue celestite (p.245), blue lace agate (p.219), blue sapphire (p.247), blue topaz (p.240), lapis lazuli (p.223), smoky quartz (p.122)
Stomach including upsets	Desert rose (p.112), chrysoprase (p.296,) (lemon is thought to be good for diarrhoea, green for stomach ulcers), obsidian (p.79, 106, 1175, 186–8, 291, 366) (is believed to help gastro-enteritis), orange aragonite (p.84), gold tiger's eye (p.107), golden topaz (p.104)
Stress	Amethyst (pp. 212, 291), angelite (p.242), aventurine (pp.76, 82, 235, 285)), herkimer diamond (p.136), blue lace agate (p.219), kyanite (pp.195, 225), jade (pp.98, 208, 220, 264–8), labradorite (p.102), purple fluorite (p.210), rose quartz (p.50)
Sunburn	Blue calcite (p.232), ox eye (p.70)
Swellings and growths of all kinds	Aqua aura (p.232), cobalt aura (p.243) or titanium aura (p.322), jet, olivine/peridot (p.282), sugilite (p.55), zebra jasper (p. 184)
Teeth and gums	Apatite (p.230), blue howlite (p.233), malachite (p.283), shark's tooth (p.368)
Throats sore and tonsillitis	Amber (p.82), aquamarine (p.218), blue calcite (p.232), blue howlite (p.233) (seen as good for recurring infections), blue lace agate (p.219), green fluorite (p. 293), turquoise (p.239)
Tissue regeneration	Rutilated quartz (p.332), golden topaz (p.104)
Thyroid	Amazonite (p.286) aquamarine (p.218), chrysocolla (p.231), emerald (p.250), mookaite (p.317)
Trauma or accidents	Amethyst (pp. 212, 291), carnelian (pp.72, 84), labradorite (p.102), mangano calcite (p.56), rainbow obsidian (p.366), rose quartz (p.50), tree agate (p.254)
Travel sickness	Aquamarine (p.218) (sea and air), amethyst (pp. 212, 291), desert rose (p.112), jade (pp.98, 208, 220, 264–8), green jasper (p.274), ocean jasper (p.299), lemon chrysoprase (p.91)
Ulcers	Green fluorite (p.295), rhodonite (p.58), tourmalinated quartz (p.132)
Varicose veins	Blue lace agate (p.219), iron pyrites (p.180), rhyolite (p.323), serpentine (p.257),
Viruses and infections	Green calcite (p.293), iron pyrites (p.180), jade (pp.98, 208, 220, 264–8), leopardskin jasper (p.109), opal aura (p.179), garnet, amber (p.82), purple fluorite (p.210)
Warts and skin or hair parasites	Desert rose (p.112), labradorite (p.102), leopardskin jasper (p.109), serpentine (p.257),
Weight loss, to achieve	Amber (p.82), kunzite (pp.51, 210, 273), lemon chrysoprase (p.91), moonstone (pp.99, 145, 237)
Weight gain, to achieve	Carnelian (pp.72, 84), unakite (p.280)
Whole mind and body health and healing/immune system	Aqua aura (p.232) , amethyst (pp. 212, 291), clear quartz (p.113), chiastolite (p.172), rutilated quartz (p.332), jade (pp.98, 208, 220, 264–8), herkimer diamond (p.136), labradorite (p.102), rainbow moonstone (pp.99, 145, 237), tektite (p.188)

The publishers would like to thank the following sources for their kind permission to reproduce the pictures in this book.

Picture Credits: L=left, R=right, T=top, B=bottom.

Alamy Images: /Arco Images: 98b, 297, /Blickwinkel: 254, /Emilio Ereza: 35, /Greg C Grace: 291, /John Lens: 214b, /Mark Schneider/ Visuals Unlimited: 241r

Barlows Gems: 102b

Better Rocks: 274

Corbis: /Ric Ergenbright: 256, /José Manuel Sanchis Calvete: 345b, / Gavin Kingcome/Science Photo Library: 336, /Sandro Vannini: 9, / Visuals Unlimited: 89b, 95b, 235r, 258r, 262, 361, 387r

Critical Eye Photography: 200l

Fawcett Hobbies: 228

Gemological Institute of America: 64, 138, 208, 220, 278, 303, 306, 385r

Getty Images: /James L. Amos: 295, /Arabian Eye: 46, /De Agostini: 93, 103r, 121, 176b, 184l, 209, 213r, 359, 362, /Yashuhide Fumoto: 85r, /Ken Hayden: 40, /Colin Keates: 281, /Alan Levenson: 21, /Mark Schneider: 105r, 347, 370, /Scientifica: 143, /Harry Taylor: 94l, 131, 180b, 189, 271b, 368r, 376

IRocks.com: 234

IStockphoto: /Matt Jeacock: 42, /Sean Locke: 44

Jack Taylor: 183

Joanne Hollingsworth: 387b

Joseph Freilich: 191

Krystal Love: 243b, 340, 345r, 346

Little Gems: 106, 227r

Manuel Beers: 387r

Natural History Museum: 71r, 108, 168, 176l, 181, 226, 250b, 271r, 351, 362b, 373r

Photolibrary.com: 29

Precious Pebbles: 211

Private Collection: 51, 109b, 149b, 214l, 244, 270, 325, 366, 383, 385b, /John Krygier: 69b. /Asta Remeikaite: 193

Rodney Fox: 67r

Roger Lang: 288

Science Photo Library: /Joel Arem: 96, 144, 298, 373r, /Michael Clutson: 111r, /Jean-Claude Revy, A. Carion, ISM: 101r, 210l, /Charles D. Winters: 128b, 352

SoMK: /somkartshop.com: 202

That Crystal Site: 289

All other photographs copyright of Carlton Books Ltd.

Every effort has been made to acknowledge correctly and contact the source and/or copyright holder of each picture and Carlton Books Limited apologises for any unintentional errors or omissions which will be corrected in future editions of this book.

Photography Credits:

Crystals on pages 2, 5, 6, 7, 8, 15, 17, 18, 19, 24, 25, 30, 31, 38, 39, 51, 43, 45 (all except for t), 48, 49, 50, 51, 52, 53 r, 54, 55, 56, 57, 60, 61, 62 r, 63, 65, 66, 67, 68, 69 r, 70, 71 l, 72, 74, 75 l, 76 l, 77, 79, 81, 82, 83, 84, 85 r, 86, 87, 89 r, 90, 91, 92, 94 r, 95, 96, 98 r, 97, 99, 100, 101 l, 103, 104 r, 105 l, 107, 109 r, 110, 111, 120 r, 128n r, 114, 115, 116, 117, 118, 119, 122, 124, 125, 126 l, 128, 129n l, 130, 132, 133, 134, 135, 136, 137, 139, 140, 141, 142, 145 r, 147, 148, 149 l, 150, 151, 152, 155, 156, 157, 158, 159, 161, 162, 163, 164, 165, 166, 167, 168, 170, 171, 172, 173, 174, 175 r, 176, 177, 178, 179 r, 182, 184 r, 185, 186, 187, 188, 195 r, 200 r, 201, 203, 204, 205, 209, 210 l, 212, 213 l, 214 r, 215, 217, 218, 219 r, 222 l, 223, 224, 225, 227, 229 l, 231, 232 l, 233, 235 l, 236 l, 239, 241 l, 242, 243 r, 244 r, 245, 246, 247, 248, 250 l, 251, 252, 253, 254 l, 257 r, 259 r, 260, 261, 262, 263, 264, 265, 266, 267, 268, 269, 272, 273, 274 l, 275 r, 277, 279, 280, 282, 283, 284 l, 285, 286, 287, 288 l, 289, 290, 291 r, 292, 293, 294 l, 295 l, 296, 298 l, 299, 300, 301, 302, 304, 305, 306 r, 307, 308, 309, 310, 311, 312, 313, 314, 315, 316, 318, 317 l, 319, 320, 321, 323 l, 324, 325, 327, 328, 329, 332, 333, 334, 335, 337, 338, 339 r, 340 l, 342, 343, 346, 348, 349, 350, 351 l, 353 r, 355, 356, 357, 358, 360, 364, 366 r, 367, 368 l, 369, 371m 372 l, 373 l, 374, 375, 377 l, 378, 379, 380, 381 r, 382, 384 r, 386 l, 388 and 389 courtesy of Charlie's Rock Shop, Unit 1 The 1929 Shop, 18 Watermill Way, Merton Abbey Mills, London, SW19 2RD, tel: 020 8544 1207, fax: 020 8544 0992, website: http://www.charliesrockshop.com/

Crystals on pages 45 t, 57, 59 l, 62 r, 68, 69 r, 70, 73, 75 r, 94 l, 120 l, 123, 126 r, 133 r, 145 l, 153, 154 l, 162 r, 179 l, 197, 199 r, 216, 219 l, 230 l, 232 r, 245 r, 238, 229 r, 237 l, 240, 249, 255, 258, 271 l, 284 r, 281, 288 r, 317 l, 322, 326, 330, 331, 338 r, 343 r, 352, 361 l, 365, 382 and 384 l, courtesy of The Crystal Healer, http://www.thecrystalhealer.co.uk.

Crystals on pages 77, 85r, 101 r, 104 l, 113, 144, 143 l, 230 r, 237 r, 276, 294 r, 297, 354, 376 l, 377 l, 381 l courtesy of Avalon Crystals, 6 Dukes Mill, Broadwater Road, Hants, SO51 8PJ, tel 01794 516644.

Crystals on pages 129 r and 275 l courtesy of Cassandra Eason.

Further Information

Charlie's Rock Shop
Unit 1 The 1929 Shop
18 Watermill Way
Merton Abbey Mills
London SW19 2RD
Tel: 020 8544 1207
Fax: 020 8544 0992
Website: http://www.charliesrockshop.com/

The Crystal Healer
Tel: 01727 866720
Website: http://www.thecrystalhealer.co.uk

Avalon Crystals
6 Dukes Mill
Broadwater Road
Hants, SO51 8PJ
Tel: 01794 516644
Website: http://www.avaloncrystals.co.uk/

Cassandra Eason
Website: http://www.cassandraeason.com/

Credits

The publishers would like to thank the following people for their assistance in the preparation of this book:

Charles Reynolds, Philip Permutt and Gary Onslow.

Publishing credits:

Copyeditor: Catherine Rubinstein

Additional editorial work: Philip Parker, Vanessa Daubney, Alice Payne, Jane McIntosh and Nicky Jeanes.

Studio Manager: Stephen Cary

Original design: Jake DaCosta

Design: Emily Clarke, Brian Flynn

Photography: Karl Adamson

Picture Manager: Steve Behan

Picture Researcher: Ben White

Production: Karin Kolbe